W9-DEU-364

# THE UNITED NATIONS

## International Organization and World Politics

### THIRD EDITION

LAWRENCE ZIRING
*Western Michigan University*

ROBERT E. RIGGS
*Brigham Young University*

JACK C. PLANO
*Western Michigan University*

WADSWORTH

THOMSON LEARNING

*Australia • Canada • Mexico • Singapore • Spain
United Kingdom • United States*

**WADSWORTH**

**THOMSON LEARNING**

*This third edition is dedicated*
*to Diether Haenicke*

**Publisher:** Earl McPeek
**Executive Editor:** David Tatom
**Market Strategist:** Steve Drummond
**Project Editor:** Katherine Dennis
**Art Director:** Burl Sloan

**Production Manager:** Diane Gray
**Cover Printer:** R. R. Donnelley, Crawfordsville
**Compositor:** G & S Typesetters
**Printer:** R. R. Donnelley, Crawfordsville

COPYRIGHT © 2000 Thomson Learning, Inc. Thomson Learning™ is a trademark used herein under license.

ALL RIGHTS RESERVED. No part of this work covered by the copyright hereon may be reproduced or used in any form or by any means— graphic, electronic, or mechanical, including but not limited to photocopying, recording, taping, Web distribution, information networks, or information storage and retrieval systems—without the written permission of the publisher.

Printed in the United States of America
2  3  4  5  6  7  05

For more information about our products, contact us at:
**Thomson Learning Academic Resource Center**
**1-800-423-0563**

For permission to use material from this text, contact us by:
**Phone:** 1-800-730-2214 **Fax:** 1-800-730-2215
**Web:** http://www.thomsonrights.com

**Library of Congress Catalog Card Number:**
99-64030
**ISBN:** 0-15-507865-8

**Asia**
Thomson Learning
60 Albert Street, #15-01
Albert Complex
Singapore 189969

**Australia**
Nelson Thomson Learning
102 Dodds Street
South Melbourne, Victoria 3205
Australia

**Canada**
Nelson Thomson Learning
1120 Birchmount Road
Toronto, Ontario M1K 5G4
Canada

**Europe/Middle East/Africa**
Thomson Learning
Berkshire House
168-173 High Holborn
London WC1 V7AA
United Kingdom

**Latin America**
Thomson Learning
Seneca, 53
Colonia Polanco
11560 Mexico D. F.
Mexico

**Spain**
Paraninfo Thomson Learning
Calle/Magallanes, 25
28015 Madrid, Spain

# PREFACE

The second edition of *The United Nations* was released following the collapse of the Soviet Union. That moment marked the end of a global rivalry between the United States and the Union of Soviet Socialist Republics that had stalked the United Nations from its inception. The end of the Cold War heavily influenced Robert Riggs and Jack Plano, who predicted a more positive future for the United Nations and anticipated more elaborate forms of cooperation from among its members. At this writing, however, some ten years after the fall of the Berlin Wall, and just eight years after the dissolution of the Soviet Union, the organization designed "to save humanity from the scourge of war" remains in an ambiguous state. As the century ends, the United Nations appears suspended somewhere between the exclusivity of its member states and the latter's obvious need for transcendent experience. We are reminded that the United Nations is the sum of its parts, and that the organization is either the composite voice of its member states or an ideal still awaiting realization.

The image of the United Nations, in contemporary times, is sometimes seen as antiquarian in an age of global economic transactions and revolutionary advances in communication. The new global order appears to center more on electronic market transfers than on classic diplomatic processes, and the central arena for interstate activity is less in the halls of the world's largest debating society than in the board rooms of transnational corporations and international financial centers. Clashes of interest at different levels of human experience would seem to require the intervention of the United Nations, and indeed the organization responded to the many crises that followed the end of the Cold War. But it did not take very long to realize that the organization, as represented by its secretariat and less so by its member states, was hardly ready to assume the responsibilities outlined in the UN Charter. This third edition of *The United Nations*, therefore, contrasts with the upbeat portrayal of the organization at the beginning of this last decade of the twentieth century.

Because of the changed global environment prevailing prior to and during its preparation, this third edition of *The United Nations* is more than an update and possesses a different overall character. Nevertheless, the reader who is familiar with the previous editions will note that the original format has been retained. So too, virtually all the historical narrative produced by Riggs and Plano, which is so fundamental to the text.

## NEW TO THIS EDITION

- Citations have been reduced to a minimum through incorporation in the narrative, creating a less distracting, more readable, and informative text
- New tables and figures have been added while others critical to the text have been updated
- The advent of co-deployment operations are explored against a background of the United Nations increasing dependence on other forms of international organization
- The efforts being made to restructure the United Nations by the office of the Secretary General in the absence of amendments to the Charter
- The central and ever more controversial role of the Secretary General
- The challenge of peacekeeping and a thorough examination of every successful and failed UN mission
- The evolution of humanitarian law and the creation of the international criminal court

- The institutional responsibilities allocated to the Security Council, the General Assembly, and the International Court of Justice are revisited with particular reference to contemporary as well as historic issues
- The new challenges posed to disarmament in the post-Cold War world, and the difficulties in preventing the spread of weapons of mass destruction
- A new section discussing self-determination in the 21st century
- An exploration of global environmental questions and the increasing influence of the non-governmental organizations
- An introduction to 21st century trading practices and the new international organizations, e.g. EU, WTO, NAFTA, EMU, etc. that are destined to shape the future
- A new concluding chapter examining the functionality and utility of the United Nations in the 21st century

Looking back to the founding of the United Nations, I am reminded of the high elation that permeated our thoughts as well as the idealism that captured our senses after the long, grueling, and costly conflict that was World War II. The chemistry of that experience made it possible to believe in both your country and the alliance that had won the war and now was charged with maintaining the peace. Admittedly, that was a far different time from that which we experience today, at the close of a century.

Whatever the changes, the United Nations remains as relevant today as the day it was conceived, and furthermore, its work is all before it. It is my hope, and I think one shared by my co-authors, that this third edition of *The United Nations* will edify the readers who were born long after the organization's founding. Hopefully they will come to recognize what the United Nations really is, what it stands for, and what it endeavors to accomplish in the fullness of a world dramatically represented by so many different nation-states.

Writing, albeit revising, a book like *The United Nations* is an all-consuming experience. If there was anyone to intrude upon my solitude, it was Sangmook Lee, my research assistant, whose dedication to this project was as great as mine and whose identification and recovery of mounds of data was nothing less than phenomenal. But assembling this presentation and preparing it for publication involves the labors of a number of people at Harcourt Brace that I must acknowledge and to whom I would like to express my gratitude. I am most appreciative to Katie Frushour, an editor of special talent, as well as to David Tatom, Executive Editor. I am also grateful to those members of the Harcourt Brace production staff who have contributed so much to the completed project: Katherine Dennis, Project Editor; Diane Gray, Production Manager; and Burl Sloan, Art Director.

Finally, I was both humbled and flattered by the request made by the original authors to revise their work. In taking on this assignment I understood it was my task to work alone and to produce a text that would not only do justice to their endeavor, but which would sustain *The United Nations* as the book of choice in exploring the life and trials of the world body. I trust I have measured up to that task; that they, and those who read this book, will find in its pages the same enlightenment that an earlier generation of readers was exposed to.

Lawrence Ziring
Western Michigan University

# TABLE OF CONTENTS

# I

# THE UNITED NATIONS IN HISTORICAL PERSPECTIVE

## PROLOGUE

International organization does not come naturally to a world of nation-states. Nations draw pride from their independence and their sovereign status suggests an unerring concern for individuality and aloofness. The exclusive aspects of the territorial states reinforce go-it-alone posturing and it is not without considerable reluctance that they seek community in organizations that transcend their unique character and peculiar stated purposes. Indeed, states behave as though they would rather not be burdened by arrangements that seem to dilute their private interests, and coalescence is a feature of state behavior only because states must live in a world of many nation-states, all of which share the same desire to be free of the restrictions that transcendent organizations require. It is only in spite of their otherwise limited inclinations that states join with other states and thus accept the limitations on their sovereignty that collective membership demands. States, after all, are seldom if ever self-sufficient, and barring costly autarkic ambitions, they cannot avoid external commitments.

In the greater realm of the nation-states, each actor is something less than the omnipotent entity it aspires to be; in the end therefore, nation-states will join with others in order to compensate for their shortcomings, to make up for their obvious and not so obvious weaknesses. International organization promises something the individual states cannot achieve in isolation, and security, development, prosperity are hardly realizable goals in the absence of cooperative arrangements. Moreover, in no arrangement is this more obvious than in the United Nations system.

Emerging from the ashes of World War II, the United Nations projected a new world order that in principle elevated international organization above that of the sovereign states. The United Nations was conceived as the answer to a world torn by license and anarchy and ravaged by the excesses of aggressive, self-centered national states. Limitations on sovereignty was a significant outcome of a world no longer divided into colonial and colonized peoples. Retreating empires left behind national actors, none of whom were capable of making it alone and all enthusiastically sought association in the organization

1

of nations that became the United Nations. The United Nations was not only called humankind's best hope for an enduring peace, it also promised a cooperative grouping of nations whose concerns centered on social and economic advances.

The new states of the immediate post-war generation saw in the United Nations a guarantee against big power aggressiveness as well as the promise of a helpful hand to those struggling to find their way in an uncharted wilderness. And although the role of the United States loomed large over the organization, the character of the colossus of the western hemisphere projected a charitable, benevolent and amiable presence. Unlike earlier super actors, the United States was prompted by a substantial portion of the international community to assume global responsibility and an overwhelming number of states applauded and welcomed its leadership and guidance. Moreover, the country that conceived a League of Nations following World War I (only to reject its own innovation) now in the changed conditions wrought by World War II, could not fail to make the United Nations central to its foreign policy.

American idealism was never so heavily tested. The nation that had contributed so much to the defeat of fascism and militarism stood alone at the apex of world power. The only major state to have emerged from World War II intact and more prosperous than when the war began, the United States addressed the need to restructure the world's economic and financial institutions; it was also only the United States that appeared capable of reviving a world that literally lay in ruins. With its forces in occupation in Japan and Germany, and with its network of military bases and installations in virtually every region of the world, the U.S. assumed the dual role of policing the defeated nations, in addition to restoring the world's socio-economic equilibrium. Not given to posturing a *Pax Americana,* however, the United States endeavored to legitimize its external policies and programs through the institutions of the United Nations system, and in so doing, it gave special credence to an experiment in international living that while not entirely new, was nevertheless as innovative as it was self-limiting.

United States membership in the United Nations involved the sublimation of national proclivities. It also meant the organization would guide the powerful as well as the weaker actors along a path requiring their accommodation to policies and programs not necessarily of their particular choosing. Such national sacrifice, however, was deemed a small price following the tragedy of World War II. In an atmosphere of relief and self-examination, in a period of heightened idealism, the joint enterprise that was the United Nations was deemed a noble undertaking, and one that promised a future far more positive and manifestly more significant than anything preceding it.

But the expectations of the architects of the United Nation's system in that heady moment of creation were not to be realized. The era that came to be known as the *Cold War* began as the dust of World War II was just beginning to settle. The bipolar conditions that positioned the United States on the one side of a conflicted geopolitical frontier and the Soviet Union on the other, imposed an enormous burden on the new international organization. More-over, the fact that both countries were made responsible for the success or fail-ure of the United Nations system, in fact had assumed primary responsibility for operationalizing the organization, only distorted UN purposes. As a conse-quence, the United Nations was handicapped from the outset, and its weakness was written large in its lack of capacity to meld and transcend national experi-ences. Even its expansion to include the newly independent states did more to heighten national, not international, organization. The peculiar characters of the different nation-states were exaggerated, hardly muted by membership in the United Nations.

In the initial years following its formation, therefore, the United Nations became an extension of U.S. foreign policy, and Washington did not hesitate in exploiting the bona fides of the organization in its contest with Moscow. The collapse of the European empires, however, forced the release of their colonies and the latter's emergence as sovereign nation-states soon altered the Ameri-can monopoly. At the same time, the Soviets freely employed their veto power against efforts that would use the United Nations to thwart Soviet ambitions. Thus, many member states were conditioned to view the United Nations as an instrument for the advancement of their exclusive policies. With the principal powers showing the way, virtually all the states endeavored to squeeze from the organization some justification for their otherwise parochial behavior. But none of the member states were more obvious in their exploitation of the orga-nization than the major powers. Almost from its inception, the United Nations was transformed into an arena of major power jousting, and the lesser states were not long in using the world body for their own largely exclusive pursuits.

Still in its infancy, the United Nations was identified with the war on the Korean peninsula but the nature of its involvement merely demonstrated the weakness of the central enforcement section of the UN Charter. The transfer-ence of peacemaking and peacekeeping functions from the Security Council to the General Assembly exposed structural weaknesses in the organization that were to carry forward through all the decades of the Cold War and beyond. The United Nations was less the instrument for denying aggression, and more a ve-hicle for the projection of unrealized national and bloc objectives. More a fo-rum for debate, many of the issues with which it was seized proved insoluble, and as a consequence, their cumulative weight only imposed still heavier bur-dens on the organization.

The United Nations received little if any credit for the termination of the Cold War, but it is not without noting that the last major incident prior to its ending was the UN sanctioned coalition that drove Iraq from Kuwait. The revival of the UN Security Council during the Persian Gulf crisis of 1990–91 appeared to breathe new life into the organization. The bridging of U.S.-Soviet differences during that episode heralded a new beginning for the interna-tional organization, but this new accommodation came just as the Soviet Union was about to self-destruct. The break-up of the communist superpower left a new Russian Federation as the Soviet Union's heir. Moreover, Russia's largely amicable approach to the United States appeared to indicate a heavier reliance on the institutions of the United Nations. The People's Republic of China also appeared inclined to play a more cooperative role in the world body, and indeed, the appearance of permanent power unity tended to alter if not reduce the leverage of the lesser states.

Given major power preference for multilateral assertiveness, the United Nations once more was deemed the primary instrument in the maintenance of international equilibrium, and pacifying numerous violent incidents became the responsibility of the organization. UN peacekeeping forces were assembled to confront conflicts within and between member states as never before, but the enthusiasm with which the United Nations assumed those tasks, often at the behest of one or more of the permanent powers, could not conceal deep divisions among the many member states. Called upon to make substantial contributions to expanded UN activities, the permanent powers were notably hesitant, or in different situations, unwilling to honor their expressed commitments. Indeed, with the end of the Cold War, the U.S. Congress refused to meet its financial obligations to the United Nations, and considerable mainstream public sentiment in the United States began to verbalize opposition to UN policies and activities.

Conversant with the basic features of the Cold War, the United Nations was unprepared for the conditions that now demanded its attention. Restructuring had been contemplated and sometimes debated, but action was slow in developing. Moreover, the need for collective action appeared to conflict with the forces of nationalism that now again heavily influenced state policy. The penchant of nation-states to pursue exclusive interests contradicted the inclusive and collective purpose of the United Nations. With the twentieth century already history, the twenty-first century may yet prove to be the century of deeper international organization, but the contest that had aroused the forces of exclusivity and particularism are still to be reckoned with.

## IN THE BEGINNING

Scholars have traced the origins and have identified features of international organization in the numerous ancient leagues and assemblies that were aimed at warding off threats posed by more formidable powers. The quest for security encouraged cooperation among the lesser states confronting the imperial power of China and Rome, but international organization was perhaps more relevant in the amphictyonic councils of the Greek city-states. Bound by a common culture and devoted to shared ceremonial temples, the different Hellenistic tribes pledged themselves to observe established rules, particularly in matters related to warfare. From the amphictyonic councils emerged the confederations of the Phocian, Akarnian and Boetian leagues, which in turn, gave rise to the Lycian and Achaean Leagues that promised even richer accommodations. By the fourteenth century more significant arrangements were developed that centered on trade and commerce, particularly among the commercial towns around the North and Baltic Seas. The formation of the Hanseatic League, drew some fifty cities together and for two hundred years their combined power not only monopolized trade and commerce, but also demonstrated considerable strategic prowess. The fading of Hanse power culminated with the emergence of a territorial, though absolutist dynastic state system that was formally acknowledged with the Peace of Westphalia in 1648. Although international organization was not made a feature of the Westphalian settlement, the assembly of great and lesser European powers heralded the opening of a new era in international relations, and indeed, Europe ushered in the epoch of the nation-states. No longer guided by mythology or priest, let alone by emperor or pope, the evolution of a secular state system necessitated cooperation no less than it projected individual sovereignty. Clearly, a traceable thread runs through the history that links these early and rudimentary efforts at accommodation to the contemporary world of the United Nations.

Despite monumental and continuing failures to eliminate war, peoples and governments continue to reach beyond existing political boundaries to build on the orderly, brotherly, and cooperative side of human nature rather than give free rein to the suspicious, destructive, dark side. The founding of the United Nations is in this tradition. While falling short of its high ideals and purposes, the UN system nevertheless represents that human outreach toward peace and cooperation. In this chapter we will place the United Nations in historical perspective by looking at the modern state system that gave rise to it, describing the emergence of earlier international institutions, and briefly reviewing events leading to the establishment of the United Nations at the end of World War II. In Chapter 2 we will discuss the structure and operation of the United Nations.

# THE STATE SYSTEM AND INTERNATIONAL ORGANIZATION

As the many separate political units created during the European feudal era were fused into larger communities, the national state, on which the contemporary UN system rests, emerged as the dominant political unit. Through conquest and annexation the number of small political entities was progressively reduced, and a Europe of nation-states began to take shape. The legal inception of the modern state system is commonly dated from the 1648 Treaty of Westphalia, which ended the Thirty Years' War and recognized the territorial state as the cornerstone of the system.

The new European state system was characterized not only by conflict and disunity but also by forces moving peoples and nations toward closer contact and agreed rules of conduct. Political and economic rivalries were the chief source of conflict, and periodic wars remained a constant testimony to the difficulty of resolving them peaceably. Nevertheless, increased contacts among the new states also brought an awakening in the realm of economic activity, and this created a need for state cooperation. In response to this need, rules were established for the adjustment of differences that inevitably arise through commercial intercourse. This resulted in a progressive elaboration of the system of international law that had begun to develop before Westphalia and in the growing use of consular interchange for the promotion and adjustment of commercial contacts. As trade competition among the new nations increased, it began to spill over into a race to acquire overseas colonies. This, in turn, produced a need for further international rules by which nations could recognize one another's titles to new lands, settle boundary disputes, and undertake joint action against piracy. Nations began to deal more directly with such problems by entering into agreements and treaties with one another. Hence rivalries and antagonisms, while continuing to grow, tended to produce countervailing forces leading to increased cooperation.

The closing decades of the eighteenth century witnessed the emergence of two powerful new ideas destined to have a profound effect on the nature of the state system. These were the two concepts of laissez-faire and democratic nationalism, each of which dramatically recognized the new role to be played by the individual in human affairs. In the economic realm, the mercantilist doctrine of state controlled economic activity for the enhancement of state power gave way to a new concept of economic liberalism that placed greater emphasis on individual choice and initiative, rather than government regulation, as the focus of activity. This philosophy of laissez-faire was buttressed by a new technology that provided the means for producing goods with machines. The ensuing Industrial Revolution not only changed the methods of economic production but also spectacularly increased the interdependence of states.

The forces of science and invention responsible for developing the new machine technology also helped shrink the world through new and better devices for communication and transportation. Steamships, railroads, telegrams, and telephones made closer contacts possible, accelerated trade expansion, and produced a new awareness in the minds of Western peoples of their common societal relationship in a larger community of nations. Thus, in a progressive and dramatic way, patterns of individual and national self-sufficiency began to erode and give way to new and rapidly developing systems of interdependence, which, in turn, produced the rudiments of a new philosophy of internationalism among Western nations.

At the same time, political developments triggered forces of individualism that were destined to have far-reaching effects on the state system. The salient events were the American and French revolutions. By producing, on a national scale, working political systems built upon principles of popular sovereignty and the importance of the individual, they ushered in an era of democratic nationalism. Democracy, as a political doctrine, presumes individuals to be rational creatures who will submit to a higher authority of their own choosing as a means of achieving order in society. Translated to the international level, democratic individualism supports a rational search for cooperative alternatives and agreed rules of state conduct. It has not been a historical accident that modern international law and institutions have been created largely at the initiative of nations enjoying the greatest measure of individual freedom.

## THE PROCESS OF INTERNATIONAL ORGANIZATION

With the onset of the machine age and the appearance of democracy in the Western world, the stage was set for the emergence of modern international organization. Democracy fosters the growth of international organization because both involve, in essence, commitment to a *consensual process*. Just as democracy in a national political setting implies a process of public decision making by consent of the governed, international organization implies a process of international action achieved through the consent of sovereign states.

The process of building international organizations is thoroughly pragmatic; most, if not all, international institutions have been created to achieve specific, practical objectives. The process assumes the multistate system as fact and seeks only to provide an effective means to reconcile the conflicts and contradictions that emerge from this system. As Dag Hammarskjöld, the second Secretary-General of the United Nations, observed,

> The United Nations is not in any respect a superstate, able to act outside the framework of decisions by its member governments. It is an instrument for negotiation among, and to some extent for, governments. It is also an instrument for concerting action by governments in support of the Charter. Thus the United Nations can serve, but not substitute itself for, the efforts of its member governments.[1]

In the absence of supranational government, only voluntary agreement can succeed in mitigating international conflicts, and international organization provides an institutionalized means for eliciting such agreement. It provides the principles, the machinery, and the encouragement, but the catalytic agent needed to bring about tangible results is the will to cooperate. When cooperation is forthcoming, great things can be accomplished by international organs and agencies; when it is lacking, they become mere "debating societies." An international organization like the United Nations is only as useful as its members want it to be.

## THE EMERGENCE OF INTERNATIONAL INSTITUTIONS

International institutions dating from the early nineteenth century represent a creative response to the need for a joint approach to common problems in such fields as commerce, communication, and transportation. The first examples of modern international organization were the river commissions in Europe. The Central Rhine Commission was created in 1804 by an agreement between France and Germany; it provided for extensive regulation of river traffic, the maintenance of navigation facilities, and the hearing and adjudication of complaints for alleged violations of the Commission's rules. The European Danube Commission was created in 1856 to regulate international traffic on the Danube River. Both river commissions function today much the same as they did when they were first established.

The development of international organization was carried a step farther with the creation of international public administrative unions in the latter half of the nineteenth century. In many cases the public unions were developed as a result of demands placed on national governments by the members of private international associations. Such demands resulted in the establishment of the International Telegraphic Union in 1865 and the Universal Postal Union in 1874. The success of these two unions paved the way for the creation of numerous international public agencies in such diverse fields as narcotic drugs, agriculture, health, weights and measures, railroads, patents and copyrights, and tariffs. The prolific growth of technical international agencies reflected the new world of science and technology that was compressing space and overcoming political boundaries. States were willing to collaborate because it was essential to business and commerce and useful in protecting the lives, health, and other interests of their citizens.

As cooperation among states increased during the nineteenth century, a pattern of organization and procedures developed. Each new international agency established institutional machinery that was unique in some respects, yet each possessed certain basic characteristics in common with its contemporaries. The following pattern was typical:

1. Membership was usually limited to sovereign states. Unless regional in scope, such an organization typically held membership open to all states without political conditions.
2. Each organization was created by a multilateral treaty. The treaty served as a constitution that specified the obligations of members, created the institutional structure, and proclaimed the objectives of the organization.
3. A conference or congress was usually established as the basic policymaking organ. The conference included all members of the organization and met infrequently, typically once every five years.
4. Decision making was based on the principle of egalitarianism, with each member having an equal vote and decisions reached by unanimous consent. In time this gave way to majoritarianism, especially in voting on procedural questions.
5. A council or other decision-making organ of an executive nature was often created to implement policies. It usually had a limited membership, and its primary responsibility was to administer the broad policy decisions laid down by the conference.
6. A secretariat was established to carry out the policies of the conference and council and to conduct routine functions of the organization. The secretariat was headed by a secretary-general or

director-general, a professional civil servant with an international reputation.

7. Some organizations, such as the river commissions, exercised judicial or quasi-judicial powers. Some created special international courts to decide controversies arising out of their administrative operations.

8. Many organizations were endowed with a legal personality enabling them to own property, to sue and be sued in specified areas, and, in some cases, to enjoy a measure of diplomatic immunity.

9. Financial support was provided by contributions from member governments, using a formula for contributions based on a principle such as "ability to pay," "benefits derived," "equality," or on a combination of such principles.

10. The competence of the organization was usually limited to a functional or specialized problem area, as set forth in its constitution. Organizations of general competence in political, economic, and social areas were not established until the twentieth century.

11. Decision making was carried on in two ways: by drafting international treaties and submitting them to member governments for ratification, and by adopting resolutions recommending action by member governments. A few organizations possessed administrative and minor policy-making powers.

An important by-product of political cooperation on technical matters was the growth of the belief that political cooperation might be equally productive in securing agreement among states in the more weighty matters of war and peace. Such thinking helped prepare the ground for the calling of two conferences at The Hague, Netherlands, in 1899 and 1907, the first general international conferences concerned with building a world system based on law and order. The first Hague Peace Conference was attended by delegates from only twenty-six nations and was largely European in complexion; the second conference, however, moved toward universality, with representatives from forty-four states, including most of the countries of Latin America. The principle of the sovereign equality of states was accepted at the conferences, with the result that the Hague system helped break the monopoly of the great powers in handling matters of war and peace and economic and colonial rivalry. The Hague system also established precedents that contributed to the later development of international parliamentarianism. Headquarters at The Hague provided international machinery to facilitate the pacific settlement of international disputes. The Hague system in effect proclaimed a new era of cooperation and indicated that a global political organization to keep the peace and promote interstate cooperation was now a possibility. But expectations and realities were not synonomous. The Hague system did not deter the empires from their more aggressive impulses, and World War I appeared to make a mockery of the idealism that underpinned it. Among other developments, the Great War had altered the game of states by demonstrating the incredible forces behind the fusion of popular nationalism and modern technology, and instead of acknowledging failure, the statesmen of the period found new urgency in structuring an international system that could prevent a recurrence of that most tragic experience. Indeed, World War I revealed something more formidable than the Hague system was needed to deal with the issues that compelled states to torment, aggress, and bloody one another.

## THE LEAGUE EXPERIMENT

Americans were living in an age of innocence when the United States declared war against the Central Powers in 1917. Both sides were then close to exhaustion, their idealism and fiery nationalism largely dissipated by nearly three years of savage fighting. In the early years of the war, the carnage in Europe produced a U.S. consensus that involvement should be avoided at all costs. But as the war dragged on, that consensus was eroded by a growing belief that the New World somehow had to save the Old World from extinction. If Europeans of all nationalities could live in peace under the U.S. system of democracy, why not apply these same principles to the international community?

The United States entered World War I fired with a holy mission to "make the world safe for democracy." U.S. idealism was summed up in President Woodrow Wilson's peace program, submitted to Congress on January 8, 1918, in which he enunciated Fourteen Points aimed at rekindling Allied idealism and determination and weakening the enemy's resolve by promising a just peace and a new world of security and democracy. In his fourteenth point Wilson declared that "a general association of nations must be formed under specific covenants for the purpose of affording mutual guarantees of political independence and territorial integrity to great and small powers alike."

The chief architect of the League, unquestionably, was Woodrow Wilson. Without his support the idea of a League of Nations would probably not have gone beyond the point of intellectual germination. While many Allied statesmen thought more cynically of how the victory won at a terrible cost could be exploited for national gain and political advantage, Wilson sought to materialize his dreams of a just world based on law and democracy. Because his program appealed to millions of Europeans emerging from the trauma of war, Allied leaders were forced by public opinion to pay more than lip service to his ideas. Wilson's vision of a just peace was focused on the building of a League of Nations, and Allied statesmen accepted his demands that the League be created as an integral part of the Versailles Peace treaty. Wilson believed that the League Covenant would support and reinforce provisions of the treaty, especially Article 10 of the Covenant, which was aimed at preserving the territorial integrity of signatory states from aggression (see Appendix A). But while Wilson's dream of a new, formally structured international organization was realized with the formation of the League of Nations, the U.S. Senate refused to ratify the Versailles Treaty, thus rejecting American membership in the world body. Decrying what it called an assault on U.S. sovereignty, the Senate opened the way for those nations that had joined the organization to violate its principles, again in the name of state sovereignty. In sum: the League of Nations, although structurally more elegant than the earlier Hague system, was no less at the mercy of the individual states and their exclusive interests.

## STRUCTURE AND FUNCTIONS OF THE LEAGUE

The League Covenant provided for the establishment of three permanent organs—the Assembly, the Council, and the Secretariat. Two semiautonomous bodies were created outside the Covenant framework—the Permanent Court of International Justice and the International Labor Organization. Their objectives were similar to those of the League, however, and the budgets of both were part of the League budget. The Council and Assembly also elected the judges of the World Court. Of greater importance than structures were the obligations that members assumed toward the organization and toward one another. Each state undertook to "respect and preserve as against external aggression the territorial integrity and existing political independence of all Members of the League" (Article 10). Members agreed to submit all of their disputes to arbitration, adjudication, or Council inquiry and in no case to resort to war until three months after a settlement was offered. If any state resorted to war in violation of the Covenant, members would apply diplomatic and economic sanctions and consider the violation an act of war against the world community. Members further agreed to work together to control national armaments and to cooperate in solving social, economic, colonial, humanitarian, and other common problems.

## LEAGUE INNOVATIONS

In its basic design and role, the League was both old and new. It was old in the sense that the system was based firmly on the sovereignty of the member states; no new obligation could be imposed on a member without that member's consent. As with earlier attempts to establish some degree of international order, the powers of the League were limited to recommendations. The Covenant, in keeping with the traditional guidelines of international law, did not seek to outlaw war but only to regulate a state's resort to this ultimate action. A special security role was accorded to the great powers, a role that they had always played (along with warmaking) in the international political system. The League's decisions were made on the basis of mutual agreements that reflected each state's particular interests, a decision-making system as ancient as the state system itself. Progress in technical, social, economic, and humanitarian fields was, as in the past, founded on common treaty actions and on recommendations for national statutory enactments. All in all, there was much in the new League of Nations system that was merely a continuation of the old traditions, customs, institutions, and decision-making procedures of the pre-League world.

But there was also much that was new, some quietly evolutionary in nature, some dramatically revolutionary in scope. The League, for example, was the first attempt to establish a permanent international organization of a general political nature with machinery functioning on a continuing basis. For the first time a community responsibility to use the collective force of the state system against an international lawbreaker was given institutional flesh and bone. Although the League could hardly be compared to a domestic political system with its superior authority, independent police force, and automatic action against lawbreakers, it was, nonetheless, a step toward internationalizing the responsibility of enforcing peace. In the past, military action against an aggressor had been a right of state; under the League Covenant it had been made a collective duty. In point of fact, however, the individual right of states to choose, judge, and act militarily remained elevated over that of the League's internationalized "collective state duties." In its approach to the problem of war, the Covenant made no general statement that war was illegal. The traditional right of states to engage in war was circumscribed in the Covenant by provisions that made it illegal in most situations, mandated delay in some cases, and prescribed community sanctions against the warmaker in others. Acknowledging this weakness in the League machinery, in 1928, the major nations, this time with the United States playing a significant and participant role, entered into a treaty that renounced war as an instrument of national policy. The Kellogg-Briand Pact, however, did little more than create false assurances that peace between the signatories could be maintained by words and solemn promises alone.

## THE LEAGUE IN ACTION

The two major functions of the League, as stated in the Preamble to the Covenant, were "to achieve international peace and security" and "to promote international cooperation." These functions were expected to be complementary. A secure world would encourage state cooperation in many fields, and a common attack on economic, social, and technical problems would help eliminate conflict by developing a sense of community among states. Of the two functions, the security function was regarded as the more pressing.

There was little agreement, however, on how the League should pursue its security objectives. In French eyes the primary responsibility of the League was to enforce the provisions of the peace treaties and guard against a resurgence of German military power. Britain, in contrast, viewed the League as an agency for fostering the peaceful settlement of disputes and protecting the vital interests of the Empire. Each member, in fact, tended to define the League's peace-preserving role largely in terms of its own national interest, so that when the League was confronted with threats to the peace, it often spoke in a cacophony rather than with a single voice.

## THE MANCHURIAN CASE

The League's first test in meeting war initiated by a great power came in 1931, when Japan, claiming Chinese destruction of its railway properties, attacked

Manchuria and occupied the capital city of Mukden. China, charging aggression by Japan, appealed to the League under Article 11 of the Covenant. Attempts by the Council to secure a cease-fire and a Japanese withdrawal were vetoed by Japan, which requested an on-the-spot inquiry into the facts before League action was undertaken.

As fighting spread in Manchuria, the Council appointed a Commission of Inquiry under Lord Lytton's direction to go to Manchuria and ascertain the facts. By the time the commission arrived in the Far East, in April 1932, the Japanese had changed Manchuria into the new independent state of Manchukuo and had begun an attack upon China proper at Shanghai. China, deeply affronted by Council procrastination, asked for transference of the dispute to the Assembly. The Assembly condemned the Japanese aggression and adopted the U.S.-initiated Stimson Doctrine of nonrecognition of new states or governments created illegally by the use of force. A voluminous report from the Lytton Commission condemning Japan's aggressive actions in Manchuria was adopted unanimously by the Assembly but was too late to affect the outcome since the conquest was an accomplished fact. The Assembly's action in fixing blame and condemning aggression, however, led to the withdrawal of Japan from the League of Nations.

The Manchurian case emphasized that situations involving overt aggression could not be successfully handled by using League procedures for peaceful settlement. Japan proved, and the lesson was not lost on potential European aggressors, that the cumbersome machinery and procedures of the League could be used to stifle effective collective action. The League suffered also because great power leadership was lacking on the Council and because the United States, the major power most concerned about Japanese aggressive tendencies, was not a League member. U.S. concern was expressed by sending to Geneva an observer who sat quietly listening to the debates and offered nothing but moral condemnation of Japan's actions. Clearly, this was not enough. The first major test found the League weak and indecisive.

## THE ETHIOPIAN CASE

A second critical test for the League was not long in coming. In the winter of 1934, League-member Italy attacked League-member Ethiopia in violation of their mutual Covenant obligations to respect each other's political and territorial integrity and to adjust their differences peacefully. Italy, following the Japanese example, launched a diplomatic offensive in Geneva, claiming that Ethiopian forces had attacked first. Ethiopia, not recognizing the Italian master plan to build an African empire, sought to negotiate and to use the power of the League facilities for conciliation rather than collective action. Under cover of negotiations, Mussolini mobilized Italian reserves for war, granting minor concessions each time it appeared that the Council would intervene. Outside the main arena of the League, a diplomatic web of intrigue developed as Britain and France, concerned more with the rising power of Nazi Germany, sought to keep Italy as a buffer to Germany. Permitting Mussolini to seize a piece of African territory seemed to the statesmen in London and Paris a small price to pay for the containment of German power. Incredibly, the United States remained aloof and President Franklin Roosevelt refused Emperor Haile Selassie's request that he call on the parties to observe their commitment under the Kellogg-Briand Pact of 1928 not to use war as an instrument of national policy.

By the autumn of 1935 Italy had completed its mobilization, and on October 2, disregarding many League resolutions and Covenant provisions, it launched a full-scale attack on Ethiopia. Ethiopia at once invoked Article 16 of the Covenant, holding that Italy's resort to war before fulfilling Covenant requirements must be considered an act of war against each League member. The Ethiopian delegate at Geneva argued that all members must honor their Covenant obligations by applying immediate economic sanctions against Italy, and he called on the Council to recommend military sanctions as well. Under an interpretation of the Covenant agreed on in 1921, however, neither the Council nor the Assembly was empowered to determine that aggression had been committed; each member state was entitled to decide for itself. The levying of economic and other sanctions was likewise controlled by each state, emphasizing the veto power held by each member under the League system. Of the fifty-four League members polled, fifty indicated that Italy was the aggressor, thus obligating them to apply economic sanctions at once and to undertake military sanctions if these were recommended by the Council.

For the first time in history, economic sanctions were levied against an international lawbreaker, with fifty member states participating. Numerous questions arose immediately concerning what kinds of materials should be embargoed, whether imports from Italy should be banned, what would happen to private long-term contracts, and whether an effort should be made to prevent nonmember states from violating the embargoes. A League consensus soon developed that economic sanctions should include an embargo on arms and a number of essential minerals (but not coal and oil), a ban on loans and other kinds of financial help, a restriction against all imports from Italy and its possessions, and mutual support among League members to minimize their economic injury from the embargoes. By November 1935 the economic sanctions were in effect, and within a period of several months the sanctions began to have a telling effect on Italy's economy. Within two months following the levying of sanctions in November 1935, Italian exports had declined 43 percent over the same month of the previous year, and imports had dropped 47 percent. In three months imports fell to 56 percent of the previous year and imports of strategic items such as iron ore, tin, and raw rubber had almost ceased. Thus, within a short period of time economic sanctions proved effective in significantly reducing Italy's economic activity.

In spite of economic sanctions, the Italian armies swept into Addis Ababa, and on May 5, 1936, Mussolini boasted that victory had been achieved. Eight months after sanctions had been imposed, the Assembly voted to withdraw all sanctions against Italy. Why had the economic sanctions failed? Why were they

terminated after Italy had completed its conquest, thus condoning the aggression? Why had the Council not recommended military sanctions? These and similar questions were aired in Assembly debates following the withdrawal of sanctions. The answers to them, incomplete as they may be, help explain the difficulties of carrying out an effective collective security action against a great power within the international milieu of that day.

Basic to the League's problem was the real-politik British and French objective of building a coalition to balance the power of Hitler's Germany. In much the same way that the East-West split weakened the great power concert on the UN Security Council during the first forty years of United Nations operations, the struggle in the 1930s to contain Nazi power replaced collective security as the prime concern of British and French statesmen.

Other nations contributed to the weak-sanctions syndrome. The United States condemned Italian aggression but avoided any cooperation with the sanctions decision other than placing both belligerents off-limits for arms shipments under the Neutrality Acts. U.S. trade, especially shipments of oil, increased sizably, with most of the increase going to the Italian African colonies, which were supply bases for the military campaign. Many Latin American countries, nearly suffocating under gluts of primary commodity surpluses, agreed in principle to sanctions but failed to apply them in practice. Four League members refused to apply any kinds of sanctions, one refused to reduce imports from Italy, and seven never applied the arms embargo. The bait of stimulating national economies stagnated by the world economic depression proved to be a more powerful motivator of national actions than idealistic considerations of collective security.

Yet, ironically, the gains of appeasement were illusory. Italy joined the Axis powers, the United States was eventually drawn into war against the dictators, and potential aggressors in Europe and the Far East were encouraged by the League's vacillation and irresoluteness. As for the League, the imposition of sanctions by an international organization for the first time in history was a signal achievement; but the Ethiopian case illustrated that it takes more to deter aggression than covenants, organizations, institutions, procedures, and decisions. In the final analysis, effective collective security depends on the states that make up international organizations and the policies they pursue. With Hitler's attack on Poland in September 1939 and the beginning of World War II, the League experiment in collective security ended.

## AN APPRAISAL: THE LEAGUE'S BALANCE SHEET

A review of the League record might be summarized as a study in utility and futility. Conclusions about the degree of success or failure attained by the League must obviously depend on the standard of measurement employed. If it is measured by what the Covenant framers intended, or what millions of people hoped for, or what the principles of the Covenant actually called for, the League fell far short. If, on the other hand, it is measured by what other international organizations in the past had accomplished, or what skeptics and critics predicted for it, or what the nature of the rivalry-ridden state system would permit, the League probably rated high. Any evaluation faces the danger of falling into the old pro-League–anti-League controversy that characterized the great American debate on the subject and kept it on a largely emotional level for twenty years.

## A CAPSULE HISTORY OF THE LEAGUE

Obviously, an appraisal of the League must recognize that its effectiveness varied in response to changes in the international environment. The peace, stability, and relative prosperity of its first decade permitted the League to make a promising start in several directions. Numerous international disputes ware settled peacefully, the complex problem of disarmament was tackled, and the Kellogg-Briand Pact of 1928 attempted to close a gap in the League Covenant by outlawing war as an instrument of national policy. Cooperation in welfare areas was explored, and foundations were laid for extensive programs that flowered during the subsequent decade.

The period from 1930 to 1935 was one of challenge and uncertainty for the League. The economic depression that started with the U.S. stock market crash in 1929 and spread across the world in a chain reaction reduced the League's carefully cultivated channels of cooperation to a shambles. Economic nationalism and ideological rivalries spawned in the depression's wake split the status quo world into hostile camps. Japanese, Italian, and German fascism posed successive political and military challenges with which the organization and its members were unwilling or unable to cope. A new wave of nationalism erased many of the gains of internationalism during the 1920s as League members became increasingly obsessed with their own limited conceptions of national security and with domestic problems. Government after government fought desperately to rescue its people from the brink of economic and financial collapse, social disintegration, and political revolution. As Germany rearmed, disarmament talks collapsed and the world witnessed the start of a new arms race. Economic and monetary conferences failed, and the world depression deepened. The world of the 1930–35 era was not of the League's making, but it was the one in which the League had to function.

The world stage was now set for the League's inevitable collapse. Nine members withdrew between 1935 and 1939, some for political reasons, others claiming financial problems. A desperate reform movement initiated by the Assembly in 1936 sought to stem the tide and refurbish the League's varnished image by updating its security provisions and by divesting the Covenant of all references to the peace treaties of World War I. The Axis powers, bent on aggression, were not interested in returning to the League, nor were other former member states, which continued to pursue independent courses. With the failure of the reform movement, the League became inoperative in the security field, except for voting the Soviet Union's expulsion because of its attack on Finland in 1939, and a majority of the members professed neutrality in the crises growing out of German annexations in Central Europe. When general war came to Europe in September 1939, the League became quiescent, a posture it retained through the six years of World War II. A shell of the League organization lived on at the Geneva headquarters through the war period, only to be ignored by the architects of a new world organization, who did not want their creation tainted by association with the League's failure.

## AN AUTOPSY

Just as friends of the League in its early years tended to exaggerate its novelty and its potential, critics have in retrospect emphasized its failures and undervalued its contributions. All evaluations, however, eventually return to the central question: Why did the League fail to keep peace? Since the maintenance of peace and security was the primary objective of the League, it is only natural that the historical verdict on the League has been delivered mainly in that area and in condemnatory terms.

In fixing blame, some observers have sought to explain the League's demise as a failure of its member states to support the principles of the Covenant. Such a rationalization fails to recognize that in the field of international organization members *are* the organization, that the League had no real existence independent of its component parts. No organization made up of sovereign and independent entities can possibly be stronger than the will and support for common action that exists within the group. Thus, to blame the members rather than the League is a circular argument. One could as well make the point that the pre-World War I balance of power worked well in keeping the peace but eventually failed because the states involved did not play their proper roles within the system.

Procedural difficulties growing out of the League's machinery have also been blamed for its failure. It is quite true that the requirement of unanimity in both Council and Assembly on most substantive questions enabled aggressor nations to veto some countermeasures. Also, because war was not effectively outlawed by the Kellogg-Briand Pact, and the League Covenant permitted members to use the provisions regulating resort to war to block serious collective responses to aggression, the use of official violence was still deemed a sovereign act of state. Covenant provisions dealing with disarmament were so loosely worded that no definite responsibility existed for members to reduce their arms. The sanctions system was weakened in the League's early years by a Covenant interpretation permitting each member to decide for itself the question of invoking an economic embargo. Many other technical deficiencies also contributed to the League's failure, but it would be inaccurate to assign organizational weaknesses a major role in the debacle since most of the weaknesses could be, and many were, overcome by interpretation and by the use of alternative pathways.

Probably the most popular explanation for the League's failure, in the United States at any rate, was U.S. defection. Unquestionably the refusal of the United States to participate in a world organization sponsored by its own president created a psychological and power vacuum that the League never fully overcame. In the security field U.S. policymakers offered only moral condemnation of aggression, while permitting U.S. businessmen to continue extensive trade with the aggressors. The popular myth that U.S. military force combined with that of other League members would have made the League successful against aggressors overlooks the fact that U.S. power during the 1920s and 1930s was only a potentiality awaiting the full mobilization of World War II. Contributions from the small, garrison-bound U.S. Army could hardly have influenced the outcome of any major military action during the League period, and Americans were psychologically unprepared for a major war effort prior to the suprise Japanese attack on the American naval base at Pearl Harbor. The U.S. defection, then, weakened the League but was not the central reason for its ultimate collapse.

Some critics of the League have sought to explain its failure as resulting from its close association with the "unjust" peace treaties of World War I. The League, it is argued, was placed in the impossible position of defending the status quo of the victors against the attempts of the vanquished to undo the peace treaties imposed on them. The League itself recognized this argument officially when it appointed a committee in the late 1930s to propose reforms that would free it from this incubus and, hopefully, regain the support of nations—especially Germany—that had been alienated. Yet the League would still have had to operate within a world based on the peace settlements even if it had in no way been associated with them. Moreover, to the League's credit, the status quo was not tenaciously defended and justice often took precedence over the status quo, as in the case of the Saar, whose people, in a League-supervised plebiscite, voted for reunion with Germany.

Finally, some groups of critics have seen in the League's failure an example of the fundamental inability of a collective security system to keep the peace. One such group rejects the League as an impractical and idealistic concept that was foredoomed to failure because it ignored the power realities of the world. Only by fostering a balance of power through military preparedness and alliances can peace be preserved, so runs the argument of these critics, and the League diverted the status quo great powers from such a course, making disaster inevitable. Another group has also criticized the League's utopianism, but its alternative is a world government with substantial powers acting directly on individuals. Since peace can be adequately preserved within nations by a federal government, this group has argued, the world scene likewise demands a world authority with a near monopoly of power. Compelling as arguments favoring world federalism may be in theory, the world of sovereign states was hardly ready then, nor is it now, to undergo such a radical metamorphosis. Moreover, if the will to resist the aggressors had been broadly based and deeply rooted, if conditions approaching a consensus had existed, the cooperation of member states could probably have done the job as expeditiously as a world federal system. Conversely, the absence of consensus under either system would have had equally deleterious results.

In conclusion, no single theory suffices to explain the League's failure. One might even conclude that bad luck had something to do with it. A combination of many factors, often appearing at inopportune times, made success in the security field a difficult and elusive quarry. Unquestionably the economic nationalism engendered by world depression created an environment uncongenial to international cooperation. And once the world had been irretrievably split between revisionist and status quo powers, the malfunctioning of the League's collective security apparatus became a matter of course.

## ORGANIZING THE UNITED NATIONS

The failure of the major nations to promote collective security following World War I meant the League of Nations would be helpless in meeting the challenges of the aggressive states determined to recast the world in their own image. The rise and popularity of fascism in Italy, Japan, and Germany was paralleled by the Bolshevik Movement in the Soviet Union, and the League, a manifestation of the imperial conditions existing before the Great War, was ill-prepared to confront a new and more bombastic expression of exclusive nationalism on the one side, and an ideological form of popular internationalism on the other. Moreover, having failed to repel aggression in Manchuria and Ethiopia, the League demonstrated it was hardly an obstacle to the ambition of a violence-prone and vengeful Hitlerian Germany. But as much as World War II was attributed to the failure of the League, and it ceased playing a role in that long and costly conflict, the central idea of collective security remained. Furthermore, the alliance that was eventually forged to defeat the Axis Powers and demand their unconditional surrender had assumed an identity as the United Nations. It was for the purpose of sustaining that alliance once the war was over that the United Nations organization was created. Energized again by the United States, and this time with a guarantee that the Americans would play a central role in United Nations operations as well as its establishment, the League of Nations was allowed to fade into history.

### THE ROAD TO SAN FRANCISCO

The UN Charter, which emerged from the San Francisco Conference on International Organization, was a product of extensive wartime planning. The seed of the idea for a new postwar world organization was planted by President Franklin Roosevelt and Prime Minister Winston Churchill in the Atlantic Charter of August 14, 1941. The date is significant because it was four months before the Japanese attack on Pearl Harbor and the entry of the United States into the war. Churchill wanted explicit endorsement of a postwar international political organization included in the joint statement of aspirations. Roosevelt, however, recognized that U.S. public opinion, still basically isolationist, might react unfavorably to such a clear-cut internationalist objective. In final form the

Atlantic Charter called for "fullest collaboration between all nations in the economic field" and hinted of the future "establishment of a wider and permanent system of general security." Even in this watered-down form it carried the clear implication that progress toward a world organization having security and economic responsibilities was a joint objective of the two leading democracies. On January 1, 1942, with the United States now in the war, twenty-six nations subscribed to a Declaration by the United Nations that reaffirmed the principles of the Atlantic Charter. This declaration established the United Nations military alliance, to which twenty-one other nations subsequently adhered, each agreeing to employ its full resources against the Axis, cooperate with one another, and not make a separate peace.

The vague references to international organization in these early war documents were made explicit in the Moscow Declaration on General Security signed in October 1943 by the foreign ministers of the Big Four (Hull, Eden, Molotov, and Foo Ping-sheung). The Moscow Declaration pledged continuance of wartime cooperation "for the organization and maintenance of peace and security" and explicitly recognized "the necessity of establishing at the earliest practicable date a general international organization." It was also the first definite commitment by the Soviet Union to support the establishment of a world organization.

## THE DUMBARTON OAKS CONFERENCE

With the three major powers diligently working on drafts of a constitution for a general international organization, the American State Department suggested to the Russian and British governments that they meet to work out a single set of proposals. After negotiations the three governments agreed that they would participate in the drafting of a proposed charter and that China should participate, although not directly with the Soviet Union, since the latter desired to preserve its position of neutrality in the Far Eastern war. The four governments met at Dumbarton Oaks, an estate in Washington, DC, in two separate phases. Conversations were held among the U.S., Soviet, and British delegations from August 21 to September 28, 1944, and among the U.S., British, and Chinese delegations from September 29 to October 7, 1944. At the conclusion of the conference, the areas of joint agreement were published as the Dumbarton Oaks Proposals.

A surprisingly large area of agreement emerged from the conference in an atmosphere that was cordial and cooperative. Although the Allies were taking the offensive on all fronts by the summer of 1944, victory was not yet assured and all four governments still felt the close attachment of nations seriously threatened by common enemies.

The Dumbarton Oaks Proposals were intended by the four governments to constitute a basis for discussions at the forthcoming general conference on international organization. The following summarizes some of the major areas covered by the Proposals:

*Purposes:* To maintain international peace and security, encourage friendly relations among nations, and achieve international cooperation.

*Nature:* To be based on the sovereign equality of its members, in the tradition of early international organizations and the League of Nations.

*Membership:* To be open to all peace-loving states, on the assumption that all states will eventually become "peace-loving," hence eligible for membership. New members to be admitted through action by the Security Council and the General Assembly.

*Organs:* To have five major organs: a Security Council including all great powers as permanent members, a General Assembly comprising all members, a Secretariat, a Court, an Economic and Social Council, plus such subsidiary agencies as might be found necessary.

*Competence:* To have primary responsibility, through the Security Council, for maintaining peace and security, with all decisions in this crucial area reached only by unanimous agreement of the permanent members.

## THE YALTA CONFERENCE

Several important topics were not settled in the Dumbarton Oaks conversations. No decision was reached on whether a new court should be established to replace the existing Permanent Court of International Justice. The question of how the new world organization would deal with the mandates system and the general problem of colonialism was avoided. More important than the omissions were the disagreements that were to prove too fundamental to settle at any but the highest levels. These disagreements were eventually resolved at the final wartime conference of the Big Three—Roosevelt, Churchill, and Stalin—meeting at Yalta in the Russian Crimea February 4–11, 1945. At Dumbarton Oaks the Soviets had demanded a comprehensive and unlimited veto power in the Security Council; at Yalta Stalin accepted a compromise that the great power veto would not apply to decisions on procedural matters and could not be invoked by a party to a dispute. At Dumbarton Oaks the Soviets had sought the admission of each of the sixteen Soviet republics as original members; at Yalta this demand was reduced to additional seats for two republics, the Ukraine and Byelorussia, and it was accepted by Roosevelt and Churchill. The term *peace-loving*, adopted at Dumbarton Oaks as a criterion of fitness for membership, was defined at Yalta to provide original membership for any state that had declared war on the common enemy by March 1, 1945, a definition that was somewhat anomalous but operational. Agreement was reached on the question of territories then governed under mandates from the League of Nations: a trusteeship system would be established, and the territories placed under it would include existing League mandates, colonial holdings from the enemy states, and other areas voluntarily placed under trusteeship. A Trusteeship Council would be established to oversee the trust system. Finally, at Yalta the Big Three agreed that the five great powers would sponsor a UN Conference on International Organization to meet on April 25, 1945. San Francisco was selected as the site of the conference.

The Yalta Conference helped resolve outstanding issues among the Big Three, but the Publication of the Dumbarton Oaks Proposals raised murmurings among the small powers. The views of some of the small states were carefully set forth, somewhat to the annoyance of the U.S. delegation, at the Inter-American Conference on Problems of Peace and War held at Mexico City in February and March 1945. These states called for universality of membership, a more powerful General Assembly, more emphasis on a world court, a special agency to promote intellectual and moral cooperation, adequate representation for Latin America on the Security Council, and the settlement of regional disputes by regional organizations, such as the Inter-American system, acting in harmony with the new organization. Clearly, the small powers were not going to accept passively great power domination in the framing of the new Chapter or in the power structure of the organization itself.

To some extent, the Dumbarton Oaks Proposals also collided with the views of informed public opinion in the United States. The wartime propaganda for a new world organization had fostered a wave of idealism bordering on utopianism among segments of the public. The Proposals, conversely, were based on the bedrock of diplomatic realism, as were the compromises reached at Yalta. Consequently, many idealists regarded the Proposals as a step backward from the League of Nations Covenant, pointing out that the principle of national sovereignty was proclaimed more strongly than it had been in 1919, that great power domination was more solidly entrenched, and that references to law and justice were vaguer. Idealists who had been thinking in terms of a world federal union were brought harshly back to reality.

The great powers, however, could not wait for the building of a full public consensus; to prolong the process of constructing the framework of the new organization might run the risk of destroying existing areas of agreement as the war drew to a close. Suggestions for revisions and improvements could be explored at San Francisco. In the words of Franklin D. Roosevelt, addressing the Congress on his return from Yalta, "This time we shall not make the mistake of waiting until the end of the war to set up the machinery of peace."

## The UN Conference on International Organization (UNCIO)

The UN Conference on International Organization opened in San Francisco on April 25, 1945, with forty-six nations represented. Four additional delegations representing Argentina, Denmark, Byelorussia, and the Ukraine were subsequently admitted to participate in drafting the Charter. The fifty nations represented, plus Poland, became the original members of the United Nations. The latter did not participate in the San Francisco Conference because the United States and Britain refused to recognize the Soviet-sponsored Provisional Government, but Poland was permitted to sign the completed Charter as an original member. The controversy over Poland's participation hinted strongly of the coming ideological conflicts within the new organization.

The process of writing the UN Charter resembled that of a democratic constituent body drafting a constitution. The Big Five provided the leadership and initiative in most of the decision making. The U.S. delegation was particularly conspicuous in its role as godfather of the new organization. Although diplomatic practice demands that the foreign minister of the host country be chosen as the presiding officer of an international conference, in the interest of great power unity the conference chose the foreign ministers of the four sponsoring governments as cochairmen. France was invited to become a sponsoring government but had declined.

The conference agenda was based on the Dumbarton Oaks Proposals as modified by the Yalta Conference. The conference rules provided for freedom of discussion, voting equality, and substantive decision making by a two-thirds vote of those present and voting. These ground rules theoretically gave the small states an opportunity to undo the work of the great powers, but in fact no substantial change in the great power position was effected. The threat of empty great power chairs at the UN table was incentive enough for the majority to defer to the few. The middle and small powers did sometimes obtain concessions on matters of secondary importance that, in total, added up to a significant modification of the Proposals. Bloc politics were also used at the conference, with the twenty Latin American states and five Arab states particularly active and effective. The Commonwealth states, however, did not join Britain in a voting bloc, preferring to provide leadership to the attempts to modify the great power position.

The completed Charter was signed on June 26, 1945, by the delegates of fifty-one nations. On the same date the delegates also established a Preparatory Commission consisting of representatives of all member states. The Preparatory Commission met in London during November to make arrangements for the first meetings of the new organization's major organs and for the transfer of certain activities from the League of Nations.

## PUBLIC SUPPORT AND RATIFICATION

After signing the UN Charter, the fifty-one signatory states undertook its ratification through their respective constitutional processes. The process of ratification varies from nation to nation, although it generally involves some measure of approval by the national legislative body. Such approval may be automatic in authoritarian nations, and it may even be perfunctory in democratic nations, but in some nations, such as the United States, it may be the crucial test for a treaty. Although the great majority of treaties submitted to the U.S. Senate over the years have received its consent, some of the most important ones, such as the Covenant of the League of Nations and the Statute of the first World Court, have been rejected. Many others have been effectively killed by remaining buried in the Senate Foreign Relations Committee.

On July 28, 1945, the Senate of the United States approved the Charter of the United Nations by a vote of 89 to 2. The lopsided vote surprised no one. Never before in U.S. history had a treaty been studied and debated so extensively both before and after its writing. Never had the Senate participated so directly in the major steps of the treaty process or had bipartisanship operated so successfully in removing a major treaty from politics. Never before, or since, had the State Department been so successful in stimulating organized group support for a major policy objective. In a very real sense the U.S. decision to participate in the United Nations was in accord with the democratic principle expounded in the Preamble of the Charter: "We the peoples of the United Nations . . . have resolved to combine our efforts . . . and do hereby establish an international organization to be known as the United Nations."

On August 8, 1945, President Truman ratified the Charter of the United Nations and the Statute of the International Court of Justice, which was annexed to it. The United Nations came into being on October 24, 1945, which has since been established as United Nations Day. At that time the Soviet Union deposited its ratification and the Secretary of State, James F. Byrnes, signed the Protocol of Deposit of Ratifications affirming that a majority of the fifty-one original signers (twenty-nine nations), including all five great powers, had deposited ratifications with the United States. All fifty-one signers of the Charter had ratified it by December 27, 1945. On January 10, 1946, with the opening of the First General Assembly, the United Nations began its work.

# NOTES

1. *New York Times Magazine,* September 15, 1957, p. 21.

# SELECTED READINGS

Armstrong, James D. *From Versailles to Maastricht: International Organization in the Twentieth Century.* New York: St. Martin's Press, 1996.

Bennett, A. Leroy. *Historical Dictionary of the United Nations.* Lanham, MD: Scarecrow Press, 1995.

Boulding, Elise. *Building a Global Civic Culture: Education for an Interdependent World.* New York: Teachers College Press, 1988.

Bretton, Henry L. *International Relations in the Nuclear Age.* Albany: State University of New York Press, 1986.

Burton, M. E. *The Assembly of the League of Nations.* Chicago: University of Chicago Press, 1943.

Churchill, Winston. *The Gathering Storm.* Boston: Houghton Mifflin, 1948.

Diehl, Paul F., ed. *The Politics of International Organizations.* Chicago: Dorsey Press, 1989.

Eagleton, Clyde. *International Government.* New York: Ronald Press, 1948.

Goodrich, L. M. "From League of Nations to United Nations." *International Organization,* February 1947, pp. 3–21.

Gorbachev, Mikhail. *Perestroika—New Thinking for Our Country and the World.* New York: Harper & Row, 1987.

Hilderbrand, Robert C. *Dumbarton Oaks: The Origins of the United Nations and the Search for Postwar Security.* Chapel Hill: University of North Carolina Press, 1990.

Hoopes, Townsend and Douglas Brinkley. *FDR and the Creation of the UN.* New Haven, CT: Yale University Press, 1997.

Hull, Cordell. *The Memoirs of Cordell Hull,* 2 vols. New York: Macmillan, 1948.

Iriye, Akira. *Cultural Internationalism and World Order.* Baltimore: The Johns Hopkins Press, 1997.

Kegley, Charles W., Jr., and Eugene R. Wittkopf. *World Politics: Trend and Transformation.* New York: St. Martin's Press, 1985.

Mangone, Gerard J. *A Short History of International Organization.* New York: McGraw-Hill, 1954.

Perlmutter, Amos. *Making the World Safe for Democracy: A Century of Wilsonianism and Its Totalitarian Challengers.* Chapel Hill, NC: The University of North Carolina Press, 1997.

Potter, Pitman B. *An Introduction to the Study of International Organization.* New York: Appleton-Century-Crofts, 1948.

Reinsch, Paul S. *Public International Unions.* Boston: Ginn, 1911.

*Report to the President on the Results of the San Francisco Conference.* Department of State Publication 2349, Conference Series 71. Washington, DC: U.S. Government Printing Office, 1945.

Reuter, Paul. *International Institutions.* New York: Rinehart, 1958.

Russell, Ruth B., and Jeanette E. Muther. *A History of the United Nations Charter: The Role of the United States, 1940–45.* Washington, DC: Brookings Institution, 1958.

Smith, S. S. *The Manchurian Crisis: A Tragedy in International Relations.* New York: Columbia University Press, 1948.

Walters, F. P. *A History of the League of Nations.* London: Oxford University Press, 1952.

Zolo, Danilo. *Cosmopolis: Prospects for World Government.* Cambridge: Polity Press, 1997.

# 2

## LEGAL FRAMEWORK, INSTITUTIONAL STRUCTURES, AND FINANCIAL REALITIES

### THE CONSTITUTIONAL STRUCTURE

Formally written and ratified as a multilateral treaty, the UN Charter became a de facto constitution with the establishment of the UN organization. Like most constitution makers, the framers had sought to create a document that would facilitate the development of an administrative substructure, allocate responsibilities, grant and circumscribe powers, demarcate jurisdictions—in short, do the jobs that are typical of a national constitution. Also common to every constitution is the enunciation, usually in hortatory language, of the principles and objectives underlying the organization. The framers fulfilled this responsibility more than adequately.

The real test of any constitution comes in the transition from principle to practice. Meeting this test is an ongoing process. Words constantly take on new meanings as different people interpret them and as changing situations and fresh problems call for solutions not in keeping with older interpretations. This is the process of constitution building; it exists because constitution makers can never fully anticipate the changes that will occur. Although the Charter is a lengthy and verbose document, its framers, whether by intent or accident, wrote much flexibility into it, as the more than fifty-year history of the United Nations indicates.

#### CONSTITUTIONAL EVOLUTION

Constitutional development for an international organization like the United Nations may closely parallel that of a national constitutional system. A comparison can be a useful enterprise if the analogy is not carried too far. Over the years the U.S. Constitution, for example, has developed largely through the process of executive, legislative, and judicial interpretation. Similarly, the Charter of the United Nations has evolved through interpretation by its members and by its major organs, particularly the General Assembly, the Security Council, the Secretariat, and the International Court of Justice. Custom and usage, where mandates are lacking or ambiguous, have been significant forces in shaping both national constitutional systems and the UN system. In both instances, when the constitutional text has been too confining, ways have been found to bypass or ignore the strict letter of the law. Formal amendments have been adopted only infrequently in U.S. constitutional history and for the United Nations as well, since there have been only three formal Charter amendments in nearly a half century. Two amendments to the Charter were proposed by the Eighteenth General Assembly in 1963, one enlarging the Security Council from eleven to fifteen and changing its voting majority from seven to nine, the other increasing the size of the Economic and Social Council from eighteen to twenty-seven. Both amendments were ratified and took effect in 1965. A third amendment, which took effect in 1973, enlarged the Economic and Social Council to fifty-four members. For a proposed amendment to take effect it must be approved by a two-thirds vote of the General Assembly and ratified by two-thirds of the members, including all permanent members of the Security Council. Each great power thus retains a veto over all *formal* changes to the Charter, but not over changes brought about by interpretation.

Constitutional development in the United Nations has been largely a political process. As a multilateral treaty, the Charter was a product of extensive international negotiations, with the precise meaning and application of many words and phrases in the Charter masked by the need for agreement at the time of negotiations. Since 1945, difficulties in translations, the vagaries of power politics, conflicts of national interests, the admission of new members, ideological rivalries, and the lack of a final judge have all contributed to the continuing problems of interpretation and development.

Like the U.S. Constitution, the Charter does not establish a definitive constitutional umpire. Who, then, shall decide what the Charter means when questions of jurisdiction, powers, competence, and procedures arise? Should the International Court of Justice as the principal judicial organ appoint itself "guardian of the UN constitutional system" and undertake a role similar to that assumed by the U.S. Supreme Court in the historic case of *Marbury* v. *Madison*? Should that guardian be the General Assembly, in which all members are represented and on which the Charter has bestowed the power to "discuss any questions or any matters within the scope of the present Charter or relating to the powers and functions of any organs provided for in the present Charter"? Should each major organ determine the nature and extent of its own jurisdiction and procedures? Should unanimity prevail, as it did traditionally with multilateral treaties, with constitutional issues resolved through agreement of all signatory governments? Or should each member interpret the Charter for itself?

The question of establishing a constitutional umpire was never resolved at San Francisco, nor was it specifically considered. The result has been that all of the preceding methods, and many others, have been used to deal with constitutional issues in the UN system. Decisions on constitutional questions have included interpretations made by presiding officers, by majority and extramajority votes in major organs and other bodies, by decisions of the Secretary-General and other Secretariat officials, by advisory opinions of the Court, and by decisions of member governments made outside the UN framework but based on interpretations of Charter provisions. Thus, most interpretations of the Charter leading to development of the UN system have been made *politically* by political organs or individuals rather than *juridically* by the International Court or some other legal body.

## CHARTER PRINCIPLES

The analogy between national constitutions and the constitutional system of the United Nations can also be extended to the realm of principles. Underlying the U.S. governmental system, for example, are basic principles that provide the philosophical underpinning and moral justification for the constitutional structure. Most of these principles are also found, explicitly or implicitly, in the UN system, supplemented by others that are more germane to an international body. Those that can be observed or implied from the operations of the United Nations include democracy, self-determination, parliamentarianism, majoritarianism, the rule of law and justice, horizontal federalism (regionalism), and the separation of powers. In addition, principles set forth in Article 2 of the UN Charter, which members accept by ratifying the Charter, include (1) the sovereign equality of all members, (2) good faith fulfillment of Charter obligations, (3) peaceful settlement of international disputes, (4) nonuse of force or the threat of force for aggressive purposes, (5) support for UN enforcement action, and (6) nonintervention by the United Nations in matters that are essentially within a state's domestic jurisdiction. Together these principles constitute basic rules of international conduct that all member states are ostensibly committed to observe. These rules are a projection into the international arena of purposes and principles already having national validity. In this sense the Charter takes a first step in the direction of an organized international community independent of the organs set up for international decision making. Even in the most democratic of states, these ideals are never perfectly realized, and certainly a great gulf exists between theory and practice in the United Nations. Nevertheless, they can provide guidelines for action and they are frequently invoked in General Assembly debates. Although these and other principles will be discussed throughout the book as they relate to the operations of the United Nations, two of them—domestic jurisdiction and regionalism—will be examined now in their constitutional context.

### Domestic Jurisdiction

In federal states such as Canada, Mexico, Germany, and the United States, a written constitution provides for a division of powers between a central government and provincial or "state" subdivisions. In a somewhat related manner, Article 2 of the Charter recognizes a dual authority when it proclaims that nothing in the Charter should be interpreted to "authorize the United Nations to inter-vene in matters which are essentially within the domestic jurisdiction of any state." The application of enforcement measures to maintain peace and security under Chapter VII is specifically excluded from the limiting clause. The domestic jurisdiction clause resembles the Tenth Amendment of the U.S. Constitution in that it makes explicit a division of powers and responsibilities between two levels of political organization and provides a limitation on the higher level to safeguard the lower from unwarranted intrusions. In effect, this Charter principle suggests that only *international* problems and issues are proper subjects for UN inquiry and action and that *national* questions remain within the complete jurisdiction of member states (unless, of course, the state consents to UN involvement). The Charter leaves open to controversy, however, the questions of who shall determine what is national and what is international, how that determination should be made, and what is meant by "intervene."

Controversy within the organization has also centered on the nature and intent of the domestic jurisdiction clause, with differences over whether it provides a *legal* limitation or merely proclaims a *political* principle. In practice, the latter has generally been accepted, with decisions made by UN organs in keeping with the political realities of the situation. Problems within the Republic of South Africa, for example, were debated extensively, and resolutions condemning the apartheid system and maltreatment of Africans were adopted despite repeated invocation by South Africa of the domestic jurisdiction clause. Most UN members took the position that South African apartheid practices constituted a threat to international peace and security and were therefore subject to UN jurisdiction. Persistence in the condemnation of apartheid practices by the United Nations eventually paid off when the practice was abandoned in 1991, and in 1994, Nelson Mandela was elected the South African president. Some states—France and Portugal, for example—invoked the domestic jurisdiction clause for many years in refusing to submit reports to the United Nations on conditions in their colonies, holding that their overseas possessions were part of their "metropolitan territory" and therefore matters of purely local concern. Granting independence to these colonies eventually solved that controversial problem.

Over the years, domestic jurisdiction has become increasingly ineffective as a deterrent to UN action. UN majorities have grown more and more inclined to define UN competence so broadly that virtually nothing is left to domestic jurisdiction. The arms inspection requirements, no-fly zones, and sanctions imposed on Iraq after the 1991 Gulf War, and again in 1994 and 1997–98, constituted a particularly intrusive invasion of Iraqi jurisdiction. Iraqi efforts to force an end to the UN-directed inspections caused the UN Secretary General to personally seek reassurance from Iraq's head of state that his country's full compliance with UN resolutions governing inspections would be honored. Seeking to head-off an American air attack in 1998, Baghdad accepted the terms offered by the UN Secretary-General. Nonetheless, by October, and after repeated violations of UN resolutions, and especially interference with the work of UNSCOM inspectors, what to do with Iraq burdened Security Council deliberations. Although military action was initially forestalled, in December 1998 the United States and Great Britain, acting alone, but assured they were complying with previous UN resolutions, launched raids against Iraqi military targets. The contest engaging Iraq and the United Nations entered still another phase in 1999, and no end to the crisis was forecast so long as Saddam Hussein remained at the head of the Baghdad government. UN involvement in internal conflict with the consent of the parties, as in Cambodia and El Salvador, has further blurred the line between domestic and international concerns. Demands for UN intervention to protect human rights, as in Croatia and Bosnia, or in the Serbian province of Kosovo in 1999, would also subordinate sovereignty to broader world order values. On the other hand, UN resolutions are generally ineffective when addressed to matters believed by nonconsenting states to be within their domestic jurisdiction except in cases where the organization is willing and able to enforce its mandates. Whether or not observed by UN majorities, the domestic jurisdiction clause reflects a world of sovereign states not yet ready to yield power to the United Nations over their internal affairs.

## Regionalism

Interstate cooperation, a halfway house in the U.S. constitutional system between the central government and the state units, has its international counterpart in the form of regionalism. The U.S. Constitution refers to this middle-level organization as "interstate relations"; in its politically activist form it is known as "horizontal federalism," connoting an extensive system of teamwork among states to solve common problems through uniform laws, joint actions, and common agencies.

International regionalism is a recognition by participating governments that not all problems are either national or global in scope. Some international problems may be confined to a geographic region; their solutions may require action by only a limited number of states, or psychological, technical, or administrative difficulties may limit the ability of international agencies to function beyond the region. International regionalism exists, therefore, because groups of states have found it to be the most appropriate means of solving some common problems.

The framers of the UN Charter, although theoretically committed to universalism, recognized the political investment in regional organizations and accepted the feasibility of decentralizing some international operations concerned with security, political action, and economic and social welfare. The framers compromised on the issue by providing that regional organizations would serve as adjuncts of the UN system subject to a measure of control and direction by it. All such arrangements and activities must also be consistent with the purposes and principles of the Charter, although no apparent means exist for enforcing this rule. Under these provisions a host of regional political, security, economic, social, and technical organizations have been established over the past fifty years in all areas of the globe.

Collective self-defense, expressly authorized by Article 51 of the Charter, has served as a basis for the construction of numerous regional alliances. The Charter further provides that regional organizations should contribute to security by making "every effort to achieve pacific settlement of local disputes . . . before referring them to the Security Council" (Article 52). The framers assumed that some disputes might be better resolved without inviting the whole world in, and this in turn would reduce the load on the United Nations. In practice both assumptions have to some extent been borne out, although a number of disputes have been referred to the United Nations as well as a regional organization. But with the volume of United Nations work at unprecedented levels following the end of the Cold War, and with the funds and capabilities needed to address world issues inadequate to meet the many challenges, in 1998, the UN Secretary-General called for greater acceptance of the "co-deployment principle" wherein states with regional organizations capable of addressing an area problem would be encouraged to play a primary role in establishing and enforcing order. Thus, regional organizations, or regional alliances (e.g., the CIS, OAU, and NATO) have assumed enforcement responsibilities generally found under Chapter VII of the Charter, while UN peacekeeping has become more a Chapter VI or peaceful resolution of disputes activity. Although no clear criteria have emerged, either in theory or in practice, there are indications a formula may yet be arrived at that would determine which level is most appropriate in dealing with threats or breaches of the peace. Co-deployment, however, in no way alters the Charter's stated purpose that the Security Council could decide to consider a dispute already handled in a regional forum.

Still another role for regional organizations involves political, economic, and social cooperation. In this regard, the concept of regionalism has sometimes been applied to limited-membership organizations such as the Organization for Economic Cooperation and Development (OECD). Although OECD is primarily Europe-based, it nevertheless includes members from other geographic regions. Thus Japan, the United States, and Canada are members of the organization. Collaboration rather than competition has characterized the relationship between the global organization and such groups as the Organization for Cooperation and Development, the Organization of American States, The Association of Southeast Asian Nations, and the European Union. Economic regionalism, in particular, has flowered as states have tried to solve their trade, balance of payments, economic development, and technical assistance problems through arrangements with neighboring or interdependent states.

Regionalism is offered as either an alternative or a complement to universalism. Debates involving the respective advantages of regionalism and universalism have usually focused on the following points.

## ARGUMENTS FOR REGIONALISM

1. Regionalism permits a sharper focus on local problems.
2. Regionalism involves fewer states than universalism and offers greater propensities for consensus because of common traditions; similar political, economic, and social systems; the regional nature of the problem to be solved.
3. Regionalism tends to produce greater support from the peoples of the participating states than universalism because of a closer identification of common interests.
4. Regionalism permits a more appropriate handling of administrative, technical, and functional problems than universalism because the organization's machinery is better matched with the nature and scope of its operations.
5. Regionalism is a necessary precursor to effective global cooperation because it lays the groundwork for a broader consensus.

## ARGUMENTS FOR UNIVERSALISM

1. Universalism is a more appropriate means for preserving peace than regionalism since peace is indivisible; a war anywhere in the world threatens to engulf all.
2. Universalism encourages a more effective pooling of resources to attack economic and social problems; a pooling of African regional resources, for example, would result only in a sharing of African poverty.
3. Universalism encourages a consensus of mankind based on universal principles; regionalism encourages conflict between rival blocs and economic groups.
4. Universalism recognizes that disease, hunger, illiteracy, and poverty are common to all regions of the world; a common attack carried on by a single organization, therefore, will avoid duplication and make the most effective use of available resources.
5. Universalism as embodied in the United Nations already exercises broader powers over a greater variety of subjects than any regional organization; hence, to speak of regionalism as a necessary precursor to universalism ignores contemporary facts.

Although the arguments on both sides have intrinsic merit, such debates tend to be detached from reality because the operational dichotomy between regionalism and universalism is largely a false one. Both types of international organization exist today; both serve useful purposes, and their functions are usually—if not always—complementary. For example, in electing members of the various organs of the United Nations, including the Secretary-General, regional factors are generally considered relevant in reaching electoral decisions.

In subsequent chapters the functioning of regional organizations will be discussed at appropriate points for comparison with the United Nations and its specialized agencies.

# INSTRUMENTS OF POLITICAL DECISION MAKING

UN operations revolve around the functions of six principal organs: the General Assembly, the Security Council, the Economic and Social Council, the Trusteeship Council, the Secretariat, and the International Court of Justice. The organization and processes of each of these major organs will be discussed in this chapter.

In addition to the six principal organs, eighteen specialized agencies and other autonomous organizations within the overall framework of the United Nations operate in various technical, economic, and social fields (see Figure 2-1). Added to the specialized agencies and related bodies are a number of major programs and organizations that have been created by the United Nations to deal with specific problem areas. These bodies have their own directors and governing boards but are not legally autonomous because they are subject to the direction of the General Assembly. The major ones are listed in Figure 2-1. Of these programs and organizations, the United Nations Relief and Works Agency for Palestine refugees in the Near East reports directly to the General Assembly, whereas the rest report to the General Assembly through the Economic and Social Council. Peacekeeping missions, which are created and disbanded as necessary, report to the Security Council. Finally, the UN system includes regional commissions, functional commissions, and a variety of committees that report to the Economic and Social Council and, indirectly, to the General Assembly.

The vast array of agencies and programs subject to supervision by the major organs of the United Nations, or at least reporting to them, testifies to the global nature of the UN *system,* as distinct from the political decision-making apparatus headquarters in New York. The latter is merely the tip of a huge organizational and bureaucratic iceberg with its operations carried on in one way or another in almost every country in the world. Isolated, indeed, is the country or society that has not been touched by one of the many UN programs. Hundreds of millions of individuals have benefited directly, and all human beings stand to gain from UN activities directed toward such objectives as reducing conflict, controlling pollution, and improving health. Specific actions and programs, problems and issues, that emerge from many of these agencies making up the UN system will be covered in later chapters.

## THE GENERAL ASSEMBLY

Central to the sprawling UN organization, resembling somewhat the British prototype Parliament at Westminster in its unifying role, the General Assembly

FIGURE 2-1    The UN System

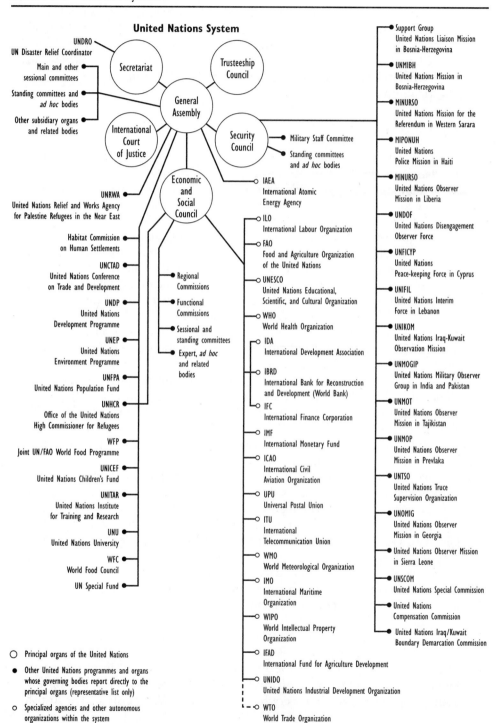

**United Nations System**

UNDRO
UN Disaster Relief Coordinator

Main and other
sessional committees

Standing committees and
*ad hoc* bodies

Other subsidiary organs
and related bodies

Secretariat

Trusteeship
Council

General
Assembly

International
Court
of Justice

Security
Council

Military Staff Committee

Standing committees
and *ad hoc* bodies

Economic
and
Social
Council

UNRWA
United Nations Relief and Works Agency
for Palestine Refugees in the Near East

Habitat Commission
on Human Settlements

UNCTAD
United Nations Conference
on Trade and Development

UNDP
United Nations
Development Programme

UNEP
United Nations
Environment Programme

UNFPA
United Nations Population Fund

UNHCR
Office of the United Nations
High Commissioner for Refugees

WFP
Joint UN/FAO World Food Programme

UNICEF
United Nations Children's Fund

UNITAR
United Nations Institute
for Training and Research

UNU
United Nations University

WFC
World Food Council

UN Special Fund

Regional
Commissions

Functional
Commissions

Sessional and
standing committees

Expert, *ad hoc*
and related
bodies

IAEA
International Atomic
Energy Agency

ILO
International Labour Organization

FAO
Food and Agriculture Organization
of the United Nations

UNESCO
United Nations Educational,
Scientific, and Cultural Organization

WHO
World Health Organization

IDA
International Development Association

IBRD
International Bank for Reconstruction
and Development (World Bank)

IFC
International Finance Corporation

IMF
International Monetary Fund

ICAO
International Civil
Aviation Organization

UPU
Universal Postal Union

ITU
International
Telecommunication Union

WMO
World Meteorological Organization

IMO
International Maritime
Organization

WIPO
World Intellectual Property
Organization

IFAD
International Fund for Agriculture Development

UNIDO
United Nations Industrial Development Organization

WTO
World Trade Organization

Support Group
United Nations Liaison Mission
in Bosnia-Herzegovina

UNMIBH
United Nations Mission in
Bosnia-Herzegovina

MINURSO
United Nations Mission for the
Referendum in Western Sarara

MIPONUH
United Nations
Police Mission in Haiti

MINURSO
United Nations Observer
Mission in Liberia

UNDOF
United Nations Disengagement
Observer Force

UNFICYP
United Nations
Peace-keeping Force in Cyprus

UNIFIL
United Nations Interim
Force in Lebanon

UNIKOM
United Nations Iraq-Kuwait
Observation Mission

UNMOGIP
United Nations Military Observer
Group in India and Pakistan

UNMOT
United Nations Observer
Mission in Tajikistan

UNMOP
United Nations Observer
Mission in Prevlaka

UNTSO
United Nations Truce
Supervision Organization

UNOMIG
United Nations Observer
Mission in Georgia

United Nations Observer Mission
in Sierra Leone

UNSCOM
United Nations Special Commission

United Nations
Compensation Commission

United Nations Iraq/Kuwait
Boundary Demarcation Commission

○  Principal organs of the United Nations

●  Other United Nations programmes and organs
   whose governing bodies report directly to the
   principal organs (representative list only)

○  Specialized agencies and other autonomous
   organizations within the system

functions as the main focus for most UN activities. "Global Parliament," "Town Meeting of the World," "Sun of the UN Solar System"—these and other catchphrases are used to sum up, perhaps somewhat inaccurately, the General Assembly's widely diffused activities and diverse roles. Unlike the Security Council, which pays homage to the elitism of great power politics, the Assembly effuses the democratic ethos of *egalitarianism, parliamentarianism,* and *majoritarianism.*

## Equality of Members

The Assembly's *egalitarian* nature should be obvious to even the casual UN visitor: The Assembly is the only one of the six principal UN organs in which all member states are equally represented, with a maximum of ten delegates and one vote for each member (see Table 2-1). Efforts by some of the great powers to push for a change to a weighted voting system have never been taken seriously by the small and middle powers. The traditional equality of all states, large and small, under international law and as participants in international conferences provides the legitimacy for retaining equal voting. The political defensiveness of the new states, some of which formed their Assembly delegations at the same time that they established their first governments, safeguards the principle. This equality permeates the work of the Assembly, including that carried on by its seven main committees, on each of which all members are represented. The seven main committees of the Assembly are the First (Political and Security); Special Political (originally an ad hoc committee, this committee has remained numberless although it is now a permanent committee); Second (Economic and Financial); Third (Social, Humanitarian, and Cultural); Fourth (Trusteeship); Fifth (Administrative and Budgetary); and Sixth (Legal). Consideration of agenda items usually begins in one of the main committees, which meet and carry on business as committees of the whole. Most matters receive their most thorough airing and consideration at this stage, since the press of time permits the Assembly in plenary session to explore extensively only the most politically explosive issues. Increasingly, as in legislative bodies like the U.S. Congress, a committee's report has been accepted in plenary session with only perfunctory debate. This trend has had the effect of creating eight assemblies with a full complement of members in each, a development that has helped keep the business of the Assembly moving forward but has also added to the general confusion of Assembly decision making. The General Assembly also utilizes various procedural committees and subsidiary bodies in carrying out its decision-making functions (see Figure 2-1).

## Parliamentary Role

The parliamentary nature of the Assembly becomes evident in observing its modus operandi. It may be, as an astute British observer has noted, that the Assembly's operations are "a far cry from anything at Westminster." The British

TABLE 2-1   **Membership of Principal UN Organs in 1999**

GENERAL ASSEMBLY—ALL UN MEMBERS

SECURITY COUNCIL

Permanent members: China, France, the Russian Federation, the United Kingdom, the United States.

Nonpermanent members (two-year term expires 31 December of the year indicated): Argentina (2000), Bahrain (1999), Brazil (1999), Canada (2000), Gabon (1999), Gambia (1999), Malaysia (2000), Namibia (2000), Netherlands (2000), Slovenia (1999).

ECONOMIC AND SOCIAL COUNCIL

Fifty-four members (three-year term expires 31 December of the year indicated): Algeria (2000), Belarus (2000), Belgium (2000), Bolivia (2001), Brazil (2000), Bulgaria (2001), Canada (2001), Cape Verde (1999), Chile (1999), China (2001), Colombia (2000), Comoros (2000), Cuba (1999), Czech Republic (2001), Democratic Republic of the Congo (2001), Denmark (2001), Djibouti (1999), El Salvador (1999), France (1999), Gambia (1999), Germany (1999), Guinea-Bissau (2001), Honduras (2001), Iceland (1999), India (2000), Indonesia (2001), Italy (2000), Japan (1999), Latvia (1999), Lesotho (2000), Mauritius (2000), Mexico (1999), Morocco (2001), Mozamique (1999), New Zealand (2000), Norway (2001), Oman (2000), Pakistan (2000), Poland (2000), Republic of Korea (1999), Russian Federation (2001), Rwanda (2001), Saint Lucia (2000), Saudi Arabia (2001), Sierre Leone (2000), Spain (1999), Sri Lanka (1999), Syria (2001), Turkey (1999), United Kingdom (2001), United States (2000), Venezuela (2001), Vietnam (2000), Zambia (1999).

TRUSTEESHIP COUNCIL

The Trusteeship Council suspended operation on November 1, 1994, with the independence of Palau, the last remaining United Nations Trust Territory, on October 1, 1994. By resolution adopted on May 25, 1994, the Council amended its rules of procedure to drop the obligation to meet annually and agreed to meet as occasion required—by its decision or the decision of its President, or at the request of a majority of its members or the General Assembly or the Security Council.

INTERNATIONAL COURT OF JUSTICE

Fifteen judges, elected individually (nine-year term ends 5 February of the year indicated): Mohammed Bedjaoui of Algeria (2006), Carl-August Fleischauer of Germany (2003), Gilbert Guillaume of France (2000), Geza Herczegh of Hungary (2003), Rosalyn Higgins of the United Kingdom (2000), Shi Jiuyong of China (2003), Pieter H. Kooijmans of the Netherlands (2006), Abdul G. Koroma of Sierre Leone (2003), Shigeru Oda of Japan (2003), Gonzalo Parra-Aranguren of Venezuela (2000), Raymond Ranjeva of Madagascar (2000), Jose Francisco Rezek of Brazil (2006), Stephen M. Schwebel of the United States (2006), Christopher G. Weeramantry of Sri Lanka (2000), Vladlen S. Vereshchetin of the Russian Federation (2006).

SOURCE: Adapted from United Nations Department of Public Information, 1999.

system's focus on a legislative program, its emphasis on responsibility, its party-whip discipline, and its organized majority and opposition are missing or hardly discernible in the Assembly Hall. Yet the agenda is adopted, debate proceeds, votes are taken, and decisions are made. Our British observer described the process in this picturesque language: "Like a herd of grazing cattle, that moves as it chews, head down, the Assembly gets through its day (or more often its morning) without any particular drive, yet not without a certain vaguely diffused sense of purpose." [1]

In a search for analogies, the Assembly's parliamentary qualities may be found to resemble the continental European parliaments, with their multiparty coalitions, ideological rivalries, and shifting centers of power, more closely than the orderly, compact British model. Or a watchful observer might note some similarities between the Assembly's operations and those of the U.S. Congress. Both are more often than not caught up in clashes of parochial interests and must attempt to harmonize regional, class, creed, and racial conflicts. Both must grapple with procedural rules that often complicate rather than expedite the process of decision making. The U.S. federal system produces an attachment to states' rights in somewhat the same manner that the sovereign states of the world with their attachments to national interests produce a loose, untidy, somewhat anarchic General Assembly. Yet a parliament's main role is concerned with freedom of debate, in which issues can be discussed, decisions made, budgets approved, taxes levied, and administrative operations supervised. The General Assembly resembles all national parliaments in these functions. Although it does not possess a direct lawmaking authority, its competence to discuss and debate extends to *any* problem of the world or of the organization itself that a majority of members regard as proper for Assembly consideration. The only exceptions to this broad power are the domestic jurisdiction clause (Article 2) and the limitation on the Assembly concerning matters under consideration by the Security Council (Article 12).

## Majority Rule

The Assembly's *majoritarian* approach to decision making is an improvement over that of the Assembly of the League, which required unanimity for most actions. Article 18 of the Charter provides that decisions on "important questions" be made by a two-thirds majority of members present and voting. All other questions require only a simple majority. "Important questions" include those mentioned in Article 18 (peace and security recommendations; elections to the three UN councils; admission, suspension, and expulsion of members; trusteeship and budgetary questions and those that the Assembly decides by a majority vote are to be considered "important").

Consensus, not overpowering majority votes, is the objective of Assembly politics. Consensus demands compromise, and compromises in the Assembly are sought through negotiations, pressures, demands, debates, promises, and other techniques of parliamentary diplomacy that, in art and form, closely resemble the "politics" that keeps the wheels turning in a national legislative body. Groups of delegates meet, plan strategy, and negotiate with other groups before decisions are made. On economic and related issues, when the issue comes to a vote, decision making is dominated by the Group of 77 (G-77), which consists of over 130 Third World countries that caucus to determine a common approach to issues that arise before the General Assembly. In recent years, however, the Assembly has decided more issues by consensus than by voting.

## Formal Organization

Regular sessions of the General Assembly are held each year, beginning usually on the third Tuesday in September. At the beginning of each session, the Assembly established a target date for adjournment, usually mid-December. A three-week period of "general debate" opens each Assembly session, with most delegations taking the opportunity to express their views on the full range of issues on the global agenda. Heads of state or government often participate. A special session may be convoked after the Assembly adjourns its regular annual session, and cannot be requested by a member state, the Security Council, or the General Assembly. The majority of special sessions have been convened by the General Assembly, given the necessary majority support of the members. When the need for Assembly action beyond the regular December adjournment date is anticipated in advance, the Assembly will recess its session and reconvene as later needed. Table 2-2 identifies the twenty Special Sessions convened from 1947 to June 1998.

In addition to General Assembly Special sessions, the General Assembly can also meet in Emergency Special Sessions. Dealing with more contentious issues of critical importance, Emergency Sessions are convoked under the 1950 Uniting For Peace Resolution. Such sessions can be convened within twenty-four hours. Between 1956 and 1997 ten emergency sessions were held. Table 2-3 lists the General Assembly Emergency Special Sessions through April 1997.

The first job facing a new Assembly each year is to elect a President and seventeen Vice Presidents who serve for one year. It has become traditional to select as President a leading international statesman from an important small- or middle-power state, usually from the Third World. The vice presidencies are allocated to the five great powers and to geographic areas of the world to ensure their representative character and a fair apportionment of prestige. In 1963, when the number of Vice Presidents was increased from thirteen to seventeen, a formula was adopted to provide for the election of seven Vice Presidents from Asia and Africa, one from Eastern Europe, three from Latin America, two from Western Europe and "other states" (Canada, Australia, and New Zealand), and one from each of the five permanent members of the Security Council. These figures total eighteen because the region from which the President is elected receives one less than the formula specifies. The President, the Vice Presidents, and the chairmen of the seven standing committees constitute

TABLE 2-2   **General Assembly Special Sessions**

| SPECIAL SESSION | DATE OF SESSION | REQUESTED OR CONVENED BY |
|---|---|---|
| 1 Palestine | 28 April–15 May 1947 | Great Britain |
| 2 Palestine | 16 April–14 May 1948 | Security Council |
| 3 Tunisia | 21–15 August 1961 | 38 member states |
| 4 UN Finances | 14 May–27 June 1963 | General Assembly |
| 5 South West Africa (Namibia) | 21 April–13 June 1967 | General Assembly |
| 6 Raw Materials and Development | 9 April–2 May 1974 | Algeria |
| 7 Development and International Economic Cooperation | 1–16 September 1975 | General Assembly |
| 8 Financing the UN Interim Force in Lebanon | 20–21 April 1978 | General Assembly |
| 9 Namibia | 24 April–3 May 1978 | General Assembly |
| 10 Disarmament | 23 May–1 July 1978 | General Assembly |
| 11 New International Economic Order | 25 August–15 September 1980 | General Assembly |
| 12 Disarmament | 7 June–10 July 1982 | General Assembly |
| 13 Africa | 27 May–1 June 1986 | General Assembly |
| 14 Namibia | 17–20 September 1986 | General Assembly |
| 15 Disarmament | 7 June–10 July 1988 | General Assembly |
| 16 Apartheid | 12–14 December 1989 | General Assembly |
| 17 Drug Abuse | 20–23 February 1990 | General Assembly |
| 18 International Economic Cooperation | 23–27 April 1990 | General Assembly |
| 19 Earth Summit+5 | 23–27 June 1997 | General Assembly |
| 20 World Drug Problem | 8–10 June 1998 | General Assembly |

SOURCE: United Nations Department of Public Information, 1998.

the General Committee, which functions as a steering committee for each session. (see Table 2-4).

Although his formal powers are limited, the President may accomplish much through his personal influence and political adeptness. Qualities desirable to abet the role of presiding officer of the Assembly include a "refusal to be bored, a memory for faces, a capacity to slough off private and national partialities, a sense of humor coupled with a concern for the dignity of his office, a ready grasp of procedural technicalities, a proper sense of pace, and a quick feeling for the sense of the meeting." [2] Seated beside the President at all Assembly

TABLE 2-3   **General Assembly Emergency Special Sessions**

| EMERGENCY SPECIAL SESSION | TOPIC | DATE OF SESSION | CONVENED BY |
|---|---|---|---|
| 1 | Middle East | 1–10 November 1956 | Security Council |
| 2 | Hungary | 4–10 November 1956 | Security Council |
| 3 | Middle East | 8–21 August 1958 | Security Council |
| 4 | Congo Question | 17–19 September 1960 | Security Council |
| 5 | Middle East | 17 June–18 September 1967 | USSR |
| 6 | Afghanistan | 10–14 January 1980 | Security Council |
| 7 | Palestine | 22–29 July 1980 | |
| | | 20–28 April 1982 | Senegal (Chairman, Palestine Rights Committee) |
| | | 25–26 June 1982 | |
| | | 16–19 August 1982 | |
| | | 24 September 1982 | |
| 8 | Namibia | 3–14 September 1981 | Zimbabwe |
| 9 | Occupied Arab Territories | 29 January–5 February 1982 | Security Council |
| 10 | Occupied East Jerusalem and the rest of the occupied Palestinian territory | 24–25 April 1997 | Qatar |

SOURCE: UN Department of Public Information, 1998.

sessions is the Executive Assistant to the Secretary-General, who, as Secretary of the General Assembly, functions as parliamentarian and adviser to the President. Although the President's formal powers to control or influence the direction of debate and action are weak and tend to resemble those of the President of the U.S. Senate or the Speaker in the House of Commons, the disarray of the Assembly demands a strong yet tactful guidance. The international reputations of the Presidents have helped each of them to weather many verbal storms and to develop the office into a respectable source of Assembly power and influence.

### Assembly Functions

Against a backdrop of politics and diplomacy, the General Assembly carries out its various roles and diverse activities, some assigned by the Charter and others assumed by the Assembly.

One frequently indulged activity is exhortation by means of resolutions aimed at member states, nonmembers, great powers, the Security Council, other

TABLE 2-4    UN Presidents of the General Assembly since the 1st Session

| SESSION | YEAR | NAME | COUNTRY |
|---|---|---|---|
| First | 1946 | Mr. Paul-Henri Spaak | Belgium |
| First special | 1947 | Mr. Oswaldo Aranha | Brazil |
| Second | 1947 | Mr. Oswaldo Aranha | Brazil |
| Second special | 1948 | Mr. Jose Arce | Argentina |
| Third | 1948 | Mr. H. V. Evatt | Australia |
| Fourth | 1949 | Mr. Carlos P. Romulo | Philippines |
| Fifth | 1950 | Mr. Nasrollah Entezam | Iran |
| Sixth | 1951 | Mr. Luis Padilla Nervo | Mexico |
| Seventh | 1952 | Mr. Lester B. Pearson | Canada |
| Eighth | 1953 | Mrs. Vijaya Lakshmi Pandit | India |
| Ninth | 1954 | Mr. Eelco N. van Kleffens | Netherlands |
| Tenth | 1955 | Mr. José Maza | Chile |
| First emergency special | 1956 | Mr. Rudecindo Ortega | Chile |
| Second emergency special | 1956 | Mr. Rudecindo Ortega | Chile |
| Eleventh | 1956 | Prince Wan Waithayakon | Thailand |
| Twelfth | 1957 | Sir Leslie Munro | New Zealand |
| Third emergency special | 1958 | Sir Leslie Munro | New Zealand |
| Thirteenth | 1958 | Mr. Charles Malik | Lebanon |
| Fourteenth | 1959 | Mr. Victor Andrés Belaúnde | Peru |
| Fourth emergency special | 1960 | Mr. Victor Andrés Belaúnde | Peru |
| Fifteenth | 1960 | Mr. Frederick H. Boland | Ireland |
| Third special | 1961 | Mr. Frederick H. Boland | Ireland |
| Sixteenth | 1961 | Mr. Mongi Slim | Tunisia |
| Seventeenth | 1962 | Sir Muhammad Zafrulla Khan | Pakistan |
| Fourth special | 1963 | Sir Muhammad Zafrulla Khan | Pakistan |
| Eighteenth | 1963 | Mr. Carlos Sosa Rodríguez | Venezuela |
| Nineteenth | 1964 | Mr. Alex Quaison-Sackey | Ghana |
| Twentieth | 1965 | Mr. Amintore Fanfani | Italy |
| Twenty-first | 1966 | Mr. Abdul Rahman Pazhwak | Afghanistan |
| Fifth special | 1967 | Mr. Abdul Rahman Pazhwak | Afghanistan |
| Fifth emergency special | 1967 | Mr. Abdul Rahman Pazhwak | Afghanistan |
| Twenty-second | 1967 | Mr. Corneliu Manescu | Romania |
| Twenty-third | 1968 | Mr. Emilio Arenales Catalán | Guatemala |
| Twenty-fourth | 1969 | Miss Angie E. Brooks | Liberia |
| Twenty-fifth | 1970 | Mr. Edvard Hambro | Norway |
| Twenty-sixth | 1971 | Mr. Adam Malik | Indonesia |
| Twenty-seventh | 1972 | Mr. Stanislaw Trepczynski | Poland |

TABLE 2-4 (*continued*)

| SESSION | YEAR | NAME | COUNTRY |
|---|---|---|---|
| Twenty-eighth | 1973 | Mr. Leopoldo Benítes | Ecuador |
| Sixth special | 1974 | Mr. Leopoldo Benítes | Ecuador |
| Twenty-ninth | 1974 | Mr. Abdelaziz Bouteflika | Algeria |
| Seventh special | 1975 | Mr. Abdelaziz Bouteflika | Algeria |
| Thirtieth | 1975 | Mr. Gaston Thorn | Luxembourg |
| Thirty-first | 1976 | Mr. H. S. Amerasinghe | Sri Lanka |
| Thirty-second | 1977 | Mr. Lazar Mojsov | Yugoslavia |
| Eighth special | 1978 | Mr. Lazar Mojsov | Yugoslavia |
| Ninth special | 1978 | Mr. Lazar Mojsov | Yugoslavia |
| Tenth special | 1978 | Mr. Lazar Mojsov | Yugoslavia |
| Thirty-third | 1978 | Mr. Indalecio Liévano | Colombia |
| Thirty-fourth | 1979 | Mr. Salim A. Salim | United Republic of Tanzania |
| Sixth emergency special | 1980 | Mr. Salim A. Salim | United Republic of Tanzania |
| Seventh emergency special | 1980 | Mr. Salim A. Salim | United Republic of Tanzania |
| Eleventh special | | Mr. Salim A. Salim | United Republic of Tanzania |
| Thirty-fifth | 1980 | Mr. Rüdiger von Wechmar | Federal Republic of Germany |
| Eighth emergency special | 1981 | Mr. Rüdiger von Wechmar | Federal Republic of Germany |
| Thirty-sixth | 1981 | Mr. Ismat T. Kittani | Iraq |
| Seventh emergency special | 1982 | Mr. Ismat T. Kittani | Iraq |
| Ninth emergency special | 1982 | Mr. Ismat T. Kittani | Iraq |
| Twelfth special | 1982 | Mr. Ismat T. Kittani | Iraq |
| Thirty-seventh | 1982 | Mr. Imre Hollai | Hungary |
| Thirty-eighth | 1983 | Mr. Jorge E. Illueca | Panama |
| Thirty-ninth | 1984 | Mr. Paul J. F. Lusaka | Zambia |
| Fortieth | 1985 | Mr. Jaime de Piniés | Spain |
| Thirteenth special | 1986 | Mr. Jaime de Piniés | Spain |
| Forty-first | 1986 | Mr. Humayun Rasheed Choudhury | Bangladesh |
| Fourteenth special | 1986 | Mr. Humayun Rasheed Choudhury | Bangladesh |
| Forty-second | 1987 | Mr. Peter Florin | German Democratic Republic |

(*continued*)

TABLE 2-4    (*continued*)

| SESSION | YEAR | NAME | COUNTRY |
| --- | --- | --- | --- |
| Fifteenth special | 1988 | Mr. Peter Florin | German Democratic Republic |
| Forty-third | 1988 | Mr. Dante M. Caputo | Argentina |
| Forty-fourth | 1989 | Mr. Joseph Nanven Garba | Nigeria |
| Sixteenth special | 1989 | Mr. Joseph Nanven Garba | Nigeria |
| Seventeenth special | 1990 | Mr. Joseph Nanven Garba | Nigeria |
| Eighteenth special | 1990 | Mr. Joseph Nanven Garba | Nigeria |
| Forty-fifth | 1990 | Mr. Guido de Marco | Malta |
| Forty-sixth | 1991 | Mr. Samir S. Shihabi | Saudi Arabia |
| Forty-seventh | 1992 | Mr. Stoyan Ganev | Bulgaria |
| Forty-eighth | 1993 | Mr. Samuel R. Insanally | Guyana |
| Forty-ninth | 1994 | Mr. Amara Essy | Côte d'Ivoire |
| Fiftieth | 1995 | Prof. Diogo Freitas do Amaral | Portugal |
| Fifty-first | 1996 | Mr. Razali Ismail | Malaysia |
| Tenth emergency special | 1997 | Mr. Razali Ismail | Malaysia |
| Ninteenth special | 1997 | Mr. Razali Ismail | Malaysia |
| Fifty-second | 1997 | Mr. Hennadiy Udovenko | Ukraine |
| Twentieth special | 1998 | Mr. Hennadiy Udovenko | Ukraine |
| Fifty-third | 1998 | Mr. Didier Opertti | Uruguay |

SOURCE: The United Nations Department of Public Information.

major organs, and even the General Assembly itself. Sometimes referred to as "manifestos against sin," these resolutions permit the Assembly to carry out what it supporters regard as the role of guardian of Charter principles and the conscience of mankind and what its detractors write off as sheer hypocrisy. Through such resolutions the Assembly has, *inter alia,* called on the permanent members of the Security Council to use the veto with restraint, the great powers to cease their war propaganda, all states to accept the maxim of peaceful coexistence, and disputants to settle their controversies peacefully.

The Assembly's quasi-legislative function, carried on through the adoption of resolutions, declarations, and conventions, goes beyond exhortation in seeking to develop and codify international law. In this role the Assembly most closely approximates the lawmaking activities of a national legislature. Assembly resolutions governing internal matters, such as procedural rules, control of funds and property, and staff regulations, have the force of law. Resolutions directed toward state conduct outside the organization are not binding of themselves, but the rules thus enunciated may have legal force if they are regarded as statements of customary international law or authoritative interpretations of the UN Charter. The Assembly may also engage in lawmaking through the drafting of multilateral treaties. Conventions adopted by the Assembly, such as the Genocide Convention (outlawing acts aimed at the destruction of a national, ethnic, racial, or religious group) or the Law of the Sea Treaty, become operative as law among the consenting parties after they have been ratified by the required number of states. The Assembly's International Law Commission is regularly engaged in the codification of rules of international law to be presented to members in treaty form. The numerous Assembly-approved treaties now in force illustrate the quasi-legislative function. When members are motivated to act, the Assembly can truly function like a world Parliament.

In its investigative role the Assembly complements its quasi-legislative functions. This role can be illustrated by frequent resolutions asking the Secretariat, or a special committee, to study a problem and report to the next General Assembly. As in a national legislature, facts are often helpful before the Assembly acts. In the settlement of disputes, investigation is an essential prelude to a determination of the issues involved and the working out of a just solution.

Although the Security Council has primary responsibility for international peace and security, the Assembly also has a role. That role was more important in earlier decades when the Security Council was often deadlocked by the veto. Commonly the Assembly has pursued peaceful settlement through discussion and recommendation, tendering good offices, mediation, conciliation, commissions of inquiry, and appointment of individual mediators. Since 1950 the Uniting for Peace Resolution has specifically authorized the Assembly to make recommendations for economic or military sanctions when the Security Council is unable to deal with a breach of the peace or act of aggression. Assembly creation of the UN Emergency Force (UNEF) in the Middle East (1956), when the Security Council was unable to act, illustrates this backup role in a very threatening situation.

The Assembly's budgetary function resembles that of a national legislature's traditional "power of the purse." All UN programs and all activities of subsidiary UN bodies come under a measure of surveillance and control since all must be supported financially. Budget decisions have on occasion become the tail that has wagged the dog of substantive actions in the United Nations, as happened during the financial crisis of the 1960s, when lack of funds forced the discontinuance of the UN Congo operation. In the 1980s and 1990s, the huge backlog of unpaid dues owed by the United States, along with smaller amounts owed by many other members, have put serious constraints on UN activities. In 1996, Secretary General Boutros Boutros-Ghali called on the General Assembly to deal with what he described as "a grave set of problems" facing the United Nations due to financial limitations, in part a product of the UN's heavier and more complex workload, and in part caused by the failure of members to pay their assessments. His successor, Kofi Annan, has sustained the effort but despite severe austerity measures that resulted in a drastic reduction in UN staff, the financial status of the organization did not improve. At the end of the century, attention was riveted on the U.S. Congress, which refused to grant the president authority to meet U.S. obligations if the world body continued to pursue family planning and population control programs.

Closely related to the Assembly's budgetary function is its supervisory role. It is to the Assembly that the Security Council, the Economic and Social Council, and the Trusteeship Council submit annual and special reports on their respective operations. Although the Security Council is not a subsidiary organ, the Charter empowers the Assembly to make recommendations to it and to call peace-threatening situations to its attention. The Economic and Social Council and the Trusteeship Council, although designated as "principal organs," are actually subsidiary and operate "under the authority of the General Assembly" (Articles 60 and 85). Decisions on economic, social, trusteeship, and related matters are made by the Assembly on recommendations from the two councils. The Secretariat is also primarily concerned with serving the Assembly and in turn is controlled by it. Decisions about the organization, work, personnel, and budget of the Secretariat are regularly made by the Assembly. Annual reports on selected activities and on the work of each organ and agency of the United Nations enable the Assembly to receive, to criticize, and, hence, to supervise the entire UN operation.

The Assembly exercises a twofold elective function. One phase involves the admission of new members into the United Nations; the other relates to the selection of the elective members of other organs. The election to membership takes place following a recommendation by the Security Council, a prerequisite affirmed by the International Court of Justice in an advisory opinion in 1950. Prospective members file an application with the Secretary-General, who transmits it to the Security Council. Before 1955 memberships were often delayed in the Security Council, sometimes for years, but once the Council has made its recommendations, Assembly action to admit has been swift. The Assembly's second elective function helps shape the outlook and decision-making capabilities of other major UN organs. Some elections are conducted jointly with the Security Council, as in selecting the judges of the International Court and appointing the Secretary-General. Others occur through Assembly action alone, as in the election of the ten nonpermanent members of the Security Council and all members of the Economic and Social Council. Annual elections to fill vacancies in various organs are preceded by extensive group consultation, which ordinarily, but not always, has prevented sharp wrangling in the Assembly over the more prestigious seats, especially those in the Security Council.

Finally, as previously noted, the Assembly exercises a constituent function in proposing formal amendments to the Charter which take effect when ratified by two-thirds of the member states, including all the permanent members of the Security Council. Amendments to enlarge the Security Council and Economic and Social Council are the only ones that have been added to the Charter.

### Assembly Decision Making

Changes in global political and economic systems have also meant significant changes in General Assembly decision making. In 1990, the forty-fifth year of

Assembly operation, for example, President Guido de Marco of Malta described it as "The first Assembly session in the post-cold-war era." The forty-fifth, he noted, was "marked by a rising tide of consensus decisions . . . with fewer meetings, fewer debates, fewer votes." This "calm," however, proved short-lived as crises erupted in several regions of the world, particularly in the former Yugoslavia, where Bosnia-Herzegovina was the scene of European conflict not experienced since the end of World War II. So too the African continent exploded in a series of civil wars that demanded the attention of the United Nations, and of which Rwanda proved to be the most tragic. Involvement in Somalia and Haiti were also of major significance. But it was the Gulf War, precipitated by the Iraqi invasion and conquest of Kuwait, that necessitated an aggressive UN response as well as a sustained policing operation that kept the lights burning at UN headquarters.

Nonetheless, the passing of the Cold War brought promise as well new problems. The democratization of Eastern Europe was begun, although tempered by the realization that integrating these countries into the world of free political expression and an open, market economy would be painful. Perhaps even more affected by revolutionary changes in the global economy were the Third World countries that found the competition for international assistance far more difficult in a world liberated from the command economies of the communist bloc. But for the first time in the history of the United Nations, the East European states no longer voted as a bloc, and the unification of the two Germanys meant the German state would be represented by one united voice. The post-Cold War period also saw the further integration of Europe as the European Community became the European Union, and in 1998 the EU agreed to establish its European Monetary Union. With the world passing through a period of dynamic change, and with enhanced cooperation a reality, the General Assembly was nevertheless far from the proverbial quiet refuge, nor could it ignore the forces and conditions that made for greater conflict. Examples of the latter were found in the General Assembly Emergency Special Session on Jerusalem and the West Bank territory in April 1997, as well as the world's reaction to the nuclear arms race between India and Pakistan in 1998.

Through the extended UN system, however, the General Assembly devotes principal attention and resources to the promotion of the development of human skills and potentials. The system's annual disbursements, including loans and grants, amounted to more than $10 billion in 1998. Examples of these activities were found in the UN Development Program (UNDP), which worked in close cooperation with over 170 member states and other UN agencies. UNDP designs and implements projects for agriculture, industry, education, and the environment. Another was the Earth Summit, the UN Conference on Environment and Development that was called by the General Assembly in 1992, and resulted in treaties on biodiversity and climate change. All attending countries adopted the "Agenda 21" blueprint promoting sustainable development, a commitment that was reaffirmed at the General Assembly's Special Session (Earth Summit+5) in June 1997. Coupled with its responsibilities in maintaining peace and security, promoting democracy and human rights, preventing nuclear proliferation, providing humanitarian assistance, strengthening international law, promoting women's rights, and scores of other issues, the General Assembly, along with the other UN organs, is a major element in the management of an increasingly more complex world.

*Proposals to Streamline the Assembly Procedures*

Despite a relatively greater harmony in recent sessions, Assembly delegations still agree as they have for years that the Assembly must somehow find the means for streamlining its procedures in order to expedite the work of the organization. The growth in membership has added a degree of urgency as the Assembly often becomes mired in procedural quicksand of its own making. Little agreement, however, has existed on the means of achieving the desired efficiency. Suggestions and recommendations over the years have included the following:

1. Reduce the time wasted during each session. Better scheduling of speakers and the relegation of those not prepared to speak at their appointed time to the bottom of the list have been suggested. Joint statements by a number of delegations with the same viewpoint and written statements instead of oral statements have been encouraged.
2. Expedite the "general debate" with which each Assembly session opens. Often speeches made by heads of government and foreign ministers during general debate are repeated by heads of delegations later in regular debate.
3. Speed up committee work, and organize it better. Committees should start their work early in each session and should coordinate their activities through the steering committee. The creation of more subcommittees might help free the main committees from the detailed work of drafting resolutions.
4. Accelerate the debate and voting processes in the Assembly and its main committees.

Many proposals to speed the deliberative process have been considered, such as placing time limits on general debate. Ultimately, the orderliness and dispatch with which a body like the Assembly conducts its procedural work depend on the proficiency of the officers and committee chairmen and on the willingness of heads of delegations to exercise self-restraint in the interest of moving along.

## THE SECURITY COUNCIL

In both the planning and writing of the UN Charter, the primacy of the Security Council was generally accepted. Nothing seemed more certain to the framers than the logic of its role: The primary responsibility of the United Nations is to keep the peace; keeping the peace is mainly a function of the great powers; ergo, the Security Council is the logical focus for this responsibility. For more than forty years, however, the Security Council did not fully measure up to the framers' hopes. Then, beginning in the late 1980s, a new spirit of great power cooperation permitted unified action to deal with crises in Afghanistan, Iran and Iraq, Cambodia, and other troubled areas. When Iraq invaded Kuwait in 1990, the Council was able to act with unanimity in condemning Iraq's aggression against Kuwait and authorizing collective military action to expel the aggressor.*

## Council Composition

The Security Council has fifteen members. Five countries—China, France, the United Kingdom, the Soviet Union, and the United States—are designated by the Charter as *permanent* members. With the demise of the Soviet Union, its permanent seat was filled by Russia. This sparked discussion of possibly adding other states, such as Japan, Germany, or India, as permanent members, but no serious attempt at Charter amendment followed. Ten (originally six) *nonpermanent* or *elected* members are chosen by the General Assembly for staggered two-year terms, five elected each year (see Table 2-1). On retirement from the Council, elected members are not immediately eligible to reelection. This provision was inserted because under the League the elective seats on the Council were controlled by the middle powers in most elections to the near exclusion of the small powers. Although all members of the United Nations other than the five permanent members are eligible for election, the Charter, as a result of pressures from the middle powers at San Francisco, stipulates that in the selection process due regard be "specially paid, in the first instance to the contribution of members of the United Nations to the maintenance of international peace and security and to the other purposes of the organization, and also to equitable geographical distribution" (Article 23). These two considerations obviously can be contradictory since states with strategic locations, economic resources, or manpower reserves are not evenly distributed about the globe.

During the early years of the United Nations, the Western powers held a majority on the Council. By virtue of a "gentlemen's agreement" in 1946, two elective Council seats were assigned to Latin America and one each to Western Europe, Eastern Europe, the Middle East, and the British Commonwealth, an arrangement that normally assured the West a majority on the Council.

In the late 1950s, pressed by demands for Asian and African representation, the United States succeeded in shifting the seat allocated for Eastern Europe to Asia. This shift proved to be only a temporary tranquilizer, however, as

---

* For further analysis of the Persian Gulf crisis see Chapter 5.

African, Eastern European, and Asian states clamored for greater representation for their areas. An amendment to the Charter, proposed in 1963 and adopted in 1965 after sufficient ratifications, emerged out of these pressures for greater representation. It provided for enlarging the Council from eleven to fifteen by increasing the elective members from six to ten, and it changed the majority needed for a decision from seven to nine. By Assembly resolution, the ten nonpermanent seats are now allotted as follows: five seats to Asia and Africa, one to Eastern Europe, two to Latin America, and two to Western European and other states. The keen competition in Assembly elections and the demands for "area representation" demonstrate that a seat at the Council table is one of the most coveted honors and crucial power positions available to members of the United Nations.

*Council Functions*

The Security Council's two main functions under the Charter are to settle disputes peacefully (Chapter VI) and to meet threats to peace with the concerted action of the organization (Chapter VII). Whenever possible the Council has handled situations under Chapter VI of the Charter as simple disputes rather than considering collective action under Chapter VII, even when both sides to the dispute have been engaged in extensive military actions. The Korean War (1950–53) and the Persian Gulf hostilities (1990–91) were two exceptions to this general rule of trying to avoid a UN military action.

Techniques employed by the Council in the application of either Chapter VI or Chapter VII vary from case to case, depending in each situation on the political considerations involved, the degree of unity on the Council, the extent of the danger to peace, and the relationship of the dispute and the disputants to Council members, particularly the permanent members. Typical techniques used by the Council in dealing with peace and security matters include deliberation, investigation, recommendation, exhortation, mediation, conciliation, interposition of a peacekeeping presence, and in extreme cases economic or military sanctions. These are discussed at greater length in Chapters 5 and 6. In Article 26 of the Charter, the Council is assigned the additional security responsibility of developing plans "for the establishment of a system for the regulation of armaments" (see Chapter 7).

Other Council functions are elective or supervisory in nature and were designed by the framers to permit the great powers to maintain some control over organizational matters. These functions are shared with the General Assembly. They include the election of a Secretary-General, the admission of new members, the election of the judges of the International Court of Justice, the deprivation and restoration of members' rights and privileges, and the expulsion of a member. In addition, the Council supervised a trusteeship system that was left in suspension after the last trust territory, Palau, was declared independent in October 1994.

## Council Procedures

Each Council member, permanent and elective, appoints a representative and an alternate to the Council. Unlike other United Nations organs, the Security Council is in permanent session and meets whenever a need exists. Under its rules of procedure, intervals between meetings should not exceed fourteen days. The President of the Council may convene it at any time on his own initiative, when requested to do so by a member of the Council, or, under circumstances prescribed in the Charter, when requested to do so by the General Assembly or the Secretary-General.

Under the Security Council's rules of procedure, its presidency rotates each month among its members. This provision, while safeguarding the Council from continuing domination or abuse by a presiding officer who is out of sympathy with its objectives, gives the organ a discontinuity that has not always been consistent with its high responsibilities. The brief two-year terms of the ten nonpermanent members add to the impromptu quality of the Council. Moreover, debates in the Council lack spontaneity and continuity because important statements must often be studied thoroughly before they are answered and because comments are often reserved until home governments can be contacted for instructions.

Although debates are carried on in the Security Council under rules of procedure established by the Council, the Charter provides that any UN member may be invited to participate in any discussion if its interests are affected by the question under debate. Also, any state, whether a UN member or not, must be invited to participate in the discussion if it is a party to a dispute being considered by the Council. In neither case does the invited state have a vote.

When debate on a measure has been completed, a vote is taken, with each member of the Council having one vote. Decisions are of two types: *procedural* and *substantive*. The Charter provides that all decisions on procedural questions be made by an affirmative vote of any nine members; thus permanent and elected members have equal voting power on procedural questions. On all other, or substantive, matters, the Charter specifies that decisions shall be made "by an affirmative vote of nine members including the concurring votes of the permanent members," except that when a member of the Council is a party to a dispute, it must abstain from voting. Although the words of the Charter clearly denote that substantive decisions require a "yes" vote of all five permanent members, in a practice based on numerous precedents, a permanent member's abstention from voting is not regarded as constituting a veto of the pending measure. To kill or "veto" a matter of substance that is supported by at least nine members of the Council, a permanent member must cast a negative vote.

The Charter does not specify how the Security Council, in the event of disagreement, decides whether a question is procedural or nonprocedural. At San Francisco the great powers agreed that the issue would be treated as a nonprocedural question and therefore subject to the veto. This meant that a permanent member could gain the right to veto any matter simply by voting against the preliminary motion to declare it procedural. In practice, this so-called double veto has not been attempted often enough to be a serious problem.

## THE ECONOMIC AND SOCIAL COUNCIL

Although afforded the status of principal organ by the Charter, the Economic and Social Council (ECOSOC) functions under the authority of the General Assembly. In many respects its activities resemble those of the main Assembly committees, and it has occasionally been accused of duplicating or competing with the work of the Second (Economic and Financial) and Third (Social) committees of the Assembly.

Originally established with eighteen members, ECOSOC was enlarged to twenty-seven in 1965 and to fifty-four in 1973. Both enlargements were implemented through Charter amendments that were the product of growing demands by the Third World bloc for a greater voice in determining economic and social policy. Members are elected by a two-thirds vote in the Assembly for staggered three-year terms. Although all UN members are equally eligible for election, in practice members representing First World countries of industrial importance have been consistently elected over the years. This practice contributed to the expansion of the Council in 1965 and again in 1973 to meet the demands of the developing countries for a more influential role in economic and social policy making. A president is elected each year from one of the small or middle powers represented on the Council. Sessions are held twice annually, the first in New York in the spring, the second in Geneva in the summer. Decisions are made by a simple majority of those present and voting.

### ECOSOC Functions

ECOSOC's mandate is very broad, and it has the power only to recommend. In all things it must defer to the General Assembly, which means that ECOSOC can scarcely be the final word on anything of importance. It can hold meetings, do research, produce studies and reports, draft multilateral conventions for submission to the Assembly, and make recommendations. It is authorized to coordinate the activities of the UN specialized agencies but is given no power to make this mandate effective. Despite a persisting gap between aspirations and reality, ECOSOC has carried on some useful if usually unspectacular work.

Recent ECOSOC agendas have included such diverse topics as housing, narcotic drug control, water resources, desertification, world population, trade, UNICEF, industrial development, literacy, refugees, the environment, science and technology, the status of women, the needs of children, and the problems of the disabled. Always on the agenda are two subjects of perennial concern and overriding importance: human rights and economic development. In these and other areas, ECOSOC has from time to time generated proposals that have affected state practice.

In the development of programs, studies usually come first. Through studies and reports ECOSOC has done much to overcome the dearth of statistical and other kinds of data on economic and social conditions in the world. In performing this function ECOSOC operates as a research agency and clearinghouse, attempting to coordinate the work of numerous committees, commissions, study groups, and private or nongovernmental organizations. The information thus gathered is vital to coming to grips with world problems, and no other agency in history has had such a broad research mandate.

Often studies and preliminary recommendations originate in ECOSOC's functional commissions or regional economic commissions. The functional commissions established by ECOSOC are Human Rights (with it subcommission on the Prevention of Discrimination and Protection of Minorities), Narcotic Drugs, Population, Statistical, Status of Women, and a Social Commission. Regional economic (or economic and social) commissions have been set up for Africa (ECA), Asia and the Pacific (ESCAP), Western Asia (ESCWA), Europe (ECE), and Latin America and the Caribbean (ECLAC).

### Decision-Making Role

Based on its deliberations and extensive studies, ECOSOC makes appraisals of its findings and, by Charter directive, may make recommendations "with respect to any such matters to the General Assembly, to the Members of the United Nations, and to the Specialized Agencies concerned" (Article 62). Sometimes ECOSOC resolutions embody a statement of general principles and require only a favorable vote in the General Assembly for implementation, such as the proclamation of the Universal Declaration of Human Rights of 1948. They may also take the form of conventions requiring affirmative action by the Assembly and subsequent ratification by a stipulated number of member states.

Drafting conventions provides a quasi-legislative role for ECOSOC because the Council is often involved in the early phases of consensus building for many UN-sponsored treaties. This resembles the national lawmaking function in that the resulting convention binds consenting states, often limits governments in their relationship to their own citizens, and makes an addition to international law. While ECOSOC cannot make law, it plays a role in helping members of the United Nations develop law. This is a much more difficult process than the mere proclaiming of principles, and some nations that voted for the Universal Declaration of Human Rights in 1948 have failed to ratify the international covenants that would make these rights enforceable.

One such covenant, the Convention on the Political Rights of Women, serves as an example of what can be accomplished in the form of international legislation when states find ground for agreement. Consensus, in that case, was not easily developed. Women's groups from many countries, banding together as an international pressure group, demanded and obtained from ECOSOC a Commission on the Status of Women. They followed this up by promoting the idea of feminine political equality in the Commission, ECOSOC, General Assembly, and national ratification stages. The Convention guarantees women the right to vote and to hold public office equally with men in all adhering states.

### Coordination Responsibilities

ECOSOC is supposed to exercise a coordination function relating to the specialized agencies of the United Nations and several autonomous organizations. The Charter charges the Economic and Social Council with bringing the specialized agencies into a relationship with the United Nations through agreements negotiated by ECOSOC and approved by the General Assembly. The specialized agencies range in nature from the highly technical and functionally specific (such as the International Civil Aviation Organization and the International Telecommunication Union) to those that are involved in highly controversial political matters (such as UNESCO and the International Monetary Fund). Each of the specialized agencies began its existence as an intergovernmental organization with its own treaty or constitution. At the initiative of the agency, negotiations are conducted between it and ECOSOC, with the resulting agreement subject to approval by the General Assembly. Sixteen agencies have gone this route (see Table 2-1) and thus are classified as "specialized agencies" of the United Nations. In addition to the specialized agencies, two other intergovernmental agencies function in a somewhat similar capacity as largely autonomous agencies within the UN system. These were the International Atomic Energy Agency (IAEA) and the General Agreement on Tariffs and Trade (GATT), which was superseded by the World Trade Organization in 1995.

Integrating the activities of eighteen diverse intergovernmental agencies that are largely autonomous in their powers, have their own organizational machinery, adopt their own budgets, select their own secretariates, and, in some cases, antedate the UN organization is no simple task. The permissive authorization given to ECOSOC in the Charter has, as a result, not proved adequate to the challenge of securing effective "coordination," although various agreements have been concluded.

The growing assertion of power by the Assembly and its main committees in the 1980s and 1990s has produced a closer working relationship between them and the specialized agencies than between the agencies and ECOSOC, but this relationship tends to involve general oversight rather then coordination. More effective coordination on a voluntary consultative basis is effected through the Administrative Committee on Coordination, a committee of high officials from the UN Secretariat and the secretariats of the specialized agencies, functioning as an international administrative cabinet. Much of the important work of the UN family is carried on by the sixteen specialized agencies, and by other UN-related bodies that report to ECOSOC or directly to the General Assembly. Most of them will be discussed in their proper context in later chapters.

## THE TRUSTEESHIP COUNCIL

Although the Charter designates the Trusteeship Council a principal organ of the United Nations, like ECOSOC, it was subordinate to the General Assembly. Its function, to supervise nonstrategic trust territories for the Assembly and strategic trusts for the Security Council, involved only recommendation powers.

Membership on the Trusteeship Council was accorded by the Charter to three types of members: (1) states that administer trust territories, (2) permanent members of the Security Council that did not administer trust territories, and (3) enough additional elected members. Elected members were eliminated when the remaining trusts were all in the strategic classification. And with the last strategic trust territory, Palau, gaining independence in 1994, the first category of membership was also eliminated. The Council's work has therefore been concluded. Its remaining permanent members have suspended meetings, and it only remains for a Charter amendment to be approved declaring the Trusteeship Council abolished.

### Trusteeship Functions

In carrying out its responsibilities the Trusteeship Council exercised power in performing a variety of functions. Two of these functions were similar to those of ECOSOC: The council deliberated on matters within its jurisdiction through studies and debates, and it made recommendations for action based on its evaluations. Its recommendations, however, related to problems of specific trust territories or their administration and, unlike those of ECOSOC, did not usually take the form of proclamations or treaties.

The council's supervisory role involved overseeing the governance of trust territories by administering states. An elaborate questionnaire drawn up by the council served as a basic supervisory tool. The council also received petitions, sometimes several hundred in a year, from individuals and groups in the trust territories seeking redress of real or imagined grievances. Reports and petitions were supplemented by periodic on-the-spot investigations by visiting missions of the Trusteeship Council, composed of two persons chosen by administering powers and two by nonadministering states. The missions evaluated economic and social conditions, examined progress toward self-government, sought answers to specific questions raised by the council and the General Assembly, and consulted a wide cross section of the population, including labor leaders, tribal chiefs, local administrative officials, and private individuals.

The information thus gathered was subjected to rigorous scrutiny in the council, forcing each trust-holding state to defend its actions or lack of them. Out of these confrontations emerged the Council's annual report to the Assembly, permitting, this time by the Assembly, another inquiry, another debate, and another evaluation of how well administering states lived up to their mandated responsibilities. Little wonder that most trust states impatiently pushed their trust territories toward independence and self-government!

The work of the Trusteeship Council will be further examined in Chapter 8.

## THE INTERNATIONAL COURT OF JUSTICE

Although the International Court of Justice functions largely outside the UN framework as a semi-independent entity headquartered at The Hague in the Netherlands, the Charter recognizes it as one of the six principal organs of the United Nations. The ICJ, or World Court, is the successor to the Permanent Court of International Justice (PCIJ), which functioned as the world's chief judicial organ from 1922 to 1946. The Charter, in Article 92, recognizes this successor status in noting that the annexed Statute for the ICJ "is based upon the Statute of the Permanent Court of International Justice."

Although some of the organization and powers of the ICJ are set forth in the Charter (Articles 92 to 96), most are contained in the ICJ Statute, a multilateral treaty that serves as its basic constitution. All members of the United Nations are automatically parties to the ICJ Statute, but a state that is not a member of the United Nations can join the Court on conditions laid down by the General Assembly following recommendation by the Security Council. Switzerland, for example, has refused to join the United Nations because of its centuries-old position of neutrality, but it has for many years been a member of the ICJ.

The fifteen judges that make up the International Court of Justice are elected by the Security Council and the General Assembly, voting separately, with five judges elected every three years for nine-year terms. Each judge is eligible for reelection. Article 9 of the Statute of the ICJ provides that judges should be selected on the basis of their individual qualifications and together should represent the main forms of civilization and the principal legal systems of the world. No two judges may be of the same nationality. Although the judges strive for objectivity, their voting behavior on the Court can often be predicted with some degree of accuracy, based on the nature of the cases and the issues involved, their records as national judges, their publications in the field of international law, their ideological persuasions, and other factors that may be calculated to affect their judicial decision making.

The Court's competence to hear and decide cases extends to all controversies submitted to it by contending parties. If there is no judge on the Court of the nationality of one or several of the parties to a case, the party or parties so deprived may under Court rules appoint a judge to participate in that case with full voting rights. While such action is unknown in national courts, the World Court provisions reflect the sovereign independence of the parties in such cases. Some states have accepted the compulsory jurisdiction of the Court in advance under the Optional Clause of the Statute (Article 36), but because of a myriad of reservations and amendments, the general rule is that only those states that are willing to have their controversies adjudicated by the Court will be parties to cases before it. Cases are decided by a majority vote, with a quorum of nine needed for voting, unless by agreement the case is submitted to a smaller panel of judges. Decisions and awards cannot be appealed. In case of a tie, the President of the Court is entitled to a "casting" (tie-breaking) vote. The Court's jurisdiction also extends to the rendering of advisory opinions on legal questions submitted to it by the principal organs of the United Nations and the UN specialized agencies.

To reach a decision, the Court interprets and applies treaties, international customs, the general principles of law, and decisions of international tribunals. Decisions of national courts and the teachings of respected international jurists can be used as subsidiary means for determining rules of international law. If the parties agree, the Court can render a decision *ex aequo et bono* (based on the Court's conception of justice and fairness rather than law).

The International Court of Justice is a symbol of the widespread yearning to replace the use of force with the rule of law. Within its scope of operation it has performed well, but its reach is necessarily limited by the willingness of all affected parties to place a dispute before it. For this reason it has had little part in resolving the major issues of peace and war and resource distribution that persistently plague the international system. The modest successes and inherent limitations of the Court in dispute settlement will be explored in depth in Chapter 7.

## THE SECRETARIAT

The UN Secretariat under Article 7 of the Charter is included as one of the six "principal organs of the United Nations." The Secretariat consists of officials and civil servants who perform administrative, budgetary, secretarial, linguistic, staff, and housekeeping functions for the other principal organs and carry out the programs of the organization. Members of the Secretariat are recruited individually and do not serve as representatives of their governments, as do those who serve as delegates to the General Assembly and the three councils. They are full-time employees of the United Nations who bring diverse skills to the organization. They are supposed to serve the entire membership of the United Nations in a politically neutral manner, although reality sometimes falls short of the ideal.

Heading the Secretariat is a Secretary-General who in Article 97 is designated "the chief administrative officer of the Organization." Appointment of the Secretary-General for a five-year term of office is the culmination of a political process that includes recommendation by the Security Council, with the veto power applicable, and appointment by a two-thirds vote of the General Assembly.

The responsibilities of the Secretary-General and his staff include preparing the agenda for major organs, providing essential services and sometimes expert advice at meetings, drawing up the biennial budget of the organization, expending funds, supervising day-to-day operations, taking the initiative in suggesting new programs, offering political leadership when requested to do so by a major organ, serving as a diplomatic agent to iron out difficulties among member delegations, and serving as the ceremonial head of the United Nations in formal affairs. The Secretary-General is the only person in the United Nations who can speak for or represent the entire organization. The Secretariat's role in the administration and politics of the United Nations will be further elaborated in Chapter 4.

# FINANCING THE UNITED NATIONS

The effectiveness of a multilateral organization such as the United Nations and the dedication of its members can often be evaluated by an analysis of its budget. The short history of international organizations reveals that many states have been penurious to an extreme and often grudging in providing financial support. This propensity of members to invest only relatively meager resources in the work of international organizations may reflect the limited character of their commitment, the poverty of their societies, or their disagreement with some of the activities carried on by these organizations. Demands by statesmen for substantial benefits from such organizations are often balanced by inclinations to contribute little more than lip service to their operations.

## ASSESSMENT PROBLEMS

When the United Nations began its work in 1946, the need to find an equitable but adequate financing formula was given high priority. The task of preparing a scale of budgetary assessments was assigned to a special Committee on Contributions under guidelines laid down by the General Assembly. The committee has since continued to provide periodic review and recommend necessary revision of the assessment scale. Members of the committee are supposed to be experienced in financial matters and drawn from states providing a broad geographic representation. In determining assessments, the committee was originally charged by the General Assembly to utilize the criterion of ability to pay as reflected by each state's total national income, per capita income, economic dislocation caused by the war, and foreign exchange earnings. These factors, with the exception of dislocation caused by war, remain the main criteria for determining assessments today, although "floor" and "ceiling" limitations have been added. The United States pays the largest assessment of the regular budget. Many of the small, poor states of the Third World are assessed the minimum payment of 0.01 percent. Assessments are paid as "contributions," but they are considered binding once the General Assembly has adopted the organization's annual budget. Unlike the technical programs of the League of Nations, whose financing was included within the League's general budget, each of the specialized agencies of the United Nations has its own budget and financial system, with Assembly oversight confined to consultation and recommendations. The UN budget system also differs from that of the League in that budgetary questions are decided in the Assembly by a two-thirds majority rather than by the unanimity rule that often came close to paralyzing League operations.

In 1946 the first scale of assessments reflected the dominant economic position of the United States in a world suffering from the aftermath of war. The U.S. assessment amounted to almost 40 percent, with the remaining 60 percent paid by the other fifty member states. Objections were raised by U.S. leaders who argued that the United States did not have that great a capacity to pay and did not wish to weaken the organization by a heavy dependence on a single source of revenue. United States opposition took the form of a demand that a ceiling be established prohibiting contributions of more than one-third of the budget by any one state, a position that was gradually accepted over a ten-year period, with the admission of new members and the economic revival of old members easing the transition. In years past, the contributions of the United States to the UN system have sometimes approached 50 percent despite its regular budget assessment portion of 25 percent, reflecting sizable U.S. support through voluntary contributions to special UN programs. These heavy U.S. contributions are less impressive if measured strictly in terms of ability to pay, since a number of members contribute a greater percentage of their gross national product (GNP) than does the United States. Moreover, in recent years U.S. voluntary contributions to UN programs have declined to about 25 percent.

The poorer states of the world prefer that budget assessments be based strictly on each state's national income and ability to pay. The use of national per capita income as a factor in the assessment scale has encountered objections from states with high national incomes and small populations. In deference to this protest, the Assembly established a rule that no state should be assessed more per capita than the largest contributor. Canada is the only state that has had its assessment reduced under this rule.

In previous years much of the debate over budgetary questions involved cold war animus and North-South frictions as well as controversies over money. The Soviet Union's share of the regular budget was 6.34 percent in 1946, but after a vigorous campaign pushed by the United States, the Soviet share was increased to 12.95 percent, a figure that included the separate assessments for the Byelorussian and Ukrainian republics. The breakup of the Soviet Union and the near collapse of the surviving Russian Federation's economy caused a reduction in its assessments from 9.41 in 1992 to 2.87 in 1998. Japan, with the world's second largest economy, was the recipient of the second largest assessment, amounting to 17.98 percent in 1998, with Germany following at 9.63 percent, France at 6.49, Italy 5.39, and the United Kingdom 5.07. The 1998–99 two-year budget was set at $2.532 billion, $51 million below the 1996–97 budget, and there was considerable complaint from the member states that the reduction as well as the overall budget had been set at a level imposed by the United States. The U.S. Congress had in fact insisted that the UN could not exceed its earlier budget. On the basis of capacity to pay, however, the poorest thirty members of the United Nations saw their assessments reduced from 0.01 to 0.001 percent in 1998. But perhaps the most heated debate resulted from a demand by the United States that its 25 percent share be reduced to 20 percent. The reaction from the other member states, especially from members of the European Union, to the U.S. demand was that the request could only be considered after Washington paid all its arrears. And when the U.S. refused to comply, its assessment was left at 25 percent. Earlier, the American ambassador had argued in the Fifth Committee that the U.S. assessment must be reduced to 22 percent by 1998 and 20 percent by the year 2000, in order to prevent serious damage of the U.S. relationship to the UN. Under the 1998–99 assessment scales, however, ten members were made responsible for 80 percent of the UN budget, with the United States, Japan, and Germany accounting for more than half. And because assessments were made on a capacity to pay arrangement, that is the country's share of the world economy, it meant that three countries with less than 10 percent of the world's population controlled more than half the world's wealth, an issue that did not go unnoted by the more numerous, less endowed states.

## BUDGET PROCEDURES AND POLITICS

Overall UN operations are divided into four major budget categories: (1) the regular budget, (2) the specialized agencies, (3) voluntary programs related mainly to economic development, and (4) peacekeeping operations.

The regular budget pays the day-to-day costs of the organization, including buildings and equipment, conferences, travel, salaries and retirement pay, and other administrative costs arising from the operations of the major UN organs. Each specialized agency has its own budget, which is presented to the General Assembly for formal approval, but is in fact arrived at independently. Economic aid and technical assistance through the UN Development Program (UNDP) is one of the larger voluntary programs. Some programs, such as the expenses of the office of the UN High Commissioner for Refugees (UNHCR), operate largely on voluntary contributions but are partly supported by the regular budget.

The United Nations two-year program budget requires the administrative staff to plan organizational goals, to establish the programs needed to achieve the goals, and to provide budgetary support for the programs. The budget process is carried on by members of the Secretariat under the direction of the Secretary-General. The Secretary-General proposes; the majority of member

FIGURE 2-2   Relationship of Assessments to Voting Strength in the General Assembly, January 1998.

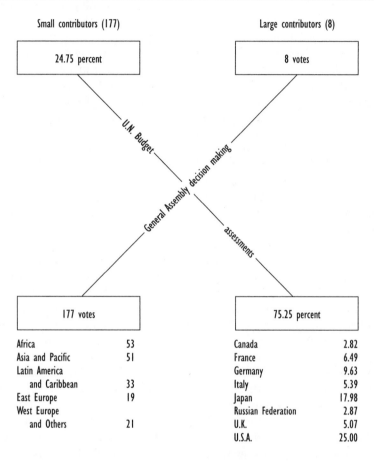

| Small contributors (177) | | Large contributors (8) | |
|---|---|---|---|
| 24.75 percent | | 8 votes | |

| 177 votes | | 75.25 percent | |
|---|---|---|---|
| Africa | 53 | Canada | 2.82 |
| Asia and Pacific | 51 | France | 6.49 |
| Latin America | | Germany | 9.63 |
| and Caribbean | 33 | Italy | 5.39 |
| East Europe | 19 | Japan | 17.98 |
| West Europe | | Russian Federation | 2.87 |
| and Others | 21 | U.K. | 5.07 |
| | | U.S.A. | 25.00 |

states dispose. This means that nations of the Third World, which pay the least, have the voting power to determine how much should be spent, and for what. The eight richest countries pay more than 70 percent of the total budget but can be outvoted by the huge Third World majority, which pays only a small portion of the remaining 30 percent (see Figure 2-2). No effective budget ceiling has ever been established; new programs and inflation adjustments for old programs have been approved regularly over the years and added to the total cost of UN operations.

In 1982 the United States, Britain, and the Soviet Union tried to halt budgetary escalation by jointly demanding that the Secretary-General set a ceiling on the 1982–83 budget and accept stringent limits on future budgets. Although the Secretary-General agreed to try budgetary restraint, he also faced pressures from Third World members to expand various programs. Neither side was happy when the budget for 1984–85 was fixed at $1,606 million, an increase of $133 million, or 9 percent over the previous biennium. The tide turned against the Third World nations after the cold war, however. The United States, chastened by lack of support in the General Assembly on numerous policy issues, exacted revenge for earlier failures to impress the majority members by withholding payment of its assessed fees, and by insisting on a greater assumption of responsibility by all the member states in paying the UN's bills. With the U.S. in a unipolar role and the dominant actor in strategic as well as economic and financial matters, this contest between the one surviving superpower and the vast majority of member states was likely to continue.

Quite apart from budget ceiling controversies, UN budgetary planning has been complicated by failure of numerous states to pay their assessed contributions. In past years some twenty-five member governments have at various times withheld portions of their assessments for political reasons. A number refused to pay their share for peacekeeping operations because they opposed the use of UN peacekeeping forces in particular situations. As of mid-July 1997, member states owed the United Nations a total of $2.3 billion—$1.6 billion for peacekeeping, $681 million for the regular UN budget, and $8.7 million for international tribunals. The U.S. debt stood at $1.4 billion for past and 1997 payments, over half of the total. This included $498 million for the regular budget and $920 million for peacekeeping. After tallying the entire UN membership in 1998, only 78 of 185 members states had paid their obligations in full.

Theoretically, continued nonpayment of compulsory assessments could lead to loss of voting right in the General Assembly. Article 19 of the Charter provides that a member shall lose its vote when its budgetary arrearage equals or exceeds its total assessment for the preceding two years. That sanction lost most of its teeth in 1964 and 1965, however, when the United States tried— and failed—to persuade the Assembly to impose the penalty on the Soviet Union for failure to pay peacekeeping assessments. The Assembly went through the entire 1964 session without taking a formal vote, rather than confront the issue. The United States finally threw in the towel, reserving to itself the right to reject compulsory assessments in the future if compelling reasons should arise. As a result Article 19 has never been used to deprive any state of a vote.

Since the mid-1980s the United States has been the greatest offender in withholding assessed contributions, stemming from funding cuts mandated by Congress. In 1985 the Congress adopted the Kassebaum Amendment, which required the United States to reduce its regular budget payments from 25 percent to 20 percent, beginning with the 1987 UN fiscal year. Under the amendment, this cut was to be continued until the United Nations adopted a system of reforms on budgetary matters by which the major financial contributors would no longer be subjected to budgetary decisions arrived at arbitrarily by the Third World majority. Additional reductions in the U.S. contribution were made necessary by subsequent congressional action.

The UN's financial crisis intensified with the end of the Cold War when it was assumed the world body would accept major responsibility for a variety and multiplicity of political, economic, and social upheavals. Indeed, the UN found itself expanding its peacekeeping and peacemaking operations, but not without considerable encouragement from its member states. As a consequence the organization was soon overextended and so heavily burdened that it became necessary to request even heavier financial commitments from the major member states, especially the United States. By 1996, the Secretary General was forced to call a special session of the General Assembly to discuss the organization's financial crisis and propose remedies. Faced with insolvency and unpaid cash flows estimated at $3.3 billion, the Secretary General declared it would be necessary to scale back the number of peacekeeping missions as well as cut a wide range of social and economic programs. Assessments for peacekeeping operations, however, were the main problem. They fell from $3 billion in 1995 to $1.3 billion in 1997 and by 1998 the UN owed some 71 countries more than $800 million for troops and equipment. The UN's two-year budget for 1998 and 1999 represented a zero-growth plan that required the Secretary General to carry on the work of the organization with $372 million less than he had for 1996 and 1997. Thus, the UN staff was reduced from 12,000 in the mid-1980s to 9,000 at the end of the 1990s, and although the U.S. approved such cuts, the U.S. Congress continued to delay meeting its financial obligations.

## FUTURE FINANCING PROBLEMS

The financing of UN operations remains a problem, given the continuing prospect of nonpayment, late payment, and selective withholding. One answer, at least in theory, is to find sources of income for the United Nations independent of its members. Although many such sources would require Charter amendment or basic changes in the UN structure, the principle of revenue production independent of members' contributions is not without precedent. Each year the organization nets several million dollars from its headquarters' businesses involving stamp sales, a gift shop, investment income, and guided tours. Although this amounts to only a small percentage of the annual regular budget, other proposals to secure independent sources of revenue could be regarded as extensions of this principle.

Suggestions for new sources run the gamut from those that would provide minor amounts of supplemental income to those that might in themselves finance most or all UN activities. As might be expected, sources that offer the greatest potential for substantial income are also the least feasible politically. Many members, of course, do not regard financial independence for the United Nations as a virtue because it would reduce their control over the organization and its activities. Potential sources for UN income might include the following:

1. Private contributions in the form of individual gifts, inheritances, and foundation grants encouraged through a joint policy of making such contributions deductible from national taxes.

2. Charges levied by UN agencies for services performed; for example, the World Meteorological Organization could charge a service fee for its weather data and the International Telecommunication Union could issue international radio licenses for substantial fees.
3. Tolls charged for various kinds of transportation and communications, facilitated in today's world by UN programs.
4. Fees for international travel imposed through levies on passports and visas or through surcharges on national customs duties.
5. Profits earned through implementation of the 1982 Law of the Sea Treaty by which a UN international investment corporation could exploit the mineral and other forms of wealth in international waters and seabeds.
6. Charters sold to private companies or governmental agencies authorizing them to exploit the resources of seabeds and Antarctica, with royalty rights reserved by the United Nations.
7. Fishing, whaling, and sealing rights in international waters, assigned to countries or private companies upon the payment of "conservation" fees to the United Nations.
8. Rights to the use of outer space, or the operation of outer space programs by the United Nations, aimed at producing revenues through communications satellites, meteorological systems, and the future development of resources on the moon and the planets.
9. Taxes levied on member states, collectible by their governments, and based on ability to pay judged by national income.
10. Taxes levied directly on individuals through the cooperation of member states, based on income and with a mild graduation of rates.
11. Issuance of an international trading currency, backed by national reserves, that could serve the dual function of financing UN programs and providing a supplementary international monetary unit to encourage greater trade.

Recent Secretaries General have addressed the serious short-term cash flow problem created by late payment of assessments, including charging interest on late payments, increasing the working capital fund, establishing a temporary Peacekeeping Reserve Fund, and authorizing the Secretary-General to borrow commercially to meet temporary cash needs. Other suggested plans include a levy on arms sales, a tax on international air travel, UN authority to borrow from the World Bank and the International Monetary Fund, and a general tax exemption for private contributions to the United Nations.

# NOTES

1. H. G. Nicholas, *The United Nations as a Political Institution,* 5th ed. (London: Oxford University Press, 1975), p. 104.
2. *Ibid.,* p. 92.

# SELECTED READINGS

Ali, Sheikh R. *The International Organizations and World Order Dictionary.* Santa Barbara, CA: ABC-CLIO, 1992.

Beigbeder, Yves. *The Internal Management of United Nations Organizations: The Long Quest for Reform.* New York: St. Martin's Press, 1997.

Boutros-Ghali, Boutros. *An Agenda for Peace.* New York: United Nations, 1992.

Feld, Werner J., and Robert S. Jordan. *International Organizations: A Comparative Approach.* 2nd ed. New York: Praeger Publishers, 1988.

Galey, Margaret E. "Reforming the Regime for Financing the United Nations." *Howard Law Journal,* vol. 31, no. 4 (1988), pp. 543–574.

Gati, Toby Trister, ed. *The US, the UN, and the Management of Global Change.* New York: New York University Press, 1983.

Goodrich, Leland M.; Edvard Hambro; and A. P. Simons. *Charter of the United Nations, Commentary and Documents.* 3rd rev. ed. New York: Columbia University Press, 1967.

Gordenker, Leon. *Thinking About the United Nations System.* Hanover, NH: The Academic Council on the United Nations, 1990.

Jacobson, Harold K. *Networks of Interdependence.* 2nd ed. New York: Alfred A. Knopf, 1984.

Kaufmann, Johan. *Conference Diplomacy: An Introductory Analysis.* 2nd rev. ed. Dordrecht: Martinus Nijhoff Publishers, 1988.

Nicholas, H. G. *The United Nations as a Political Institution.* 5th ed. London: Oxford University Press, 1975.

Riggs, Robert E. *Politics in the United Nations.* Urbana: University of Illinois Press, 1958. Reprinted by Greenwood Press, 1984.

Russell, Ruth B. *A History of the United Nations Charter: The Role of the United States, 1940–1945.* Washington, DC: Brookings Institution, 1958.

Schachter, Oscar, ed. *United Nations Legal Order.* Cambridge: Cambridge University Press, 1995.

Stoessinger, John G., and Associates. *Financing the United Nations System.* Washington, DC: Brookings Institution, 1964.

Van Dervort, Thomas R. *International Law and Organization.* Thousand Oaks, CA: Sage Publications, 1997.

Yoder, Amos. *The Evolution of the United Nations System.* New York: Crane Russak, 1989.

# 3

## THE UN POLITICAL PROCESS

The United Nations provides a setting for the practice of international politics. The principal participants are representatives of governments, secretariat officials, representatives of other international organizations, and spokesmen for nongovernmental interests. The UN political process is the sum of their efforts to influence the making and implementing of international decisions. This chapter will examine the several types of UN participants, how their interaction is affected by the UN institutional setting, and the consequences that flow from this process.

## PARTICIPANTS IN THE UN DECISION PROCESS

### MEMBER STATES

The chief participants in any intergovernmental organization are the official representatives of member states. When decisions are made by voting, these representatives are ordinarily the only ones entitled to vote. They also control most of the resources essential for implementing decisions. What the organization does is thus heavily dependent on its members, their interests, and their capabilities.

Today membership in the United Nations is virtually universal, a reflection of the global scope and character of its objectives. This was not so in the beginning. The organization took its name from the wartime United Nations, a coalition formed to defeat the Berlin-Rome-Tokyo Axis, and Charter membership provisions were designed to permit at least temporary exclusion of former enemy states by requiring that members be "peace-loving." Thus the original membership consisted of states that had demonstrated their "love" of peace by declaring war on the Axis powers prior to March 1, 1945. Membership, under Article 4, paragraph 1, of the Charter was subsequently to be

> open to all other peace-loving states which accept the obligations contained in the present Charter and, in the judgment of the Organization, are able and willing to carry out these obligations.

Such a judgment was not meant to be taken lightly, since favorable action required an affirmative decision of the Security Council, including the acquiescence of all five permanent members, and a two-thirds majority vote in the General Assembly.

During the first ten years of the United Nations, admission was granted grudgingly—only nine new members were added to the original fifty-one. The reasons had little to do with World War II or love of peace but rather were a product of the emerging cold war. As East-West lines hardened, the U.S.-led majority denied the necessary seven Security Council votes to applicants from the Soviet bloc and the Soviet Union used the veto to block the admission of most other applicants. Understandably, the Soviet Union hoped to use its veto as leverage to secure the admission of its own protégés.

The break in the stalemate came in 1955 with the relaxation of cold war tensions that followed the Korean Armistice and the death of Joseph Stalin. In this new atmosphere the United States and the Soviet Union agreed on a package deal for the admission of sixteen new members, including several Communist applicants. Since then, UN membership has been available virtually for the asking. Table 3-1 shows the present UN member states by years of admission.

The principal exceptions to the new open-door policy were the partitioned states of Germany, Vietnam, and Korea, a persisting legacy of the cold war and the internal politics of the divided countries. Political détente led to the admission of both German states in 1973, and a single Vietnam was admitted in 1977 in the aftermath of the Vietnam War. Problems associated with partition kept the two Koreas outside the organization until 1991, when the end of the cold war and softened Korean attitudes on both sides of the thirty-eighth parallel boundary permitted the United Nations to recognize the two sovereign Korean governments.

An exception of a different kind is Switzerland, the former seat of the League of Nations and the present site of UN European headquarters, which has voluntarily remained aloof out of conviction that membership is incompatible with Swiss neutrality. This reflects Swiss public opinion as well as governmental policy. When the issue of UN membership was put to a national referendum in March 1986, Swiss voters rejected it by a margin of three to one. Switzerland, along with Monaco and the Holy See, presently maintain "Permanent Observer" status at the United Nations.

A different problem was presented by China. An original member of the United Nations, China also became a "partitioned" state in 1949, when the People's Republic won the civil war on the mainland and the Nationalist government fled to the island of Taiwan. Because neither China would officially admit the reality of two Chinas, the issue was treated as one of representation rather than of admission to membership. Each year from 1950 to 1971, the General Assembly was forced to decide whether China should be represented by delegates from the mainland or from Taiwan. The string of Nationalist voting victories, made possible by vigorous support from the United States, was finally broken in November 1971, when the General Assembly recognized the

TABLE 3-1   Growth of UN Membership, 1945–January 1999

| YEAR | FOUNDING MEMBERS |
|------|------------------|
| 1945 | Argentina, Australia, Belarus, Belgium, Bolivia, Brazil, Canada, Chile, China, Colombia, Costa Rica, Cuba, Denmark, Dominican Republic, Ecuador, Egypt, El Salvador, Ethiopia, France, Greece, Guatemala, Haiti, Honduras, India, Iran, Iraq, Lebanon, Liberia, Luxembourg, Mexico, Netherlands, New Zealand, Nicaragua, Norway, Panama, Paraguay, Peru, Philippines, Poland, Russian Federation, Saudi Arabia, South Africa, Syria, Turkey, Ukraine, United Kingdom, United States, Uruguay, Venezuela, Yugoslavia |

| YEAR | MEMBERS SUBSEQUENTLY ADMITTED |
|------|-------------------------------|
| 1946 | Afghanistan, Iceland, Sweden, Thailand |
| 1947 | Pakistan, Yemen |
| 1948 | Myanmar |
| 1949 | Israel |
| 1950 | Indonesia |
| 1955 | Albania, Austria, Bulgaria, Cambodia, Finland, Hungary, Ireland, Italy, Jordan, Lao People's Democratic Republic, Libyan Arab Jamahiriya, Nepal, Portugal, Romania, Spain, Sir Lanka |
| 1956 | Japan, Morocco, Sudan, Tunisia |
| 1957 | Ghana, Malaysia |
| 1958 | Guinea |
| 1960 | Benin, Burkina Faso, Cameroon, Central African Republic, Chad, Congo, Côte d'Ivoire, Cyprus, Democratic Republic of the Congo (formerly Zaire), Gabon, Madagascar, Mali, Niger, Nigeria, Senegal, Somalia, Togo |
| 1961 | Mauritania, Mongolia, Sierra Leone, United Republic of Tanzania |
| 1962 | Algeria, Burundi, Jamaica, Rwanda, Trinidad and Tobago, Uganda |
| 1963 | Kenya, Kuwait |
| 1964 | Malawi, Malta, Zambia |
| 1965 | Gambia, Maldives, Singapore |
| 1966 | Barbados, Botswana, Guyana, Lesotho |
| 1967 | Equatorial Guinea, Mauritius, Swaziland |
| 1970 | Fiji |
| 1971 | Bahrain, Bhutan, Oman, Qatar, United Arab Emirates |
| 1973 | Bahamas, Germany |
| 1974 | Bangladesh, Grenada, Guinea-Bissau |
| 1975 | Cape Verde, Comoros, Mozambique, Papua New Guinea, São Tomé and Principe, Suriname |
| 1976 | Angola, Samoa, Seychelles |
| 1977 | Djibouti, Vietnam |
| 1978 | Dominica, Solomon Islands |
| 1979 | Saint Lucia |
| 1980 | Saint Vincent and the Grenadines, Zimbabwe |

TABLE 3-1 (*continued*)

| YEAR | MEMBERS SUBSEQUENTLY ADMITTED |
|---|---|
| 1981 | Antigua and Barbuda, Belize, Vanuatu |
| 1983 | Saint Christopher and Nevis |
| 1984 | Brunei Darussalam |
| 1990 | Liechtenstein, Namibia |
| 1991 | Democratic People's Republic of Korea, Estonia, Latvia, Lithuania, Marshall Islands, Micronesia (Federated States of), Republic of Korea |
| 1992 | Armenia, Azerbaijan, Bosnia and Herzegovina, Croatia, Georgia, Kazakhstan, Kyrgyzstan, Moldova, San Marino, Slovenia, Tajikistan, Turkmenistan, Uzbekistan |
| 1993 | Czech Republic*, Slovak Republic*, The Former Yugoslav Republic of Macedonia**, Monaco, Eritrea, Andorra |
| 1994 | Palau |

* Czechoslovakia was an original member of the UN in 1945. On January 1, 1993, Czechoslovakia ceased to exist, and its former constituent parts received separate membership.

** The General Assembly admitted "The former Yugoslav Republic of Macedonia" on April 8, 1993 pending settlement of differences that had arisen over its name. By April 1999 there were 185 member states in the United Nations.

People's Republic as the legitimate holder of the China seat. Other UN organs quickly followed the lead of the Assembly, and Nationalist representatives departed the UN scene. Although the Beijing government purports to speak for all of China, including Taiwan, that island nation remains unrepresented in the United Nations.

The few exceptions aside, essentially all states have valued the status of UN membership. The United Nations now welcomes all comers. For a time some members agonized over the ministate problem—the admission of new states with equal voting rights in the General Assembly but without the population or resources to contribute much to UN programs (or, indeed, to exercise much influence in any aspect of international affairs). But the admission of Antigua and Barbuda, the Seychelles, Dominica, the Marshall Islands, Micronesia, Liechtenstein, and San Marino—all with less than 100,000 population—and more than thirty other states with populations less than one million indicates that no state is too small to qualify for membership.

The policy of unrestricted admission has made membership in the United Nations virtually universal and in the process has changed the character of the organization. With the growth in membership coming primarily from newly created states in Africa, Asia, and the Caribbean (see Table 3-2), Western (and specifically U.S.) dominance of the United Nations gave way to the numerical dominance of the Third World. The new states have differed from the Western industrialized world in their needs and priorities, and they have not hesitated to redefine UN priorities according to their own vision. The changes, of course, have been more profound in the General Assembly, where all members have a voice and a vote, than in the Security Council with its great power veto.

TABLE 3-2    UN Membership and Geographic Region, 1945–January 1999

| DATE | WESTERN EUROPE[1] | EASTERN EUROPE | ASIA AND PACIFIC[2] | AFRICA | LATIN AMERICA & CARIBBEAN | OTHERS[3] | TOTAL |
|------|-------------------|----------------|---------------------|--------|---------------------------|-----------|-------|
| 1945 | 9  | 6  | 8  | 4  | 20 | 4 | 51  |
| 1950 | 11 | 6  | 15 | 4  | 20 | 4 | 60  |
| 1955 | 17 | 10 | 20 | 5  | 20 | 4 | 76  |
| 1960 | 17 | 10 | 23 | 26 | 20 | 4 | 100 |
| 1965 | 18 | 10 | 27 | 37 | 22 | 4 | 118 |
| 1970 | 18 | 10 | 29 | 42 | 24 | 4 | 127 |
| 1975 | 19 | 11 | 36 | 47 | 27 | 4 | 144 |
| 1980 | 19 | 11 | 39 | 51 | 30 | 4 | 154 |
| 1985 | 19 | 11 | 41 | 51 | 33 | 4 | 159 |
| 1993 | 21 | 19 | 51 | 52 | 33 | 4 | 180 |
| 1998 | 23 | 20 | 52 | 53 | 33 | 4 | 185 |

[1] Includes Turkey

[2] Includes Israel as well as the former Soviet Republics that are geographically located in Asia

[3] Includes Australia, Canada, New Zealand, and the United States

The addition of new members has changed the United Nations by enlarging the cast of characters who make decisions. Developments within member countries, particularly changes in national leadership and national policies, also affect UN politics by placing new actors on the stage and giving them new lines to speak. No more striking example can be cited than the shift in Soviet policy under Mikhail Gorbachev, which made international cooperation through the United Nations an important Soviet priority, ended the cold war, and led ultimately to the breakup of the Soviet Union and the admission of its former republics as members of the United Nations.

## PRIVATE INTEREST GROUPS

While states are the central actors, the twentieth century has seen a very significant meshing of activity by private interest groups ("non-governmental organizations" or "NGOs" in UN parlance) with the processes of intergovernmental bodies ("international governmental organizations" or "IGOs"). Profit-making private organizations are often called BINGOs (business international nongovernmental organizations), or TNCs (transnational corporations), or MNCs (multinational corporations). An international organization having both governmental and nongovernmental members is sometimes categorized as IQUANGOs (international quasi nongovernmental organizations). Although much of the contact is informal in nature, like the lobbying activity of domestic special interest groups in democratic states, a great deal of interest group consultation now takes place in all international organizations.

The International Labor Organization has gone the farthest in this direction, allowing participation with full voting rights to representatives of private interests. The ILO permits each member state to send four delegates to its general conference—two representing the government, one representing employer interests, and one chosen in consultation with national labor organizations. This combination of public and private interest representation dates from the formation of the ILO in 1919 and is still unique, but consultation without right of participation in debate and voting has become common in other intergovernmental bodies.

The UN Economic and Social Council, under Article 71 of the Charter, is authorized to "make suitable arrangements for consultation with nongovernmental organizations." The Council acknowledges the right of these organizations to express their views and accepts that they often possess special experience or technical understanding vital to its work. Over 1,500 nongovernmental organizations had consultative status with the Council in the closing years of the twentieth century, and these were classified into three categories: Category I, organizations having consultative interests that coincide with those of the Council. Category II, organizations having special competence in specific areas. And Category III, which includes a designation called roster organizations, which are judged worthy of making occasional contributions to the Council or its subsidiary organs, or other United Nations bodies. NGOs with consultative status may send observers to public meetings of the Council and its subsidiary organizations and may also submit written statements relevant to the Council's work. They are also permitted to consult with the UN Secretariat on matters of mutual concern.

The General Assembly has no formal consultative arrangements separate from the ECOSOC system, but representatives of NGOs try to make their presence felt in corridors, lounges, and meeting halls while the Assembly is in session. In 1978, during the tenth special session devoted to disarmament, the Assembly broke precedent by allowing representatives from a number of private organizations to address the assembled delegates.

Observer status was officially granted to the Palestine Liberation Organization (PLO) as the representative of the Palestinian people and to the South West Africa People's Organization (SWAPO) prior to Namibian independence. The African National Congress (ANC) was also an observer in debates on South African questions.

The significance of UN recognition is illustrated in the subsequent achievements of these different movements. The PLO was transformed into the Palestine Authority (PA) when Israel granted it political and administrative responsibility over most of the urban areas in the West Bank. In July 1998, the UN General Assembly voted to upgrade the status of the Palestinians to that of a virtual state. The Assembly voted 124 in favor and only 4 against, with 10 abstentions, to give the Palestinian Observer Group the new status of a nonvoting member in the 185-member assembly. With the new designation, Palestinian representatives could raise issues, co-sponsor draft resolutions, and have a right to reply. The Palestinian representative, however, could not vote or put forward candidates for UN committees. In affirming the resolution, it was stated that the Palestinians already enjoyed membership in the Arab League, the Group of 77, and other regional organizations. Finally, the resolution noted that the Palestinian Authority had been established on part of the occupied Palestinian territory. Only the United States, Israel, Micronesia, and the Marshall Islands voted against the resolution, thus paving the way for full Palestinian membership. Many of the member states already assumed the PA represented the 186th member of the United Nations. That official status, however, had yet to be bestowed. In the case of SWAPO, its observer status was transformed into full membership when Namibia achieved statehood in 1990. The ANC discarded its observer status when it gained control of the South African government following its popular victory at the polls in 1994.

Most intergovernmental organizations have formal or informal arrangements for consultation with private groups. The volume of contacts frequently depends on the perceived capacity of the organization to affect group interests. The European Union, for example, is lobbied heavily because it has extensive power to regulate, reward, and punish the conduct of private groups and individuals. On a lesser scale, UNESCO is also an important focus of private group activity. Private groups and individuals are involved directly in many of its programs for educational, scientific, and cultural interchange; and UNESCO can reward some of them with fellowships and scholarships, contracts for writing and publication, and subsidies to support private international societies fostering such interchange. UNESCO maintains additional private contracts through the national UNESCO commissions that have been formed in many member countries.

Private groups have been particularly active in the environmental field. Such groups are influential nationally in many countries, and they have extended their efforts to the international arena as the global scope of environmental issues has come to be recognized. The United Nations Environmental Program (UNEP) has been effective in building links with national and international groups through which it cultivates support for programs to preserve the environment. Private groups also play an important and growing role in IGO activities relating to human rights and development assistance.

A notable increase in private group activity has been stimulated by the practice of holding special world conferences under UN auspices. As early as 1963, and again in 1970, the FAO-sponsored World Food Congresses designed primarily for NGOs as a means of publicizing and enlisting support for FAO objectives. Since the 1972 Stockholm Conference on the Environment, the more common pattern has been to hold intergovernmental conferences on special subjects with informal participation and sometimes "parallel" conference activities by NGO representatives. Conferences that attracted widespread interest and vigorous NGO participation were the Conference on Environment and Development held in Rio de Janeiro (1992), the Conference on Women's

Issues assembled in Beijing (1996), the Conference on Climate Change and Global Warming convened in Kyoto (1997), the Rome Conference concerned with the Establishment of an International Criminal Court (1998), and the General Assembly Special Session on the World Drug Problem (1998).[1]

Participation at world conferences includes the usual forms of lobbying at meetings and, often, working with secretariat officials or national governments in preparation for the conference program. Increasingly it has included appeals to the media and their mass public audiences. NGOs lobby media representatives at international conferences, hoping to influence the reporting of what is done. Many NGO representatives themselves hold press accreditation from local newspapers or broadcasting stations and send out their own news reports. Such NGO activity has carried over to General Assembly special sessions on economic development and on disarmament.

Generalizing about the role of private interest groups is difficult. There is wide variation from one intergovernmental organization to another, and it is all too easy to equate activity with influence. UN officials often tend to view NGOs as vehicles for building public support for IGO programs rather than as coparticipants in UN decision making. Speeches delivered by NGO representatives (where permitted) or papers submitted to ECOSOC or some other UN body are easily ignored, and most have little impact beyond the satisfaction felt by the NGO representatives in expressing their points of view. The same, of course, can be said of most speeches delivered by governmental delegates.

In other contexts, NGO influence may be significant. Where NGO cooperation is essential or helpful in carrying out IGO programs—refugee relief, cultural exchange, or programs for economic and social development, for example—influence on details of administration may be considerable. NGOs with influential national constituencies may also affect policy decisions through their influence on positions taken by national governments. Groups that have political clout with governments are likely to have the ear of international secretariats as well, especially if the interests of the group and the secretariat are convergent. When secretariat officials recognize the need for NGO involvement, group input can be substantial in developing position papers and documentation for UN conferences. Environmental groups, for example, have been politically influential in the United States, Western Europe, and some other countries and, as a result, have been able to work closely with the staff of international agencies in the environmental field to promote common goals. Advice and support of environmental groups was extensively utilized by the international staff assigned to prepare for the 1992 United Nations Conference on Environment and Development (UNCED).

As in the national arena, the intensity of lobbying by private groups is affected by the group's resources and the stakes involved. Thus vigorous lobbying can be expected in a setting such as the European Union, where supranational agencies have a capacity to promote—or injure—private interests in a direct and substantial way. Many of the affected groups, including large national and multinational corporations, have resources to conduct extensive lobbying with community organs and member governments and do not hesitate to use those resources when important interests are at stake.

Sometimes special circumstances enhance the influence of a particular group. In preliminary negotiating sessions preceding the June 1992 UNCED meetings, the United States took a strong stand against including in the global warming treaty any reference to achieving environmental goals by reducing economic consumption in the North. In retaliation the developing countries proposed to remove from the treaty all reference to slowing population growth. This opened the way for vigorous and effective lobbying by the Vatican, a political force in many countries, against inclusion of provisions that might be inconsistent with the church's position on birth control.

Even groups with limited lobbying resources can sometimes have an impact through a piece of high-quality research or a good idea proposed at the right time. Once a resolution or recommendation has been adopted, NGOs may serve as gadflies to the international body politic, monitoring compliance by governments and subsequent follow-up by secretariat officials. This is particularly evident in the area of human rights where private humanitarian groups have been very active in finding facts on human rights violations and making them public. With the growth of extensive national and transnational group networks having international interests, NGO participation in international organization must be regarded as a significant part of the political process.

How significant the NGOs have become was dramatized in 1997–98, when Secretary-General Kofi Annan proposed sweeping reforms aimed at preparing the United Nations for its twenty-first century role. Although a description of these reforms is reserved for the following chapter, it is important to cite Annan's strategy to more heavily enlist the services of the NGOs and to make them "welcome partners" in UN efforts dealing with humanitarian causes. UN coordination efforts in 1997–98 assumed new significance after directives were issued from the Secretary-General to the Office of the UN High Commissioner for Refugees, the United Nations Children's Fund, and the World Food Program, calling on these agencies to work "in close concert" with the NGOs in all regions around the world, but most notably in the People's Democratic Republic of Korea, and the Great Lakes region of Africa that suffered from severe famine, as well as Iraq, where UN sanctions had imposed a special burden on the country's young and infirm.

## THE INTERNATIONAL OFFICIAL AS POLITICAL PARTICIPANT

The political functions of international secretariats will be discussed in a subsequent chapter, but a description of participants in the political process would be incomplete without a brief reference to the international civil servant. The executive head of an international secretariat is often in a position to have an effect on policy. In organizations with large budgets for operational programs, this executive is likely to be the most influential individual participant, and may initiate proposals as well as joining actively in formal and informal discussion of matters to be decided by members of the organization. Influence will of course vary with the type of organization, the nature of the issue, and the individual attributes of the incumbent. All UN Secretaries-General have felt a responsibility to bring the weight of their office to bear on issues confronting the United Nations, some with more success than others.

Secretariat influence on the political process is not restricted to the activities of the chief administrative officer. Others farther down the hierarchy participate as well. Experience and expertise may qualify secretariat officials for the role of counselor or informal adviser to delegates whose respect and friendship they have earned, or sometimes for an intermediary's role when compromise is required. Many seasoned secretariat members, steeped in the practice of an agency, provide an indispensable institutional memory that is relied upon by many member states. Formal reports or opinions prepared by secretariats provide part of the informational base for some decisions. Decisions relating to the operation of agency programs often depend on information from the officials who administer the programs. Nor can one overlook the substantial policy implications of budget preparation, a task regularly performed by secretariats, albeit with careful supervision by representatives of member states.

## INTERNATIONAL ORGANIZATIONS AS PARTICIPANTS

The participation of international organizations in the decisions of other international organizations, including organizations outside the UN system, is now a pervasive feature of international relations. Representatives of the European Union speak for the community in international tariff negotiations, and the World Trade Organization maintains contact with Union authorities in Brussels. Members of the European Union frequently address economic matters in UN forums through a common spokesman. In the UN Development Program the participating intergovernmental organizations jockey vigorously to influence the allocation of available funds. At a different level of policy making, coordination of technical assistance sponsored by different international organizations is facilitated by interagency committees of secretariat officials. Representatives of UN specialized agencies regularly participate in the work of ECOSOC, and regional organizations frequently collaborate with UN bodies in dealing with common problems. The General Assembly has adopted resolutions granting formal consultative status to a number of regional organizations, including the Commonwealth of Nations, the European Union, the Islamic Conference, the League of Arab States, the Organization of African Unity, the Organization of American States, and the Caribbean Community. The International Committee of the Red Cross, a hybrid IGO/NGO, also participates as an Assembly observer. Such arrangements illustrate an often ignored political fact—that international organizations are more than mere channels for national diplomatic activity. An international organization with permanent institutions is itself a political entity capable of participating in the political processes of the international system.

## UN DECISION MAKING

National interest and power may ultimately determine who gets what in the international arena, but perceptions of interest and use of power are modified by the institutions through which power is exercised. The most significant questions that can be asked about international organization relate to the ways in which participation modifies national perceptions of interest and affects the exercise of national power. Definitive answers have not been found—and perhaps never will be—but the questions should be asked. The following sections present information that may be helpful in framing tentative answers.

### NATIONAL ORGANIZATION FOR UN PARTICIPATION

Membership in the United Nations requires countries to adopt positions on a multitude of issues ranging in diversity from war in the Middle East to stabilization of world prices for copper and cotton to refugee relief in Africa. Many countries feel compelled to formulate policy on specific issues that never would have concerned them except for their participation in the United Nations. There is, of course, a wide variation in the thoroughness of preparation for UN discussions. States with substantial resources and broad foreign policy interests are likely to prepare detailed instructions for their UN representatives. Delegates from tiny states with limited interests and meager resources may have little guidance beyond the country's general foreign policy orientation, level of development, bloc affiliations, and the known predilections of its leaders.

The United States illustrates a very extensive adaptation to UN participation. Within the State Department, a Bureau of International Organization Affairs (IO) is concerned exclusively with coordinating U.S. policy in the United Nations and other multilateral agencies. The IO Bureau does not do it alone, however. Every major unit of the State Department is involved in preparation for UN meetings because the agendas run the full range of U.S. foreign policy interests. Indeed, every major department of government has interests in the activities of one or more international agencies, and officials from every department participate in international conferences. Interagency clearances are utilized to make sure that all relevant governmental interests are represented and, hopefully, to bring consistency to U.S. representation at different international meetings. Perfect consistency is usually an unattained ideal because of the varying agency perspectives (health, labor, commerce, defense, etc.) and the different personnel representing the United States in different international organizations. Other countries have the same problems of coordinating their own policies, often to a greater degree.

If an issue is to come before the United Nations, the IO Bureau has responsibility for clarifying the possible policy alternatives and preparing position papers to guide U.S. representatives in the UN. This, again, is not a self-contained operation. It is usually accomplished through a small working group—a temporary interoffice committee including representation from geographic and other interested bureaus—which does the groundwork and makes the initial policy recommendations. Position preparation may also require coordination with other executive departments through an interdepartmental coordination committee. This is a far cry from the behavior of a microstate, which may send no instructions at all to its UN representatives, but it shows the extent to which a major state must adapt its governmental machinery to the needs of UN participation.

## Missions and Delegations

Nearly all UN members maintain permanent missions to the United Nations in New York. Most also have permanent representation at the UN European Office in Geneva. The mission chief, or permanent representative, usually holds the diplomatic rank of ambassador. Mission size varies with the interests and resources of the state. The smaller missions may have only one or two persons of diplomatic rank plus a couple of clerical employees, whereas the United States maintains a permanent staff of about 150. In times past the size of the Soviet mission approached 300 (including personnel assigned to the ostensibly separate missions for the Ukraine and Byelorussia), but the Russian mission now maintains a staff comparable to that of the United States.

The permanent mission represents a country's interests in the United Nations much as an embassy represents its interests in a foreign capital. The functions of the permanent mission differ in many respects from those of the traditional diplomatic mission, however, because the UN is a multilateral organization rather than a government. Members of the permanent mission perform the traditional diplomatic functions of representation, negotiation, information gathering, and reporting. But at the UN this is done multilaterally with more than 180 states rather than bilaterally with one. Although bilateral and multilateral contacts occur among diplomats assigned to any national capital, such contacts are incidental to the primary mission of representation to the host government and not the fundamental object. The UN diplomat, on the other hand, deals constantly with many national viewpoints and policies and often operates through procedures more congenial to national parliaments than to chanceries and foreign offices. The UN diplomat also deals with a broader spectrum of issues, frequently of a technical nature. This, as Finger observes, "promotes a greater degree of autonomy for the mission, as few governments can keep track of so many details and the government is more dependent on the mission for relevant information."[2]

Permanent representation at the United Nations is essential for the fifteen members of the Security Council, which, under Article 28 of the Charter, must "be so organized as to be able to function continuously." Most other countries also find it useful for a variety of reasons. The Assembly is in session for at least three months of every year. The fifty-four states elected to the Economic and Social Council generally hold one five to six week long substantive session each year, alternating between New York and Geneva, and one organizational meeting in New York City. The substantive session includes a high-level special meeting, attended by Ministers and other high officials, who discuss major economic and social issues. The year-round work of the Council is carried out in its subsidiary bodies—commissions and committees—which meet at regular intervals and report back to the Council. Numerous other UN committees, commissions, and subsidiary bodies hold meetings in New York as well. (See Figure 3-1 for a typical calendar of UN meetings.) For states that have no current meeting in session, there is continuing need to prepare for forthcoming meetings, engage in preliminary negotiations, maintain working relations with the UN Secretariat, monitor the operation of UN activities, and stay in contact with other UN missions.

Diplomatic discussions in New York are by no means limited to matters on a UN agenda. The existence of so many diplomatic missions in one location makes the United Nations the world's busiest center for bilateral diplomacy. Most UN members are small states that cannot afford to maintain embassies in very many other countries. If they are geographically distant from one another, the volume of contacts among their government and citizens does not justify the expense. Yet they may have some common interests, and the United Nations provides a setting where they can exchange views and carry on diplomatic contact, whether or not the matter is a subject of UN discussion.

The United Nations is not the only alternative to exchanging ambassadors. Other possibilities range from unilateral representation (receiving but not sending an ambassador) to multiple accreditation (accrediting an ambassador in one country to others in the area), to third-country representation (communicating with a second country through the embassy of a third), to joint representation (two governments accrediting a single envoy). Permanent representation at the United Nations is helpful but in normal circumstances it is not absolutely essential, especially where the smaller states are concerned. UN representation in fact does not replace direct representation in countries that are vital to the functioning of small states, but the UN nevertheless provides states with the opportunity to dramatically assert their sovereignty, and, not to be overlooked, it also provides lesser as well as larger powers with two representatives in the United States. In sum, the United Nations is a useful channel of communication. Moreover, contacts made at the United Nations may be particularly helpful for states confronted with hostile challenges or threats, and for whom the normal channels of communication may not be fully adequate.

A "delegation" in UN parlance consists of personnel accredited to represent a country at a particular UN meeting or series of meetings. For the General Assembly, each state is entitled by the Charter to five representatives and five alternates, with no constitutional limitation on the clerical or advisory staff,

Figure 3-1   **Sample Calendar of Special Events at UN Headquarters in 1998**

| | |
|---|---|
| 2 January | Military Staff Committee |
| 19 January–6 February | Committee on the Elimination of Discrimination Against Women, 18th Session |
| 26 January–6 February | Special Committee on the Charter of the United Nations and on the Strengthening of the Role of the Organization |
| 3 February–27 March | Advisory Committee on Administrative and Budgetary Questions |
| 19–27 February | Commission on Population and Development |
| 23 February–6 March | Commission on Sustainable Development |
| 5–6 March | UNIS/UN Student Conference |
| 10–19 March | Committee on Natural Resources, Fourth Session |
| 23 March–9 April | Human Rights Committee, Sixty-Second Session |
| 6–28 April | Disarmament Commission |
| 18–22 May | Meeting of the States Parties to the United Nations Convention on the Law of the Sea |
| 18–29 May | Committee on Non-Governmental Organizations |
| 26–29 May | Commission on Human Rights–Working Group on Enforced or Involuntary Disappearances, Fifty-Fourth Session |
| 1–12 June | United Nations Commission on International Trade, Thirty-First Session |
| 13–15 July | United Nations Board of Auditors |
| 31 August–4 September | Commission on the Limits of the Continental Shelf, Fourth Session |
| 10 September | Eighteenth Meeting of States Parties to the International Covenant on Civil and Political Rights |
| October/November | United Nations Administrative Tribunal |
| 30 November | Committee on the Exercise of the Inalienable Rights of the Palestinian People—Special Meeting in Observance of the International Day of Solidarity with the Palestinian People |
| 1–8 December | Panel of External Auditors of the United Nations, the Specialized Agencies and the International Atomic Energy Agency |
| December | Advisory Committee on the United Nations Program of Assistance in the Teaching, Study, Dissemination and Wider Appreciation of International Law, Thirty-Third Session |

Source: UN Department of Public Information, 1998.

which usually consists of permanent mission personnel as well as officials from foreign offices, diplomatic posts or other agencies of government. It is customary for the permanent representative to be one of the delegates, but he is often outranked on the delegation by his foreign minister—and occasionally his head of state or head of government—who may attend part of a session. Some states send a full delegation of professional diplomats, while others include persons from other ministries of government. Many, including the United States, send one or more members of the national legislature and prominent persons from private life.

The UN delegate is akin to both legislator and diplomat. This duality is recognized by use of the term *parliamentary diplomacy* to designate what goes on at meetings of the United Nations and other international organizations. Procedures for agenda setting, debate, and decisions by vote are not unlike those in a national legislature. So also are the informal activities of discussion, persuasion, and compromise in drafting resolutions embodying areas of common interest sufficient to command a voting majority.

But the delegate is still a diplomat. She comes as a representative of her government to negotiate agreements rather than as a representative of her constituency to enact laws. Except for procedural and organizational matters, General Assembly resolutions are not legally binding on states. As a governmental agent, the delegate must act not only in the interest of her country but also in conformity with her government's instructions. There are, of course, vast differences in the quality of instructions from one delegation to another. Some delegations are given lengthy and detailed instructions that severely limit their freedom to maneuver. Some governments instruct their delegations in terms of the positions of other governments, i.e., vote like . . . or if . . . votes 'no,' abstain. Some governments provide no instructions at all, leaving matters to the discretion of the delegation. Instructions are likely to be more detailed on questions of great importance to a government, such as a conflict in which it is involved, and more general in matters of lesser interest.

Even the most meticulous instructions do not rule out all freedom of action. Like any diplomat, the UN delegate can influence the content of his instructions by the information and advice he sends to his foreign office. The degree of influence depends on his political standing at home, as well as on the force of his arguments. If a government has a strong interest in the United Nations as an institution, it may be more willing to listen to members of the delegation or the permanent mission. On the other hand, if a particular issue touches important interests of a country, the UN representative's margin for maneuver and his ability to influence policy may be reduced.

The UN setting virtually demands some leeway for the delegate because no government can fully anticipate every twist and turn of UN parliamentary diplomacy. All delegations have a large measure of discretion as to tactics, and at least some discretion to make minor adjustments of substance. If changed instructions are desired, the delegation's judgment will be given weight because of its position on the UN firing line. The bottom line, nevertheless, is the government's control over its diplomats. Notwithstanding the freedom of action and policy influence entailed by the parliamentary setting, delegations to international meetings have a responsiveness to their governments that is unmatched by any ordinary relationship of a national legislator to a voting constituency or, in democratic societies at least, to a political party.

## THE INSTITUTIONAL SETTING OF UN DECISION MAKING

National interest and national power supply the dynamics of the political process in international organization, but the outcome is also affected by the institutional setting. One obvious institutional constraint is the subject matter competence of the organization. Limited-purpose organizations such as the UN specialized agencies are confined by their charters to a specific subject area, such as the promotion of world health, development funding, or regulation of maritime transport. Regional organizations, by reason of membership as well as constitutional prescription, focus on matters of particular concern to states of the region. The United Nations, by its nature as a general international organization, is much less restrictive in scope. Its legal purview extends to virtually everything under the sun except matters "essentially within the domestic jurisdiction" of a state. Never very limiting, the domestic jurisdiction restriction has grown smaller as human rights, the environment, and other formerly domestic concerns have become the subject of extensive international action. In practice, UN members discuss any subject they wish, since the issue of jurisdiction has always boiled down to who has the votes to put an item on the agenda or keep it off.

Two other institutional features must be considered in greater detail because they so profoundly affect the perception of national interests and the exercise of national power within the United Nations. One is the body of rules and practices that govern voting and formal decision making in the organization. The other consists of the formal and informal communication structures that characterize the UN's political process. Each will be examined in the pages that follow.

### Voting in the International Arena

If decision-making procedures within an international organization accurately mirror the actual distribution of national power, the effect of procedure on the exercise of power is minimal. But such a congruence seldom obtains. This is because power is not easily measured, power patterns change over time, less powerful states are generally unwilling to accept rules that clearly reflect their impotence, and larger states have learned to live with rules that emphasize sovereign equality above national power. In practice, the three most common decision rules of modern international organizations are decision by vote, one vote per member state, and majority rule. When these three rules are combined in an organization of wide membership, an imbalance between internal and external power relationships is unavoidable.

Voting has become so common on the international scene that one can easily forget its recent origins. Modern international organizations date only from the nineteenth century, and voting as a means of international decision making is a product of that development. The international conferences of an earlier period were primarily negotiating bodies without "action" responsibilities. Their function was to negotiate agreements to be embodied in treaty form for ratification by the respective national governments. Voting implies a process of deciding—and the final right of decision belonged to governments individually, not to representatives of states gathered at an international meeting. The principles of national sovereignty and sovereign equality demanded nothing less than complete dispersal of decision-making authority among national units.

With the development of international organizations having permanent secretariats, organizational budgets, and special subject matter competences, a new dimension was added to interstate relations. The organizations themselves became entities with legal personalities distinct from those of their member states. Budgeted funds, though raised primarily through national contributions, were disbursed by the organization, and secretariats did the bidding of the collectivity—not of the individual members. A growing number of decisions of international organizations became operative immediately, without referral to the treaty ratification process. Voting, a time-honored practice in domestic politics, was readily transferred to the new setting.

The shift of real, if limited, decision-making power to international organizations placed unavoidable strain on national sovereignty and equality. In a strictly juridical context states may be equal in their legal rights and duties with respect to the world community. In any other context, including that of international organizations, state equality is pure fiction. States have neither equality of interest in the substance of organizational decisions nor equal capacity to implement them. Sovereign equality suggests that each state should have an equal voice in the decisions of the organization. But this can only result in divorce of power to decide from responsibility for implementing the decision.

The principle of sovereignty gives rise to the further implication that no state can be bound without its consent. Carried to a logical conclusion, this could mean that decisions should be taken only by a unanimous vote. The problem is practical rather than legal. If a state joins the United Nations, it consents to the decision rules of the organization. Thus it is not bound without its consent. In practice, however, states are very reluctant to assume particular obligations to which they object even if they have given general assent to the voting procedures. But such hesitation or reluctance strikes at the capacity of the organization to produce meaningful decisions, and the United Nations often is compelled to seek something less than unanimity on controversial issues. If unanimity is insisted upon decisions may never be made on subjects of vital interest to the international community. It is also true that decisions taken without full support of the member states may result in the dilution of the action so that nothing of substance is agreed upon. Some decisions, of course, cannot be carried out very effectively without the concurrence of the states most directly connected. Economic aid programs will falter without the support of the wealthier contributors. Resolutions will not achieve their aims without acceptance by the targeted governments. But many decisions, certainly those involving joint action among states disposed to cooperate, can be made and acted on without the concurrence of other states having little practical interest in or responsibility for the matter.

International organizations presently display varying kinds of compromise between principle and practicality. Equality of voting rights is the general rule, although its impact has been blunted in several ways and it has been rejected by a few organizations in favor of a distribution of voting rights more accurately reflecting differences in national interests and the distribution of power. This is true of some organizations whose primary function is the handling of money— the International Bank, the International Monetary Fund, the International Finance Corporation, and the International Development Association—where voting power is governed by amount of contribution. Commodity councils, such as the wheat and sugar councils, allot votes according to the volume of imports and exports of the commodity. Still another form of unequal or weighted voting is found in the Central Commission for the Navigation of the Rhine, where voting rights, for certain purposes, are roughly proportional to river frontage. These illustrations suggest that weighted voting is most feasible where the weighting principle can be tied to a single measurable criterion directly related to the primary function of the organization.

When weighted voting is not acceptable, organizations often recognize differences among states by the creation of special executive or deliberative bodies of limited membership on which representation can be granted according to some rough approximation of interest and power. Thus the five largest states in the wartime UN coalition were made permanent members of the Security Council, ten of the twenty-eight governmental seats on the ILO Governing Body are allotted to states of "chief industrial importance," states of "chief importance in air transport" are given preference in the election of the ICAO Council, and eligibility for selection to the Council of the International Maritime Organization is determined by a state's interest in shipping and maritime trade. As further recognition of their special status, the five permanent members of the Security Council are always represented on the UN Trusteeship Council, ECOSOC, and most other UN bodies on which they desire membership. A national of each permanent member is usually chosen to sit on the fifteen-member International Court of Justice.

If sovereign equality has been somewhat eroded by schemes of weighted voting and unequal representation on limited-membership bodies, the rule of unanimity has suffered a more far-reaching eclipse. Unanimity still governs some organizations of limited membership, including the NATO Council, the Arab League Council, and the Council of the Organization for Economic

Cooperation and Development (OECD), but most international organizations now can act by a simple or a qualified majority. Even in the UN Security Council, which retains the principle of unanimity for permanent members, decisions require only nine of fifteen votes.

Majority voting, with its inherent derogation from sovereign prerogatives, is the price paid for some degree of organizational efficiency. The spread of majority voting in international organizations does not necessarily mean the triumph of "majority rule" in international affairs, however. To pass a resolution by majority vote is one thing; to take action that is practically effective and legally binding on all members is quite another. A careful examination of the law and practice of international organizations reveals that majorities have much more authority to recommend than to command and that their authority to command is largely limited to matters eliciting a high degree of consensus or not seriously impinging on the vital interests of states. The Universal Postal Union, for example, can alter certain postal regulations by a two-thirds majority vote. This is possible because of the substantial consensus on UPU objectives. Most international organizations can adopt binding rules governing the operations of their secretariats, the filling of electoral offices, the expenditure of budgeted funds, and other housekeeping activities. Although such "law-making" power is important, it does not ordinarily affect the vital interests of states.[3]

Except for power over internal operations, one looks almost in vain for authority to make binding decisions in any of the policy-making organs of the United Nations. The General Assembly, the Economic and Social Council, and the virtually defunct Trusteeship Council are clearly limited to nonbinding recommendations. Under Chapter VII of the Charter, members are obligated to assist with military, economic, and diplomatic sanctions imposed by the Security Council in dealing with a "threat to the peace, breach of the peace, or act of aggression." However, the Security Council's authority to make binding decisions for the use of military force has thus far remained dormant for lack of special agreements, under Article 43, on the composition of forces to be available on call for UN use. And, until the 1990s, a majority in favor of compulsory nonmilitary sanctions has been a rarity. For most purposes the Security Council, like the General Assembly, has been limited to exhortation rather than command.

*Voting in the General Assembly*

General Assembly decision procedures combine the elements of sovereign equality and majority voting with persistent reluctance to let majorities legislate. Each member state is allotted one vote, regardless of size or capacity to contribute to the purposes of the organization. Decisions on "important questions" require a two-thirds majority of members present and voting. Certain types of "important questions" are specified in the Charter. As enumerated in Article 18, such questions include:

recommendations with respect to the maintenance of international peace and security, the election of the nonpermenant members of the Security Council, the election of members of the Economic and Social Council, the election of members of the Trusteeship Council . . . , the admission of new members to the United Nations, the suspension of the rights and privileges of membership, the expulsion of Members, questions relating to the operation of the trusteeship system, and budgetary questions.

Other matters are decided by a simple majority vote, including the decision to designate other questions or categories of questions as "important" enough to require a two-thirds majority. In calculating the existence of a required majority, the General Assembly has adopted the practice of excluding abstentions as well as absences from the count of states present and voting. With a large number of abstentions, even an important measure can be adopted by considerably fewer than a majority of the total membership. Decisions in the Economic and Social Council, the now-suspended Trusteeship Council, and subordinate UN committees and commissions are made by simple majority of the members present and voting, but their decisions are all subject to review by the General Assembly, with its two-thirds requirement for important questions. Just a few categories of decisions require a majority based on total membership. These include an absolute majority for election to the International Court of Justice, under Article 10 of the ICJ Statute, and a two-thirds majority for the proposal of Charter amendments as provided in Article 109 of the UN Charter.

In the decades since the framing of the UN Charter, dissatisfaction with Assembly voting rules has frequently been voiced. Equality of voting rights has been the most persistent source of concern. The expansion of the United Nations to include many small states created since 1945 has multiplied the voting disparity of small states over large. Third World states now have the voting strength to obtain a two-thirds majority on any issue of importance to them. Mathematically, a two-thirds vote could even be mustered by states collectively representing less than 15 percent of the world's population. This extreme case does not occur, however, because the prevailing Third World majority usually includes such populous countries as China, India, and Indonesia.

Even in the days of U.S. ascendance, the Assembly was prone to adopt resolutions that were totally unacceptable to states in the minority whose cooperation was essential to achieving the purposes of the resolutions. Today, with voting dominance of mostly small and poor developing countries, the gap between the power to decide and the power to implement decisions has further increased. The readiness of small states to use their collective voting power to influence UN outcomes is understandable. It is a form of political leverage. It can sometimes be used to win meaningful compromises from industrialized states. It can in any event be used to win parliamentary victories. But major power disenchantment with equality of voting rights is also understandable. And the effectiveness of the organization is diminished when groups of states, through frustration with the slow pace of negotiations or enthusiasm for a parliamentary cause, resort to an empty display of voting power that cuts short the hard search for genuine agreement. Various forms of weighted voting have been suggested as a remedy to this problem, but no one has yet devised a plan acceptable to a majority of states, not to mention the two-thirds majority required for Charter amendment. Small states, certainly, are unlikely to voluntarily relinquish the advantage they enjoy under the present system. The remedy, if any, must lie in national self-restraint.

Even though formal amendment of UN voting arrangements has not been possible, the members have come to recognize the need for alternatives to deciding by majority vote. The result has been extensive use of a "consensus" approach to decision making. Instead of taking a vote on a proposed resolution, a procedural decision, or some other matter, the presiding officer simply announces his understanding that the measure commands general support and is hence to be considered adopted by consensus. This expedites the decision procedure when there is genuine consensus on an agreed text. It is also useful when general agreement has been reached on action to be taken, but drafting a specific text might prove difficult. Approving the chairman's more-or-less vague summation averts possibly extensive wrangling over details. Sometimes the consensus procedure is used when substantial disagreement exists, but the meeting is willing to adopt a particular text without a vote. This permits a decision without forcing a defeated minority to make its opposition or abstention part of the permanent public record, although some members may still choose to express their objections or reservations to the adopted text. In some sessions of the Assembly, decisions by consensus have outnumbered decisions by majority vote. For example, of 387 resolutions and decisions adopted by the 1990 General Assembly, 297 (77 percent) were decided without a vote, that is, by consensus.[4]

### Voting in the Security Council

At the 1945 San Francisco conference the great powers insisted that their special responsibility for maintaining international peace and security should be recognized in the voting procedures of the Security Council. Thus China, France, the United Kingdom, the United States, and the Soviet Union were made permanent members of the Security Council and each was given a veto over "nonprocedural" matters. The issue involved far more than mere concern for great power status. Without the concurrence of all the major powers, the United Nations could conceivably find itself in the position of starting enforcement action that it could not finish for lack of cooperation from an essential collaborator. Worse yet, a decision to use force in the name of the United Nations over the objection of a state controlling large military forces could be the means of turning localized conflict into world war. The veto was intended to avoid such situations and, above all, to preclude initiation of enforcement action directly against one of the major powers. In the words of one of the architects of the Charter, "This would be the equivalent of a world war, and a decision to embark upon such a war would necessarily have to be made by each of the other nations for itself and not by any international organization."[5]

TABLE 3-3    Vetoes in the Security Council, 1946–1997

| Period | China | France | Britain | U.S. | USSR/Russia | Total |
|---|---|---|---|---|---|---|
| 1946–55 | 1 | 2 | — | — | 79 | 82 |
| 1956–65 | — | 2 | 3 | — | 26 | 31 |
| 1966–75 | 2 | 2 | 10 | 12 | 7 | 33 |
| 1976–85 | — | 9 | 11 | 34 | 6 | 60 |
| 1986–95 | — | 3 | 8 | 24 | 2 | 37 |
| 1996 | — | — | — | — | — | — |
| 1997* | 1 | — | — | 2 | — | 3 |
| Total | 4 | 18 | 32 | 72 | 120 | 246 |

* until 21 March 1997
SOURCE: Compiled by Joanna Franco from information prepared by Solange Habib, Senior Research Assistant, Office of the ASG for the Security Council, 1997.
NOTE: No vetoes were tabulated in 1998, but in February 1999 China cast a veto preventing the continuation of a UN peacekeeping mission.

In practice, the United Nations has not had the important military enforcement role envisioned by the framers, but the veto has still served a useful purpose in preventing the organization from overreaching itself by treading too heavily on the toes of the great powers. All of the permanent members continue to value its protection. From 1946 to 1969, the Soviet Union cast 105 vetoes and the United States none. Between 1976 and 1997, however, the United States cast sixty vetoes to only eight by the USSR/Russia. Since the founding of the United Nations to 1997, the United States had cast a grand total of seventy-two vetoes to 120 for the USSR/Russia. Of the 246 vetoes cast by all the permanent members from 1945 to 1997, China had registered four, France eighteen, and Great Britain thirty-two (see Table 3-3). In 1999, however, a new and disturbing use of the veto was registered when China cast a negative vote against the continuation of the United Nations Preventive Deployment Force (UNPREDEP) in The Former Yugoslav Republic of Macedonia. UNPREDEP was the first preventive peacekeeping operation in UN history, a force meant to quell conflict before it erupted. Moreover, China's veto of UNPREDEP was used because Macedonia had recognized the Republic of China (Taiwan) in return for its economic assistance. Given the tenuous condition in the immediate region of The Former Yugoslav Republic of Macedonia, China's use of its veto power cast a long shadow over over UN efforts at avoiding future conflict. The closing of the UNPREDEP mission, however, did not mean the withdrawal of all the peacekeeping forces. NATO forces that had been assigned to the UN mission had in fact been increased and formed into an extraction force, to be used if required, to assist in the removal of UN, OSCE, and other observer monitors in Kosovo, across the Macedonian border. In fact the monitors were ordered out of Kosovo after Serbia rejected a NATO plan for settling the strife in the Serbian province. Thus when NATO commenced its air campaign against

Serbia in March, the NATO extraction force was given still another mission, that is, providing a modicum of assurance to the host state that its territorial integrity would not be violated by Serbian forces intent on spreading the conflict. Moreover, the allied bombing of Serbia had accelerated Belgrade's ethnic cleansing pogrom in Kosovo. Serbian military and paramilitary forces moved aggressively against not only their nemesis, the Kosovo Liberation Army (KLA), but against the entire population of Albanian Kosovars. The result was a flood of refugees, forcibly removed from their land and homes and sent fleeing into the neighboring countries of Macedonia, Albania and Montenegro. NATO did not stem the human tide, nor did it alter Belgrade's policy of eliminating the Albanian presence in Kosovo. Ethnic balances in Montenegro, and especially in Macedonia were significantly disturbed with dire portents. The UN, having failed in its effort to prevent the intensification of the conflict over Kosovo, was now challenged by the codeployment principle which envisaged a still heavier NATO role in the region. Unable to secure the peace, the world organization assumed the enormous task of tending to the needs of the Kosovar Albanian refugees as well as the nations that were called upon to provide them with sanctuary.

Vetoes have been a source of irritation to states on the opposite side of the issue but up to 1999 did not seriously hamper the United Nations in performing its security functions. Fifty-one of the Soviet vetoes, all before 1960, were used to deny approval of UN membership applications that had been pressed to a vote over Soviet objection. All of the vetoed applicants were subsequently admitted, most of them in 1955. Other vetoes have been almost frivolous or inconsequential in their practical effects. In 1949 the Soviet Union vetoed a resolution of official congratulations to the Netherlands and Indonesia upon successful conclusion of their negotiations for Indonesian independence. In 1963 the Security Council was not permitted to utter official condemnation of the murder of two Israelis in an incident along the Syrian border. Still other vetoes have been circumvented through action by the General Assembly. This was notably true of the Korean War, the 1956 Suez crisis, and the 1960 UN Congo operation. It has also been true of numerous resolutions of condemnation or censure first vetoed in the Security Council and subsequently adopted, with perhaps some change in wording, by the General Assembly. Assembly resolutions disapproving Soviet intervention in Hungary and Afghanistan, U.S. intervention in Nicaragua, Grenada, and Panama, and many Israeli actions in the Middle East are examples of the practice. Generally speaking, only a few of the vetoes cast since the inception of the United Nations have been concerned with vital international security issues. Between 1946 and 1997, fifty-nine vetoes were cast to block admission of member states. Forty-three vetoes were used to prevent nominations for the office of the Secretary-General, although these latter vetoes were cast in closed sessions of the Security Council and are not included in Table 3-3. China's veto of the continuing deployment of UNPREDEP in The Former Yugoslav Republic of Macedonia, however, involved a vital security matter, especially given instability in neighboring Kosovo. If Security

Council peacekeeping missions are rejected as a consequence of purely domestic issues having no bearing on the mission itself, the UN's future capacity to buttress world security could be significantly reduced. China's veto of the continuing deployment of UNPREDEP in The Former Yugoslav Republic of Macedonia may not have been a major factor in the intensification of the conflict over Kosovo in March and April 1999, but the use of the veto by a permanent power for reasons having nothing to do with the peacekeeping mission signalled still new difficulties for the United Nations in its role as the world's chief peacekeeper.

Some vetoes, of course, have achieved their purpose of preventing UN action opposed by one or more of the permanent members. British and U.S. vetoes successfully fended off mandatory UN sanctions against South Africa, except for an arms embargo. China's veto in 1981 denied a third term as Secretary-General to Kurt Waldheim, and the U.S. veto barred the election of Tanzanian Salim A. Salim. The 1961 Soviet veto of a resolution calling for a cease-fire and withdrawal of Indian forces from Goa was never contradicted by the Assembly, and Soviet vetoes of cease-fire resolutions in December 1971 left India uninhibited in its military action against Pakistan, which secured the independence of East Pakistan (now Bangladesh). Likewise, the British veto of a call for cessation of hostilities in the Falklands permitted the fighting to be resolved on British terms before the Assembly, meeting later in the fall of 1982, could intervene.

Thus the veto has given protection to the interests of the permanent members but has seldom prevented UN action in a situation where effective UN action was possible. When action has been feasible and desired by member states, the General Assembly has usually found a way to act. If a UN resolution will not alter any state's behavior for the better, a veto of that resolution can scarcely be considered a disservice to the organization or to the cause of peace. The veto simply prevents the Security Council from undermining its own authority by issuing orders that cannot be carried out.

Viewed in another perspective, the veto may be crucial to UN viability as a world organization. During the years of Western dominance in the General Assembly, the Soviet Union might have left the United Nations altogether if it had been forced to accept the will of the Western coalition in the Security Council. Through hard diplomatic times the Soviet Union stayed, perhaps in part because the veto provided an institutional power base that could not be shaken by numerical majorities. From the 1960s onward the Soviet Union was no longer politically isolated in either the Assembly or the Security Council. But the United States, often confronted with hostile Third World majorities in the Assembly, welcomed the protection of the veto in the Security Council, and for example blocked resolutions dealing with Israel (May 1990) and the U.S. invasion of Panama (January 1990).

The veto has also had the salutary effect of promoting the search for consensus. The same forces that encourage consensus in the Assembly are at work in the Security Council, but the veto provides an additional incentive. If the Council is to act at all, it must have the concurrence—or at least the abstention—of each permanent member. The need for great power consensus was the fundamental assumption underlying the UN security system, and the veto was the institutional embodiment of that assumption. The passing decades have demonstrated both the correctness of the assumption and the utility of the veto as an incentive to reach consensus.

### The United Nations as a Communications Network

Voting procedures set important constraints on decision making. The flow of information among the participants that precedes the voting is even more important in determining the kinds of decisions that will be reached.

The United Nations generates a constant stream of information that must be evaluated by foreign offices. The United Nations also stimulates a heavy flow of information directly between governments. The approach of a General Assembly session, for example, is always the signal for increased intergovernmental consultations both through regular diplomatic channels and in New York. Members with a special interest in an issue use presession discussion to obtain the widest measure of support for their positions. On issues in which they have no special interest, they consult to obtain the information necessary to appraise their own policies intelligently in the light of positions held by others.

Whatever the scope of presession consultations, the beginning of an Assembly session brings a new phase in the communication process. National governments now become sources of information flowing into and through the UN system.

The UN provides both formal and informal channels for the flow of information. Formal debate in committee and plenary session has symbolic importance but usually does little to facilitate agreement on disputed questions. A public address may dramatize or occasionally clarify positions, but a committee of 185 members is too large for useful document drafting or for working out detailed compromise. Furthermore, reconciliation of differences requires give-and-take in a more private setting. This can occur among smaller groups of states in vacant rooms of the UN building or perhaps in delegation offices. Social gatherings also have their part in the communication process. Although casual meetings in a UN bar or lounge, luncheon engagements, cocktail parties, or formal receptions are unlikely settings for resolution drafting, they can provide occasion for significant exchanges of views and information.

### UN "Groups"

The private, ad hoc interchange between delegates drawn temporarily together by their common interest in an issue is a persistent and inevitable part of the UN process. But other forms of interchange occur on a more routinized basis. The least formal may include the regular luncheon engagements of two friendly delegates sharing a range of common interests. At a higher level of activity and significance are organized groups having more-or-less regular meeting times, established routines for the conduct of discussion, and secretarial assistance drawn from one or more of the delegation staffs.

Groups have formed at the United Nations for the obvious purpose of achieving common objectives through concerted action. Consultation within regional groups received its initial impetus from electoral contests in the General Assembly. By seeking agreement beforehand, groups of members might hope to obtain an "equitable share" of Assembly officers and elective positions on the Security Council, ECOSOC, and other UN bodies with rotating membership. This ultimately led to agreed arrangements for allotting such positions among geographic regions and permitting regional groups to nominate candidates to fill the allotted positions. For electoral purposes nearly every UN member is assigned to one of five regional groups—the African group, the Asian group, the Latin American group, the Eastern European group, and the Western European and Others group, which includes Australia, Canada and New Zealand (see Figure 3-2). Israel does not meet with a regional group. The United States is not a member of any group but consults with Western Europe on electoral matters.

The formal geographic groups exist primarily for elections and exchange of relevant information, but other groups, sometimes called caucusing groups, are concerned with policy matters. Such groups reflect common interests, and often organizational ties, developed outside the United Nations. Thus members of the Commonwealth of Independent States, the Organization of Security and Cooperation in Europe, the League of Arab States, the Organization of African Unity, the Organization of American States, the Association of Southeast Asian Nations, the European Union, the Organization for Economic Cooperation and Development, the Nordic Group, the Contact Group, the Group of 77, the G-7 (with Russia G-8), the Islamic Conference, and others, meet periodically, or as their interests dictate, to exchange views and canvass the prospects for common action.

Occasionally an issue may call for consultation among members of the North Atlantic Treaty Organization or the Commonwealth. Not infrequently a group appoints a common spokesperson to represent its views in debate on a particular issue. No group matched the voting unity of the East European states during the years of Soviet domination there, but coordination of policy initiatives and UN voting has been a frequent product of group consultation, with considerable effect on voting outcomes. The overlapping membership of various groups is shown in Figure 3-3.

During the past two decades two interrelated groups have held a special preeminence among groups in UN politics. One is the Group of 77, representing the interests of the Third World countries, which are the vast majority of UN members. The other is the Non-Aligned Movement (NAM). Although Third World does not suggest an institution or an organized lobby, the Non-Aligned Movement (NAM), and more notably, the Group of 77, does speak for the less developed states that achieved independence after World War II. The term "Third World" is believed to have been coined in France during the 1950s,

FIGURE 3-2    UN Membership Regional Groups, 1999

Much of the work of the United Nations is done after consultations within five regional groups. These groups have not been created by the General Assembly, but have evolved over the years for many practical reasons. Two countries—Israel and the United States—are not members of any regional grouping. For election purposes the United States is considered under "Western European and Other States."

AFRICAN STATES

Algeria, Angola, Benin, Botswana, Burkina Faso, Burundi Cameroon, Cape Verde, Central African Republic, Chad, Comoros, Congo, Djibouti, Egypt, Equatorial Guinea, Eritrea, Ethiopia, Gabon, Gambia, Ghana, Guinea, Guinea-Bissau, Ivory Coast, Kenya, Lesotho, Liberia, Libyan Arab Jamahiriya, Madagascar, Malawi, Mali, Mauritania, Mauritius, Morocco, Mozambique, Namibia, Niger, Nigeria, Rwanda, São Tomé and Principe, Senegal, Seychelles, Sierra Leone, Somalia, South Africa, Sudan, Swaziland, Togo, Tunisia, Uganda, United Republic of Tanzania, Zaire, Zambia, Zimbabwe.

ASIAN STATES

Afghanistan, Bahrain, Bangladesh, Bhutan, Brunei Darussalam, Cambodia, China, Cyprus, Democratic People's Republic of Korea, Federated States of Micronesia, Fiji, India, Indonesia, Iraq, Iran, Japan, Jordan, Kuwait, Lao People's Democratic Republic, Lebanon, Malaysia, Maldives, Marshall Islands, Mongolia, Myanmar, Nepal, Oman, Pakistan, Palau, Papua New Guinea, Philippines, Qatar, Republic of Korea, Samoa, Saudi Arabia, Singapore, Solomon Islands, Sri Lanka, Syrian Arab Republic, Thailand, Turkey,* United Arab Emirates, Vanuatu, Vietnam, Yemen.

EASTERN EUROPEAN STATES

Albania, Armenia, Azerbaijan, Belarus, Bosnia and Herzegovina, Bulgaria, Croatia, Czech Republic, Estonia, Georgia, Hungary, Kazakhstan, Kyrgyzstan, Latvia, Lithuania, Poland, Republic of Moldova, Romania, Russian Federation, Slovak Republic, Slovenia, Tajikistan, Turkmenistan, Ukraine, Uzbekistan, Yugoslavia, the former Yugoslav Republic of Macedonia.

LATIN AMERICAN STATES

Antigua and Barbuda, Argentina, Bahamas, Barbados, Belize, Bolivia, Brazil, Chile, Colombia, Costa Rica, Cuba, Dominica, Dominican Republic, Ecuador, El Salvador, Grenada, Guatemala, Guyana, Haiti, Honduras, Jamaica, Mexico, Nicaragua, Panama, Paraguay, Peru, Saint Kitts and Nevis, Saint Lucia, Saint Vincent and the Grenadines, Suriname, Trinidad and Tobago, Uruguay, Venezuela.

WESTERN EUROPEAN AND OTHER STATES

Andorra, Australia, Austria, Belgium, Canada, Denmark, Finland, France, Germany, Greece, Iceland, Ireland, Italy, Liechtenstein, Luxembourg, Malta, Monaco, Netherlands, New Zealand, Norway, Portugal, San Marino, Spain, Sweden, Turkey,* United Kingdom.

* Turkey, which is in the Western European Group for election purposes, is also a member of the Asian group.

FIGURE 3-3   Regional and Other UN Groups: Overlapping Membership, 1999

**1**

**3** Albania    Latvia
    Armenia    Lithuania
    Azerbaijan    Moldova
    Bosnia and    Poland
      Herzegovina    Russian Federation
    Belarus    Slovak Republic
    Bulgaria    Slovenia
    Croatia    Tajikistan
    Czech Republic    The Former
    Estonia       Yugoslav Republic
    Georgia       of Macedonia
    Hungary    Turkmenistan
    Kazakhstan    Ukraine
    Kyrgyzstan    Usbekistan

Romania

**2** Antigua and Barbuda    Haiti
    Argentina    Honduras
    Brazil    Mexico
    Costa Rica    Paraguay
    Dominica    St. Kitts and Nevis
    Dominican Republic    St. Vincent
    El Salvador    Uruguay

**4** Yugoslavia

Bahamas   Ecuador   Peru
Barbados   Grenada   St. Lucia
Belize   Guatemala   Suriname
Bolivia   Guyana   Trinidad and
Chile   Jamaica    Tobago
Colombia   Nicaragua   Venezuela
Cuba   Panama

**Key to group numbering**
1. Group of 77
2. Latin America and
   Caribbean group
*3. Eastern European group
4. Non-aligned movement
5. African group
6. Islamic conference
7. Arab group
8. Asian group
9. Western Europe and
   other states
10. European Union
11. Nordic group

**5**

Angola    Democratic Republic   Liberia    Sao Tome
Benin      of the Congo   Madagascar   Seychelles
Botswana    Equatorial Guinea   Malawi    South Africa
Burundi    Eritrea   Mauritius    Swaziland
Cape Verde    Ethiopia   Mozambique   Tanzania
Central African Republic   Ghana   Namibia    Togo
Congo    Kenya   Nigeria    Zambia
Cote d'Ivoire    Lesotho   Rwanda    Zimbabwe

**6**

Burkina Faso   Guinea Bissau
Cameroon   Mali
Chad   Niger
Comoros   Senegal
Gabon   Sierra Leone
Gambia   Uganda
Guinea

**7** Algeria    Morocco
    Djibouti    Somalia
    Egypt    Sudan
    Libya    Tunisia
    Mauritania

**8**
China
Japan

Bangladesh   Malaysia
Brunei   Maldives
Indonesia   Pakistan
Iran

Bahrain   Qatar
Iraq   Saudi Arabia
Jordan   Syria
Kuwait   United Arab Emirates
Lebanon   Yemen
Oman

Fiji
Korea,
Republic of
Marshall Islands
Micronesia
Myanmar
Philippines
Samoa
Solomons
Thailand

Turkey

**9**
Andorra
Australia
Austria
Canada
Liechtenstein
Monaco
New Zealand
San Marino

Afghanistan   Nepal
Bhutan   Palau
Cambodia   Papua New Guinea
Cyprus   Singapore
India   Sri Lanka
Korea, D.R.   Vanuatu
Laos   Viet Nam
Mongolia

Malta

**10**
Belgium   Netherlands
France   Luxembourg
Germany   Portugal
Greece   Spain
Ireland   United Kingdom
Italy

**11**
Denmark   Finland
       Iceland
       Norway
       Sweden

Member of no group
Israel
United States

All of the former Soviet Republics were technically
still members of the Eastern European group,
although several of them are in Asia. Moreover,
NATO's expansion program includes Poland, Hungary,
and the Czech Republic, thus giving some East European
States (3) association with Western Europe (10).

more or less to describe those nations emerging from the tutelage of colonialism. And because the majority of these nations are found in the southern hemisphere, they are also described as the "South," as in the "North-South" dialogue. The Group of 77 was actually formed at the 1964 inaugural meeting in Geneva of the UN Conference on Trade and Development (UNCTAD), which was attended by 77 Third World nations. It was during that conference that the developing countries agreed to form an organization through which they could better represent their economic and trade problems at future UNCTAD sessions, as well as within the UN General Assembly and the entire United Nations system. The membership of the Group of 77 expanded to include almost double that number in subsequent years, but the original description, that is, G-77, has nonetheless been retained.

Organizationally, the G-77 has no secretariat but is formally divided into African, Asian, and Latin American groupings and creates committees and working groups as the need arises. The group has been the driving force in the United Nations for promoting developing countries' interests in trade, aid, investment, technical cooperation, and related matters. Developed countries have come to expect position papers or other statements from the Group of 77 at most UN meetings, and draft resolutions are frequently submitted on behalf of the whole group by the state holding the current chairmanship.

The Group of 77 has maintained a fair degree of cohesiveness on issues of economic development, although significant divisions have emerged in recent years. Unity is greatest in formulating broad statements of principle or general concepts reflecting the interests of developing countries vis-à-vis the industrialized states. On specific issues, differences in levels of development and particular economic interests have often made negotiation of a common position difficult. At the UN Law of the Sea Conference, for example, members of the group were frequently divided on the basis of their differing maritime interests, their locations as landlocked or coastal states, or their positions as importers or exporters of certain minerals.

The Group of 77 has the voting strength to override all opposition in the United Nations, and sometimes it does. Since meaningful action often depends on voluntary cooperation from industrialized states, however, the group has shown an increasing tendency to negotiate consensus decisions. In the negotiation process the numbers and unity of the group provide political leverage but are far from determinative. Occasionally negotiations with the industrialized states break down and end in a display of raw voting power. At other times a degree of genuine consensus can be reached.

The decline of East-West tensions reduced the leverage of the group because it could no longer play off East against West. The retreat from socialist economics in Eastern Europe, and the obviously superior performance of the Western market economies, had the further effect of undermining the economic presuppositions of some developing countries that relied heavily on state economic management. Moreover, the states of the former Soviet bloc became competitors for economic aid that might otherwise go to the Third World. None of this changed the basic needs of the Third World or the drive for development. It did, however, make developing countries more receptive to market-oriented solutions suggested by the United States and other Western industrialized countries, and this in turn moved the G-77 into a more conciliatory position on some economic matters. It has also led the G-77 to emphasize the "environmental card"—that is, to make a case that developing states cannot afford the cost of controlling industrial pollution, preserving the rain forests, and other environmental measures without more assistance from the rich countries. This was an underlying theme at the 1992 Conference on Environment and Development.

The Non-Aligned Movement was organized separately from the Group of 77, although the two shared economic goals and reinforced each other on matters of common interest. The NAM had a somewhat smaller membership than the Group of 77, 105 states and the PLO (representing "Palestine"). The Non-Aligned Movement dates from a 1961 summit conference in Belgrade, convoked by Marshal Tito for the purpose of exploring a common foreign policy independent of the superpowers. Summit meetings were held approximately every three years (except 1967), with annual meetings of foreign ministers during the fall meeting of the UN General Assembly and meetings of specialized lower-level representatives as necessary. The NAM had no headquarters or permanent secretariat.

The NAM took positions on a broader range of issues than the Group of 77. In addition to being concerned with economic development, the NAM was highly active on issues pertaining to the Middle East and southern Africa, as well as other political questions. Its anticolonial, anti-Western bias frequently put the movement at odds with the United States. In its summit pronouncements and UN voting, the NAM was far less likely to make common cause with the United States than with the Soviet Union, which for years maintained a posture of general support and encouragement for the NAM. In 1983 the U.S. permanent representative to the United Nations called the NAM "the most important bloc of all" because of it size and effectiveness.

But with East and West no longer strategic rivals, with NATO expanding to include some of the former Warsaw Pact states of Eastern Europe, and with Russia a member of the U.S.-inspired Partnership For Peace (PFP), G-8, and Contact Group, the notion of non-alignment has become anachronistic, and the NAM has been forced to redefine its role. As a movement the NAM always had internal divisions, and group discipline was difficult to attain. Exceptions perhaps were found in UN votes on the issue of apartheid in South Africa, or the Palestinian question in the Middle East, but on many other matters there were always significant defections. Indeed, the termination of apartheid and South Africa's rebirth under black majority leadership, as well as the Palestine Liberation Organization's several agreements with the state of Israel, has further divided and confused the organization's members. So too on economic questions where the G-77 is a more dominant actor, the NAM more and more finds its purpose ambiguous, and in many instances, redundant. And because the NAM never established a permanent secretariat or official headquarters it appears likely to fade away, its work assumed by other, more formal organizations.

Opinions differ on whether the group system has a salutary effect on UN politics. On the negative side, the group system introduces elements of rigidity into the political process. When a group has agreed on its position, the need for constant reference back to the group may make negotiation of compromise solutions more difficult. An individual member of the group also loses flexibility when pressures to conform to the group position prevent the public expression of any misgivings that the member may have. The dilemma may be excruciating when an individual spokesperson for a group passes off his or her own extremist views as the group position or when the group position in fact represents the views of its more extremist elements. The group system has the further disadvantage of fostering power relationships within the United Nations that are at variance with the actual distribution of national power. Large groups of small states can dominate voting, but they may have little power to carry out the mandates they have issued.

The system nevertheless has a positive side. For the smaller or less developed countries, which constitute the majority of UN members, groups play a very useful role in promoting shared interests—most notably in dealing with issues of economics and anticolonialism. For new and smaller members, the groups perform an important socializing function, helping new governments and delegates to find their roles in the UN community. For nearly all members, the groups provide additional channels of communication and a forum for harmonization of views. Such discussions are an important means of building consensus at the group level, in some instances eliminating the need for an extensive series of bilateral negotiations. If the formulation of group positions adds rigidity to UN decision making, that rigidity is mitigated by the trend toward consensus decisions in UN meetings generally. As a further benefit, the group system saves time in meetings by permitting speaking assignments to be filled by one or a few delegates from a group in place of the many who might otherwise speak.

## UN DECISIONS: WHO WINS?

Action by the General Assembly or the Security Council, as in most other intergovernmental bodies, is symbolized by the adoption of a resolution. The winners, in a parliamentary sense, are those who vote for a resolution that succeeds or against a resolution that fails. When the political process works at its best, an adopted resolution is the expression of a common interest among states having the will and the ability to do whatever its implementation requires. At other times the "win" is purely parliamentary.

### Pressure and Influence

Most resolutions are the product of extensive negotiation and compromise. The frequent adoption of resolutions by consensus indicates that this process can be successful in finding the requisite area of common interest (or at least in watering down the resolution so that no one is seriously offended). Often, however, opinion in the Assembly is strongly divided, so that adoption of a resolution is a victory for some and a defeat for others. In such a situation the delegations most directly interested will lobby vigorously to achieve victory or avoid defeat.

An example of massive lobbying was the successful U.S. campaign in December 1991 to secure the repeal of the General Assembly's 1975 resolution equating Zionism with racism. The groundwork was laid months in advance, first by consulting close allies and subsequently extending the contacts to other states as possible co-sponsors of the measure. Advance contact was also made with moderate Arab states that might be persuaded not to oppose repeal. In early December, when the U.S. concluded that prospective support was sufficient to justify a repeal attempt, State Department telegrams went out to every U.S. embassy in the world. Each ambassador was instructed to solicit not only the foreign government's support of the repeal but also co-sponsorship. In some cases, the United States sought a further commitment to lobby for repeal so that the campaign would appear more than a U.S.-Israeli effort. The initial area of focus was Europe, East and West, and reluctance had to be overcome in both places. Moscow hung back at first, out of concern for antagonizing the Muslim republics in Central Asia, but eventually gave in. Many Latin American states were reluctant as well until Argentina and Mexico agreed to co-sponsor. Eventually a list of 86 sponsors was obtained from every regional group, a product of great persistence and personal contacts, including letters and telephone calls from President George Bush, Vice President Dan Quayle, and Secretary of State James Baker. At the final vote 111 states supported repeal, 25 opposed, 13 abstained, and 15 were absent. No Arab state supported the repeal or abstained, but seven chose to be absent when the vote was taken.

What is the content of "pressure" when a country decides to turn it on? For the most part it is insistence, persistence, and finding ways to neutralize objections. The lobbying is most effective where there is an important relationship between the parties concerned—ties of friendship, military security, cultural homogeneity, or economic dependence. Regional and group solidarity have become especially important in UN meetings, particularly for the small or less developed countries whose parliamentary strength lies in unity. On many issues group pressures are determinative. As between individual governments, pressure may consist not so much in what is said as in how it is said. When reluctant delegates are repeatedly buttonholed in New York and their governments subjected to insistent appeals at home, the pressure is noticed. In this context an appeal for "good relations" carries a hint that relations may be strained by failure to cast an appropriate vote. For a large country merely to communicate a strong opinion to a smaller dependent country may constitute pressure. If no more is said, the smaller country is left to weigh the uncertain consequences of taking a position displeasing to its more powerful patron. Such interchanges constitute a kind of diplomatic pressure and are a common occurrence in connection with UN meetings.

The crasser forms of threat or promise are seldom used because they are too costly to invoke often. Threats arouse resentment, and bribes do not build

TABLE 3-4   Regional Group Voting Agreement with the United States: Forty-Sixth General Assembly, 1991 (70 recorded votes on which the U.S. voted "yes" or "no")

| GROUP | PERCENT IDENTICAL VOTES | PERCENT OPPOSING VOTES | PERCENT ABSTENTIONS |
|---|---|---|---|
| Western Europe and Others | 41.9 | 28.3 | 29.8 |
| Eastern Europe | 35.2 | 33.8 | 31.0 |
| Latin America and the Caribbean | 22.2 | 68.9 | 8.9 |
| Asia and the Pacific | 18.5 | 74.5 | 7.0 |
| Africa | 18.4 | 77.8 | 3.8 |
| Arab States | 15.3 | 83.4 | 1.3 |
| Israel | 70.0 | 19.0 | 20.0 |
| All UN Members | 24.5 | 63.5 | 12.0 |

SOURCE: U.S. Department of State, *Voting Practices in the United Nations 1991*, Report to Congress submitted pursuant to Public Law 101-167, March 31, 1992, pp. 8–21.

mutual esteem and respect over the long run. Most Assembly decisions are not important enough to justify the threat to alter levels of foreign aid or to take other forms of retaliatory action. Seldom do the stakes of UN action appear to justify strong bilateral pressures. Undoubtedly the occasions when such pressures would bring a favorable vote are even fewer. Another form of pressure, exerted primarily as a deterrent to action, is the threat of noncooperation with proposed UN programs. This kind of bargaining power is still important for a country like the United States, whose cooperation may be essential to the effective functioning of particular economic programs.

The discussion of pressure tactics may convey the picture of a great power using its muscle to induce small states to vote the way the larger power wants. Within Eastern Europe this once was true, but East bloc solidarity was not enough to win an Assembly vote. The Soviet Union never had enough reliable friends to constitute anything close to a UN majority, and the days of a dependable U.S.-led majority are also long gone. As Table 3-4 indicates, except for Western Europe, no regional group of states votes with the United States on contested votes even half of the time. In point of fact, neither Russia nor the United States consistently votes with the majority as often as most members. A tabulation of majority agreement scores for seventy-nine resolutions adopted by roll-call votes during the 1954, 1959, and 1962 sessions of the Assembly shows that the United States voted in the minority more often than did 93 of the 110 member states and that only four members had a poorer win-loss record than the former Soviet Union. Since the early years of the Cold War U.S. agreement with the majority on contested roll-call votes has grown much worse, falling below 15 percent in the 1980s, while the Soviet (now Russian) score has improved markedly. The U.S. decline and the corresponding rise in Soviet agreement with the Assembly majority are shown in Table 3-5 and Figure 3-4. The improved Soviet position was not the result of Soviet leadership initiatives

TABLE 3-5    U.S. and Soviet Union Percentage
Agreement with the Majority, UN General
Assembly Roll-Call Votes, Regular Plenary
Sessions, 1946–90

| PERCENT AGREEMENT WITH MAJORITY | | |
|---|---|---|
| YEARS | UNITED STATES | SOVIET UNION |
| 1946–50 | 74.0 | 34.1 |
| 1951–55 | 60.1 | 52.4 |
| 1956–60 | 72.5 | 47.2 |
| 1961–65 | 54.5 | 54.7 |
| 1966–70 | 43.9 | 59.4 |
| 1971–75 | 38.9 | 65.1 |
| 1976–80 | 32.6 | 67.4 |
| 1981–85 | 14.3 | 79.3 |
| 1986–90 | 12.3 | 93.0 |

SOURCE: Inter-University Consortium for Political Re-
search, Ann Arbor, Michigan, for years 1946–85; United
Nations, *Index to Proceedings of the General Assembly,*
ST/LIB/SER. B/A. 41–46, Part I (1987–91).

or of pressures effectively exerted on smaller states. It reflected mainly the General Assembly dominance of the Third World majority, with which the Soviet
Union was able to make common cause.

This state of affairs led a Reagan-appointed U.S. ambassador to the United
Nations to observe that the United States had no influence at all in the General
Assembly (see Table 3-5). Continuing frustration with the United Nations, as
expressed by some American government officials, as well as segments of the
lay public, is traced to the changing patterns of UN membership, and the one
state, one vote principle that provided the Third World nations with a figura-
tive veto over U.S. policy in the General Assembly. The more determined United
States use of the veto in Security Council deliberations in the latter years of the
Cold War was a reflection of this frustration. Moreover, this dissatisfaction
with the UN carried over and into the post-Cold War era. Public opinion in
the United States had become demonstrably divided between those favoring a
larger role for the UN and those vehemently opposed to it. Washington's failure to meet its financial obligations to the world organization, and Congressional statements adverse to United Nations-sponsored programs, however,
appeared to cause more distress in United Nations headquarters than in individual member states.

Clearly, the United States does not have a monopoly of pressure tactics or
influence within the United Nations. And given the leverage enjoyed by Third
World nations in the General Assembly, the U.S. Congress will continue to

FIGURE 3-4 Graph of U.S. and Soviet Union Percentage Agreement with the Majority, UN General Assembly Roll-Call Votes. Regular Plenary Sessions, 1946–90

**Percent agreement**

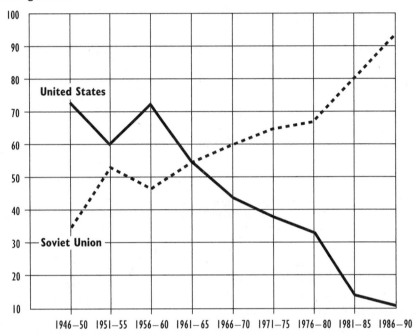

SOURCE: Roll call voting data obtained from Inter-University Consortium for Political Research, Ann Arbor, Michigan, for years 1946–85; and United Nations, *Index to Proceedings of the General Assembly*, ST/LIB/Ser. B/A. 41–46, Part I (1987–91), for years 1986–90.

promote NATO over that of the UN in security matters. It is interesting to note that in votes in the American Congress in 1998, the enlargement of NATO received almost unanimous support, whereas the same body could not muster the necessary majority to pay the country's back dues to the UN.

On the one side, the United States represents the only surviving, and indeed flourishing superpower. On the other, however, it is not just the Third World nations that find the Americans too eager to display their prowess in strategic as well as economic matters. Even U.S. allies are distressed by what they judge to be an overbearing and demanding American posture. American hegemony was to be resisted and nowhere was this more obvious than in the United Nations General Assembly. Washington's enthusiasm for NATO expansion therefore was in sharp contrast to its reluctance to grant permanent power status on the Security Council to additional countries.

TABLE 3-6   Security Council Voting Behavior, 1987–94

| Year | Meetings | Resolutions Considered | Resolutions Adopted | U.S. Vetoes |
|------|----------|------------------------|---------------------|-------------|
| 1994 | 160 | 78 | 77 | 0 |
| 1993 | 171 | 95 | 93 | 0 |
| 1992 | 129 | 74 | 74 | 0 |
| 1991 | 53 | 42 | 42 | 0 |
| 1990 | 69 | 40 | 37 | 2 |
| 1989 | 69 | 25 | 20 | 5 |
| 1988 | 55 | 26 | 20 | 6 |
| 1987 | 49 | 15 | 13 | 2 |

SOURCE: U.S. Department of State, *Voting Practices in the United Nations, 1994, Report to Congress* Submitted Pursuant to Public Law. 101–167, March 31, 1995.

The voting dynamics in the Security Council are significantly different from that in the General Assembly, and here the United States is more likely to find itself voting with the majority (see Table 3-6). If 1994 is taken as a pivotal year in the escalation of UN activity following the end of the Cold War, it also reveals a marked increase in Security Council cooperation. While the number of formal meetings and resolutions adopted were slightly lower than in 1993, there were more than in any other previous year. More significantly, the number of consensus agreements were extremely high. Moreover, the Council had become involved even more deeply in the world community's efforts to resolve intra as well as international conflicts.

The Security Council authorized new operations in Haiti, Tajikistan, and the Aouzou strip border between Libya and Chad. It also began the closing down of operations in Mozambique, South Africa, Somalia and El Salvador. Nevertheless, it responded to acts of genocide in Rwanda, and it sought peaceful solutions to disputes in the Persian Gulf, Georgia, Liberia, Angola, Burundi, and Cyprus. Measured against the popularity contest in the General Assembly, it was the Security Council that more accurately reflected the realities of UN voting behavior. Of the seventy-seven resolutions adopted by the Council in 1994 (only one was rejected), three were approved without a vote and sixty-two won unanimous approval. Of the twelve resolutions adopted without unanimous approval, the United States voted in favor of eleven and abstained in one. Russia was the only permanent member to cast a veto in 1994, its first since the collapse of the Soviet Union.

## The Structure of General Assembly Coalitions

The makeup of winning coalitions differs in detail with the nature of the issue, but UN membership patterns now guarantee that any majority in the General

Assembly must depend heavily on votes from African, Asian, and Latin American countries. The large powers win when they can find common ground with the developing, non-Western majority. On many issues the larger and wealthier states have important leverage in the negotiation process because their cooperation is essential to carrying out proposed resolutions.

In economic matters the majority understandably favors proposals for redistributing the world's wealth. Assembly majorities routinely vote anti-Israel and anticolonial. On Middle East issues, the United States and Israel frequently stand alone on the losing side of the vote, with a few U.S. allies abstaining. Before the breakup of the Soviet empire, the UN majority purported to be nonaligned but their speeches and votes indicated more suspicion of the United States than of the Soviet Union.

The cohesiveness of the majority is shown by the extreme rarity of close votes. The African, Asian, and developing countries simply overwhelm the opposition when agreement cannot be negotiated. The division of ninety-three to twenty-seven with thirty-seven abstaining that occurred during the Forty-Sixth Assembly (1991) on a vote demanding immediate and complete Israeli withdrawal from occupied territories was a close decision by UN standards. More typical examples from the same session were the vote of 104 to two with forty-three abstaining setting forth principles for a Middle East peace that were unacceptable to Israel (opposed only by Israel and the United States), and a resolution calling for the return or restitution of cultural property to the countries of origin, which drew twenty-three abstentions but no opposing votes. Winning coalitions thus have a remarkable quality of sameness. Nothing can pass that does not minimally satisfy the Third World. The fact that Western industrialized states, East European states, and individual Third World states slide in and out of the majority is almost incidental to the outcome. With small, poor, developing states winning far more often than large, rich, developed states, the UN General Assembly appears to be a place where, to parody Thucydides' maxim, "the weak do what they can and the strong suffer what they must."

But that is not the whole story. In recent years the United States has prepared an annual report on General Assembly voting practices for the purpose of identifying how frequently other UN members vote with the United States. One feature of the report is a congressionally mandated discussion of "votes on issues which directly affected important United States interests and on which the United States lobbied extensively." [6] Of the twelve decisions in the 1991 Assembly meeting these criteria, the United States prevailed on eight. These included defeat of an Iraqi proposal to recondemn Israel for its 1981 attack on an Iraqi nuclear reactor; commending the International Atomic Energy Agency for monitoring Iraqi violations of its nuclear non-proliferation obligations; providing a registry of conventional arms transfers; urging support of the United Nations Relief and Works Agency in Palestine; repealing the 1975 resolution equating Zionism with racism (two recorded votes); focusing international attention on Iraqi human rights violations in Kuwait; and streamlining UN procedure for providing electoral assistance to countries requesting it. The United States unsuccessfully opposed resolutions calling for discontinuance of all nuclear testing, proposing a Middle East peace settlement on terms unfavorable to Israel (two decisions), and deploring "coercive measures" against developing countries by some developed states (a Cuban initiative aimed at the United States). Although the United States voted with the majority on about 15 percent of all contested issues in the Forty-Sixth Assembly, the U.S. position prevailed on two-thirds of the twelve important votes. This outcome indicates that the United States can still win when it is willing to lobby intensively for a position not diametrically opposed to interests of Third World states.

The picture of small states routinely outvoting the large ones is further blurred by the growing tendency to make decisions by consensus. In its report on voting in the 1991 Assembly the United States rated fifteen of the consensus resolutions as "important." If these are added to the twelve "important" recorded votes, the United States was with the majority in twenty-three of twenty-seven important decisions, or 85 percent of the time. Furthermore, when decisions by consensus are taken into account, the United States has voted with the majority most of the time in recent years. In 1984 the proportion of Assembly decisions by consensus was 55 percent; in 1987 it rose to 61 percent; and in 1991 more than 78 percent of all decisions (272 of 348) were by consensus. With 272 consensus decisions and ten recorded votes in which the United States joined the majority, the overall majority agreement score for the United States in 1991 was 81 percent.[7] This was a lower score than for any other UN member except Israel, but nevertheless it was indicative of a reasonable level of satisfaction with Assembly actions.

The voting power of the Third World clearly does not make the General Assembly either a useless or a dangerous place for the others. Even when a resolution objectionable to some states is adopted, it has only the force of a recommendation. A parliamentary victory of one group over another may induce temporary euphoria in the winners, and even have some weight as an expression of world opinion, but no dissenting state is bound to comply. Also not to be overlooked is the UN function of harmonizing differences and promoting action in the common interest. The large and growing number of resolutions adopted without objection demonstrates that differences are usually harmonized, at least at the verbal level, and widely approved UN programs in such disparate areas as peacekeeping, economic development, and refugee relief indicate that the agreement often extends beyond rhetoric. The Assembly undoubtedly could accomplish more if its members behaved better, but it has utility for all of them. Even apart from the decisions reached, it is a good place for listening and learning.

## THE CONSEQUENCES OF UN ACTION

The UN political process normally focuses on the adoption of a resolution. But what are the consequences of this action? Will the resolution be enforced, ignored, or acted on in any way? There is no single answer to these questions because UN resolutions are not all alike and much depends on the circumstances.

Partial answers will be supplied as particular UN activities are examined in subsequent chapters. Here we will present a more general framework for identifying and explaining the differing consequences of differing UN actions. In developing this analysis, an examination of conditions that give weight to the decisions of national governments will be helpful. These include the sanction of physical force, the authority of law, customary obedience, and the economic and human resources available to carry out programs.

Physical force is important, primarily as a deterrent to law violation. Without it society would be at the mercy of the deviant lawbreaker, vulnerable to a general breakdown in order and respect for law. Physical coercion works best when its use is the exception rather than the rule. A government that habitually resorts to violence to obtain compliance with its rules is unstable at best. In a well-ordered state people obey the law because it is the law. The law is respected because it is legitimate; that is, the people accept the government's right to make it. The legitimacy of the law is also reinforced by customs of compliance, While the state's coercive power may lurk in the background, the daily homespun of obedience is woven from threads of habit, legitimacy, underlying consensus on the goals of the state, and rational recognition that obedience to law is in the general interest. The viability of a state and its government rests heavily on the capacity to command widespread compliance without the necessity of physical coercion.

The protective and regulatory functions of government require general obedience to law. Governments also perform service functions, and these are dependent not so much on the obedience of the citizenry as on the availability of material resources and of administrative apparatus for application of the resources to the task at hand. All governments have the power to raise money by various forms of compulsory levy, and all have some type of administrative machinery. Given a satisfactory level of obedience to law, the effectiveness of government action is closely correlated with the availability of taxable resources and the efficiency of public administration. The states of Western Europe and North America, for example, have effective governments not only because of general obedience to law but also because their resources are adequate and their administrative machinery is relatively efficient. In contrast, some of the smaller, poorer countries lack resources, administrative capacity, and even an adequate level of obedience to law.

To what extent can the United Nations draw on the sources that give force to decisions of national governments? On its face the UN Charter appears to confer on the United Nations a legal monopoly of the right to use physical coercion in international affairs, with the exception of self-defense. In practice, however, states—individually and through alliances—have retained control over the instruments of coercion. The United Nations neither has a monopoly of such force nor makes any grandiose claim to it. At best, the United Nations can serve as a catalytic agent for mobilizing force for UN objectives when enough members are willing to cooperate.

Most UN decisions also lack the force of law. The organization has much authority to recommend but little to command. Recommendations might be effective if they were supported by a strong tradition of customary obedience, but the United Nations has not yet developed such a tradition. Some UN specialized agencies do much better. The regulations of the Universal Postal Union, for example, are observed with a regularity that would do credit to national administrations. All the elements of customary obedience are there—habit legitimacy, broad consensus on goals, and recognition of a common interest in international postal operations. As one moves away from purely technical activities to the more political subjects debated by the General Assembly and other UN organs, the degree of customary obedience declines markedly. States have not yet developed habits of indiscriminate compliance with General Assembly recommendations. As a result, compliance is left to rest on a coincidence of national interests in particular UN policies and programs. The action of a UN majority may sometimes create political pressure in favor of compliance, but that is no substitute for the kinds of forces that induce voluntary compliance with national laws.

International organization also stands in a different position from that of national governments in its ability to command financial and other resources. Although budgetary assessments are usually paid, international organizations are ultimately dependent on the resources that individual states are willing to supply, not on what majorities are moved to demand. This should not suggest that the sums raised by contribution are inconsequential. The regular UN budget for 1997 was significantly reduced from five years earlier, due in part to a failure of the United States to meet its financial obligations, but also as a consequence of the organization's overextension in dealing with world problems following the end of the Cold War. From a budget of $2.39 billion in 1992–93, the 1997 budget, including UN core functions in New York, Geneva, Nairobi, Vienna, and five regional commissions, was a mere $1.3 billion, about 4 percent of New York City's annual budget and nearly $1 billion less than the yearly cost of Tokyo's fire department. As the United Nations public relations office notes, the UN budget was considerably less than the $3.7 billion of the New York State University system. The figure given for UN peacekeeping operations in 1996 was $1.4 billion, or less than 1 percent of the U.S. military budget, and hardly 0.2 percent of worldwide military spending. Eighty percent of the work of the UN system was still devoted to helping developing countries improve their economies, but also to encourage them to build democratic institutions and protect human rights. No other organization was so deeply involved in administering to needy children, in warding off infectious disease, or assisting refugees and disaster victims, let alone those exposed to land-mine dangers. Granted organizations like UNICEF, UNDP, UNFPA and WFP spend an additional $4.6 billion, but even this figure only represents the equivalent of 80 cents per human being. In 1994, by contrast, the world's governments spent approximately $778 billion on their armed forces, the equivalent of $134 per human being. In all of this the U.S. share of the 1997 UN budget was $312 million, and the assessment for peacekeeping was another $400 million, down from $1 billion in 1995. In spite of the diminished costs, and even though U.S. citizens held more UN secretariat positions than any other member state, more top posts at

UNICEF, the UN Development Program, the World Bank, the World Food Program, and the Universal Postal Union, the U.S. Congress demanded still more drastic reductions in a UN workforce already cut 25 percent by 1997.

In 1998 the United Nations regular budget was reduced still further, to $1,190 billion and the estimated peacekeeping budget from July 1998 to June 1999 was pegged at $860 million, down from $992 million in the same period for 1997–98. But even these reductions did not cause the organization's delinquents to pay their full share. As of October 31, 1998 the total amount owed the UN was $2,281,725,084. Of this amount $650,594,871 involved the regular budget, $20,951,563 was for the operations of international tribunals, and $1,630,178,650 was for the peacekeeping program. The nations most delinquent as of 1999 were the United States ($1,477,107,967), Ukraine ($223,310,477), Russian Federation ($131,826,307), Japan ($96,558,681), Belarus ($56,251,700), and Brazil ($46,820,811).

The United Nations must depend on the willingness of members to provide funds. The sale of UN publications and postage stamps does not yet constitute an important source of independent income, and substantial revenues from resources of the common seabed area are yet in the distant future. The remaining condition of effective action, administrative capability, will be discussed in more detail in the following chapter. Here we may observe that the UN Secretariat has performed reasonably well the administrative tasks imposed on it, whereas decisions dependent on member state compliance have frequently been dead letters.

Given UN capabilities as we have assessed them, the consequences of UN action may be briefly summarized. Where UN resolutions have initiated programs to be administered by the Secretariat and members are willing to contribute the necessary resources, the consequences of UN action have been significant. The United Nations has solid accomplishment in areas ranging from research studies to development assistance to peacekeeping operations. On the other hand, where resolutions have depended on compliance by member states, the record is very checkered. In many instances members comply because they are in sympathy with the resolution. Occasionally states are moved to compliance, or a show of compliance, by a desire not to appear out of step with a large UN majority. In numerous other instances UN recommendations are flatly ignored by governments that perceive no self-interested basis—however broadly or narrowly construed—for compliance. No UN majority could persuade the Soviet Union to withdraw its troops from Afghanistan or induce the United States to pull out of Grenada before either was ready. In the absence of rules having the force of law, compelling habits of obedience, and physical sanctions to support the rules, the United Nations must rely on a convergence of national interests to secure compliance.

There is still another way in which UN resolutions affect international politics, without the expenditure of financial resources and even without the voluntary cooperation of states to which a resolution may be directed. More than two decades ago Inis L. Claude, Jr. observed that the United Nations "has come to be regarded, and used, as a dispenser of politically significant approval and disapproval of the claims, policies, and actions of states." [8] He called this phenomenon "collective legitimization" and argued that statesmen took it seriously. "A state may hesitate to pursue a policy that has engendered the formal disapproval of the Assembly," he suggested, "not because it is prepared to give the will of that organ priority over its national interest, but because it believes that the adverse judgment of the Assembly makes the pursuit of that policy disadvantageous to the national interest." Former UN Ambassador Jeane J. Kirkpatrick, a persistent critic of UN decision making, made a similar point in explaining why UN decisions have significance for the conduct of foreign affairs: UN votes define "world opinion" on major issues. Since there are no other arenas in which all the countries of the world express their opinions on policy, the decisions of the U.N. bodies are widely taken as the most valid expression of "world opinion." [9]

United Nations' resolutions, by the very fact of their adoption, become intangible resources for their supporters and liabilities for their opponents. United Nations' decisions may not confer the legitimacy of law, but they do confer the legitimacy of majority approval in a body representing virtually every sovereign state. The legitimizing force of a resolution varies according to the size and composition of the voting majority and the forcefulness and clarity of the language used. Specificity cuts sharper than ambiguity. A unanimous Security Council resolution is weightier than one on which several permanent members abstain (and even more so if it is a "decision" under Article 25, which members have agreed to "accept and carry out"). Overwhelming approval in the Assembly is more convincing than a two-vote margin. A series of resolutions reaffirming a position will have more impact than an isolated case. Repeated UN reaffirmations of support for decolonization, aid to developing countries, and human rights have helped to make such concepts almost articles of faith (if not of unfailing practice) in the global system. Even states that deny the validity of particular UN pronouncements are sometimes reluctant to violate them, or appear to violate them, in tacit recognition of the significance of collective legitimization.

The United Nations is not a supergovernment. Its resources are limited; its words are seldom law. Its mandates can be enforced against an unwilling state only if members are willing to use the necessary coercion. But its decisions do make a difference. Funds are raised and expended; economic and social programs are launched; peacekeeping missions are maintained; disputes are sometimes settled. Much voluntary cooperation is encouraged. And no state can disregard UN processes without paying some penalty, or losing some benefit, in its relations with other states.

# NOTES

1. Some others include the UN world conferences on Population (1974), Food (1974), International Women's Year (1975), Human Settlements (1976), World Employment (1976), Water (1977), Desertification (1977), Racial Discrimination (1978), Technical Cooperation among Developing Countries (1978), Agrarian Reform and Rural Development (1979), Science and Technology for Development (1979), UN Decade for Women (1980), Energy (1981), Outer Space (1982), Palestine (1983), Racial Discrimination (1983), Population (1984), Fisheries (1984), Status of Women (1985), Sanctions against South Africa (1986), Peaceful Uses of Nuclear Energy (1987), Disarmament and Development (1987), Children (1990), Education for All (1990), Environment and Development (1992), Human Rights (1993), Population and Development, and Women (1995).
2. Seymour Maxwell Finger, *Your Man at the UN* (New York: New York University Press, 1980), p. 20.
3. See Robert E. Riggs, "The United Nations and the Politics of Law," in *Politics in the United Nations System,* ed. Lawrence S. Finkelstein (Durham: Duke University Press, 1988), pp. 41–74.
4. U.S. Department of State, *Report to Congress on Voting Practices in the United Nations 1990,* submitted pursuant to Public Law 101-167, March 31, 1991, p. 61.
5. Leo Pasvolsky, "The United Nations in Action," in *Edmund J. James Lectures on Government* (Urbana: University of Illinois Press, 1951), pp. 80–81.
6. For example, U.S. Department of State, *Voting Practices in the United Nations 1991,* Report to Congress submitted pursuant to Public Law 101-167, March 31, 1992, p. 33.
7. The percentage figures for Assembly consensus voting, 1976 through 1991, are found *ibid.,* p. 63. For 1984 the figures are taken from U.S. Department of State, *Report to Congress on Voting Practices in the United Nations,* submitted pursuant to Public Law 99-190 and Public Law 98-164, May 20, 1985, p. 3. The ten recorded votes in which the United States was with the UN majority are found in *Resolutions and Decisions Adopted by the General Assembly during the First Part of Its Forty-Sixth Session,* United Nations Press Release GA/8307, 21 January 1992.
8. Claude, *The Changing United Nations* (New York: Random House, 1967), p. 73, 93.
9. "Testimony of U.S. Permanent Representative to the United Nations Jeane J. Kirkpatrick before the Senate Foreign Operations Subcommittee of the Senate Appropriations Committee, March 25, 1985," reproduced in U.S. Department of State, *Report to Congress on Voting Practices in the United Nations,* submitted pursuant to Public Law 98-151 and Public Law 98-164, May 30, 1985, p. 3.

# SELECTED READINGS

Alker, Hayward R., and Bruce M. Russett. *World Politics in the General Assembly.* New Haven: Yale University Press, 1965.
Ameri, Houshang. *Politics and Process in the Specialized Agencies of the United Nations.* Aldershot, Eng.: Gower Publishing, 1982.

Baehr, Peter R. *The Role of a Delegation in the General Assembly.* Occasional paper no. 9. New York: Carnegie Endowment for International Peace, 1970.

Bailey, Sydney D. *The Procedure of the United Nations Security Council.* 2nd ed. Oxford: Clarendon Press, 1988.

Chiang Pei-Heng. *Non-Governmental Organizations at the United Nations.* New York: Praeger Publishers, 1981.

Cox, Robert W.; Harold K. Jacobson; et al. *The Anatomy of Influence: Decision Making in International Organization.* New Haven: Yale University Press, 1973.

Finger, Seymour Maxwell. *American Ambassadors at the U.N.: People, Politics, and Bureaucracy in Making Foreign Policy.* New York: Holmes & Meier, 1988.

Hovet, Thomas, Jr. *Bloc Politics in the United Nations.* Cambridge, MA: Harvard University Press, 1960.

Jackson, Richard L. *The Non-Aligned, the UN and the Superpowers.* New York: Praeger Publishers, 1983.

Kaufmann, Johan. *United Nations Decision Making.* Alphen aan den Rijn: Sijthoff & Noordhoff, 1980.

————. *Conference Diplomacy: An Introductory Analysis.* 2nd rev. ed. Dordrecht: Martinus Nijhoff Publishers, 1988.

McConnell, W. H., and Wheeler, Ron, eds. *Swords and Plowshares: The United Nations in Transition.* Toronto: Canadian Scholars Press, 1997.

McWhinney, Edward. *United Nations Law Making.* New York: Holmes & Meier Publishers, 1984.

Mortimore, Robert. *The Third World Coalition in International Politics.* Boulder, CO: Westview Press, 1984.

Peterson, M. J. *The General Assembly in World Politics.* Winchester, MA: Allen & Unwin, 1986.

Rajan, M. S., et al, eds. *The Nonaligned and the United Nations.* Dobbs Ferry, NY: Oceana Publications, 1987.

Riches, Cromwell A. *Majority Rule in International Organization.* Baltimore: Johns Hopkins University Press, 1940.

Riggs, Robert E. *Politics in the United Nations: A Study of United States Influence in the General Assembly.* Urbana: University of Illinois Press, 1958. Reprinted Greenwood Press, 1984.

Rosenau, James N. *The United Nations in a Turbulent World.* International Peace Academy, Occasional Paper Series. Boulder, CO: Lynne Rienner Publishers, 1992.

Sauvant, Karl P. *The Group of 77: Evolution, Structure, Organization.* Dobbs Ferry, NY: Oceana Publications, 1981.

Sloan, Blaine. *United Nations General Assembly Resolutions in Our Changing World.* Los Angeles: Transnational Publishing Co., 1991.

Sonnenfeld, Renata. *Resolutions of the United Nations Security Council.* Dordrecht: Martinus Nijhoff Publishers, 1989.

Stoessinger, John G. *The United Nations and the Superpowers.* 4th ed. New York: Random House, 1977.

Whittaker, David J. *United Nations in Action.* Armonk, NY: M. E. Sharpe, 1995.

Willetts, Peter, ed. *The Conscience of the World: The Influence of Non-Governmental Organizations in the UN System.* Washington: The Brookings Institution, 1996.

Willetts, Peter, ed. *Pressure Groups in the Global System: The Transnational Relations of Issue-Oriented Nongovernmental Organizations.* London: Frances Pinter, 1982.

Williams, Marc. *Third World Cooperation: The Group of 77 in UNCTAD.* New York: St. Martin's Press, 1991.

# 4

## POLITICS AND THE UN SECRETARIAT

"I am a free man; I feel light as a feather." These words captured the exhilaration and the relief of Javier Pérez de Cuéllar as he left UN headquarters in the early hours of New Year's Day 1992. His tenth and final year as UN Secretary-General had just drawn to a close, only minutes after the completion of lengthy negotiations leading to a cease-fire agreement between El Salvador's contending factions. A compromise candidate for the Secretary-Generalship in 1982, he had assumed office when UN fortunes were at a low ebb. In 1992 he departed an organization much closer to the center of world politics and an office with a greatly enlarged role in the promotion of world peace and security. Entering the office without great expectations, this bland, determined diplomat-professor from Lima made his exit with a standing ovation from the General Assembly and a nomination for the Nobel Peace Prize.

Pérez de Cuéllar did not create the world climate that made possible this new prominence for the United Nations and its Secretary-General, but he was able to take advantage of the changed climate to help propel the organization into the mainstream of world politics. Such a role for the United Nations was not inevitable, and without the Secretary-General and his staff it would have been impossible.

The importance of an international secretariat to the functioning of international organizations is hard to exaggerate. It is fair to say that modern international organization did not, indeed could not, exist until the invention of the permanent international secretariat. Without a staff to administer its affairs between meetings, an international organization is little more than a series of conferences. With a permanent secretariat, the organization is no longer just an arena where states and other actors play out their roles but is itself an actor on the international scene. A permanent staff creates the capacity to gather and disseminate information, monitor state compliance with rules and recommendations of the organization, and provide services to member states and their people. These functions comprise an awesome range of activities for the Secretariat and its economic, social, and technical agencies. Lending money, giving advice on agricultural questions, fighting AIDS, reducing illiteracy, improving meteorological services, regulating labor standards, promoting human rights, safeguarding the environment, and providing refugee relief are just some of the

UN activities that come within the purview of the UN Secretariat. Within its sphere of operation, the organization becomes a continuing influence on states in their relations with one another and often in their domestic policies.

Secretariat employees perform many tasks that have little direct effect on the substance of UN decisions or the relations of states. Internal housekeeping activities, such as personnel management, financial administration, property maintenance, and supply procurement are important institutionally but usually politically neutral. So also are conference servicing activities. Hundreds of language specialists are employed to interpret speeches at UN meetings, often simultaneously, into each of six official languages—English, French, Russian, Spanish, Chinese, and Arabic—and to prepare documentation in the same six languages. The designation of "official" and "working" languages became a political issue in the early years of the United Nations. Initially, the UN had five "official" languages but only two "working" languages—English and French—into which all documents were routinely translated. Arabic was subsequently added to the official languages. All the official languages later were declared working languages, thus satisfying a large number of members, but also considerably increasing the cost of producing documentation.

The United Nations Secretariat conducts its own postal service, including the issuance of postage stamps, and maintains a large-scale publishing operation to supply the world with reports, records of meetings, and other UN publications. But secretariats also do much that is politically significant. At meetings of the United Nations and other international agencies, the staff is concerned not only with translation and documentation but also with the substantive problems being discussed. Whether the subject is human rights, social welfare, disarmament, environmental protection, or the pacific settlement of disputes, staff members are assigned duties of information gathering, research, and reporting. Staff reports are often the basis for discussion and decision in meetings of UN bodies. Specialists in economic development, international law, or specific political problem areas must be prepared to advise the Secretary-General and, on occasion, national delegates. Countries lacking qualified experts available for service with national UN delegations sometimes rely heavily on the expertise of secretariat officials. In organizations whose principal business is supplying technical assistance and other services to member states, the budget proposal prepared by the secretariat dominates the organization's agenda.

Even internal matters such as staff recruitment can become intensely political as member states intervene to secure secretariat positions, especially high-level positions, for their nationals. Budgeting in any international agency is also an intensely political process. Staff members and governmental representatives consult extensively in negotiating a budget that will satisfy their special interests and yet win the necessary majority of votes. Budget battles are ultimately resolved by governments, but secretariats are intimately involved in the political give-and-take.

Beyond advising, reporting, budgeting, and otherwise influencing organizational decisions, the Secretary-General and other high level secretariat officials may become intimately involved in the politics of the world as intermediaries in the settlement of international disputes. The services of Pérez de Cuéllar and his deputies were utilized widely in the closing years of his administration to help resolve conflict in Afghanistan, Iran and Iraq, El Salvador, Western Sahara, Angola, and elsewhere, often with considerable success. In such situations UN representatives become political actors, on a par with ambassadors and foreign ministers in their capacity to effect desired outcomes. Their effectiveness is often enhanced by their unique character as agents of an international rather than a national constituency.

Before considering the political role of the UN Secretariat in detail, this chapter will briefly examine the origin of the international civil service and some of the special problems that it raises for those who serve in it. The discussion will then turn to the UN Secretariat, with emphasis on political problems associated with personnel recruitment and preserving staff independence from national influences. A final section will elaborate the principal theme of the chapter—the role of secretariats in organizational decision making and their impact on international politics. The discussion will center on the United Nations and its Secretary-General, but a broader perspective will be added by occasional comparison with other international organizations.

# THE INTERNATIONAL CIVIL SERVICE

## ORIGIN

The international civil service dates only from the establishment of the League of Nations and the International Labor Organization at the close of World War I. Before that time the permanent bureaus or secretariats of such technical organizations as the Universal Postal Union were not international in composition. The personnel were typically citizens of the headquarters host state, and often they were national officials on temporary leave from their normal assignments with the home government.

The League Covenant made no express provision for internationalization of the staff. It simply stated, "The Secretariat shall comprise a Secretary-General and such secretaries and staff as may be required." To Sir Eric Drummond, first Secretary-General of the League, goes the credit for insisting on a truly international secretariat. The decision to establish a multinational civil service recruited individually rather than as contingents of national representatives has been called, in an authoritative history of the League, "one of the most important events in the history of international politics." [1] The secretariat of the International Labor Organization, under the leadership of Albert Thomas, adopted a similar concept of an international civil service.

Codifying the experience of the League and the ILO, the UN Charter expressly provided for a Secretariat that was to be appointed by a Secretary-General as its administrative head, recruited individually on the basis of merit, and responsible in official conduct only to the organization. These provisions embodied the ideals of the international civil service—*efficiency, loyalty* to the organization, *independence* from national pressures, and *impartiality* toward all member states. Wide geographic distribution of appointments was recognized as an important subsidiary principle. Other intergovernmental organizations have looked to these standards and have applied them to an ever-growing international public service. At their peak the staff of the League and ILO together numbered scarcely more than a thousand. Although the United Nations Secretariat employs significantly more people, when judged by its greater complexity, and the number of specialized international agencies that have emerged in the more than half century that followed World War II, its overall workforce is very modest, indeed McDonald's hamburger chain employs three times as many people. The worldwide UN system in 1998, that is, the Secretariat and twenty-eight other organizations (e.g., UNICEF, and including its specialized agencies and related intergovernmental organizations) employed 53,300 people. Of this number, the Headquarters Secretariat in New York City enjoyed the services of 4,700. Tough new standards introduced in 1997 cut the overall Secretariat staff (which includes those based in Geneva, Nairobi, and Vienna) from 12,000 to 9,000 employees. Further cuts are forecast as the reform effort enters its second phase, which involves the consolidation of several Secretariat bodies, the streamlining of management, and the shifting of resources from administration to development programs.

## PROBLEMS OF DIVERSITY AND POLITICAL SUPPORT

An international secretariat faces the problems that bureaucracies face everywhere—problems of internal decision making, communication, lines of authority and responsibility, and recruitment and retention of competent personnel. But compared with national civil services, an international secretariat has special problems stemming from its political environment.

One obvious challenge is to integrate within a single administrative machine the diverse attitudes, tongues, backgrounds, and abilities of personnel recruited from the four corners of the earth. The central problem here is the absence of a shared political culture. A national civil service operates within a relatively homogeneous value framework. There is broad consensus on the functions of government, the means by which political decisions are reached, and the limits of legitimate governmental authority. With no shared global political culture, the secretariat lacks both the guidelines that would make its own choice of actions easier and the legitimacy that would make its functions acceptable to its clientele. In any governmental system the conduct of administration requires some bargaining and negotiation with the clientele to be served or regulated. In international administration the lack of shared political values greatly widens the range of issues that must be negotiated. Even when norms for specific activities are developed through practice, such as standards for technical assistance programs, the process is complicated by the need to adapt standards to differing national contexts.

The international secretariat also lacks sustaining links with sources of political support that national civil services enjoy. At the apex of the national administrative structure is a president or prime minister who is himself a very influential figure. In the United States the president draws power from his constitutional prerogatives, his control of the executive branch, his electoral mandate, and his relationship with his political party and other influential groups within the society. The administrative departments work under his direction and draw political support from that relationship. Parliamentary systems have the further advantage of a chief executive who speaks for a dominant political party or coalition within the national legislature. In addition, administrative agencies often receive support from groups within the community that benefit from agency services.

In contrast, the links that join an international secretariat to sources of power within the international system are more fragile and tenuous. The typical secretary-general or director-general has very limited political prerogatives, no significant ties with a public constituency, no broad electoral mandate, and scarcely anything resembling leadership of a dominant political party or legislative coalition. The executive head can cultivate the support of governments within his organization. But governments change, as do their UN representatives, and governments are motivated very little by a sense of loyalty, obligation, or feelings of support for a UN Secretary-General.

Sometimes international bureaucracies can develop important ties of mutual interest with their counterparts in national ministries of government. Periodic personal contacts at international meetings and regular communication between staff of national and international agencies concerned with similar problems can lead to mutually supportive behavior. Thus officials in national ministries of health may feel a vested interest in the work of the World Health Organization, or national finance ministries may provide support for the work of the International Monetary Fund. Such relationships are more likely to be developed in technical, relatively noncontroversial fields and in economic and social activities rather than matters affecting national security.

Some international secretariats, such as UNESCO, the International Labor Organization, the United Nations Environmental Program, the International Civil Aviation Organization, the World Bank, and even the United Nations, have mutually beneficial relationships with private groups; but in range and intensity of support, they cannot be compared to the agency-clientele relationships that sustain national bureaucracies.

## THE UN SECRETARIAT

The United Nations Secretariat is undergoing major reforms that are proposed to meet the demands of the twenty-first century with far less financial support. The Secretariat of the future will be smaller, better trained, more versatile, and more integrated than any before it. The average age of the UN staff at the end of the century was 49, with only 14 percent below the age of 40, and fewer than

5 percent under 35. Within the next decade almost half of the secretariat staff are expected to retire, and the opportunity will exist to refashion the organization so that it better represents geographic and gender representation. Moreover, some member states are still not represented, and less than 20 percent of senior level posts are filled by women. Indeed, women were less than 36 percent of the total secretariat staff. In 1998–99 budget projections, UN Secretariat personnel was cut by 1,000, or by more than 20 percent. The administrative budget was also reduced by one-third. Scrutinized as never before, the UN Secretariat of the future will be much leaner, more efficient, less concerned with internal personnel matters, and more geared for external development.

## RECRUITING THE UN OFFICIAL

The UN Secretariat, like a national bureaucracy, faces the constant problem of recruiting competent employees to fill available positions. For support staff positions, the problems of recruitment are much the same as those faced by other employers. Such jobs are commonly filled by local recruitment without regard to geographic distribution and mostly with nationals of the host country. About two-thirds of the employees at UN headquarters in New York and Geneva fall into these categories.

For higher-level employees, the search for talent is limited to persons with the necessary language skills and the willingness to live in an alien environment. There is also the very serious problem of reconciling competence with the demands of wide geographic distribution. This applies to positions at the professional level and higher, except for language specialists. These professionals are mandated to do all the substantive work of analyzing global and regional developments in the political, security, disarmament, economic, social, human rights, and environmental areas. They also are authorized to direct peacekeeping and other emergency operations, and prepare the Secretary-General's reports to the General Assembly, Security Council, the Economic and Social Council, as well as their related organs and agencies. Finally, the professional staff oversees the implementation of works programs and other detailed assignments. The Secretariat's professional-level civil service numbering 2,514 in 1996, are listed in Table 4-1 with an emphasis on gender distribution.

According to Article 101 of the UN Charter, the "paramount consideration" in recruitment and conditions of service should be "the necessity of securing the highest standards of efficiency, competence, and integrity." Article 101 further provides that "due regard shall be paid to the importance of recruiting the staff on as wide a geographical basis as possible," but the Charter makes this clearly secondary to the merit principle. In practice, the Secretary-General has tried to place efficiency first, with substantial support from the United States and countries of Western Europe, which have always been heavily represented in the UN Secretariat. Areas less well represented, especially Eastern Europe and the newer states of Asia and Africa, have fought for the principle of equitable geographic distribution as though it were the paramount consideration.

TABLE 4-1    United Nations Secretariat Professional Staff, 1996

| DEPARTMENT OR OFFICE | TOTAL MEN | TOTAL WOMEN | GRAND TOTAL | PERCENT WOMEN |
|---|---|---|---|---|
| Administration and Management | 14 | 17 | 31 | 54.8 |
| Human Resources Management | 36 | 41 | 77 | 53.2 |
| Interorganization Body | 3 | 3 | 6 | 50.0 |
| Public Information | 131 | 128 | 259 | 49.4 |
| Policy Coord. and Sustainable Dev. | 47 | 44 | 91 | 48.4 |
| Joint Staff Pension Fund | 18 | 15 | 33 | 45.5 |
| UN Environmental Program | 11 | 9 | 20 | 45.0 |
| Program Planning Budget 7 Accounts | 51 | 40 | 91 | 44.0 |
| UN Center for Human Rights | 33 | 25 | 58 | 43.1 |
| Dev. Support & Management Services | 49 | 37 | 86 | 43.0 |
| UN Office in Geneva | 55 | 38 | 93 | 40.9 |
| UN Drug Control Program | 27 | 18 | 45 | 40.0 |
| Political Affairs | 84 | 52 | 130 | 38.2 |
| Legal Affairs | 49 | 30 | 79 | 38.0 |
| International Oversight Services | 31 | 18 | 49 | 36.7 |
| Eco. & Soc. Information & Analysis | 83 | 42 | 125 | 33.6 |
| Conference Services | 91 | 46 | 137 | 33.6 |
| Peacekeeping Operations | 53 | 26 | 79 | 32.9 |
| Office of the Secretary General | 17 | 8 | 25 | 32.0 |
| Eco. & Soc. Comm. for Western Asia | 50 | 22 | 72 | 30.6 |
| Eco. & Soc. Comm. for Asia & Pacific | 93 | 40 | 133 | 30.1 |
| Eco. Comm. for Latin Amer. & Carib. | 101 | 38 | 139 | 27.3 |
| Humanitarian Affairs | 33 | 12 | 45 | 26.7 |
| UN Office in Vienna | 38 | 13 | 51 | 25.5 |
| Regional Commissions | 3 | 1 | 4 | 25.0 |
| Center for Human Settlements | 34 | 11 | 45 | 24.4 |
| Economic Commission for Europe | 68 | 20 | 88 | 22.7 |
| UN Comm. on Trade and Development | 157 | 46 | 203 | 22.7 |
| Economic Cooperation Administration | 128 | 36 | 164 | 22.0 |
| Peacekeeping-Field Adm. & Logistics | 39 | 6 | 45 | 13.3 |
| UN Compensation Commission | 5 | 0 | 5 | 0.0 |
| Total* | 1632 | 882 | 2514 | 35.1 |

SOURCE: UN Department of Public Information, Gender Distribution of United Nations Staff, 1996.

* 797 of the total of 2,514 represents the highest grades of Under Secretary-General, Assistant Secretary-General, Directors, and top professional staff.

TABLE 4-2    UN Staff in the Professional Category and above in posts subject to geographical distribution by region and gender as of 30 June 1997

| REGION | WOMEN | MEN | TOTAL | PERCENT WOMEN |
|---|---|---|---|---|
| Africa | 87 | 284 | 371 | 23.45 |
| Asia and the Pacific | 193 | 240 | 433 | 44.57 |
| Europe (Eastern) | 28 | 211 | 239 | 11.72 |
| Europe (Western) | 214 | 358 | 572 | 37.41 |
| Latin America | 76 | 129 | 205 | 37.07 |
| Middle East | 39 | 81 | 120 | 32.50 |
| North America & Caribbean | 261 | 247 | 508 | 51.38 |
| Others | 3 | 10 | 13 | 23.08 |
| Total | 901 | 1560 | 2461 | |

SOURCE: UN Office of Human Resources Management, 1998.

They contend that efficiency in the broader sense is not possible unless all national viewpoints are adequately represented in the Secretariat.

Initially the principal basis for geographic distribution was budgetary contribution. In 1962 the General Assembly adopted a formula that took into account membership (one to five per member state regardless of other factors) and population, in addition to budgetary contribution. Desirable ranges for each country and region, derived from the formula, were to serve as a guide to the Secretary-General in the recruitment of staff. Since then, greater weight has been given to the membership factor, which now places the minimum desirable range at two to fourteen. The majority of UN members, being small and poor, fall within the range of two (or three) to fourteen. The distribution of such posts, by geographic region, is presented in Table 4-2. Most governments have come to regard the ranges as entitlements rather than guidelines, and some have generated great political pressure on the Secretary-General to conform. Even for regions within or very close to their desirable ranges, merely maintaining the balance is a drag on recruitment by merit, and individual countries continue to press the Secretary-General for the maximum number of posts. The Assembly has kept up the pressure by setting targets for the appointment of candidates from underrepresented countries. Ironically, the most grossly overrepresented countries are themselves from developing areas. This is possible because no hiring disadvantage is imposed on overrepresented states from underrepresented regions.

As might be expected, the developing countries have not been content with overall geographic equity but have sought a proportionate share of senior and policy-formulating posts as well. There is ample precedent for politicizing recruitment among top echelon UN administrators. The initial distribution of top-level posts was determined by informal agreement among the permanent members of the Security Council to have a national of each of them appointed as an Assistant Secretary-General. The Soviet Union was specifically awarded the top post in Political and Security Council affairs and held it thereafter, except for a few years in the mid-1950s. In 1992 this informal claim fell to Russia. France, Britain, the United States, and China have also staked their respective claims to a position at the highest administrative level.

Intimately related to geographic distribution is the problem of the fixed-term appointment to posts subject to geographic distribution. Short-term appointments are appropriate for positions at the highest levels where some rotation is desirable, for needed specialists who are not willing to make a career of UN service, and for posts that are temporary because of the nature of the work (for example, technical assistance projects). Nevertheless, a career service is the heart of the international civil service ideal. With the large-scale admission of new members after 1955, the career ideal came into conflict with the principle of equitable geographic distribution. Many new members did not have a large pool of qualified candidates whom they could afford to lose permanently; but they wanted to be "represented," and they were willing to send persons who would return after a short period, often better qualified because of the UN experience. Thus fixed-term appointments of one to five years became a tool for achieving desired geographic distribution of UN jobs. Not all short-term appointments are inconsistent with a career system. A two-tier five-year contract may provide a probationary period before a career appointment is granted. Some fixed-term appointments are followed by career appointments, and others become de facto career vehicles by virtue of periodic renewal. The result was an increase in the percentage of fixed-term appointments from about 10 percent in 1955 to about 25 percent in 1965 and 36 percent in 1985. A reversal of the trend began in the late 1980s, reducing the percentage of fixed-term appointments to less than 25 percent.

The developing countries do not bear the sole responsibility for the large percentage of fixed-term appointments. Until recently East European states, with the exception of Yugoslavia, insisted on fixed-term appointments for their nationals. They rejected the civil service ideal of placing loyalty to international organization above loyalty to country, and they were unwilling to run the risk that national ties might become attenuated through long residence abroad. They also opposed a career service on principle, insisting that an international civil servant is less effective if he has lost touch with life in his own country. With the breakup of the East European bloc and the splintering of the former Soviet Union, these countries became more receptive to the principle of career appointments. The proportion of East European nationals with fixed-term appointments in posts subject to geographic distribution was reduced from 99 percent (1986) to 66 percent (1992). This was still more than twice as high as for Africa, the region with the second highest proportion of fixed-term appointments (25 percent).

Although the Secretary-General has ultimate responsibility for Secretariat recruitment, geographic considerations and government pressures often lead to the hiring of government-sponsored candidates with little effort to canvass

TABLE 4-3 Distribution by gender of UN staff in posts with special language requirements as of 30 June each year, 1987–97

| YEAR | MEN | WOMEN | TOTAL | PERCENT WOMEN |
|------|-----|-------|-------|---------------|
| 1987 | 652 | 323 | 975 | 33.13 |
| 1988 | 639 | 316 | 955 | 33.09 |
| 1989 | 624 | 324 | 948 | 34.18 |
| 1990 | 598 | 317 | 915 | 34.64 |
| 1991 | 586 | 299 | 885 | 33.79 |
| 1992 | 574 | 306 | 880 | 34.77 |
| 1993 | 572 | 308 | 880 | 35.00 |
| 1994 | 555 | 304 | 859 | 35.39 |
| 1995 | 582 | 317 | 899 | 35.26 |
| 1996 | 574 | 327 | 901 | 36.29 |
| 1997 | 561 | 317 | 878 | 36.10 |

SOURCES: Reports of the Secretary-General on the Composition of the Secretariat (A/42/636, A/43/659, A/44/604, A/45/541, A/46/370, A/47/416, A/48/559, A/49/527, A/50/540, A/51/421) and Office of UN Human Resources Management, 1998.

the field of available applicants. Announcements of vacancies are commonly sent to governments, universities, professional societies, and other agencies where persons with needed qualifications may be contacted. But if a department already has a particular person in mind for the job, the distribution of announcements my be limited to UN permanent missions and a few international organizations. Some appointments are made with no circulation of a vacancy announcement at all.[2] This is more likely to be the case with senior posts. For positions at the lowest professional levels, candidate screening is frequently done through publicized national competitive examinations.

The recruitment of able personnel is also affected by conditions of service. Staff salaries thus far have been maintained above national levels, but large-contributor efforts to hold the line on budgetary increases have reduced career advancement prospects through periodic hiring freezes and staff reductions in some areas. UN pay rates, however, for matching grades at the professional level, average higher than pay rates for comparable federal civil service positions in Washington, DC. Recruitment of the most able candidates has also been hampered by the politicization of personnel decisions. Promotion prospects for the career civil servant are necessarily limited if many higher level positions are filled from outside the organization in response to government pressures and geographic considerations. When extraneous factors of national origin and political influence determine promotion, the whole concept of a career service is undermined.

## LOYALTY, INDEPENDENCE, IMPARTIALITY

The international civil service ideal requires that national loyalties be transcended by a primary professional loyalty to the international organization and the cause of international cooperation. In practice the ideal has not always been attained. Most UN officials have put international interests above the interest of any single state or group of states. But some have not, and the UN record clearly demonstrates that observance of the international ideal declines when it is undermined by the conduct of member states.

The elements of international loyalty, set forth in Staff Regulation 1.4, are integrity, impartiality, and independence. From the viewpoint of the individual, *integrity* is the key. A person of integrity will not be false to his own standards or his responsibility to others, including his oath to put the interests of the organization first. *Impartiality* requires the UN official to act neutrally toward all states, except as the interests and objectives of the United Nations dictate. Since appearances are important, impartiality embodies an element of prudence in not publicly taking sides on controversial matters. The ideal of impartiality probably goes no farther than integrity requires, and it does not presume that an international official must or will free himself from all cultural bias or previously developed political values and attitudes.

*Independence* in a Secretariat official is the ability to act without regard to political pressure from any national government or any group of countries. The Charter (Article 100) states that the Secretary-General and his staff "shall not seek or receive instructions from any government or from any other authority external to the Organization." Members, on their part, undertake "to respect the exclusively international character of the responsibilities of the Secretary-General and the staff and not to seek to influence them in the discharge of their responsibilities." Independence is thus a two-way street. It requires determination by the official to be independent and a willingness of governments, particularly his own government, to let him be independent.

Unfortunately, governmental pressures have sometimes been hard to resist. During the League days the governments of Nazi Germany and Fascist Italy attempted, with some success, to control their nationals on the Secretariat. Until the demise of the Communist regimes in the Soviet Union and Eastern Europe, these states followed the same practice in the United Nations. Their policy of national control has now begun to change. Other states have also made inroads on the ideal of independence. From 1953 to 1986 the United States subjected its nationals to a loyalty check before their appointment to the UN Secretariat. The practice was discontinued following a federal court decision that the loyalty program violated the First Amendment rights of speech and association. A number of other governments screen their nationals informally, which is less obvious but equally incompatible with Secretariat independence.

Other practices may be even more inimical to Secretariat independence. Some governments make supplementary payments to their nationals on the Secretariat, in clear violation of the Staff Regulations, which prohibit acceptance of "any honour, decoration, favour, gift or remuneration from any Government excepting for war services." The dangers of creating dependence on the government making the payment are obvious. Independence is similarly threatened when an initial appointment or a subsequent promotion results from government intervention an behalf of the candidate.

The relatively large proportion of fixed-term appointments to key positions also has implications for staff independence, since persons with a career stake in the United Nations may have more incentive to serve the organization single-mindedly. Many fixed-term employees do in fact measure up to the international civil service ideal, and the threat to independence is probably more acute with seconded employees, that is, national civil servants on temporary duty with the UN who anticipate returning to government service when the UN appointment expires. Even in such cases, personal integrity and government respect for the Secretariat's role may preserve the official's independence of action, but the risk of partiality and special influence is undoubtedly magnified by secondment.

# THE UN SECRETARIAT IN THE POLITICAL PROCESS

Every aspect of international administration is affected by its political milieu, and the UN Secretariat is far more a creature of its environment than a controller. Nevertheless, secretariats do affect political outcomes through initiative and leadership in the administration of programs, participation in the decisions of policy-making organs, and the practice of quiet diplomacy. The following pages will examine each of these avenues of influence.

## POLICY THROUGH ADMINISTRATION

Administration is the process of carrying into action the commands of policy-making bodies. Some legislative commands are more specific than others, but nearly all leave room for administrative discretion in the application of rules to particular cases. Sometimes commands are stated so broadly that important decisions of substance must be made by administrators. During the 1956 Suez War and the 1960 Congo crisis, for example, Dag Hammarskjöld was given very wide latitude in creating and directing the operations of UN peacekeeping forces. Since the Hammarskjöld years, the Security Council has maintained closer control of the Secretary-General's political and security activities but in many situations, including peacekeeping, a large amount of secretariat discretion is unavoidable. In economic and social matters, broad mandates for the Secretary-General are quite common.

Administration also becomes entwined with large policy decisions in less direct ways. Research studies and reports prepared by UN Secretariat officials add to the information base for government policy. A League historian estimates that the monumental *Nutrition Report* issued in 1937 by a special committee of the League Assembly had far-reaching effects on the attitudes of governmental officials and private groups in many countries by calling attention to the abysmally low levels of nutrition in most parts of the world. A 1987 report of an independent commission established by the General Assembly, *Our Common Future,* helped focus global interest on the interrelationship of environmental preservation and economic development.[3] Nearly every international organization can point to reports drafted by expert UN Secretariat personnel that were the basis for subsequent action by policy-making bodies.

Successful performance of assigned duties by UN Secretariat personnel can lead to requests for more of the same. The UN Emergency Force had to be built almost from the ground up when the Suez crisis arose in 1956, but that precedent made a peacekeeping force the logical UN response to subsequent outbreaks of violence in the Middle East, the Congo, Cyprus, Croatia, Central America, Cambodia, and elsewhere. On the other hand, ineffective administrative performance may lead to modification or abandonment of programs.

## SECRETARIAT PARTICIPATION IN DECISION MAKING

International officials participate directly in the decision-making processes of their governing bodies. Among existing international organizations, probably no secretariat enjoys greater influence than the staff of the World Bank, which not only frames the program for discussion by its executive directors and governing board but generally secures their approval for what the bank president and his staff recommend. Governments are of course closely consulted in the preparation of the recommendations. The UNESCO secretariat also fixes the agenda and prepares a program of action for its governing body. Although the UNESCO General Conference is sometimes disposed to alter the program, the director-general is undoubtedly the most important decision-maker in the organization. The European Union represents yet a different relationship. By constitutional fiat, policy-making authority is divided between the Council of Ministers, which speaks for governments, and the Commission, which head the administrative establishment. Some types of decisions are made by the Commission alone, some by the Council alone, and others of considerable importance by the concurrent action of both.

These organizations are to be contrasted with the UN General Assembly, where most agenda items are proposed by member states, or mandated by previous resolutions, and simply compiled by the Secretariat in a preliminary agenda. Although the Secretary-General may suggest additional items, he does not submit a legislative program, as is done in some other international agencies. However, most items represent continuing business from a previous session and are usually accompanied by a Secretariat report that helps shape consideration of the issue. Where the issue involves programs administered by the Secretariat, the recommendations of the Secretariat have considerable weight, especially since the views of member states are likely to have been solicited in formulating the Secretariat positions.

The Secretary-General is also responsible for preparation of the biennial UN budget. His estimates are, for the most part, based on the amounts required to carry out programs already authorized by the policy-making bodies, but the choice of figures nevertheless involves discretion. The Secretary-General is normally required to defend his budget vigorously and usually loses something to the budget cutters. Large contributors put great pressure on the Secretary-General to produce a "no-growth budget," even though many smaller members would like to see continuing expansion of UN programs of special benefit to them. In this tug-of-war the more heavily taxed member states carry the greater influence, but the Secretary-General's negative-growth budget for 1998–99 also proposed a Revolving Credit Fund, while a new Office of Development Financing was designed to utilize a smaller member "Development Dividend" that would be drawn from resources heretofore used for other more generalized administrative purposes.

Whether or not the secretariat of an international agency has a large role in initiating program proposals, other avenues of participation in the policy process are open. Executive heads are usually authorized to take part in formal discussion and debate of agenda items. All UN policy-making organs have provision for hearing the Secretary-General. Other UN officials conduct their own lobbying operations with varying degrees of directness. Individual civil servants are often consulted by national officials because of their expertise in a subject, and the Secretary-General will certainly be consulted if members are seriously considering the proposal of new functions or responsibilities for the Secretariat. On some questions the Secretary-General may be drawn into informal negotiating processes because he represents a relatively neutral and impartial viewpoint on an issue or because he can serve as a useful channel of communication. At a tactical and procedural level, Secretariat officials are storehouses of information on such policy-relevant matters as the conduct of meetings, the drafting of resolutions, and tactics of effective advocacy.

## THE PRACTICE OF DIPLOMACY

International officials affect organizational policy and the larger international system in important ways by means of "quiet diplomacy." Here we refer to the Secretariat's role in promoting agreement among states through quiet discussion and reconciliation of differences, as contrasted with public discussion and voting.

Opportunities for quiet diplomacy are presented in a wide variety of situations. Continuing diplomatic activity is required to carry out the programs of an organization and to obtain compliance with its resolutions. Establishing and maintaining a UN peacekeeping mission, for example, requires a pivotal role for the Secretary-General both as administrator and diplomat. He has responsibility to write its terms of reference, appoint the commander, negotiate necessary arrangements with affected states, and deal with the many diplomatic problems that arise in the course of its operation.[4] No peacekeeping mission can be launched without extensive negotiations with countries supplying the troop contingents and necessary matériel, as well as with the host country and any other country directly involved with the underlying threat to peace. No mission is maintained without continuing negotiation to resolve problems and differences as they arise. The same is true of other operating programs of international organization. Every technical assistance project is the product of extensive and detailed interchange among governments and the responsible international agency. Programs for refugee relief often require negotiation among representatives of one or more international organizations, the host country, the countries supporting the refugee program, and private organizations that cooperate in the relief activities.

When UN resolutions call for government action rather than establishing operating programs, Secretariat officials may perform a diplomatic function in seeking compliance from member states. The object of the negotiation is as varied as the subject matter of the resolutions—from urging financial support of UN development programs to observance of human rights to support of UN economic sanctions.

Another form of diplomatic activity is the resolution of controversy between states. The role of mediator, conciliator, and consensus-builder often appears in the quiet negotiations that occur behind the scenes of conference diplomacy. While government representatives often fill that role, not a few compromises later embodied in a resolution have been forged with the help of a timely suggestion or the mediatory services of a secretariat official. The expertise, impartiality, and continuity of secretariats become especially important in negotiating issues that persist over a long period of time within the UN framework, such as arms control or economic development.

The UN Secretary-General and his staff may also mediate particular disputes between countries.[5] Frequently this involvement comes through a mandate from the Assembly or the Security Council. The diplomatic services of the Secretary-General, acting personally or through his representatives, have been enlisted by the Assembly or Council in such diverse problem areas as the Iran-Iraq war, Afghanistan, Namibia, the Falkland Islands, Lebanon, the Arab-Israeli conflict, Grenada, Cambodia, the former Yugoslav Republic of Macedonia, Bosnia and Herzegovina, Kosovo, Georgia, Rwanda and Burundi, Guatemala, Iraq and Kuwait, Liberia, Cyprus, East Timor, the Western Sahara, Tajikistan, Angola, and the Slovonia region of Croatia.

Sometimes Secretaries-General have not waited for the Council or Assembly to act but have attempted a mediating role on their own initiative. Dag Hammarskjöld initiated a successful mediation effort in 1958 in a dispute arising from Thailand's military occupation of territory claimed by Cambodia. U Thant attempted, with less success, to be a mediating influence in the Vietnam War, as did Kurt Waldheim in the Soviet invasion of Afghanistan and the Iranian hostage crisis. Perez de Cuellar's successful mediation through his emissary, Diego Cordovez, brought the withdrawal of Soviet forces from Afghanistan in 1988–89, and in his final act as Secretary-General, he helped bring an end to the internal conflict in El Salvador. Boutros Boutros-Ghali, his successor, was not nearly as successful, however, in major part because during his tenure the United Nations assumed a heavier responsibility in pacifying troubled nations and regions. His successor, Kofi Annan, nevertheless, sustained the Secretary-General's practice of personal diplomacy. His use of former U.S. Secretary of State James Baker in the protracted Western Sahara conflict produced measured results, so too his own intervention in the politics of Angola where he tried to convince the opposition UNITA to fulfill its commitment to work with a new government of national unity. But Annan's most dramatic negotiation was his February 1998 visit to Iraq. Meeting with Saddam Hussein, he obtained assurances that the UN inspection team (UNSCOM), which had been authorized by the Security Council to identify and destroy Iraq's weapons of mass destruction, would be permitted to complete its work. Saddam's renewed defiance of UN resolutions, however, negated the Secretary General's efforts, and American and British aircraft again struck Iraqi targets.

## THE SECRETARY-GENERAL AND POLITICAL LEADERSHIP

Political leadership and initiative cut across all avenues of secretariat influence—administration, policy-making, and diplomacy. In the United Nations the focus of political leadership within the Secretariat must necessarily rest on the Secretary-General as the "chief administrative officer" of the organization. In contrast to all subordinate UN civil servants, the Charter makes his appointment subject to a uniquely political process. Under Article 97, he is "appointed by the General Assembly upon the recommendation of the Security Council." Since the Security Council recommendation is a nonprocedural matter, the recommendation is subject to all the hazards of great power politics. In practice, whenever the Security Council has been able to agree on a candidate, the General Assembly has hastened to add its formal approval.

Agreement in the Security Council has not always come easily. In 1950, when Trygve Lie's first five-year term was about to expire, the Soviet Union vetoed Lester Pearson of Canada and Paul-Henri Spaak of Belgium, and the United States then threatened to veto any candidate other than Lie. In this impasse the Secretariat was prevented from going leaderless only by the constitutionally questionable expedient of extending Lie's term an additional three years by General Assembly resolution. Since then, the appointment of a Secretary-General has sometimes gone to several ballots in the Security Council, but disagreement has never forced such an extra-constitutional extension of tenure. In 1981 the Council was deadlocked for more than six weeks. Through sixteen straw ballots China vetoed Kurt Waldheim's bid for an unprecedented third five-year term, while the United States blocked his Tanzanian challenger, Salim A. Salim. When these two candidacies were finally withdrawn, Javier Pérez de Cuéllar was nominated on the first formal ballot from a list of nine Third World hopefuls. The process of selecting Pèrez de Cuéllar's successor, the 69 year old Boutros Boutros-Ghali of Egypt, went more smoothly. In the Security Council the field was narrowed by a number of straw votes, which permitted Boutros-Ghali to be approved unanimously on the only formal vote taken by the Council. The General Assembly, as expected, gave its approval by consensus. Boutros-Ghali, however, was not allowed to seek another term. The United States had rated Boutros-Ghali a failure in dealing with the Somalia and Bosnia problems. Washington also was unhappy with the Secretary-General's budget reforms. After a lengthy struggle, Boutros-Ghali's supporters were forced to acknowledge defeat, especially after the U.S., using its prerogatives in the Security Council, cast the only vote in opposition to his reappointment. Kofi Annan, one of four African candidates to succeed to the office of the Secretary-General, and a long time international civil servant at the United Nations, was the identifiable frontrunner. Thus, when Boutros-Ghali announced the suspension of his candidature, Kofi Annan received the unanimous support of the Security Council, and the General Assembly elected him the seventh UN Secretary-General.

Given the political considerations that surround the appointment, it is not surprising that all successful candidates have come either from small, neutral European countries or from the Third World: Norway (Trygve Lie), Sweden (Dag Hammarskjöld), Burma (U Thant), Austria (Kurt Waldheim), Peru (Javier Pérez de Cuéllar), Egypt (Boutros Boutros-Ghali), and Ghana (Kofi Annan) (see Table 4-4). The election of Pérez de Cuéllar in 1981 undoubtedly reflected his personal reputation for fairness and ability, acquired as Peruvian permanent representative to the United Nations and as Undersecretary-General to Kurt Waldheim. It also indicated that Peru and other Latin American countries had come to be identified in the United Nations as part of the Third World—states of the South rather than the West.

Boutros-Ghali's appointment, likewise, owed something to geography— in particular, the insistence of African states that the selection be made from their region. This claim had the backing of the Non-Aligned Movement, which reportedly agreed to vote in the General Assembly against any non-African candidate. The United States, Britain, and the Soviet Union were reluctant to recognize any claim to the office based on geography. They also questioned whether Boutros-Ghali might have the energy (at age 69) to handle the pressing problems of peace and security, economic development, the environment, and internal finance and administration that the Secretary-General must address. Ultimately they found him acceptable, and Boutros-Ghali became the first African and Arab to fill the office of Secretary-General. His successor, Kofi Annan, sustains the focus on the African continent, but gives particular attention to its sub-Saharan region. Born in 1938, Annan was seen as possessing more energy than his predecessor, and as the first international civil servant to hold the post, he was more familiar with the operations of the United Nations than any Secretary-General preceding him. Annan also brought significant academic credentials to the position, completing his undergraduate work in economics at Macalaster College in St. Paul, Minnesota, and having served as a Sloan Fellow at the Massachusetts Institute of Technology where he received a Master of Science Degree in Management. He also had undertaken graduate studies at the Institut Universitaire des Hautes Etudes Internationales in Geneva.

TABLE 4-4   UN Secretaries-General, 1946–99

| Secretary-General | Nationality | Term of Office | Previous Experience |
|---|---|---|---|
| Trygve Lie | Norway | 1946–53 | Norway Foreign Minister at time of appointment; head, Norway delegation to San Francisco Conference (1945); former Minister of Justice, Commerce; politician and trade union negotiator |
| Dag Hammarskjöld | Sweden | 1953–61 | Minister of State (Finance) of Sweden at time of appointment; former chairman, Bank of Sweden; high-level civil servant, academic (political economy) |
| U Thant | Burma (Now Myanmar) | 1961–71 | Permanent Representative of Burma to United Nations at time of appointment; former government press director, freelance journalist, high school teacher |
| Kurt Waldheim | Austria | 1972–81 | Permanent Representative of Austria to United Nations at time of appointment; former foreign minister, ambassador to Canada, foreign service officer; unsuccessful candidate for President of Austria (1971) |
| Javier Pérez de Cuéllar | Peru | 1982–91 | Representative of UN Secretary-General in Afghanistan at time of appointment; former UN Undersecretary-General; Representative of UN Secretary-General in Cyprus; Permanent Representative of Peru to United Nations; ambassador to Switzerland, Poland, Venezuela; foreign service officer, professor of international law and relations |

*(continued)*

TABLE 4-4   *(continued)*

| SECRETARY-GENERAL | NATIONALITY | TERM OF OFFICE | PREVIOUS EXPERIENCE |
|---|---|---|---|
| Boutros Boutros-Ghali | Egypt | 1992–96 | Deputy Prime Minister of Egypt at time of appointment; Egypt's minister of state for foreign affairs; diplomat, law professor, author, journalist |
| Kofi Annan | Ghana | 1997– | UN Undersecretary-General for Peacekeeping Operations at the time of his appointment; he had served the UN as an international civil servant for more than thirty years, having served in UN offices in Addis Ababa, Cairo, Geneva, Ismailia, and New York City |

The Charter appointment process assures that the new incumbent will have the support—or at least the acquiescence—of all permanent members and of a UN majority. This is a political asset, but leadership demands that he continue to seek support wherever he can—primarily among governments but also with private interest groups and the general public. Since governments are the principal clients of the Secretariat and the direct beneficiaries of most of its service, earning their goodwill begins with trying to serve them well. It also requires careful counting of costs before taking action or assuming a public stance that will antagonize influential members. Lie's outspoken endorsement of UN action in Korea totally alienated the Soviet support he had formerly enjoyed. Hammarskjöld's handling of the Congo crisis also enraged the Soviet Union, but his cultivation of Afro-Asian support paid off handsomely in that crisis. U Thant's efforts at mediation in the Vietnam conflict brought a significant cooling in his relations with the United States, and his withdrawal of the UN Emergency Force from Egypt in May 1967 under Egyptian pressure brought severe criticism from many sides—especially after it proved a prelude to a new outbreak of war. Waldheim made no implacable enemies during two terms in office, but his bid for an unprecedented third term was blocked by China's veto. The Chinese position reflected a strong preference for a Third World candidate rather than antagonism to him personally. Pérez de Cuéllar, the beneficiary of a more hospitable political environment, concluded his service at the end of 1991 with general approbation from the world community he had served.

Secretariat links with private groups can also be a source of support. Private groups supply helpful information, and some have field operations that can be harnessed to UN objectives in such areas as refugee and disaster relief or development assistance. Private groups may also lobby national governments and mobilize public opinion in favor of UN programs. The UN Department of Public Information maintains liaison with many national and international groups having an interest in the work of the United Nations. UN staff also try to inform and accommodate the numerous nongovernmental organizations that hold consultative status with the Economic and Social Council. Individual units and programs established by the United Nations, such as UNICEF, the UN Population Fund, the UN Environment Program, and the UN Development Program, also maintain ties with national and international groups that may provide political support for their operations. UN specialized agencies and other intergovernmental organizations do the same.

The general public is cultivated as well. In New York and Geneva, busy information clerks and smartly uniformed tour guides minister to the throngs of people who visit the UN headquarters each year to see the sights and observe UN public meetings. The United Nations reaches out to a vast world audience through a constant stream of news releases from New York, Geneva, and UN information centers around the world. Publications range from documentary reports of proceedings and Secretariat research to slick brochures lauding the accomplishments of the United Nations and its related agencies.

The object of building a power base is to influence the affairs of the organization and the larger political community. Kofi Annan's eclectic abilities and his long domicile in New York City has sensitized him to the importance of a variety of groups and organizations, many of which are located in the private sector. His emphasis on civil society is symbolized by his recommendation that a People's Millennium Assembly be organized around the General Assembly session in year 2000 to ensure the greater participation of the world's ordinary people who have a positive opinion of the United Nations. Moreover, soon after assuming his new responsibilities, he reached out to the private business sector whose assistance he sought in fighting poverty and injustice worldwide. In response to this appeal, Time-Warner chairman Ted Turner, in September 1997, announced he would contribute $1 billion of his personal wealth to the United Nations.

All incumbents have considered themselves spokesmen for the world community and have not hesitated to take positions in support of UN purposes and principles. Lie, as he later recalled in his memoirs, "was determined that the Secretary-General should be a force for peace."[6] Hammarskjöld also insisted on the right to take a stand on international issues whenever it could "be firmly based on the Charter and its principles."[7] Thant, Waldheim, Pérez de Cuéllar, Boutros-Ghali and Annan have continued to defend the Secretary-General's right to speak out, whether the issue be Vietnam, Iran, Afghanistan, the Falklands, the Middle East, the Balkans, Somalia, Iraq, human rights, economic development, the environment, or the staffing of the Secretariat.

The Secretary-General's opinion carries more weight if the Secretariat has special expertise or interest in the issue, other than his role as global community spokesman. Matters of administrative structure and budget fall into this category. So also do programs administered by the Secretariat, where the Secretary-General and his agents are closer to the facts of the issue than the representatives of most governments, and his arguments weigh accordingly. The same is true where the Secretary-General is engaged in mediatory activities, either in person or through an appointed mediator.

In taking political initiatives, the Secretary-General has certain formal powers of office on which to draw. He enjoys the privilege of speaking to UN deliberative bodies or placing items on their agendas. Under Article 99 of the Charter, he is specially authorized "to bring to the attention of the Security Council any matter which in his opinion may threaten the maintenance of international peace and security." While this right has rarely been exercised— almost always some member state will raise an issue if it is appropriate for Security Council consideration—Article 99 clearly stamps the office as one of political as well as administrative functions. A seemingly innocuous clause in Article 98, authorizing the Secretary-General to "perform such other functions as are entrusted to him" by the other major organs, has also been interpreted as an important grant of power. For Dag Hammarskjöld it was a mandate to do whatever he found necessary to implement directives from the General Assembly and the Security Council relating to the Middle East, the Congo, and other problem areas.

Hammarskjöld went even farther in finding broad political responsibilities inherent in the office of Secretary-General. When deadlock in the Security Council prevented enlargement of the UN Observer Group in Lebanon in the summer of 1958, he enlarged it on his own initiative, explaining to the Security Council that under the Charter he "should be expected to act without any guidance from the Assembly or the Security Council should this appear to him necessary towards helping to fill any vacuum that may appear in the systems which the Charter and traditional diplomacy provide for the safeguarding of peace and security." Hammarskjöld's assumption of such authority was bold, almost audacious; but in another perspective it was simply part of the ongoing process of Charter evolution, through interpretation, as the foundation for a global constitutional system.

U Thant continued the practice of taking independent political initiatives. The UN temporary executive authority in West New Guinea (1962), the observer mission in Yemen (1963), and the UN plebiscite in North Borneo and Sarawak (1963) were instigated by Thant on his own responsibility, although each action was subsequently approved by the General Assembly or the Security Council. At the height of the 1962 Cuban missile crisis, Thant's appeal for a voluntary suspension of Soviet arms shipments to Cuba and of American quarantine measures provided a formula that helped avert a direct confrontation at sea. After 1964 he made various attempts, all unsuccessful, to assume a mediating role in the Vietnam conflict. Waldheim actively sought a solution to the Afghanistan crisis, likewise without success.

Pérez de Cuéllar also, quietly but with dedication, asserted the powers of his office as international peacemaker. His efforts to mediate conflict in Lebanon, the Falklands, the Iran-Iraq War, Grenada, and elsewhere during his first term were largely unavailing, By contrast his second term saw genuine progress in peacemaking. Internal changes in the Soviet Union, the coincident thaw in the cold war, the unexpected Soviet embrace of the United Nations in 1987, and a somewhat more positive U.S. view of the United Nations that emerged near the end of the Reagan administration created a favorable setting for UN action. In the Persian Gulf conflict, weariness in both Iran and Iraq provided the local ingredient for successful action, and in 1988 the Secretary-General and his aides were able to arrange an end to the fighting in this eight-year-old war. The same year a second major diplomatic breakthrough, brokered by UN Undersecretary-General Diego Cordovez, led to Soviet troop withdrawal from Afghanistan. These achievements were followed by further mediations of conflict in Central America, Cambodia, and Western Sahara, and, in 1991, the UN-negotiated release of most Western hostages in Lebanon. On the negative side, the 1991 Gulf War underscored the continuing reality that peaceful resolution of conflict does not inevitably follow intervention by the Secretary-General.

Boutros-Ghali added to the precedent of political activism set by his predecessors. In the first year of his incumbency he provided a mediator for Afghanistan's internal warring factions; took initiatives to resolve continuing disputes in Cyprus, East Timor, and elsewhere; recommended new peacekeeping forces in Yugoslavia, Somalia, and Mozambique; proposed a wide-ranging overhaul of UN enforcement capabilities; and persistently urged stronger measures of enforcement in the Balkans and Somalia. The vigor with which he pursued his objectives may have been surprising to some, but it was consistent with his past experience as a diplomatic trouble-shooter in Africa and a key participant in the Camp David talks leading to the 1979 peace accord between Egypt and Israel.

Kofi Annan has followed in this tradition. Moreover, as UN Undersecretary-General for Peacekeeping Operations prior to his election, he was already well-schooled in the diplomatic arts. Annan was expected to bring his expertise in conflict resolution to bear in the most pregnant world crises, and he did not disappoint his observers. Shortly after assuming his high office he revived the peace process in a number of intractable conflicts. The Secretary-General's pet phrase summed up his attitude toward diplomacy: "it is not an event, but a process," he said. The long time international civil servant was a remarkably patient individual. Frustrating those seeking a quick fix to complex problems, Annan counseled patience and fortitude. Where a desire for unconditional surrender was sought, he insisted on compromise and confidence building. Nowhere was this style more dramatized than in his decision in the Winter of 1998, with Security Council approval, to go to Baghdad just as the United States, also in the name of the United Nations, made preparations to launch a heavy blow against Iraqi military targets because its leadership continued to block UN-authorized inspections of suspected weapons sites. Annan's discussions with Saddam Hussein and his lieutenants were declared successful when the Secretary-General revealed Iraq would abide by all UN resolutions. The flip side of that agreement, however, emphasized respect for Iraq's sovereignty, and critics of the Secretary-General questioned how one objective could be realized without doing damage to the other. To all of this Annan noted that it was not the agreement (i.e., the "event") that was important, but the "process."

The tradition of political initiative by the Secretary-General is thus well established, but limits are fixed by political realities. The free-wheeling, vigorous assertion of political prerogative characteristic of the late Hammarskjöld years gave way to a more restrained approach to political leadership by his successors, at least until Boutros-Ghali. This was in part a matter of personality, but it was also a result of lessons learned from that experience. If Hammarskjöld opened new vistas of executive action, his clash with the Soviet Union—like that of Lie—plainly marked its limits. The Security Council has also held tighter rein on the Secretary-General in political matters, and more great power agreement on the scope of appropriate UN action in political crises has left fewer occasions for either the General Assembly or the Secretary-General to exercise broad discretion.

Because the support of governments is so crucial to the successful outcome of mediation or other political initiative, the Secretary-General takes a serious risk in making any major political move without first consulting members of the Security Council, formally or informally. When the Secretary-General appeals for UN action (or stronger action) in a given situation, he may simply be calling members to a sense of their responsibilities to the global community. On the other hand, without advance consultation, it may appear as carping, scolding, or criticizing the policies of governments whose support he needs. Boutros-Ghali's public statements regarding the Balkans, Somalia, and other problem areas crossed over the line. The negative reaction of some of the larger states, especially the United States, seemed to confirm the proposition that effective political leadership by the Secretary-General lies primarily in the area of quiet diplomacy. Kofi Annan appears to fill that requirement, but the criticism levelled against him by important members of the U.S. Congress shortly after his return from Baghdad illustrated the impossibility of meeting everyone's expectations in any act of diplomacy. Moreover, repeated Iraqi violations of its agreement with the Secretary-General that resulted in U.S. air strikes on Iraq's military installations in December 1998 further undermined the Secretary-General's pursuit of a diplomatic solution and hardened opposition to his actions among members of the United States Congress. However, Kofi Annan's somewhat muted reaction to the December bombing of Iraq, as well as his January 1999 response to the fighting in Kosovo, that NATO might indeed be justified in using force against Serbia in order to gain Belgrade's compliance to human rights questions, was an indication that the Secretary-General may have shifted his ground on the use of force.

## THE BASIS OF SECRETARIAT INFLUENCE

International secretariats and their executive heads have extensive involvement in the political processes of international organizations. But involvement and effectiveness vary from one organization to another, and even within a single organization, over a period of time. What accounts for these differences? Although an adequate answer to that question would require a book in itself, some of the reasons will be briefly summarized here.

## Legal Powers

The charter of an organization gives the executive head certain rights, powers, and duties that help define the office. Others may be conferred by action of the organization's governing bodies. The UN Charter gives more authority to the Secretary-General than did the League Covenant. The constitutional grant of authority to the Commission of the European Union, as contained in relevant treaties, is still greater. Legal rights are a source of positive influence.

## An Administrative Organization

A secretariat is a working organization, often embracing hundreds or, in the case of the United Nations, thousands of employees. It can perform or withhold service. Its programs affect the welfare of numerous people. The ability to control such an organization is a source of power to the secretary-general, or whoever is in charge.

In some secretariats, perhaps most, the executive head is never fully in charge. This may be because he lacks the personal skills to administer effectively. In part it results from the inherent unwieldiness of large bureaucracies. In some instances geographic distance from headquarters, or the support of governmental clients, or the strong personality of an able subordinate, may reduce the secretary-general's control over particular units of the staff. A higher-level official who owes his appointment primarily to the political influence of his government may feel some independence from the executive head. Within the United Nations the General Assembly has been prone to create special programs, such as the UN Development Program, the UN Children's Fund (UNICEF), the UN High Commissioner for Refugees, and the UN Relief and Works Agency for Palestine Refugees in the Near East, for which the Secretary-General has little or no administrative responsibility. In addition, the Assembly frequently creates committees, consisting of national representatives, to carry out some of its mandates. The work of the staff assigned to these committees is subject to the control of the committee rather than the secretary-general. With such bodies as the Special Committee against Apartheid, the Committee on the Exercise of the Inalienable Rights of the Palestinian People, or the Special Committee to Investigate Israeli Practices Affecting the Human Rights of the Palestinian People and Other Arabs of the Occupied Territories, a secretary-general who wishes to mediate in these areas might find a portion of his staff working at cross-purposes to him by supporting a much harder committee line. When an executive head lacks full control, his administrative power is thereby diminished.

*Information*

Many states rely on the secretariat to provide reliable information and advice on a wide variety of subjects. This "information power" may result from the technical expertise of secretariat personnel, continuity of service and depth of experience, or access to sources of information not directly available to governments. Sometimes the balance of influence as between government representatives and international civil servants hinges on relative expertise, particularly if the organization performs primarily technical functions. If government representatives possess the technical expertise, they will certainly dominate the policy process. If secretariat officials are more technically qualified, their prospect of influencing policy will be greater.

*Neutrality*

However difficult the achievement of absolute neutrality in international affairs, one source of secretariat strength is the secretariat's position as spokesman for the whole community. A reputation for neutrality, impartiality, and integrity increases trust and thereby the prospect for successful mediation of disputed questions.

*Personal Qualities of the Incumbent*

Each executive head brings his own talents and interests to the office. He may be a good administrator or a good politician, or both, or neither. He may be interested in administration or in politics. He may be more adept, or less adept, at building coalitions of support among governments and private groups and at inspiring his staff to a sense of unity and purpose.

Albert Thomas, first Director-General of the ILO, was a promoter of causes, heavily involved in broad questions of organizational policy. This presumably reflected his background as a politician, a trade unionist, a social campaigner and reformer. On the other hand, Sir Eric Drummond brought to the League the self-effacing anonymity of the British civil servant who, while leaving center stage to others, exerted his influence through management, counsel, and negotiation behind the scenes. Trygve Lie, like Thomas, delegated administration to deputies and emphasized the political function of the UN Secretary-General both as a public figure and as a quiet negotiator. Dag Hammarskjöld appeared in many ways to combine the best aspects of both the Lie and Drummond types—concern for administrative detail, mastery of quiet diplomacy, and zealous advocacy of secretariat initiative.

Hammarskjöld's successors have preserved the political functions of the office, although their personal qualities as well as their circumstances have dictated a less assertive approach. U Thant by nature was calm, self-assured, not prone to giving needless offense. He spoke out on principle, however, and did in fact give offense to the United States by his criticisms of the Vietnam War. Kurt Waldheim, whose reputation has since been tarnished by revelations of his Nazi connections during World War II, was more polished, correct, and formal. He was less inclined to criticize member states in ways that would diminish his personal influence and thus opted for quiet diplomacy. Pérez de Cuéllar, also in the quiet mold, was genuinely self-effacing. Integrity, persistence, optimism, and a sense of humor contributed to his success in the political arena.

Boutros-Ghali, the first Secretary-General to serve after the Cold War, was neither a successful administrator nor politician. Distancing himself from the career members of the Secretariat, he failed in his management of a complex international bureaucracy. In political matters, he often said the wrong thing in the wrong place, under the wrong circumstances. He clearly fell out with the UN's most prominent member, and he had the misfortune of running afoul of the U.S. Congress when it shifted from a Democratic to a Republican majority in 1994. Moreover, American isolationism reappeared with the passing of the Cold War, and isolationist policies had long been associated with Republicans. If President Clinton was credited with the undoing of Boutros-Ghali, his decision to withhold American support was in major part prompted by political sentiment in the Congress and in the public at large that showed a diminished interest in international affairs. Kofi Annan inherited the legacies of all the previous Secretaries-General, but none weighed upon him more than that of his immediate predecessor. With the United States playing a heavy hand in UN and other world matters, the Secretary-General was called upon to satisfy American demands without at the same time compromising his role as the world's most prominent international civil servant.

## The Organizational Task

The nature of the organizational task has important consequences for secretariat influence on policy. Highly technical tasks usually generate less controversy than broad political questions and hence provide safer subjects for secretariat initiative. An organization that administers programs is likely to have greater staff influence on policy than one that makes rules for state behavior or tries to settle international disputes. Within the United Nations one should expect more secretariat influence on the form of technical assistance programs than on the outcome of resolutions dealing with conflict in the Middle East. If task performance generates its own financial resources, as with the lending operations of the World Bank, the reduced dependence on member states for funds is almost certain to give the staff a greater policy role.

## The Political Environment

The political environment of an organization may be the most important variable affecting secretariat influence and, indeed, every other aspect of international organization. One kind of environmental impact consists of unplanned events that may frustrate organizational goals or, contrarily, offer new opportunity for initiative and constructive accomplishment. Another is the persistent influence of government attitudes, preferences, and control of resources that set limits on any attempted secretariat initiative. The environment, far more than the skills of the executive head, determines the support that may be available from governments and nongovernmental groups. Attitudes can of course change, and sometimes the process of participation precipitates change. But environment, even a changing environment, controls the organization, and not vice versa.

## REVITALIZING THE UNITED NATIONS

Confronted with the challenges of a new era, the United Nations is experiencing a significant restructuring of its Secretariat and associated institutions, agencies, and administrative units. Led by Secretary-General Kofi Annan, the 1998 General Assembly was described as the "Reform Assembly" and it gave Annan a clear mandate in meeting the twenty-first century objectives of the organization. Determined to give concrete expression to the centrality of the United Nations in issues of concern to the international community, especially peace and security, Annan stressed making the peacekeeping operations more effective. Thus, in 1997–98 the peace process was revived in the Western Sahara, East Timor, Cyprus, Tajikistan, Afghanistan, and Angola. In Iraq, Annan obtained agreement from the Security Council to increase the oil-for-food program, and pledged an end to UN-imposed sanctions once Baghdad had demonstrated full compliance with UN resolutions and opted for peace with its neighbors. UN peacekeeping operations also successfully monitored elections in Liberia and in the Eastern Slavonia region of Croatia, where in January 1998 the UN completed the handing over of its administrative responsibilities to local authorities. The UN also completed peacekeeping operations in Haiti, where only a small contingent of police advisers remained to help in the fashioning of democratic institutions.

No less important was the restructuring of the UN administrative system. The General Assembly welcomed Kofi Annan's plan to create a Department of Disarmament Affairs in the UN Secretariat that would consider a reduction in conventional as well as weapons of mass destruction. The Secretary-General also stressed the need to ban landmines, and sought to override the lack of enthusiasm from some of the major world actors by drawing support from the nongovernmental organizations. At the signing ceremony of the new Convention on the Prohibition of the Use, Stockpiling, Production and Transfer of Anti-Personnel Mines and on Their Destruction, in Ottawa in December 1997, Annan paid tribute to the "union of governments, civil society, and international organizations" for the drafting and acceptance of the Convention. Citing the spreading importance of the non-governmental organizations in humanitarian affairs, the Secretary-General called for greater cooperation and coordination between all public and private institutions, and at his order the UN High Commissioner for Refugees, the United Nations Children's Fund, and the World Food Program, were brought into intimate relationship with specific NGOs.

Human rights abuses also were given closer scrutiny. Citing a degree of helplessness in investigating human rights violations in the Democratic Republic of the Congo and the continuing slaughter of the innocent in Algeria, the Secretary-General reaffirmed the UN's commitment to people threatened by indiscriminate violence. Addressing the Organization of African Unity in Harare, he declared "human rights are African rights, not an imposition or plot by the industrialized West." He followed this performance with a speech at the Tehran Conference on Human Rights Day, where he noted "human rights are foreign to no culture and native to all nations, and lie at the heart of all that the United Nations aspires to achieve in peace and development." Noting the fiftieth anniversary of the Universal Declaration of Human Rights, Kofi Annan articulated an "all human rights for all" theme for that special event. Acting on this principle, the Secretary-General combined the Geneva-based programs on human rights into a single office to ensure greater coordination and strength of purpose, and he appointed the President of Ireland, Mary Robinson, as the new UN High Commissioner for Human Rights.

Annan's reorganization and upgrading of the different UN institutions paralleled the appointment of a number of outstanding international personalities. The former German Environment Minister, Klaus Toepfer, was named head of the UN Environment Program. Italian Senator Pino Arlacchi was appointed head of a new Vienna-based Office of Drug Control and Crime Prevention. A senior UNHCR official, Sergio Viera de Mello, was made Emergency Relief Coordinator. Olara Otunnu, head of the New York-based International Peace Academy, assumed the role as Special Representative for Children in Armed Conflict. Jayantha Dhanpala, the former Sri Lankan ambassador to the United States who presided over the Review and Extension Conference that focused on the renewal of the Nuclear Non-Proliferation Treaty in 1995, agreed to become Undersecretary-General of the newly created Department of Disarmament Affairs. Malaysia's Rafiah Salim assumed the duties of the Assistant Secretary-General in the UN Human Resources Office, and Angela King of Jamaica became Annan's Special Adviser on Gender Issues.

Annan's proposal, and the General Assembly's approval of the new post of Deputy UN Secretary-General, was testimony to his considerable negotiating skills. Long discussed but never acted upon by other secretaries-general, Annan's long experience with the United Nations convinced him that the work of the office was more than one administrator could manage. Louise Frechette, Canada's Deputy Minister of National Defense, was Annan's choice for the position, and the Secretary-General made it clear she would be the number one person in the UN in all matters related to development. Never in the history of the United Nations had so many highranking positions gone to women, but Annan was less influenced by gender, and more concerned with enlisting the services of the most talented people. The Secretary-General had in fact assembled a team of experts, who like himself, were devoted to international public service, and who like him, were totally committed to the mission of the United Nations.

Annan had assumed the leadership of the United Nations at a time of high controversy, a period in which the United Nations had lost considerable stature, and where its major sponsor, the United States, had lost interest in the collective character of the organization. With the United States significantly behind in its payments to the world organization, the Secretary-General was compelled to cut administrative costs in order to secure more funds for development programs. Annan proposed the first negative-growth budget in the world organization's history in 1998–99, and collapsed the three departments involved in economic and social development into a single Department of Economic and Social Affairs. In fact, within a year of assuming his new responsibilities, Annan rearranged some thirty UN units, grouping them into four thematic areas for greater efficiency and cost-savings. These areas were: peace and security; economic and social affairs; development operations; and humanitarian affairs. Moreover, all UN funds and programs, including development operations, were brought together in a UN Development Group that functioned on the basis of common goals. (See Table 4-5).

The consolidation of conference support services into a Department of General Assembly Affairs and Conference Services dovetailed with the upgrading of the Department of Political Affairs and its linkage with the new Secretariat Department of Disarmament Affairs. The Secretariat also tightened its procurement services by streamlining procedures, expanding electronic procurement and the use of documents in electronic form, and by developing a single service to provide information technology and telecommunication infrastructure. All this was accomplished with a budget savings of $200 million and a staff 25 percent smaller than the one Annan had inherited from his predecessors.

The larger reform package, still in the planning stage, involved a new concept of trusteeship now that the work of the Trusteeship Council had been completed. Also on the agenda was the formation of a Special Commission at the ministerial level, to examine possible changes in the constitutional relationship between the organization and the autonomous specialized agencies within the UN system. Indeed, much of Annan's long-range thinking was expected to be on the table for Assembly action by the time of the Millennium Assembly and the companion People's Assembly that he planned to convene in the year 2000.

TABLE 4-5   Renewing the United Nations: A Program For Reform*

| PEACE AND SECURITY | |
|---|---|
| DPA | Department of Political Affairs |
| DPKO | Department of Peace-keeping Operations |
| DDAR | Department for Disarmament and Arms Regulation |

| UN DEVELOPMENT GROUP | |
|---|---|
| UNDP | United Nations Development Programme |
| UNICEF | United Nations Children's Fund |
| UNFPA | United Nations Population Fund |

| HUMANITARIAN AFFAIRS | |
|---|---|
| ERC | Emergency Relief Coordinator |
| UNHCR | United Nations High Commissioner for Refugees |
| WFP | World Food Programme |
| UNRWA | United Nations Relief and Works Agency for Palestine Refugees in the Near East |

| ECONOMIC AND SOCIAL | |
|---|---|
| DESA | Department of Economic and Social Affairs |
| Regional Comissions | Includes: Economic Commission for Europe, Economic and Social Commission for Asia and the Pacific, Economic Commission for Latin America and the Caribbean, Economic Commission for Africa, Economic and Social Commission for Western Asia. |
| UNCTAD | United Nations Conference on Trade and Development |
| UNEP | United Nations Environment Programme |
| Habitat | United Nations Centre for Human Settlements |
| ODCCP | Office of Drug Control and Crime Prevention |
| UNU | United Nations University |

| GENERAL SERVICES | |
|---|---|
| OLA | Office of Legal Affairs |
| DM | Department of Management |
| GAACS | Department of General Assembly Affairs and Conference Services |
| DPI | Department of Public Information |
| OIOS | Office of Internal Oversight Services |

SOURCE: United Nations Website (http://www.un.org/reform/track2/initiate.htm#newun)

* This chart places the various UN entities under the sector to which they principally contribute. A number of entities contribute to the work of more than one. Human Rights (comprising the Office of the High Commissioner and the Centre for Human Rights) is introduced in the chart as a distinct sector but also constitutes an integral dimension of all sectors.

# NOTES

1. F. P. Walters, *A History of the League of Nations* (New York: Oxford University Press, 1952), p. 76.
2. Maurice Bertrand, "The Recruitment Policy of United Nations Staff," in *International Administration: Law and Management Practices in International Organizations,* ed. Chris de Cooker, for United Nations Institute for Training and Research (Dordrecht: Martinus Nijhoff Publishers, 1990), pp. I.2/3–4. See also Theodor Meron, *The United Nations Secretariat* (Lexington, MA: D. C. Heath, 1977), p. 57.
3. *Our Common Future,* World Commission on Environment and Development (Oxford: Oxford University Press, 1987).
4. For a good sketch of the Secretary-General's role in peacekeeping, see Kjell Skjelsbae, "The UN Secretary-General and the Mediation of International Disputes," *Journal of Peace Research* 28, no. 1 (1991), pp. 112–113.
5. See Indar Jit Rikhye, "Critical Elements in Determining the Suitability of Conflict Settlement Efforts by the United Nations Secretary General," in Louis Kriesberg and Stuart J. Thorson, eds., *Timing the De-Escalation of International Conflicts* (Syracuse, NY: Syracuse University Press, 1991), pp. 58–82.
6. Trygve, Lie, *In the Cause of Peace* (New York: Macmillan, 1954), p. 42.
7. Address in Copenhagen, May 2, 1959, reprinted in *United Nations Review 5* (June 1959), p. 25.

# SELECTED READINGS

Barros, James. *Office without Power: Secretary-General Sir Eric Drummond, 1919–1933.* New York: Oxford University Press, 1979.
———. *Trygve Lie and the Cold War: The UN Secretary-General Pursues Peace, 1946–1953.* DeKalb: Northern Illinois University, 1989.
Bercovitch, Jacob. *Resolving International Conflicts: the Theory and Practice of Mediation.* Boulder: Lynne Rienner, 1995.
de Cooker, Chris, ed. *International Administration: Law and Management Practices in International Organisations.* United Nations Institute for Training and Research. Dordrecht: Martinus Nijhoff Publishers, 1990.
Finger, Seymour M., and John Mugno. *The Politics of Staffing the United Nations Secretariat.* New York: Ralph Bunche Institute on the United Nations, 1974.
Fisher, Julie. *Nongovernments: NGOs and the Political Development of the Third World.* West Hartford, CT: Kumarian Press, 1997.
Gordenker, Leon. *The UN Secretary-General and the Maintenance of Peace.* New York: Columbia University Press, 1967.
Graham, Norman A., and Robert S. Jordan, eds. *The International Civil Service: Changing Role and Concepts.* New York: Pergamon Press, 1980.
Jordan, Robert S., ed. *Dag Hammarskjöld Revisited: The UN Secretary-General as a Force in World Politics.* Durham, NC: Carolina Academic Press, 1983.
Langrod, Georges. *The International Civil Service.* Leyden: A. W. Sijthoff, 1963.
Lie, Trygve. *In the Cause of Peace: Seven Years with the UN.* New York: Macmillan, 1954.

Loveday, Alexander. *Reflections on International Administration.* Oxford: Clarendon Press, 1956.

McLaren, Robert I. *Civil Servants and Public Policy: A Comparative Study of International Secretariats.* Waterloo, Ont.: Wilfrid Laurier University Press, 1980.

Marks, Edward. *Complex Emergencies: Bureaucratic Arrangements in the UN Secretariat.* Washington: National Defense University Press, 1996.

Meron, Theodor. *The United Nations Secretariat: The Rules and the Practice.* Lexington, MA: D. C. Heath, 1977.

Mouritzen, Hans. *The International Civil Service, A Study of Bureaucracy: International Organizations.* Aldershot, Eng.: Dartmouth, 1990.

Pérez de Cuéllar, Javier. *Pilgrimage for Peace: A Secretary-General's Memoir.* New York: St. Martin's Press, 1997.

Pitt, David, and Thomas G. Weiss, eds. *The Nature of United Nations Bureaucracies.* Boulder, CO: Westview Press, 1986.

Ranshofen-Wertheimer, Egon F. *The International Secretariat: A Great Experiment in International Administration.* New York: Carnegie Endowment for International Peace, 1945.

Reymond, Henri, and Sidney Mailick. *International Personnel Policies and Practices.* New York: Praeger Publishers, 1985.

Rovine, Arthur W. *The First Fifty Years: The Secretary-General in World Politics, 1920–1970.* Leyden: A. W. Sijthoff, 1970.

Royal Institute of International Affairs. *The International Secretariat of the Future.* London: Oxford University Press, 1944.

Russett, Bruce, ed. *The Once and Future Security Council.* New York: St. Martin's Press, 1997.

Thant, U. *View from the UN.* Garden City, NY: Doubleday, 1978.

Urquhart, Brian. *Hammarskjöld.* New York: Alfred A. Knopf, 1972.

———, and Erskine Childers. *A World in Need of Leadership: Tomorrow's United Nations.* Uppsala, Sweden: Dag Hammarskjöld Foundation, 1990.

Weiss, Thomas G. *International Bureaucracy: An Analysis of the Operation of Functional and Global International Secretariats.* Lexington, MA: D. C. Heath, 1975.

Zacher, Mark W. *Dag Hammarskjöld's United Nations.* New York: Columbia University Press, 1970.

# 5

## Security through Collective Action

Safeguarding international peace and security was the primary reason for the establishment of the United Nations in 1945. The aspiration "to save succeeding generations from the scourge of war" is enshrined in the opening lines of the UN Charter. Maintaining peace and security appears first in the Charter's statement of purposes and principles. UN functions are not narrowly limited to promoting military security, but even the non-military functions are justified in the Charter by their potential contribution to peace. The rationale for international economic and social cooperation, for example, as set forth in Article 55 of the UN Charter, is "the creation of conditions of stability and well-being which are necessary for peaceful and friendly relations among nations." Peace and security also figure prominently in Articles 73(c) and 76(a) for dependent territories and peoples.

The great frequency of armed conflict since 1945 testifies that the UN security system has not worked as intended. Security is still the central concern of all states, but the United Nations has been less central to the security of its members than the Charter might indicate. States rely primarily on their own might and that of their allies to deter aggression against themselves and, should peace fail, to vindicate their interests by force of arms. Lack of centrality does not mean irrelevance, however, and the United Nations has in many situations affected the way states pursue their security interests. The UN role in dispute settlement, arms control, and establishment of the economic and social foundations for peace will be discussed in succeeding chapters. This chapter will examine efforts through the United Nations to prevent and limit war and to organize coercive sanctions against states that violate Charter norms.

The UN war-prevention role has often been called "collective security," although in practice the United Nations has been largely an adjunct to the operation of local and global balances of power. Before examining UN activities in detail, this chapter will present a brief historical and theoretical analysis of the balance of power and collective security concepts. A second section will discuss the generally unsuccessful efforts of the United Nations to achieve the collective security ideal. A third section recounts the evolution of UN "peacekeeping" as a means of war limitation that depends, not primarily on coercion, but on the willingness of the affected states to accept a pacifying UN presence.

142

# BALANCE OF POWER AND COLLECTIVE SECURITY

## ALLIANCES AND THE BALANCE OF POWER

Historically, the most common security arrangement among independent political entities has been the military alliance. The book of Genesis gives accounts of alliances and wars among rival groups of kings in the days of Abraham. Thucydides' *History of the Peloponnesian War* is the story of alliances and counteralliances among contending groups of Greek city-states. The modern state system has followed the same pattern from its inception, and even today arrangements for military cooperation among two or more states—secret or open, simple or highly organized—maintain undiminished popularity.

*Balance of power* is the term usually applied to a system in which states rely on international alliances to promote their individual security interests. However, what passes for a balance of power system in a world of independent nation-states, each of whom are mindful of, and in pursuit of exclusive national interests, is more a condition rather than an operative mechanism. Alliance arrangements are methods in the balance of power and generally give tangible form to a perceived balance, but the balance of power operates even in the absence of formal alliances, and oftentimes in spite of them. Although the outbreak of World War I was attributed to the failure of the balance of power, and statesmen like Woodrow Wilson called for its abandonment, it was not the balance of power that failed to sustain the peace, but the changing assumptions and perceptions of those responsible for the making of critical decisions. The central premise of any balance of power system is the assumption of those involved with its operation that their adversary or rival has the capacity to do them particular damage and that prudence requires their dispelling conditions that might precipitate a costly conflict. The mutual over-estimation of the capability and will of one's adversary to engage in war, and the rational decision to avoid such conflict, gives meaning to a balance of power system. In other words, if the balance of power is working effectively, what nations generally describe as "peace" is preserved. Thus, the balance of power is not concerned with the righting of wrongs, or the purification of political systems, let alone the establishment of preferred governments. To the contrary, if the balance of power is anything, it is the acceptance of the status quo by the state actors. The balance of power, therefore, is a diplomatic, not a military exercise, and it is when the diplomats are no longer able to manage the "peace" that the balance breaks down and soldiers make war—at least until that time when still another balance permits the diplomats to construct a new "system."

The outbreak of World War I, therefore, irrespective of those who argued its black eminence, was not a consequence of the balance of power system, but the gross failure of key European decisionmakers. Otto von Bismarck had demonstrated the successful use of the balance of power system, but his dismissal by Kaiser Wilhelm, and the latter's determination to establish Germany as both a major land and naval power had elevated the threshhold of threat and provoked the guarantor of the balance, notably Great Britain, to abandon its role as the "balancer" and engage itself in the crosscutting rivalries that eventually produced the Great War. If World War I had proved anything it was the need for a more credible balance of power system, albeit for a more successful demonstration of international diplomacy.

The victors of World War I could not ignore the epic transformation in warfare that occurred during 1914–18. Citing the technological advances made in weapons and munitions and the terrible loss of life as a consequence of their almost casual employment, the statesmen who assembled at Versailles to fashion a new world order were primarily concerned with preventing a repeat performance of this human tragedy. As they saw the situation it was a matter of restricting the use, or even eliminating what then could be described as weapons of mass destruction. But disarmament was hardly a realistic pursuit when the political issues underlying the Great War had not been satisfactorily addressed. Some empires had been defeated and dissolved but imperialism remained the central feature of international politics, and as time would demonstrate, national or popular imperialism was exponentially more aggressive than its traditional, aristocratic cum-commercial predecessor.

Unfortunately, the world leaders who met at Versailles to restore world equilibrium failed to grasp the realities of the time. Confronted with the dilemmas created by the Great War and imposed upon by an American President whose forces had helped to turn the tide of battle, the European statesmen yielded to their transatlantic counterpart and agreed with him that serious concern had to be given to the creation of an international organization that would ensure the continuance of the wartime alliance—not as a prop for the creation of a more formidable balance of power, but as a substitute for it! Hence the emphasis given to collective security as the essential and only workable substitute for the balance of power. But whereas the balance of power acknowledged the sovereign independence of the nation-states, collective security called for a diminution in exclusive state behavior, while requiring an almost abstract commitment to matters of world concern. The U.S. Senate's rejection of Versailles, the League of Nations, and more so, of collective security, was seemingly justified on the basis of a loss of sovereignty, albeit a loss of national control over critical events. For the American senators who damned the League, the issues that the international organization could be called upon to address were judged too distant from U.S. national interests. Although the Americans rejected both a role in the balance of power as well as collective security, the latter was largely kept alive by the more idealistic of the European leaders. Lacking the necessary support, however, collective security failed to prevent World War II. Moreover, in the absence of a resilient diplomacy that was capable of managing the balance of power, global conflict was repeated with even more devastating results.

## THE ADVENT OF COLLECTIVE SECURITY

The task of finding a workable substitute for the balance of power was undertaken by the Paris peacemakers in 1919, under the prodding of President Woodrow Wilson. The available precedents for bringing two or more states within a common security system were not promising. The principal historical precedents were conquest, political federation, and, at a lower level of integration, the military alliance. Conquest was a wholly unacceptable model, and voluntary extinction of separate sovereignties through political federation was not feasible, given deep-seated nationalisms and global diversity in economic development, social organization, and political values. The military alliance made few inroads on national sovereignty, but as a security system it was discredited by the onset of World War I.

Another nineteenth-century precedent was the Concert of Europe, a loose-knit system of great power consultation spawned by the Napoleonic Wars and continued sporadically to the eve of World War I. The Concert was more a state of mind than an organized security system, and it was only indifferently effective. When the Serbian crisis arose in the summer of 1914, the Concert technique of great power consultation was not even called into play. In addition to the Concert, there was the legacy of the 1899 and 1907 Hague Conferences and the considerable experience of organized international cooperation in economic and social fields. Although suggestive of organizational forms and procedures, the international conference and the public administrative union were not security systems. The hard fact was that nothing in history constituted a working precedent for an effective system of security within a community of sovereign states.

The peacemakers thus were forced to innovate. They took the ideal of a universal security system, hitherto the domain of political dreamers, and fused it with nineteenth-century international organization, using in the process much of their own ingenuity to forge the essential compromises between ideals and realities. The result, appearing as the first twenty-six articles of the Versailles Treaty, was the League of Nations Covenant—the world's first major attempt at "collective security."

## THE NATURE OF COLLECTIVE SECURITY

The rejection of the League of Nations by the United States and that organization's failure to meet its collective security obligations heralded its end even before the outbreak of World War II. Nevertheless, as a concept "collective security" survived the war, and the statesmen of the post-World War II period, again led by an American president, recognized the need to give it another try. The alliance forged in World War II to defeat the aggressive forces of fascism and ultranationalism, although comprised of discordant actors, nevertheless acknowledged the need to sustain their association. Appalled by the horrors and destructiveness of modern warfare as well as their own capacity for unlimited and unrestrained violence, and arguably more realistic than their predecessors after World War I, the framers of the United Nations Charter were determined to avoid the pitfalls of the League. Indeed, they gave still another interpretation to the meaning of collective security. What it means, however, varies with the context. The term *collective security* had been applied indiscriminately to almost any arrangement among two or more countries that involves the possibility of joint military action. After World War II it was used to describe military alliances such as NATO in order to give them more respectability. In this context it became almost a synonym for a "good" or a "defensive" alliance, as contrasted with a "bad" (someone else's) alliance, which might be used for "aggressive" purposes. The terms *collective defense* or *collective self-defense* (see Charter Article 51), rather than collective security, have been applied to multilateral alliances aimed primarily at threats to security created by countries outside the coalition.

In its more specialized and correct meaning, collective security is an arrangement among states by which all are committed to aid any country threatened with armed attack by any other country. The object is to deter aggression by confronting a potential aggressor with the power of an overwhelming coalition and, should war nevertheless occur, to bring the aggressor quickly to heel. A collective security system is synonomous with a balance of power system, but modifies the traditional conception of alliances. While an alliance is geared to threats from foes of the alliance, collective security focuses on threats arising within the larger balance of power system. Among the states involved, there are no predetermined alignments. All of them, presumably, are "friends" until one of them chooses to become an aggressor. That state then becomes the "enemy" of all the others until the threat of aggression has been removed.

As originally conceived, collective security was intended to be worldwide in scope. In theory, however, a collective security system might include any smaller number of states as long as preponderant power could be marshaled against any one of them. Some regional organizations have collective security aspects. The Inter-American Treaty of Reciprocal Assistance (the Rio Pact) makes explicit provision for resisting possible aggression by one Latin American state against another. NATO, the Organization of African Unity, and the Arab League have all tried to deal with armed conflict among their own members. The Commonwealth of Independent States that emerged from the breakup of the Soviet Union has not displayed a collective interest in a common security arrangement, but NATO's enlargement in 1998 to include Poland, Hungary, and the Czech Republic raises the prospect that the CIS could follow a similar course. For the time being, however, CIS cooperation with the Organization of Security and Cooperation in Europe (OSCE) sustains the idea of a collective security dimension. Although these organizations and combinations fall short of the collective security ideal, they nevertheless are either regarded as collective security alliances or collective self-defense expedients. Indeed, their utility is demonstrated in the growing number of cooperative associations with United Nations peacekeeping operations.

The essential elements of an effective collective security system are *consensus, commitment,* and *organization.* At the minimum level of *consensus,* states must agree that peace is indivisible and that threats to peace anywhere are the concern of all. But more is required. There must be a *commitment* to act in accordance with the collective security principle. The commitment has both a positive and a self-denying aspect. States are bound affirmatively to combine their force to meet any threat to the security of the world community. They are also committed to refrain from unilateral use of force to achieve purely national objectives. Ideally, the commitments should be so binding and so widely embraced that attempts to change the *status quo* by violence are considered unlawful and subjected to overwhelming force. Without this commitment consensus remains a meaningless abstraction. But commitment, too, may fail in time of crisis if there is no *organization* to make it effective. Every such commitment is necessarily a generalized commitment until a specific crisis arises. If each state is then free to decide how and when its commitment will be honored, enforcement may be highly selective. An effective collective security system requires a central decision-making organ that is empowered to say how and when collective force is to be used, with adequate military forces available on call to carry out that decision.

For practical purposes collective security has a fourth prerequisite. Power should be widely enough dispersed that no state can hope to challenge all the others. The effectiveness of the system depends on its capacity to deter most potential violators and to defeat an actual aggressor in short order. If one state is substantially stronger than the rest, it may be willing to act militarily in defiance of the system. Even though the collectivity may ultimately put down the aggression, the system fails if protracted or devastating war occurs.

## THE LEAGUE SECURITY SYSTEM

The League of Nations did not satisfy any of the conditions for effective collective security, except perhaps the last. During the interwar period no country was strong enough to defy all the others if the others were united. But League members, and the United States as the major nonmember, were not sufficiently convinced that every war anywhere was a threat to them. And certainly they lacked commitment to use their combined force against any and every case of aggression, regardless of who the aggressor might be.

The League Covenant did not even require such a commitment. Far from it. In disputes coming before the League, the Covenant expressly permitted aggressive war against a state that refused to comply with recommendations unanimously endorsed by the Council and against any party to a dispute on which the Council was divided. These so-called gaps in the Covenant were widely deplored, but even more enfeebling was the absence of obligation to act when unauthorized aggression occurred. Article 10 of the League Covenant declared unequivocally that "the Members of the League undertake to respect and preserve as against external aggression the territorial integrity and existing political independence of all Members of the League." Yet Manchuria, Ethiopia, and ultimately a host of other members fell victim to violence without a shot being fired in their defense in the name of the League and without any state being obligated by the Covenant to fire such a shot.

Article 11 seemed to embody both the necessary consensus and commitment in its grand assertion that "any war or threat of war, whether immediately affecting any of the Members of the League or not, is hereby declared a matter of concern to the whole League, and the League shall take any action that may be wise and effectual to safeguard the peace of nations." But when the obligations were spelled out in greater detail, League decisions to take military action had only the force of recommendations (Article 16). Even the supposedly automatic "severance of all trade or financial relations" was vitiated by League resolutions adopted in 1921 emphasizing the right of each state to determine for itself how and when to apply economic sanctions. The League was also hampered by its rule requiring a unanimous vote for most decisions. Whenever the League was moved to action against threats to the peace during the troubled 1930s, it was almost always too little and too late. In short, the League system did not work well because the disposition of members to view their own security as separable from that of others was reinforced by weak legal commitments and ineffective decision-making procedures.

## THE UNITED NATIONS AND COLLECTIVE SECURITY

### The Charter Framework

The framers of the UN Charter were not willing to abandon the collective security concept of peace enforced by the community of nations. Although they recognized the need for some compromise with the ideal, they hoped that improved institutions and a new will to cooperate would succeed where the League had failed.

Taking a cue from the 1928 Pact of Paris, the UN Charter commits all members to "refrain in their international relations from the threat or use of force against the territorial integrity or political independence of any state, or in any other manner inconsistent with the Purposes of the United Nations" (Article 2, section 4). The only exceptions to the use of force are (1) self-defense, individual or collective (Article 51); (2) action against "enemy" states of World War II (Article 107); (3) joint action by the Big Five on behalf of the organization, pending the availability of troops under Article 43 (Article 106); (4) any other use of force authorized by the Security Council, including enforcement by regional organizations (Article 53). The Charter does not ban internal armed revolt and civil wars which, strictly speaking, are not concerned with the use of force in "international relations."

Equally important was the attempt to put sharper teeth into the Charter. Instead of economic sanctions that were automatic in theory but discretionary in practice, the Security Council was given the right to impose nonmilitary sanctions, with all members obligated "to accept and carry out the decisions of the Security Council." In place of the League Council's right to recommend military sanctions, the Security Council was to have earmarked troops supplied by prior agreement with members and awaiting only the Council's call to action. Abandoning the unanimity requirement, the Security Council was empowered to take military action by vote of seven of eleven (now nine of fifteen) members, including the concurring votes of the five permanent members.

The retention of a great power veto was, admittedly, a conscious compromise with the principle of collective security, but one dictated by common sense. Critics had constantly pointed out that collective security treated all wars as incipient world wars, with the practical danger of turning localized wars into global war if powerful forces were ranged on both sides. The veto was intended to prevent such an eventuality. With the great powers all committed to collective enforcement through the organization, the prospect of quickly squelching an outburst of violence would be very good indeed.

On paper the UN Charter seemed a reasonable approach to collective security, subject to the limitation of the veto. The Charter registered broad consensus that peace is indivisible and that any threat to international peace and security is the concern of all. Members were legally committed to accept and carry out Security Council decisions, and the Council could make binding decisions (not just recommendations) to impose both military and nonmilitary sanctions. Here then was consensus, commitment, and central decision-making machinery merged in a coherent collective security system.

## THE DEMISE OF MANDATORY MILITARY SANCTIONS

The Charter system did not work as intended. The root problem was lack of genuine consensus and commitment to match the paper responsibilities. Even while the United Nations was being planned, leaders of the Big Three questioned the collective security concept or the efficacy of particular institutional arrangements. Roosevelt, Churchill, and Stalin all regarded new rivalries as inevitable. Churchill and Stalin hoped to stabilize international conditions by recognizing spheres of influence in areas of special interest to them—particularly the Balkans. Roosevelt looked more to a "Four Policemen" concept (including a rehabilitated China) modeled after the old Concert of Europe as a means of providing order in the system. Great power cooperation, i.e., the balance of power, not collective security, was the answer. Roosevelt ultimately accepted the UN concept, but the germ of his Four Policemen idea was preserved in the provision for permanent members of the UN Security Council.

Events subsequently confirmed President Roosevelt's judgment about collective security, if not his optimism about the prospects for East-West cooperation. Wartime collaboration quickly degenerated into cold war, revealing discordant national security interests that could not be harnessed to the collective security requirement of all for one and one for all. Soviet-American rivalry was reflected in the Security Council, where a Western majority was held in check by the Soviet veto. But the veto was only a symptom. Fundamental divergence of interest was the underlying problem.

One of the early institutional casualties was the UN security force envisioned by Charter Article 43. The capacity of the Security Council to take military action on its own initiative was dependent on the subsequent negotiation of special agreements with member states to make standby military forces and facilities available to the Council at its call. Each such agreement required ratification by the states concerned according to their respective constitutional processes. The ratification requirement meant that member states, in accepting the Charter, had made only a moral commitment to support UN military sanctions, while postponing to a later day any limitation on the right to control their own military forces. In fact, no Article 43 agreement ever reached the ratification stage, because the major powers could not agree on the size and character of their respective national contributions or on where the units should be based. The Security Council and its Military Staff Committee (Articles 46, 47) were never able to resolve their differences.

Without agreement on guidelines for UN military forces, no special agreements under Article 43 could be negotiated. The broad Charter commitment to collective security was not translated into a specific commitment to supply troops and matériel. Despite the intent of the Charter, members retained the right to decide for themselves, according to the circumstances of each case, how their military forces should be used. If collective military action were to be taken at all, it would be on a voluntary basis.

While the Security Council was struggling with Article 43, the General Assembly embarked on the project of defining aggression. Nearly thirty years later, in 1974, the Assembly approved a compromise definition embodying a fair degree of international consensus but containing enough ambiguities to leave the identification of aggression in many situations still an ad hoc political act. The Assembly determined that an act of aggression must be considered "in light of all the circumstances of each particular case." Article 1 of the definition proscribes "the use of force against the sovereignty, territorial integrity or political independence" of another state and labels it "aggression." Article 2 makes "the first use of force by a State in contravention of the Charter" *prima facie* evidence of aggression, subject to Security Council determination that the act in question did not constitute aggression. Article 3 lists several other acts that may be labeled aggression, subject again to Security Council decision to the contrary. Article 7 specifically excludes from the definition of aggression acts by and in support of peoples struggling to achieve "self-determination, freedom and independence" from "colonial and racist regimes or other forms of alien domination."

## Korea and Collective Action

Korea provided the first major test of voluntary collective security under UN auspices. In a number of respects, the conditions for voluntary UN enforcement action were highly favorable. When fighting broke out in June 1950, a UN observation group already in South Korea was able to provide immediate confirmation that an armed attack by North Korean troops had in fact occurred. The absence of the Soviet delegate, in protest against the continued seating of Nationalist China, eliminated the prospect of a veto and allowed a quick Security

Council endorsement of the U.S. request for military aid to South Korea. In Japan and Okinawa the United States had troops that could be quickly moved to the scene of the fighting. Thus the "UN" action was commenced, relying almost totally on American initiative and resources.

When the return of the Soviet delegate in August snuffed out the Security Council's capacity to act, the issue was removed from the Security Council to the General Assembly. At first, the Assembly was able to act on crucial issues with some dispatch. As the months wore on, however, Chinese intervention, military stalemate, and rising concern about touching off a third world war brought division and dissension to the United Nations. Nearly all members breathed a sigh of relief when the Korean Armistice was arranged in July 1953.

UN action helped preserve the independence of the Republic of Korea, but it brought no renewed enthusiasm for collective security, on a voluntary basis or otherwise. At first seen as the rebirth of collective military action, the Korean War proved almost the opposite. The reasons are now fairly clear, and most of them speak to characteristics of the world and of the United Nations that persist to the present time.

One reason is the ambiguous form in which armed conflict has occurred since Korea. Civil wars, revolutions, guerrilla warfare, clandestine infiltration and subversion, and foreign intervention in the guise of assistance to contending domestic factions are the common forms of violence that have ruptured the peace of the world. In such situations there is often no clearly identifiable aggressor to make the object of a collective military response. The probability that the Korean experience may have encouraged the subsequent use of more covert forms of aggression in place of overt military invasion does little to enhance the usefulness of collective military sanctions in meeting the kinds of threats that do exist.

The Korean War also highlighted basic defects of the United Nations as an instrument for launching collective military sanctions. Without consensus among its permanent members, the Security Council could not take decisive action in times of crisis. Only the absence of the Soviet delegate made the initial Security Council action possible, and the Security Council was immobilized by the Soviet return. When responsibility for decisions was then shifted to the General Assembly, that body proved too large, too unwieldy, and too divided in counsel to direct a military operation effectively.

Korea further revealed the disadvantages of dependence on voluntary commitment of forces in time of crisis. Just twenty-two of the sixty member states offered military forces, and only sixteen of the offers were of usable size and quality. The United States contributed more than half of the ground forces, 85 percent of the naval forces, and nearly 95 percent of the air force contingents, with South Korea providing most of the remaining personnel. Less than 10 percent came from the other contributors. This means that the Korean War was largely an American operation. It was directed by a unified command, a euphemism generally understood to mean U.S. command. The unified command reported to the United Nations, but only what the United States saw fit to report. The United Nations undoubtedly provided a valuable political cover for U.S. operations in Korea, but a collective response so heavily dependent on a single great power, and so closely tied to its national interests, is a questionable kind of collective security.

If UN institutions and member response fell short of the collective security ideal, in one respect the Korean action exceeded the carefully delimited bounds of the Charter. The United Nations wielded arms against the interests of a permanent member of the Security Council, with all the explosive potential for a third world war that the veto had been designed to prevent. Korea did not lead to a direct military confrontation of the giants and to world war, but at times the thread by which the Damoclean sword hung suspended seemed perilously slender. The enduring lesson of the Korean venture was not that it repelled aggression but that it was too risky to try again—at least in the absence of great power agreement.

Korea also demonstrated the absence of a fundamental precondition for effective collective security: consensus on the kind of world that is to be made secure. Enforcement of peace in a national political system is possible because of general agreement on political goals and the existence of machinery for the peaceful settlement of most disputes as they arise. Collective security, by attempting to outlaw violent change, assumes that existing methods of peaceful change and dispute settlement are adequate to resolve international differences and satisfy legitimate national aspirations. The unreality of this assumption is well illustrated by the Korean War, where the only settlement possible was an agreement to exchange prisoners and to stop fighting along a line roughly corresponding to the status quo ante. A divided Korea was perpetuated, and the underlying problems that precipitated the crisis remained unresolved. Without greater agreement on the kind of world that was to be made secure, the nations were not ready for collective security.

One enduring institutional legacy of the Korean conflict was the Uniting for Peace resolution, adopted by the Assembly in early November 1950, when total UN victory seemed imminent.[1] The resolution was a U.S. proposal intended to make the United Nations more efficient in dealing with future threats to the peace. The UN system had worked reasonably well in repelling North Korean aggression (or so it appeared at the time), but only because of fortuitous circumstances (the Soviet boycott and nearby U.S. forces).

The Uniting for Peace resolution formally affirmed the responsibility of the General Assembly for dealing with international violence when the Security Council was unable to act, including the right to recommend collective military action. It established a procedure for calling the General Assembly into "emergency special session" by a vote of any seven (now nine) members of the Security Council or on request of a majority of UN members. In addition, it created a "Peace Observation Commission" to send observers to tension-laden areas on request, authorized a "Collective Measures Committee" to study and report on methods of strengthening international peace and security, and urged members to earmark national military units for use by the United Nations. The last three provisions of the resolution quickly fell into disuse, but the emergency special session procedure survived. It was invoked in the Suez and Hungarian crises of 1956, the Lebanon crisis of 1958, the 1960 Congo crisis, and the 1967 Suez War. After a period of disuse, it was revived again to deal with Afghanistan (1980), Palestine (1980, resumed 1982), Namibia (1981), and the Occupied Arab Territories (1982). The Uniting for Peace system was originally sponsored by the United States as a means of facilitating UN action in security matters when the Soviet veto immobilized the Security Council. Ironically, the last three emergency special sessions of the cold war were made possible by the votes of the Soviet Union and Third World countries, over the objection of the United States.

The attempt to apply the full force of Chapter VII of the UN Charter in Korea, and, in effect, to give genuine meaning to collective security, failed as a consequence of the ideological rivalry existing between the United States and the Soviet Union. The success of Chapter VII is read in an "all against the aggressor" principle that is the hallmark of collective security. And although North Korea was deemed to be an "aggressor" against the South, Cold War differences negated the unity necessary to meet the high standards of collective security actions. The passage of Council responsibilities to the Assembly with the Uniting for Peace Resolution enabled the United States to sustain its military effort in Korea under the aegis of the United Nations, but the demands on UN member states were considerably reduced. Where the Security Council under Chapter VII provisions could "order" the full membership of the United Nations to assist in beating back the aggressor, once the matter was transferred to the General Assembly the capacity to "order" had been downgraded to a "recommendation." Thus, the member states were left to determine for themselves the extent of their commitment, and whether or not it was in their interests to pursue a war that not only involved North Korean forces but also those from Communist China. In sum: The United Nations General Assembly, following the Korean experience, would send other forces into emergency situations under different aspects of the Uniting for Peace Resolution, but with a limited presence on the part of both the United States and the Soviet Union. Chapter VII of the UN Charter, therefore, could not be applied in its collective security mode during the decades of the Cold War, and indeed it was only revived when Mikhail Gorbachev voiced renewed interest in its application.

## WAR IN KUWAIT—REBIRTH OF COLLECTIVE SECURITY?

On August 2, 1990 an Iraqi army crossed the border into the Kingdom of Kuwait, quickly subdued its defenders, forced the flight of its ruler and government, and left the small country at the mercy of Iraq's leader, Saddam Hussein. Kuwait was not only conquered by the Iraqi assault, it was eliminated as an independent, sovereign state and given new status as the nineteenth province of Iraq. Coming as it did hardly two years after a ceasefire had been arrived at in the very costly Iraq-Iran war, this Iraqi aggression was attributed to the

?|  machinations of Iraq's leader, whose ambition, it was said, centered on domi-
nating the Arab world, controlling its oil reserves, toppling its remaining mon-
archs, and eventually, doing successful battle with Israel. Although the United
States had earlier tilted toward Iraq in its war with Iran, Washington reacted
most unfavorably to this act of aggression against a sovereign member of the
United Nations. The Soviet Union too, now under the leadership of Mikhail
Gorbachev, condemned the Iraqi invasion and called upon Iraq to withdraw its
troops or risk threatening the relationship forged between their two countries
since the late 1950s. Given the effectiveness of the Iraqi military campaign, however, the only recourse was to bring the matter before the UN Security Council, which for the first time since the war on the Korean peninsula, appeared
ready to apply the collective security provisions under Chapter VII of the UN
Charter.

Unlike the Korean War, the United States had no military forces in the area
capable of offering serious resistance. In other respects, however, the conditions
for UN action were favorable. The Iraqi invasion was readily identifiable as
a violation of the UN Charter prohibition of the use of force (Article 2, paragraph 4) against "the territorial integrity or political independence" of another
state. It was not in the ambiguous mold of clandestine infiltration and subversion, or intervention in aid of a domestic rebellion. Still more important, the Soviet foreign policy turnabout under Gorbachev had brought a Soviet-American
rapprochement that made the Security Council a workable instrument of collective action. Perhaps most important, as in Korea, the United States perceived
its threatened interests in the Middle East (oil, Saudi influence, Israeli security)
as something worth fighting for.

The Security Council reacted quickly. On August 2, the day the attack began, the Security Council condemned the invasion and demanded an immediate unconditional withdrawal, citing as authority Articles 39 (determining the
existence of a breach of international peace) and 40 (provisional measures).
Four days later the Security Council ordered mandatory economic sanctions, as
provided in Article 41, barring all trade with Iraq except "supplies intended
strictly" for medical and humanitarian purposes. Over the next five months
the Security Council adopted ten additional resolutions to deal with the crisis,
including a request for the Secretary-General to seek a diplomatic solution.
Council action culminated in Resolution 678, adopted November 29, setting
January 15, 1991, as a deadline for Iraq's withdrawal and authorizing member
states "to use all necessary means" to force compliance if Iraq did not withdraw voluntarily.

While the Security Council was tightening the screws, the United States
worked feverishly to build U.S. ground, air, and naval strength in the area, at
first for the defense of Saudi Arabia and eventually for an assault on Iraqi positions in Kuwait. With equal fervor the United States moved to forge a military
coalition against Iraq, particularly among states of the Middle East. All attempts at a negotiated withdrawal failed, including last-minute initiatives by
the United States and the UN Secretary-General. On January 16, the day after
the deadline, coalition forces commenced massive aerial and naval bombard-

ment of targets in Kuwait and Iraq. An all-out ground offensive was launched on February 24, with such devastating effectiveness that President Bush was able to proclaim a provisional cease-fire on March 6. At the commencement of the air attack, U.S. troops in the Persian Gulf theater were estimated at 425,000. Before the buildup ceased U.S. forces numbered 540,000. In addition to this massive U.S. contribution, twenty-seven countries contributed an additional 250,000. They were: Argentina, Australia, Bahrein, Bangladesh, Belgium, Czechoslovakia, Canada, Denmark, Egypt, France, Germany, Greece, Italy, Kuwait, Morocco, Netherlands, Niger, Norway, Pakistan, Oman, Qatar, Saudi Arabia, Senegal, Spain, Syria, United Arab Emirates, and the United Kingdom.

Ousting the armies of Saddam Hussein from Kuwait served to vindicate the United Nations in its stand against armed aggression and removed Iraq, at least temporarily, as a serious military threat to the stability of the Middle East. A United Nations Iraq-Kuwait Observation Mission (UNIKOM) was established to monitor a demilitarized zone along the boundary between the two countries. As a condition of a permanent cease-fire, the Security Council demanded the destruction of all Iraqi chemical and biological weapons, long-range missiles, and facilities for producing nuclear weapons. UN inspection teams (UNSCOM) were sent to Iraq to monitor compliance.

In spite of the punishment inflicted on Iraq by the UN coalition, Saddam Hussein and his government prevailed and in fact had sufficient military capacity to crush both a Shiite Muslim rebellion in the southern area of the country and a Kurdish insurrection in the north. The Security Council decision to halt the fighting was in part predicated on the belief that Saddam would be swept aside by his Iraqi opposition, as well as the knowledge that the Americans, who carried major responsibility for the ground war, were reluctant to move on to Baghdad. Saddam, however, surprised the pundits. He not only survived the war but appeared to gain in strength as one by one his internal enemies, as well as would-be enemies, were liquidated. Nevertheless. Saddam's regime was forced to suffer the embarrassment of defeat, and more significantly, the obtrusive scrutiny of UNSCOM, the special commission concerned with identifying and destroying Iraq's weapons of mass destruction, as well as the facilities capable of manufacturing them. Moreover, until it could be demonstrated that Iraq was no longer a threat to its neighbors and the world, the UN-imposed economic sanctions remained in place. Furthermore, as a consequence of Baghdad's assault on the Kurds, the United Nations secured an enclave in northern Iraq where Kurds uprooted from their homes could find a minimum degree of security. To protect this enclave from Iraqi airstrikes, the U.S., under UN authorization, established a no-fly zone in the northern region of the country, thus denying Iraqi aircraft use of airspace over their own country.

In the years that followed the war, the Iraqi government sought to reassert its sovereign power in both the south and north. In the south, it acted as though it would again invade Kuwait, and when it was also disclosed that Baghdad had plotted to assassinate former President Bush (who had been succeeded by President William (Bill) Clinton in January 1993), the new American president ordered cruise missile strikes against a limited number of Iraqi targets, and extended the no-fly zone to include the southern area of the country. In the northern region, however, Iraq successfully took advantage of a conflict between rival Kurdish factions, and Saddam moved his forces into a portion of the UN-protected enclave. Nothing was done to reverse this action.

Given the continuing tug-of-war with Saddam Hussein, the United Nations punitive resolutions remained in place and the sanctions imposed on Baghdad prevented the country from selling its oil or entering into normal commerce with other nations. While Saddam's government weathered these limitations on its sovereignty and power, the Iraqi people, especially its children, confronted dire circumstances. Reports by international agencies, amplified by the Iraqi government, cited the death of thousands of children as a direct consequence of the embargo on Iraqi trade. Bolstered by international opinion that argued for greater flexibility in the acquisition of food and medicine, Baghdad was allowed to sell some of its oil on the open market, but it also began to impede the work of the UNSCOM inspection teams. The authorities blocked access to suspected sites and generally harassed the investigators. After six years of UNSCOM's intrusive behavior the Iraqi government declared it had had enough and it demanded an end to its activities.

Pressured by the United States, the Security Council insisted UNSCOM's work was not yet done because Saddam's regime continued to possess, and could still manufacture, weapons of mass destruction. Baghdad was warned to obey all the UN resolutions, which meant unfettered access to all suspected weapons sites, or face the consequences of a military response. In a not-uncommon display of defiance to this threat, Baghdad ordered the American members of UNSCOM to leave the country. In spite of the U.S. intention to target Iraq, the Americans were forced to leave the country. They were followed by the entire UNSCOM team. The United States reinforced its military units in the region, despite divided opinion on the Security Council. To avert a renewal of hostilities between the United States and Iraq, the UN Secretary-General flew to Baghdad in an effort to get the Iraqis to allow UNSCOM to resume its inspections. Meeting with Saddam Hussein and members of his cabinet in February 1998, Kofi Annan managed to convince the Iraqi leaders to readmit the Americans and to open all sites to UNSCOM inspection. UNSCOM activities were revitalized soon thereafter, but in June, reporting to the Security Council on the mission's progress, the head of the UN operation questioned the Baghdad government's credibility and indicated that the work of the inspectors was not yet at an end. Nevertheless, Iraq continued to press for the termination of economic sanctions, for the withdrawal of UNSCOM, as well as for the full restoration of Iraq's sovereignty and territorial integrity.

If Saddam Hussein's strategy was to prevent the reformation of the 1991 coalition, he certainly succeeded in neutralizing almost all the Arab states. If he also sought to paralyze or fracture the Security Council, he had at least begun a process that revealed serious divisions among the permanent members of the Security Council. If he expected to gain international sympathy for the Iraqi people, he also achieved that objective. Saddam believed time was on his side and he may have judged correctly. But what did the prolonged crisis in the Gulf mean to the United Nations?

The answer to that question was not long in coming. In spite of the promises made to Kofi Annan in Baghdad, on August 6, 1998, the Security Council again cited Iraq's failure to allow UNSCOM inspectors unfettered access to the country's facilities that were deemed capable of producing weapons of mass destruction. Calling Baghdad's behavior "totally unacceptable," the Council appeared ready to force compliance with its resolutions, however, if that was the expectation it was not to be realized. Russia and France, and to a lesser extent China, were more inclined to ease further, or lift the sanctions against Iraq altogether. For their part, the United States and Britain refused to support such efforts, and it was they, virtually alone, who insisted on the need to again punish Iraq if it insisted on holding to its position. Observing the division among the permanent members of the Security Council, Baghdad announced it would no longer cooperate with the arms inspectors and would only allow video and other technical surveillance to continue. In the face of this challenge, UNSCOM sent a letter to the Security Council that it was no longer confident that Iraq was not restarting prohibited weapons programs. Not since the Gulf War had Saddam Hussein taken such a clear step to block UNSCOM inspections. And as expected, the Iraqi parliament unanimously adopted a resolution calling for an immediate halt to the UN intrusion. Citing the failure of the UN and the United States to act forcefully against Saddam Hussein, a prominent American member of the UNSCOM inspection team, Scott Ritter, quit the organization to publicize his views. Embraced by members of the U.S. Congress, Ritter warned of the dire consequences if Saddam was allowed to avoid intensive scrutiny. Describing Saddam's "breakout scenario," Ritter warned that Iraq would be able to reconstitute its biological and chemical weapons capability and deliver a weapon of mass destruction within six months of the end of the UN inspection program. Although Ritter was criticized for his outspokenness, his message could not be ignored. The U.S. Congress was galvanized to authorize funds for use in overthrowing the Iraqi regime, and in September the United States and Britain introduced a draft resolution to the UN Security Council that was aimed at punishing Iraq if UNSCOM operations were again not allowed to proceed. Still seeking to head off an American air attack on Baghdad, the Security Council agreed to suspend its review of the 1991 sanctions, but otherwise members continued to bicker over the requisite course of action.

The tug-of-war between Iraq and the Security Council continued through October and into November when Baghdad declared it was severing all relationships with UNSCOM. The Council called Iraq's continuing defiance a "flagrant violation" of its resolutions and total disregard of promises made to Kofi Annan in February. The Council, however, insisted on pursuing the matter through diplomatic channels and only the United States and Britain urged the need for a military response. With UNSCOM inspectors leaving Iraq, Baghdad demanded the firing of Richard Butler, the head of the special UN commission, accusing him of collaborating with the American CIA and Israeli intelligence. By November 11 virtually all UNSCOM inspectors were ordered out of Iraq, followed by all UN humanitarian workers as well. Appealed to by the UN Secretary-General and under threat of an immediate American assault, on November 14 Saddam again backed down, and once more invited the UNSCOM observers to return to the country. At this juncture President Clinton declared he would refrain from using force but that if Iraq again impeded the work of UNSCOM there would be no warning and no further resort to diplomacy. UNSCOM teams resumed their searches in mid-November, but Iraq refused to submit documents on its biological weapons program, and on December 10 one team sought admission to Iraqi Baath Party headquarters, and was denied entry. This time the crisis could not be avoided.

On December 17, with the UN having again withdrawn all its personnel from Iraq, the United States with cooperation from Great Britain—and despite the criticism levelled against it by Russia, France, and China—authorized Operation Desert Fox, a four-day intensive air campaign against targets described as central to the government and military establishment of Saddam Hussein. Unmanned cruise missiles and bomber aircraft hit scores of Iraqi military installations, including several of Saddam Hussein's palaces as well as barracks of his elite Republican Guard. Although capable of delivering a punishing blow against Saddam's weapons of mass destruction, it was decided to avoid hitting targets believed to house chemical and biological weapons because their destruction could release deadly toxins and microbes into the atmosphere. President Clinton declared the raids were aimed solely at the regime of Saddam Hussein and were not meant to inflict more harm on the Iraqi people. The attacks, however, appeared to terminate the work of UNSCOM, and in the circumstances there was little likelihood that the UN inspectors would again operate inside Iraq. Given this reality, Washington argued that UNSCOM had long been prevented from carrying through its mission, and that in the absence of an assured UN monitoring institution, the United States was prepared to "contain" Saddam until that day when the Iraqi opposition deposes him.

Not yet prepared to yield to the increased American pressure, Baghdad ordered the United Nations to cancel the visit of UN military observers, members of the UN Iraq-Kuwait Observer Mission who since 1991 had patrolled the border between the two countries. Baghdad also renewed its claim to Kuwait in what was seen as still another act of defiance. By the end of December Iraq announced it would more aggressively challenge the no-fly zones patrolled by American aircraft, and almost immediately Iraqi antiaircraft batteries began targeting American planes. The American reaction was immediate. Authorized to defend themselves, the patrolling aircraft attacked the Iraqi sites and thus began a train of events wherein Iraqi ground defenses, or in some instances, Iraqi fighter aircraft repeatedly attempted to intercept and shoot down the American planes.

Citing the illegality of the American actions, Saddam called upon his Arab neighbors for support in Iraq's effort to "regain its sovereignty." At the same time Saddam lashed out against those Arab leaders, notably in Kuwait, Saudi Arabia, and Egypt, who he claimed worked in harmony with the Americans. Calling for their overthrow, Saddam's actions and statements were judged to be those of a desperate man, unable to put an end to his isolation. Nonetheless, on January 14, 1999, Iraq declared all "Kuwaiti land and coastal regions belong to the Iraqi people" and that the border between the two countries was "a bombshell that may explode in the future." Almost simultaneous with this declaration, articles appearing in the U.S. press suggesting a conspiracy against Iraq by UNSCOM and Washington provided succor for Saddam Hussein, but caused Kofi Annan and Richard Butler some embarrassment. Nevertheless, the struggle to contain Iraq was apparently just beginning.

With Saddam Hussein wounded but nevertheless defiant, and with no hint of a change in government in Baghdad for the foreseeable future, it was the United Nations that appeared to pay the heaviest price for the unfinished contest in the Gulf. Informed observers were convinced it was United Nations collective security responsibilities, not Saddam Hussein, that was diminished by the failure to write an end to the drama.

## LESSONS OF THE GULF CRISIS

The Gulf War countered overt aggression. The invading forces were defeated and Iraq's capacity for further aggression was substantially reduced. The Security Council, immobilized by the veto during the Korean War, proved resolute, united, and effective. The Gulf War did not necessarily portend a greatly enlarged role for collective military sanctions, however. A forthright and overwhelming UN response was possible in 1991 because Saddam's open use of naked force against Kuwait's independence and territorial integrity was a clear, universally recognizable case of armed aggression. Iraq departed from the common postwar practice of using a neighbor's domestic upheavals as the cover for military intervention, resorting instead to old-fashioned military conquest. This stark, undisguised violation of the UN Charter permitted mobilization of an international consensus against Iraq that would not have been possible in a more ambiguous situation. Given the collective response, Iraq's experience may deter others from the more overt forms of aggression. To the extent that it encourages potential aggressors to desist, rather than merely modifying their tactics, the result should be applauded. As with national defense strategies, deterrence is the better part of collective security.

Apart from the possible deterrence dividend of the Gulf crisis, the nature of the UN military response may justify only two cheers for this reincarnation of collective security. The economic sanctions were mandatory, on the authority of Article 41 of the Charter, but the military action remained voluntary. Without forces made available in advance under Article 43, the Security Council was dependent on volunteers. As the legal basis for Resolution 678 authorizing the use of "all necessary means" against Iraq, the Council referred to Chapter VII but cited no specific article. Chapter VII deals with "Threats to the

Peace, Breaches of the Peace, and Acts of Aggression." Given the voluntary nature of the military coalition then being assembled in opposition to Iraq, and the nonexistence of any Article 43 forces, the Council must have been making a "recommendation" under Article 39. Presumably, also, it was authorizing the coalition to exercise "the inherent right of individual or collective self-defense" under Article 51.

As in Korea, the United Nations had to rely on a convergence of UN objectives with the national interests of states capable of supplying the necessary military power. In both instances the initiative and bulk of the power came from the United States. This is the same limited kind of collective security displayed in Korea. It may be comforting to the United States to know that such actions will not be undertaken without its approval, but that assurance was already embodied in the UN Charter in the form of the Security Council veto. The other side of the coin is more sobering: No major enforcement action will occur unless the United States is willing to shoulder the lion's share of the burden. But other states cannot be highly enthusiastic about a collective security that is invoked only when U.S. national interests are heavily engaged.

Nor is this the only problem implicit in the collective security decision process. During the Korean War, UN Policy was formulated through the General Assembly's cumbersome and ultimately unmanageable process. UN decision making went more smoothly during the Gulf War because of close collaboration among the permanent members of the Security Council. This too, however, was a source of frustration to other UN members who felt left out of the consultation or inadequately consulted. Included among the frustrated states were the other ten members of the Council, developed countries such as Germany and Japan, which were expected to pay a substantial part of the cost, and most other UN members (other than the coalition) who were given no voice at all. The problem of broadening the consultative process while retaining the necessary speed and flexibility in decision making has yet to be resolved.

Still more disturbing to some was the free hand exercised by the United States, with the acquiescence of other coalition members, in battlefield decisions. In effect the authorization of "all necessary means" proved to be a blank check to be filled in as expedient. Destruction of Iraq's infrastructure through massive aerial bombardment undoubtedly weakened its military capability. So too the limited land invasion that inflicted heavy casualties on Iraqi military personnel and destroyed a substantial array of weapons. But the decision to refrain from destroying Saddam's regime, based as it was on a number of scenarios that ranged from the human cost in overrunning and policing Baghdad, to the breakup of Iraq and the consequences to Turkey and its own Kurdish problem, or to Iran, which still had visions of spreading the Shiite version of Islamic revolution in the direction of Basra, caused President Bush to order a halt to the American-led coalition's advance. Had the military action against Iraq been a more chaste use of the UN Charter, the campaign might have ended differently. As it was, however, the war in the Gulf was tailored to American objectives, the most immediate of which was the liberation of Kuwait, the security of Saudi Arabia, and the assurance that oil would flow uninterrupted from the region.

Thus, the UN was compelled to assume a protracted role in the Gulf, and especially in Iraq. Saddam Hussein was not to be trusted and given his demonstrated capacity to crush his opposition, it was grudgingly concluded that he would continue to rule Iraq for some time to come, and therefore would have to be monitored by the international community. Having used chemical weapons against the Iranians earlier, and again against his own Kurdish citizens, Iraq's stockpiling of chemical, and now too biological, weapons had to be prevented. Moreover, Iraq's long history in attempting to build atomic weapons, only interrupted by the 1981 Israeli airstrike against its Osirak reactor, had to be thwarted. This then was made the responsibility of the United Nations with UNSCOM its major instrument.

UNSCOM therefore had the task of sustaining the collective security arrangements originally agreed to by the permanent powers at the end of the Gulf war. But the disbanding of the coalition soon after the war left only the threat of renewed collective military action should Iraq violate the earlier agreements. Iraq's efforts in the years that followed the end of the war were directed at bringing to a conclusion the UN intrusion. Moreover, the intrusion was more and more associated with U.S. policy, a policy not necessarily shared by the other members of the Council. Kofi Annan's meeting with Saddam Hussein in Baghdad in February 1998 was aimed at least in part in clarifying the UN operation against Iraq. Unlike the United States, which had targeted Saddam Hussein, Annan was more inclined to depersonalize the struggle, and in so doing, to pose the United Nations (with notable support from Russia, China, and France) as a disinterested party in the matter of who governs Iraq. The UN, he stressed, was solely concerned with establishing the conditions that allow for threat reduction and confidence-building. The mission of the UN, noted the Secretary-General, was ensuring the peace, not making war.

In effect, the UN was first and foremost a diplomatic institution, and with Article 43 of the Charter in abeyance, only in the most critical circumstances could it be considered a warmaking body. Unlike the United States, which continued to insist the Iraqi government could not be trusted, Annan believed he spoke for the vast majority of UN member states when he intimated UNSCOM's operations should be ended as soon as it could be concluded Iraq was no longer in possession of weapons of mass destruction. Annan's effort at bringing UN operations in Iraq to a satisfactory conclusion, however, was frustrated by Saddam Hussein, who never intended to cooperate with the UNSCOM inspectors. By exploiting divisions within the Security Council, as  well as the goodwill of the Secretary-General, Saddam sought to end the UN intrusion on his own terms. And indeed, were it not for the determination of the United States he would have succeeded in eliminating the restrictions imposed on his government. As it was, Saddam's defiance brought still another test of wills in December 1998 when the U.S. struck at Iraqi military installations following UNSCOM's failure to gain unfettered access to Iraqi weapons sites. While UNSCOM remained an organ of the Security Council, few observers believed its activities inside Iraq could be resumed. Moreover, France put forth an alternative program for a more remote monitoring of Iraqi military ventures, while the U.S. continued to emphasize its intention to "contain" Iraq within the context of resolutions previously approved by the Security Council. How the situation impacted the United Nations' collective security role remained unclear. Nor could it clarify the meaning of Chapter VII in the UN Charter.

## THE UNCERTAIN FUTURE OF UN ENFORCEMENT ACTION

The problem of ensuring UN control over UN enforcement actions could undoubtedly be overcome by the negotiation of Article 43 agreements and assigning real responsibility to the UN Military Staff Committee as provided in Article 47. The Secretary-General proposed such action in June 1992 (to the applause of some states but with a cool reception by the United States and some European powers). If the agreements were actually concluded they would, presumably, solve the problem of ready availability, because Article 43 provides for "armed forces, assistance, and facilities" to be made "available to the Security Council, on its call. . . ." On the other hand, the existence of an Article 43 force would not guarantee small states a voice in their utilization, nor would it do anything to alter the reality that UN military sanctions would still be exercised only at the behest of a major-power dominated Security Council.

Other questions also arise regarding the use of such a force. The UN could act quickly, but under what circumstances would it and should it act? The Article 43 force, as proposed by the Secretary-General, would not be large enough to respond to a threat of the magnitude posed by Saddam Hussein in Kuwait. In such event the UN would be thrown back on the Korean or Gulf War model. That may not be a serious concern because a repeat of such naked, unrelenting, cross-border aggression by the armies of any country is unlikely.

The most likely occasions for the use of a ready enforcement capability would be UN intervention to suppress violent internal conflicts, to prevent gross violations of human rights (such as the mass killings in Cambodia during the 1970s), or, as in Somalia in the 1990s, to combat internal chaos that threatens widespread death and suffering to civilian populations. The targets would ordinarily be small states. Except in the most unusual circumstances, large states could not feasibly be the objects of military intervention. Even with small states, forcible intervention would be fraught with peril. Military setbacks could occur, creating a need for reinforcements and escalating the conflict beyond what was originally contemplated. UN forces would in any event incur persisting hostility among factions on the other side. Assuming that initial military objectives were achieved, the UN force could still face sporadic conflict with irregular forces should the intervention prove unpopular with large elements of the local population. If the violence is spawned by ethnic conflict rooted in centuries-old antagonisms, departure of UN forces could lead to renewed violence. A substantial political and economic rebuilding task would remain on completion of military operations. The problems of achieving internal stability would seem no less if the purpose of the intervention were to halt government oppression of its own citizens as in the former Yugoslavia.

These and other questions surrounding the coercive use of force by the United Nations describe an issue that is complex and far from resolved, and they suggest that the decision to authorize the use of UN military force, with or without Article 43 agreements, will continue to be decided on a case-by-case basis as the specific interests of Security Council members dictate. In the post-cold-war system there may be more agreement than before on the kind of world that is to be made secure, but many practical obstacles to a functioning collective security system remain.

## NONMILITARY SANCTIONS

Like the League Covenant, the UN Charter provides for nonmilitary sanctions against states that threaten the peace. Article 41 authorizes the Security Council to enforce its decisions through "complete or partial interruption of economic relations and of rail, sea, air, postal, telegraphic, radio, and other means of communication, and the severance of diplomatic relations." Moral condemnation is also available as a sanction for noncompliance.

Moral condemnation, although frequently invoked, has seldom been very effective in getting states to comply with UN directives, at least in the short run. In the longer term the mobilization of shame can sometimes have productive results, as in the Human Rights Commission. Certainly, alleged violators do their best to tone down or eliminate phraseology that condemns their behavior. States may sometimes act with an eye to avoiding UN condemnation, but UN scolding after the fact is more likely to harden positions than evoke repentance. Israel has been the constant object of UN railing, with little discernible effect on its policies. China was totally undeterred by the "aggressor" label attached to its Korean intervention, and UN censure did nothing to hamper Soviet suppression of the 1956 Hungarian revolt or the Soviet repression in Afghanistan. Nor has the United States responded penitently to UN disapproval of its support for Israel or such ventures as the 1983 invasion and occupation of Grenada and the December 1989 invasion of Panama.

Diplomatic and economic sanctions have had somewhat greater effect when kept in place over a long period of time, but they have seldom had the desired political effect in the short run. The more notable examples of UN nonmilitary sanctions include actions taken against Rhodesia, South Africa, Iraq, Libya, and Serbia.

### Sanctions against Rhodesia

Modest success might be claimed for UN efforts to topple Ian Smith's white minority regime in Rhodesia though use of nonmilitary sanctions. The initial

Security Council response to Rhodesia's 1965 unilateral declaration of independence from Britain was to apply a limited range of voluntary economic and diplomatic measures. This was followed in 1966 with the first-ever UN *mandatory* sanctions under Chapter VII of the Charter. Although limited at first to an embargo of arms, oil, and motor vehicles and a boycott of Rhodesian exports, the sanctions were expanded in subsequent years to include a ban on most economic intercourse with Rhodesia. The sanctions contributed to Rhodesia's economic deterioration, despite nonobservance by a number of states. They were lifted in 1980 when power was transferred to the black majority and Rhodesia was renamed Zimbabwe. This outcome was attributable primarily to the pressures of internal civil war, combined with persistent British efforts to promote a settlement, but the UN sanctions linked with general delegitimization of the Rhodesian regime by the world community undoubtedly had some effect.

*Sanctions against South Africa*

South Africa had been the most frequent target of UN nonmilitary sanctions, which were aimed at altering its racial policies and securing the independence of Namibia. With Namibian independence achieved in 1990 and the repeal of apartheid laws in 1991, some success for the sanctions policy can be claimed. The process has required more than three decades, however—not exactly a quick fix. Beginning in 1962 the General Assembly repeatedly called for severance of economic and diplomatic relations as well as an embargo on arms and war materials. The arms embargo was endorsed as a voluntary measure by the Security Council in 1963 and eventually made mandatory under Chapter VII in 1977. The UN sanctions were not well observed during those years and did not substantially affect the economic and military strength of South Africa or its racial and colonial policies. South Africa occasionally made modest concessions to satisfy its Western friends but was quite contemptuous of the UN majority.

South African relations with the world entered a new phase in 1985 and 1986, when the white government's stern reaction to internal dissent induced a number of countries to take a hard look at their own policies toward South Africa. The Security Council at last endorsed voluntary economic sanctions, and a number of countries—including the United States and other important trading partners of South Africa—adopted new or strengthened sanctions. Private multinational firms also moved toward disinvestment in South Africa under the watchful eye of UN monitoring groups.

The combined effects of internal troubles and increased external economic pressures induced a substantial weakening of the South African economy, and this was a factor in South Africa's decision at last to seek fundamental change. In December 1988, with U.S. prodding, South Africa signed a protocol on the independence of Namibia leading to the creation of the new state in March 1990. Dismantling of apartheid was a little slower in coming but in early 1990, under the leadership of its new President F. W. de Klerk, South Africa began a gradual process of healing internal divisions and eliminating discriminatory practices. In December 1991 the UN General Assembly responded by voting to restore international sporting, cultural, scientific, and academic ties with South Africa. The Assembly also suggested that states might consider lifting other restrictive measures as South Africa moved toward a new multiracial government and a democratic constitution. Many influences, both external and internal, were at work, but the salutary changes in South Africa undoubtedly owed something to the weight of economic sanctions. However slow in achieving their result, the sanctions imposed by the United Nations achieved their most positive result when Nelson Mandela, leader of the African National Congress, was released from an imprisonment that had extended over a twenty-eight year period. Moreover, apartheid was officially abandoned in 1994 and that same year, in South Africa's first open election, Mandela was elected president of the country, ending a sustained period of all-white rule.

*Sanctions against Iraq*

Iraq's invasion of Kuwait triggered the most extensive economic sanctions yet imposed by the United Nations. Beginning in August 1990 the Security Council ordered a mandatory trade and arms embargo (with exceptions for medical supplies and humanitarian foodstuffs) and severance of all financial relations with Iraq. It subsequently authorized member states to cut off maritime shipping to and from Iraq and imposed a cargo-related air transport embargo. The sanctions received general compliance and had a severe effect on the Iraqi economy, which depended heavily on proceeds from oil exports. The sanctions also had serious economic repercussions in countries having close economic relations with Iraq and Kuwait. Jordan, Lebanon, and Yemen were especially hard hit, along with several states of South Asia that supplied migrant laborers to the Gulf region and in turn received substantial remittances from them. Twenty-one countries claimed economic hardship resulting from the sanctions and exercised their right under Article 50 of the UN Charter to seek Security Council assistance in alleviating the problem. In most instances no significant relief was available.

Although widely observed, the economic sanctions did not achieve their intended effect of securing Iraqi troop withdrawal and restoring the independence of Kuwait. Military action was required for that. Whether economic sanctions would have succeeded over a longer period of time is uncertain. Rhodesia took fifteen years, South Africa thirty. Withdrawal from Kuwait by the year 2020 would scarcely be a vindication of UN sanctions. The sanctions against Iraq were more comprehensive than previous efforts, and Iraq was more vulnerable, but Saddam Hussein was both durable and obdurate. After the military operations were terminated, the economic sanctions remained in effect. This was necessary because Iraq, even in military defeat, proved slow to comply with UN demands to accept liability for damage inflicted by the war and to submit to nuclear, biological, and chemical weapons disarmament.

The lifting of the UN sanctions became a major objective of the Iraqi government in the years following the Gulf war. Claiming that the embargo denied Iraq the opportunity to meet the basic needs of its citizens, and asserting the sanctions had caused the death of thousands of Iraqi children, the UN was hard-pressed to sustain the restrictions. Efforts were launched by some UN members to at least reduce the harshness of the sanctions. Oil for food arrangements were therefore pressed through the Security Council, and in 1997 and again in 1998, Iraq was permitted to expand the sale of its petroleum in return for increased food and medical supplies. Not satisfied with such UN flexibility, however, and determined to have the sanctions lifted altogether, Iraq drew even more attention to its position by blocking the work of UNSCOM inspection teams. In the crisis that resulted only the United States and Great Britain were steadfast in perpetuating the sanction policy. And with the UN Secretary-General seeking to avoid another demonstration of violence in the Gulf, Iraq appeared to have gained the needed leverage to bring the sanctions to an end.

### Sanctions against Libya

In April 1992 the United States, Britain, and France persuaded the Security Council to impose mandatory sanctions on Libya, consisting of a ban on airline traffic and arms sales and a reduction in the size of Libyan diplomatic missions abroad. The sanctions went into effect when Libya refused to surrender for trial two suspects in the December 1988 bomb explosion on board Pan American flight 103 over Lockerbie, Scotland, which resulted in the death of 288 persons. Libya attempted to nullify the sanctions by an appeal to the International Court of Justice, but the Court concluded that the Security Council sanctions took precedence over any rights Libya might claim under the 1971 Montreal Convention for the Suppression of Unlawful Acts against the Safety of Civil Aviation, under which the two men might be tried in Libya. Libya subsequently called for direct negotiations with the United States, Britain, and France about a possible compromise location for a trial of the two suspects. In 1998, however, with the sanctions still in force, the International Court of Justice agreed to hear a Libyan complaint concerning the venue for the trial of the alleged perpetrators of the PanAm bombing. Subsequently, with an agreement developed by Libya, the Netherlands, the United Kingdom, and the United States, Tripoli, in April 1999 finally transferred the suspects for a trial to be held in the Netherlands under Scottish law. As a consequence of these actions, the UN imposed sanctions were automatically lifted.

### Sanctions against Serbia

The dissolution of Yugoslavia in 1991 provoked fighting between Serbia and Croatia, which spilled over into Bosnia-Herzegovina and presented Europe with its first episode of major conflict since the end of World War II. Serbia and Montenegro were the only units of the old federation to cling together, while the Serb inhabitants of the other states found themselves in a struggle for survival. Belgrade's attempt to assist these distant remnants of "greater Serbia" provoked violent clashes among the different ethnic groups, especially in Bosnia where the Serb population attempted to seize a portion of the territory in a campaign that came to be described as "ethnic cleansing." In the quasi-civil war that ensued, more than 200,000 casualties were recorded and Europe was again confronted with a vast and complex human tragedy. The United Nations Security Council, as early as September 1991 imposed a general and complete embargo on all deliveries of weapons and military equipment to all the regions of the former Yugoslavia. In 1992 that resolution was followed by another that reaffirmed the arms embargo applied to all areas of the collapsed state. By May 1992, it was determined that the Republic of Yugoslavia (FRY), comprising Serbia and Montenegro, was the principal purveyor of violence in the Balkans and a full trade embargo was imposed. The FRY was also denied participation in all international sporting and cultural events, and in November 1992 a further resolution blocked the transshipment through the FRY of petroleum, coal, steel, and other products. In April 1993 these latter sanctions were strengthened, and in September 1994, Bosnian Serbs were singled out when their officials and leaders were prohibited from traveling to other states. The same resolution curtailed trade with the Bosnian Serbs and froze Bosnian Serb financial assets held abroad. In 1994, the Security Council suspended sanctions against the FRY for an initial period of 100 days when it was reported Serbia had closed its border with the Bosnian Serbs. The lifting of the sanction permitted the resumption of civilian air flights to and from Belgrade, allowed for the reinstatement of ferry services to Italy, and cancelled the ban on participation in international events. In 1995 and 1996, following the Dayton Accords, and the establishment of a ceasefire under NATO supervision, the Security Council removed the arms embargo and other sanctions that had been imposed on all the parties. Following certification by the Organization of Security and Cooperation in Europe (OSCE) of the September 14, 1996 elections in Bosnia-Herzegovina, all sanctions against the Federal Republic of Yugoslavia and the Bosnian Serbs were terminated.

Given the 1998 extension of NATO's mandate in policing the Bosnian ceasefire, efforts were made at restoring normalcy in the region, but conditions in Kosovo, claimed by Serbia as an integral part of FRY territory, deteriorated. Kosovo's overwhelmingly Albanian population expressed self-determination sentiments and a Kosovo Liberation Army assaulted the Serb minority in the province. Belgrade's response was immediate and violent, with regular FRY forces ordered to clear a western strip of the separatist region. The killing of several hundred Kosovars and the flight of still more refugees was answered by the European Union and the United States, which imposed new sanctions on Serbia in June. Serbia called these sanctions arbitrary and unjustified. According to Belgrade, Kosovo was an integral portion of Serbia and therefore the government had a duty to quell the unrest. The Serbs were even more incensed that the sanctions had been levelled against them and not the FRY as a whole. Judged a more explosive problem than that in Bosnia, it was feared the Kosovo fighting could spread to Albania and Macedonia, and if not contained, to Greece, Bulgaria, and possibly Turkey. And because it was the NATO intervention, not the sanctions that brought a semblance of peace to Bosnia, few believed these sanctions on Serbia would be sufficient without again a forceful response from the world's most formidable military alliance. Serbia's suppression of the Kosovo Liberation Army had had a spillover affect on the civilian population, and Serbian "ethnic cleansing" operations raised new, more fearful questions for the European community. Fearing genocide, NATO's Supreme Commander, General Wesley Clark, was sent in October 1998 to meet with Slobodan Milosovic in Belgrade. General Clark warned the Serbian leader that NATO was poised to take military action if he continued to press his violent campaign against the people of Kosovo. Milosovic promised General Clark he would withdraw his forces, but by January 1999, given the uncovering of more atrocities, Clark again gained an audience with Milosovic. This time, however, the Serbian leader refused to yield to pressure, and even Kofi Annan was forced to acknowledge NATO's right to use force against Serbian positions.

Confronted with an intensifying dilemma, the Contact Group, led by the United States insisted on a Dayton-like conference between the leaders, or their representatives, of the Belgrade government and the Kosovo Liberation Army (KLA). Under considerable pressure from NATO, whose planes were marshalled for an assault on Serbian forces and military installations, the parties grudgingly agreed to the meeting which took place in Rambouillet, France in February 1999. With the American Secretary of State present for most of the proceedings, the deliberations, or proximity talks wherein the parties did not actually face one another, were difficult and protracted. Several deadlines were allowed to pass to give the participants more opportunity to accept the terms laid out by the Contact Group, but most significantly by the major NATO actors. The Contact Group's plan envisaged an autonomous but not an independent Kosovo, policed by NATO forces similar to those in Bosnia. But because the draft agreement was a take it or leave it proposition, the deliberations at Rambouillet were without result. The Serb delegation under orders from Belgrade rejected the introduction of NATO troops in Kosovo, arguing such a force would be a violation of Serbia's sovereignty. The Kosovar delegation, under pressure, eventually accepted the Rambouillet draft, but Belgrade used the hiatus provided by the deliberations to reinforce its military units in the province. Determined to obliterate the KLA, the Serbs intensified their campaign of ethnic cleansing in defiance of repeated NATO warnings. Forced to follow through on its threats, in March 1999 NATO aircraft struck Serbian military infrastructure and installations. The Serbs responded by accelerating their actions against the Kosovars, and NATO, reluctant to use ground forces, could not prevent the forced removal of hundreds of thousands of ethnic Albanian inhabitants of Kosovo. The Belgrade government not only ignored the renewed sanctions imposed upon it, it also refused to yield to NATO's increasingly deadly bombing campaign. With Russia in search of a viable media between the

Serbs and NATO, by May a compromise formula that would include an international presence in Kosovo under United Nations supervision loomed as a possibility.

## SANCTIONS: A SUMMARY

Collective sanctions failed during the era of the League of Nations, and the United Nations has compiled only a slightly better record. Despite the numerous sanctions imposed on Iraq, Baghdad has not altered any of its policies. Unilateral sanctions have had no better record. The United States grain embargo against the Soviet Union in 1980 did not force Moscow to withdraw from Afghanistan, nor have strenuous efforts aimed at pressuring Cuba to alter its political ways resulted in the desired change. Sanctions are often circumvented by governments, or undermined by business interests that are more concerned with making profits wherever they may be found. In this regard, economic sanctions can sometimes do more harm to local commercial interests than the targeted country. Generally speaking, the United Nations Security Council has been reluctant to use sanctions, and in the initial forty-five years of the United Nations only two sanctions regimes were imposed. Both were against white governments in Africa, i.e., Southern Rhodesia (now Zimbabwe) in 1966, and South Africa in 1977. Both were subsequently withdrawn. More stringent sanctions were brought to bear against South Africa outside the United Nations in the 1980s, and in 1989, the U.S. Congress approved a sanctions bill that was opposed by the Bush administration. Nevertheless, American maritime and longshoremen unions, in cooperation with United Nations agencies, helped to expose corporations doing business with the apartheid government, and in time many were pressured to cease their operations in the country. It is believed these economic sanctions, unlike those imposed on other nations, reduced South Africa's GNP by approximately 5 percent, and therefore played a role in forcing the regime to end its racial practices and introduce democratic reforms.

Of the more than 120 cases of sanctions since 1914, the United States has initiated about 70 percent, but less than 15 percent have been applied in a collective manner. In fact, it is only in the 1990s that the United Nations adopted sanctions as a major instrument in dealing with international questions. Starting with Iraq in 1990, the Security Council authorized sanctions against the former Yugoslavia in 1991, Libya, Somalia, Haiti, and Angola in 1993, Rwanda in 1994, Liberia in 1995, Sudan and Burundi in 1996, and Sierra Leone in 1997. Pressure used by the United States to force the Security Council to sanction India and Pakistan for their tests of nuclear devices in 1998 did not succeed, and even when American sanctions were imposed, complaints by domestic agricultural interests forced the U.S. Senate to exempt food exports, the most painful economic penalty that Washington had inflicted. Given other situations, especially regarding Cuba, however, the United States imposed unilateral sanctions that went into effect in 1962, and were further embellished in 1996 when the Helms-Burton Act imposed penalties on third parties doing business with the island nation. Condemned for its original action by many of the world's leading nations, the Helms-Burton legislation embittered Canada, Mexico, and the European Union countries, which lodged a formal protest with the World Trade Organization. In fact the Organization of American States declared that the legislation was "not in conformity with international law." Following the OAS action, in 1996 the United Nations General Assembly condemned the U.S. embargo of Cuba and the Helms-Burton law by a vote of 117 to 3 with 38 abstentions. No less a humanitarian organization than the Red Cross added its voice to the condemnation of sanctions, especially those directed at Iraq, which it argued could only continue to harm the people least responsible for the policies of the Baghdad government. Given the climate of world opinion at the end of the century, there was sufficient evidence to suggest the United Nations would be most reluctant to use economic sanctions against its members and that the practice would remain an instrument to be used by individual countries acting in their own interest. Indeed, the United Nations was eager to lift sanctions imposed on Libya when in April 1999 Tripoli yielded for trial the two individuals charged in the bombing of Pam Am 103 over Lockerbie, Scotland, in 1988. The United States, however, while acknowledging the Libyan government's action, reserved judgment on the matter of sanctions until after the trial of the defendants.

## THE REGIONAL ALTERNATIVE

The UN Charter places primary responsibility for international peace and security on the Security Council, with regional organizations playing a secondary role. The principal proponents of regionalism at the San Francisco Conference were delegates from the American states who wished to preserve the developing Inter-American security system, and the relevant provisions, Articles 51–54, are a compromise. These provisions focus on three central issues—peaceful settlement, self-defense, and enforcement action (the use of diplomatic, economic, or military sanctions). Regional associations are expressly encouraged to take the initiative in settling local disputes (Article 52). Article 51 recognizes an "inherent right of individual or collective self-defense" against armed attack, but all action taken in self-defense must be immediately reported to the Security Council and that body retains authority to take any concurrent action it finds necessary. The Security Council's predominance with respect to enforcement action is even more forcefully established. With the exception of measures against the enemy states of World War II, the Charter states categorically that "no enforcement action shall be taken under regional arrangements or by regional agencies without the authorization of the Security Council" (Article 53).

In practice, the roles were reversed. Because of bitter East-West rivalries the Security Council never acquired its military capability, and members utilized Article 51 to expand collective self-defense arrangements out of all proportion to the puny enforcement arm of the general system and, in some instances, to justify outright aggression. The United States led the stampede to regional security and autonomy. From the Pact of Rio de Janeiro (1947) to NATO

(1949) to ANZUS (1951) to SEATO (1954) to CENTO (1955) and numerous bilateral military pacts, the United States became the hub of the most complex and extensive system of alliances the world had ever known. Other states followed suit in a more modest way with such arrangements as the Arab League, the Warsaw Pact, and the Organization of African Unity, as well as a host of bilateral alliances.

Much of this system has since disintegrated. The Southeast Asian component of the U.S.-sponsored system (SEATO) was formally abandoned in 1977, and CENTO, the Middle East segment, in 1979. New Zealand's participation in ANZUS was effectively suspended in 1986 because of that state's refusal to let U.S. nuclear-powered or nuclear-armed ships into its ports. The Rio Pact experienced severe strains because of revolutionary regimes in Cuba and Nicaragua, U.S. support of Britain in the Falklands War, and other sources of disunity. With the breakup of the Soviet Union and its East European empire, members of the Warsaw Treaty Organization agreed on July 1, 1991, to dissolve the pact entirely. While East-West alliances were casualties of peace, the Arab League was a casualty of war. The Gulf War, pitting Arabs against Arabs, was a blow to Arab unity.

Although alliance systems appeared less functional with the end of the Cold War and the dissolution of the Soviet Union, the North Atlantic Treaty Organization, at first judged destined for the ash heap of history, dramatically took on new importance. NATO operations in war-torn Bosnia were necessitated by the failure of the United Nations UNPROFOR peacekeeping mission. Article 51 of the Charter retained its relevance and the NATO alliance enjoyed a life after the Cold War. NATO possessed the military capacity and the will, so long as the United States was agreeable, to intrude itself in violent situations. The United Nations, by contrast, neither had the forces nor the strategy to regulate civil conflict. NATO did. Moreover, NATO's role, whether in Bosnia or in the Kosovo conflict, was still another example of the alliance's functionality. And not to be overlooked, the Partnership for Peace that was formed in 1994 linking the former Warsaw Pact countries with NATO, as well as NATO's enlargement in 1998 to include Poland, Hungary, and the Czech Republic, attested to its utility and importance in the overall UN security system. It also hinted at a changed role for alliances in the twenty-first century.

## THE PEACEKEEPING ALTERNATIVE

Collective security as envisioned by the Charter never became a reality, and even the voluntary version of military enforcement action has been attempted sparingly. Nevertheless, the United Nations has found other ways to remain relevant to the control of international violence. The most significant and innovative is UN "peacekeeping." In a UN context the term *peacekeeping* was first used to describe the work of the UN Emergency Force (UNEF), created by the

General Assembly during the 1956 Suez War to take temporary control of the Suez Canal area and encourage the withdrawal of invading Anglo-French and Israeli forces from Egyptian territory. It has since become the generic term for a UN nonfighting field operation, usually involving military as well as civilian personnel, undertaken to maintain or restore peace in an area of conflict.[2]

Peacekeeping, as heretofore practiced, contrasts sharply with the collective military sanctions contemplated by Article 41. Instead of acting to deter or defeat an aggressor, the UN peacekeeping mission is deployed against no identified enemy. Its purpose is to help maintain peace when tension is high but no party is determined to pursue armed conquest. It does this by such means as observing border violations, policing a cease-fire or truce line, serving as a buffer between hostile forces, supervising troop withdrawal, and helping to monitor elections and maintain domestic order during a transition period. A peacekeeping force is deployed only with the consent of the sovereign of the territory where it operates, and usually with the consent or acquiescence of all major parties to the conflict. While large UN peacekeeping forces are normally armed, military observer units commonly are not. If weapons are carried they are to be used only in self-defense and not to enforce the UN will on any of the contending parties. In practice, UN peacekeeping operations have seldom been large enough to enforce order against serious military opposition. The largest UN forces thus far have served in the Congo (20,000), Cambodia (19,500), and Yugoslavia (23,000).

Secretary-General Dag Hammarskjöld, at least in retrospect, viewed UNEF as part of a UN strategy to prevent local disputes or power vacuums from becoming extensions or inciting escalations of the cold war. This concept, fathered and nurtured by the Secretary-General, became known as "preventive diplomacy." During the cold war era most UN peacekeeping missions embodied a large element of preventive diplomacy, defined as filling power vacuums with a UN presence in order to insulate the conflict from cold war antagonisms.

Over the years, preventive diplomacy has acquired a broader meaning and now commonly connotes any diplomatic action aimed at preventing potential or actual conflict from getting worse. In a report issued in June 1992, Secretary-General Boutros-Ghali characterized preventive diplomacy as a means "to ease tensions before they result in conflict—or, if conflict breaks out, to act swiftly to contain it and resolve its underlying causes." The report gave a new prominence to the concept of preventive diplomacy and called for an ambitious program of measures to build confidence between contending states (such as exchange of military missions and monitoring arms agreements), a system for early warning of potential threats to peace, preventive deployment of UN forces to forestall the outbreak of violence, and creation of demilitarized zones before rather than after armed conflict arises.

UN Peacekeeping forces were generally deployed after a conflict had arisen, rather than before it happened, but in 1997, the combined efforts of the member states, the Secretary-General, and the Department of Peacekeeping Operations (DPKO) acknowledged the need for more rapid and more efficient deployment. By Security Council resolution a Standby High Readiness Brigade (SHIRBRIG) was authorized to address the question. SHIRBRIG aimed at improving the Secretariat's reaction capacity, while DPKO also was provided with a Mission Planning section, Standby Arrangements Systems and a Rapidly Deployable Mission Headquarters. According to its sponsors, SHIRBRIG ready-alert status enabled the international community to intervene swiftly and effectively to a crisis before it intensified. Organized outside the auspices of the UN, SHIRBRIG fell under Chapter VI of the Charter. It was to include a headquarters of its own, ready infantry battalions, reconnaissance units, engineer and logistics support, and a common pool of military instruments, weapons, and vehicles. Established formally in Denmark, the Nordic countries were the first to commit between 4,000 and 5,000 troops to its operation. SHIRBRIG in fact followed the 1994 creation of a Standby Arrangements System for the Department of Peacekeeping Operations, to which approximately 70 countries identified a total of 88,000 troops for future peacekeeping missions. The latter provided DPKO with a database that gave the UN body significant information about the availability of personnel and equipment for future missions. Essential to DPKO's operation was its capacity to respond quickly to a crisis. Thus, a Mission Planning Service (MPS) was created and charged with the constant study of potential problem areas. Given this restructuring of the UN security system, there was little doubt the UN peacekeeping role had become a major element in the containment of critical international matters. Past and present UN peacekeeping missions—their size, function, and duration—are shown in Table 5-1. A brief description of each follows.

## EARLY UN EXPERIMENTS

Early UN experiments with a nonfighting military presence occurred in Greece, Indonesia, Kashmir, and Palestine. Two of these missions, in Greece and in Indonesia, were never included in official UN lists of UN peacekeeping operations because they were not organized and administered by the UN Secretariat. Nevertheless, these initial missions became the forerunners of those that followed in subsequent years. From 1947 to 1952, a UN Special Committee on the Balkans (UNSCOB) kept a small observer team (up to thirty-six) along the northern frontiers of Greece to monitor border violations by Soviet bloc states in support of leftist Greek rebels. Another temporary field mission was conducted in Indonesia from 1947 to 1951. UN military observers associated with the UN Commission for Indonesia (UNCI) and its predecessor Good Offices Committee aided Security Council peacemaking efforts in the Indonesian war for independence from the Netherlands and observed the subsequent repatriation of Dutch forces. Two observer missions dating from the pre-UNEF period proved to be more than temporary. The UN Truce Supervision Organization (UNTSO), established in 1948 to police a truce between Israel and its Arab neighbors, grew to nearly 600 in number before armistice agreements were concluded in 1949. The size of UNTSO has since fluctuated with events, but lack

TABLE 5-1   Principal UN Peacekeeping Missions, 1947–98

| MISSION | DATE | PEAK FORCE SIZE | FORCE SIZE (MARCH 1998) | FUNCTION |
|---|---|---|---|---|
| UNSCOB | 1947–52 | 36 | — | Monitor violations of Greek border |
| UNCI | 1947–51 | 63 | — | Observe Indonesian cease-fire and Dutch troop withdrawal |
| UNTSO | 1948–present | 572 | 169 | Report on Arab-Israeli cease-fire and armistice violations |
| UNMOGIP | 1949–present | 102 | 42 | Observe Kashmir cease-fire |
| UNEF I | 1956–67 | 6,073 | — | Observe, supervise troop withdrawal and provide buffer between Israeli and Egyptian forces |
| UNOGIL | 1958 | 591 | — | Check on clandestine aid from Syria to Lebanon rebels |
| ONUC | 1960–64 | 19,828 | — | Maintain order in the Congo, expel foreign forces, prevent secession and outside intervention |
| UNSF | 1962–63 | 1,576 | — | Maintain order during transfer of authority in New Guinea from Netherlands to Indonesia |
| UNYOM | 1963–64 | 189 | — | Supervise military disengagement in Yemen |
| UNFICYP | 1964–present | 6,411 | 1,197 | Prevent internal conflict Cyprus, avert outside in intervention |
| DOMREP | 1965–66 | 2 | — | Report on cease-fire between domestic factions |
| UNIPOM | 1965–66 | 96 | — | Observe India-Pakistan border |
| UNEF II | 1973–79 | 6,973 | — | Supervise cease-fire and troop disengagement, control buffer zone between Egypt and Israel |
| UNDOF | 1974–present | 1,450 | 1,032 | Patrol Syria-Israel border |
| UNIFIL | 1978–present | 7,000 | 4,473 | Supervise Israeli troop withdrawal, maintain order, help restore authority of Lebanese government |
| UNGOMAP | 1988–90 | 50 | — | Monitor Geneva Accords on Afghanistan and supervise Soviet withdrawal |

TABLE 5-1   *(continued)*

| Mission | Date | Peak Force Size | Force Size (March 1998) | Function |
|---|---|---|---|---|
| UNIIMOG | 1988–91 | 399 | — | Supervise cease-fire and mutual withdrawal of forces by Iran and Iraq |
| UNAVEM I | 1989–91 | 70 | — | Verify withdrawal of Cuban troops from Angola |
| UNTAG | 1989–90 | 4,493 | — | Assist Namibia's transition to independence, ensure free and fair elections |
| ONUVEN | 1989–90 | 120 | — | Monitor Nicaraguan elections |
| ONUCA | 1989–92 | 1,098 | — | Verify compliance by Costa Rica, El Salvador, Guatemala, Honduras, and Nicaragua with agreement to disarm and neutralize irregular forces in the area |
| ONUVEH | 1990–91 | 260 | — | Observe elections in Haiti |
| UNIKOM | 1991–present | 1,440 | 1,088 | Monitor demilitarized zone between Kuwait and Iraq |
| UNAVEM II | 1991–95 | 476 | — | Verify compliance with Peace Accord to end civil strife in Angola |
| ONUSAL | 1991–95 | 1,003 | — | Monitor cease-fire and human rights agreements in El Salvador's civil war |
| MINURSO | 1991–present | 375 | 283 | Conduct referendum in Western Sahara on independence or union with Morocco |
| UNAMIC | 1991–92 | 380 | — | Assist Cambodian factions to keep cease-fire agreement |
| UNPROFOR | 1992–95 | 21,980 | — | Encourage cease-fire in Croatia and Bosnia-Herzegovina, protect relief programs |
| UNTAC | 1992–93 | 19,500 | — | Demobilize armed forces of Cambodian factions, supervise interim government, conduct free elections |
| UNOSOM I | 1992–93 | 550 | — | Monitor cease-fire between Somali parties, protect shipments of relief supplies |

*(continued)*

TABLE 5-1    *(continued)*

| MISSION | DATE | PEAK FORCE SIZE | FORCE SIZE (MARCH 1998) | FUNCTION |
|---------|------|-----------------|-------------------------|----------|
| ONUMOZ | 1992–94 | 7,500 | — | Supervise internal peace accord in Mozambique, disarm combatants, establish a non-partisan army, hold national elections, conduct humanitarian program |
| UNOMIG | 1993– | 120 | 120 | Verify ceasefire agreement, with Abkhazia, observe CIS peacekeeping force |
| UNOMUR | 1993–94 | 100 | — | Observer mission in Uganda-Rwanda, monitor arms shipments |
| UNOSOM II | 1993–95 | | — | UN mission in Somalia, peacemaking operations |
| UNAMIR | 1993–96 | 5,500 | — | Stop the massacre of the defenseless population of Rwanda, assist refugees, report atrocities |
| UNMIH | 1993–96 | 900 | — | Mission in Haiti, pacification and monitor elections |
| UNOMIL | 1993–97 | 91 | — | Observer group in Liberia monitor OAS peacekeeping |
| UNASOG | 1994 | 25 | | Observer group in Aouzou Strip, Libya-Chad border |
| UNMOT | 1994– | 24 | 24 | Investigate ceasefire violations and work with OSCE and CIS missions in Tajikistan |
| UNMIBH | 1995– | 1,584 | 1,584 | Monitor law enforcement in Bosnia and Herzegovina |
| UNPREDEP | 1995–99 | 1,150 | 1,150 | Preventive deployment force Former Yugoslav Republic of Macedonia |
| UNCRO | 1995–96 | 20 | — | Confidence restoration in Croatia |
| UNAVEM III | 1995–97 | 5,560 | — | Angola verification Mission of the Peace Accords (1991), the Lusaka Protocol (1994), and relevant Security Council resolutions |
| UNMOP | 1996– | 28 | 28 | Monitor demilitarization in Prevlaka Peninsula, Croatia |
| UNTAES | 1996–98 | 5,257 | — | Facilitate demilitarization in Eastern Slavonia (Croatia) |

TABLE 5-1    *(continued)*

| MISSION | DATE | PEAK FORCE SIZE | FORCE SIZE (MARCH 1998) | FUNCTION |
|---|---|---|---|---|
| UNSMIH | 1996–97 | 1,549 | — | Support Mission in Haiti |
| UNTMIH | 1997 | 300 | 300 | Transition Mission in Haiti |
| MINUGUA | 1997 | 155 | 155 | Verification Mission in Guatemala |
| MIPONUH | 1997– | 290 | 290 | Civilian Police Mission in Haiti |
| MONUA | 1997–99 | 5,560* | 5,560 | Observer Mission in Angola and a follow on to UNAVEM III |
| MINURCA | 1998– | 1,350 | 1,350 | Help maintain and enhance security and stability in the Central African Republic |
| UNOMSIL | 1998– | 109 | 41 | To observe and report to the Security Council military conditions in Sierra Leone |

SOURCE: United Nations Peacekeeping Operations, *Police, Troops and Military Observers— Contributors by Mission and Country,* UN Peacekeeping Home Page, January 1998; Center for International Relations, *Current UN Peace-Keeping Operations,* Zurich, Switzerland, PKO webmaster, Jan. 1998.

* The force identified with UNAVEM III is the same force operating under MONUA.

of permanent peace in the area has made its continuance necessary. UNTSO currently maintains about 225 observer personnel to monitor situations in Lebanon, the Golan Heights, and the Sinai. The UN Military Observer Group in India and Pakistan (UNMOGIP) has experienced a similar longevity. Set in operation in January 1949 to help curb the fighting in Kashmir, it continues to monitor the ceasefire line. Nevertheless, it has never convinced the parties to resolve their differences diplomatically, nor has it prevented them from attacking one another. The war that erupted in 1965 when Pakistan attempted to take the mountain state by force, or subsequently, in 1971 when India attacked Pakistan in eastern Bengal, but also struck blows all along the West Pakistan frontier, including Azad Kashmir (under Pakistani control), did little to enhance UNMOGIP's credibility. UNMOGIP's helplessness in the face of renewed unrest in the Kashmir valley did not serve the cause of the international community. By the late 1990s, Indian army and paramilitary units, estimated at several hundred thousand, were unleashed against rebellious Kashmiris, who, New Delhi declared, were aided by the Pakistan government. The small UN observer force, which had been reduced from a peak of 102 several decades earlier, to 42 by 1998, continued to monitor the situation and make periodic reports to headquarters in New York. The testing of nuclear weapons by both India and Pakistan in May 1998, however, suggested that the Kashmir dispute required more than patience from the United Nations.

## UN EMERGENCY FORCE I (UNEF)

UNEF, like the earlier observer missions, was a nonfighting UN military presence designed to help bring international violence under control. The violence in this case was precipitated by an October 1956 Israeli invasion of Egypt, launched in coordination with Anglo-French seizure of the Suez Canal, which Egypt had nationalized the previous July. Security Council action was prevented by the British and French veto but the General Assembly, responding to an initiative by Canadian Foreign Minister Lester Pearson, called for a ceasefire and authorized Secretary-General Hammarskjöld to prepare a plan for an international emergency force. Because of the large hostile armies and the extent of the area to be patrolled, UNEF went far beyond any previous UN peacekeeping operation in size and function. UNTSO at its largest had numbered under six hundred; UNEF fielded six thousand troops from ten countries. Earlier missions had been concerned largely with observation and reporting. UNEF was intended not only to observe, report, and supervise troop withdrawal but also to serve as a buffer between the contending forces and to keep order in the areas under its control.

Primarily concerned with neutralizing the strategic Sinai location of Sharm al-Shaykh astride the Gulf of Aqaba, Israeli withdrawal from the Sinai was predicated on Tel Aviv's demand that it be permitted to transit Aqaba to the Israeli port of Eilath. Heretofore, Egyptian forces had blocked the waterway. Now, however, Israel insisted on its right to use its only outlet to the Red Sea. UNEF forces were therefore stationed at Sharm al-Shaykh in return for the Israeli promise of withdrawal, which it did in March 1957. During the next ten years Israel used the UNEF presence to expand its port operations at Eilath and it became central to the nation's trade with Asian countries insofar as the Jewish state was still prohibited from using the Suez Canal. Secretary-General U Thant's decision in 1967 to acquiesce when Egypt's leader Gamal Abdul Nasser demanded the removal of UNEF from Sharm al-Shaykh therefore created an instant crisis. U Thant took the action without consulting the Security Council or the General Assembly, and Israel, sensing a major challenge to its security, quickly mobilized its forces and attacked Egyptian airfields and military installations, and again sent its forces into the Sinai peninsula. Despite the renewed hostilities, UNEF had demonstrated its significance and what was learned from that experience would be applied to other peacekeeping operations in the years that followed. Among the more important principles learned were the following:

1. A peace force should be established only by authorization of the General Assembly or the Security Council.

2. While responsible to the organ that established it, the force should be administratively integrated with the UN Secretariat under the political control of the Secretary-General.
3. Troops from the great powers should not participate in the force.
4. The force should remain politically neutral as between the various contending parties.
5. The force should be limited to nonfighting functions—those that could be performed with the consent or acquiescence of all the governments concerned—but weapons might be used in self-defense.
6. Troop-supplying states should pay the costs that would be incurred if the military units remained in national service; all other costs should be borne by UN members in accordance with the normal UN scale of contributions.

These principles have continuing validity with two principal exceptions: (1) UN assessments for the more costly peacekeeping missions are now based on a scale that minimizes developing country contributions, and (2) with the decline of East-West antagonisms, troop contributions from the United States and Russia are no longer excluded. The last peacekeeping force acting under General Assembly authorization was the UN security force in West New Guinea, created in 1962. Since then the establishment of peacekeeping missions has become the prerogative of the Security Council.

## THE CONGO FORCE (ONUC)

When the Congo crisis erupted in July 1960, the United Nations turned without hesitation to the UNEF model even though conditions in the Congo were quite different from conditions in the Middle East. The Congo had achieved independence from Belgium on June 30 with obviously inadequate preparation for statehood. Widespread rioting, tribal disorders, and mutiny in the Congolese army broke out almost immediately, and Belgium intervened militarily on July 8 to protect the lives and property of its nationals. Three days later the mineral-rich province of Katanga seceded to form an independent state with economic ties to Belgium. Faced with breakdown of internal order, outside intervention, and secession, the government of the Congo appealed to Secretary-General Hammarskjöld for UN military assistance. The Security Council authorized Hammarskjöld to prepare a plan for military and technical aid and thereafter approved his proposal for a UN Operation in the Congo (ONUC, using the French acronym). The ONUC peacekeeping force eventually reached a strength of twenty thousand troops from twenty-nine countries, cost more than $400 million in its four-year existence, and, with its massive civilian aid component, helped restore a measure of internal stability to the Congo.

In the chaotic situation of the Congo operation, several of the UNEF rules for peacekeeping were bent or broken. The U.S.-Soviet consensus that permitted initial authorization of ONUC quickly evaporated, and responsibility shifted from the establishing organ to the General Assembly. Political neutrality also suffered. A fair degree of neutrality with respect to outside powers was maintained (the Soviet Union thought otherwise), but internal factions were not treated evenhandedly. Early actions of the force tended to favor an anti-Soviet faction over a leftist faction striving for control of the central government. Later on, ONUC supported the central government in its struggle to prevent the secession of Katanga. Support for the government also meant abandonment of ONUC's nonfighting role, since the Katanga secessionists and their foreign mercenaries could be suppressed only by the use of force. Throughout the Congo operation the principle of financing by assessment of all UN members was maintained, but the Soviet Union, France, and some other countries refused to pay. The skyrocketing deficit brought financial and political crisis to the United Nations and ultimately forced the premature withdrawal of ONUC before internal stability had been fully achieved.

Whatever its shortcomings under extremely trying circumstances, ONUC had notable accomplishments to its credit. The Belgian troops, mercenaries, and foreign military advisers were gone; the secession of Katanga and other areas of the Congo had been forestalled; and a modicum of law and order had been maintained. The civilian side of the operation had kept essential public services in operation—transport and communication, health, education, public administration—while providing needed technical training for Congolese personnel and supplying emergency relief throughout the country. The threat of intervention by foreign governments was substantially reduced, and the Congo was insulated from the worst effects of cold war rivalry. The UN intervention, however, was not without its costs. Among the casualties in the campaign was UN Secretary-General Dag Hammarskjöld, who died when his aircraft crashed during a mission to the war zone.

## UN FORCES IN WEST NEW GUINEA AND CYPRUS

The UN Security Force (UNSF) in West New Guinea (West Irian) and the UN Peacekeeping Force in Cyprus (UNFICYP) were both initiated while the Congo operation was still in progress. They followed the UNEF/ONUC organizational pattern in most respects, with some differences in the force composition. Of some 1,600 UNSF personnel in West Irian, more than 1,500 were Pakistani troops and the others were U.S. and Canadian air force personnel assigned to an air contingent for supply and liaison activities. The Cyprus force was much larger, about 6,400 in the initial stages. It was more widely international in composition, but the largest contribution came from one of the large powers— the United Kingdom—for reasons of direct interest and immediate availability. Both UNSF and UNFICYP departed from precedent in their mode of financing, in recognition of the growing impasse over the financing of peacekeeping forces by mandatory assessment on the regular UN budgetary scale. The Netherlands and Indonesia—the two parties directly involved in the West Irian dispute— agreed to share all UN expenses equally. UNFICYP has been financed by the countries supplying troops, the government of Cyprus, and voluntary contributions, largely from the states of the Atlantic Community.

UNSF, unlike the other peacekeeping forces, came into being as the result of prior political settlement between the disputants. After years of dogged resistance to Indonesian claims, the Dutch government finally agreed to give up West Irian and to use the United Nations as a convenient mechanism for the transfer. An August 1962 agreement committed the Netherlands to turn over the administration of the territory to a UN Temporary Executive Authority (UNTEA) on October 1. UNTEA, in turn, was to transfer governmental authority to Indonesia after May 1, 1963, subject to the right of the native Papuans to determine their own political fate by a plebiscite before the end of 1969. The Security Force was created by the General Assembly to maintain the authority of UNTEA and supplement existing Papuan police in preserving law and order.

The UN Force in Cyprus was created to cope with conflict between Greek and Turkish communities in Cyprus and the threat of military intervention by Greece and Turkey. A British dependency since 1878, Cyprus was granted independence in 1960 under a constitution drafted as a compromise minimally acceptable to the United Kingdom, Greece, Turkey, and the local Cypriot leaders. Under the constitution, majority rule—which would have meant rule by leaders of the Greek Cypriots constituting 80 percent of the island's 600,000 population—was modified by placing a legislative veto in the hands of the Turkish minority. In the absence of good faith, goodwill, and rational behavior, all of which were in short supply, the constitution was scarcely workable. And without consent of the Turkish minority and of the British, Greek, and Turkish governments, it could not lawfully be amended.

Not surprisingly, the machinery of government stalled, the Greek Cypriot majority set about to amend the constitution unilaterally, and domestic violence ensued. Bloodshed and the formation of rival terrorist groups on Cyprus brought Greece and Turkey to sword's point once more, with Britain in the middle as mediator, peacemaker, and policeman. Unable to quell the violence, Britain turned to the Security Council, which established UNFICYP in March 1964.

The UN force has been on duty in Cyprus ever since, though its initial strength of 6,400 has been scaled down to a present force of under 1,200. The initial function of UNFICYP was to create a buffer between Greek and Turkish communities in Cyprus but not to interfere with freedom of movement throughout the island. Subsequently its functions included resolving conflicts between the two groups, adjudicating local disputes, and, with the assistance of a special UN civilian police force, helping to maintain local order. A new crisis erupted in 1974 when a military coup in Cyprus and the prospect of closer military ties between Greece and Cyprus prompted Turkey to invade the island. UNFICYP became involved in the fighting and suffered a number of casualties before a cease-fire could be arranged. The result was a *de facto* territorial division strongly favoring the Turkish community, followed by a resumption of UNFICYP functions along a now distinct dividing line.

UNFICYP has competently performed its mandate to curb violence and contribute to the maintenance of law and order. The original Security Council resolution authorized the Secretary-General to appoint a mediator to assist the parties with a political settlement, but such efforts have been fruitless. No better result has been accomplished by a personal representative of the Secretary-General, serving at the request of the governments of the United Kingdom, Greece, Turkey, and Cyprus since January 1964. UNFICYP, through repeated Security Council extensions of its mandate, performs a useful and perhaps indispensable function in maintaining order, but the political issues remain impervious to solution.

## Observer Missions after UNEF

The invention of the large peacekeeping force did not make small observer missions obsolete. Besides perpetuating UNTSO and UNMOGIP, the UN deployed new observer teams during the 1958 Lebanese crisis and in Yemen and India-Pakistan during the mid-1960s. A token UN observer presence was also sent to the Dominican Republic in 1965 to report on U.S. military intervention there and observe a cease-fire agreement between internal factions.

The largest of the three small observer missions was the UN Observation Group in Lebanon (UNOGIL), a mission of six hundred men that was established in June 1958 at Lebanese request to check on clandestine aid from Syria to rebel groups in Lebanon. UNOGIL reported only minor border infiltration, but in July the border problem was completely overshadowed by a violent pro-Soviet coup in Iraq that raised fears of a similar upheaval in Lebanon. UNOGIL appeared wholly inadequate to cope with this new threat, and fourteen thousand U.S. troops were rushed to Lebanon at the request of the Lebanese president. In retrospect, the U.S. intervention was an overreaction. The external threat to Lebanon had been exaggerated, and domestic strife declined markedly after the July 31 election of a new president. UNOGIL's presence, however, continued to serve a useful purpose by providing a diplomatic rationale for the early withdrawal of U.S. troops. The UNOGIL mission was terminated in December, having played a significant role in relieving a potentially serious crisis.

The UN Yemen Observation Mission (UNYOM) had a more difficult mandate to fulfill. It was established in July 1963 to observe a military disengagement agreement between parties to Yemen's civil war, which posed a serious international threat because of intervention by Egypt and Saudi Arabia on opposite sides. UNYOM's small team, never more than 189 observers, exerted a modest restraining influence on hostilities in the area, but repeated violations of the disengagement agreement led to its withdrawal in September 1964.

Political conditions permitted a happier conclusion to the work of the UN India-Pakistan Observation Mission (UNIPOM), which supplemented UNMOGIP in observing a cease-fire between India and Pakistan from October 1965 to February 1966. The Tashkent Agreement of January 1966 led to mutual troop withdrawal and to the disbandment of UNIPOM with its work successfully completed. Of the three observer missions, UNIPOM and UNOGIL were financed by regular budget assessments. The expenses of UNYOM, however, were jointly shared by Saudi Arabia and Egypt.

The Mission of the Representative of the Secretary-General in the Dominican Republic (DOMREP) consisted of a three-man team sent at the request of the Security Council to report on the situation. No more than two observers were on duty at one time, and DOMREP's role was very limited because of non-cooperation by the United States and other parties. DOMREP served mainly to confirm the proposition that UN peacekeeping during the cold war period was unlikely to be viable within the regional sphere of a superpower.

## Peacekeeping in the 1970s—Middle East Focus

From 1965 to 1973, no new peacekeeping missions were established, although UNTSO, UNMOGIP, and UNFICYP continued to function under repeated extensions of their mandates. In 1973 an attack on Israel by Egypt and Syria made UN peacekeeping again seem a necessary collective response to crisis. The Security Council authorized a UN Emergency Force (UNEF II) of seven thousand men to supervise a cease-fire and troop disengagement on the Egyptian front and subsequently to control a UN buffer zone between the combatants. On the Syrian front military action persisted until May 1974, when a disengagement agreement was signed at Geneva by Syria and Israel, with provision for a UN peacekeeping force. Pursuant to the agreement, the Security Council established a UN Disengagement Observer Force (UNDOF) of approximately 1,450 to supervise disengagement and patrol the border area. UNEF II and UNDOF initiated the practice of financing peacekeeping through a specially scaled budgetary assessment designed to reduce the proportionate share of the developing countries.

Both UNEF II and UNDOF performed their assignments successfully and kept hostile incidents to a minimum. Warming relations between Egypt and Israel culminated in the 1978 Camp David accords and the March 1979 treaty of peace, the first political settlement between Israel and any Arab country, which included agreed withdrawal of Israeli forces from the Sinai, to be completed by April 1982. Both parties requested that UNEF II be reconstituted to serve within the framework of the peace agreement, but Soviet and Arab opposition to the treaty made continued UN involvement impossible. UNEF II was terminated in 1979 through nonrenewal of its mandate, leaving a few UNTSO observers as the only UN presence in the Sinai. The gap was filled temporarily by expanding the duties of the U.S. Sinai Field Mission (staffed by civilians, most under private contract), which had been established in 1976 to monitor two strategic passes within the UNEF II buffer zone by means of highly sophisticated electronic surveillance equipment. In 1982 a Multinational Force and Observers (MFO) was created outside the United Nations to monitor the final stages of Israeli troop withdrawal and serve as a continuing border watch. Its 2,500-man force has included troops from the United States and ten other countries, with 60 percent of the cost defrayed by the United States.

UNDOF was not a precursor of a Syria-Israel settlement, but it continues to keep peace by patrolling a forty-seven-mile-long corridor separating opposing forces in the Golan Heights area. That tenuous peace has survived the Syrian occupation of large parts of Lebanon, a 1981 exchange of threats over Syrian missiles in the nearby Bekaa Valley, Israeli annexation of the Golan Heights, Israeli invasions of Lebanon in 1978 and 1982, the maintenance by Israel of a six-mile wide "security zone" in southern Lebanon since 1985, and numerous military incidents initiated by both Israel and Lebanese military groups.

A third peacekeeping force, the UN Interim Force in Lebanon (UNIFIL), was a Security Council response to the 1978 Israeli invasion of Lebanon. UNIFIL was given the broad mandate of "confirming the withdrawal of Israeli forces, restoring international peace and security, and assisting the Government of Lebanon in ensuring the return of its effective authority in the area." This mission proved impossible for its seven thousand troops to carry out. Although Israel eventually withdrew under heavy international pressure, UNIFIL lacked the resources to maintain order among the numerous armed Christian and Muslim groups or to restore government control over southern Lebanon. Israel complained that UNIFIL was unable to prevent continued PLO raids across the border, while Israel itself continued to make retaliatory strikes against PLO forces both within and beyond the UNIFIL area. UNIFIL troops frequently came under fire, suffered many casualties, and—though a "defensive" force— sometimes had to initiate preventive military action against one or another of the domestic military groups.

UNIFIL was brushed aside by Israeli forces in the June 1982 invasion of Lebanon, but it subsequently resumed its efforts to provide a buffer and reduce violence in the area. At the conclusion of the 1982 hostilities, a non-UN Multinational Force consisting of British, French, Italian, and U.S. contingents was established to monitor withdrawal of PLO forces from Beirut (MNF I) and to help maintain domestic order (MNF II). MNF II was unable to remain neutral in the ensuing civil war. U.S. and, to a limited extent, French troops found themselves fighting not only in self-defense but in support of the Lebanese army against Druze, Shiite, and Palestinian militias. Their position proved untenable, as illustrated by the October 1983 truck bombings that killed 299 U.S. and French troops. MNF II withdrew in early 1984, unable to provide for even its own security. UNFIL, however, remained in place through numerous civil and cross-border conflicts as well as random acts of terror. Still mandated to confirm Israeli withdrawal from southern Lebanon, to assist in the restoration of peace and security in the region, and to assist the Government of Lebanon in regaining control of the area, UNFIL's force of 4,473 in 1998 represented one of the enduring, larger peacekeeping missions of the United Nations. UNFIL's work apparently will not end until Syria, which after the 1991 Gulf war exerted major influence in Lebanese political affairs, and Israel, which continues to emphasize its security in the face of Syrian and Iranian sponsored terror organizations in southern Lebanon, reach agreement on matters of mutual concern.

## A NEW ERA OF UN PEACEKEEPING

After the creation of UNIFIL in 1978, a decade elapsed before the United Nations fielded another peacekeeping mission. This was the low tide of UN fortunes, the nadir of UN prestige. Although a half dozen "peacekeeping" operations were launched during this period, all were outside the United Nations. The world did not lack situations appropriate for UN peacekeeping but the United Nations was not called in. Hobbled by East-West and North-South divisions, and a general image of ineffectualness, the organization awaited better days.

The better days arrived, perhaps to be dated from Mikhail Gorbachev's September 1987 address to the General Assembly announcing a new (and as it turned out, genuine) commitment to the United Nations and to "the idea of a comprehensive system of international security."[3] The extent of the internal changes then underway in the Soviet Union were not yet fully appreciated, but Soviet leaders had clearly come to grips with the cost, the danger, and the futility of the ruinous cold war competition. Shifts in U.S. policy were less dramatic, but President Ronald Reagan experienced a notable softening toward the United Nations during the closing months of his administration. His successor, George Bush, already had a concept of UN possibilities based on his earlier service as U.S. Ambassador to the United Nations (1971–73).

The implications for peacekeeping soon became apparent. The Soviet Union began to pay its peacekeeping assessment arrearages, and the United Nations Good Offices Mission in Afghanistan and Pakistan (UNGOMAP) was created in May 1988 to monitor Soviet troop withdrawal from Afghanistan. This was soon followed by a major peace initiative in the stalemated war between Iran and Iraq, leading to a cease-fire and establishment of the United Nations Iran-Iraq Military Observer Group (UNIIMOG) in August 1988.

Most UN operations have been relatively small observer missions with a staff of 500 or fewer, but all have had important assignments. The United Nations Good Offices Mission in Afghanistan and Pakistan (UNGOMAP) was commissioned to help implement the Geneva Accords of 1988 which brought an end to more than eight years of Soviet military intervention in Afghanistan and reduced tensions between Afghanistan and Pakistan. Pakistan had provided a haven to an estimated three million Afghan refugees and, with U.S. assistance, was channeling aid to Afghan guerrillas fighting the Soviet-supported government. UNGOMAP's fifty military observers successfully monitored Soviet troop withdrawal and somewhat less successfully kept watch on unauthorized Afghan-Pakistani border crossings. When UNGOMAP withdrew in

March 1990, the internal strife still continued but the international tensions were greatly reduced. The civil war abated in 1992 with the triumph of the rebel forces, only to be followed by conflict between rival rebel groups.

The United Nations Iran-Iraq Military Observer Group (UNIIMOG) was also a response to major armed conflict. It helped bring an end to a devastating war that took nearly a million lives and lasted almost eight years. The combatants had repeatedly rebuffed UN efforts to mediate the conflict, but in 1988 the new unity on the Security Council and war weariness on both sides provided a setting for successful peace intervention. UNIIMOG's 399 military observers faithfully patrolled the 850-mile cease-fire line until February 1991 when the exigencies of the war in Kuwait led Iraq to make a formal peace settlement with Iran. UNGOMAP was small enough to be financed as a part of the regular UN budget. UNIIMOG was financed from the special peacekeeping account raised by assessments falling more heavily upon the wealthier states and the permanent members of the Security Council.

Two observer missions were required to deal with Angola's troubled domestic and international situation. After gaining independence from Portugal in 1975, Angola became a base for the South West Africa People's Organization (SWAPO) to carry on its armed struggle against South African authorities in Namibia. At the same time, South Africa was giving aid to the National Union for the Total Independence of Angola (UNITA), an armed insurgent group within Angola. The picture was further complicated by 50,000 Cuban troops stationed in Angola since 1975 to prop up its left-leaning government. The international aspects of the situation were resolved by a U.S.-engineered agreement between Cuba, Angola, and South Africa in December 1988, linking Cuban troop withdrawal with a South African commitment to accept Namibia's independence. UNAVEM I, the United Nations Angola Verification Mission, utilized seventy military observers to verify the withdrawal of Cuban troops from Angola over a two-year period from 1989 to 1991.

This left Angola with a serious internal problem that was addressed by UNAVEM II, a force of 350 military observers and 126 police observers enlisted to monitor a peace settlement between the Angolan government and UNITA. UNAVEM II commenced operation in June 1991, and its size was temporarily augmented by some 400 election observers for a general election held in September, 1992. UNAVEM II was supposed to be disbanded after the election, but UNITA cried fraud following electoral defeat and the UN was faced with the task of negotiating a new cease-fire.

Having assisted in reconciling UNITA with the elected Angolan government, the work of UNAVEM II was completed in 1995, but almost immediately differences again developed between the parties and UNITA forces once more took to the field, striking at government positions and generally disrupting the country's governance. Again the United Nations was called upon to interpose itself between the conflicted parties, and UNAVEM III was authorized to pick up where UNAVEM II had left off. UNAVEM III was comprised of troops from 32 countries, which in 1997 totalled 5,560 police, military personnel, and observers, including more than 4,900 armed soldiers. UNAVEM III was transformed into MONUA in June 1997. MONUA was to assist the government of Angola and UNITA to consolidate peace and national reconciliation on the basis of the peace accords of 1991 and the Lusaka Protocol of 1994. Unlike UNAVEM III, MONUA was altered from a strict verification force to an observer mission and was authorized to monitor the normalization of state administration throughout the country, observe and verify the activities of the Angolan National Police, oversee security for UNITA leaders, investigate offensive troop movements, monitor the dismantlement of checkpoints and UNITA command posts and promote human rights. Deeply concerned by the failure of UNITA to comply with its obligations and Security Council resolutions, the Council imposed travel restrictions on UNITA personnel in August 1997. This sanction was extended and expanded to include the closure of UNITA offices. Following the shooting down of two UN aircraft by UNITA forces, however, the Security Council decided against putting unarmed observers at continuing risk, and in February 1999 it was decided to allow the peacekeeping force mandate to expire. MONUA was liquidated and the Secretary General's office was authorized to work with the Angolan government on how the United Nations might maintain a presence in the country.

No more successful in quelling the internal war in Liberia, UNOMIL, an observer mission, was sent to Liberia in 1993 to monitor a ceasefire agreement and the Cotonou Peace Agreement, which called for an embargo on the delivery of arms, in addition to the disarmament and demobilization of the combatants. It was also authorized to train ECOMOG engineers for mine clearance and the removal of unexploded bombs. When the parties to the conflict made the carrying out of these responsibilities impossible, UNOMIL was assisted by forces from the Organization of African Unity and ECOWAS, which subdued the fighters, but that nevertheless did not provide an environment in which UNOMIL could pursue its mandate. The UN peacekeepers were withdrawn in September 1997, leaving the policing of Liberia to the OAU. The first new UN peacekeeping mission to be established in Africa since 1993, MINURCA was authorized by the Security Council to take over peacekeeping responsibilities from the Inter-African Mission to Monitor the Bangui Agreements (MISAB) in the Central African Republic in March–April 1998. MINURCA again demonstrated the UN commitment to Africa, and in addition to maintaining security it was called upon to train local police and security forces as well as monitor the elections of August–September 1998.

Called to manage dilemmas in Tajikistan where civil strife had erupted soon after it achieved independence in 1991, UNMOT was mandated to accomplish similar tasks. A joint commission composed of the representatives of the Tajik government and the Tajik opposition was to monitor an agreement entered into in 1994, and to investigate reports of ceasefire violations. UNMOT was created to work parallel with the Joint Commission and to report to United Nations headquarters on the progress made in providing good offices. Here as elsewhere the UN peacekeepers were called upon to work with other international organizations that had committed considerable resources to ease the suffering of the innocent. Given the strife in Georgia and Abkhazia, the Commonwealth of Independent States, and particularly Russia was committed to mollifying the parties. The Organization of Security and Cooperation in Europe (OSCE) also became involved. Nevertheless, UNMOT's mandate was extended by the Security Council in 1997 with the expectation that the peacekeepers would be successful in getting the United Tajik Opposition (UTO) to accept integration in the Tajik armed forces and yield their bases in Afghanistan.

The United Nations Advance Mission in Cambodia (UNAMIC) was established in November 1991 with a staff of 380 military and civilian personnel to prepare the ground for a much larger UN peacekeeping operation projected for 1992. The larger objective was to assist contending Cambodian factions to end years of civil strife and foreign intervention, punctuated by unspeakable atrocities, and erect a government all could live with. In fulfillment of its mandate, UNAMIC provided a line of communication between the military headquarters of each of the contending Cambodian parties, monitored cease-fire violations, and conducted a mine-awareness program to help the public avoid injury from hidden mines and booby traps. It was terminated in 1992 when UNTAC (see below) became operational.

Two additional missions, having at least a kinship with peacekeeping, were established for the express purpose of observing national elections in Nicaragua and Haiti. The UN Observer Group for Verification of Elections in Nicaragua (ONUVEN) and the UN Observer Group for Verification of Elections in Haiti (ONUVEH) completed their tasks without serious incident and ceased operations in February 1990 and January 1991, respectively.

The United Nations Mission for the Referendum in Western Sahara MINURSO) was established in September 1991. MINURSO originally involved 375 military and civilian observer experts. This figure was reduced to 283 in 1997 but expected to increase again if the long postponed referendum on the status of the Western Sahara can be conducted. MINURSO's task in the interim was to monitor the ceasefire between Morocco and the Polisario Front, which sustained its demand for self determination and independence for the region. A settlement agreed to in 1988 had promised a reduction of Moroccan forces in the Western Sahara. MINURSO was authorized to monitor compliance, ensure the release of political prisoners, oversee the exchange of prisoners of war, as well as register qualified voters and organize and ensure a free referendum. MINURSO was given final responsibility for proclaiming the results of the election, but the divergent views and different interpretations of key elements contained in the settlement plan made conforming to an earlier timetable impossible. The 1998–99 timetable was not any more realistic.

Two larger observer missions were established in Central America. The United Nations Observer Group in Central America (ONUCA) was created in November 1989 to help verify implementation of the Esquipulas II Agreement dealing with border violations affecting Costa Rica, El Salvador, Guatemala,

Honduras, and Nicaragua. The border problems had resulted from activities of the Nicaraguan Resistance ("Contras") and, to a lesser extent, from the Salvadoran civil war. The Agreement bound the parties to prevent arms trafficking in the area, cease aid to insurrectionist forces, and deny use of each state's territory for attacks on another state. At first consisting of 260 military observers, in addition to an air wing and a naval unit, the observer corps was expanded to a peak of nearly 1,100 in May 1990 when its mandate was extended to include assistance with the voluntary demobilization of the Contras. The termination of hostilities in Nicaragua and the establishment there of a democratically elected government brought a substantial reduction in border violations, and ONUCA was disbanded in January 1992.

The remaining ONUCA observers, about 160 in number, were transferred to the United Nations Observer Mission in El Salvador (ONUSAL). ONUSAL was created in July 1991 as part of a UN-brokered attempt to end a protracted civil war between the Salvadoran government and the insurgent Frente Farabundo Martí para la Liberación Nacional (FMLN). With an initial strength of 135 military and civilian staff, ONUSAL's task was to help reduce human rights abuses through monitoring human rights activities, investigating specific complaints, and making recommendations to eliminate violations. By the end of the year its staff had grown to 260 and, in January 1992, the Security Council authorized a force of 372 military personnel and 631 police to monitor a cease-fire to take effect on February 1. Besides monitoring the separation of forces and cease-fire, and continuing to check on human rights violations, ONUSAL was given the complex assignment of supervising the creation of a new national police force that might administer even-handed protection free from past antagonisms. ONUSAL's success allowed the Security Council to withdraw the observers and terminate the mission in April 1995.

A third large observer mission, subsequently reduced in size and still in operation, was a product of the 1991 Gulf War. The United Nations Iraq-Kuwait Observation Mission (UNIKOM) was put into the field in April 1991 to monitor the Khawr' Abd Allah waterway between Iraq and Kuwait and to deter violations of a demilitarized zone established along the Iraq-Kuwait land boundary. At its inception the force included 1,440 troops and unarmed military observers. The troops were withdrawn in June 1991 leaving 300 observers to patrol the area. Given the sustained crisis conditions in the region, the United Nations continued to augment its UNIKOM force, and because of boundary violations and the threat of hostile action from Iraq, in February 1993 the Security Council again added a military component and extended its terms of reference to include a capacity to take physical action to prevent violations of the DMZ and of the newly demarcated boundary between Iraq and Kuwait. As of March 1997 UNIKOM was staffed with a tripwire detachment of 891 soldiers drawn from thirty-three different countries. One hundred and ninety-seven observers were also assigned to the operation, which was paid for from assessments in respect of the UN special account.

*UN Forces in Namibia and Cambodia*

In addition to observer teams ranging in size from fifty to as many as 1,400, peacekeeping operations also numbered in the thousands. Of these the United Nations Transition Assistance Group (UNTAG) was the most obviously successful. It had the responsibility of supervising Namibia's transition from South African colonial rule to independent statehood, and this was accomplished in thirteen months from February 1989 to March 1990. At peak strength the mission consisted of approximately 4,500 troops, 1,500 civilian police, and 1,000 election observers. Although its basic mandate was to ensure a fair election process, the need to create preconditions for free and uncoerced choice involved UNTAG in a variety of tasks, including some not usually associated with peacekeeping missions. It observed the cease-fire between South African forces and those of the South West Africa People's Organization (SWAPO). It supervised not only the November 1989 elections but also the registration process. It presided over South African military withdrawal, monitored the conduct of South West African police, and encouraged SWAPO forces to honor their agreement to remain in designated base areas. It also assisted the return of large numbers of refugees, ensured the repeal of racially discriminatory laws, and generally attempted to create an atmosphere in which people subjected for a hundred years to repressive and discriminatory colonial rule might exercise a genuine act of self-determination. UNTAG's mission was accomplished when Namibia declared its independence as a new sovereign entity on March 21, 1990. The total cost was $383 million, assessed to member states according to the special scale for peacekeeping.

A larger peacekeeping force began operation in March 1992 when the first contingents of UN troops arrived in Cambodia. Preparations for the United Nations Transitional Authority in Cambodia (UNTAC) had been laid by the 380 military liaison officers and civilian staff of UNAMIC, established the previous October to help maintain the cease-fire between warring factions in Cambodia. UNTAC at full strength included 21,900 troops, 3,600 police monitors, and 2,400 civilian administrators. The largest UN peacekeeping force since the Congo operation, UNTAC had the mammoth task of preserving order and providing transitional governance until a new freely elected government could assume control. In addition it had to disarm the military forces mobilized by the four warring domestic factions in Cambodia. Elections were initially scheduled for April 1993 and the dissolution of UNTAC by July 1993. Led by Yasushi Akasi, UNTAC was to be a catalyst for the assembly of a government of reconciliation. It also was slated to operate at least five of Cambodia's ministries, but faced with resistance, UNTAC confined its tasks to providing basic medical services and distributing food. Unable to bring the different factions together and no match for the profiteers or the Khmer Rouge, the UN mission was closed down on schedule. The venture cost the international community approximately $2 billion between 1992 and 1994, but there was little to show for it given the worsened social conditions, the enormous peasant displacement, and widespread official corruption. Cambodia was left to its own designs and although a formula was initially found to bind the competing groups in common endeavor, shared responsibility was not Cambodia's strong suit. In 1997, the government divided again, and although the country confronted renewed fighting, sufficient calm prevailed to conduct new elections in the summer of 1998.

## UN Forces in the Former Yugoslavia and Somalia

The initial mission of the United Nations Protection Force (UNPROFOR) in Croatia was to supervise a cease-fire between Croats and Serbs, the latter supported by the Serb-dominated Yugoslav army. UNPROFOR's authorized force of 14,400 troops, police, and observers found the cease-fire difficult to maintain in the face of the underlying ethnic conflict. When serious fighting also broke out in neighboring Bosnia-Herzegovina, the Security Council was reluctant to authorize another large, expensive peacekeeping force. However, on the understanding that countries supplying the troops (primarily Britain, France, Italy, and Canada) would pay the additional costs, UNPROFOR was expanded to well over 23,000 by the end of the year, making it the largest UN peacekeeping force to date. Irrespective of its size UNPROFOR was not a success story for United Nations peacekeeping. The bulk of the force was stationed in Bosnia and made responsible for protecting humanitarian agencies that were involved in the distribution of food and medicine. The force had air support provided by NATO, as well as airlift capability for food and medicine drops in battle areas cut off from normal supply routes. Indeed, these airdrops were described as the most ambitious in history. UNPROFOR was supposed to interpose itself between the warring factions, its lightly armed status meant to convince the combatants of its peaceful intentions. Not called upon to take sides, UNPROFOR was supposed to slow and reduce the level of combat so that the peace process might go forward. The largest contingents for the peacekeeping operation were drawn from France (3,493), Britain (3,283), Pakistan (2,973), Malaysia (1,539), the Netherlands (1,485), Turkey (1,468), Spain (1,402), and Bangladesh (1,239). Ten other countries also contributed forces.

In spite of its declared neutrality and peaceful representation, UNPROFOR was attacked militarily, politically, verbally, and psychologically. Spread over a vast area and operating in small units the troops were easy targets for the warring groups, especially the Serbs, who in 1995 seized more than 300 UNPROFOR troops and declared them to be prisoners of war. UNPROFOR could neither protect itself nor the victims of indiscriminate aggression and ethnic cleansing pogroms. Moreover, the mission took a considerable number of casualties, and the Security Council was forced to consider withdrawing the troops before more were killed. Sensing an opportunity to be rid of the UN presence, in 1995 defiant Bosnian Serbs threatened a bloodbath on UN forces. But no longer prepared to stand by defenseless, without UN authorization, France, Britain, and the Netherlands organized a Rapid Reaction Force of 10,000 fully armed combatants. Deploying the RRF as security for UNPROFOR, the

Europeans insisted they were not taking sides, merely trying to protect their forces in UNPROFOR. The United States remained somewhat hesitant, refusing to become more involved in what Washington believed was a European problem. With the exception of the NATO airlift, to which the Americans were a major contributor, the U.S. practiced a hands-off policy. Moreover, Washington, claiming strict neutrality, had refused to arm the Bosnian Muslims who were challenged by a far better equipped Bosnian Serb army.

The seizure of UNPROFOR hostages, however, did register among Americans, and President Clinton ordered some very limited airstrikes against select Serbian targets. Deemed to be of token value, the U.S. again hesitated when the areas delimited as "safe havens" were made free fire zones by the Bosnian Serbs. Seldom had so many large nations been so humiliated by so few renegades. In fact it was only when Croatian forces scored a series of victories against Serbian units in the Krajina region of Croatia that the United States galvanized a significant NATO response to what Washington now judged was unacceptable Serbian aggression.

A largescale NATO air campaign commenced on August 30, 1995, and was slated to continue until the Serbs had removed their artillery from around Sarajevo and the other safe havens. Given the ferocity of the bombing, in October 1995, the Bosnian Serbs agreed to accept ceasefire terms. Diplomatic negotiations went forward under arrangements pressed by the United States. UNPROFOR's role was made dysfunctional and the force was quickly phased out. In its place was a 60,000-person NATO force fully armed and ready to do battle with those who would reignite the conflict. Unlike UNPROFOR, the NATO force was comprised of mainline American units that were totally removed from UN control. Thus, with NATO providing a counterweight to the Bosnian Serbs, other UN peacekeeping missions were authorized for Bosnia-Herzegovina (UNMIBH), the Former Yugoslav Republic of Macedonia (UNPREDEP), both in 1995, as well as Eastern Slavonia, Baranja and Western Sirmium (UNTAES) and Prevlaka (UNCRO) in 1995, followed by (UNMOP) in 1996. All of these missions were in one way or another related to the fighting in the former Yugoslavia. UNMIBH was made responsible for monitoring the re-establishment of political and juridical activity in Bosnia. It was called upon to train police personnel and help develop and improve law enforcement institutions.

The introduction of NATO forces gave the United States a more direct role in pacifying the region. Washington also engineered the Dayton Peace Agreement between the presidents of Serbia, Bosnia, and Croatia, but it was the UN that was given responsibility for developing an International Police Task Force. UNPREDEP was the preventive deployment force that was sent to monitor conditions in Serbia's neighbor, the former Yugoslav Republic of Macedonia. Fear that the civil unrest in Serbian Kosovo province might spill over into Macedonia prompted the UN action. Included in the 600-man military unit that was dispatched to the Balkan state were 300 American troops. Worsening conditions in Kosovo in 1998, and Washington's demand that Serbia end its brutal repression of the majority Albanian population, gave significance to the importance of the region but the bloodletting in Kosovo also revealed the precarious nature of the UNPREDEP mission. Indeed, at a time when conditions in Macedonia were even more disturbed by the flight of thousands of Kosovo refugees seeking safe havens in the neighboring state, UNPREDEP lost its mandate when China cast a veto in the Security Council. The vote to extend the United Nations' first preventive peacekeeping force was thirteen to one with Russia abstaining. Although China argued its vote was in opposition to a mission that it believed had fulfilled its responsibility, the underlying reason for the negative vote was Beijing's dissatisfaction with Macedonia over its recognition of the Republic of China (Taiwan). But whatever the explanation, the Chinese veto came at a critical time and further handicapped United Nations' capacity to play an effective role in bringing peace to the Balkans.

The Security Council authorized UNCRO and its successor UNMOP to monitor the demilitarization of the Prevlaka peninsula in Croatia, and UNTAES, which performed a similar role in another area of Croatia that had been won from Serbia. UNTAES supervised and oversaw the voluntary return of refugees and displaced persons to their original homes in Eastern Slavonia, and contributed to the maintenance of peace and security in a region inhabited by Croats and Serbs. UNTAES also organized elections to local bodies of government and monitored compliance with prior commitments to respect the highest standards of human rights and fundamental freedoms, irrespective of ethnic origin. Demining programs were also constituted. The success of UNTAES was read in its withdrawal from the region in 1998, and demonstrated that the UN, unlike earlier failures, was capable of satisfying its mandate given the relative goodwill of the parties. Nevertheless, by Resolution 1145 in December 1997, the United Nations Security Council authorized a police support group (UNPSG) to assume the task of UNTAES. The function of the Police Support Group, formally instituted in January 1998, was to continue monitoring the performance of the Croatian police in the Danube region and especially to monitor the return of displaced persons. The strength of the force was pegged at 114 and it was drawn from eighteen countries, including the United States, Russia, Finland, and even Switzerland, a non-member of the UN. In October 1998 UNPSG completed its mission and its responsibilities were assumed by the Organization for Security and Cooperation in Europe (OSCE). UNCRO was authorized to operate from March 1995 to January 1996, after which UNMOP assumed a similar charge. Functioning under the security umbrella provided by NATO in Bosnia, UNCRO and UNMOP monitored compliance with the ceasefire agreement of 1994 and an economic agreement also arranged in 1994. Especially concerned with checking the flow of weapons and military personnel across the Serbian, Croatian, and Bosnian frontiers, the missions continued humanitarian assistance to Bosnia-Herzegovina. Thirty-eight countries provided personnel for UNCRO and UNMOP, which for all intents and purpose had replaced UNPROFOR, but with a vastly reduced force.

UNPROFOR's lack of success was somewhat masked by the NATO intervention and the subsequent work of UNMIBH, UNCRO, UNMOP, and UNTAES, but nothing could remove the blemish suffered by the United Nations in

Somalia. The Somalia story began in April 1992 when the Security Council created a small mission (UNOSOM) of fifty unarmed military observers to monitor a ceasefire in Somalia's civil conflict, while several hundred Pakistani soldiers were assigned responsibility for protecting the distribution of food and medicine to a population cut off by the fighting. Failure to manage this effort, however, caused the United States to send a major military force into the country, with the expressed objective of feeding and caring for a people confronted with famine on a vast scale. The earlier overthrow of the long-time ruler of Somalia, Siad Barre, had resulted in armed bands, led by individual regional leaders, to struggle over the spoils. No government could be created in the circumstances, and as a consequence the people of Somalia faced mass starvation as well as a complete breakdown in services.

President George Bush, moved by photo-reports of the desperate millions of Somalia, ordered American forces into the country on what was called a humanitarian mission. The U.S.-led Unified Task Force (UNITAF) quickly opened the principal port of Mogadishu and its airfield in order to mount a major relief program. Quickly gaining compliance from the warring parties, a conference of reconciliation was held in 1993, and United Nations Secretary-General Boutros Boutros-Ghali, sanctioned by Security Council resolutions, expanded the UNOSOM mission. UNISOM II involved a major change from peacekeeping to peacemaking. Boutros-Ghali, apparently impressed with UNITAF's initial success, now urged the United Nations to take up the task of creating a government for Somalia. To pursue this objective, the Secretary-General called for the disarming of the different militias, and with the United States now under the presidency of William (Bill) Clinton, the UNITAF mission was authorized to serve the objectives stated by the Secretary-General. In effect, UNITAF was subsumed under UNOSOM II in May 1993.

Somali leaders, however, opposed the more blatant UNOSOM role and in June 1993, twenty-three Pakistani members of the UN force were ambushed and killed while attempting to search for a weapons depot controlled by the militia of Mohammad Farah Aidid. The response of the Security Council was still another resolution, this time calling for the apprehension and punishment of the Somali headman. Aidid's forces responded by attacking a small contingent of Americans from the UNITAF force, killing them and dragging their naked bodies defiantly through the streets of Mogadishu while television cameras caught the sequence for transmission around the world. The U.S. and UN forces mounted a major effort to locate Aidid following this incident, but without result. In the meantime, Congressional criticism was directed at the Clinton administration, which, it was said, had succumbed to the "mission creep" of the United Nations and its Secretary-General.

Clinton, under pressure from his many critics, decided to end the American presence in Somalia and UNITAF was withdrawn. Arguing that the humanitarian mission had succeeded, Washington declared it was not its responsibility to create a government for Somalia. Following the American withdrawal, the Security Council passed Resolution 865, which specified the withdrawal of UNOSOM II and the termination of the UN activity in Somalia by March 1995. UN peacekeeping and peacemaking suffered a grievous setback in Somalia and the humiliating retreat from the east African nation had consequences in other UN missions as well, notably in Bosnia. The Somalia experience also altered the American perception of the United Nations as well as thinking on the subject of U.S. responsibility in matters not directly concerned with the country's national interests. Subsequent U.S. failure to meet its financial obligations to the United Nations, and Washington's insistence that Boutros-Ghali should not be allowed to serve an additional term as UN Secretary-General, can be traced to the Somalia fiasco.

## Proliferation of Peacekeeping Missions

The Security Council granted the Secretary-General's request to establish yet another large peacekeeping force—the United Nations Operation in Mozambique (ONUMOZ)—to assist Mozambique's transition to internal peace. After years of civil war, a peace accord between the government and the Renamo insurgent group was signed, and the United Nations was invited to supervise the implementation of the agreement. The UN agenda included demobilizing troops on both sides, helping to establish a new nonpartisan army, organizing elections by the end of 1993, and carrying on a large-scale humanitarian program. A force of some 7,500, plus civilian staff, was projected to accomplish these tasks. A more successful operation during this period, ONUMOZ completed its work and was disbanded on schedule in 1994.

The extent and geographic range of UN peacekeeping has broadened remarkably since 1988. One other notable feature has been the focus on internal conflict rather than conflict between sovereign states. Of the thirty-five missions authorized from 1988 through 1998, only five were sent to deal with exclusively interstate conflict—UNIIMOG (Iran-Iraq), ONUCA (Central America), UNIKOM (Iraq-Kuwait), UNOMUR (Uganda-Rwanda), and UNASOG (Libya-Chad). UNGOMAP was concerned with withdrawal of Soviet troops from Afghanistan and also with incidents along the Pakistan border, but the roots of the problem, as the continuing civil war demonstrated, were internal to Afghanistan. The UNAVEM I mission in Angola was aimed at both internal and external conflict. The withdrawal of Cuban troops from Angola was South Africa's price for ceasing military aid to UNITA (the Angolan insurrectionist movement) as well as a precondition to moving ahead with Namibian independence. UNOMIG, authorized in 1993, was mandated to verify compliance with the ceasefire agreement between Georgia and breakaway Abkhazia. Called upon to investigate reports of violations, it was also instructed to mediate the parties. With a force of 120 observers, UNOMIG operated in the midst of a CIS (Commonwealth of Independent States) peacekeeping force that was primarily responsible for separating the opposed armies and limiting their weapons deployment. UNOMIG was called to monitor protection for the city of Sukhumi and to verify the withdrawal of Georgian troops from the Kodori valley. It was required to make regular reports to the Secretary-General, who in turn kept the Security Council informed of developments in the conflicted region.

UNOMUR was also authorized in 1993 and yielded to UNAMIR the following year. Charged first with monitoring the Uganda border with Rwanda, it was supposed to confirm that Uganda was not being used to funnel weapons into Rwanda. Three African nations (among a group of eight) provided observers for a mission that did not total more than 100 peacekeepers. After the killing of the Presidents of Rwanda and Burundi on April 6, 1994, militant members of the Hutu majority in Rwanda launched attacks against the Tutsi minority, moderate Hutu politicians, and UNAMIR positions. When major contributors began withdrawing their contingents, the Security Council elevated UNAMIR to a combat unit and the Secretary-General requested a force of 5,500 soldiers from member states. Member states, however, showed little willingness to provide the necessary troops. Given this indifference, the Hutu-induced massacres in Rwanda went on unabated and UNAMIR was paralyzed by a lack of capacity to respond. France's willingness to deploy its troops, but outside the UN orbit, ended some of the carnage. French actions also downgraded the UNAMIR mandate, which was now confined to providing assistance to Rwandan refugees. Although thirty-nine countries later gave UNAMIR the force requested by the Secretary-General in 1994, the peacekeeping operation was judged a failure. UNAMIR never quite provided the necessary security for the city of Kigali, but it did monitor the ceasefire agreements, assisted in land mine clearance and the repatriation of Rwandese refugees as well as their resettlement. It also investigated reports of atrocities and aided the UN in the establishment of an International Tribunal to try those accused of genocide. UNAMIR was terminated in 1996, after a Tutsi-led coalition successfully routed the Hutu perpetrators of the massacres and established a government of reconciliation. The plight of the Hutu refugees, however, remained a complex matter that continued to burden UN and NGO relief workers.

In November 1994, the UN Secretary General appointed a Special Envoy to work with the Organization of African Unity (OAU) and the Economic Community of West African States (ECOWAS) that were seeking to mediate a peaceful resolution between rival factions in Sierra Leone. Parliamentary and presidential elections were held in 1996 and Alhaji Dr. Ahmed Tejan Kabbah was made president of the country. The election results, however, were not accepted by the Revolutionary United Front (RUF) which had been insisting on its right to govern Sierra Leone since 1991. Nevertheless, an agreement was reached between the parties through the good offices of the Ivory Coast, the United Nations, the OAU, and the Commonwealth, and it was anticipated life in Sierra Leone could be normalized. In May 1997, however, highranking army officers led a coup d'etat against the government and an Armed Forces Revolutionary Council was formed. Citing the overthrow of an elected government, the United Nations Security Council imposed sanctions and an oil embargo on the country and authorized ECOWAS to ensure their strict implementation.

Shortly thereafter an agreement was arrived at with the junta and ECOWAS dispatched a Military Observer Group (ECOMOG) to the area and called upon it to work with the UN military observers already in the country. At this juncture a large, heavily armed ECOMOG force launched an attack on rebel units, and after gaining the advantage, it returned President Kabbah to office. The Security Council welcomed the change in events and lifted the sanctions and the embargo. The RUF and former members of the military junta were not pacified, however, and by the Spring and Summer of 1998 they had succeeded in brutalizing the populations coming within their sphere of operations. The rebel campaign led to the displacement of approximately 450,000 people, many of them fleeing to neighboring Ivory Coast, Gambia, Senegal, Guinea and Liberia. UNOMSIL was thus authorized by the United Nations Security Council to work with ECOMOG in the effort at restoring a semblance of normalcy to Sierra Leone. At a summit meeting in London in October-November 1998, the UN mission reaffirmed its determination to work in tandem with ECOMOG, but in spite of all these efforts the security situation in Sierra Leone did not improve. Moreover, the government's execution of twenty-four ranking military officers, for alleged complicity in the coup, only intensified the struggle. Atrocities and massacres of the innocent intensified in those regions occupied by the Revolutionary United Front. In spite of their considerable number and dedication ECOMOG forces were hardpressed to maintain order, but none of the peacekeepers were prepared to yield to the insurgents. In January 1999 the Security Council extended the mandate of UNOMSIL, and urged the parties to find a way out of their impasse.

The UN was pressed into service in behalf of western hemispheric interests in 1993. The first elected president of Haiti, Jean-Bertrand Aristide, had been ousted from office shortly after his inauguration by a military coup. Disturbed by this act of undemocratic behavior in a region of vital importance to the United States, Washington used considerable diplomatic pressure to force the junta to meet with Aristide—in exile in the United States—in order to work out an understanding that would allow the president to resume his duties. The Governor's Island Agreement was a consequence of this effort, and pledges were made by the junta for Aristide's return and reinstatement. Subsequent violation of this agreement caused the U.S. to threaten the de facto government with military force, and only when airstrikes were readied and an American invasion force was poised for attack did the military leaders of Haiti relent. Their departure from the country made it possible for Aristide to return and although the United States sent several thousand troops to the island nation, it was the United Nations that was called upon to assume responsibility for politically reforming Haiti.

The U.S. force disassembled the military/police organization that had dominated the country and terrorized its population, but UNMIH was given responsibility for stabilizing the political environment, professionalizing the Haitian armed forces, forming an entirely new police establishment, and arranging for free and fair elections to succeed Aristide, who was prevented from seeking another term. UNMIH was to consist of 6,000 soldiers and police, 2,500 drawn from the United States and 3,500 from Pakistan, Bangladesh, Nepal, France, Canada, Honduras, Algeria, Argentina, Austria, Benin, Belize, Antigua and Barbuda, and Bahamas. UNMIH was given an initial six-month mandate that was subsequently extended to almost three years, during which time the U.S. withdrew most of its forces but left enough in place to deal with untoward events. In 1995 Haiti experienced new elections, and in 1996 UNMIH was dissolved in favor of UNSMIH, the United Nations Support Mission in Haiti. The major combat force was removed from the island and replaced by 300 civilian police personnel and 600 troops who were charged with overseeing the development of police and economic institutions. Given the need to eliminate its peacekeeping presence, UNSMIH was phased out in July 1997 and in August UNTMIH, still another mission, was authorized to focus exclusively on the professionalization of the Haitian National Police.

UNTMIH provided the necessary protection for UN personnel, and the mission was ended four months later. Military personnel were drawn from Canada and Pakistan, while civil police trainers came from Argentina, Benin, Canada, France, India, Mali, Niger, Senegal, Togo, and the United States. UNTMIH was comprised of 250 civilian police and fifty military personnel for security purposes. UNTMIH was authorized to assume all the assets of UNSMIH. The transition to greater Haitian self-government centered on economic rehabilitation and the reconstruction of the Haitian government, a program that was deemed impossible without substantial international assistance given Haiti's reputation as the poorest country in the western hemisphere. With the end of UNTMIH's mandate in November 1997, still another mission, MIPONUH, was authorized in December of that same year. MIPONUH, the United Nations Civilian Police Mission in Haiti, was described as a follow-on mission to UNTMIH and it was specifically directed to work with the Government of Haiti in the further development of its National Police establishment. The training of special units and the monitoring of police performance was of major concern. Moreover, unlike previous missions, MIPONUH was not to undertake patrolling missions. Composed of 290 police officers, including a ninety-man special police unit to protect mission personnel and installations, MIPONUH was further authorized to carry personal weapons. The mandate was for one year and drew personnel from Argentina, Benin, Canada, France, India, Mali, Niger, Senegal, Togo, Tunisia, and the United States. Although the United Nations peacekeeping operations had come a long way in a relatively short period, Haiti's problems were legion. Nevertheless, the several missions had accomplished what they could in a country only recently self-governing, and still desperately impoverished.

Haiti, of course, was not the only country in Latin America to draw UN assistance. A United Nations Observer Group (ONUCA) had functioned in wideranging activities in central America from 1989 to 1992. In a 1960s mission, DOMREP, a representative of the Secretary-General was sent to the Dominican Republic to oversee the stabilizing of the country following the conflict that provoked an American invasion of the island. ONUSAL had also performed a significant task helping restore stability to El Salvador after many years of civil strife. And then there was the Guatemala mission, MINUGUA, created in January 1997 and terminated in May. MINUGUA was a UN Verification Mission that was called upon to monitor the Comprehensive Agreement on Human Rights, which had been signed by the Government of Guatemala and the Unidad Revolucionaria Nacional Guatemateca (UNRG) in Mexico City in March 1994. The agreement required the Guatemalan authorities to follow up complaints of human rights violations and to carry out thorough investigations in accordance with human rights norms. Both sides had agreed to a definitive ceasefire and had requested the UN to deploy military personnel to verify implementation of their agreement. MINUGUA had the distinction of becoming a full peacekeeping operation under the terms of the agreement. When its mandate ended in May 1997, it nevertheless remained in place, although it ceased to be a full undertaking of the United Nations. At its height MINUGUA was authorized a force of 155 military observers and requisite medical personnel.

## THE UN PEACE FORCE: RETROSPECT AND PROSPECT

In a world overshadowed by cold war conflict, the UN peacekeeping force emerged as a creative alternative to the coercive enforcement action contemplated by the Charter. During a difficult and dangerous period, UN peacekeeping enabled the United Nations to play a constructive role in matters of global security when the large powers saw a common interest in the termination of hostilities and the maintenance of order. Despite U.S.-Soviet hostility, violence was curbed through UN intervention in such diverse places as Indonesia, the Middle East, Kashmir, and Cyprus without resort to international military sanctions. When Soviet and American interests converged, the peace force proved a highly useful instrument for performing local police functions while a settlement was being effected or, in the more usual case, for encouraging restraint and separating combatants in a volatile situation where the parties accepted peace without settlement.

In the later stages of the cold war, lack of the requisite Soviet-U.S. cooperation and U.S. disenchantment with the United Nations left UN peacekeeping in a holding pattern. Military conflict occurred in many parts of the world—Afghanistan, Cambodia, the Falkland Islands, Grenada, Panama, Iran-Iraq—but the United Nations was largely irrelevant to it.

Judged in terms of political feasibility, the future of peacekeeping, as one looks beyond the 1990s, appears significant in spite of the setbacks. Major power cooperation in the Security Council now permits timely and forthright decisions, and states beset with turmoil have become more willing to accept UN assistance—in part, perhaps, because of the organization's increased moral and political stature. This does not remove all political obstacles to effective UN peacekeeping, including the problem of obtaining cooperation from warring ethnic groups and other internal factions. Still, the limits of political feasibility have been considerably broadened.

Financial feasibility, of course, remains an ever-present constraint. In the past the financial problem was in large part a political problem resulting from disagreement over the establishment, control, and functioning of peacekeeping operations. Today the issue is primarily one of financial priorities—how much are governments willing to spend on UN peacekeeping in relation to other domestic and international demands on their resources? In recent years the costs have escalated. In 1987 UN peacekeeping assessments totaled $233 million; in 1991 members were asked to pay $421 million for peacekeeping; for 1992, with over 40,000 UN personnel in the Balkans and Cambodia, the estimated cost was more than $2 billion. In 1995 UN peacekeeping costs were $2.8 billion, which reflected the expenses incurred in the former Yugoslavia. Peacekeeping costs fell with the termination of the UNPROFOR mission to $1.4 billion in 1996, and in 1997 a further decline was registered when peacekeeping costs came to $1.3 billion. The 1997 figure represented the first time in many years that peacekeeping costs were less than the yearly cost of the regular budget. From July 1997 to June 1998 the UN peacekeeping budget was approximately $1 billion. The U.S. share of the peacekeeping budget in 1997 was 30.39 percent, and its actual payment schedule decreased from about $1 billion in 1995 to $400 million in 1997, or less than one-quarter of 1 percent of the annual U.S. military budget. In 1998 member states owed the UN $1.6 billion for peacekeeping missions.

The UN Secretary-General suggested that member states treat peacekeeping costs as part of their defense budgets rather than as foreign affairs expenditures. Typically, national defense budgets are much larger than the budgets of foreign ministries, and contributions to UN peacekeeping could rationally be regarded as serving the interests of national security. If adopted (and national defense establishments may resist a new demand on their resources), this alteration in national budgetary practice could make it politically more acceptable for some countries to allot funds to UN peacekeeping. Generally, domestic support is greater for "national defense" than for "foreign aid" or "international organizations." By comparison with amounts spent by governments on their national defense the few hundred millions spent each year by UN peacekeepers is a very small price in the effort to build international cooperation and integrity.

Nevertheless, with the United States counting the costs, and Russia seriously stressed in meeting its assessed 4.3 percent (1998) of the peacekeeping budget, UN peacekeeping must continually confront the issue of financial feasibility. The peacekeeping expertise of the UN Secretariat and its cadre of peacekeepers in the field is a valuable international asset. In past years this resource was underutilized. In the new United Nations the demands for UN peacekeeping services may be greater than the members are willing to support. With limited resources the United Nations cannot intervene everywhere it is invited, or everywhere serious violence is threatened. It must make choices, which means that setting priorities and guidelines for future UN peacekeeping is one of the more compelling questions now facing the organization. This is particularly true in view of proposals to use "peacekeeping" forces in situations where the consensual basis for the UN mission breaks down, or perhaps never existed, and military force must be used. Peacekeeping will undoubtedly play a central role in the UN security system of the twenty-first century, but the challenge to adapt to changing needs remains.

Peacekeeping is a difficult and often thankless activity. It needs reminding that since the United Nations began assisting nations challenged by extreme deprivation, insecurity, threat, and aggressive intent, more than 1,500 peacekeepers have sacrificed their lives in strange places they barely knew. Often in harm's way, with little to protect them other than the blue beret that marks their impartiality, they are at the mercy of those who have created the conditions they seek to temper. From 1948 to 1999 there have been forty-eight peacekeeping operations, thirty-five of these between 1988 and 1999, and fourteen were operational in 1999. Several of the peacekeeping missions span the years of the United Nations itself. In the fifty years of peacekeeping approximately 750,000 military and civilian police personnel, and thousands of other civilians, have given their services. (See Table 5.1 and Figure 5.1)

It is important to note, however, that while the Secretary-General is usually at the center of each peacekeeping operation, it is the Security Council, the institution with primary responsibility for the maintenance of international peace and security, that sets each operation in train. Indeed, given the veto power of the permanent members, a mission can be rejected by any one of them. By the same token, ultimate command and control of a nation's peacekeepers remains with the contributing government, and a force can be withdrawn by that authority at any time and for any reason. Up to 1999, 110 nations had contributed personnel to different UN missions, and seventy remained actively involved. The countries contributing the largest number of peacekeepers in the decade of the 1990s have been Pakistan, Bangladesh, Jordan, Poland, the Russian Federation, and Canada, in that order. Moreover, the South Pacific island of Fiji, as well as Canada, have taken part in virtually every UN peacekeeping operation.

Having noted that peacekeeping is linked more to diplomacy than to warfare, the activity rests on a foundation of good faith, not military capability. Thus peacekeeping must be separated from and contrasted with enforcement that is so often confused with it. Peacekeeping requires the consent of all the parties, that is, from the peacekeeping contributors, and most important, the countries where the forces are deployed. Enforcement procedures follow a different course. Consent is not required and the United Nations has used it sparingly, e.g., Bosnia, Somalia, Rwanda, Haiti, and Iraq. Clearly, contributing governments are more prepared to provide forces for peacekeeping than for enforcement purposes. For example, considering the threat posed to the "safe havens" in Bosnia, UN efforts that were aimed at raising the necessary force to

FIGURE 5-1    Completed and Ongoing Peacekeeping Missions

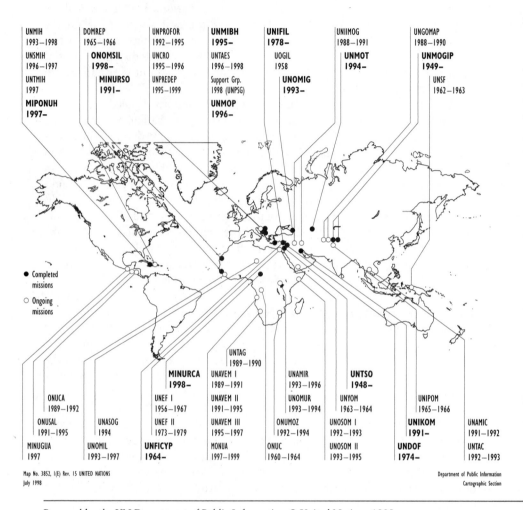

| UNMIH | DOMREP | UNPROFOR | UNMIBH | UNIFIL | UNIIMOG | UNGOMAP |
|-------|--------|----------|--------|--------|---------|---------|
| 1993–1998 | 1965–1966 | 1992–1995 | 1995– | 1978– | 1988–1991 | 1988–1990 |
| UNSMIH | ONOMSIL | UNCRO | UNTAES | UOGIL | UNMOT | UNMOGIP |
| 1996–1997 | 1998– | 1995–1996 | 1996–1998 | 1958 | 1994– | 1949– |
| UNTMIH | MINURSO | UNPREDEP | Support Grp. | UNOMIG | | UNSF |
| 1997 | 1991– | 1995–1999 | 1998 (UNPSG) | 1993– | | 1962–1963 |
| MIPONUH | | | UNMOP | | | |
| 1997– | | | 1996– | | | |

● Completed
  missions

○ Ongoing
  missions

| | | | UNTAG | | | |
|---|---|---|---|---|---|---|
| | | | 1989–1990 | | | |
| | | MINURCA | UNAVEM I | UNAMIR | UNTSO | |
| | | 1998– | 1989–1991 | 1993–1996 | 1948– | |
| ONUCA | | UNEF I | UNAVEM II | UNOMUR | UNYOM | UNIPOM |
| 1989–1992 | | 1956–1967 | 1991–1995 | 1993–1994 | 1963–1964 | 1965–1966 |
| ONUSAL | UNASOG | UNEF II | UNAVEM III | ONUMOZ | UNOSOM I | UNIKOM | UNAMIC |
| 1991–1995 | 1994 | 1973–1979 | 1995–1997 | 1992–1994 | 1992–1993 | 1991– | 1991–1992 |
| MINUGUA | UNOMIL | UNFICYP | MONUA | ONUC | UNOSOM II | UNDOF | UNTAC |
| 1997 | 1993–1997 | 1964– | 1997–1999 | 1960–1964 | 1993–1995 | 1974– | 1992–1993 |

Map No. 3852, I(E) Rev. 15 UNITED NATIONS
July 1998

Department of Public Information
Cartographic Section

Prepared by the UN Department of Public Information © United Nations 1998

protect them were unsuccessful. Instead of the 35,000 troops authorized by the Security Council, only 7,600 were made available, and that smaller number took a whole year to assemble. Similarly, genocide was not unanticipated in Rwanda and the Security Council was unanimous in its call for 5,500 troops to avert the tragedy. Nevertheless, it took six months to mobilize the needed force and by the time it was deployed the bloodletting had already run its course.

Chastened by these tragic events, the United Nations of the twenty-first century will stress the need for cooperation with regional organizations. Co-deployment with other international organizations such as the Organization of

American States (OAS), The Organization of African Unity (OAU), the Economic Community of West African States (ECOWAS), the Organization of Security and Cooperation in Europe (OSCE), the Commonwealth of Independent States (CIS), and the North Atlantic Treaty Organization (NATO) will be emphasized. Operations such as the Unified Task Force (UNITAF) and the Implementation Force (IFOR) and Stabilization Force (SFOR) of NATO, and CIS Collective Peacekeeping forces, will more and more assume Chapter VII enforcement responsibilities, while UN peacekeeping will focus attention on matters requiring more even-handed Chapter VI socio-political and economic issues.

It needs to be repeated that while the United Nations peacekeeping activities are freely criticized and ridiculed for being "inept," and, as in the Bosnian conflict, were made to defer to NATO, or in Rwanda, to France, the appearance of ineptness is more a consequence of an international organization trying to do the world's work in an arena of particular and exclusive nation-states.

## PEACEKEEPING AND HUMANITARIAN LAW

The United Nations is both an asset and a challenge to the world of nation-states. No less significant, it is the instrument whereby those charged with the governance of peoples are measured and judged. Unlike nation-states and those who officially act in their behalf, the United Nations and the people who perform its functions are not shielded from ethical scrutiny. The Machiavellian logic that is the foundation of nation-state behavior does not suffice for the United Nations. The nation-state's exclusive character has given its performance an amoral caste; not so the United Nations. The world organization aspires to a higher standard. Self-preservation and the maximizing of advantages in an aggressively competitive world describes the individual sovereign states, not the United Nations. The UN Charter amply describes a transcendent organization, one that rises above the need for self-glorification or aggrandizement. Focused on the weakest members of the global community, the United Nations makes the symbolism of state equality a reality. Made responsible for the maintenance of world peace in the immediate aftermath of World War II, the United Nations was assigned this task by the very states that acknowledged their own inability to assure still another miasmic display of international anarchy. It was in this context that collective security was reinvigorated, and it was this task that became the hallmark of the organization.

The United Nations remains in its international form. It is first and last an organization between and among the nation-states, not above them. Nowhere is this more obvious than in the matter of collective security and what has come to be understood as peacekeeping. While the individual states continue to pursue their peculiar interests, it is the United Nations that seeks to moderate their excesses. In many ways the United Nations has evolved into a more complete experience than that represented by its constituent member states. The

United Nations must deal with the inchoate aspects of nation-state development while at the same time accepting that nation-state integrity and sovereignty is paramount.

Acting as the conscience for the world of nations, the United Nations has now moved to still another plateau in its evolutionary cycle. Redefining its tasks in terms of peaceful settlement rather than enforcement, UN peacekeeping has raised the bar of national and international performance. So too it is the United Nations that attempts to represent individual persons, both singularly and collectively. And it comes as no surprise that the United Nations gives credence to the question of international humanitarian law. Drawing upon the experience at the Nuremberg War Crime Trials that followed World War II, in May 1993 the Security Council established the International Criminal Tribunal for the Former Yugoslavia (ICTY) at The Hague in the Netherlands and in November 1994, it created still another juridical agency, the International Criminal Tribunal for Rwanda (ICTR) in Tanzania. Citing the commission of "crimes against humanity" and the violation of the four Geneva Conventions of 1949 as well as the Convention on the Prevention and Punishment of the Crime of Genocide of 1948, the United Nations was authorized to apply international humanitarian law and to hold responsible those found violating fundamental human rights.

The ICTY was mandated to prosecute persons responsible for serious violations of international humanitarian law committed in the territory of the former Yugoslavia from 1991 to 1995. Eleven judges were drawn from a variety of countries, along with a chief prosecutor and deputy prosecutor. The tribunal began its work in 1995, and by 1997 had rendered twenty public indictments against seventy-four individuals. Twenty-six of the accused were in custody, several were undergoing formal trial, and two were sentenced to long prison terms for violating the laws or customs of war as well as crimes against humanity. In May 1998, citing the difficulty and resources required in trying all the accused, the ICTY announced it had withdrawn charges against fourteen Bosnian Serbs and thereafter would pursue only the highest level cases or those where the evidence reveals "exceptionally brutal or serious offenses."

The Rwandan tribunal was linked with the formation of a United Nations Human Rights Force (HRFOR), which functioned in concert with the UN High Commissioner for Refugees (UNHCR). A more complex situation and on a larger scale than that of the former Yugoslavia, the ICTR was concerned with not only bringing the perpetrators of the 1994 genocide (in which an estimated 500,000 to 1 million lives were lost), but also the continuing assaults on refugees and displaced persons. HRFOR was charged with assisting the tribunal with the identification of those connected with the bloodletting, a momentous task, given the detention of approximately 92,000 persons who were believed responsible for the slaughter. By 1997 HRFOR had more than 130 human rights observers deployed in Rwanda who were either recruited by the United Nations or UN volunteers. The vastness of the undertaking is seen in the eleven HRFOR offices that covered all the prefectures of Rwanda.

Spurred by these proceedings, but nevertheless, in train since the end of World War II, a conference was convened in Rome from mid-June to mid-July 1998 for the expressed purpose of giving reality to a global Nuremberg principle, that is, to the creation of a permanent International Criminal Court where individuals accused of atrocities and genocide could be tried and punished, irrespective of the safeguards provided by their official positions. Attending the conference were delegations from 160 countries, seventeen intergovernmental organizations, fourteen specialized agencies and funds of the United Nations, and 124 NGOs. In the course of the month-long conference, debate swirled around the issues of jurisdiction and accountability, with the United States eager to rein in the proposed court's prosecutorial scope. Although the United States argued the need to try personalities like the late Pol Pot of Cambodia and Saddam Hussein of Iraq as war criminals, the Americans were reluctant to provide the court with unlimited powers to charge and prosecute its own citizens, especially its soldiers, sailors, and airmen who served in stations around the world.

The United States, originally joined by China, Russia, and France, insisted on the Security Council having the final say in all prosecutory judgments. But despite major power opposition, fully one-third of the participants argued in favor of the court's total independence. Supporting these nations were the non-governmental organizations and human rights associations, many of them American-based, who argued most forcefully for an unrestricted criminal court. In the course of the month-long discussions, numerous concessions were made, and delegates were called upon to alter their positions with each innovation. The United States, however, could not be accommodated. Efforts by the United States to seek more time, and to delay a vote on the issue, failed to receive any significant support. On July 17, 1998, more than 100 countries overwhelmingly approved the statute that formally established the court. The final vote was 120 for and only 7 against, with 21 nations abstaining. Joining the United States in opposing the treaty were Algeria, China, Iraq, Libya, Qatar, and Yemen. At the request of the United States the vote was officially listed as non-recorded, however.

Following the adoption of the text whose formal title was the Rome Statute of the International Criminal Court, the treaty and the Final Act of the Conference were opened for signature at the headquarters of the Food and Agriculture Organization, and subsequently, at a ceremony hosted by the Mayor of Rome. The new International Criminal Court was slated to commence operations in The Hague as soon as the structure and personnel were in place. The court was given authority to bring to justice individuals accused of genocide, crimes against humanity, war crimes, and acts of aggression, but the treaty specifically omitted nuclear weapons. Established as an autonomous organ, the tribunal was made independent of the United Nations, and therefore could act even when the international community was divided on a matter. Having been denied veto powers, the United States was not expected to join the court. Moreover, by approving the treaty, signatory states revealed they were willing to risk loss of aid (which the United States had threatened in the course of the debates). Even Germany had been warned that it risked endangering key military alliances if it voted to support the treaty.

The creation of the International Criminal Court was a long time in coming, although its arrival was notably different from that envisaged by the Nuremberg trials. Nevertheless, the International Criminal Court was intended to be a permanent court with the power to investigate and bring to justice individuals who commit the most serious crimes of concern to the international community, such as genocide, war crimes, and crimes against humanity. And while the court had its origin in World War II, it was only in 1992 that the United Nations General Assembly had directed the International Law Commission to elaborate a draft statute for an International Criminal Court. That work was accelerated by the Security Council's establishment of the criminal tribunals for the former Yugoslavia in 1993 and for Rwanda in 1994. In December 1994, the Assembly formed an ad hoc committee of all the member states and members of specialized agencies to review the final version of the International Law Commission's draft statute. In December 1995, the Assembly created a preparatory committee for the purpose of discussing the substantive and administrative issues involved in the creation of the court. The first sessions of the preparatory committee were held in 1996, and the General Assembly extended its mandate, setting 1998 for the international conference. The Preparatory Committee's draft consisted of thirteen parts and 116 articles, which generated controversies on no less than 1,500 matters. The adoption of the statute, therefore, was no small accomplishment. And while many delegations acknowledged that the final version was far from a perfect document, the vast majority conceded that it represented a major international achievement.

## GLOBAL SECURITY AND THE UNITED NATIONS

In the fall of 1961, the United States submitted to the General Assembly a plan for "General and Complete Disarmament." An integral part of the plan was a proposal to build a "United Nations peace force" strong enough, ultimately, to "deter or suppress any threat or use of force in violation of the purposes and principles of the United Nations." In the final stage of disarmament, the force would be so strong that no state would have the military power to challenge it. The proposal was breathtaking, to say the least, if it could be taken seriously. It went much farther along the road to collective security than anything the peace architects of Versailles and San Francisco had dreamed of. The proposal created a noticeable ripple on the UN diplomatic pond, but the reaction was in no way commensurate with the drastic alteration of the conditions of international life that it contemplated. Most observers regarded it as lip service to collective security that would bring no more practical result than preceding proposals. This episode illustrates the paradox of global security today. People cherish the ultimate ideal of an orderly, peaceful world made secure by force wielded in the common interest, but their actions often negate the notion of a common interest.

The UN has often been characterized as the mythological Sisyphus, forever commanded to roll a stone uphill and never permitted to reach the top. But perhaps the plight of world organization is not so eternally void of hope as that of Sisyphus. No one can feel very confident about getting to the top, but occasionally the stone is rolled upward to a new plateau that marks a gain over previous efforts to promote world peace and security. The establishment of the League of Nations was such an advance, for all the League's inability to stave off aggression and a catastrophic world war. If international security arrangements had changed very little from the days of Abraham to the assassination of the Austrian Archduke at Sarajevo, the creation of the League of Nations interjected a new and lasting element into the international system. The League symbolized widespread acceptance of the principle of common interest in the maintenance of peace and security, and it was an institutional embodiment of the principle. Even World War II could not wipe out this concept; the United Nations reflected the same sense of common interest.

This development, of course, is no more than a step toward world order. If twentieth-century international organization marks a plateau in the ascent toward world peace and security, it is still very far from the top. Note, for example, the end of the century war between NATO and Serbia over Kosovo. It is all too obvious that international organizations whose goals are the formation of a more integrated and tranquil planet must still manage in a world where national armaments, alliances, and some form of balance of power remain the chief reliance of states in their quest for security. Nevertheless, that which passes for a global balance of power at the dawn of a new millennium remains dependent on the services provided by international organizations, and especially the United Nations, which promises enhanced communication, mediation, and judious, and essentially neutral intervention in time of international crisis. Contemporary events have demonstrated that conflicts internal to a state may yet be ameliorated by a pacifying UN presence. Resolving internal conflict indeed has merit in itself, notably in humanitarian matters, and the promotion of domestic stability more often than not also makes regional and global systems more stable. Therefore the increased convergence of security interests among the larger powers that makes all this possible may be a sign that the world is reaching an even higher plateau in the difficult ascent toward peace and universal understanding.

## NOTES

1. General Assembly Resolution 377 (V), November 3, 1950.
2. The United Nations has defined peacekeeping as "an operation involving military personnel, but without enforcement powers, undertaken by the United Nations to help maintain or restore international peace and security in areas of conflict." United Nations, *The Blue Helmets: A Review of United Nations Peacekeeping* (New York: United Nations Department of Public Information, 1990), p. 4.
3. Mikhail Gorbachev, "Realities and Guarantees for a Secure World," reprinted in Richard A. Falk, Samuel S. Kim, and Saul H. Mendlovitz, eds., *The United Nations and a Just World Order* (Boulder, CO: Westview Press, 1991), p. 13.

## SELECTED READINGS

Ayoob, Mohammed. *The Third World Security Predicament: State Making, Regional Conflict, and the International System.* Boulder: Lynne Rienner, 1994.

Benton, Barbara, ed. *Soldiers for Peace: Fifty Years of United Nations Peacekeeping.* New York: Facts on File, 1996.

Bowett, D. W. *United Nations Forces: A Legal Study.* London: Stevens and Sons, 1964.

Boyd, Gavin. *Regionalism and Global Security.* Lexington, MA: D. C. Heath, 1984.

Claude, Inis L., Jr. *Power and International Relations.* New York: Random House, 1962.

Damrosch, Lori Fisler, and David J. Scheffer, eds. *Law and Force in the New International Order.* Boulder, CO: Westview Press, 1991.

Daniel, Donald C. F., et. al. *Coercive Inducement and the Containment of International Crises.* Washington, DC: U.S. Institute of Peace Press, 1999.

Dinan, Desmond. *Encyclopedia of the European Union.* Boulder: Lynne Rienner, 1998.

Doxey, Margaret P. *International Sanctions in Contemporary Perspective.* New York: St. Martin's Press, 1987.

Durch, William J., ed. *UN Peacekeeping, American Politics, and the Uncivil Wars of the 1990s.* New York: St. Martin's Press, 1996.

———, and Barry M. Blechman. *Keeping the Peace: The United Nations in the Emerging World Order.* Washington, DC: The Henry L. Stimson Center, 1992.

Finkelstein, Marina S., and Lawrence S. Finkelstein, eds. *Collective Security.* San Francisco: Chandler Publishing, 1966.

Goodrich, Leland M., and Anne P. Simons. *The United Nations and the Maintenance of International Peace and Security.* Washington, DC: Brookings Institution, 1955.

Gordenker, Leon, and Thomas G. Weiss, eds. *Soldiers, Peacekeepers and Disasters.* London: Macmillan, 1991.

Higgins, Rosalyn. *United Nations Peacekeeping, Documents and Commentary.* 4 vols. London: Oxford University Press, 1969–81.

Ishiyama, John T., and Marijke Breuning. *Ethnopolitics in the "New Europe."* Boulder: Lynne Rienner, 1998.

James, Alan. *Peacekeeping in International Politics.* London: Macmillan in association with the International Institute for Strategic Studies, 1990.

Lepgold, Joseph, and Thomas G. Weiss, eds. *Collective Conflict Management and Changing World Politics*. Albany: SUNY Press, 1997.

Mackinlay, John. *The Peacekeepers: An Assessment of Peacekeeping Operations at the Arab-Israeli Interface*. London: Unwin Hyman, 1989.

Mills, Susan R. *The Financing of United Nations Peacekeeping Operations*. Occasional Paper No. 3. New York: International Peace Academy, 1989.

Murphy, John F. *The United Nations and the Control of International Violence: A Legal and Political Analysis*. Totowa, NJ: Allanheld, Osmun, 1982.

Otunnu, Olara A., and Michael W. Doyle. *Peacemaking and Peacekeeping for the New Century*. Lanham, D: Rowman and Littlefield Publishers, 1998.

Rhodes, Carolyn. *The European Union in the World Community*. Boulder: Lynne Rienner, 1998.

Rikhye, Indar Jit. *The Theory and Practice of Peacekeeping*. London: C. Hurst and Company for the International Peace Academy, 1984.

———, and Kjell Skjelsbaek, eds. *The United Nations and Peacekeeping: Results, Limitations and Prospects—The Lessons of 40 Years Experience*. New York: St. Martin's Press, 1991.

Rosner, Gabriella E. *The United Nations Emergency Force*. New York: Columbia University Press, 1963.

Royal Institute of International Affairs. *International Sanctions*. London: Oxford University Press, 1938.

Skogmo, Bjorn. *UNIFIL: International Peacekeeping in Lebanon, 1978–1988*. Boulder, CO: Lynne Rienner Publishers, 1989.

United Nations. *The Blue Helmets*. 2nd ed. New York: UNDPI, 1990.

———. *The United Nations and the Maintenance of International Peace and Security*. United Nations Institute for Training and Research. Dordrecht: Martinus Nijhoff Publishers, 1987.

Urquhart, Brian. *A Life in Peace and War*. New York: Harper & Row, Publishers, 1987.

Wainhouse, David W. *International Peace Observation: A History and Forecast*. Baltimore: Johns Hopkins University Press, 1966.

Weiss, Thomas. *The United Nations and Civil Wars*. Boulder: Lynne Rienner, 1995.

Weiss, Thomas G., and Jarat Chopra. *United Nations Peacekeeping: An ACUNS Teaching Text*. The Academic Council on the United Nations System, Reports and Papers 1992–1.

Wesley, Michael. *Casualties of the New World Order: The Causes of Failure of UN Missions to Civil Wars*. New York: St. Martin's Press, 1997.

White, N. D. *The United Nations and the Maintenance of International Peace and Security*. New York: Manchester University Press, 1990.

# 6

## THE SETTLEMENT OF
## INTERNATIONAL DISPUTES

Collective security was never seen as the answer to all global problems of peace and security. Whatever the deterrent effect of UN enforcement machinery, many underlying sources of international tension and conflict would still exist. Countries would continue to have disputes with one another, with the ever-present possibility that some of them might get out of hand and lead to violence. The UN Charter acknowledges this problem by encouraging states to use existing methods of peaceful settlement and by providing additional options through the United Nations.

Before examining the UN role in the pacific settlement of disputes, this chapter will briefly describe the traditional settlement procedures that have become an accepted part of international law and practice and through which most disputes are settled. We will then look at UN practice to see what it has added to the procedures and machinery already available. This includes an appraisal of the International Court of Justice, which technically is a principal organ of the United Nations but renders decisions independent of the other organs. A subsequent section will examine a sampling of disputes before the General Assembly and Security Council to illustrate how the system operates in practice, including its capabilities and limitations. A concluding section will render judgment on the UN's performance in dispute settlement.

## PROCEDURES FOR SETTLING
## INTERNATIONAL DISPUTES

The international norm of peaceful settlement is set forth in Article 2, paragraph 1, of the UN Charter, which states, "All Members shall settle their international disputes by peaceful means in such a manner that international peace and security, and justice, are not endangered." On its face the injunction to settle appears obligatory, but in fact no UN organ has authority to require states to settle a dispute or to accept any particular form of settlement. A dispute could go unresolved indefinitely without constituting a Charter violation. The obligation, rather, is to *try* peaceful settlement and, in any event, not to seek resolution of a controversy by use of violence.

Most of the common procedures for settlement of international disputes are cataloged in Article 33, paragraph 1, of the Charter:

> The parties to any dispute, the continuance of which is likely to endanger the maintenance of international peace and security, shall, first of all, seek a solution by negotiation, enquiry, mediation, conciliation, arbitration, judicial settlement, resort to regional agencies or arrangements, or other peaceful means of their choice.

All of these techniques of dispute resolution were embodied in international law and practice well before the advent of the United Nations. The Charter merely recognizes their existence and encourages their use. The procedure of "good offices," to be discussed shortly, is another time-honored approach to dispute settlement. Unlike the procedures listed in Article 33, which parties to a dispute are urged to use, good offices depends entirely on the initiative of third parties.

Except for negotiation, each of the procedures requires the assistance of third parties, that is, persons not directly involved in the dispute. Most are also *political* rather than *judicial* modes of settlement, in the sense that parties are left free to accept or reject proposed settlements, as their interests dictate and their capacities permit. Third-party assistance is concerned primarily with finding some common ground where agreement can be reached. Arbitration and judicial settlement, however, are in the judicial mode because (1) the basis of decision is supposed to be international law rather than national interest and power, and (2) the decisions are legally binding on the parties that accept these settlement procedures in a particular case.

*Negotiation* among parties to a dispute is older than the state system and is the most common method of settlement. It involves direct discussion by official representatives of the states concerned, for the purpose of reaching agreement on matters at issue. Successful negotiation normally requires a good faith effort to achieve compromise solutions that serve the national interests of all parties.

*Good offices* (not mentioned in Article 33) is the name given to friendly assistance rendered by a third party for the purpose of bringing disputants together so that they may seek to reach a settlement. Good offices may be tendered by a state (through an official representative), a group of states, or even an individual of international standing such as the UN Secretary-General. The third-party representative meets with each disputant separately but may, with consent, convey messages between them. Technically, good offices are limited to facilitating negotiation by the states directly concerned and do not include discussion of substantive issues. Good offices are particularly useful where the disputing parties have broken off diplomatic relations or where negotiations have been interrupted and neither side takes the initiative to resume them, out of pride or out of fear that such action would be an indication of weakness.

*Mediation* occurs when the third party actively participates in the discussion of substantive issues and offers proposals for settlement. If the disputants are not speaking, the mediator may also tender good offices as a prelude to mediation. The mediator may meet with the parties either separately or jointly and is expected to maintain an attitude of impartiality throughout. She can expect little success unless she enjoys the confidence of all parties. Her proposals are suggestions only, with no binding force on any party. Disputants are of course free to reject an offer to mediate.

*Enquiry,* or *inquiry,* may be used when the disputing parties are unable or unwilling to agree on points of fact relating to a controversy but are willing to let an impartial commission investigate and report on the facts. The parties need not accept the findings of the inquiry, but they usually do. The inquiry is limited to findings of fact and does not include proposed terms of settlement. Many international disputes hinge on disputed questions of fact, and inquiry may be a means of lowering tensions as well as reducing the area of disagreement.

*Conciliation* is a procedure for settling a dispute by referring it to a commission, or occasionally a single conciliator, charged to examine the facts and recommend a solution that the parties are free to accept or reject. Conciliation is more formal and less flexible than mediation. Whereas mediation is a continuing process of assisting negotiations among parties to a dispute, conciliation involves formal submission of the dispute to a conciliation body in anticipation of a final report containing the conciliator's findings and recommendations for settlement. The boundaries between the two tend to blur in practice because the conciliator usually confers informally with the parties, hoping to find an area of agreement. Moreover. in UN parlance, such terms as mediation, conciliation, and good offices are frequently used without careful reference to the legal distinctions among them. Thus a UN conciliator may in reality be a mediator who also finds it necessary to render good offices and never has occasion to publish a formal recommendation for settlement.

*Arbitration* is a procedure by which disputants agree to submit a controversy to judges of their own choosing, who render a legally binding decision based on principles of international law. Commonly each side names one or two arbitrators, and those two or four designate one additional arbitrator to complete the panel. The essential characteristics of arbitration are (1) free choice of judges (arbitrators), (2) respect for international law, and (3) obligation to comply with the award. The parties frequently stipulate in the arbitral agreement (*compromis*) the particular rules of law or equity, or even special rules, that are to be applied. The parties are relieved of their obligation to accept or carry out the award only if the arbitrators disregard instructions laid down in the *compromis*. Arbitration is at least as old as the Greek city-states, and within the modern state system it enjoyed a substantial renaissance during the nineteenth and early twentieth centuries. Since 1945 arbitration has been used extensively in resolving trade and investment disputes but less frequently to resolve political disputes between states. Some exceptions may be noted, however. The Rann of Kutch arbitration between India and Pakistan in 1965–66 brought a peaceful end to a violent confrontation over a swampy borderland near the Arabian Sea. Iran's seizure in 1979 of the United States embassy in Tehran and the confinement of its staff for forty-four months, caused a severe rupture in the relations of the two nations. The release of the American hostages in 1981, however, led to the establishment of the U.S.-Iran Claims Tribunal, which subsequently arbitrated hundreds of claims. By 1990, the Tribunal had awarded more than $6 billion to U.S. citizens, corporations, and banks, while more than $1 billion was paid to the government of Iran and its citizens. Still another contentious dispute between Chile and Argentina was resolved through a Vatican-assisted arbitration when in 1984 Argentina accepted Chilean sovereignty over islands in the Beagle Channel. Chile in turn yielded to Argentina's claim on the Atlantic side of Cape Horn, thus ending their 100-year-old controversy.

*Judicial settlement* or *adjudication,* like arbitration, produces legally binding awards or judgments based on rules of international law. Unlike arbitration, however, the judges are not chosen by the parties for their particular case but are members of a preconstituted international tribunal. Settlement of disputes by international courts is based on voluntary acceptance by the parties, either through advance agreement to accept the jurisdiction of the court in special types of cases or through agreement at the time the dispute is submitted. The same is generally true of arbitration. The International Court of Justice (ICJ) and its predecessor from League of Nations days, the Permanent Court of International Justice, provide the principal examples of judicial settlement at the global level. The League Court was not widely used, and the ICJ docket has until recently been even less crowded. Decisions have generally been carried out, but no effective means have been available to enforce Court decisions against a few recalcitrants that have ignored their obligation to comply. Noncompliance is most common in cases involving controversies over the Court's jurisdiction. At the regional level the Court of Justice of the European Union has been an extensively used and highly successful organ of judicial settlement.

## UN PRACTICE

The Charter provides broad authorization for UN involvement in any dispute serious enough to threaten international peace and security. Although the Security Council is given preeminence, the General Assembly is also authorized to consider peace and security questions. The Assembly may not, however, make any recommendation as long as the Security Council is exercising jurisdiction over a question. A dispute may be submitted to the Council or the Assembly by one of the parties, by any member of the United Nations, or by the Secretary-General. Neither body can *impose* a final settlement on any party to a dispute, but the Charter places no limits on UN organs in *recommending* procedures or terms of settlement.

UN organs utilize most of the traditional techniques of dispute settlement, and submission of a dispute to the Security Council or the Assembly has something in common with the procedure of conciliation. The United Nations becomes a third party that examines the facts of the dispute and renders a decision that the parties are free to accept or reject. But the UN political setting and procedures make the process considerably different from traditional forms of conciliation. Recourse to conciliation generally assumes that both sides are willing to submit the issue to an impartial commission in hope of finding an acceptable compromise. Most disputes before the United Nations, however, come not as agreed submissions but as complaints brought by one party against another or by a third state without necessarily obtaining the consent of either party to the dispute.

The United Nations, moreover, is not always impartial toward the disputes brought before it. Its members can be highly partisan and are often bitterly divided. Complaints are frequently brought there, not for the purpose of seeking an agreed compromise, but to legitimize the position of one side or the other. The parties themselves participate in the discussion and may be more interested in scoring debating points before the bar of world opinion than in honestly seeking common ground for agreement. Such exchanges may widen the gulf between them, harden their positions, and inflame rather than repair relations. The public nature of UN debate facilitates the appeal to world opinion but often at the expense of viable compromise that might emerge from the privacy and quiet deliberation of traditional conciliation.

The UN process thus is *sui generis,* a new approach to dispute settlement having strengths as well as weaknesses. The public debate pattern is only part of the picture, and even that is not wholly negative. Public debate makes UN members aware of the conflicting positions and sometimes helps clarify facts. Although speeches and supporting documentation submitted by the parties are mostly self-serving versions of the case, they can be informative as well. Public debate also provides governments with a way to "blow off steam," particularly in situations where an objectionable act has been committed, no redress is in sight, and retaliation is not feasible. When Soviet troops occupied Afghanistan, and when Soviet aircraft shot down a civilian airliner over the Sea of Japan, denunciation in the United Nations was a way for the United States to express outrage, uphold principle, and score a few propaganda points at little cost or risk. When the *USS Vincennes* mistakenly downed an unarmed Iranian airbus over the Strait of Hormuz, Iran had the satisfaction of publicly excoriating the United States before the Security Council. Giving and receiving public denunciation is of course not limited to large states.

On a more positive note, UN consideration serves the further purpose of legitimizing the involvement of other states that may sometimes be able to exert a moderating influence on the disputants. In the days before the UN anticolonial majority became automatic, the United States frequently used its influence in the United Nations to steer parties to colonial disputes away from extreme positions.

## THE SECURITY COUNCIL

The Security Council has firmly established its preeminence among UN organs in the field of peace and security. During the early postwar years the United

States was the prime mover in an effort to enhance the security role of the General Assembly as a means of overcoming the Soviet veto in the Security Council. The effort was so successful that during the early 1950s the Council sometimes went months without discussing a substantive question. The shift of activity away from the Council was only temporary, however. The growing numbers and solidarity of Third World countries undermined U.S. dominance in the Assembly and made the Security Council a relatively more attractive forum for the United States. It became clear that U.S. as well as Soviet interests might require the protection of the great power veto. These developments paved the way for the reemergence of the Security Council as the central security organ of the United Nations. This resurgence was hastened by the Council's inherent advantages over the Assembly stemming from its smaller size, its capacity to function continuously, and the primacy assigned to it by the UN Charter.

Although the United Nations appears to thrive on the high visibility of public debate, the more significant work of the organization is conducted in quiet consultation and negotiation, and this is certainly true in the case of the Security Council. The delegates tend to follow working procedures that involve prudent and careful preparation, and the day to day contact between members allows for a range of interactions that are both formal and informal. Moreover, the assistance provided by staff and senior members of the Secretariat, sometimes, even by the Secretary-General, has proven of vital importance in the conduct of effective diplomacy. Much of the Security Council's work involves such quiet diplomacy and if the parties to a dispute are prepared to seek counsel, they generally find Council members agreeable to procedures that are aimed at avoiding embarrassment and maximizing results.

The Security Council is not obligated to discuss every complaint that a state chooses to submit to it, and potentially inflammatory debate may sometimes be avoided by prior consultation and informal decision not to place an item before the Council. Occasionally the Council has discussed a proposal to inscribe an item on its agenda but failed to obtain the necessary votes to do so. A decision by the Council to discuss a peace and security matter is considered a "procedural question" and thus not subject to the veto.

When the Security Council decides to consider a dispute or a threatening situation, numerous techniques are available for dealing with it. Whatever is said in the debating chamber, members of the Council usually approach the parties quietly to explore the possibilities for agreed settlement. Sometimes debate is adjourned, at least temporarily, while exploratory discussions are conducted. Quick agreement on a solution to the underlying substantive dispute is uncommon, but an understanding is frequently reached as to the appropriate limits of Security Council action. The understanding may be that the Council will adjourn without adopting a formal resolution, or will simply urge the parties to seek a solution by negotiation or other peaceful means. However, this was not done following India and Pakistan's testing of nuclear weapons in May 1998. Meeting in an emergency session in June, the Council ignored all the subtleties of diplomacy when it demanded, by unanimous vote, that both countries refrain from further testing, that they halt their weapons programs, and that they sign with due haste the nuclear control agreements, i.e., the Nuclear Non-Proliferation Treaty and the Comprehensive Nuclear Test Ban Treaty. Moreover, the Security Council resolution denied both India and Pakistan legal status as nuclear powers, hence preventing the two countries from acquiring the legal and formal status as nuclear weapons powers under terms of the 1970 nonproliferation treaty. India's indignation was obvious when it quickly denounced the Security Council resolution, calling it "coercive and unhelpful." The Indian foreign ministry said the Security Council action was "grotesque" and it questioned how an organ of the United Nations could address India in so condescending a manner. The Pakistan government was no less outspoken, accusing the major powers of using the nuclear treaties "to legitimize their own possession of huge nuclear arsenals," while denying others the same sovereign right. The Pakistani delegation informed the Council that nonproliferation is no longer an issue in South Asia. The "real danger" now, was not proliferation but "nuclear conflict," and no amount of "sermonizing and lamentations can rectify or reverse" what was now a reality. Although approving the resolution, a number of non-nuclear states were moved to support the argument made by the South Asian nations that it was time for the permanent members of the Security Council, all of whom were nuclear weapons powers, to seriously reduce their own stockpiles. Seldom had the Security Council been so challenged, nor was it lost on all the major actors that the entire system of global nuclear controls was threatened and that an arms race more unpredictable and more deadly than any experienced during the Cold War was in the offing. In the superheated environment, the Pakistan ambassador to the United Nations insisted his country reserved the right to deter aggression by conventional or non-conventional means, and the Security Council was urged to accept the reality of a new worldwide power equation and alter its procedures accordingly.[1]

Sometimes more than discussion and resolutions are called for by the situation or demanded by members of the Council. The Secretary-General can be authorized to appoint a mediator or to consult with the parties and mediate himself as circumstances permit. The Council may occasionally create a special commission of inquiry or conciliation body to deal with the problem. Alternatively, the dispute may be referred to an appropriate regional organization, such as the Organization of American States or the Organization of African Unity. If hostilities seem imminent, the Council or its President may urge the parties to refrain from taking any action that might aggravate the dispute. Should fighting break out, the Council will in all likelihood issue an order for a cease-fire. If one party has occupied the territory of another, the cease-fire order may be accompanied by an order for troop withdrawal. In a number of situations the Security Council has authorized peacekeeping forces and observer missions to help police a cease-fire and prevent violence that might further aggravate the dispute.

When the Security Council speaks, the disputants do not always listen. In his 1982 report on the work of the United Nations, Secretary-General Pérez de Cuéllar lamented that the Council's resolutions "are increasingly defied or ignored by those that feel themselves strong enough to do so." [2] Although respect for the Council's authority has grown since then, there is still substance to this lament. Israel, perhaps the most frequent target of Security Council censure, has repeatedly disregarded Council resolutions that were in conflict with its national interests. South Africa did the same for many years, as have many other countries in pursuit of their own interests. For example, in the spring of 1982 Argentina ignored a Security Council demand for a cease-fire in the Falklands; and, until 1988, Iraq and Iran persistently flouted Council requests to terminate hostilities. In the 1990–91 Gulf crisis, Iraq rejected numerous Security Council calls for withdrawal from Kuwait, yielding only to superior military force.

Nevertheless, disregard of Security Council recommendations is not undertaken lightly. This is true even of states that sometimes disregard them. According to a former director-general of Israel's Foreign Ministry, Israeli actions in times of crisis have been heavily influenced by anticipation of what the Security Council might do. In his words,

> Throughout the thirty years of conflict the estimated timing of intervention by the Security Council in the fighting had engaged the closest attention of the military planners of both sides. Strategists and field commanders planned and conducted their campaigns virtually with an eye on the ticking of the United Nations clock. They accelerated the advance or slowed down the retreat of their forces in synchronization with the movements of the clock's hands. The ringing of the Security Council bell was never absent from their mind because they knew that military means would not finally decide the outcome of the conflict. [3]

Israel's concern was no doubt justified by the history of active Security Council intervention in the Middle East, as well as Israel's dependence on U.S. support, which might be alienated if Israel ignored Council actions taken with the approval of the United States. Argentina, Iran, and Iraq, on the other hand, anticipated that Council intervention in their wars would go no farther than harsh words. In its Kuwait adventure Iraq proved badly mistaken. And, certainly, words alone would never have dislodged Saddam Hussein from Kuwait. But even words can sometimes have an impact. To disregard them risks disapproval of the international community, which no state wantonly invites.

## THE GENERAL ASSEMBLY

The General Assembly has also been extensively involved in disputes among UN members, but since it is a very large public forum, its debates and decisions are better adapted to legitimizing the position of one side or another than to promoting a negotiated settlement. During the first ten years of the United Nations, the Assembly overshadowed the Security Council as a forum for airing disputes and threats to the peace. This enhancement of the Assembly's security role occurred mainly as a U.S.-led response to Soviet vetoes in the Security Council. Even then, the most obvious function of the Assembly was legitimizing U.S. and Western positions rather than promoting agreed settlement of the issues.

Although the Assembly has since relinquished its primacy to the Security Council, security questions still make up a substantial part of its agenda. Issues relating to the Middle East and southern Africa have predominated from year to year, but conflicts in Cambodia, Grenada, Central America, the Falkland Islands, Afghanistan, Bosnia, Croatia, Kosovo and elsewhere have found their way to the Assembly as well as to the Security Council. Now, however, the Assembly tends to legitimize Third World positions rather than Western positions on the issues when the two are in conflict. In nearly all instances it lends legitimacy to demands for peaceful settlement.

The legitimization approach to dispute settlement, whether indulged in by the Security Council or the Assembly, is often more than a propaganda exercise or a shouting match. If consensus is high, the offending party may look for ways to bring its conduct more into line with the views of the majority without compromising its vital interests. Numerous disputes arising out of the decolonization process have been considered by the Assembly, and progress toward self-government and independence was undoubtedly hastened by diplomatic pressures mobilized in the Assembly.

Occasionally the Assembly has been able to play a third-party role extending beyond legitimization. It authorized peacekeeping operations that helped defuse the 1956 Suez crisis, for example, and it facilitated West Irian's transition from Dutch to Indonesian rule in 1962–63. It took over control of the UN Congo force in 1960 when the Security Council became deadlocked. It fielded a border watch team in Greece from 1947 to 1952 and in Korea prior to the outbreak of the Korean War. Since the West Irian mission, however, the authorization of field missions for security purposes has become the exclusive province of the Security Council.

The Assembly can enlist the services of its President or one of its officers in promoting quiet negotiations among disputing parties. It can formally appoint a UN mediator to assist the parties in reaching agreement, as it did in the early stages of the Arab-Israeli conflict, although mediation is now more likely to be undertaken by the Secretary-General and the Security Council. Like the Security Council, the Assembly has authorized and supported the Secretary-General's peacemaking efforts in the Falklands War, Afghanistan, the Iran-Iraq War, southern Africa, Cyprus, Palestine, Lebanon, and other conflict situations. The convening of the General Assembly each year also provides occasion for high-level diplomatic representatives of most countries to gather in New York and, if they choose, to meet privately for the exchange of views and the resolution of differences.

## THE SECRETARY-GENERAL

The Secretary-General—at the direction of the Council or the Assembly, on his own initiative, or at the request of a party—is a very important UN dispute settlement resource. His operations as a third-party intermediary, acting personally or through a special representative or mediator, are generally carried on without the disadvantages of great publicity and public debate. His purposes are also more exclusively focused on settlement, in contrast to the substantive biases that frequently motivate governmental representatives to UN bodies. Where there is genuine room for agreement, the Secretary-General can perform an effective third-party role. The political role of the Secretary-General was discussed in Chapter 4.

## THE UNITED NATIONS AND REGIONAL DISPUTE SETTLEMENT

The United Nations was not expected to handle every international dispute that might endanger international peace and security. Article 33 of the Charter urges disputants first to "seek a solution" through "peaceful means of their own choice," including "resort to regional agencies or arrangements." Since 1945 regional organizations have become an important supplement to UN procedures for pacific settlement. A 1987 study found that four regional agencies— the Organization of American States, the Organization of African Unity, the Arab League, and the Council of Europe—had dealt with a total of 90 disputes from 1945 to 1984, compared with 159, for the United Nations during the same period.[4]

There are no clear guidelines for determining whether a dispute should be handled by a regional organization or by the United Nations. A dominant state within a region might prefer to have intraregional disputes settled locally, where it has greater control, but one of the parties often sees a political advantage in appealing to the United Nations. Until the mid-1960s the United States had considerable success in keeping hemispheric disputes within the Organization of American States. Thereafter inter-American controversies began to appear frequently on UN agendas, usually over a U.S. objection. Since 1988, the United States has accepted a greater UN role in the Americas and supported the establishment of UN observer missions in Central America. The Arab League has always had trouble keeping its quarrels at home because the issues have been so divisive. The Organization of African Unity, embracing the vast expanse of the African continent and its associated islands, also finds consensus difficult to achieve.

The techniques of dispute settlement used by regional organizations do not differ significantly from those used by the United Nations. Good offices, inquiry, informal mediation, conciliation, formal debate, adoption of resolutions, cease-fire pleas—the whole gamut of approaches is available. Regional organizations have even resorted to various forms of "peacekeeping" by a military presence. The Organization of American States authorized a peacekeeping force in the

1965 Dominican crisis, although the OAS action was largely a post hoc ratication of U.S. military intervention. The Arab League established a peacekeeping force in Kuwait from 1961 to 1963, mostly Egyptian and Saudi Arabian troops, to ward off the threat of an Iraqi attack. In 1976, the Arab League legitimized Syrian intervention in Lebanon's civil strife by creating an Arab League force dominated by Syrians. The Organization of African Unity fielded an abortive peacekeeping force in Chad for two months in early 1980 and for a six-month period in 1981 and 1982. The force was withdrawn with no appreciable effect on the shifting tides of revolution and outside intervention in Chad. In 1990 the Economic Community of West African States sent a peacekeeping force of 7,000 to curb the violence of Liberia's civil war. ECOWAS and the Organization of African Unity continued to operate alongside UN peacekeeping observers from 1993 to 1997, when the latter mission was phased out. ECOWAS and the OAU, however, continued their patrols of the country. Commonwealth of Independent States (CIS) forces were deployed in Georgia and Tajikistan following the break-up of the Soviet Union, and the subsequent civil strife in those new republics. Given the volatility in both countries, CIS presence was anticipated to carry into the twenty-first century. Perhaps the most noted intervention by a regional organization, however, was NATO's replacement of the United Nations UNPROFOR mission in 1995. NATO's sustained role in Bosnia in the late 1990s was supposed to provide the kind of security UNPROFOR had failed to accomplish, and NATO's role was formally acknowledged and sanctioned by the Security Council. By the same token, the Organization of Security and Cooperation in Europe offered its good offices in a desperate but futile attempt at reconciling Serbian and native Albanian demands in Kosovo province. In 1998 NATO injected its presence into the Kosovo dispute as a last resort. Although Kosovo, unlike Bosnia, was considered an integral part of Serbia, NATO was called upon by the American and European governments to help ensure a diplomatic settlement in the region. Neither NATO diplomacy or threats impressed the Milosovic government in Belgrade, and with the situation in Kosovo deteriorating, in March 1999 NATO launched widespread and sustained air strikes against Serbian targets. NATO force proved no more successful in forcing a quick settlement. In fact the Serbs accelerated their ethnic cleansing campaign against the Kosovar Albanians, and by May almost one million had been forced to take refuge in neighboring countries. The Security Council was now seriously divided on the use of codeployment and its jurisdiction and legality. Moreover, the accidental NATO bombing of China's Belgrade Embassy in May deeply divided the Council's permanent members and put the codeployment principle to its most severe test.

## JUDICIAL DISPUTE SETTLEMENT

As noted in Chapter 2, the International Court of Justice is named in the UN Charter as one of the six principal organs of the United Nations, its budget is included within the regular UN budget, and its fifteen members are selected by action of the Security Council and the General Assembly. All UN members are ipso facto parties to the ICJ Statute. The Court nevertheless performs its judicial duties independently of the other UN organs and is supposed to reach its decisions on the basis of international law rather than international politics. Although its decisions apply only to the parties and do not constitute precedents binding on others, its opinions—like those of the League Court before it—have been recognized as important statements of existing international law. Only states may apply to and appear before the Court. The states members of the United Nations (numbering 185 in 1999), and two states not members (Nauru and Switzerland) that have become parties to the Court's Statute, are also entitled to use the Court.

The procedure followed by the Court in contentious cases is defined in its Statute, and in Rules of the Court that have been adopted under the Statute. The Rules currently in force were adopted in April 1978. Court proceedings include a written phase in which the parties file and exchange pleadings, and an oral phase consisting of public hearings at which agents and counsels address the Court. Because the Court functions in two official languages (English and French), whatever is written or presented orally must be translated into one or the other. Following the oral proceedings, the Court deliberates privately and later will deliver its judgment in a public proceeding. The Court's judgment is final and without appeal, and a state or states that fail to comply may have the matter of their noncompliance brought before the Security Council by the party favored by the judgment. The Court operates as a full Court, but at the request of the parties it may establish a special chamber. The Court constituted a special chamber in 1982 for the first time, and followed with another in 1985, and two more in 1987. A Chamber of Summary Procedure, however, is elected every year by the Court in accordance with its Statute. In July 1993 the Court also established a seven-member Chamber to deal with any environmental cases falling within its jurisdiction.

In twenty-five years of its existence, 1921–46, the League Court rendered decisions in thirty-two cases and gave twenty-seven advisory opinions at the request of League organs. This was not a heavy caseload and the ICJ has been no busier. From 1946 through March 1998, the Court entertained just sixty-nine "contentious" cases (actions by one state against another). Thirty-four cases were filed from 1947 to 1960, but only twelve more in the next twenty years. A modest resurgence occurred after 1980, with twenty-three additional filings between 1981 and March 1998. The total number of Court judgments on disputes concerning *inter alia* land frontiers and maritime boundaries, territorial sovereignty, the non-use of force, non-interference in the internal affairs of states, diplomatic relations, hostage-taking, the right of asylum, nationality, guardianship, rights of passage, and economic rights, was sixty (with nine pending) by March 1998.

In addition, since 1946 the Court has been called to issue twenty-three advisory opinions at the request of UN agencies. The advisory procedure is open solely to international organizations, and the only bodies currently authorized to request advisory opinions are the six principal organs of the United Nations and the sixteen specialized agencies of the UN system. Requests for advisory opinions can be made in writing or orally, and the Court's procedures follow that used in contentious cases, as well as applicable law. Unlike judgments in contentious cases, the Court's advisory opinions are consultative and hence not binding. Advisory opinions can be made binding, however, if the instruments or regulations that call for the advisory opinion contain specific advance notification. The twenty-three advisory opinions rendered by the Court up to March 1998 were concerned *inter alia* with admission to UN membership, reparation for injuries suffered in the service of the United Nations, the territorial status of South-West Africa (Namibia) and the Western Sahara, judgments rendered by international administrative tribunals, expenses of certain United Nations operations, and the applicability of the United Nations Headquarters Agreement. Two advisory opinions were made in July 1996 in response to a request made by the World Health Organization (WHO) on the *Legality of the Use by a State of Nuclear Weapons in Armed Conflict,* and a request made by the United Nations General Assembly on the *Legality of the Threat or Use of Nuclear Weapons.* Another in 1998 unanimously called upon the United States to postpone the execution of a Paraguayan citizen who had been sentenced to death in Virginia. The argument was that the defendant's government had not been consulted and thus was denied the opportunity to provide legal counsel under terms of established international treaty law. In the latter, the U.S. and the state of Virginia, although acknowledging the government had *not* complied with the Vienna Convention aimed at protecting nationals charged with crimes in other countries, ignored the ruling and proceeded with the execution. A somewhat similar case was brought before the Court by Germany in March 1999. Germany charged the United States with violations of the Vienna Convention on Consular Relations (1963) after the state of Arizona executed a German national and was about to put another, a brother of the deceased, to death. The two brothers had been charged and found guilty of killing a bank manager in the course of a robbery in Arizona. Germany maintained that the two men were tried and sentenced without being advised of their rights to consular assistance, as required by the Vienna Convention. Germany argued the failure to provide the required notification precluded it from protecting its nationals' interest in the United States at both the trial and the appeal level in the state courts. The German action did not spare the life of the second brother who was executed on schedule, but the German government insisted on pressing its case against the United States, and cited Article 1 of the Vienna Convention's Optional Protocol which states the International Court of Justice had the jurisdiction to resolve the dispute between the United States and Germany on the interpretation or application of the Convention.

There are a number of reasons why the World Court has been used so sparingly. The most obvious reason is its limited jurisdiction. Only states—not individuals or organizations—can be parties to a dispute before the Court. A private claimant cannot be represented there unless he can persuade his own government to plead his cause. Requests for advisory opinions may be submitted only by the General Assembly, by the Security Council, or by other UN organs or specialized agencies previously authorized by the Assembly to make such requests on legal questions pertaining to their activities. Thus the number of entities entitled to invoke the jurisdiction of the Court is strictly limited.

A still more stringent limitation on use of the Court is the requirement that all parties consent to the Court's jurisdiction. The complaining state (the "applicant") signifies consent by its act of submitting the dispute to the Court, and the respondent state may of course consent at that time by special agreement or by filing a response accepting jurisdiction. But agreed submissions to the Court after a dispute has arisen are not numerous. Few defendants in a civil suit would appear in national courts if they were not required to do so, and very few plaintiffs would file lawsuits if the courts could not compel the defendant to respond. Lacking any general compulsory jurisdiction, the World Court is in precisely that position: Few applications are filed because the country complained against can usually ignore the Court if it wishes.

The docket would be even shorter if the Statute did not provide for methods of consent conferring a limited degree of compulsory jurisdiction on the Court. This is done by permitting states to give consent *before* a dispute has occurred, through treaty or other agreement accepting the Court's jurisdiction for a specified class of cases that might arise in the future. For example, an optional protocol to the 1961 Vienna Convention on Diplomatic Relations provides that disputes arising out of the interpretation or application of the Convention fall within the compulsory jurisdiction of the Court. Any party to the protocol may invoke the jurisdiction of the Court against any other party in that class of cases. This optional protocol allowed the Court in 1979 to entertain the U.S. claim that Iran had violated the Vienna Convention by holding U.S. diplomatic personnel hostage in the Tehran embassy. Iran denied the Court's jurisdiction at the time of the U.S. application, but the Court nevertheless took jurisdiction because of Iran's prior consent in ratifying the protocol. The United States also claimed jurisdiction for the Court under a bilateral treaty between the United States and Iran because the treaty had a dispute settlement clause conferring jurisdiction on the Court. Other bilateral or multilateral treaties similarly confer jurisdiction on the Court, although they are seldom invoked.

The ICJ Statute provides a further avenue for states to grant compulsory jurisdiction to the Court by depositing a declaration to that effect with the Secretary-General of the United Nations. Because no state is required to do so, this provision (Article 36, Section 2) is commonly known as the "optional clause." It applies only between states that have made the optional declaration, but for them it extends the Court's jurisdiction to a very broad range of cases. In the words of the Statute, it includes

all legal disputes concerning

a. the interpretation of a treaty;
b. any question of international law;
c. the existence of any fact, which, if established, would constitute a breach of an international obligation;

d. the nature or extent of the reparation to be made for the breach of an international obligation.

As of March 1998, the requisite declaration was in force for fifty-nine parties to the Statute.

In accepting the optional obligation, many states have given with one hand and taken away with the other by attaching reservations that substantially limit the scope of the jurisdiction accepted. The most common reservation is to exclude disputes within the domestic jurisdiction of the state concerned. An extreme form of this reservation is illustrated by the U.S. declaration of acceptance in 1946, which excepted "disputes with regard to matters which are essentially within the domestic jurisdiction of the United States *as determined by the United States of America.*" The italicized phrase, added on the floor of the U.S. Senate as the so-called Connally amendment, greatly weakened the acceptance by allowing the United States rather than the Court to determine the existence of domestic jurisdiction. Because of the reciprocity principle recognized by the Court, other states could invoke the same exception against the United States if the United States brought an action against one of them. Several other countries have adopted similar "self-judging" reservations. For the United States, the reservation became moot on April 7, 1986, when the United States officially withdrew its declaration of acceptance following a six-month notice of termination. Its withdrawal was prompted by the Court's decision to entertain Nicaragua's complaint of U.S. intervention in support of the Nicaraguan Contras.

Another reason for the Court's scanty caseload is the expensive, time-consuming, and highly public nature of the Court's proceedings. Settling a dispute by quiet negotiations between the parties is much preferred. If the World Court is involved, the parties can expect at least a two-year wait between submission of the case and final judgment, and often longer. Legal action entails the time and expense of preparing memorials (legal briefs), exhibits, counter-memorials, replies, and supporting documents, as well as conducting a formal hearing with witnesses, expert testimony, and oral argument. The parties may then wait many months for the Court to render its decision. If preliminary decisions on jurisdictional questions or provisional orders are necessary, this argumentation process may occur more than once. The costs of legal counsel can run high, especially when—as is commonly done—private counsel is hired to assist with an ICJ proceeding. Common sense suggests settling in some quicker, cheaper way if at all possible. In recognition of this difficulty, the UN Secretary-General in 1989 established a trust fund to aid states lacking funds to employ expert legal counsel. On the other hand, even if the finances are available to press the case, if the dispute is not already a matter of serious public concern, submission to the Court might not only be an unnecessarily costly venture, it also could further disadvantage the state making the submission, especially if the controversy is between otherwise friendly states.

In the decades immediately following World War II, Third World states and the former Communist-bloc countries had additional reasons for avoiding the Court. International law evolved to accommodate the needs of a state system that was dominated by Europe and oriented to the status quo. Many new states believed that the international legal system inherited from European practice did not adequately reflect their needs and perspectives. The distinction was probably less one of geography than one of vested interests. Law tends to protect established rights and thus to work against demands for change by states in a less favored position. (See Table 6-1). Most cases brought before the Court during its first three decades were initiated by the Western states, but since that period, it has been the Third World nations that have found the Court an important instrument in their dealings with other, sometimes more powerful, states. The contentious cases brought before the Court since 1976 by the Third World countries far exceeds those originating with the more developed countries. The significance of this reversal in the use of the Court was dramatized in 1998 when the Court agreed to hear the complaint registered by the Government of Libya, which had resisted a United States and United Kingdom interpretation and application of the 1971 Montreal Convention arising from the aerial incident that caused the destruction of PanAm 103 over Lockerbie, Scotland, in December 1988. The United States and the United Kingdom, concerned with a loss of control over the decision process, and already pressing the international community to impose and sustain sanctions against Libya for its failure to yield for trial the persons accused of causing the incident, were clearly disturbed by the Court's action. Thus, because important interests are in conflict between the states, and because the stakes are usually judged to be very high, governments are most unwilling to risk an unfavorable decision by the Court. Although the ICJ continued to register the Libyan case on its docket, in April 1999, Tripoli finally yielded the two persons accused of perpetrating the bombing after a prior compromise agreement between Libya, the United Kingdom, the Netherlands, and the United States allowed the men to be tried in the Netherlands by Scottish jurists, operating under Scottish law.

Prolonging a dispute may be preferable to a settlement on unsatisfactory terms. In nonlegal approaches to dispute settlement, the parties remain the final judges of settlement terms, and matters of primary national interest are not compromised. In legal settlements, a majority of the judges make the decision, which is binding on the parties. In extreme circumstances a state might reject the award of the Court, but, given the legal obligation to comply with the decision, this can be done only at considerable diplomatic cost by any state that wishes to be known as law-abiding.

The unpredictability of judicial decisions is one aspect of the problem. Not all international law is uncertain, but the disputes most likely to be brought before an international court are those in which the relevant law or facts are uncertain. The numerous dissenting opinions reflect a wide divergence of opinion on the Court in many cases. Moreover, uncertainty in the law increases the

TABLE 6-1   International Court of Justice

*Current docket of the Court*

LIST OF PENDING CASES BEFORE THE COURT AND CURRENT STATUS

 1. Maritime Delimitation and Territorial Questions between Qatar and Bahrain *(Qatar v. Bahrain)*

 2. Questions of Interpretation and Application of the 1971 Montreal Convention arising from the Aerial Incident at Lockerbie *(Libyan Arab Jamahiriya v. United Kingdom)*

 3. Questions of Interpretation and Application of the 1971 Montreal Convention arising from the Aerial Incident at Lockerbie *(Libyan Arab Jamahiriya v. United States of America)*

 4. Oil Platforms *(Islamic Republic of Iran v. United States of America)*

 5. Application of the Convention on the Prevention and Punishment of the Crime of Genocide *(Bosnia and Herzegovina v. Yugoslavia)*

 6. Gabčíkovo-Nagymaros Project (Hungary/Slovakia)

 7. Land and Maritime Boundary between Cameroon and Nigeria *(Cameroon v. Nigeria)*

 8. Kasikili/Sedudu Island (Botswana/Namibia)

 9. Sovereignty over Pulau Ligitan and Pulau Sipadan (Indonesia/Malaysia)

10. Ahmadou Sadio Diallo *(Republic of Guinea v. Democratic Republic of the Congo)*

11. LaGrand *(Germany v. United States of America)*

12–21. Legality of the Use of Force ( *Yugoslavia v. Belgium, Canada, France, Germany, Italy, Netherlands, Portugal, Spain, United Kingdom, United States.* )

Registry of the Court Website, http://www.icj-cij.org/icjwww/idocket.htm

---

probability that a judge, consciously or unconsciously, may be influenced by political considerations.

But unpredictability is only half the problem. If uncertainty discourages advance acceptance of the Court's jurisdiction, certainty as to the applicable law may also discourage submission by the side with the weaker legal position. In either situation, loss of control over the outcome of the dispute, and consequent risk of injury to important interests, discourages submission to the Court. Under these circumstances the limited use of both the ICJ and its League predecessor is wholly understandable.

With such formidable deterrents to the use of the Court, one may reasonably ask why it is used at all. A close look at the cases submitted since 1945 reveals that the motivations are almost always intensely practical, having to do with specific questions of national interest rather than generalized allegiance to the ideal of a world governed by law. Recourse to the Court is often merely an incident in a larger process of bargaining and political conflict. A strong legal position can give the application some deterrent or harassment value against an antagonistic state, even if the Court ultimately fails to establish jurisdiction. This probably helps explain U.S. resort to the Court in three aerial incidents of the 1950s in which the Soviet Union twice and Bulgaria once were charged with illegally shooting down foreign aircraft. Undoubtedly it was also a factor in Nicaragua's 1984 decision to seek ICJ action on its complaint against the United States for mining Nicaraguan harbors and aiding Nicaraguan rebels, although the Court subsequently found jurisdiction in that case and, indeed, ruled in favor of Nicaragua.

Among friendly states, recourse to the Court may be a means of isolating a dispute to prevent it from tainting otherwise cordial relations. Australia and New Zealand had this consideration in mind when they asked the Court in 1973 to declare that French atmospheric nuclear testing in the South Pacific was illegal. That objective was largely achieved, even though France never admitted the competence of the Court to hear the case. France continued its testing during 1973 and again in 1995 before announcing its compliance with the Comprehensive Test Ban Treaty of 1996.

The outcome of the nuclear testing cases suggests another reason for initiating litigation—to encourage a negotiated settlement. Resort to the Court by Australia and New Zealand came only after ten years of unsuccessful bilateral negotiation and UN debates on the subject. A similar motivation has accompanied numerous other applications to the Court. The United Kingdom and West Germany, for example, brought suit against Iceland in 1972, primarily to communicate the seriousness of their determination to resolve their longstanding dispute over Iceland's unilateral extension of its fishing boundaries. The Court rendered a judgment favoring the applicants' position, but a more important effect of the litigation was to encourage subsequent negotiation among the parties. In 1973 Pakistan found the Court helpful in breaking a stalemate with India in negotiations over the release of Pakistani prisoners of war taken during the hostilities in East Pakistan (now Bangladesh) in 1971. The application was filed in May, negotiations were resumed in July, the case was withdrawn from the Court in December, and a final agreement for release of the prisoners was signed in April 1974.

A variety of other reasons may enter into the calculations of an applicant state in deciding for judicial settlement. If settlement of a dispute among friendly states is slow in coming, the bargaining process may reach a point where finding a settlement is more important to both sides than striking a particular kind of bargain. In the North Sea continental shelf cases (1967–69) pitting Denmark and the Netherlands against West Germany, the controversy was submitted by agreement of all the parties because just such a plateau had been reached. The Court decision broke the deadlock over the division of the oil-rich shelf, although final resolution of all the disputed issues required still further negotiation and a compromise settlement. One additional motive for the agreed submission, at least on the part of Denmark, was to "save face" with domestic public opinion. If territorial concessions were the price of settlement, a Court judgment would make them more politically acceptable.

Much more than saving face was connected to The Belgrade government's decision in April 1999 to bring ten separate but joined cases against the NATO countries most involved in the air war against it. The Yugoslav cases were based upon Article 36, paragraph 2 of the Statute of the International Court of Justice, with Belgrade charging ten NATO countries, but particularly the United States and the United Kingdom of violating international obligations banning the use of force against another state, the obligation not to intervene in the internal affairs of another state, the obligation not to violate the sovereignty of another state, the obligation to protect the civilian population and civilian objects in wartime, the obligation to protect the environment, the obligation related to free navigation on international rivers, the obligation regarding fundamental human rights and freedoms, the obligation not to use prohibited weapons, and the obligation not to deliberately inflict conditions of life calculated to cause the physical destruction of a national group.

# CASE STUDIES IN UN CONFLICT RESOLUTION

Disputes before the United Nations have had a variety of causes, but most frequently they have involved East-West controversies, conflicts produced by the decolonization process, territorial and boundary questions, and disputes arising from intervention by one or more states in the internal quarrels of another. In addition, the United Nations has recently been asked to resolve disputes stemming primarily from internal conflict rather than external intervention. The following pages present case studies illustrating the range and difficulty of the disputes placed on UN agendas throughout the history of the organization.

## SOUTH AFRICA AND THE UNITED NATIONS

South Africa's racial policies dominated UN discussions and debates more than any other issue through the 1980s. Some twenty subsidiary UN offices, committees, or funds were centered solely on South African issues. In one General Assembly session in the 1980s, antiapartheid agitation occurred in sixty-two of 111 plenary meetings. Moreover, the white South African government was made the target of criticism in one-fifth of all UN resolutions adopted during that period.

South African discrimination against minorities first came before the General Assembly in 1946. The complaint was brought by India, alleging South African violation of the Capetown Agreements of 1927 and 1932, which guaranteed equality of treatment for each other's resident nationals. The Indian complaint was never resolved, and it was a perennial subject of Assembly discussions and resolutions until it was merged in the 1950s with a broader attack on South African racial discrimination, focusing on the policy of apartheid, or separation of whites from the non-white majority.

The major objective of sustained UN condemnation of apartheid was to isolate South Africa from the world community, and ultimately, to force the Afrikaner government to abolish the practice. In 1962 the Assembly created a Special Committee against Apartheid to gather information about apartheid and make sure the issue remained on the front burner in the Assembly and the world at large. When South Africa persistently refused to heed Assembly demands to abandon its apartheid policies, the Assembly responded with increasingly bitter denunciations. The UN body repeatedly urged members to cut all political and economic ties with South Africa and called on the Security Council to impose mandatory sanctions. In 1973 an International Convention on the Suppression and Punishment of the Crime of Apartheid was opened for signature, and in 1976 the Assembly began explicitly to advocate "armed struggle" in South Africa as a means of eradicating the evil.

Action on apartheid by the Security Council was more restrained because harsh measures were subject to U.S. and British vetoes. The Council first addressed the issue in 1960, criticizing South African behavior in the Sharpesville incident in which police killed sixty-seven people during an antiapartheid demonstration. Three years later the Council called for a voluntary embargo on the sale of arms to South Africa, and in 1977 it made the embargo mandatory. The 1977 resolution also banned nuclear cooperation with South Africa. Third World and East European states called for much stronger measures, including a total severance of economic relations with South Africa, but the Western members of the Council were never quite ready to cut all ties. In 1985, with Britain and the United States abstaining, the Security Council recommended nonmandatory economic sanctions against South Africa. In 1986 the U.S. Congress adopted economic sanctions over a presidential veto, and the European Community also decided to impose economic sanctions, including an oil embargo. Many private multinational businesses undertook voluntary disinvestment in South Africa.

Through the decade of the 1980s the apartheid system remained largely intact. In 1982, in response to growing external pressures, South Africa introduced modest reforms, including a tricameral legislature with separate chambers for whites, Indians, and coloreds (persons of mixed race). The changes gave no political rights to blacks and left the white minority firmly in control. Meanwhile the government used the full force of the criminal law, including the death penalty, against internal opponents of apartheid. Members of the antiapartheid African National Congress (ANC) were the most frequent targets. Externally, South African forces periodically raided neighboring countries harboring ANC guerrillas and unabashedly gave aid to insurgents seeking the overthrow of leftist governments in Angola and Mozambique. During all these years South Africa remained a perpetual affront to UN ideals and majority interests, unflinching in its defense of racial separation.

The first major crack in the South African stone wall came in December 1988 with an agreement to accept Namibian independence in exchange for the withdrawal of Cuban troops from Angola. Other hopeful signs followed. In

February 1989 P. W. Botha was succeeded by F. W. de Klerk as head of the ruling Afrikaner-dominated National Party. De Klerk, though conservative, was seen as more open to change. In March the Dutch Reformed Church, the largest denomination in South Africa and traditionally a supporter of racial separation on biblical grounds, publicly reversed its position and condemned apartheid as contrary to Christian teaching. These events occurred against the background of severe economic decline, induced in part by the international sanctions and domestic unrest. Taking hope from these developments, the UN General Assembly held a special session in December 1989 to enunciate guidelines for negotiating a peaceful dismantling of apartheid.

The initiative came at the right moment. F. W. de Klerk, now President of the Republic, had seen the light and was prepared to embark on a course that would change the history of South Africa. In February 1990 he lifted the country's political ban on the ANC and other antiapartheid groups. Within days he ordered the release of ANC leader Nelson Mandela after twenty-seven years in prison. This was followed by the release of other political prisoners and, in the ensuing months, the repeal of most antiapartheid legislation. The new policy brought vocal protest from internal opponents of change, but in a national referendum of white voters held in March 1992, a majority of 68.7 percent gave de Klerk their support. Though uncertain and even fearful of the future, South Africa's white population preferred integration and sharing power with a black majority to the alternative prospect of renewed international isolation, civil war, and economic collapse. The way was thus cleared for the most difficult task of all—negotiating a new constitution for a democratic, multiracial society.

The world reaction was approving but cautious. The General Assembly removed a ban on South African participation in international sporting, scientific, and cultural activities and advised members to consider ending other sanctions as circumstances warranted. The European Community scrapped its oil embargo, and the United States ended restrictions on economic contact with South Africa.

Sustained diplomatic pressure and economic sanctions were deemed successful when political reforms were introduced in the country, permitting elections in which each adult South African, white and black, voted in 1994 for a government of his or her choice. Nelson Mendela's victory and inauguration as president, as well as his leadership of a government of both races, marked the end of a long, tedious campaign. The United Nations role in the transformation of South Africa was pivotal. The lifting of all sanctions and the recognition of the new government of South Africa by all members of the United Nations marked a new era for the country. It also was a major milestone in the maturation of the international organization.

## NAMIBIA

Closely related to apartheid was the issue of South African rule in Namibia. Large (half the size of Europe), arid, rich in uranium, and small in population (about 1.5 million), Namibia borders South Africa to the northwest. A German colony prior to World War I the territory (known as South West Africa until the late 1960s) was invaded and occupied by South Africa in 1915 and governed by South Africa as a League of Nations mandate after 1920. Unlike other holders of League mandates, South Africa refused to accept UN supervision under the trusteeship system at the end of World War II but instead took steps to integrate the territory with South Africa and impose its apartheid system there.

The General Assembly responded to these developments with alarm, criticism, attempted negotiation, and legal action against South Africa. A 1950 advisory opinion of the International Court of Justice ruled that the South West African mandate should be subject to UN supervision, but this opinion was totally ignored by South Africa. Subsequently the Assembly encouraged Ethiopia and Liberia, as former League members, to file an ICJ action against South Africa to obtain a binding legal decision on the former mandate. This effort failed when the Court in 1966 determined that Ethiopia and Liberia had insufficient legal interest to pursue the claim. According to the Court, the right to sue in such a cause belonged to the League, as distinct from its individual members, which left no legal remedy since the League had ceased to exist.

The General Assembly then acted unilaterally to terminate the mandate and declare Pretoria's continued occupation of Namibia illegal. This position was subsequently endorsed by the Security Council and by advisory opinions of the International Court of Justice. In 1967 the Assembly created an eleven-member Council for South West Africa, subsequently renamed the UN Council for Namibia, to take over administration of the territory from South Africa. The Council for Namibia was never permitted to serve in that capacity, but it became a center for constant UN agitation against South African occupation of Namibia. Many UN members blamed the failure of UN efforts on the United States and its Western allies because their vetoes in the Security Council prevented tougher sanctions against South Africa.

In addition to external UN pressures, South Africa faced growing opposition within Namibia. The principal opposition organization, the South West Africa People's Organization (SWAPO), was formed in 1960 and began guerrilla warfare in 1966. In 1973 the General Assembly recognized SWAPO as the "authentic" representative of the Namibian people.

For years hostility between South Africa and the UN majority disabled the United Nations from serving as an effective third party or a forum for negotiations. The Secretary-General was designated as a UN representative to negotiate with Pretoria, but his office had little credibility there. In 1977 the five Western members of the Security Council, called the "contact group," succeeded in promoting dialogue between South Africa and SWAPO. This led to a proposal for Namibian independence that was accepted by both South Africa and SWAPO and subsequently embodied in Security Council Resolution 435 (1978). The UN Secretariat prepared an elaborate plan for a UN Transition Assistance Group (UNTAG) including a 7,500-man peacekeeping force to supervise elections and oversee the transition to independence. South Africa persistently balked at the details for implementation, however, and beginning in 1981 the issue was further complicated by the efforts of the United States and South Africa to link a Namibian settlement to agreement for withdrawal of the 50,000 Cuban troops stationed in neighboring Angola. This linkage was not totally without factual underpinning, since Angola was providing a haven for SWAPO guerrillas, but most UN members regarded the linkage as a ploy to postpone settlement.

The long awaited break in the impasse occurred in December 1988 against a background of increased U.S.-Soviet cooperation in finding a solution. South Africa agreed to cease hostilities against Angola and grant Namibian independence, while Angola and Cuba agreed that Cuban troops would be withdrawn from Angola. In addition to the great power pressure for a settlement, the cost to South Africa of continued presence in Namibia, including military operations that extended into Angola, had come to exceed the benefits. With Angola a sanctuary for SWAPO units, and Cuban troops supporting the Angolan government, the prospects for victory were slim. On the rebels' side, war weariness was taking its toll, and signs were clear that Soviet support of the Angolan war effort would be reduced.

The December 1988 protocol on the independence of Namibia was a signal for the activation of UNTAG, heretofore a paper force in the files of the UN Secretariat. The first troops arrived in April 1989; the last departed in March 1990, leaving behind an independent Namibia with SWAPO leader Sam Nujoma the duly elected president. The settlement had been long in coming, and not wholly peaceful, but the United Nations played a critical role in bringing it to a conclusion.

## ARAB-ISRAELI CONFLICT

The Arab-Israeli conflict has been a perennial concern of the United Nations almost from the beginning of the organization. It was first placed before the United Nations in 1947 and has been there ever since. Diaspora Jews, residing mostly in Eastern Europe, and reacting to their persecution by Christian societies (and oftentimes their governments), formed the World Zionist Organization under the leadership of Theodor Herzl, in the latter segment of the nineteenth century. Calling for a Jewish homeland or state where Jews would be free to practice their traditions, the movement centered its attention on a "return to Zion," and an agency was organized that purchased land from absentee Arab landlords in the territory that was deemed to be the Jewish people's ancestral home. Prior to World War I, that region was known as Greater Syria and was administered by the Ottoman Turks. World War I proved to be the catalyst for the crystallization of the Zionist "dream." On the one side, European Jewry identified with the British cause, while on the other, the Ottomans were defeated in the war and lost control of their empire. The British and French filled the vacuum left by the Ottomans, and "Palestine" was created as a separate entity and made a British mandate. In 1917, the British government had declared its intention to establish a formal Jewish homeland in Palestine (the

Balfour Declaration), and with the war over, the Zionists anticipated the British would honor their commitment. But the British had also promised Arab leaders, notably the Sherif of Mecca, who had sided with the British, that after the war the Arabs would be granted rule over the territories heretofore dominated by the Turks. These two promises could not be reconciled, especially in the case of Palestine where Jewish settlements appeared to negate the creation of an independent Arab state. With the Jewish settlers of Palestine caught between rival Arab aspirations and British imperial machinations, the period following World War I was turbulent and costly to all concerned. World War II further aggravated the situation. The British, under pressure from the Arabs, issued a series of white papers denying the further settlement of Jews in Palestine at a time when Nazi Germany had launched an all-out campaign to destroy European Jewry. The Zionists of Palestine attempted to save as many Jews as they could and both during and following the war, they struggled against what they judged to be the inhumane tactics of the British Palestine authority. Using hit-and-run tactics and random acts of terror, the Jewish settler community demanded unlimited immigration to Israel for those Jews surviving the Holocaust. The Arab states, however, now more independent, reacted adversely to this idea, and they pressured the British to reject all Zionist demands. Unable to stem the influx of Jews to Palestine, and lacking the will to reconcile the parties, the British announced their departure from the region, and the matter became the responsibility of the United Nations.

The General Assembly at first recommended partition of the mandate into separate Arab and Jewish states, each politically independent but forming an economic union. When Arab opposition thwarted peaceful implementation of the partition plan, the United Kingdom terminated the mandate on May 15, 1948, and the Jewish groups by force of arms secured their own independence over a territory extending well beyond the boundaries specified in the UN partition plan. Through the offices of a UN mediator appointed by the General Assembly and a Truce Commission authorized by the Security Council, a cease-fire, truce, and four armistice agreements were concluded.

Since that time no annual session of the Assembly has been free from the Arab-Israeli problem in its many aspects. Among the specific issues have been refugee relief and resettlement, Arab property rights in Israel, human rights violations, Israeli withdrawal from conquered territories, the status of Jerusalem, the creation of an independent Palestinian state, and a host of security questions ranging from specific acts of terrorism to military border clashes and full-scale war.

The Security Council has also been heavily involved in the Arab-Israeli conflict. Scarcely a year passed without one or more Palestine security questions appearing on its agenda, and major hostilities erupted in nearly every decade since the 1948–49 war for Israeli independence. In 1956 Egyptian nationalization of the Suez Canal provided the occasion for an invasion of Egypt by Israel, Britain, and France (the Suez War). In 1967 (the Six-Day War) Israel launched a preemptive military strike against Egypt in a bold attempt to remove the threat to its security and borders. In 1973 (the Yom Kippur War) Egypt and

Syria struck the first blow against Israel in hope of regaining lost territory. In 1978 and again in 1982, Israeli forces initiated major hostilities in Lebanon in response to Palestinian raids into Israel over the Lebanese border.

Security Council resolutions have established certain principles to which all the participants repeatedly refer in Middle East negotiations. Security Council Resolution 242, adopted unanimously on November 22, 1967, in the aftermath of the Six-Day War, is by far the most important. Its two cardinal principles, often reaffirmed, are (1) Israeli withdrawal "from territories occupied in the recent conflict" and (2) "respect for and acknowledgement of the sovereignty, territorial integrity, and political independence of every State in the area and their right to live in peace within secure and recognized boundaries." The two points were intended to be mutually dependent. Unfortunately, agreement in the 1967 Security Council did not produce agreement among the parties to the conflict and Israel interpreted the withdrawal provision of Resolution 242 as though it read "some but not all" occupied territories.

The 1967 war had established Israel as a formidable actor in Middle Eastern affairs, and Arab declarations about destroying the Jewish state ceased to carry the weight of earlier years. Awareness of Israeli military prowess registered on Anwar el-Sadat, who became president of Egypt following Gamal Abdul Nasser's death. It was Sadat who initiated the 1973 war against Israel, but his objectives were directed more at achieving diplomatic leverage than a knockout blow. Just a few years after that conflict Sadat took it upon himself to fly to Jerusalem and for the first time since Israel's proclaimed independence, an Arab leader acknowledged the need to find a settlement acceptable to both sides. Sadat's action angered as well as frustrated the other Arab states, especially as Egypt represented the most important Arab nation and had shouldered the major burden in all the Arab wars with Israel. Shouts of betrayal, however, failed to deter Sadat, who with the good offices provided by President Jimmy Carter, met with his Israeli counterpart at Camp David in the United States. The outcome of those meetings in 1978 was the Egypt-Israel Peace Treaty of 1979, which was signed on the lawn of the White House. Sadat's peacemaking efforts were little appreciated back home, however, and in 1981 he was assassinated while viewing a military parade. Succeeded by another military officer, Hosni Mubarak, the treaty with Israel was sustained but it was also paralyzed by Israel's assault on PLO positions in Lebanon in 1982.

The United Nations General Assembly failed to reflect these dramatic turns in the Arab-Israeli conflict. Over the years the role of the General Assembly had changed from that of a relatively evenhanded third party to that of a shrill partisan of the Arab cause. In subsequent years, as the third world nations increased their influence, the Assembly substituted condemnation for any genuine attempt at settlement. The Assembly therefore abdicated its role in attempting to mediate the Arab-Israeli dispute, and what headway could be made was accomplished outside the United Nations. The passing of the Cold War did not change this equation. The Assembly continued its assault on Israeli policies and actions, and the *intifadah,* or uprising of Palestinian youth on the West Bank and in the Gaza Strip, only provided more fuel for the passionate speeches in the General Assembly. The United Nations continued to reflect the views of the majority Arab states that had rejected the existence of Israel, not the views or actions of those seeking a diplomatic solution. The war in the Gulf in 1990–91, pitting some Arab states against others, however, offered new opportunities.

Iraq's aggression against Kuwait divided the Arab world; it also made it possible for the United States to pressure the General Assembly to repeal its 1975 resolution (72-35, with 32 abstentions) that equated Zionism with racism. In December 1991 the Assembly voted 111-25 with 13 abstentions to withdraw that original resolution. The Palestine Liberation Organization, led by Yasir Arafat, found itself on the losing side during the Gulf War, and one immediate consequence was the loss of its financial support from the Arabian states, especially Saudi Arabia and Kuwait. Sensing its isolation, and unwilling to abdicate its role as the leader of the Palestinian Arabs, in October 1991 Arafat was forced to join the Madrid peace conference, which was convened by the United States, with the Soviet Union a co-sponsor. Attended by Egypt, Syria, and Lebanon in addition to the PLO and Israel, the conference was opened by Presidents George Bush and Mikhail Gorbachev. Although it did not produce new settlements, the Madrid Conference expanded the dialogue and set the stage for more confidential meetings between high representatives of the PLO and Israel in Oslo, Norway. In September 1993, Arafat entered into an agreement with Yitzhak Rabin, and the Israelis turned over the administration of the Gaza Strip and the West Bank city of Jericho to the PLO in return for a Palestinian promise to cease the violence against the Jewish state. As a consequence of these successes, Jordan also entered into a peace treaty with Israel in 1994. Still another accord between Israel and the PLO was entered into in September 1995 when Israel agreed to withdraw from six additional West Bank cities as well as 450 towns and villages. The subsequent formation of a Palestinian ruling council, and with Yasir Arafat elected president of the Palestinian Authority, the PLO assumed the role of a quasi-government.

Dissatisfaction on both the Israeli and Arab sides, however, prevented an end to the violence. Confronted by disgruntled elements, peacemaking was seriously impacted by the assassination of Yitzhak Rabin at the hands of an Israeli zealot. Although Rabin was succeeded by Shimon Peres, a staunch peacemaker of the Israeli Labor Party, given an escalation in the use of terror against innocent Israeli citizens by a variety of extremist organizations, the Israeli elections that followed Rabin's death resulted in an electoral shift to a more conservative political coalition. The conservatives, led by Benjamin Nethanyahu, were reluctant to follow the lead of the Labor Party and the subsequent delay in the peace process only added more ammunition to the arsenal of the rejectionists on both sides. Arafat soon became trapped between Arab extremists and his own disaffected organization members. In the circumstances there was little the United Nations could do but monitor the situation.

Undaunted, however, U.S. government envoys did not allow the parties to forget their peacemaking pledges, and Washington maintained its pressure, especially on Prime Minister Nethanyahu. Nevertheless, like Arafat, Nethanyahu had to answer to a constituency that sustained his authority. And although the

Israeli leader associated himself with the peace process, indeed cited its irreversibility and had withdrawn Israeli troops from sensitive areas such as Hebron, he was equally adamant on Jerusalem's status as the Israeli capital. He also refused all demands to forego construction of Israeli settlements in Arab Jerusalem. Thus, although the peace process had moved along a somewhat progressive path since the end of the Gulf war, the outstanding issues—the permanent security of Israel, the status of Jerusalem, the total withdrawal of Israeli forces from the West Bank, the acknowledgement of self determination for the Palestinian Arabs, as well as the return of the Golan Heights to Syria—were still far from resolution. Moreover, the UN General Assembly's decision in July 1998 to elevate the PLO from its longstanding observer status to "near membership," raised additional questions of statehood that further complicated the peace process. Given Israeli reluctance to sustain the flow of the peace process with the Palestinian Authority and fearing more delay would complicate the diplomatic situation beyond remedy, President Clinton pressured the principals to reinvigorate their efforts and arranged for a meeting in Wye, Maryland, not far from Washington, in October 1998. Brought together under difficult circumstances, Prime Minister Netanyahu and PA leader Yasir Arafat deliberated for a number of days but failed to reach an understanding. Obviously in need of good offices, President Clinton requested King Hussein of Jordan, who was receiving medical treatment in the United States, to join in the discussions. Along with the U.S. president, King Hussein was able to convince the parties that an accord was in everyone's interest, and on October 24, these efforts were crowned by an agreement signed in the White House by the four leaders. The Wye River Accord provided for a series of intricately linked steps over a three-month period that called for Israeli withdrawal from an additional 13 percent of West Bank territory. In return, the Palestinian Authority agreed to abrogate that section of the Palestinian National Covenant calling for the destruction of Israel. Arafat also pledged a crackdown on alleged Palestinian terrorists and hence greater security for Israel. The central purpose at Wye was confidence-building between the parties, but the accord left in question the PA threat to unilaterally declare an independent Palestinian state by May 1999, the status of Jerusalem that the PA claimed as its capital, the future of Israeli settlements on the West Bank, the return to the West Bank of Palestinian refugees residing in other Arab nations, and the division and control of the region's water supply.

Unable to effectively neutralize opposition to the Wye agreement in both Israel and the West Bank, and with acts of terror and protest demonstrations directed against Israel continuing, the Netanyahu government failed to meet the January 1999 withdrawal deadline detailed in the accord. The PA also infuriated the Israeli government by releasing alleged terrorists. With Arafat once more expressing a desire to declare the independence of his state, tensions were again on the ascendant. Moreover, the death of King Hussein on February 7, 1999, left a cloud over future deliberations. The Kingdom of Jordan's geostrategic position astride the West Bank and Israel was never more pronounced than at the funeral of the king, which was attended by more than forty heads of state, including President Clinton (accompanied by former presidents Carter, Ford, and Bush), Prime Minister Netanyahu, the presidents of the Russian Federation and France, the prime minister of Great Britain, the Chancellor of Germany and almost all key Arab leaders, not the least of which was Yasir Arafat. Seizing the opportune moment to reinvigorate diplomacy, in the May 1999 elections Israelis chose Yitzhak Rabin's disciple, Ehud Barak, to succeed Nathanyahu as Prime Minister of the Jewish state.

## INDIA-PAKISTAN

Territorial and other disputes between India and Pakistan have been a periodic feature of the UN landscape. The India-Pakistan issue first came before the Security Council in January 1948 at the complaint of India. When the two countries gained independence in August 1947, more than 500 princely states of the subcontinent were given the choice of joining one or the other. For most, the choice was easily made on the basis of geographic proximity and predominance of Muslim or Hindu populations. But Kashmir (also called Jammu and Kashmir) with its Hindu Maharaja, predominantly Muslim populace, and geographic contiguity with both India and Pakistan, faced a difficult choice. Invading tribesmen from Pakistan, allegedly supported by the Pakistani government, forced the Maharaja's hand, and he sent out a plea for help with the announcement that he had decided to join India. Indian troops moved to protect the new accession, Pakistani forces formally entered the fray, and Kashmir became the scene of large-scale armed combat.

The Security Council appointed a UN Commission on India and Pakistan (UNCIP) to investigate and mediate the dispute. After months of negotiation, UNCIP was able to secure a truce and cease-fire, effective January 1, 1949, and an acceptance in principle of a plebiscite to resolve the accession question. A UN military observer group (UNMOGIP) was established to supervise the cease-fire. The proposed plebiscite was never held, primarily because India occupied the larger part of Kashmir and regarded this *fait accompli* as preferable to a free vote in which the Muslim majority would in all likelihood opt for union with Pakistan.

In August 1965 renewed fighting shattered the truce, but prompt Security Council action, mediation by the Secretary-General, and close coordination of diplomatic efforts by the Soviet Union and the United States brought a cease-fire in September. The UN observer group helped make the cease-fire effective. In 1971 serious conflict again broke out, although the major hostilities were in East Pakistan, where Indian armies intervened in support of Bengali separatists fighting for independence from Pakistan. The Soviet Union vetoed a Security Council call for a cease-fire, and a similar resolution adopted by the Assembly was ignored by India until the creation of an independent Bangladesh was assured.

UNMOGIP was organized in 1949 to monitor the cease-fire line in Jammu and Kashmir, not to do diplomacy. Indeed, UN diplomatic efforts in the region were virtually non-existent after 1958. Nor did the Indo-Pakistani wars of 1965 or 1971 cause the United Nations to take more aggressive action to resolve the Kashmir dispute. Thus, by the 1990s, non-governmental diplomacy attempted to fill the vacuum. Confronted by renewed fighting in Kashmir, and sensing a lack of will in New Delhi and Islamabad, let alone in the United Nations, university academicians and working journalists tried to breathe life into an almost expired peace process. Representing the intelligentsia from both countries, they engaged in conversations that were aimed at finding a solution for the decades-old problem. Identified as the "Third Generation," and detached from the traumatic events of their elders, their deliberations seemed to point to the rebirth of diplomacy in the region. By August 1997, several "summer school" meetings had been arranged, notably in Sri Lanka and in the United States. This effort at freelance diplomacy was just beginning to show positive results, when in May 1998, New Delhi, without warning, tested several nuclear devices. Moreover, the Indian prime minister's public declaration that his country now possessed the "big bomb" was not intended to ease the work of the unofficial negotiators. Nor were the Pakistani authorities prepared to be intimidated by the Indian action. Within weeks, Pakistan demonstrated it too was a nuclear weapons power. With the two governments exchanging verbal threats, and now too, brandishing their weapons of mass destruction, the United Nations Security Council was forced into emergency session. The Council called upon both governments to cease their tests, and more important, to accept the terms of the NPT as well as the comprehensive nuclear test ban treaty. Attention was also given to the Kashmir dispute, but in the course of the debate none of the council members appeared ready to engage in serious diplomacy. Sanctions were also discussed, but here too there was no agreement and individual countries were left to implement their own policies. It did appear, however, that IMF and World Bank assistance would be more difficult to obtain. Fearful that renewed fighting in Kashmir could escalate into a nuclear exchange, the Security Council acknowledged the need to encourage conversations between the two governments, but India held to its position that Kashmir was a permanent unit within the Indian union, and the government of Pakistan continued its demand that the 1949 UN resolution that called for a plebiscite in Kashmir be honored. In effect, in spite of the serious escalation in tension and the threat of a tragic encounter, the decades-old Kashmir question was no nearer to solution at the century's end.

## UN DISPUTE SETTLEMENT

For more than forty years the United Nations existed in a cold war environment that severely hampered its peacemaking role. Since 1987 a fundamental transformation has occurred in the conditions of global politics that may make the UN more successful in dispute settlement. Some of the successful efforts during the cold war period are presented in the cases that follow.

## The U.S. Airmen

The release of U.S. air force personnel imprisoned by China in violation of Korean Armistice arrangements is an early instance of successful UN dispute settlement from the Hammarskjöld era. The issue arose in November 1954, when the Peking government unexpectedly announced that eleven crewmen of a B-10 bomber shot down near Korea in January 1953 had been tried by a military tribunal and sentenced to long prison terms for espionage. Four U.S. jet pilots were already known to be similarly detained. The United States immediately appealed to the General Assembly, which in this case proved surprisingly effective. At the request of the Assembly, Dag Hammarskjöld departed for Beijing in early January, and shortly after his visit Beijing announced that relatives of the airmen would be permitted to visit China. Four months later, in a letter to the Secretary-General sent through the Swedish ambassador in Beijing, the Chinese government informed Hammarskjöld that the four jet pilots would be deported. In August the eleven crewmen were freed. Whatever the motivation of the Chinese, the United Nations played an important mediating role in obtaining release of the fliers.

## Thailand-Cambodia, Equatorial Guinea, Bahrain, and Greenpeace

In 1958–59 and again in 1962–64, a representative of the Secretary-General was instrumental in resolving border disputes and hostile incidents between Thailand and Cambodia. The representatives were sent at the request of both parties, which undoubtedly helps explain the success of the missions. The second UN mission remained on the scene for two years, with expenses jointly shared by the two governments. The Secretary-General's personal representative was also successful in assisting the peaceful withdrawal of Spanish troops from Equatorial Guinea (a former Spanish colony) in the spring of 1969. Again, the assistance was requested and received with cooperation by the parties.

A potentially much more explosive situation was defused by a representative of the Secretary-General in the 1970 controversy over the status of Bahrain, a small, oil-producing British protectorate off the coast of Saudi Arabia in the Persian Gulf. Iran's claims to sovereignty over Bahrain were disputed by Britain, and the good offices of the Secretary-General were enlisted to help resolve the controversy. All of the parties subsequently accepted a report by the personal representative of the Secretary-General, reinforced by UN consultation in Bahrain, that the islands should become independent. The report was unanimously endorsed by the Security Council, and Bahrain became a member of the United Nations the following year.

Considerably less threatening to international peace, but nevertheless irritating to the parties, was the Greenpeace incident. In that case Secretary-General Pérez de Cuéllar successfully mediated a controversy between France and New Zealand arising from the clandestine bombing of the Greenpeace ship

*Rainbow Warrior* by French agents while the ship was in Auckland harbor. Greenpeace had planned to use the ship to protest French underground nuclear tests on a South Pacific atoll. One life was lost as a result of the incident, and two French agents were convicted of manslaughter by a New Zealand court. The agreed settlement, announced in July 1986, Called for $7 million compensation to New Zealand, an apology by France, and the lifting of a French embargo on the import of food from New Zealand. New Zealand, in return, released the two agents on the condition that they be transferred to a French military garrison in the South Pacific for a period of three years.

### The Cuban Missile Crisis

The United Nations played a modest part in the resolution of the 1962 Cuban missile crisis, potentially one of the most serious East-West confrontations of the postwar period. The crisis arose from the presence of Soviet missiles and jet bombers in Cuba, discovered by a U-2 spy plane surveillance mission over Cuba in the fall of 1962. Agreement on dismantling the missile sites and removing the missiles and bombers from Cuba was reached primarily through great power negotiation, but the UN contribution is not to be discounted.

The UN link most obvious at the time was U.S. use of the Security Council as a forum to display evidence that missiles were indeed being installed in Cuba. Aerial photographs laid before the world made Soviet denials no longer credible. The United Nations also had a part in the less public negotiation processes. Both superpowers used their UN ambassadors to channel informal suggestions and semiofficial messages that supplemented more direct communication. At various times during the crisis, Secretary-General U Thant served personally as an intermediary. After the acute stage of the crisis had passed, the United Nations was the site of extensive negotiations on means of verifying the weapons withdrawal. At this stage U Thant was the principal point of contact between Castro and the superpower representatives in New York.

Another important UN contribution to settlement was a face-saving formula that gave Soviet Premier Nikita Khrushchev an excuse to call for the return of Soviet freighters bearing additional missiles to Cuba, and ultimately to agree to withdrawal of all missiles and equipment. At a crucial moment in the Khrushchev-Kennedy dialogue, Secretary-General U Thant offered a proposal for a voluntary suspension of Soviet arms shipments to Cuba in return for a voluntary suspension of the American naval quarantine. This suggestion was quickly accepted by Khrushchev as an excuse for Soviet freighters already under way with a missile cargo and a submarine escort to steer clear of the quarantine fleet, even though Kennedy's reply to Thant made suspension of the quarantine contingent on removal of offensive weapons already in Cuba. At this point the UN role may have been crucial. Kennedy could scarcely have made such a proposal, and if he had, Khrushchev could not easily have accepted it. But Thant, as impartial spokesman for a community of states, was able to elicit a degree of restraint that neither of the parties could have exercised under pressure from the other.

## Decolonization

The United Nations has been involved in numerous disputes arising from the decolonization process. The important UN contribution to the overall process of decolonization is examined in Chapter 8. The end of Namibia's colonial status has already been discussed as a post-cold-war UN success story, but much earlier the United Nations played a third-party role in colonial disputes that ultimately turned out well. Indonesia was one of the first to elicit extensive UN involvement. During the course of the Indonesian struggle for independence from the Netherlands, 1945–49, a Security Council Good Offices Committee (later reconstituted as the UN Commission for Indonesia) arranged cease-fires in the field, maintained a small truce observation team, and assisted with negotiations. At UN headquarters, debates and resolutions kept continual pressure on the Dutch to grant Indonesian independence. When the United States finally took sides in the controversy, the United Nations helped legitimize U.S. diplomatic and economic pressures on the Dutch. The final agreement on independence, in December 1949, owed much to UN involvement. As noted in Chapter 5, the subsequent controversy over Western New Guinea (West Irian, now Irian Jaya), which the Netherlands refused to relinquish to Indonesian rule in 1949, was also resolved with UN assistance when the Dutch were finally ready to deal. The terms of the transfer of West Irian to Indonesia were arranged by a UN mediator and executed with the help of the UN Temporary Executive Authority and the UN Security Force.

The United Nations also peacefully resolved the fate of the former Italian colonies of Libya, Eritrea, and Italian Somaliland. France, the Soviet Union, the United Kingdom, and the United States had agreed in the World War II treaty of peace with Italy to let the UN General Assembly decide the future status of the colonies if the powers were unable to agree among themselves by September 1948. Disagreement prevailed, and the decision fell to the Assembly. The question occupied several sessions of the Assembly, but ultimately Libya was granted independence (proclaimed in December 1951), Somaliland was placed under Italian trusteeship until independence was achieved in 1960, and Eritrea was associated in a federal arrangement with Ethiopia, but achieved independence in 1993.

## Cold War Era Failures in Dispute Settlement

UN successes in dispute settlement sometimes came after the outbreak of violence between the parties, and some of the partial successes in curbing violence left the controversy still unresolved. Other conflicts, often entailing death and destruction of major proportions, seemed impervious to UN settlement attempts. Although failures of dispute settlement will not be examined in detail here, they should be mentioned to keep the UN role in perspective. They include the two most devastating international wars of the period—the Vietnam conflict and the Iran-Iraq War. The Vietnam War, largely because of the U.S. attitude, proved totally resistant to UN attempts at mediation. The Iran-Iraq conflict eventually succumbed to persistent UN mediation but only after eight years of war and the onset of the cold war thaw. Soviet military intervention in Afghanistan created another major crisis that could not be resolved while the cold war continued. Military actions on a lesser scale that eluded UN efforts at mediation included the Argentine attack on the British-held Falkland Islands, U.S. intervention in Grenada, and Nicaragua's conflict with U.S.-backed insurgents and the neighboring states that harbored them. Among the serious internal conflicts that resisted settlement was civil strife in Cambodia, where the Khmer Rouge reign of terror during the late 1970s took the lives of an estimated one to three million Cambodians.

The UN record of dispute settlement has improved since 1987. The limits and possibilities of UN accomplishment have always been set by its environment, and in recent years both have been extended outward by the termination of the cold war.

### Afghanistan

UN-monitored Soviet troop withdrawal from Afghanistan was one of the first tangible fruits of the cold war thaw. In December 1979 the Soviets sent 85,000 troops into Afghanistan, later increased to 115,000, to ensure that a factional fight there would not bring an anti-Soviet government to power. With the United States channeling aid to Afghan insurgents through Pakistan, the internal fighting expanded into a full-scale guerrilla war against the government and its Soviet backers. Early in 1980 the General Assembly issued the first of many unheeded calls for Soviet troop withdrawal, and the following year UN Secretary-General Kurt Waldheim appointed Javier Pérez de Cuéllar as his personal representative to seek a diplomatic solution. When Pérez de Cuéllar became Secretary-General in 1982, he named UN Under-Secretary-General Diego Cordovez as his successor in that assignment.

Through skill and persistence Cordovez kept the negotiations alive until a fundamental change in Soviet foreign policy goals dictated an end to the intervention. Agreement was reached in April 1988 through the Geneva Accords, which committed the Soviet Union to early troop withdrawal under UN supervision. The United States and Pakistan, along with the Soviet Union, also agreed to cease intervention in the Afghan civil war. By this time the Soviet Union had come to recognize the war as unwinnable, and a reconsideration of the costs of its aggressive foreign policies was undoubtedly an important factor in the Soviet decision to moderate the cold war.

*The Iran-Iraq War*

Continuation of the war between Iran and Iraq, like Soviet intervention in Afghanistan, represented a failure of pre-1988 UN peacemaking. Like the intervention in Afghanistan, it also was brought to a halt in the new world climate of 1988.

Iraq commenced the war in September 1980 in the aftermath of the Iranian revolution, hoping for a quick victory that would nullify Iran's support of Shiite revolution in Iraq, gain control of the Shatt al Arab waterway, and establish Iraqi dominance in the Persian Gulf area. Iraq miscalculated. Although the tides of battle periodically shifted, the overall result was a stalemate. After years of fighting, Iraq became readier than Iran to end a war entailing hundreds of thousands of casualties, material losses running to billions of dollars, severe economic damage to both countries from drastically reduced oil production and shipment, and war-caused oil leaks that threatened to pollute large sections of the Gulf coast.

Security Council cease-fire appeals were regularly rejected by Iran, and sometimes by Iraq. Several mediation missions by a representative of the Secretary-General, acting under the Security Council's authorization, proved fruitless. A fact-finding mission dispatched by the Secretary-General in May 1983 was praised by Iran for its objectivity but brought the war no closer to an end. The General Assembly also called for an end to the fighting, but Iran refused to support any resolution that did not brand Iraq as an aggressor. In June 1984, in response to an appeal by the Secretary-General, the two combatants agreed to stop deliberate attacks on civilian population centers. The agreement was generally, if imperfectly, observed. Conciliation efforts by the Islamic Conference, the Gulf Cooperation Council (formed for this purpose by Saudi Arabia and five small Arab states bordering the Persian Gulf), and the Non-Aligned Movement were totally without avail.

Years of war were sapping the military and economic capabilities of both sides, however, and in 1987 the United Nations undertook a renewed effort. In July the Security Council unanimously adopted a resolution offering a new peace plan and repeated its demand for a cease-fire, with the implicit threat of a mandatory arms embargo against any party that refused to comply. The threat was primarily aimed at Iran, which had shown the greater aversion to a cease-fire. The United States added to the pressure on Iran by reflagging Kuwaiti-owned tankers as U.S. merchant vessels and providing naval escorts through the Gulf waters. The effect of these measures was not immediate, but they gained force from the increased Soviet-American unity that developed in subsequent months. Secretary-General Pérez de Cuéllar personally conducted negotiations with the two warring countries, and the fighting was brought to an end in August 1988 with an agreed cease-fire supervised by a UN peacekeeping force (UNIIMOG). Comprehensive peace negotiations between the parties were begun in Geneva and mediated by the Secretary-General, but settlement proved elusive. A final peace agreement came in February 1991 when Iraq, faced with turmoil at home and military defeat in Kuwait, accepted Iranian terms.

*Central America*

In one respect the most remarkable UN peacemaking ventures in the new era occurred in Central America. The United States has traditionally regarded security in this area as a U.S. responsibility and, with the major exception of the Cuban missile crisis, has treated UN involvement as superfluous at best. Nevertheless, when the Sandinista government in Nicaragua decided to make peace with the Contras and agreed with four neighboring states on the need for UN assistance in policing the arrangement, the United States went along.

There, as elsewhere, until the parties were ready to stop fighting, the United Nations could do little. In 1989 the parties were ready. Nicaragua was a country riven by civil war, its economy in shambles, and aid from its erstwhile Soviet patron was shrinking as a result of new Soviet policies. The Sandinistas wanted peace and were willing to pay for it with free and fair UN-monitored elections. Nicaragua's neighbors also were tired of the border violations and ready to end them. The Bush administration, impressed with recent UN peacemaking success and perceiving growing domestic opposition to its Contra policy, acquiesced. ONUCA was sent to patrol the border areas and demobilize the Contras, while ONUVEN observed the elections from which the Sandinistas emerged as the minority party. The ONUCA mission was phased out in January 1992.

One success apparently deserved another. With the barriers to UN peacemaking in the Americas removed, the Secretary-General was encouraged to try his hand in El Salvador, where both sides in the civil war were growing weary of the struggle and sickened at the human consequences of their deeds. Through a personal representative, the UN Secretary-General negotiated an agreement in July 1990 to end human rights violations. After months of further negotiation the parties agreed to a UN observer mission to monitor the human rights agreement. ONUSAL's 135 observers took up their positions in July 1991. The civil war continued sporadically, but in late December Pérez de Cuéllar personally negotiated a cease-fire agreement as the last official act of his administration. ONUSAL was subsequently enlarged to monitor the cease-fire and help maintain internal order as the Salvadorans pursued the difficult unfinished business of creating a new constitution and government.

ONUSAL's success was demonstrated in its dissolution in April 1995, leaving only the MINUGUA peacekeeping mission in Guatemala. The last remaining conflict in Central America, MINUGUA oversaw compliance with the peace agreement entered into by the parties in December 1996. Already involved in policing human rights violations, MINUGUA was given responsibility for monitoring the demobilization of the combatants, a task that was accomplished under a sixty-day deadline. In the brief period it operated in

Guatemala, MINUGUA assisted in making improvements in the electoral system and in permitting wider citizen participation. Although originally scheduled for termination in May 1997, a scaled-back version of MINUGUA was extended to the year 2000. Similar United Nations activity obtained in Nicaragua, where, with the cooperation of the government, the UN sustained its efforts in disarming the combatants and in promoting socio-economic reintegration after long years of civil strife.

UN successes in Central America also were echoed in the UN operation in Haiti where the mission began with UNMIH from September 1993 to June 1996, to UNSMIH from June 1996 to July 1997, to UNTMIH from August 1997 to November 1997, and finally to MIPONUH, which in 1998 was solely concerned with the professionalization of the Haitian National Police. The UN began its task in Haiti following U.S. intervention in behalf of an elected government that it reinstated despite the efforts of a military junta to dominate the country. The several United Nations missions stabilized the political environment, assisted in the reorganization of the Haitian armed forces and organized free elections. Acknowledging the need to maintain law and order in an atmosphere of mistrust and a general lack of popular confidence, and citing the difficulties in resurrecting a society long subject to official abuse, the task of the United Nations was hardly a simple one, but was nonetheless assumed with considerable enthusiasm and purpose.

### Cambodia

In 1990 the United Nations assumed the task of bringing peace to Cambodia. Achieving independence from France in 1953, Cambodia was governed by the neutralist Prince Norodom Sihanouk until 1970 when he was overthrown in a right-wing coup led by Lon Nol. Despite substantial aid from the United States, the Lon Nol regime was in turn ousted by Marxist Khmer Rouge forces under Pol Pot in 1975. Incident to Pol Pot's brutal Marxist and anti-Western reforms, an estimated one to three million Cambodians were killed by disease, starvation, and mass execution. Khmer Rouge military forays into Vietnam led to a Vietnamese invasion of Cambodia in December 1979, the defeat of Pol Pot, and the installation of a new government styled the People's Republic of Kampuchea (PRK). This initiated a civil war pitting the Vietnam-backed government against several resistance groups, the Khmer Rouge being militarily the strongest.

This troubled scene continued until the late 1980s when the Soviet Union, in the process of reducing its financial commitments to leftist movements around the world, began to encourage Vietnam and the PRK to resolve the civil war by sharing power with the insurgents. In August 1989 the various Cambodian factions convened a Paris International Conference on Cambodia, while contemporaneously Vietnamese forces were being withdrawn. When the parties were unable to reach a compromise settlement, competition was renewed on the battlefield.

In early 1990 the five permanent members of the Security Council decided to assume a more active part in the peacemaking. Drawing on Secretariat expertise, they drafted proposals for a settlement which became the basis for discussion when in mid-1991 the five permanent members succeeded in bringing the opposing domestic factions to the peace table. The talks led to an agreement on cease-fire, the creation of UNAMIC to monitor the cease-fire, and the subsequent establishment of UNTAC to facilitate the establishment of a new constitutional system. UNAMIC completed its mission in March 1992 and UNTAC was withdrawn in September 1993, but Cambodia's problems did not cease. In spite of the limited success in establishing a government of national reconciliation the regime could not be sustained. Conflict between Hun Sen, a leftist ideologue, and his co-premier, the monarchist Prince Norodom Ranariddh, could not be resolved. In 1997, their mutual antagonism degenerated into open warfare with Hun Sen proving himself to be the stronger of the two. Ranariddh found refuge in the Cambodian hinterland where he sustained attacks on the government in Phnom Penh, and although efforts were made by Pacific-Asian nations to moderate the dispute, in March 1998, Hun Sen's high court sentenced Ranariddh, in absentia, to thirty years imprisonment. The continuing rivalry between Cambodia's key political personalities was only somewhat muted by the subsequent death of Pol Pot, who in the end, successfully evaded punishment for his major role in the killing fields of the 1970s. The demise of Pol Pot nevertheless marked an end to the long period of civil conflict. In the new circumstances, and although differences between the major Cambodian actors had not not been reconciled, the parties, including Hun Sen, agreed to holding a new round of popular elections. Moreover, given the presence of scores of international observers, elections were conducted in July 1998 that seemed to promise a new beginning for the beleaguered nation. Hun Sen and Ranariddh were not reconciled, but the sentence imposed on the latter was lifted, and both men again indicated a desire to work toward improving conditions within Cambodia.

## The Balkans

The 1990s focused particular attention on the Balkans, and especially the events leading up to and following the disintegration of Yugoslavia. The self-declared independence of Croatia and Slovenia in 1991 received instant recognition from a newly reunified Germany while other western European states hesitated to certify an action that had such explosive potential. Indeed, Serbia, seeking to perpetuate the Yugoslavian federation, was propelled into a war with Croatia, a war that quickly spilled over into Bosnia-Herzegovina. No longer able to sustain the unity of the old Yugoslavia, Serbia attempted to make the most of a difficult situation by moving against areas of Croatia inhabited by Serbs, as well as in Bosnia, whose Muslim population formed the largest segment of the population. These actions caused the different ethnic groups to form themselves into rival armies, with the most significant fighting occurring in Bosnia-Herzegovina.

The Security Council of the United Nations was among a number of international bodies that sought to prevent the intensification of the fighting, and the despatch of the UNPROFOR mission, totalling several thousand troops drawn from countries around the world, was authorized to interpose itself between the warring parties. While UNPROFOR was deployed in the most conflicted regions, diplomatic efforts were launched through the good offices of the United Nations, the European Union, the Organization of Security and Cooperation in Europe, and numerous other agencies, to stem the tide of battle. All these efforts failed amid the viciousness of the combat, which had become known as "ethnic cleansing." Serbia was judged the principal culprit in the intensification and prolongation of the fighting, and pressure was brought to bear on its leader, Slobodan Milosevic, to cease his country's involvement, and at the same time to restrain the Bosnian Serbs who were determined to carve out a Serb state from Bosnia-Herzegovina.

UNPROFOR's failure to tranquilize the parties, in fact the vulnerability of the force, proved an embarrassment to the United Nations. Eventually yielding its peacemaking role to more aggressive NATO forces, the United States, in cooperation with the United Nations, urged a diplomatic settlement on the parties. The three leaders representing Serbia, Croatia, and Bosnia-Herzegovina were invited to participate in a peace conference in Dayton, Ohio, in 1995, the outcome of which were the Dayton Accords and a general agreement to terminate the fighting. Although the accords did not bring an end to all the fighting, the scene had been set for the introduction of NATO ground forces, which were described as a Stabilization Force. UNPROFOR was dissolved and a UN International Police Task Force (UNMIBH) took its place alongside NATO troops.

The United Nations Transitional Administration for Eastern Slavonia, Baranja and Western Sirmium (UNTAES) also assisted in the demilitarization of Serb forces and in facilitating elections in April 1997. Moreover, a United Nations Preventive Deployment Force (UNPREDEP) was despatched to the former Yugoslav Republic of Macedonia to protect that state from the spillover effects of the conflict in Bosnia, and more significantly, from conditions in Kosovo where conflict had erupted when the minority Serbs sought to sustain their domination over the majority Albanian Muslim population. Other UN missions continued to monitor demilitarization in the Croatian Prevlaka peninsula (UNMOP), and until 1996, UNCRO focused on the restoration of confidence between Bosnia, Croatia, and the Federal Republic of Yugoslavia (Serbia and Montenegro). UNCRO also monitored the peaceful integration of Eastern Slavonia, Baranja and Western Sirmium into Croatia. At the end of the century, however, Kosovo and the plight of its Albanian population provoked NATO to take forceful action against Serbia. The outcome of that clash was likely to determine the future of Balkan peace efforts into the twenty-first century.

*Caucasus and Central Asia*

The United Nations sent peacekeeping forces to the Caucasian state of Georgia. Heretofore a republic within the Soviet Union, Georgia's territorial integrity and national unity was tested soon after it declared its independence. Abkhazian citizens of Georgia declared their desire to establish a separate state and in the ensuing conflict, Russia led a Commonwealth of Independent States (CIS) peacemaking force into the new nation. UNOMIG was authorized to work with the CIS in monitoring compliance with a cease-fire agreement of 1993, and a separation of forces agreement signed in Moscow in 1994. Given the volatility of the situation in Georgia, UNOMIG was destined to remain in Georgia into the next century. A similar disturbance destabilized newly independent Tajikistan, and in 1994 the United Nations was called upon to monitor a 1994 agreement entered into by the government and the Tajik opposition. Here too the CIS sent a sizeable military force, while a mission from the Organization of Security and Cooperation in Europe (OSCE) attempted to mediate the dispute. Nevertheless, it was the UN mission known as UNMOT which played an important role in inducing the parties to sign a Moscow peace agreement in June 1997. In November 1997, the Security Council extended the mandate of UNMOT and expanded the number of military observers.

*Africa*

UN efforts at achieving peaceful settlements in Africa following the end of the Cold War have not been easy. The several missions despatched to Angola between 1989 and 1997 were largely responsible for the restoration of civil order, and indeed the verification missions—of which UNAVEM III was the last in a series—were recalled when it was assumed the conflicted parties had given sufficient assurances of forming a government of reconciliation. Renewed fighting, however, between the government and the forces of Joshua Savimbi destabilized the government in 1998 and a smaller mission (MONUA) sustained the UN presence and was authorized to help bridge factional differences as well as monitor violations of human rights. Savimbi, heavily supported by the United States during the cold war years, still believed he was the only genuine representative of the Angolan nation. His struggle with a government whose roots are traced to the Cuban intervention of the 1970s has never ceased. And in the absence of a diplomatic coup that would give him sole control of the government, his forces apparently were prepared to sustain the fighting. Savimbi's forces were accused in December 1998 and January 1999 of shooting down two transport aircraft of the UN mission in Angola. The mortal danger this posed to MONUA members of the UN mission signalled a new and more desperate turn of events and brought into serious question the continuing feasibility of the operation. MONUA was phased out in February 1999.

The situation in Liberia was hardly better. UNOMIL operated in Liberia from 1993 to 1997, and in conjunction with Organization of African Unity (OAU) and ECOWAS peacekeepers it sought to restore a semblance of order to the war-torn nation. Not different from the anarchy that overwhelmed Somalia, Liberia was unable to find a government to unify the many tribes and factions that surfaced after the destruction of the longstanding Tubman regime. As a source of instability in western Africa, neighboring states took it upon themselves to correct the situation and an agreement was orchestrated by the OAU that the United Nations attempted to reinforce. Promising humanitarian relief, and seeking a return of the refugees that had flooded adjoining countries, the United Nations offered assistance in disarming the combatants, in clearing mines, as well as in removing unexploded bombs and artillery shells. Absorbing the demobilized fighters into a more congenial system proved extremely difficult, however, and it was with mixed emotions that the UN peacekeeping operation was ended following elections in the summer of 1997. After September 1997, the ongoing problem of Liberia was made the exclusive concern of ECOWAS and the OAU.

But if Angola and Liberia were something less than outstanding UN achievements, the bloodletting in Rwanda in 1996–97 was a total disaster. Although UNOMUR had been sent to police the Uganda border with Rwanda in 1993, no one was prepared for the genocide that the Hutus visited upon the Tutsi. Pleas by the United Nations Secretary-General to member states to help thwart the slaughter went unanswered and were it not for the French intervention, there is no telling how many more tens of thousands would have lost their lives. Although the military situation in Rwanda was subsequently managed by indigenous African forces, and a Tutsi-dominant government assumed power in the country, the United Nations offered technical assistance, refugee relief, and training for the judiciary and communal police through UNAMIR. UNAMIR ended its mission in April 1996, but the United Nations then was involved with the formation of an International Criminal Tribunal for Rwanda. Citing crimes against humanity, the UN assumed the awesome task of bringing the perpetrators of genocide to justice.

Somalia was still another publicized setback for the United Nations. The intervention in Somalia was prompted by the United States, which had cited a humanitarian emergency. The immediate need was to save hundreds of thousands of innocent Somalis who were threatened by famine. The United Nations was enlisted in this effort and thus began the deployment of UNOSOM and UNOSOM II, the last of which represented a force of some 28,000 military and police personnel. Functioning with more than $1.6 billion, it assumed the tasks of UNITAF, the multinational force organized by the United Nations earlier. Authorized to use "all necessary means" to establish a secure environment for humanitarian relief operations, UNOSOM II also was mandated to rebuild the political, economic, and social life of Somalia. Compelled to make war on local warlords who blocked the formation of a central government, UNOSOM's humanitarian resettlement operations became demonstrations of force. In the violent struggles that ensued, the United States declared it was unwilling to sustain additional casualties (a number of Americans had been killed in attempting to apprehend a Somali warlord) and it withdrew its troops. The Security Council therefore again reversed UNOSOM's role, and in March 1995, it declared the peacekeepers had completed their humanitarian work and they were withdrawn.

UN peacekeepers also operated in the Aouzou Strip between Chad and Libya, where a small staff of nine military observers and six civilians verified the withdrawal of Libyan forces from the region in accordance with a ruling by the International Court of Justice. A coup in Sierra Leone in 1997 ousted the elected government, but the Security Council hesitated in responding to that problem. A resolution of concern was voted on 26 February 1998 but it did little to relieve the situation. Seizing the initiative, ECOWAS, and especially Nigeria, sent troops into Sierra Leone. They forced the coup leaders to flee the country, after which they also reinstated the original government. Tranquility, however, did not come to Sierra Leone. Rebel forces continued to battle the ECOWAS force, now known as ECOMOG, and in spite of the latter's determined efforts the killing was perpetuated. The UN Security Council authorized the dispatch of an observer force, UNOMSIL in 1998, and gave its support to ECOMOG, but the fighting did not end. Although UNOMSIL was slated to be withdrawn by the end of the year, given sustained turbulence in the East African nation, in 1999 its mandate was renewed.

## South Pacific

UN concerns for the people of East Timor were somewhat reduced when Indonesia's post-Suharto government ceased its aggressive campaign against the Timorese people. In the summer of 1998, Jakarta removed its troops and agreed to conduct elections in an effort to restore tranquility and self-government to the island. Seizing the opportunity to press for a resolution of the Timorese problem, Secretary-General Kofi Annan named a Personal Representative on East Timor to work with the parties. In March 1999 the representative, Jamsheed Marker, reported progress in his negotiations and an agreement to hold a direct ballot in Timor was obtained from the Indonesian government. In effect, the people of East Timor were to be given the option of accepting or rejecting an autonomy proposal. Secretary Annan cited his continuing concern but welcomed the positive atmosphere of the negotiations as well as the statements by the parties that their objective was peace and stability on the island.

## Perspective

The changed global political climate has not eliminated the political, economic, and sociological roots of conflict, nor has it enabled the United Nations to settle every dispute brought before it since 1987. The Middle East is still a volcano waiting for the next eruption. In Cyprus the underlying conflict between Greek and Turkish communities remains unresolved after nearly three decades of UN settlement efforts. In Croatia, Bosnia-Herzegovina, Kosovo, Azerbaijan, Armenia, Georgia, and elsewhere, political ambitions combine with ancient ethnic antagonisms to produce continuing threats to the peace. In a number of Third World countries, of which Somalia was the most obvious example, internal divisions and lack of governmental institutions provide a setting for persisting violence and disorder.

*Looking Ahead*

Citing the difficulties in making UN peacekeeping operations more effective as well as more cost efficient, also noting the greater likelihood in the post Cold War era of other-organization involvement in peacekeeping, Secretary-General Kofi Annan called for a re-examination of the co-deployment principle. Georgia, Tajikistan, Liberia, Sierra Leone, and the former Yugoslavia provided insight for the development of doctrine and guidelines that might better prepare the United Nations for more frequent partnerships with regional organizations. Annan digressed on the need to ensure that humanitarian strategies as well as longer term development aims are fully integrated in an overall, sustainable peacekeeping program. The building of a collective security system for the twenty-first century, he noted, should center on preventive diplomacy and the avoidance of armed conflict. The UN system, as never before, must learn to meld its activities with regional IGOs as well as purposeful NGOs concerned with military security, civil law and order, human rights, refugees and displaced persons, elections, local administration, ensuring public utilities, health, education, finance, reconstruction, and the creation of civil society. All international institutions are significant and all must be enlisted in the cause of peace and development, he opined, but no organization demonstrated more experience or greater scope and universality than the United Nations. Thus, in spite of its obvious weaknesses and shortcomings, the Secretary-General left little doubt that there was no real substitute for the UN system.

# CONCLUSIONS ON DISPUTE SETTLEMENT

Most states settle most of their disputes with one another most of the time without resort to force and without need for assistance from third parties. The vast bulk of day-to-day transactions between nationals of different countries and their governments are mutually beneficial, and all parties have an interest in peacefully resolving differences that may arise. Most differences between governments are settled by diplomatic negotiation without recourse to courts, the United Nations, or complicated procedures and pose no threat to international peace and security. The United States alone concludes perhaps two hundred treaties and executive agreements with foreign governments every year, each of which settles some disputed question. Major states annually settle scores or even hundreds of disputed matters with other states through letters and memoranda, without resorting to the formality of a treaty. If one could identify and count all of the disputes between governments that have been peacefully resolved, the statistical evidence in support of peaceful settlement as an international norm would be overwhelming.

By contrast, the UN record of peaceful settlement is statistically not strong. Although people may reasonably differ in their judgment of UN impact on particular disputes, knowledgeable observers agree that during the cold war era the United Nations contributed to the settlement of many fewer than half of the disputes brought before it. Table 6-2 presents findings of Ernst Haas in a study of disputes considered by the United Nations from 1945 to 1984. During that time, by his methods of calculation, 137 disputes were referred to the United Nations for settlement. Of this number, the United Nations helped settle just thirty-four. In eleven of the disputes, the organization's contribution to settlement was judged substantial; in the other twenty-three it was significant but nevertheless modest in relation to other influences working toward settlement.

An additional forty disputes, for a total of seventy-four, were in some degree ameliorated because of UN efforts at conflict management. *Conflict management,* as Haas defines the term, includes not only settling disputes but also abating the conflict (reducing its intensity), isolating the conflict (inhibiting third parties from intervening diplomatically or militarily in support of the disputants), and stopping armed hostilities. United Nations' success in conflict management was characterized as "great" in thirty-two cases and "limited" in the other forty-two. If the concept of pacific settlement is expanded to embrace Haas's definition of conflict management, the UN success level through 1984 rises to just 54 percent, including cases in which the organization made only a limited contribution.

No similar study has covered the period since 1984, but the cases discussed earlier in connection with UN peacekeeping and dispute settlement indicate that UN performance has not improved since 1987. The United Nations would undoubtedly do better if it had the legal right and the practical capability to enforce settlements. In this respect the United Nations mirrors the shortcomings of the larger international system, which lacks sufficient sense of community to support central coercive institutions. In peacefully settling most of their bilateral disputes with one another, states also operate within the constraints of the existing system, but that is an unfair comparison because the United Nations never deals with routine disputes susceptible of ready compromise. Bilateral negotiation has already failed in most disputes brought to the United Nations, and parties have often resorted to the threat or use of force. In many UN cases, one or more of the parties is willing to settle only for the complete capitulation of the other side. Not all UN disputes are this intractable, but as a class the disputes that reach the United Nations are the most difficult to resolve. Viewed in this light, the spotty UN settlement record is understandable. Given the nature of the disputes that come to the United Nations, one may presumably conclude that a contribution to the settlement of any of them is noteworthy.

The United Nations' ability to settle disputes has always been closely correlated with the existence within the United Nations of a consensus having links

TABLE 6-2    UN Success in Conflict Management, 1945–1984

| TIME PERIOD | NUMBER OF DISPUTES REFERRED TO UNITED NATIONS | GREAT UN SUCCESS NUMBER | % | LIMITED UN SUCCESS NUMBER | % | GREAT OR LIMITED UN SUCCESS NUMBER | % |
|---|---|---|---|---|---|---|---|
| 1945–50 | 20 | 8 | 40.0 | 5 | 25.0 | 13 | 65.0 |
| 1951–55 | 12 | 3 | 25.0 | 1 | 8.3 | 4 | 33.3 |
| 1956–60 | 16 | 6 | 37.5 | 6 | 37.5 | 12 | 75.0 |
| 1961–65 | 26 | 5 | 19.2 | 5 | 19.2 | 10 | 38.5 |
| 1966–70 | 14 | 4 | 28.6 | 5 | 35.7 | 9 | 64.3 |
| 1971–75 | 12 | 3 | 25.0 | 2 | 16.7 | 5 | 41.7 |
| 1976–80 | 24 | 3 | 12.5 | 13 | 54.2 | 16 | 66.7 |
| 1981–84 | 13 | 0 | 0 | 5 | 38.5 | 5 | 38.5 |
| Total | 137 | 32 | 23.4 | 42 | 30.7 | 74 | 54.0 |

SOURCE: Ernst B. Haas, "The Collective Management of International Conflict, 1945–1984," in *The United Nations and the Maintenance of Internal Peace and Security,* United Nations Institute for Training and Research (Dordrecht: Martinus Nijhoff Publishers, 1987), Tables 5, A, E, and F, pp. 63, 67–68.

with effective centers of power outside the organization. At the inception of the United Nations, the necessary consensus in the Security Council was available only on the rare occasions when Soviet and U.S. interest converged. For a number of years U.S. leadership was able to engineer the needed consensus in the General Assembly on many issues, and that consensus was given practical effect by U.S. world influence. The organization was seldom effective in resolving conflicts between opposing cold war coalitions, but promoting settlement between an aligned and a nonaligned state was often possible. The United Nations was quite effective in dealing with decolonization disputes, perhaps the typical case of aligned versus nonaligned.

After 1960 U.S. leadership in the Assembly was replaced by Third World dominance. The new majority readily mustered a united front on issues of Western colonialism, on Israel and South Africa, and usually on opposition to superpower military interventions. But the remaining vestiges of vanished colonial empires became a declining portion of the UN agenda, and when a superpower opposed the consensus, the prevailing majority lacked the power to carry out its mandates. This often led to name-calling and denunciation in place of a genuine search for settlement. Other serious quarrels and threats to peace occurred within the Third World, and here the requisite consensus was often lacking. Thus, whereas Israel, South Africa, and the remaining colonial enclaves evoked strong UN disapproval, the Third World majority was much less decisive in dealing with disputes between nonaligned votes, such as those arising from the

1975 Indonesian conquest of East Timor, Vietnamese military occupation of Cambodia, China's 1979 incursion into Vietnam, the Iraqi attack on Iran, and Indian aid to secessionist Bangladesh.

Since 1987 U.S.-Soviet (now Russian) cooperation has brought new consensus to the Security Council. Remarkably, even China—sometimes grudgingly or by abstention—goes along. More than ever before, a UN consensus is linked with effective centers of world power. The Charter framers at San Francisco never contemplated that the United Nations would abolish differences of interest among states. They did believe that international disputes should be kept within peaceful bounds and that the United Nations could help with this task. In this they were not wrong or mistaken. Peaceful settlement of international disputes is still a worthy goal, and the United Nations has been a helpful adjunct to other settlement techniques. No war of global extent, no conflict severe enough to threaten the system of independent states has emerged since the United Nations was established. To this conflict containment, the United Nations has made a contribution. The persistence of unresolved disputes and the occurrence of numerous local wars still leave the world far short of the peaceful settlement ideal. One may regard such conflict at the periphery as a reasonable price to pay for stability at the center if that is in fact the trade-off. But if the framers were right in believing that no war is necessary, it represents a persisting challenge to extend the reach of peaceful settlement procedures.

# NOTES

1. *The New York Times,* June 6, 1998.
2. "Report on the Work of the Organization," *UN Chronicle* 19, no. 9 (October 1982), p. 2.
3. Gideon Rafael, *Destination Peace: Three Decades of Israeli Foreign Policy* (New York: Stein & Day, 1981), p. 235. This subject is elaborated in Istvan S. Pogany, *The Security Council and the Arab-Israeli Conflict* (Aldershot, Eng.: Gower Publishing, 1984).
4. Ernst B. Haas, "The Collective Management of International Conflict, 1945–1984," in United Nations Institute for Training and Research, *The United Nations and the Maintenance of International Peace and Security* (Dordrecht: Martinus Nijhoff Publishers, 1987), pp. 58–59, note 3.

# SELECTED READINGS

Bailey, Sydney D. *The Procedure of the U.N. Security Council.* 2nd ed. New York: Oxford University Press, 1988.

———. *How Wars End: The United Nations and the Termination of Armed Conflicts, 1946–1964.* 2 vols. New York: Oxford University Press, 1982.

Berridge, G. R. *Return to the UN: UN Diplomacy in Regional Conflicts.* New York: St. Martin's Press, 1991.

Boudreau, Thomas E. *Sheathing the Sword: The U.N. Secretary-General and the Prevention of Inter-Nation Conflict.* Westport, CT: Greenwood Press, 1991.

Boyd, Andrew. *Fifteen Men on a Powder Keg: A History of the United Nations Security Council.* New York: Stein & Day, 1971.

Brus, Marcel, Sam Muller, and Serv Wiemers, eds. *The United Nations Decade of International Law: Reflections on International Dispute Settlement.* Dordrecht: Martinus Nijhoff Publishers, 1991.

Childers, Erskine, ed. *Challenges to the United Nations: Building a Safer World.* New York: St. Martin's Press, 1995.

Deng, Francis M., and I. William Zartman. *Conflict Resolution in Africa.* Washington, DC: Brookings Institution, 1991.

Diehl, Paul. *The Politics of Global Governance: International Organizations in an Interdependent World.* Boulder: Lynne Rienner, 1996.

Hillen, John. *Blue Helmets: The Strategy of U.N. Military Operations.* Washington: Brassey's, 1998.

Lall, Arthur S. *Multilateral Negotiation and Mediation.* New York: Pergamon Press, 1985.

McWhinney, Edward. *Judicial Settlement of International Disputes: Jurisdiction, Justiciability, and Judicial Law-Making on the Contemporary International Court.* Dordrecht: Martinus Nijhoff Publishers, 1991.

Merrills, J. G. *International Dispute Settlement.* 2nd ed. Cambridge: Cambridge University Press, 1991.

Niedermayer, Oskar, and Richard Sinnott, eds. *Public Opinion and Internationalized Governance.* New York: Oxford University Press, 1995.

Nicol, Davidson. *The United Nations Security Council: Towards Greater Effectiveness.* New York: UNITAR, 1982.

———, ed. *Paths to Peace: The UN Security Council and Its Presidency.* New York: Pergamon Press, 1981.

Peck, Connie, and David A. Hamburg. *Sustainable Peace: The Role of the UN and Regional Organizations in Preventing Conflict.* Lanham, MD.: Rowman and Littlefield Publishers, 1998.

Roberts, Adam, and Benedict Kingsbury. *United Nations, Divided World.* Oxford: Clarendon Press, 1988.

Rosenne, Shabtai. *The World Court: What It Is and How It Works.* 4th rev. ed. Dordrecht: Martinus Nijhoff Publishers, 1989.

Singh, Nagendra. *The Role and Record of the International Court of Justice.* Dordrecht: Martinus Nijhoff Publishers, 1989.

United Nations. *The United Nations and the Maintenance of International Peace and Security.* United Nations Institute for Training and Research. Dordrecht: Martinus Nijhoff Publishers, 1987.

Urquhart, Brian. *A Life in Peace and War.* New York: Harper & Row, Publishers, 1987.

Weiss, Thomas G., and James G. Blight, eds. *The Suffering Grass: Superpowers and Regional Conflict in Southern Africa and the Caribbean.* Boulder, CO: Lynne Rienner Publishers, 1992.

Woodhouse, Tom, Robert Bruce and Malcolm Dando, eds. *Peacekeeping and Peacemaking: Towards Effective Intervention in Post-Cold War Conflicts.* New York: St. Martin's Press, 1998.

Yost, David S. *NATO Transformed: The Alliance's New Roles in International Security.* Washington, DC: US Institute of Peace Press, 1999.

# 7

# DISARMAMENT AND ARMS CONTROL

Although the UN Charter does not include disarmament in its statement of purposes and principles, arms control negotiations have been fostered by the United Nations since it came into being. For decades the results were meager. A few limited arms control measures were agreed to, but the growth of national armaments and the development of new and more destructive technologies continued apace. Hundreds of proposals and thousands of meetings brought disarmament no closer. Disarmament was always a mirage—visible at a distance but fading away on close approach.

Then the cold war ended. The world Communist threat dissolved. The Warsaw Pact was terminated, unilateral actions to reduce armaments were undertaken in Eastern Europe, and NATO reciprocated by a reduction in forces. The collapse of Communist economics and the splintering of the Union of Soviet Socialist Republics (USSR) into fifteen independent states made continued arms competition with the West totally unfeasible. These developments engendered hope that at last East-West disarmament might become a reality. Hope was tempered, however, by the persisting specter of nuclear proliferation, the burgeoning arms trade to less developed states, and the uncertainties of the road ahead.

This chapter will explore the prospects for disarmament by surveying the history of arms negotiations, evaluating the accomplishments to date, analyzing the obstacles to successful arms control, and examining a number of possible approaches to the disarmament problem. Such a broad-based analysis of the theory and practice of arms control is necessary to place UN actions in their global and historical context and to identify both the promise and the problems of the future.

## DISARMAMENT IN HISTORICAL PERSPECTIVE

Pursuit of disarmament through international negotiation is largely a phenomenon of the twentieth century. In centuries past such visionaries as Immanuel

Kant, Jean-Jacques Rousseau, and William Penn had postulated the ideal of a completely disarmed world, but these utopian notions had little impact except in intellectual circles. Through most of the nineteenth century, various proposals for arms reduction by European leaders aroused little interest, and the only real success of that period was the Rush-Bagot Agreement of 1817 by which the United States and Great Britain limited naval armaments on the Great Lakes. The first major conference with disarmament as its objective was called by Czar Nicholas of Russia at The Hague in 1899. His action was motivated by desire to reduce the economic burden of armaments and keep his rivals from equipping their armies with new and improved artillery. Although no agreement was reached on the limitation of armaments and war budgets, the First Hague Conference was able to codify some of the laws of war and produced a Convention for the Pacific Settlement of Disputes. A second Hague Peace Conference called in 1907 was similarly ineffective in halting the arms race, which climaxed in the maelstrom of World War I.[1]

## DISARMAMENT EFFORTS DURING THE LEAGUE YEARS

The Covenant of the League of Nations followed the prescription advocated by Woodrow Wilson in one of his Fourteen Points. It provided that armaments, as a recognized cause of war, should be "reduced to the lowest point consistent with national safety" but retained in sufficient quantities to provide for "the enforcement by common action of international obligations." Implementation of Covenant provisions awaited general agreement on arms limitation, but Germany was immediately subjected to disarmament under the terms of the Versailles Treaty, and the Rhineland was completely demilitarized. This was effective in the short term, but neither the League nor the Allied powers were able to halt German remilitarization in the 1930s when Hitler came to power. Meanwhile, the League's approach was to sponsor disarmament studies and conferences aimed at implementing Covenant provisions.

The first major postwar effort to limit arms by voluntary agreement took place outside the League framework. In 1921 the Washington Naval Conference—called by the United States and attended by representatives of Britain, France, Italy, and Japan—set the pace for arms limitation negotiations. A treaty signed the following year limited the size of warships, restricted the construction of battleships and aircraft carriers for ten years, limited new construction thereafter by a ratio agreement (United States, 5; Britain, 5; Japan, 3; France, 1.67; and Italy, 1.67), and imposed limitations on naval bases in the Pacific. Subsequently some of the parties violated the spirit and others the letter of the treaty. Britain and the United States engaged in a "cruiser race," Japan devised ingenious variations of the prohibited vessels to nullify the intent of the treaty, and France refused to implement any limit in the absence of a general European security arrangement. The record of violations and subterfuge that followed the

Washington Naval Arms Limitation Treaty, and the countermeasures under-taken in response to evasions, call attention to the difficulty of implementing a disarmament agreement without international inspection and enforcement machinery.

The League was even less successful in its efforts to promote a general re-duction in armaments. A Temporary Mixed Commission of nongovernmental experts, appointed by the Assembly to formulate a plan for consideration by the Council, labored from 1921 to 1924 without producing an acceptable pro-posal. In 1925 the Assembly decided to try the world conference approach and established a Preparatory Commission composed of governmental representa-tives to lay the groundwork. After five years of sporadic effort, the Commission prepared a Draft Convention in 1930 that reflected mostly the inability of its members to reach accord on limiting their armed forces. The main provisions of the Draft Convention called for the reduction of military budgets, modest re-ductions in naval armaments, and the establishment of a Permanent Disarma-ment Commission. The Preparatory Commission's experience did not augur well for arms limitation agreement, although the deepening economic depres-sion raised the possibility that the struggle to preserve fiscal solvency might force some states to curtail arms production unilaterally.

The World Disarmament Conference was finally convened at Geneva in 1932, with sixty-one states represented. Each of the major nations in turn of-fered its scheme to a skeptical group of delegates. The French plan envisaged a comprehensive security system that included qualified disarmament, an in-ternational control system, compulsory arbitration, and an international police force under League jurisdiction to guarantee security. Britain offered a plan that would outlaw the use of "offensive" weapons through a reinforced League se-curity system, provide for disarmament by stages over a five-year period, and outlaw weapons of mass destruction. Germany demanded equality with France in any disarmament program. The United States proposed a uniform reduction in forces so that each nation would retain the same arms ratio with all other na-tions that it had before the agreement.

There was never much chance for agreement, but the last flicker of hope was extinguished when Adolf Hitler was appointed Chancellor of Germany in 1933 and withdrew his country from the conference and the League. The conference, immobilized almost from the start by the basic conflict between German demands for arms equality and the French insistence on arms superi-ority over Germany, finally adjourned in 1934 without agreement on an arms limitation treaty. The conference may have been a useful learning experience, however. Agreement on broad principles, though never formalized, indicated a general revulsion against the use of chemical and bacteriological weapons, a consensus that arms should be reduced and military budgets curtailed, and a general acceptance of the idea that an international authority should be estab-lished to supervise any disarmament agreement that could be reached. Debates at the conference and in the League's Assembly over a period of twenty years undoubtedly helped prepare the world for the next round in the disarmament cycle under the United Nations.

## THE UNITED NATIONS AND DISARMAMENT

Disarmament negotiations since 1945 have been more persistent than during the League era and have been driven by a greater sense of urgency. The explosion of an atom bomb over Hiroshima just six weeks after the signing of the Charter alerted the world to the potential of a calamity far greater than the destructiveness of World War II. The ensuing cold war, accompanied by full-scale rearmament, rival alliances, perpetual crises, and the development of intercontinental missiles with thermonuclear warheads—all occurring within a setting of ideological hostility—forged a link in some minds between disarmament and sheer survival. Third World peoples, unheard from during the 1930s, joined the disarmament chorus not only from fear of nuclear destruction but in the hope that resources diverted from armaments might be channeled to economic development.

The Charter framers did not assign disarmament a prominent role in pursuing the primary goal of peace and security. In the Charter scheme, the use of collective force against international lawbreakers, rather than disarmament, was the key to maintaining a peaceful world. Specific mention of "disarmament" in the Charter occurs only twice. Under Article 11, the General Assembly is authorized to consider and make recommendations concerning "the general principles of cooperation in the maintenance of international peace and security, including the principles governing disarmament and the regulation of armaments." The other reference appears in Article 47, which authorizes the Military Staff Committee to advise the Security Council on "the regulation of armaments and possible disarmament."

The failure of the UN founding fathers to stress the need for disarmament can be ascribed in part to their ignorance of the atomic device that American scientists were secretly preparing to test at the very time the Charter was being written. Added to this, the frustrations of the League period and the emphasis on the use of an international army to maintain peace and security through community force influenced the framers against setting forth extravagant disarmament goals that would probably be unrealizable.

Unlike the League Covenant, which had called for an outright *reduction* in arms, the Charter merely proclaims the objective of arms *regulation*. Regulation implies the need for a strategically balanced ceiling on armaments so that the collective security machinery of the United Nations can function in a world not obsessed with fear of an imminent and massive attack. The close relationship between the two objectives—arms regulation and collective security—led the framers to assign responsibility for both functions to the Security Council aided by the Military Staff Committee (Articles 26 and 46, respectively). Giving the same bodies the responsibility of formulating plans for arms regulation *and* the use of military forces offered no contradiction for the framers, who considered progress in both areas essential to the maintenance of peace and security.

Despite the difficulties and frustrations encountered in the area of disarmament during the years of the Cold War, the United Nations never lost sight of its goal of a world less prone to arms races. The General Assembly has six committees dealing exclusively with disarmament and international related issues, of which the First Committee, consisting of all member states, focuses on disarmament and security questions and recommends draft resolutions to the Assembly. The Disarmament Commission is still another body that addresses key areas, notably nuclear-free-weapon-free zones, and the reduction and limitation of conventional weapons. The Secretary-General was also made responsible for overseeing activities concerned with arms reduction, especially in the matter of weapons of mass destruction. A United Nations Institute for Disarmament Research (UNIDIR) was established in Geneva and made an integral part of the UN Secretariat. In 1978, an Advisory Board on Disarmament Matters was created by action of the General Assembly and made functional in 1982. The Board on Disarmament advised the Secretary-General on various aspects of research in the area of arms limitation. It also served as the Board of Trustees for the UNIDIR and assisted in the dissemination of the UN Disarmament Information Program.

In 1997 the Board examined the reorganization of the UN disarmament sector proposed by Kofi Annan, and cited the new security challenges facing the world body in the twenty-first century. The 1997 conference focused attention on both weapons of mass destruction and conventional arms and emphasized the need to have member states register conventional arms in their arsenals, as well as the desire to develop norms for the implementation of agreements related to weapons of mass destruction. A most important action of the UN disarmament organs was the 1995 Nuclear Non-Proliferation Treaty conference, which was convened at UN Headquarters in New York City for the purpose of extending indefinitely the NPT treaty that had gone into force in 1970. After twenty-four days of difficult negotiations, agreement was achieved when the acknowledged nuclear powers, the United States, Russia, China, Britain, and France, assured the non-nuclear states that a comprehensive test-ban treaty would be entered into during the following year, and that they were determined to significantly reduce their nuclear stockpiles over the next twenty years. On the subject of conventional weapons, notably those described as "excessively injurious" or having "indiscriminate effects," the UN sought to outlaw the use of blinding laser weapons and land mines. The success of these ventures was illustrated in protocols calling for their abandonment in 1995, 1996, and again in 1997. (See Figure 7-1)

FIGURE 7-1   **Major International Instruments on Disarmament and Related Issues**

Protocol for the *Prohibition of the Use in War of Asphyxiating, Poisonous or Other Cases,* and of Bacteriological Methods of Warfare, 17 June 1925

*Geneva Convention (I)* for the Amelioration of the Condition of the Wounded and Sick in Armed Forces in the Field, 12 August 1949

*Geneva Convention (II)* for the Amelioration of the Condition of Wounded, Sick and Shipwrecked Members of Armed Forces at Sea, 12 August 1949

*Geneva Convention (III)* Relative to the Treatment of Prisoners of War, 12 August 1949

*Geneva Convention (IV)* Relative to the Protection of Civilian Persons in Time of War, 12 August 1949

Convention for the *Protection of Cultural Property* in the Event of Armed Conflict. *Final act* of the intergovernmental conference on the protection of cultural property and *Protocol,* 14 May 1954

The *Antarctic* Treaty, 1 December 1959

Treaty Banning Nuclear Weapon Tests in the Atmosphere, in Outer Space and Under Water (*Partial Test Ban Treaty*), 5 August 1963

Treaty on Principles Governing the Activities of States in the Exploration and Use of *Outer Space,* Including the Moon and other Celestial Bodies, 27 January 1967

Treaty for the Prohibition of Nuclear Weapons in Latin America (*Tlatelolco Treaty*), 14 February 1967

Treaty on the *Non-Proliferation of Nuclear Weapons,* 1 July 1968

Convention on the Prohibition of the Development, Production and Stockpiling of *Bacteriological (Biological) and Toxin Weapons* and on their Destruction, 10 April 1972

Treaty between the United States of America and the Union of Soviet Socialist Republics on the *Limitation of Anti-Ballistic Missile Systems,* 26 May 1972; and *Protocol,* 3 July 1974

Treaty Between the United States of America and the Union of Soviet Socialist Republics on the Limitation of Underground Nuclear Weapon Tests (*Threshold Test Ban Treaty*), 3 July 1974; and Protocol, 1 June 1949

Convention on the Prohibition of Military or any Other Hostile Use of *Environmental Modification Techniques,* 10 December 1976

Protocol I Additional to the Geneva Conventions of 12 August 1949, and Relating to the *Protection of Victims of International Armed Conflict,* 8 June 1977

Protocol II Additional to the Geneva Conventions of 12 August 1949, and Relating to the *Protection of Victims of Non-International Armed Conflict,* 8 June 1977

Guidelines for Nuclear Transfers Adopted by the 15-Nation Nuclear Suppliers' Group (*London Guidlines*), 21 September 1977

Agreement Governing the Activities of States on the *Moon* and other Celestial Bodies, 18 December 1979

Convention on Prohibitions or Restrictions on the Use of Certain *Conventional Weapons* Which May be Deemed to be Excessively Injurious or to Have Indiscriminate Effects, 10 October 1980; and Additional Protocol (IV) on *Blinding Laser Weapons,* 12 October 1995

South Pacific Nuclear Free Zone Treaty (*Treaty of Rarotonga*), 6 August 1985

FIGURE 7-1   *(continued)*

---

Convention on the Prohibition of the Development, Production, Stockpiling and Use of *Chemical Weapons* and on their Destruction, 13 January 1993

Guidelines for transfers of nuclear-related dual-use equipment, material and related technology (*Warsaw Guidelines*), 3 April 1992

Guidelines for Nuclear Transfers (*Revision of NSG London Guidelines* of 1977), 1 April 1993

Decisions and Resolution Adopted by the 1995 *Review and Extension Conference* of the Parties to the Treaty on the Non-Proliferation of Nuclear Weapons, 11 May 1995

Treaty on the Southeast Asia Nuclear-Weapon-Free Zone (*Bangkok Treaty*), 15 December 1995; *Annex* and *Protocol*

Treaty on the Nuclear-Weapon-Free Zone in Africa (*Pelindaba Treaty*), 11 April 1996; and *Cairo Declaration*

Comprehensive *Nuclear-Test-Ban Treaty*, 10 September 1996

---

SOURCE: UN Website: http://www.unorg.ch/frames/disarm/distreat/warfare.htm

# ARMS NEGOTIATIONS IN THE UN ERA

## EARLY FAILURES

Initial efforts in the disarmament field were undertaken by the UN Atomic Energy Commission, established in January 1946, and by the Commission for Conventional Armaments, created the following year. With the devastating consequences of the first atomic explosions still fresh in every mind, control of atomic weapons was given the higher priority. In recognition of the great potentialities for peaceful uses of atomic energy, as well as grave dangers for all of mankind, the Assembly rather than the Security Council was chosen by the great powers to create and empower the Commission. By its first-adopted resolution, the Assembly called on the Commission to develop "with the utmost dispatch" a plan to provide for (1) the exchange of scientific knowledge for peaceful purposes, (2) the control of atomic energy to limit its use to peaceful purposes, (3) the elimination of atomic and other weapons of mass destruction, and (4) the establishment of an inspection and enforcement system to safeguard against evasions.

At the first meeting of the Atomic Energy Commission, the United States, with a monopoly of atomic weapons, offered a plan that would eventually provide for a sharing of its atomic secrets under an international control system. The proposal, based on recommendations made in the Acheson-Lilienthal Report, was presented by elder statesman Bernard Baruch. In its fundamentals the Baruch Plan provided for a transition to peaceful atomic control by stages, with each stage dependent on the successful implementation of the preceding stage before further progress would be attempted. It called for the creation of an International Atomic Development Authority that would operate an elaborate inspection and control system under Security Council direction unhampered by the veto power. All atomic weapons would be destroyed once the control system became operational, and the manufacture of new atom bombs would be outlawed. The Authority would then exercise exclusive ownership of atomic raw materials, control all atomic activities, encourage their beneficial use by all nations, hold a monopoly on research and development in the field of atomic explosives, and license national atomic research for peaceful purposes. In sum, the plan would establish a world federal government in the field of atomic energy.

The Soviet Union emphatically rejected the U.S. proposal, calling instead for the immediate outlawing of all atomic weapons followed by the establishment of a minimum system of control. In the Soviet view, each state should accept responsibility for the peaceful development of atomic power and for the policing of the prohibition against atomic weapons within its borders, subject to periodic oversight by an international authority. Enforcement action would be undertaken by the Security Council against violators, but only with the agreement of all permanent members. Thus the first confrontation between the United States and the Soviet Union produced basic disagreements over the timing (which comes first, complete disarmament or an inspection and control system?), peaceful development (by national or international authority?), inspection (what powers should the international authority possess, and how frequently should it conduct inspections?), and control (should the veto power apply to action against violators?).

The Soviets, placed on the defensive by the Baruch Plan and outnumbered on the Atomic Energy Commission, attempted to retrieve the initiative by proposing to the 1946 Assembly a plan for "general and complete disarmament," including both conventional and nuclear weapons. The proposal apparently was an effort to overcome the propaganda advantage gained by the United States in offering to relinquish its atomic monopoly and to contribute its know-how to the peaceful development of atomic power for mankind. The Soviet Union obviously preferred to discuss the broad, innocuous subject of general disarmament while carrying on a crash program to develop an atom bomb to offset the U.S. advantage. In 1949 the Soviets tested their first atom bomb, and thereafter the arms race was converted into a race between superpowers.

The inexorable development of new technologies produced new complexities and dangers. In 1952, the United States exploded its first hydrogen bomb, a fission-fusion device whose output of explosive power was measured in megatons or millions of tons of TNT equivalents. In 1953, the Soviets successfully exploded a hydrogen bomb, and the U.S.-Soviet nuclear arms race was on in earnest. This dangerous competition produced not only the new and more powerful warheads but new delivery systems as well, including new types of manned bombers, intercontinental ballistic missiles, and missiles with multiple warheads capable of striking multiple targets (the MIRV, or multiple independently targeted re-entry vehicle). The rivalry also extended to short-range delivery systems, down to the level of artillery shells with nuclear devices. Despite repeated attempts at negotiation and occasional agreement on subsidiary issues, the nuclear rivalry continued almost unabated through the 1980s.

## The Search for Effective Forums

Early failures did not terminate the discussion of arms control issues, although legitimization of national positions rather than agreed limitations often appeared to be the primary objective. The arms control dialogue was carried on through a succession of specialized disarmament forums created in an attempt to reconcile the needs of effective negotiation with political demands for representation.

### UN-Related Forums

From 1946 to 1952 the principal negotiating bodies were the twelve-member UN Atomic Energy Commission, including the eleven Security Council members and Canada, and an eleven-member Commission for Conventional Armaments. In 1952 these were combined into a single twelve-person Disarmament Commission. From 1954 to 1957 the main negotiating body was a five-member Subcommittee of the Disarmament Commission, consisting of the United States, the Soviet Union, the United Kingdom, France, and Canada. Beginning in 1957 the Soviet Union boycotted the Disarmament Commission and its subcommittee, demanding that Eastern bloc states be represented on the committee in equal numbers with the West. In hope of luring the Soviet Union back to the table by steps short of East-West parity (which the United States opposed in principle for any UN body), the Assembly enlarged the Commission to twenty-five members in 1958 and, in 1959, to include the entire membership of the Assembly. Thus enlarged, the Disarmament Commission became too unwieldy for serious negotiation and it virtually ceased to meet.

The impasse was ultimately resolved by creating disarmament bodies ostensibly outside the framework of the United Nations, where the United States could accept parity of representation. Thus in 1958 two conferences of experts were convened to deal with the technical problems of detecting nuclear testing (four Western states and four Soviet-bloc states) and guarding against surprise attack (five Western, five Eastern). Beginning in 1958 the United States, Britain, and the Soviet Union began three-nation nuclear test-ban talks at UN headquarters in Geneva. In 1959 a Ten Nation Committee on Disarmament (five Western, five Eastern) was established by agreement among the Big Four foreign ministers. In 1961, under pressure from the Third World for its failure to achieve disarmament results, the ten-nation body was enlarged into an Eighteen-Nation Disarmament Committee (ENDC) by the addition of eight nonaligned countries. Third World representation was further increased in 1969 when the ENDC was replaced by a twenty-six-member Conference of the Committee on Disarmament (CCD).

In 1979, at the request of the General Assembly, the CCD was expanded to forty in the hope that additional members could apply greater pressures on the nuclear powers to reach agreement. The body was reduced to thirty-nine members in 1991 with the reunification of Germany and is currently called the Conference on Disarmament (CD). It meets in Geneva about six months a year as a forum for the negotiation of multilateral arms control and disarmament issues. The CD, like its predecessors, preserves the fiction of independence from the United Nations, even though the question of parity has lost all relevance with the ending of the cold war. In practice, the CD functions almost as a UN suborgan, utilizing UN conference services at UN expense (a personal representative of the UN Secretary-General serves as secretary-general of the conference), reporting regularly to the Assembly, and accepting general guidance from it.

The Disarmament Commission, which had not held a meeting since 1965, was revived in 1978 by the General Assembly's first Special Session on Disarmament as a means of involving more member states in the arms control dialogue and generating world public pressures for disarmament. Unsuited for negotiation because of its large size, it was intended to be a forum for consciousness-raising and the elaboration of ideas. The commission now holds annual meetings of two to four weeks to discuss general issues of disarmament and make recommendations to the General Assembly.

Among some of the items brought to the attention of the General Assembly by the Disarmament Commission in 1997 were the notification of nuclear tests (March); the convention on the prohibition or restriction of certain conventional weapons, notably land mines (July, September, October); establishment of a nuclear weapon-free region in the Middle East, and another in Asia (both in August); the reduction of military budgets and the development of programs of weapons transparency (August); the registration of conventional arms (October, November 1997 as well as January and March 1998); nuclear disarmament (October); and the Comprehensive Nuclear Test Ban Treaty (October). In addition to these continuing efforts, the Commission scored a most significant achievement in December 1997, when the Conference on Disarmament, meeting in Ottawa, Canada, resulted in the signing of the Convention on the Prohibition of the Use, Stockpiling, Production and Transfer of Anti-Personnel Mines, and on Their Destruction. In the wake of this success, Secretary-General Kofi Annan called for and the General Assembly approved the creation of a Department of Disarmament Affairs in the United Nations Secretariat, and in January 1998 he made an Under-Secretary-General its chief officer.

Although a priority item in matters before the United Nations, disarmament in the form of arms control has been more successfully performed by states in direct relations with one another. Special disarmament sessions of the General Assembly were called in 1978 and again in 1982. Each extended over a period of approximately five weeks, but they did little more than encourage the member states to give greater consideration to the urgency of arms reduction. The 1982 session in fact provoked a World Disarmament Campaign that energized disarmament activists who proceeded to demonstrate against the sustained emphasis on weapons dependency. The questionable results of these special conferences, especially the platform they provided for pacifist propaganda, made governments more reluctant to hold subsequent meetings, and as of 1999, the Disarmament Commission was unable to reach agreement for the holding of still another special session on disarmament.

## Non-UN Forums: SALT and START

From the beginning of UN arms control efforts, there has been a general recognition that little progress was possible without major power agreement. Many of the key issues were essentially bilateral in nature and not well suited to negotiation in a large, cumbersome forum. In 1969 at Helsinki, the United States and the Soviet Union recognized this fact of life by initiating Strategic Arms Limitation Talks (SALT). The original SALT negotiations were envisaged as a series of agreements in which incremental reductions in nuclear weapons production and deployment would eventually produce levels that were less threatening as well as less costly to the rival superpowers. The success of SALT I led to SALT II, but the latter was scrapped by the U.S. Senate following the Soviet Union's invasion of Afghanistan in 1979. Ronald Reagan and his Soviet counterparts re-energized the process some years later as the Strategic Arms Reduction Talks (START), but a START treaty was not approved until July 1991. Under its terms, stockpiles of strategic weapons (numbering about 10,000 each) were to be reduced to approximately 8,550 for the United States and 6,450 for the Soviet Union. Other provisions identified specific categories of strategic weapons and established an extensive system of verification. Treaty ratification was delayed by the abortive anti-Gorbachev coup and the subsequent collapse of the Soviet Union. In May 1992 the United States signed a protocol with the government of Russia, and the new republics of Belarus, Ukraine, and Kazakhstan, making them all parties to START I. Ratification for START I was subsequently acquired from all the states. In addition, all four sovereign states agreed to accede to the Nuclear Non-Proliferation Treaty that had been signed in 1968 and put into force in 1970. Furthermore, Belarus, Ukraine, and Kazakhstan opted for the dismantling of their nuclear weapons and the transfer of their warheads to Russia. They subsequently renounced their status as nuclear powers, given United States and Russia guarantees of their security. Moreover, the United States assisted all three countries in the liquidation of their nuclear capabilities.

Seizing upon what was believed to be an opportune moment, on January 3, 1993, the United States and the Russian Federation signed a START II agreement that was aimed at further reducing their land-based, strategic nuclear stockpiles. START II would reduce the United States stockpile of strategic weapons to 3,500 and Russia's to 3,000 by the year 2003. The Russian parliament (Duma), however, registered alarm with START II, asserting it placed Russia at a gross disadvantage vis à vis the United States. Russia's parliamemtary leaders indicated a desire to extend the START II time frame beyond 2003 so that the country's nuclear weapons need not be withdrawn before they reached the end of their designed life-cycle. The Russians also showed displeasure that the disarmament agreement had not reduced sea-based weapons where the United States was perceived holding a distinct advantage. Nor did START II apply to the Chinese, British, and French nuclear arsenals. Finally, the Duma was suspicious of American maneuvers that called for the enlargement of NATO, and Russian legislators cited U.S. Congressional actions in 1998, approving NATO admission for Poland, the Czech Republic, and Hungary. Although Boris Yeltsin continued to publicize his support for START II and urged the Duma to ratify the treaty, as of 1998 the Carnegie Endowment for World Peace reported that Russia still held some 7,000 strategic weapons to 8,000 for the United States. France was said to possess 482 weapons while China had 284 and Britain 100. To highlight that the world was still a very dangerous place after the Cold War, it was noted that Russia and the United States continued to hold an additional several thousand theater-type or tactical nuclear weapons. Moreover, differences with Russia on a range of issues, not the least of which was the American decision in January 1999 to proceed with the development and deployment of an anti-missile defense, and in apparent conflict with the anti-ballistic missile treaty, made it even less likely that the Duma would agree to ratify START II any time in the near future.

## DISARMAMENT AND ARMS CONTROL— A BALANCE SHEET

The pursuit of security in a dangerous nuclear world over a period of five decades has produced no assurance to the global community that Armageddon can be avoided. Yet progress has been made in a number of arms control and related fields. These fields include (1) achieving demilitarization and denuclearization of specific geographic areas, (2) halting nuclear proliferation, (3) banning nuclear weapons tests, (4) avoiding a nuclear weapons race in outer space, (5) limiting or reducing nuclear warheads and delivery systems, (6) developing confidence-building and communication measures to avoid accidental war, (7) banning chemical and biological weapons, and (8) reducing tension by economic and political policies. Each of these fields will be examined briefly.

### DEMILITARIZATION AND DENUCLEARIZATION

If global disarmament is beyond reach in the contemporary world, disarmament within specific geographic areas may still be possible. The first arms control agreement to emerge after World War II provided for the complete demilitarization of the Antarctic continent. The Antarctic Treaty of 1959, signed by twelve governments, developed into the Antarctic Treaty System (ATS), which subsequently included more than forty countries, representing 70 percent of the world's population. Larger than China, India, or the United States and Mexico combined, Antarctica accounted for 10 percent of the planet's land surface and 30 percent of all the land in the Southern Hemisphere. Because Antarctica is believed to possess vast mineral deposits, especially in platinum, petroleum, and natural gas, a protocol on environmental protection established a permanent ban on their mining and exploitation. ATS sought to maintain the frozen continent as a region open to all nations that wish to join in its preservation and scientific discovery. The treaty centers on the following provisions:

1. The use of the region for military activities of any kind is forbidden.
2. Each signatory has the right to inspect the installations of the others to ensure that no treaty violation has occurred.
3. Territorial claims on the continent remain unrecognized, and no new claims may be made.
4. No nuclear explosions or dumping of radioactive wastes is permitted.
5. Disputes under the terms of the treaty will be settled peacefully.
6. The signatories will cooperate in scientific investigations in the region.

The Antarctic Treaty provides a model for the potential demilitarization of other regions in the world. No known violations have occurred, and the right of national inspection has been fully acknowledged. Although no joint arrangements exist for governing the area, Antarctica is at least partially "internationalized" by the voluntary system.

Other proposals aimed at reducing the threat of nuclear war through denuclearization of various regions of the world have since been presented in the General Assembly or developed by regional groups. Third World scholars and diplomats have demonstrated a continuing concern about the impact of a great power war on the peoples of Africa, Asia, and Latin America, and have frequently called for a demilitarization and denuclearization of their regions (without, however, showing much concern for reducing their own national armaments).

The prototype nuclear-weapons-free zone was concluded in the Treaty of Tlatelolco in 1967. This Treaty on the Prohibition of Nuclear Weapons in Latin America was originally signed by twenty-one countries. The number swelled to twenty-five in 1980, and in 1995, Cuba also became a signatory to the treaty. The treaty created an operational body known as OPANAL (Agency for the Prohibition of Nuclear Weapons in Latin America), which oversees enforcement of treaty provisions. Two protocols supplement the treaty and guarantee that the region will remain denuclearized, as well as lend assurances that neither the United States, Russia (the successor state to the Soviet Union), Britain, China, or France will deploy nuclear weapons in the region.

Other regions also have tried to establish nuclear-weapons-free zones. A resolution adopted by the General Assembly in 1961, for example, requested all countries to "consider and respect the continent of Africa as a denuclearized zone." The Organization of African Unity (OAU) followed up by adopting a Declaration on the Denuclearization of Africa, which led the General Assembly to call for an African nuclear-weapons-free zone. This and similar calls, however, have yet to produce a treaty that follows the Latin American precedent.

In 1987, a number of states including Australia, New Zealand, Indonesia, the Soviet Union, and several island nations in the South Pacific, notably Fiji, signed the Treaty of Rarotonga, which declared the region of the South Pacific to be a nuclear-free zone. The United States did not sign the treaty, nor did France, which maintained a nuclear test site near Tahiti. Although the treaty was centered on declaring the region off limits to nuclear weapons deployment and testing, U.S. nuclear-armed vessels continued to operate in the area (even though denied port calls in New Zealand), and in 1995, Paris resumed testing of nuclear weapons in defiance of the provisions of the Rarotonga Treaty. In spite of threats of economic and political retaliation from Australia and New Zealand, France proceeded with its testing program, arguing that it would be the last of its kind. Only a month earlier France had agreed to an indefinite extension of the Nuclear Non-Proliferation Treaty, and this action by Paris disturbed and angered nations around the world.

### The Growing Brotherhood of the Bomb

Closely related to the concept of regional denuclearization has been the issue of nuclear proliferation. That problem arose in 1949 when the Soviet explosion of an atomic device ended the U.S. postwar monopoly of atomic weapons. Three years later Britain exploded a fission bomb, followed by France in 1960 and China in 1964. Each member of the "nuclear club" also exploded test fusion warheads thousands of times more powerful than the Hiroshima fission bomb. India became the first Third World country to join the brotherhood of the bomb in 1974, when it successfully tested a "peaceful nuclear explosive." At least ten nations having the scientific and technological capability to join the club are perhaps debating whether or not to expend the effort and the money necessary for membership. As many as ten additional nations may in time have that capability. Moreover, the spread of nuclear power for peaceful uses involves a risk that fissionable materials may be diverted for military purposes, and more than fifty countries now have nuclear reactors. A number of European countries and Canada, Australia, New Zealand, and Japan have the capability to develop nuclear weapons but have refrained from doing so. Several nations, such as North Korea and Israel, have secretly developed a nuclear weapons capability.

Long-standing efforts to create a nuclear-weapons-free zone in South Asia was most unsuccessful. India's detonation of a nuclear device in 1974, ostensibly as a signal to China, which had gone nuclear earlier, registered more particular impact upon neighboring Pakistan, which was prompted to accelerate its efforts at developing similar capabilities. Although the world seemed to little notice India's nuclear program, Pakistan came in for special scrutiny. The United States was especially concerned over the possibilities of a nuclear arms race in South Asia, notably because of the sustained hostility between the subcontinent's two most prominent states. Neither India nor Pakistan accepted the Nuclear Non-Proliferation Treaty, and they again refused to become signatories following the treaty's indefinite extension in 1995. By the same token neither country agreed to sign the 1996 Comprehensive Nuclear Weapons Test Ban Treaty. Moreover, despite strenuous American efforts at dissuading other nations from assisting Pakistan's nuclear program, by 1997 various intelligence circles had concluded Pakistan was nuclear capable. Thus, when India decided to shock the world by exploding five additional nuclear devices on May 11 and 13, 1998, few were truly surprised that Pakistan followed the Indian lead with six tests of its own, not three weeks later. Although India justified its actions as necessary to balance off the threat posed by nuclear China, Pakistan cited the threat to its security from its immediate neighbor. The Indo-Pakistani actions reminded the world how fragile the edifice of peace was in the years after the cold war. More significant, the nuclear tests had seriously damaged United Nations efforts at preventing the proliferation of nuclear weapons.

The Middle East countries were most immediately impacted by the nuclear explosions in South Asia. Arab-Israeli hostility was undoubtedly the principal reason for the failure to ensure a nuclear-weapons-free region. Israel began developing atomic weapons in the 1950s and by the 1990s was believed to possess a formidable nuclear arsenal. Several Arab countries had also been identified with nuclear weapons programs, but none more so than Iraq. In 1981, Israel made a surprise and daring raid on Iraq's nuclear facility at Osirak, destroying it before it was ready to manufacture nuclear weapons. Although a violation of international law and Iraqi sovereignty, as well as an audacious act that was without precedent, Israel's action had nonetheless delayed Baghdad's quest for the bomb. Iraq's attempt to develop atomic weapons was sustained through the 1980s, but its invasion of Kuwait in 1990 again exposed its nuclear facilities, this time to the U.S.-led coalition, which liberated the small Arab kingdom. Baghdad's surrender in 1991 opened Iraq to United Nations inspection teams, which were authorized to identify and destroy the country's facilities for the development and deployment of all weapons of mass destruction, whether nuclear, chemical, or biological.

From 1980 to 1988, Iraq had made war on its larger neighbor, Iran, and during that long and brutal campaign Baghdad had used chemical weapons, not only against its Iranian adversaries, but against its own Kurdish population, who were suspected of aiding the enemy. The Halabjah atrocity perpetrated by Baghdad in March 1988, in which cyanide and mustard gas was used to destroy an entire Iraqi Kurdish village, confirmed the worst fears of the international community. Compelled to contemplate Iraq's future use of chemical and/or biological weapons, as well as its determination to become a nuclear weapons power, the United Nations Security Council authorized a special commission whose task it was to inspect and verify the destruction of all weapons stockpiles as well as Iraqi installations that could manufacture weapons of mass destruction.

Iraq's defeat at the hands of the UN coalition in 1991 did not bring an end to the regime in Baghdad. Thus, following Iraq's surrender, the UN Security Council sustained the resolutions imposed on Iraq during and following the conflict, and along with safeguarding the integrity of Kuwait, efforts were launched to destroy Iraq's remaining weapons of mass destruction. In addition to the imposition of sanctions that limited Iraqi access to the world around it, by resolution 687 of April 3, 1991, the Security Council spelled out the limitations on Iraqi sovereignty. Section C of this resolution centered on the elimination, under international supervision, of Iraq's weapons of mass destruction as well as its ballistic missiles with a range greater than 150 km. Their related production systems were also authorized for destruction. The resolution also called for measures to ensure that the acquisition and production of prohibited items would not be resumed. A Special Commission (UNSCOM) was set up to implement the non-nuclear provisions of the resolution and to assist the International Atomic Energy Agency (IAEA) in nuclear areas.

Iraq formally accepted the terms of the resolution in April 1991 and the Secretary-General authorized UNSCOM, making Swedish Ambassador Rolf Ekeus its executive chairman. Members of UNSCOM were drawn from twenty countries (Australia, Austria, Belgium, Canada, China, the Czech Republic, Finland, France, Germany, Indonesia, Italy, Japan, the Netherlands, Nigeria, Norway, Poland, the Russian Federation, the United Kingdom, the United States, and Venezuela). In 1997, Richard Butler of Australia replaced Ekeus and assumed the role of Executive Director.

UNSCOM was mandated by the Security Council to carry out on-site inspections of Iraq's biological, chemical, and missile capabilities, and to seize and render harmless all biological and chemical weapons as well as all stocks of agents and related components used for research, development, support, and manufacturing. Furthermore, UNSCOM was required to verify Iraqi compliance and Baghdad's agreement not to use, develop, construct, or acquire any items connected with weapons of mass destruction. UNSCOM also assisted the Director General of the IAEA in denying Iraq nuclear weapons capability. UNSCOM was given full authorization to inspect any and all sites of its own choosing to ensure the fulfillment of the mandates given the Commission and IAEA. All UNSCOM and IAEA inspectors were provided privileges and immunities, and unrestricted freedom of entry and exit to and from Iraq. They also were granted unrestricted freedom of movement to all sites without advance notice, and enjoyed the right of unimpeded access to any site or facility for the purpose of on-site inspection, whether such sites were above or below ground. The right to take photographs from the ground and air was also acknowledged, and the work of the Commission would not cease until it alone was assured Iraq no longer possessed or intended to develop weapons of mass destruction.

UNSCOM's work proved to be a protracted affair and in spite of the Commission's success in destroying significant stores of Iraqi weapons and facilities between 1991 and 1997, its mandate was not ended. The sustained sanctions and the obtrusive nature of UNSCOM's work bridled Saddam Hussein, and following considerable worldwide publicity about the plight of the Iraqi people and especially the country's children, the Iraqi president sought a way out of his dilemma. In the fall of 1997 Saddam demanded the expulsion of the American members of UNSCOM, asserting they were spies whose sole purpose was the destruction of his nation. UNSCOM's work was made impossible by the Iraqi action and with the departure of the Americans the entire force was ordered out of the country by its leader, Richard Butler. Butler reported to the Secretary-General and the Security Council that Iraq continued to manufacture chemical and biological weapons, but the Council was divided on the necessary action. Moreover, the Council had voted to allow Iraq to sell more of its oil in exchange for food and medicine, and considerable sympathy was expressed for the Iraqi nation by France, Russia, and China. The United States, however, with British support, ignored differences in the Council and arguing that the resolutions in force were sufficient, Washington ordered the buildup of military forces in the Gulf.

By January 1998, with renewed fighting just over the horizon, UNSCOM inspectors, including Americans, returned to the country. Baghdad, however, refused to permit the UNSCOM teams access to specific sites, described generally as presidential palaces. In a period of high tension, and with traditional diplomacy at an impasse, it was only the decision of Secretary-General Kofi Annan to go to Iraq that offered the possibility of avoiding a violent showdown. Meeting with Saddam Hussein and members of his government in Baghdad in February, Kofi Annan negotiated an arrangement that permitted UNSCOM unfettered access to all sites, including the presidential palaces heretofore declared off limits. UNSCOM was re-energized as a consequence of this agreement, and except for the fact that diplomats selected by the Secretary-General were to accompany each team of investigators, the work of the special commission proceeded without interference. By April even the eight presidential sites had been inspected. A report was issued by the United Nations declaring Iraq free of nuclear weapons or their development. The matter of chemical and biological weapons, however, remained. UNSCOM therefore continued to perform its tasks while American forces sustained a near but reduced presence. In June 1998, Butler again reported to the Security Council that although Iraq's nuclear capability had been neutralized, Baghdad was still active in the development of chemical and germ warfare.

Baghdad was angered by the Butler Report. Arguing it had satisfied all UN resolutions and demands, and determined to widen the divisions among the permanent members of the Security Council, Saddam's government again petitioned for the early withrdrawal of the sanctions as well as the dissolution of UNSCOM. The United States, however, was just as determined to keep the pressure on Iraq, and the contest was seen as one less affecting Iraq and the United Nations than one between the Iraqis and the Americans. By the fall of 1998 Saddam's soldiers again impeded UNSCOM operations and once more Baghdad demanded the removal of the special commission's American members. Thus, before the end of 1998 the United States again threatened Iraq with air attacks, and once again Baghdad appeared to pull back from the brink. This time Washington declared it would hold its hand, but only so long as it could confirm Iraq's full compliance with UNSCOM operations. In December, judging Iraq had not complied, the United States, supported by Great Britain, launched an intense four-day air campaign against military installations. Although unable to defend the target areas, Baghdad sustained its defiance and refused to readmit UNSCOM. Anticipating differences in the Security Council would prevent the United States from sustaining the attacks, Iraq misread American resolve.

With UNSCOM no longer able to operate on Iraqi soil, the United States increased its vigilance in the no-fly zones that had been established in northern as well as southern Iraq. Flying almost daily reconnaissance flights over the zones, Iraqi radar units and gun batteries threatened the American and British planes which responded by attacking a wide range of military sites deemed to be of importance to Saddam's regime. Opposition to these continuing strikes emerged from within the United Nations Security Council as well as Arab and other Muslim states, but Washington was not deterred. Moreover, whatever the opposition to the raids in 1999, it appeared they would cease only when UNSCOM was allowed to resume unfettered operations, or, if and when Saddam Hussein's government was swept from power.

### The Threat of Proliferation

What happens if the number of nuclear states expands to fifteen or to twenty-five? Would the threat of a major war be greater, or would nuclear proliferation reduce the danger of conflict? What role should the United Nations play in reducing or stopping the expansion of the nuclear club? Could an international control system help prevent additional states from "going nuclear"? While the answers to such questions are not altogether clear, there is general agreement that nuclear proliferation does pose a threat to world peace and security.

The debate over proliferation has tended to polarize. One group regards nuclear diffusion as an obvious danger that will increase the possibility of nuclear war, probably more than proportionally to the addition of each new state. The other group views the dissemination of nuclear weapons as dangerous but inevitable and wants major consideration given to the problem of how to manage a multinuclear world.

The process of expanding the nuclear club tends to be self-propelling as is witnessed in the Indian and Pakistani test explosions in 1998. Both countries justified their behavior on national security grounds but it was New Delhi that was most outspoken on its right to possess nuclear weapons so long as the United States, Russia, China, Britain, and France did not destroy their own stockpiles. India in effect argued the world either would be totally nuclear free or it had every reason to expect an equal position alongside the other nuclear states. Such argument was fuel for still other would-be nuclear powers, and India and Pakistan's intrusion into the "select" nuclear club obviously strengthened the political and strategic motivations of other states to follow their example.

As the nuclear club expands, nuclear weapons may be increasingly viewed as an acceptable means for waging war, and the probability that they will be used by design or accident mounts with each additional finger on the trigger. States caught up in the nuclear race will also find it far more difficult to meet other priorities, such as financing economic development. The result may be a growing internal instability and revolution-proneness in Third World states that could encourage rash or even irrational actions by their leaders. Worst of all, a "catalytic war" could be touched off by a small power that surreptitiously uses an atom bomb to destroy a major U.S., Russian, Chinese, British, or French city. This is unlikely, but in the nuclear age all dangerous possibilities must be recognized and collective efforts undertaken through UN machinery to deal with such threats.

## Efforts to Halt Nuclear Proliferation

Despite the termination of the cold war and its beneficent effects on the arms race, the problem of nuclear proliferation remains real and urgent. Indeed, with the break-up of the Soviet Union and the loss of central control over weapons located in the former Soviet republics, the dangers of proliferation have increased.

The principal multilateral approach to the problem, the 1968 Treaty on the Non-Proliferation of Nuclear Weapons, was approved by the General Assembly in 1968. A product of seven years debate and negotiation in the Eighteen-Nation Disarmament Committee and the Political and Security Committee of the General Assembly, the treaty aimed to solve the problem of proliferation by preventing it. The main provisions of the eleven-article treaty are found in the first two articles, which assign obligations to nuclear and nonnuclear states as follows.

Article I
Each nuclear-weapon State Party to this Treaty undertakes not to transfer to any recipient whatsoever nuclear weapons or other nuclear explosive devices or control over such weapons or explosive devices directly, or indirectly; and not in any way to assist, encourage, or induce any non-nuclear-weapon State to manufacture or otherwise acquire nuclear weapons or other nuclear explosive devices, or control over such weapons or explosive devices.

Article II
Each non-nuclear-weapon State Party to this Treaty undertakes not to receive the transfer from any transferrer whatsoever of nuclear weapons or other nuclear explosive devices or of control over such weapons or explosive devices directly, or indirectly; not to manufacture or otherwise acquire nuclear weapons or other nuclear explosive devices; and not to seek or receive any assistance in the manufacture of nuclear weapons or other nuclear devices.

The treaty also obligates each nonnuclear state to enter into an agreement with the International Atomic Energy Agency to provide safeguards, through verification by the Agency, to prevent any diversion of nuclear energy from peaceful uses to nuclear weapons. Other provisions of the treaty call for cooperation in the development of nuclear energy for peaceful purposes and for the nondiscriminatory transfer of nuclear explosive devices to nonnuclear states for peaceful purposes. Each of the parties to the treaty also agrees "to pursue negotiations in good faith on effective measures relating to cessation of the nuclear arms race."

The major obstacle to the treaty in the Assembly debates had been the fear prevalent among nonnuclear states that renouncing their right to acquire nuclear weapons might leave them open to nuclear blackmail. To meet this problem, three of the nuclear powers—Britain, the Soviet Union, and the United States—in Article 6 of the Non-Proliferation Treaty agreed to guarantee the security of nonnuclear states against such actions or threats. This guarantee was underwritten by the Security Council when it adopted a resolution affirming the decision of three of the four nuclear powers on the Council to provide "immediate assistance, in accordance with the Charter, to any nonnuclear-weapon State that is a victim of an act or an object of a threat of aggression in which nuclear weapons are used." [2]

More than 140 states ratified the original Non-Proliferation Treaty, although France and China—two of the five original nuclear powers—did not agree to sign the document until 1991. A number of states with potential nuclear capability still refused to adhere, including Argentina, Brazil, India, Israel, North Korea, and Pakistan. In 1991, however, Argentina and Brazil entered into a Joint Safeguards Agreement with the International Atomic Energy Agency that provided comparable safeguards against diversion of fissionable materials to military uses.

A new problem of nuclear proliferation arose with the dissolution of the Soviet Union because nuclear weapons were located in many of the constituent states. With Moscow no longer at the pinnacle of the command and control system, the use and disposal of such weapons now devolved upon the leaders of numerous independent units not necessarily subject to the constraints previously observed by the Soviet government. While Russia attempted to reduce the uncertainties through negotiation and agreement with the former Soviet republics, the United States also offered assistance. Recognizing the urgency of the problem, the United States Congress in 1991, with bipartisan support, enacted the "Soviet Nuclear Threat Reduction Act of 1991" to make financial and technical aid available to the new states in regard to the handling of their nuclear weapons. The program dealt with the storage, transport, and destruction of nuclear warheads and the creation of safeguards against proliferation among the newly independent states of the Soviet Union. It also addressed the need to protect against sales of nuclear weapons, critical materials, and technological know-how to other nations.

Nuclear weapons, originally stored and deployed in Belarus, Ukraine, and Kazakhstan were dismantled in accordance with a series of agreements and their warheads were transported to the Russian Federation where the United States was a party in their destruction. Nevertheless, rumors continued to circulate that nuclear warheads and delivery systems had found their way to third countries, and the fear persisted that some weapons may have been acquired by would-be terrorists. The problem of how to control the spread of nuclear weapons proved to be far more complicated with the end of the Cold War. U.S. Defense Secretary William Perry had stated that "the fewest nuclear weapons in the fewest hands" was a central objective of his government, and that even the use of one nuclear bomb, by miscalculation, by terrorists—whether state-sponsored or transnational—was intolerable. In the quest for a truly nuclear-free world, the nuclear powers, especially the United States, Russia, and China, required a common policy. Deterrence, that is, the threat to inflict overwhelming damage on a nuclear armed enemy, no longer sufficed. Following India's decision to demonstrate its nuclear capability, there was no longer room to maneuver based on exclusive national interest. The time seemed to call for a new international security structure, a structure with adequate confidence-building measures, and above all, that centered on total transparency.

## Limiting Nuclear Testing

Elimination of nuclear testing has been high on UN agendas for many years, but to date the principal limitation on testing remains the Limited Test-Ban Treaty of 1963. Although underground nuclear testing is still permissible, the 1963 treaty has been well observed and has been a notable contribution to a safer environment. The treaty was a product of years of negotiation and became possible only when conditions had so ripened that the three negotiating parties—Britain, the United States, and the Soviet Union—regarded it as fully complementary to their respective national interests. Both the United States and the Soviet Union had exploded bombs of immense power and had perfected sophisticated devices for both strategic and tactical nuclear weapons. The bombs had reached such a magnitude of power that testing more powerful ones had become dangerous and nonsensical. Levels of radioactive fallout from Soviet and U.S. tests in the early 1960s had reached proportions that might pose a health threat to present and future generations. In addition, the rising clamor of world opinion demanding a cessation to nuclear testing had become increasingly difficult to ignore. This was a setting for agreement.

Under the 1963 treaty, each state adhering to the treaty agrees

to prohibit, to prevent, and not to carry out any nuclear test explosion, or any other nuclear explosion, at any place under its jurisdiction or control . . . in the atmosphere; beyond its limits, including outer space; or underwater, including territorial waters or high seas.

Because of the seismological problem of detecting underground nuclear tests and distinguishing them from natural earth tremors, subsurface tests were not prohibited by the 1963 agreement. The Soviet Union and the United States carried out numerous underground tests after the treaty took effect.

Although there was a clear implication that the "limited" nature of the test ban would be made complete as soon as technology had advanced to the point of ensuring the detection of all nuclear tests, negotiations lagged behind scientific advances. The treaty was also "limited" in another equally significant respect: Two nuclear powers—France and China—did not sign it, and both powers conducted atmospheric tests. In 1991 China declared a moratorium on further testing as did France the following year, but China subsequently broke the moratorium in 1992 and France did likewise in 1995 by conducting major atmospheric tests.

United Nations' disarmament bodies continued to press for agreement on a Comprehensive Test-Ban (CTB) treaty, however, advocates for nuclear weapons perceived a clear relationship between testing and the development of new weapons systems. The United States had taken a position against a Comprehensive Test-Ban treaty, on the ground that it would not be possible to assure the safety and reliability of existing nuclear stockpiles without periodic testing. Russia in 1991, however, came out unequivocally in favor, and in 1990 both countries ratified agreements limiting underground testing and other nuclear explosions to devices not exceeding a yield of 150 kilotons.

The 1963 Limited Test-Ban Treaty was an acknowledgment by the three major nuclear states that the dangers of an uncontrolled arms race outweighed the risk that the other side might not honor the agreement. At the time it represented a substantial compromise of the U.S. position against entering into any disarmament or arms control agreement without the safeguards of inspection, verification, and control. Although the treaty did not seriously restrict either side's military efforts in the arms race, it greatly reduced the level of radioactive fallout around the globe. With the subsequent Russian decision to unilaterally suspend all testing, increasing pressure was placed on the United States to follow suit.

The United States agreed to follow the Russian example with the indefinite extension of the Nuclear Weapons Non-Proliferation Treaty in 1995. Linked to that extension, and in order to meet the concerns of the non-nuclear states, Washington was the first of 149 nations to sign the Comprehensive Nuclear-Test Ban Treaty in 1996. On doing so, President Clinton announced the United States had ceased testing all nuclear weapons. The treaty created a Comprehensive Nuclear Test-Ban Treaty Organization (CTBTO), and on November 19,

1996, the original signatory states established a Preparatory Commission to oversee its implementation. In 1997, the Preparatory Commission appointed an Executive Secretary and established a Provisional Technical Secretariat in Vienna, in the same physical complex that housed the International Atomic Energy Agency. The Technical Secretariat was given full responsibility in forming the global verification system to guarantee compliance. Neither the UN agency nor the United States detection services, however, were successful in forecasting the Indian explosions of 1998, and the elaborate machinery available for such purposes proved inadequate in the face of a determined effort by a nuclear weapons state to defy the international community. India's action appeared to make a mockery of major power efforts to forego and prevent future tests. The precedent was not lost on Pakistan, nor was it likely to escape the attention of other states with similar ambitions.

## PEACEFUL USES OF OUTER SPACE

The launching of the first earth satellite in 1957 by the Soviet Union added another dimension to the disarmament problem—that of preventing military exploitation of outer space. The General Assembly took an initial action the following year, when it established a special Committee on the Peaceful Uses of Outer Space to draft a set of principles governing national conduct in the new environment. After early failures and a long deadlock over legal issues, the United States and the Soviet Union reached agreement within the committee. The General Assembly thereupon (1961) unanimously adopted the committee's draft in the form of a Declaration of Legal Principles Governing the Activities of States in the Exploration and Use of Outer Space.

Major principles to guide states in using and exploring space were enunciated in the declaration. Outer space and celestial bodies were "internationalized"; international law was made applicable to them; states were made internationally responsible for their activities in outer space; and the responsibility of rendering emergency assistance to astronauts and their vehicles and of returning them safely to their country of origin was proclaimed. The declaration also endorsed the exchange of scientific information on space programs and the establishment of a world "weather watch" under the sponsorship of the World Meteorological Organization.

From 1958 to 1963, the General Assembly adopted six other resolutions relating to outer space. These resolutions affirmed several additional guidelines for space activity:

1. The exploration and use of space should be "only for the betterment of mankind."
2. All states, regardless of their scientific or economic development, should benefit from space activities.
3. The United Nations should serve as a center for coordinating space activities and for the exchange of information regarding such activities.

4. International cooperation in space activities will foster closer relations between nations and peoples.

Space cooperation between the United States and the Soviet Union got off to a good start with bilateral agreements in 1962 and 1964. These provided for a coordinated weather satellite program and for joint satellite communications tests. Subsequent activities by both countries pointed to the potential military use of space and dramatized the need for agreement on a space treaty. In December 1966 a consensus was finally achieved and a draft treaty was approved by the General Assembly without a dissenting vote. The following year, a decade after the launching of the first Soviet Sputnik, the Outer Space Treaty came into force, with the United States and Soviet Union included among the eighty-four signatory nations.

The main provisions of the treaty (1) prohibit placing nuclear or other weapons of mass destruction in orbit or on the moon and other bodies in outer space, (2) ban military bases on the moon and the planets, (3) reject all claims of national sovereignty in outer space, (4) require that explorations and uses of outer space benefit all countries, and (5) provide for international cooperation in exploring space, in rendering assistance to astronauts and space vehicles, and in exchanging scientific information. The treaty culminated ten years of negotiations aimed at avoiding a military space race and achieving the internationalization of space.

The Outer Space Treaty succeeded only partially in its basic objective of avoiding a military space race. Both the United States and the Soviet Union sought to develop antisatellite weapons that could destroy each other's orbiting communication and reconnaissance systems. This opened a new and dangerous phase of the superpower arms race. For many years efforts by the General Assembly to mitigate the more hostile aspects of the space race found neither the United States nor the Soviet Union particularly receptive. In 1983 President Ronald Reagan gave new impetus to the space race with his Strategic Defense Initiative (SDI, popularly known as "Star Wars") aimed at development of new laser and other weapons into an ultimate outer space defense system. Following the dissolution of the Soviet Union, Russian leader Boris Yeltsin called for joint development of outer space defense systems and suggested bilateral cooperation in research and development for the Strategic Defense Initiative. Although the Yeltsin initiative remained dormant, the U.S. Congress, still concerned with the threat of nuclear weapons, in 1999 authorized the continuing development of a modified SDI program, thus heightening Russian and other government's suspicions.

## CONTROL OF NUCLEAR WARHEADS AND DELIVERY SYSTEMS

As previously noted, bilateral discussions between the United States and the Soviet Union, known as the Strategic Arms Limitation Talks (SALT), began in

1969 in Helsinki. The discussions bore fruit in the 1972 ABM Treaty (SALT I Treaty), which limited each country to the development of two antiballistic missile (ABM) defense systems. The treaty was subsequently ratified by both parties. A 1974 protocol to the ABM Treaty limited the number of ABM systems to one for each country rather than two as previously agreed. A second agreement was also reached in 1972, providing a five-year limitation on the number of missile-delivery systems with nuclear warheads.

A new round of talks (SALT II) was begun in 1973 with the broad objectives of (1) achieving permanent ceilings on offensive strategic forces, (2) controlling the size and number of warheads, and (3) ultimately carrying out a mutual reduction of strategic forces. Over a period of several years the negotiators were able to reach agreements on numerical limits for missile delivery systems, including specific limits on multiple independently targeted reentry vehicles (MIRVs), or warheads with more than one explosive device. The U.S. Senate, however, rejected these agreements. SALT II also produced a 1974 Threshold Testban and Protocol and a 1976 Underground Peaceful Nuclear Explosion Ban and Protocol that limited nuclear explosions and tests and other peaceful explosions to a magnitude of 150 kilotons. These treaties were ratified by both parties in 1991.

In 1981 supplementary Intermediate-Range Nuclear Forces (INF) bilateral negotiations were undertaken at Geneva by the United States and the Soviet Union. The objective was to reach an agreement that would reduce or eliminate the threat of Soviet missiles directed against Western Europe and to avoid the deployment of U.S. intermediate-range missiles aimed at the Soviet Union and Eastern Europe. Early inability to reach agreement was followed by deployment of U.S. Pershing II and cruise missiles in Europe. The Soviet Union retaliated by placing intermediate-range missiles in several Eastern European states and stationing missile-carrying submarines off the coast of the United States. The negotiations were eventually resumed, however, and a softening on both sides, incident to the new cordiality of the Gorbachev era, led to agreement in December 1987 for the gradual elimination of all ground-launched, intermediate-range (300–3,400 miles) nuclear weapons from their arsenals. The key concession was Soviet acceptance of on-site inspection. The treaty was quickly ratified by both parties. It stands out in the history of disarmament negotiations as the first agreement to provide for on-site verification, the first to actually reduce the number of nuclear missiles, and the first to eliminate an entire class of nuclear weapons.

While the INF negotiations were in progress, a new phase in the strategic arms dialogue began in 1982 under title of Strategic Arms Reduction Talks (START in place of SALT). The progress of the talks fluctuated with the state of U.S.-Soviet relations, but growing trust between the two countries led to the signing of a START treaty (START I) in July 1991. The modest achievements of START I produced START II, which was entered into by the United States and the successor to the Soviet Union, the Russian Federation, on January 3, 1993. The latter treaty eliminated all multiple warhead vehicles and reduced the overall total of warheads for each side to a range of 3,000 and 3,500. Russia, however, later questioned its commitment, arguing that the United States would reap an unacceptable advantage from the agreement. The Russians also complained about the high costs involved in dismantling and destroying the weapons. They also registered concern that the treaty shifted the focus from land to sea-based weapons where the U.S. and its alliance partners retained advantages. The Russian Duma (parliament) therefore insisted that the date for compliance that had been established for 2003 be extended to 2007, an arrangement that was subsequently agreed to in Helsinki. But given lingering concerns, and provoked by NATO enlargement up to the Russian border, by 1999 the Russian Duma still had not ratified START II.

Believing Russian compliance eventually would be forthcoming, however, the United States pressed ahead with START III proposals that were to reduce nuclear weapons arsenals in both countries below 1,000 by 2009, and projected the destruction of all non-strategic nuclear weapons by the end of 2010 or 2111. Looking well into the future, START IV fixed a goal of 100 to 200 warheads, and called upon China, Britain, and France to join in this program with START V. The target date for START V goals was 2012. These forecasts were made in 1998, but prior to the India and Pakistan nuclear tests. The proposals envisaged a world in 2015 where the United States and Russia possessed no more than 100 to 200 strategic weapons, and all non-nuclear weapons states would agree to forgo programs to obtain such devices. Moreover, the START projections were in accordance with Article VI of the Nuclear Non-Proliferation Treaty. Thus, motivated by the end of the Cold War, the demise of the Soviet Union, the anticipated success of the NPT, and the Comprehensive Nuclear Test-Ban Treaty, strategic thinkers envisioned a world without nuclear weapons. It was this optimistic projection that was jeopardized by the Indian and Pakistani nuclear tests in May 1998, as well as the Russian delay in ratifying START II.

### Confidence Building

One important outcome of the post-Cold War condition is the improvement in communications between the United States and the Russian Federation, and their significantly changed attitudes toward arms control and something approaching eventual nuclear disarmament. During the first forty-five years of disarmament negotiations, the biggest obstacle to agreement was verification. In the 1990s, by contrast, that problem was reduced to a relatively minor one. The Russians, in fact, requested technical and financial help in dismantling their nuclear weapons system, with U.S. technicians invited to participate on site in the process. In effect, Russia requested that the two become active partners in the weapons destruction process.

Such cooperation is to be welcomed, but realism suggests at least a degree of caution in assessing the future. In 1991, a coup d'etat was attempted by a group from within the Communist Party aimed at retaining communism in the

Soviet Union. Its failure led to the breakup of the Soviet Union and the emergence of a more democratic Russia receptive to deep arms cuts. Such an outcome was not guaranteed and a subsequent coup, not totally to be discounted, could be more calamitous. Domestic upheaval is commonly associated with severe economic distress, and Russia's economic woes are substantial. Even if revolution is avoided, military leaders, scientists, and technicians—suffering from loss of their good life and perhaps their livelihoods—may be tempted to sell their know-how and even their weapons to countries aspiring to nuclear weapons capability. Major Russian political figures in fact issued warnings about the willingness of members of the former Soviet scientific community to sell weapons, materials, know-how, or even themselves to the highest bidder. Arguing that roles must be found for such persons, and that they be employed and appropriately remunerated, has been suggested as an answer to the dilemma. Continuing economic and financial distress in the Russian Federation had clearly weakened the resolve of the country's scientists and technicians, whose personal needs appeared to outweigh their concern for nuclear proliferation.

An example of how to purchase your way out of a nuclear weapons problem was the agreement developed between North Korea, the United States, South Korea, and Japan in 1994. A 1993 CIA report revealed that North Korea had violated its earlier acceptance of the Nuclear Non-Proliferation Treaty by developing a number of atomic weapons. Moreover, North Korea had also demonstrated missile delivery capability, which made the matter even more urgent. When International Atomic Energy Agency officials tried to investigate treaty violations, North Korean authorities refused to permit their entry. In an atmosphere of considerable tension, and with the threat of a renewed war on the Korean peninsula, the United States advanced a proposal that eased the confrontation and produced a diplomatic conference. As a consequence of intense negotiations, in 1994, a treaty between the United States, North Korea, South Korea, Japan, and Russia, pledged North Korea financial benefits, as well as substitute energy-producing nuclear reactors. The agreement specified that North Korea would dismantle its nuclear fuel enrichment facilities, and Japan and South Korea, with assistance from the United States, would construct light-water facilities for the generation of electricity. The treaty also called for the transfer to the North of 500,000 tons of heavy oil annually. Following the signing of the agreement, the first shipment of fuel oil arrived in North Korea in January 1995. Seoul and Tokyo agreed to pay the major portion of the total package, and in return North Korea also promised to halt development of its graphite-moderated reactors and dismantle those already in operation. Although North Korea retained the nuclear weapons in its inventory, the realization that further bombmaking would cease was judged a major breakthrough in confidence-building. The agreement not only hinted at a change in attitude in the North Korean government following the death of Kim Il-sung, it also created conditions in which to restart the peace and unification talks between North and South Korea. Not insignificant, crop failures in the country's agricultural region forced the North Korean government to seek substantial assistance from South Korea, Japan, and the United States. Several million people were at risk in the affected area, and all three aid-giving countries acknowledged the humanitarian character of the North Korean request. Subsequent developments in late 1998 and 1999 threatened the improved diplomatic atmosphere as well as the previously entered into agreement, however. North Korea's tests of longer range ballistic missiles over Japan, and its sustained bellicose posturing, raised serious questions about the efficacy of the confidence-building measures with the still isolated communist nation.

## AVOIDING ACCIDENTAL WAR

Atomic weapons were exploded over Hiroshima and Nagasaki in August 1945 to hasten the end of World War II. Since then nuclear weapons have not been detonated in anger, and their primary function has been that of deterrence. Because of the prospect of mutual destruction, a nuclear attack against another nuclear power or one of its allies has been viewed as an irrational action. Over the years each superpower suspected that the other was developing a first-strike capability, but in fact no nuclear weapons were ever used. For whatever reasons, the possessors of nuclear weapons since World War II have thus far been deterred from using them.

Although first use of nuclear weapons has never been invoked as a viable strategy, the fear has persisted that nuclear war may come about by a means other than a planned attack—by misinterpretation of the other side's actions, by electronic or mechanical error, or by human derangement. The Soviet Union was for many years particularly concerned about the human element, recognizing that in the U.S. system of government one individual, the president, has the power as commander in chief to order a nuclear attack—a unique power, since in all the other nuclear weapons states there is collective decision making in the nuclear field. But whatever the causes of a nuclear attack, the consequences could be deadly for all concerned.

The 1962 Cuban missile crisis dramatized the need in the nuclear age for some means of direct and rapid communication between the leaders of states with nuclear weapons, especially the Soviet Union and the United States. To reduce the possibility of a great power clash through miscalculation, accident, or failure of communication, the two governments in 1963 set up a Teletype system, called the "hot line," directly linking the Kremlin in Moscow to the White House in Washington. Subsequently hot lines were established between Paris and Moscow and between London and Moscow. Although most observers hailed this communications link as a major step forward in reducing the threat of accidental war, some expressed amazement that no such precautionary arrangement had existed between the two governments during years of major crises. At the height of the Cuban missile crisis, for example, President Kennedy had to fall back on commercial facilities to communicate with the Kremlin.

The main danger of war through misunderstanding occurs during a crisis, when each side's preparations *against* a surprise attack may appear to the other to be a preparation *for* an attack. Between crises, the hot line may help to explain or moderate the effects of otherwise threatening incidents. For example, radar distorted by meteors or other natural phenomena could lead one state to believe that an attack is under way, or a major city may be destroyed through human or mechanical error in launching a missile. If a large city were suddenly vaporized in a mushroom cloud, would the leaders of the stricken country begin an immediate full-scale retaliatory attack, or would they first communicate with the leaders of the country from which the weapon of mass destruction had been launched? The former action could lead to the complete destruction of both countries, with untold casualties; the latter action might prevent an all-out nuclear exchange and lead to negotiation of "compensation" for the accidental destruction.

The changed atmosphere of the 1990s diminished the likelihood that either Russia or the United States would mistake an accidental missile flight, much less a meteor or a flock of geese, as the first shot in a planned nuclear attack against the other. Recognition of the dangers led members of the Commonwealth of Independent States to negotiate among themselves regarding nuclear security, and it also led to unilateral actions aimed at avoiding accidental war. The Bush administration, for example, quietly ended what for twenty-nine years had been referred to as "doomsday flights" of Air Force planes equipped to direct a nuclear war if a Soviet attack on the United States occurred. Doomsday planes had been in the air continuously since the crisis in 1961 that led to the building of the Berlin Wall. The decision to discontinue such flights was based on budgetary considerations as well as the thaw in the cold war. Similar unilateral initiatives were also undertaken by the Soviet Union and, after 1991, by Russia.

## Banning Chemical and Biological Weapons

Ever since chemical weapons were used with devastating results in World War I, the world community has sought to ban them. This objective was achieved in the Geneva Protocol of 1925, which incorporated a legal ban on the *use* of chemical and biological or bacteriological weapons. Although most existing states ratified the Protocol during the interwar years, the United States and Japan rejected it. Japan accepted it after World War II and the United States tardily gave approval in 1975. Despite the treaty, both the United States and the Soviet Union were able to build and maintain substantial stockpiles of chemical agents, since the Geneva Convention prohibited their first use but not their production or stockpiling. The United States no longer produces "offensive" biological weapons but continues to develop counteractive defensive agents.

Since 1969 the issue of chemical and bacteriological or biological weapons has been included annually on the agenda of the UN General Assembly, with the two types of weapons considered separately since 1971. As a result of UN efforts, a Convention on the Prohibition of the Development, Production, and Stockpiling of Bacteriological (Biological) and Toxin Weapons and on Their

Destruction was signed in 1972 and entered into force in 1975. The United States accepted the convention in that same year. Previously, U.S. objections to both the 1925 Geneva Protocol and the Biological Convention had been based on the position that outlawing these specific weapons should be part of a general disarmament treaty rather than treated separately. Banned by the treaty are pathogenic agents, such as bacteria and viruses, and toxins from microbes, plants, and animals.

In 1972 the General Assembly urged the drafting of a treaty that would also ban the development, production, and stockpiling of chemical weapons, as well as their use, and that would require the supervised destruction of existing stockpiles and production facilities. Although the United States and the Soviet Union had by far the largest supplies of chemical weapons, the problem became increasingly widespread as the technology for chemical weapons began to find its way to the Third World. In 1984 the Security Council issued a declaration condemning the use of chemical agents in the Iran-Iraq war. Evidence made it clear that Iraq had used such weapons, and Iraq's possession of chemical agents was confirmed by UN inspectors after the Gulf War.

Throughout the 1970s and 1980s mutual suspicion of the superpowers, along with reluctance to relinquish the chemical weapons bargaining chip, prevented serious progress in UN-sponsored negotiations on a new chemical weapons treaty. These roadblocks dissolved with the decline of East-West hostility and the new urgency afforded the issue by Iraq's possession and use of chemical weapons in the Gulf War. As a result the Conference on Disarmament was able to approve a treaty outlawing production and stockpiling (as well as use) of chemical weapons and providing a stringent system of on-site, short-notice inspection. The treaty was approved by the General Assembly at its 1992 session and in January 1993, the Secretary-General opened the convention for signature. In 1996, Hungary became the sixty-fifth country to ratify the Convention on the Prohibition of the Development, Production, Stockpiling and Use of Chemical Weapons and Their Destruction, and it entered into force on April 29, 1997, 180 days after Hungary deposited its instrument of ratification. The chemical weapons ban was given unlimited duration and included an extensive verification system. The treaty represented the first multilateral disarmament agreement that would eliminate an entire category of weapons of mass destruction. A technical headquarters was established at The Hague and it was given responsibility for carrying out the verification provisions of the convention.

## TENSION REDUCTION THROUGH POLITICAL AGREEMENT

A variety of agreements and policies have contributed to a lessening of tension among the nuclear powers. The expansion of East-West trade and the opening of China to Western trade, including the granting of most-favored-nation status to China, have clearly contributed to better relations, although other irritants have frequently tended to negate the gains achieved from closer economic ties.

Perhaps the main instrument of East-West tension reduction during the cold war years was the Conference on Security and Cooperation in Europe (CSCE) in the 1970s and the Helsinki Accord or Final Act that it produced in 1975. Divided into four sections or "baskets," the Helsinki Final Act included provisions for (1) security in Europe, including the development of confidence-building political and military measures (Basket I); (2) cooperation in economics, science and technology, and the environment (Basket II); (3) cooperation in promoting human rights, cultural exchanges, education, and the free flow of people, ideas, and information throughout Europe (Basket III); and (4) the holding of review conferences "to continue the multilateral process initiated by the Conference" (Basket IV).

The Helsinki Accord included no provisions for disarmament or arms control, but it was a major effort to reduce hostility between the East and West by getting all the nations of Europe plus the United States to accept the post-World War II status quo in Europe. Programs of cooperation and understanding, it was believed, would engender a relaxed atmosphere that would encourage good relations and perhaps promote demilitarization in Europe. Although the Final Act was a diplomatic agreement and not a binding lawmaking treaty, the signatories were expected to honor the spirit as well as the letter of the agreement. Periodic review conferences aimed at goading them into meeting that expectation. With the Cold War ended, the CSCE became in important forum for fostering cooperation among all the countries of Europe, East and West, but notably for Russia and the East European states. Reformed as the Organization for Security and Cooperation in Europe in 1996, now the OSCE assumed the role of a formal organization whose central purpose was the alleviation of socio-political pressures likely to culminate in conflict. Alongside Commonwealth of Independent States (CIS) peacekeeping forces, OSCE has attempted to ease tensions in Kosovo-Yugoslavia, Bosnia-Herzegovina, Georgia, Armenia, Azerbaijan, as well as in Central Asian Tajikistan.

# OBSTACLES TO DISARMAMENT

The UN objective in seeking disarmament through agreement—in contrast to the more pragmatic objectives of arms control—is to build a peaceful world by ridding it of weapons of war. This solution is so simple, so obvious, and so preferable to its alternative that an impartial observer from another planet might think that only a dedicated warmonger or a potential aggressor could resist its logic. Yet the historical record of efforts to achieve disarmament through agreement reveals appallingly few and mostly short-lived examples. Why have the United Nations and its members failed to achieve this almost universally acclaimed objective? There are many reasons—some technical, others related to the nature of the state system, and still others rooted in human nature. What follows is an analysis of some of the major problems that help explain the disarmament impasse.

## SECURITY QUESTIONS

The difficulty of securing disarmament can perhaps be understood best if it is related to the question of why nations arm in the first place. If an arms race causes war, what causes the arms race? Obviously, the building of weapons of war is related to the objectives of states, especially national survival. Nations arm for security to protect their existence, but they also arm to pursue political and economic objectives. For centuries arms have provided the means for states to carry out national policies. As long as leaders regard military capacity as essential to the fulfillment of their state's vital interests, the abandonment of that capability through international agreement is unlikely. Some, such as many ethnic groups in the former Soviet Union and Yugoslavia, have found that lack of military preparedness in today's world can spell disaster when they are attacked by a rival ethnic group.

The pursuit of security through the arms race is based on the ancient Roman maxim: *Si vis pacem, para bellum* (If you seek peace, prepare for war). In today's nuclear world, however, efforts to increase security by building more and more deadly weapons tend only to produce greater insecurity. Therein lies the paradox of United Nations efforts to end the contemporary arms races in different parts of the world. Too many countries in all regions of the globe are feverishly developing new weapons systems and bolstering older ones in their search for security. The idea of security through a general disarmament remains only a theoretical abstraction.

## SOVEREIGNTY AND NATIONALISM

The search for explanations of the failure to achieve disarmament leads to the heart of the disarmament dilemma. Controversies over means and details are only symptomatic of the basic contradiction between international needs and national prerogatives that has stymied most disarmament efforts. Two forces that emerged early in the history of the modern state system—state sovereignty and nationalism—constitute the major legal and emotional barriers to the idea of reaching agreement with "foreign" elements. A disarmament agreement, by its very nature, would limit the sovereign power of a state to exercise full control over the area most vital to its security. The ardent nationalist resents the access, free movement, and "snooping" within his state that must accompany a disarmament enforcement system in the form of on-site inspections.

An effective disarmament arrangement in the contemporary world must be based on some form of effective international control. For example, in formulating the Acheson-Lilienthal proposals that became the basis for the Baruch Plan, Dean Acheson insisted that inspection would be inadequate if the production of fissionable materials remained under national control and that enforcement would be insufficient unless a veto-free international body could punish a violator. The question of the feasibility of disarmament essentially boils down to this question: Is the world ready for a measure of world government? The answer seems clear: There is as yet no consensual support for it in any country. The sovereign state system may be obsolete when it is objectively evaluated within the context of intercontinental missiles and thermonuclear weapons systems, but in the minds of human beings nationalism and sovereignty still offer the best approach to security.

## Vested Interests

Disarmament in today's world must take into account the armaments that nations already possess. How can the arms race be reversed in a world in which enormous amounts are spent each year for military purposes, millions of people serve in the armed forces, and other millions are engaged in military production? There may well be too many vested interests in the world of armaments and the military services to challenge the status quo successfully.

The economic consequences of disarmament are viewed ambivalently in some states. Total disarmament would permit states to devote the huge savings to economic betterment. Many observers, however, fear that it would result in a loss of jobs and profits or a dislocation of the national economy. Communists have long argued that capitalism depends on the artificial stimulus provided by arms production and war. Although little evidence exists to substantiate that charge, many Americans have reacted adversely to the closing of defense plants and the cancellation of procurement contracts in economy moves. The military-industrial complex functions as a powerful force to challenge any disarmament proposal that threatens a loss of status or income. A successful disarmament plan, therefore, would have to take economic consequences into full account.

## Threats of Deception

The technological revolution that has dramatically changed the mode of warfare has also increased the difficulty of disarmament. Arms reduction in a world of conventional weapons might mean that one side could achieve an initial advantage through deception. Though this advantage is not likely to be decisive, a violation in these circumstances could give the attacking state a significant edge. With the advent of thermonuclear, chemical, and biological weapons, however, treachery in a disarmament agreement could be decisive. Moreover, the ability to deceive has increased; it is far easier to hide a few intercontinental rockets and their thermonuclear warheads than to conceal several divisions of troops or a fleet of battleships. Fear of deception has led the United States to insist that an effective system of on-site inspection be operational *before* any disarmament measures are implemented.

Deception may also relate to intentions and the fear of a surprise attack. The world has not yet forgotten the immediate military advantages seized by the armies of Adolf Hitler in their June 1941 invasion of the Soviet Union, and by the Japanese attack on Pearl Harbor in December 1941. Although both attacks were eventually reversed, the advantage of surprise was great.

## IDEOLOGICAL AND ETHNIC RIVALRY

A world of conflicting values offers a poor milieu for reaching agreement on disarmament. When one side in an ideological or ethnic struggle becomes convinced that the other is bent on conquest or destruction, any proposal for a reduction in arms is regarded as a devious inducement for a nation to weaken itself, providing the enemy with an opportunity to attack. Any disarmament agreement must depend on some minimal amount of good faith and a belief that the other side will live up to its terms. But a deep gulf between ideological and ethnic enemies makes trust a rare commodity.

During most of the postwar years, ideological hostility between the Soviet Union and the United States tended to create a "deaf man's dialogue" in disarmament negotiations. Both sides favored the reduction of arms and proposed various schemes to accomplish it, but each side was wary of the proposals of the other side because it feared a trap. Each believed its plan was logical and responsible and that if the other side were sincerely interested in disarmament, it would have ceased its diversionary tactics and accepted the plan. In the early 1990s, the ideologies of communism and state socialism were replaced by those of democracy and capitalism in the independent states that were formerly parts (republics) of the Soviet Union. Immediately, the long-stalled negotiations for major disarmament agreements became a meaningful exercise.

Ethnic rivalry, however, provided a new and very difficult challenge, especially among the former republics of the Soviet Union and among the newly independent states that formerly were part of Yugoslavia. In some cases, war—not disarmament and peace—became the consequence of the demise of communism.

## FULL PARTICIPATION NEEDED

A meaningful world disarmament agreement requires the participation of all affected states. If one or several states with sizable military strength were not included, the delicate balance of power provided by a carefully worked-out schedule of arms reductions would be in constant danger of being upset. It is difficult to get all the major powers to support disarmament, because one or several may prefer an independent policy or may regard the existing power distribution in the world as favorable to their national interests. Between World War I and World War II, for example, France was interested in maintaining arms superiority over Germany, not in a general disarmament. Both China and France refused for many years to participate in nuclear disarmament negotiations. It is doubtful that the United States and Russia will agree to deep cuts in nuclear weapons or subject them to substantial control without the participation of all nuclear powers. Although the nonproliferation treaty has been widely ratified, some states still hesitate to sign because their rivals have not yet done so.

## THE PROPAGANDA BARRIER

The appeal of disarmament to millions of human beings has made it a prime subject of psychological warfare. Diplomats confident that the other side will reject their proposals are free to advance radical schemes designed to make their country appear to be avant-garde in its search for peace. In the United Nations both East and West often drafted their proposals to appeal to the great mass of nonaligned states rather than to the negotiators sitting across the table. Sweeping Soviet proposals for general and complete disarmament, with control machinery to be established *later,* were often matched by U.S. plans providing for a maximum of elaborate international inspection and enforcement but deemphasizing such problems as overseas bases and German rearmament, which were central to Soviet security considerations.

Pressures for great power agreement on disarmament emanated regularly from the majority of the states in the General Assembly, challenging both sides to find new platitudes they could safely endorse while tabling concrete proposals "for further study." Each side tried to preserve its image—that of a peace-loving, humanitarian, but horrendously powerful nation that would gladly lay down its arms and contribute the savings to economic development but for the intransigence and uncompromising hostility of the other side. It is noteworthy that one of the most significant agreements in the arms control field during the past forty years—the Limited Nuclear Test-Ban Treaty of 1963—was reached through closed negotiations among U.S., British, and Soviet diplomats and that the SALT I and SALT II agreements and the first START treaty were the products of bilateral great power negotiations. The end of the cold war has seen a great diminution in the global propaganda war. More cooperation between Russia and the United States, along with the rejection of communism and a favoring of capitalism and democracy, muted much of the war of words and improved the climate for exchanges on arms control and reciprocal reductions in the development of weapons of mass destruction. But as the war in Kosovo revealed, significant differences over the use of force can increase tensions and reinvigorate old suspicions.

## THE SPEED OF CHANGE

An increasingly significant factor working against consensus to end the global arms race is the realization that much scientific research and development for peaceful purposes can be related to weaponry; hence no disarmament agreement can really stop progress in military technology. The development of a decisive new weapon that could upset the agreed balance of arms is a potential danger that both sides would have to assume in any arms control or disarmament agreement. No inspection or control system could offer full protection against such an eventuality. In an age of intensive exploration of the atom and of new ventures with particle beams and lasers in outer space, any disarmament agreement could be rendered obsolete within a short period of time unless it provided for periodic updating. It may be that the day has already passed when disarmament through agreement was rationally practicable.

Over the years disarmament negotiators have faced a basic dilemma: As scientific knowledge grows and technology changes with revolutionary speed, disarmament agreements become increasingly dependent on trust; but trust is vitiated by the fear of new, secret weapons spawned by advancing technology. Science and technology, the very forces that have made it necessary to end the arms race in order to save the human race from destruction, are the forces that appear to make agreement to disarm too dangerous for national security interests.

## TIMING PROBLEMS

There is a pervasive tendency for nations caught up in an arms race to procrastinate in the belief that the future will offer a more propitious time for entering into a disarmament agreement. That right moment never seems to occur. Instead, new weapons, military confrontations and other crises, and burgeoning military capabilities increase the need for disarmament but decrease its likelihood.

The Western-Soviet arms race 1945–90 illustrates the point. When the military rivalry commenced, both sides had just finished fighting a major war and were faced with critical problems of recovery. One side had suffered the destruction of its cities and calamitously high civilian and military casualties. The other side had a monopoly of nuclear weapons that it offered to sacrifice in return for a world security system. In retrospect, those first few years following World War II appear to have been an ideal time for disarmament, yet negotiations fostered by the United Nations failed dismally. Thereafter, the cold war developed, alliance systems and overseas bases were established, new weapons of mass destruction were perfected, both sides became peripherally or directly involved in local wars, and there was a proliferation of nuclear weapons and delivery systems. The grounds for insecurity and fear were no longer hypothetical or based on a future potentiality; mass extermination became a proximate danger. Yet each side continued for forty-five years to manufacture "overkill" capacity in a vain effort to achieve a preferred position in disarmament negotiations.

The cycle can of course be broken. Since 1990 the East-West arms race has subsided, without an intervening major war as a catalyst. But the change came about only after revolutionary internal change in Eastern European countries. Arms build-ups in other parts of the world have not undergone a corresponding decline. The time, apparently, is seldom right without a fundamental change in circumstances.

## RATIO PROBLEMS

During arms control negotiations the future power relationship among the parties becomes a matter of grave concern. Each nation seeks a minimum goal of maintaining parity and a maximum advantage of arms superiority from a prospective agreement. Because power and security are never absolute but always relative, each proposal must be carefully weighed to determine its potential impact on all the parties. The result is an unending series of calculations by military tacticians who prefer to err on the conservative side, in keeping with their general distaste for disarmament as a security objective. The problem of balancing different categories of forces (strategic versus tactical, air versus naval, nuclear versus conventional) provides an additional complication.

General and complete disarmament supervised by the United Nations or a system of enforcement by regional police forces might overcome the fear of giving advantage to another state, but it would raise a new threat to national freedom of action from the central police. Even if the world government implications of UN-enforced general disarmament could be accepted, the not inconsiderable difficulty of phasing out arms through stages would remain. At each stage, no party can be left relatively weaker than at an earlier point and each strives to compare more favorably with its power rivals. Since it is impossible to achieve complete parity, each state must be led to believe that it will be advantaged by successive stages of disarmament. The difficulty in successfully pulling off this sleight-of-hand maneuver is evidenced by the forty-five year disagreement between the United States and the Soviet Union over the numbers and types of forces to be disarmed at each stage and the ratio of forces that would remain. The problem of ratios, however difficult to resolve, is central to any disarmament scheme and must be faced.

## INSPECTION AND ENFORCEMENT

From the earliest postwar discussions of the Baruch Plan in 1946, disarmament talks have been dominated by issues of "inspection and control." American proposals consistently offered to exchange arms reduction for a verifiable system of safeguards against clandestine arms buildups and surprise attack. During most of this period the Soviet Union accepted the general proposition that inspection and control are necessary, but attempts to work out the details often resulted in little more than an exchange of recriminations. The highly detailed inspection provisions of the START treaties, with their comprehensive multiple systems of on-site inspection, reveal how far Russia and the other nuclear republics have moved from this position since 1990.

An effective inspection system to verify disarmament accords must resolve such issues as (1) the extent of access to each country's territory; (2) the frequency of on-the-spot surveillance; (3) the timing—whether inspection arrangements are to go into effect before or after the disarmament measures that they will verify; (4) the nature of aerial and ground reconnaissance to guard against the possibility of a surprise attack; (5) the means of detecting weapons in outer space; (6) the determination of what constitutes a weapon or a potential weapon; (7) the selection of the areas to be included in a progressive territorial demilitarization; and (8) the composition, powers, and number of inspection teams. In addition to discouraging treaty violations, proper verification could make it more difficult for a future government to reverse the disarmament agreement, inhibit efforts of insurgent forces to gain control of weapons in their territories, limit the possibility of nuclear materials and other high-tech weapons finding their way into Third World states, and establish confidence essential to future arms reductions.

The technical aspects of detecting violations lead to a second and equally difficult set of issues that involve the political and military consequences of a violation once it has been detected. To what extent, for example, will world opinion contribute to enforcement and sanctions? What role should the injured state or states play if they detect an evasion? What kind of enforcement mechanism should be set up, and what should be the nature of its sanctions? Should the injured state be entitled to undertake "restorative measures" following a detected violation to restore the military balance that would have existed without a disarmament agreement? Arms control agreements are entered into, presumably, on the theory that parties will honor their commitments. But realistically, the possibility of violations must be taken into account in framing any agreement.

## APPROACHES TO THE DISARMAMENT PROBLEM

Arms and security are inseparably intertwined, but they frequently exhibit a catch-22 relationship. Armaments are regarded by nearly all states as essential to their national security. When one state's armaments are perceived as a threat to the security of another state, however, the second state may resort to an arms program that threatens the security of the first. This is not a necessary consequence of national armaments. Canada, for example, does not view the huge U.S. military establishment as a threat to its own security. Undoubtedly a history of peaceful relations and a disarmed boundary stemming from the 1817 Rush-Bagot Agreement contribute to this happy situation. The catch-22 is readily apparent, however, in India-Pakistan relations, the Middle East, and most of the postwar history of East-West dealings. In these and other situations where arms and security are in tension with one another, the challenge is to make arms reduction compatible with the security of each state. A small sampling from the profusion of approaches offered by statesmen and scholars to overcome the dilemma or afford a partial remedy will be examined here.

### THE DIRECT APPROACH

Identifying a useful approach to disarmament starts with the question of whether the major effort should be placed on reducing arms or on developing security. Those who advocate a "direct" approach regard the arms race itself as the main source of fear and insecurity. The solution they offer is simple: "The way to disarm is to disarm." These words have reverberated through the chambers of the League and the United Nations on many occasions. As arms are reduced, so holds the theory, the familiar cycle that produces the upward spiral in the arms race (increased arms produce greater fear and insecurity, which, in turn, produce greater expenditures on arms, and so on) will be reversed. Reduced international tensions will follow in the wake of disarmament, encouraging agreement in other areas of controversy. Most Third World nations have been vocal proponents of the direct approach during the UN era, for others if not for themselves; the United States and Britain, which supported the direct approach during the League period, have changed since 1946 to the indirect approach.

## THE INDIRECT APPROACH

Proponents of an indirect approach regard armaments as a reflection of the deep insecurities of the state system. Disarmament, therefore, should be recognized for what it is—a fundamentally *political* problem that involves the totality of relations among the nations caught up in the arms race. Disarmament becomes the secondary, not the immediate, objective. Major political conflicts must first be ameliorated, an effective collective security system must be established, and carefully planned inspection, verification, and sanctions arrangements must be made operational. Disarmament cannot be feasible, therefore, until there is a convergence of national policies on these issues.

The 1990s offer some assurance that the indirect approach to disarmament works, and with the end of the cold war and improved relations between Russia and the United States, arms control negotiations appear to have a sound foundation. Deliberations between the two powers are likely to continue to produce positive results if the two governments focus their attention on confidence-building measures, but domestic turmoil in Russia is cause for concern since foreign policy decisions are more often than not consequences of prevailing national conditions.

## UNILATERAL DISARMAMENT

Some disarmament advocates offer the novel strategy of one-sided initiative to secure an arms reduction breakthrough. Once such an action has started the disarming process, reciprocation would theoretically give it the motive power necessary to accelerate its momentum. Underlying unilateral disarmament theories is an assumption that the reduction of arms is really a matter of common interest but that inertia, tension, mistrust, fear, and habit make it appear to be beyond realization.

Several religious groups advocate a complete unilateral disarmament. If the other side uses the opportunity to impose its control, a Gandhian passive resistance would be employed against the conqueror. While no one can be certain that utopian schemes of this nature would fail, they are impracticable because neither side in the arms race would be likely to place its national security or way of life in the hands of its opponent.

Disarmament theoreticians have worked out unilateral schemes that depend on reciprocal initiatives and responses rather than an abject surrender of retaliatory power. Unilateral initiatives are not posited as a substitute for bilateral negotiations but only as a "psychological primer" to reverse the trend of the arms race by demonstrating good intentions. If the other side fails in due time to reciprocate or tries to take advantage of the unilateral reductions or withdrawals, such plans call for a return to a hard-line policy.

Although partial unilateral disarmament would be unlikely to threaten the security of a state that has the power to destroy its opponent many times over, it violates the injunction not to encourage a potential aggressor through signs of weakness. The history of the superpower arms race presents evidence both for and against the efficacy of voluntary restraint. Neither participant strained its capabilities to the utmost in developing its arsenal, preferring some semblance of balance to an all-out drive for a massive superiority. Moreover, periods of lessened tension during the cold war reduced the rate of growth in arms on both sides. On the other hand, new crises had a tendency to boost the rate of arms production in both the United States and the Soviet Union to more than counterbalance previous cuts. The Soviet Union, on several occasions, stopped testing nuclear weapons for several years and invited the United States to do the same. The United States, however, was never willing to stop its testing program in the development of new weapons systems.

Unilateral arms control initiatives by Soviet President Mikhail Gorbachev and Russian President Boris Yeltsin have contributed to relaxation of tensions and paved the way for the conclusion of important arms reduction treaties. A notable example was Russia's unilateral decision in 1992 to cease nuclear targeting of U.S. cities and military installations.

Experience of the postwar period suggests that unilateral disarmament initiatives are more likely to be reciprocated in periods of low rather than high international tension. Although unilateral disarmament schemes may be rational enough in their inherent logic, in most high tension arms race situations neither side is willing to accept the risk of taking the first step. If one side does, the other may be too suspicious or too fearful to reciprocate. In periods of decreasing threat, however, unilateral initiatives appear less risky and may invite reciprocation because they appear more genuine to the other side.

## TOTAL DISARMAMENT

At differing times during the cold war era both the United States and the Soviet Union presented proposals to the United Nations for "general and complete disarmament." There is little evidence that either side either wanted or expected the outcome they were proposing. Various commentators, however, have seriously advocated total disarmament, and in particular total nuclear disarmament, as the only real hope for human survival on the planet.

That contemporary weapons of mass destruction offer at least the possibility of human extinction can no longer be doubted. At the Hiroshima kill-ratio of approximately four deaths per ton of explosive power, the billions of tons of TNT equivalent in the combined nuclear arsenals of the United States and Russia have the capability to destroy the entire population of the earth many times over. Even if START V goals are reached, the capability will still exist in both arsenals. When the deadly effects of radioactive fallout and of chemical and biological weapons of mass destruction plus the nuclear weapons capability of other states are added to this estimate, only the most imperturbable optimist can talk about a meaningful aftermath should a nuclear war occur.

Although cataclysmic global destruction is a possibility not to be disregarded, state behavior since the dawning of the nuclear age does not indicate that this is a necessary, or even a probable, consequence of the possession of nuclear weapons.[3] The "balance of terror" was an effective mutual deterrent during the cold war years, and nuclear weapons undoubtedly continue to figure in the deterrence calculus of states possessing them. Total elimination of all nuclear weapons would by hypothesis remove the possibility of nuclear war, but nuclear technology would still remain widely available and some nuclear weapons are relatively easy to hide. The present nuclear powers will be quite reluctant to destroy all nuclear weapons knowing it might leave them at least temporarily vulnerable to a rogue nation or insurgent group that had managed to secrete or clandestinely construct nuclear devices.

The infeasibility of total disarmament does not gainsay the desirability of reducing armaments far below current levels and placing more stringent controls on their production and dissemination. For Russia and the United States, a case for massive disarmament could be made on economic grounds. Everywhere in the world the diversion of resources from military uses to the production of economic wealth would bring a substantial increase in human welfare. With verified mutual reductions it could also enhance security. The dramatic changes in East-West relations augur well for this possibility between great powers, but the challenge remains to extend it to other parts of the world.

## CONCLUSION

The problem of controlling armaments is fundamentally a problem of creating a secure world. Any general disarmament agreement must operate within some broader framework for maintaining global security. The major nuclear powers have shown a proclivity to return to the UN framers' concept of collective security to keep the peace in a disarmed world, but states are unlikely to go all the way—that is, to give up their arms without some alternative guarantee of national security.

Nor is disarmament a problem that can be isolated from the development of an international legal, political, economic, and social system. Armaments will become obsolete, if ever, only when the bonds of world community, which depend on progressive evolution in each of these fields, become strong enough to moderate the conflicts and tensions that make armaments seem necessary. The transformation of international relations from a system exuding power, tension, fear, and conflict to one of cooperation, understanding, and common action may be an impossible undertaking. But small gains are better than none, and managing armaments more rationally can be a step in that direction.

# NOTES

1. A lively account of the personalities and issues involved in the two Hague Peace Conferences can be found in Barbara W. Tuchman, *The Proud Tower* (New York: Macmillan, 1962), pp. 229–88. For a more detailed discussion of arms limitations efforts in the century before the first World War, see Merze Tate, *The Disarmament Illusion* (New York: The Macmillan Company, 1942).
2. For a verbatim copy of the treaty and an extensive record of the process leading up to the writing of the treaty and its adoption, see the documentary work published by the United States Arms Control and Disarmament Agency titled *Arms Control and Disarmament Agreements—Texts and Histories of the Negotiations*, 1990 edition, pp. 89–106.
3. Kenneth E. Boulding, in a provocative and widely circulated 1962 essay, insisted that it was: "I believe the present international system to be one which has a significant probability built into it of irretrievable disaster for the human race. The longer the number of years we contemplate such a system operating, the larger this probability becomes. I do not know whether in any one year it is one per cent, ten per cent, or even fifty percent. I feel pretty sure, however, that it is of this order of magnitude, not, shall we say, of the order of magnitude of .01 per cent." Boulding, "The Prevention of World War III," *The Virginia Quarterly Review* 38, no. 1 (Winter 1962), pp. 1–12, reprinted in Richard A. Falk and Saul H. Mendlovitz, *The Strategy of World Order* I (New York: World Law Fund, 1966), p. 5. As a solution Boulding advocated not only total national disarmament but world government as well.

# SELECTED READINGS

*Arms Control and Disarmament Agreements—Texts and Histories of the Negotiations.* Washington, DC: United States Arms Control and Disarmament Agency, 1990.

Caldwell, Dan. *The Dynamics of Domestic Politics and Arms Control: The Salt II Ratification Debate.* Columbia: University of South Carolina Press, 1991.

Cohen, Roberta and Francis M. Deng, *Masses in Flight: The Global Crisis of Internal Displacement.* Washington, DC: Brookings Institution Press, 1998.

Craig, Paul P., and John A. Jungerman. *Nuclear Arms Race—Technology and Society.* New York: McGraw-Hill, 1986.

Crocker, Chester A. and Fen Osler Hampson, eds. *Managing Global Chaos: Sources of and Responses to International Conflict.* Washington, DC: U.S. Institute of Peace Press, 1996.

Elliot, Jeffrey M., and Robert Reginald. *The Arms Control, Disarmament, and Military Security Dictionary.* Santa Barbara, CA: ABC-CLIO, 1989.

Falk, Richard A., and Saul H. Mendlovitz, eds. *The Strategy of World Order.* Vols. 1–4. New York: World Law Fund, 1966.

Glynn, Patrick. *Closing Pandora's Box: Arms Races, Arms Control, and the History of the Cold War.* New York: Basic Books, 1992.

Harris, John B., and Eric Markusen, eds. *Nuclear Weapons and the Threat of Nuclear War.* New York: Harcourt Brace Jovanovich, 1986.

Jacobson, Harold Karan, and Eric Stein. *Diplomats, Scientists, and Politicians: The United States and the Nuclear Test Ban Negotiations.* Ann Arbor: University of Michigan Press, 1966.

Kanet, Roger E., and Edward O. Kolodziej, eds. *The Cold War as Cooperation: Superpower Cooperation in Regional Conflict Management.* Baltimore: Johns Hopkins, 1991.

Larsen, Jeffrey A. and Gregory J. Rattray, eds. *Arms Control Toward the 21st Century.* Boulder: Lynne Rienner, 1996.

Levine, Herbert M., and David Carlton. *The Nuclear Arms Race Debated.* New York: McGraw-Hill, 1986.

Levine, Robert A. *Still the Arms Debate.* Brookfield, VT: Dartmouth Publishing Company, 1990.

Lund, Michael S. *Preventing Violent Conflicts: A Strategy for Preventive Diplomacy.* Washington, DC: U.S. Institute of Peace Press, 1996.

Myrdal, Alva. *The Game of Disarmament.* New York: Pantheon Books, 1982.

Ravenal, Earl C. *Designing Defense for a New World Order: The Military Budget in 1992 and Beyond.* Washington, DC: CATO Institute, 1991.

Smoke, Richard. *National Security and the Nuclear Dilemma.* Reading, MA: Addison-Wesley, 1984.

Sokolski, Henry. *Fighting Proliferation: New Concerns for the Nineties.* Washington, DC: U.S. Government Printing Office, 1997.

Van Creveld, Martin. *The Transformation of War.* New York: Free Press, 1991.

Woolsey, R. James, ed. *Nuclear Arms—Ethics, Strategy, Politics.* San Francisco: ICS Press, 1983.

# 8

## THE REVOLUTION OF
## SELF-DETERMINATION

During the past half century the international system has been transformed by the disintegration of colonial empires and the rise of independent states in their stead. More than half of the present UN members were colonial dependencies before World War II. In this vast revolution of self-determination, the United Nations has played an integral part. While the League of Nations was content to exercise minimal supervision over the administration of a few ex-enemy territories, the United Nations became an advocate of self-government for colonial peoples everywhere. Decolonization would have come in any event, but the United Nations helped reinforce the anticolonial mood and hasten the transition process. This chapter will examine the evolution of international concern for dependent peoples from the League mandate system to the UN trusteeship system and UN involvement with the broader process of decolonization. Although decolonization is largely history, it provides a striking case study of the impact of international institutions upon state behavior.

## MANDATES UNDER THE LEAGUE

At the end of World War I, the European imperial system was still alive and well. Despite an earlier wave of anticolonial revolution in North and South America, and more gradual emancipation in Canada, Australia, New Zealand, and South Africa, European powers still held fast to vast territories in distant lands inhabited by native peoples rather than settlers of European stock. The empires of the European Allies emerged from the war intact, and the victors fully expected to extend their rule to German and Turkish possessions by right of conquest. Some of the Allies had already concluded secret wartime agreements to this effect among themselves.

Disposition of the defeated enemies' colonies proved not to be that simple. Direct annexation was not acceptable because it conflicted with often repeated claims that the war was being fought for the rights and freedoms of peoples and for the defense of democracy. In the waning months of the war, the British Labour Party and the French Socialist Party had publicly urged that German colonies be placed under the trusteeship of the proposed League of Nations. More important was the position of President Woodrow Wilson at the Paris Peace Conference. Determined that the war he had fought for principle should not now appear as an imperialist venture, he steadfastly opposed the annexation that the other leading Allies preferred. Another theoretical option, restoration of the conquered territories to their former masters, was not viewed with enthusiasm by any of the Allies. There was also general agreement that most of these territories were not ready for self-government.

Such a situation called for inventiveness, and the resulting compromise among the peacemakers, based on a proposal by Jan Smuts of South Africa, had a touch of political genius. The territories were parceled out among the victors, but control was to be exercised subject to League of Nations supervision. Article 22 of the Covenant declared to the world that the "well-being and development" of the peoples in the conquered territories was "a sacred trust of civilization" accepted by certain "advanced nations" serving "as Mandatories on behalf of the League." This doctrine had something in common with the still more patronizing notion of the "white man's burden," but the recognition of an international trust for conquered territory undoubtedly represented a step forward from the days of the old imperialism. For the first time in the history of the state system, the relationship between some imperial powers and their subject peoples was subjected to international supervision.[1]

The impact of compromise is also evident in the classification of the conquered territories into three groups, subsequently known as Class A, B, and C mandates, on the basis of their political development, geographic location, economic conditions, and "other similar circumstances." The relative political sophistication of the Arabs, and British wartime commitments to them, made the Turkish dominions candidates for the Class A mandate. According to Article 22, their status as independent nations could be "provisionally recognized subject to the rendering of administrative advice and assistance by a Mandatory until such time as they are able to stand alone." The tutelage stage lasted longer than the local peoples desired, but Iraq gained independence in 1932 and the other mandated areas of the Middle East achieved full statehood in the wake of World War II without undergoing a period of UN trusteeship (see Table 8-1).

At the other extreme were the Class C mandates—South West Africa and the German Pacific islands, which were to be "administered under the laws of the mandatory as integral portions of its territory." Sparse population, small size, and "remoteness from the centres of civilization" were mentioned in the Covenant as reasons for this classification. Unmentioned was the political constraint: Class C status was the maximum degree of internationalization that annexationists in Australia, New Zealand, and South Africa (the mandatory states) would gracefully accept. Class C mandates were thus linked directly with the government of the mandatory power, and their peoples were not regarded as subjects for self-government in the foreseeable future. The remaining German territories in Africa were placed in Class B. They were not to be

TABLE 8-1   Territories Placed under League Mandate and UN Trusteeship

| Territory | Class of Mandate | Administering Authority (League of Nations) | Administering Authority (United Nations) | Present Status |
|---|---|---|---|---|
| Iraq | A | United Kingdom | — | Independent (1932) |
| Palestine | A | United Kingdom | — | Independent, Transjordan (Jordan) (1946), Israel (1948) |
| Syria and Lebanon | A | France | — | Independent, Syria (1946), Lebanon (1946) |
| Cameroons | B | France | France | Independent, Cameroon (1960) |
| Cameroons | B | United Kingdom | United Kingdom | Part merged with Nigeria, part with Cameroon (1961) |
| Ruanda Urundi | B | Belgium | Belgium | Independent, Rwanda (1962), Burundi (1962) |
| Tanganyika | B | United Kingdom | United Kingdom | Independent (1961); merged with Zanzibar as United Republic of Tanzania (1964) |
| Togoland | B | United Kingdom | United Kingdom | Merged with Gold Coast as Ghana (1957) |
| Togoland | B | France | France | Independent, Togo (1960) |
| Nauru | C | Australia, New Zealand, United Kingdom | Australia, New Zealand, United Kingdom | Independent (1968) |
| New Guinea | C | Australia | Australia | Independent, Papua New Guinea (1975) |
| North Pacific Islands | C | Japan | United States | Independence for Marshall Islands (1991), Micronesia (1991); commonwealth status for Northern Marianas (1991); independence for Palau (1994) |
| South West Africa | C | South Africa | — | Mandate terminated (1966); independent, Namibia (1990) |
| Western Samoa | C | New Zealand | New Zealand | Independent (1962) |
| Somaliland | — | — | Italy | Independent, merged with British Somaliland as Somalia (1960) |

administratively annexed but were nevertheless to be governed as colonies without explicit provision for ultimate independence or self-government.

The means of enforcing Covenant obligations were minimal. Article 22 provided for a "permanent Commission . . . to receive and examine the annual reports of the Mandatories and to advise the Council on all matters relating to the observance of the mandates." This Permanent Mandates Commission consisted of nine (subsequently ten) persons appointed by the League Council as private experts rather than governmental representatives. A majority were drawn from nonmandatory states, but nearly all came from countries with colonial possessions, which enabled them to understand the problem faced by the mandatory countries. They were, for the most part, able people who took their international responsibilities seriously.

Being only advisory, the commission had no power to affect the policies of the mandatory states other than through persuasion and publicity. Its principal means of supervision consisted of reviewing annual reports submitted by the mandatories and making recommendations to the Council. The commission developed comprehensive questionnaires to facilitate uniform and complete reporting, and a representative of each mandatory participated in all commission discussions of its mandate. Written petitions were also entertained, but petitions from indigenous inhabitants had to be routed through the mandatory and all other petitions were sent to the mandatory for comments. The majority of petitions came from the Class A mandates.

The Permanent Mandates Commission made its recommendations to the Council rather than directly to the mandatory. Although the Council usually agreed with the commission, it was a political body not prone to giving needless offense to the mandatories and, in any event, it had no more legal authority than the commission to coerce a mandatory that failed to honor its "sacred trust." The Assembly, without any special authorization in the Covenant, also developed the practice of making recommendations each year on some aspect of mandate administration. Like the commission and the Council, it too was limited to exhortation and the sanction of publicity.

Given the political milieu from which the mandate system emerged, its record of accomplishment was bound to be spotty. Its greatest achievement probably lay in establishing the principle of international accountability for dependent territories. It is doubtful that prevailing attitudes toward the treatment of colonial peoples would have been altered so rapidly in the past half century without the conditioning effect of the League's mandate system. Administration of the conquered territories was also improved in some details as a result of suggestions from the commission. The mandatories, for example, generally refrained from mass naturalization of mandate peoples and did not enlist them for general military service—two practices specifically disapproved by the commission. The mandate system fell short of idealistic hopes and expectations, but there is wide agreement that the League's methods of friendly persuasion helped fix the welfare of indigenous peoples as the standard of administration.

# THE IMPACT OF WORLD WAR II

The League's mandate system was a symbol of change in world attitudes toward colonialism, but it left European imperialism untouched in most parts of the world. The great catalyst for change was World War II, which destroyed the political balance that had made imperialism viable. The war severely weakened the colonial powers and for a time brought total or partial severance of contacts with their overseas possessions. The war also stimulated the growth of existing native nationalist movements.[2] The quick collapse of Belgium, the Netherlands, and France, and Britain's hurried retreat to a beleaguered island, destroyed at a stroke Europe's long-standing image of invincibility in the eyes of colonial peoples. The immense loss of respect for Europe was most apparent in Southeast Asia, where the ease of Japanese conquest revealed the weakness of the former white masters and exploded the myth of racial superiority. The Japanese victory was clear proof that the West no longer enjoyed the monopoly of technological and military potential that had been the basis of its dominance.

Japanese occupation physically eliminated European administrative and economic personnel and systematically destroyed existing colonial institutions. Japan did not encourage nationalist aspirations for autonomy, but the necessity of entrusting high administrative responsibilities to local elites, which previously had been systematically confined to lower-grade positions, provided training for independence. At the close of the war, native nationalists in Indonesia and Vietnam took advantage of the sudden collapse of Japan to seize control of abandoned ammunition stocks and proclaim independence. Independence did not come to Indonesia until 1949 and to Vietnam until much later, in both cases only after a protracted struggle with the former colonial powers. But the nationalist movements ultimately could not be denied.

The termination of World War II also speeded decolonization in areas not occupied by the Japanese. The Philippines had been overrun by Japan early in the conflict and its scheduled independence under terms of the 1934 Tydings-McDuffie Act was delayed, but nevertheless granted by the United States on July 4, 1946. Moreover, one colony, namely India, received special treatment and status when in recognition of its contribution to the war effort, it was invited to participate in the 1945 San Francisco conference as a founding and charter member of the United Nations even before it achieved its independence. Made an original member of the United Nations in 1945, India did not achieve independence until August 1947. Pakistan, however, which was also cut from Britain's Indian colony, followed the normal procedural channels in becoming a member of the United Nations. The independence of Britain's other South Asian colonies, i.e., Burma (Myanmar) and Ceylon (Sri Lanka), followed.

In the Middle East, wartime pressures and Arab nationalism brought the early termination of the British and French mandates. Syria, Lebanon, and

Jordan (at the time known as Transjordan) became independent in 1946. Syria and Lebanon had been the responsibility of France, whereas Transjordan was a creation of the British, who in 1923 split their Palestine mandate along the Jordan River, the eastern terrritory becoming the Emirate of Transjordan. After achieving full independence, and after battlefield successes in the 1948–49 war with Israel, in 1950 Transjordan was transformed into the Kingdom of Jordan. Jordanian troops occupied the west bank of the Jordan, and the region was incorporated within a new kingdom that now spanned both sides of the river. Israel, which had its origin in a UN resolution of 1947, declared itself independent in 1948 when that resolution was rejected by the Arab states. In the war that ensued between Israel and its Arab neighbors, Israel came to occupy the remaining area of the former British mandate of Palestine, less the west bank under Jordanian occupation, and the Gaza Strip, which had been seized by Egypt. Still another consequence of World War II was the development of nationalist movements in French North Africa, where Morocco and Tunisia gained their independence in 1956, but where Algeria, which the French had every intention of retaining as an extension of metropolitan France, was forced to fight a long and bloody war with the colonial power. That war raged with great intensity from 1955 until 1962 when the French acknowledged the futility of their effort and yielded to Algeria's desire for independence.

World War II also intensified nationalist fervor and accelerated demands for self-determination in sub-Saharan Africa. The first black African country to achieve independence was Ghana in 1957. Guinea followed in 1958, and sixteen more African countries acquired their independence and became members of the United Nations in 1960. The decolonization movement by this time had become worldwide and was acknowledged to be irreversible.

# UN TRUSTEESHIP

## TRUSTEESHIP AT SAN FRANCISCO

At the UN San Francisco Conference, meeting in April 1945, the new currents were being felt but were not fully appreciated. Although no state seriously objected to continuing the League mandate system in some form, proposals to extend the principle of trusteeship to the whole colonial system met with vehement opposition from Britain, France, Belgium, the Netherlands, and South Africa. The United States, so enthusiastic for self-determination in 1919, wavered in support of international supervision, in part because of a growing security interest in the Japanese-mandated Pacific islands.

Other forces, however, compensated for the foot-dragging of the colonial powers and the waning of Wilsonian zeal in the United States. At San Francisco the anticolonial viewpoint had new and vigorous spokesmen from Egypt, Syria, Iraq, India, and other former dependencies, which loudly trumpeted the cause of fellow nationalists still under colonial domination. The Soviet Union, unrepresented at Versailles, was another forceful anticolonialist voice. The trusteeship cause was also aided by a growing belief that the just treatment of colonial peoples and their evolution toward self-government were connected with the maintenance of international peace and security. In the League Covenant the "well-being and development" of colonial peoples provided the rationale for League action. In the UN Charter, by contrast, the first objective of the trusteeship system is "to further international peace and security."

The states supporting wider involvement of international organization were able to achieve a modest increase in its power and responsibilities. A strengthened trusteeship system replaced the mandate system, and a declaration on non-self-governing territories committed members to submit economic and social information on all of their colonies. A greater departure from the League Covenant was the announced goal of ultimate "self-government or independence" for trust territories and "self-government" for all other dependencies. Although the consequences of these changes may not have been fully anticipated in 1945, they constituted the opening wedge for what subsequently became a broadside attack in the United Nations on the old colonialism in all its manifestations.

## THE NATURE OF THE TRUSTEESHIP SYSTEM

Despite the shift in goals, the new machinery of trusteeship made full allowance for the interests of the administering powers. The Trusteeship Council, as successor to the Permanent Mandates Commission, was composed of government representatives instead of private experts, with equal representation for administering and nonadministering states (UN Charter, Article 86). Each trust territory was to be brought within the system by an agreement drawn up by the administering member and approved by the General Assembly. Although the Assembly could reject a proposed agreement, the alternative was no trusteeship at all. Once the trusteeship was agreed on, both the Assembly and the Trusteeship Council were limited to information gathering, discussion, and recommendation, with no legal powers of coercion.

The Trusteeship Council was given means of inquiry into the conduct of trust administration superior to those of the League system. The practice of the annual report, based on a comprehensive questionnaire, was borrowed from the Permanent Mandates Commission. To this was added the right to receive petitions directly, without relying on the administering power as intermediary, and the right to send visiting missions to gain firsthand knowledge of conditions in trust territories. The administering powers thus matched their effective control of the trust territories against the organization's capacity to publicize, criticize, and mobilize the weight of diplomatic opinion.

The United States obtained an additional safeguard against UN interference with its administration of the Pacific Islands trusteeship. If an administering authority, in the trusteeship agreement, chose to designate all or part of a trust territory as a "strategic area," all matters relating to the area became the province of the Security Council, where the veto could forestall any adverse recommendation. The Trust Territory of the Pacific Islands under U.S. supervision was so designated.

## THE FUNCTIONING OF TRUSTEESHIP

The Class A mandates were not candidates for trusteeship because they were scheduled for early independence, but all of the Class B and C mandates except South West Africa were placed under trusteeship through agreements approved in 1946 and 1947. The Charter also made trusteeship an option for territories "detached from enemy states as a result of the Second World War," as well as any other colonies a state might choose to place within the system. No state accepted the latter invitation, although Italian Somaliland, which had been taken from Italy during the war, was given a period of trusteeship under Italian administration. The legal evolution of the territories placed under mandate and trusteeship is shown in Table 8-1.

By 1975 ten of the eleven trust territories had achieved the promised independence or were united, on the basis of a UN-approved plebiscite, with an adjoining independent country. Only the Trust Territory of the Pacific Islands, with 150,000 inhabitants scattered over 2,141 islands and atolls, remained within the system. Composed of four separate political entities—the Northern Mariana Islands, the Federated States of Micronesia, the Marshall Islands, and Palau—it also was beset by the winds of self-government. In 1975 the Northern Marianas voted to become a U.S. commonwealth when trusteeship was ended. In 1983 the other three jurisdictions, through UN-sponsored plebiscites, approved association agreements providing local autonomy while leaving defense responsibilities with the United States. The plebiscites in Micronesia and the Marshall Islands ultimately became the basis for independence, but the Palau plebiscite was ruled invalid by the Palau court because the association agreement permitted the stationing of nuclear weapons on the island in violation of the Palau constitution. A proposal to remove this prohibition from the constitution failed for lack of the required 75 percent majority. In six subsequent plebiscites through 1991, support for the amendment ranged as high as 73 percent, but it was always short of the required majority. In November 1992, however, the voters of Palau approved a proposal to reduce the constitutional majority from 75 percent to 50 percent, and Palau, the last of the trust territories, was declared independent in 1994.

The Charter's goal of independence or self-government for trust territories has been reached—an achievement for which the United Nations may claim considerable credit. Criticism in the Trusteeship Council and the General Assembly spurred the administering authorities to put the best possible face on their conduct of territorial affairs. This in turn affected administration of the territories, as policies were formulated with an awareness that the United Nations was watching. Occasionally specific government practices were modified in response to council recommendations.

Petitions and visiting missions permitted detailed scrutiny of trust administration and thereby increased the pressure on administering authorities to justify their policies. At the height of its activity, the Trusteeship Council received several hundred written petitions annually and considered as many as 250 in a session, besides granting an occasional hearing to an oral petitioner. Aside from the informational function, the petitioning procedure made administering authorities more alert to the legitimate grievances of the local populace and sometimes resulted in direct relief to the complainant. In one instance two inhabitants of the Pacific Islands accomplished through oral petition what three years of direct negotiation with the United States had failed to achieve—a settlement of their claim against the government for property taken without just compensation.

Visiting missions, conducted every three years, also proved a valuable source of information as well as an outlet for native views and grievances. Reports of the visiting missions appeared to receive serious attention from the administering authorities and in some instances foreshadowed policy changes. Australia, for example, took steps to give the New Guinea territorial legislature an elective majority in response to the recommendations of a 1962 visiting mission. In several territories the United Nations sent plebiscite teams and election observers during the final stages of preparation for self-government, which increased the international acceptability of the regimes thereby established.

Considered as a whole, trusteeship helped raise standards of administration in the trust territories and hastened the coming of independence. Suggestions and criticisms from the Trusteeship Council and the Assembly strengthened progressive elements within the administering authorities and kept them mindful of their obligations to the peoples of the territories. Trusteeship encouraged more articulate native demands for national independence and may have fostered some increased readiness for self-government. Given the growth of nationalism, the changes in power relationships wrought by two world wars, and the increasing economic liabilities of the colonial system, independence would have come to most of these areas without the intervention of the United Nations. Nevertheless, the system provided a more orderly and peaceful process of change. In none of the trust territories was the transition to independence marked by serious violence.

Trusteeship must be seen in perspective as but one aspect of a much wider movement for decolonization. Several African and Asian dependencies of France and Britain became independent before the first trust territories achieved that status in 1960. While ten trust territories were gaining independence from 1960 to 1975, several times that number of former colonies were undergoing the same transformation outside the trusteeship system. Trusteeship contributed to a climate of world opinion congenial to decolonization, but the system itself was swept along in the broader current.

The trusteeship system never achieved the scope that its more enthusiastic supporters at San Francisco had envisioned. Except for Somaliland, it did not expand territorially beyond the League mandates, and South West Africa (now

Namibia) never came within its purview. The UN Charter's option of placing other dependent territories under trusteeship appears never to have been seriously considered by any colonial power. In meeting the larger problem of colonialism, the United Nations has consistently turned to other means.

## THE UNITED NATIONS AND TOTAL DECOLONIZATION

Unlike the League Covenant, the UN Charter went beyond prescribing conditions for mandated territories and extended its concern to dependent peoples everywhere. In the Declaration regarding Non-Self-Governing Territories, contained in Chapter XI of the Charter, the colonial powers acknowledged a "sacred trust" to promote the well-being and self-government of all their dependencies. They were not willing to make independence a goal for their colonies or to accept international supervision, but they agreed to submit data "of a technical nature relating to economic, social, and educational conditions in the territories" for "information purposes." There was general accord at San Francisco that the declaration embodied only moral commitments, dependent on the good faith of the colonial powers for their fulfillment and involving no UN right to intervene in what was regarded by the colonial powers as a matter of domestic jurisdiction.

Today the picture is drastically altered. Independence has become not merely a goal but an accomplished fact for the vast majority of the colonial peoples of 1945. Within the United Nations the original Charter's assumption "that each colonial power should at its own discretion and in an unhurried way lead its dependent peoples to well-being and self-government" soon gave way to the proposition that colonialism is "an intolerable and illegitimate abuse to be done away with as speedily as possible by the international community."[3] This revolutionary change in ideology was accompanied by an organizational assault on the whole structure of colonialism; it erased any essential distinction between trust territories and other non-self-governing areas. The change mirrored new global realities, but it amounted to a Charter amendment without the niceties of ratification.

### THE COMMITTEE ON INFORMATION

The first step toward establishing UN responsibility for all dependent territories occurred in 1946 with the establishment of a Committee on Information from Non-Self-Governing Territories. Its purpose was to examine the information transmitted by the administering authorities and make recommendations to the Assembly. In composition it was modeled on the Trusteeship Council, having an equal number of administering and nonadministering members. It had no provision for permanent representation of the Big Five, however, and the Soviet Union and China generally did not hold membership on it. Like the Trusteeship Council, the committee prepared a questionnaire to guide members in reporting.

With the built-in moderation arising from its composition, the Committee on Information was not an aggressive instrument of anticolonialism. Its original terms of reference debarred it from examining "political" information, although such information was voluntarily submitted by some countries. Even on economic and social matters, the committee could make recommendations of general application but could not single out individual territories. It was not given the right to accept petitions or send out visiting missions.

Because of the committee's limited powers, the anticolonial initiative remained largely with the General Assembly and its Fourth Committee, which soon requested governments to include political information in their annual reports. Later the Assembly began to demand that administering authorities submit sufficient information on constitutional changes in the territories to enable it to determine whether self-government had in fact been attained. The Assembly's right to make such a determination was a much more sensitive issue than its demand for information, and the colonial powers vehemently rejected the idea.

The admission of Spain and Portugal to UN membership in 1955 raised the related question of who decided when and whether new members must begin to transmit information. The question was far from academic since Spain and Portugal, both of which had overseas dominions, assured the United Nations that they had no "non-self-governing territories." In 1960 the Assembly resolved the question by informing both states of their obligation to transmit information. Spain capitulated to the pressure, but Portugal refused to comply.

## SELF-DETERMINATION AND POLITICAL CRISIS

While the Assembly was attempting to turn all non-self-governing territories into quasi-trusteeships, the United Nations was also faced with a series of political crises arising from the breakup of colonial empires. During the early years the alignment of colonial and anticolonial forces was not sharply drawn, and the issues were sometimes perceived as having a complexity inconsistent with the taking of doctrinaire positions. The question of Palestine came before the United Nations in 1947 at the initiative of a harassed mandatory power that was no longer willing to bear the impossible burden of reconciling Arab and Jewish claims to the Holy Land. The issue was not whether self-determination should be granted but how and by whom it should be exercised. In the Indonesian struggle for independence from the Netherlands, mediated in part by the Security Council from 1947 to 1949, the continuation of colonial rule was more clearly at issue, but the threat to international peace and security was the Security Council's foremost concern. Assembly debates on the former Italian colonies of Libya, Eritrea, and Somaliland, from 1949 to 1951, were also relatively free from the kind of anticolonial diatribe that subsequently came to characterize UN debates on colonial questions.

Assembly debates on Morocco and Tunisia brought the anticolonial position more sharply into focus during the early 1950s, but a two-thirds majority was never available for anything stronger than a call for "free political institutions" and continued negotiations among the parties. Both states were granted independence from France in 1956.

The emergence of anticolonial dominance in the United Nations is illustrated by its handling of the Algerian question. The General Assembly considered Algeria each session from 1955 through 1961. In 1955 no action at all was taken; in 1956 the Assembly expressed the hope that a peaceful, democratic, and just solution in conformity with the Charter would be found. In 1957 the Assembly went so far as to urge negotiations, but in 1958 and 1959 no recommendation was able to command a two-thirds majority. This stalemate reflected the unwillingness of the anticolonial bloc to support a weak statement and its inability to obtain a strong one. In 1960, with the admission to UN membership of seventeen former colonies, the inhibitions of the earlier period vanished. The right of the Algerian people to "self-determination" was vigorously asserted, despite France's bitter objection to discussing the matter at all. A year later the Assembly demanded nothing less than full "self-determination and independence." These resolutions may have had no greater influence on the French decision to grant Algerian independence in 1962 than on the granting of independence to Morocco and Tunisia in 1956, but the temper of the Assembly was plainly different.

## ANTICOLONIALISM TRIUMPHANT

By 1960 the anticolonial revolution was rapidly approaching its zenith. Four decades of mandate and trusteeship had established the principle of international accountability for the administration of a select group of territories, with independence as the ultimate goal. Fifteen years of gradually expanding activity under the Charter Declaration Regarding Non-Self-Governing Territories had gone far to establish the principle of international accountability for the well-being and self-government of all colonial peoples. Repeated recourse to the United Nations in crisis situations had established at least a *prima facie* connection between colonialism and the periodic outbreak of violence. Within the world community the day of colonialism was rapidly passing. Thirty-five territories that had achieved full independence since 1945 were now members of the United Nations. Most other dependencies of any substantial size were moving toward independence with the consent and cooperation of their colonial overseers.

### An Anticolonial Manifesto

Amid these signs of a revolution well on its way to completion, the General Assembly in 1960 took a step of unusual symbolic importance. In previous years the anticolonial forces had been forced to compromise in their attack on the old colonial order. With domination of the Assembly now assured, they turned the organization into an instrument for the complete legitimization of their cause. In a historic Declaration on the Granting of Independence to Colonial Countries and Peoples, the General Assembly proclaimed that the subjection of any people to alien domination was a denial of fundamental human rights, contrary to the UN Charter, and an impediment to world peace and that all subject peoples had a right to immediate and complete independence. With General Assembly Resolution 1514 (XV) of December 14, 1960, it was formally declared that: (1) alien domination is contrary to the UN Charter; (2) all peoples have a rights to self-determination; (3) inadequacy of political, economic, social, or educational preparedness is no excuse for delaying independence; (4) all repressive measures against dependent peoples should cease so that they can freely exercise their right to complete independence; (5) all powers of government should be immediately transferred to the remaining dependent peoples; and (6) disruption of the national unity or territorial integrity of a country is contrary to the UN Charter. The power of the resolution was read in the unanimity of the vote. Not a single member state voted in opposition to the declaration. It is important to note, however, that nine countries abstained, and included among them were some of the world's more prominent colonial powers. The abstainers were Australia, Belgium, Dominican Republic, France, Portugal, Spain, South Africa, Great Britain, and the United States. The old imperial order that had resisted Woodrow Wilson's call for the self-determination of peoples following World War I was forced to sound its final retreat after World War II. By the 1960s, the once all-consuming age of colonialism had given way to a vibrant and exuberant new age of worldwide national independence. Moreover, given the admission of numerous former colonial states to membership in the United Nations, the work of the world organization became more centered on anticolonial issues. The General Assembly, therefore, unlike the Security Council where the major powers remained dominant, reflected more and more the concerns of the newly independent countries.

As long as colonial rule prevailed in any territory, the declaration provided a rationale for efforts to undermine or overthrow it. The anticolonial principle was carried to its logical conclusion when India, on invading Portuguese Goa in December 1961, assured the Security Council that the invasion was an "embodiment of the principles" in the declaration and a "new dictum of international law." Some Western states were unconvinced that an Assembly resolution, which was legally binding on no country, could create international law that overrode express Charter prohibitions on the use of force. But the basic issue, as the Indian representative admitted, was moral, not legal. Portugal's centuries-old occupation of Goa constituted "permanent aggression," and India was justified in "getting rid of the last vestiges of colonialism. Charter or no Charter, Council or no Council." [4] Like the U.S. Declaration of Independence, the Declaration of 1960 was an appeal to a higher law to which all lesser claims were subordinate.

## The Special Committee

Within the United Nations the declaration presaged a more vigorous assault on the last bastions of colonialism. In 1961 the Assembly expanded the role of the Committee on Information by authorizing it to discuss political information and to make recommendations specific to particular regions. The Fourth Committee also broke new ground by granting, for the first time, a hearing to petitioners from two non-self-governing territories.

Of considerably more importance for the future was the creation of a Special Committee on the Situation with Regard to the Implementation of the Declaration on the Granting of Independence to Colonial Countries and Peoples. Known as the Committee of Seventeen (increased to twenty-four in 1962), it was assigned to study the declaration and make appropriate recommendations for its implementation. Parity of representation was discarded as the Assembly packed the special committee with an anticolonial majority. For its terms of reference, the committee was given a blank check—a mandate to do whatever it was able to do in implementing the 1960 declaration. Under this broad grant of authority, the committee assumed powers to hear petitions, send missions to the field, and make recommendations directed at specific territories—powers that the Trusteeship Council had exercised but that had been denied to the Committee on Information. By 1963 the Committee of Twenty-four had so plainly overshadowed the Committee on Information in its systematic harassment of the colonial powers that the latter was formally abolished.

### The Demise of the Old Colonialism

The United Nations was able to launch its massive assault on colonialism because colonialism was already in full retreat. The Committee of Twenty-four was engaged mainly in a mopping-up operation. In its 1963 report to the Assembly, the committee listed sixty-four colonies, mandates, and trust territories that had not yet achieved self-government. Only ten of these could claim as many as a million inhabitants, and the total population of all sixty-four was less than fifty million. Forty of the sixty-four were British, consisting, as one writer put it, mostly of "little islands scattered about the face of the globe, representing the days when Britain was an indefatigable collector of scraps of empire."[5]

Rhodesia (Zimbabwe), Namibia, and the Portuguese African colonies of Angola, Mozambique, and Guinea were significant exceptions to the "scraps of empire" characterization. Rhodesia's white minority government unilaterally declared independence from Britain in 1965 and endured fifteen years of international ostracism, UN economic sanctions, and internal strife before finally accepting majority rule in 1980 and receiving admission to the United Nations as the state of Zimbabwe. Portugal's hard-line policy collapsed in 1974 under the weight of colonial wars that had absorbed nearly half of the Portuguese national budget. The Caetano dictatorship fell victim to an internal coup, and Portugal's African policy fell with it. Portuguese Guinea (now Guinea-Bissau) became independent in 1974, and Mozambique and Angola followed in 1975. Namibia, the former South West Africa mandate, achieved independence in 1990.

At the century's end the Special Committee's list totalled seventeen dependencies, the majority being small islands with tiny populations (see Table 8-2). In a more controversial category are Gibraltar, Western Sahara, and East Timor

TABLE 8-2    Territories to Which the Declaration on the Granting of Independence to
Colonial Countries and Peoples Continues to Apply

|  | TERRITORY | ADMINISTERING AUTHORITY | AREA (SQ. KM.) | POPULATION (EST.) |
|---|---|---|---|---|
| Africa | Western Sahara | Spain | 266,000 | 147,000 |
| Asia | East Timor | Portugal | 14,925 | 737,000 |
| Atlantic and the Caribbean | Anguilla | United Kingdom | 96 | 7,200 |
|  | Bermuda | United Kingdom | 53 | 59,000 |
|  | British Virgin Islands | United Kingdom | 153 | 12,400 |
|  | Cayman Islands | United Kingdom | 260 | 25,900 |
|  | Falkland Islands (Islas Malvinas) | United Kingdom | 12,173 | 2,000 |
|  | Montserrat | United Kingdom | 103 | 12,000 |
|  | St. Helena | United Kingdom | 412 | 5,500 |
|  | Turks and Caicos Islands | United Kingdom | 430 | 13,500 |
|  | U.S. Virgin Islands | United States | 343 | 103,200 |
| Europe | Gibraltar | United Kingdom | 6 | 29,700 |
| Pacific and Indian Oceans | American Samoa | United States | 197 | 39,900 |
|  | Guam | United States | 540 | 127,700 |
|  | Caledonia | France | 19,103 | 164,200 |
|  | Pitcairn | United Kingdom | 5 | 60 |
|  | Tokelau | New Zealand | 12 | 1,700 |

(an island territory of 5,700 square miles). Britain has been engaged in continuing negotiations with Spain on the future of Gibraltar. Western Sahara was relinquished by Spain in 1975, and the present controversy pits Moroccan claims to sovereignty against those of an indigenous nationalist movement called the Polisario Front. East Timor presented a still thornier problem. In 1976 East Timor was annexed by Indonesia following intervention in a civil war that broke out during the transfer of authority from Portugal to local entities. The annexation was never approved by the United Nations, but Indonesia firmly established its own rule there—in the process showing little respect for the human rights of the native inhabitants. While the United Nations continued to recognize Portugal's claim as the administering power, Indonesia expanded its military presence on the island and during the long reign of President Suharto it inflicted terrible penalties on the Timorese people. The United Nations tried without success to pressure the Indonesian government to relax its grip on East Timor, but it was not until Suharto's forced resignation in 1998 that the successor government agreed to look favorably on the Timorese demand for self-determination. Given renewed efforts by the UN Secretariat, in March 1999 Jakarta revealed it would seriously consider granting the Timorese either autonomy, or possibly even independence. With the UN Secretary-General's

Personal Representative playing a more aggressive role, it seemed the protracted dispute might yet end in a negotiated settlement acceptable to all the parties. Puerto Rico has also been before the special committee with great regularity. Puerto Rico is technically not on the list of non-self-governing territories, and the U.S. Congress' vote in 1998 to offer the island the choice of statehood would appear to close off UN debate on its status, that is, pending a decisive referendum of the Puerto Rican people. In fact, on August 12, 1998, the House of Representatives agreed to a local referendum to decide whether the island should become the fifty-first state or keep its commonwealth status. Then, on December 13, the people of Puerto Rico voted to hold to their current status, defeating the other options that ranged from independence to independence with free association to statehood.

## THE UN ROLE: AN APPRAISAL

Decolonization, after more than four hundred years of colonial rule, is one of the great revolutions of our century. It was brought on by forces that were neither generated nor controlled by international organizations. But the League of Nations and the United Nations have contributed to the speed and direction of the movement and, in some instances at least, have helped promote a more peaceful transition to independence and self-government. The League gave respectability to the principle of international accountability in a limited area of colonialism and moderated some of the worst abuses of the system. Since 1945 the United Nations has done much more. It provided a forum where anticolonial spokesmen could articulate their position; it greatly expanded the principle of international accountability; and it developed more effective instruments for international supervision of colonial administration. Above all, it gave an element of legitimacy to independence movements everywhere in the world. By holding aloft the standard of self-determination, it served as a reminder to Western colonial countries that such demands were basically consonant with enduring values in their own political tradition. When violence occurred, the United Nations sometimes intervened to curb hostilities, as in Indonesia, Kashmir, and Palestine. In the end, the United Nations hastened acceptance of the new order by legitimizing its tenets.

The UN record on colonial problems has not been without blemishes. In some instances the United Nations at least inadvertently encouraged a resort to violence by native nationalists who felt that creating a threat to peace and security was the best way to gain the attention of the organization. The 1960 Declaration has frequently been used to justify violence, including India's attack on Goa in 1961, and Argentina's abortive attempt in 1982 to seize the Falkland Islands by force.

A good case can also be made that the United Nations pushed many territories to premature independence and encouraged independence for ministates when association with a larger entity would have produced an economically and politically more viable state. Statehood and full membership in the United Nations were attained by many new nations woefully lacking in trained personnel to administer government and economic institutions. In most of the new states, independence was not followed by hoped-for gains in economic welfare. This led many former colonies to complain that the old colonial system had merely been replaced by neocolonialism in the form of economic exploitation by the developed countries.

The benefits of decolonization were unquestionably oversold, although the United Nations can be held only partly responsible for that. Independence was in principle a good thing, and it brought immediate benefits to those who were able to seize the levers of political and economic power in the new states. But removal of the foreign master did not everywhere bring greater respect for democratic values and individual rights. Indigenous leaders often adopted government techniques as repressive and demeaning as those formerly attributed to colonialism. Racial, tribal, and political minorities have sometimes fared ill at the hands of the new rulers. A notable example is the "killing fields" of Cambodia under the Khmer Rouge regime. Nor has decolonization done much to bring peace and security to former colonial domains. The preindependence era was marked by armed conflict in many dependent areas, but the era of independence has also witnessed internal wars and rebellions, outside interventions, and outright military aggression in many of these same lands.

The United Nations did not create all the ills of decolonization any more than it produced all the benefits, but a fair appraisal requires recognition that decolonization has its down side as well as its positive aspects. In retrospect, the most important UN contribution may have been to encourage acceptance of the new order before relations between colonial masters and subject peoples became impossibly embittered.

## SELF-DETERMINATION IN
## THE TWENTY-FIRST CENTURY

Self-determination is far from a completed process and all indicators point to a new round of demands that will carry well into the twenty-first century. Moreover, the United Nations, on the one side, will be at center of such developments, while on the other, state sovereignty will continue to argue a hands-off policy. Events in Kosovo in 1997–99 are illustrative of the former, while those that overwhelmed Chechnya in 1996–97 represent the latter. Kosovo's autonomous status within the Yugoslav Federation was withdrawn when Slobodan Milosovic won control of the country in 1989. By 1998, given Serbian efforts at crushing the Kosovar Albanian culture, and finally forcing thousands of Kosovars to flee to neighboring states, a Kosovo Liberation Army (KLA) emerged to challenge the Serbian forces. The KLA's call for self-determination had few outside supporters, but the fighting could not be ignored. Aware of a maturing problem and fearing the conflict could destabilize southeastern Europe, the

United Nations, European Union, and OSCE, all attempted to restore order to the region. When they failed to temper the conflict, NATO was energized. It was only when NATO's diplomacy also failed that the alliance began its bombing campaign against Serbian targets. Serbia argued the Kosovar matter was an internal problem and therefore outside NATO's area of jurisdiction. NATO acknowledged Kosovo's inclusion in the Yugoslav Federation, but it made the counter argument that Belgrade's sovereignty had been compromised by the atrocities committed against its own citizens. NATO insisted it was not promoting self-determination for the Kosovar Albanians, but its actions clearly demonstrated it had placed human rights over sovereign rights. On the other hand, Chechnya's declaration of independence from the Russian Federation had been met by a swift and violent response from Moscow. The intensity of the fighting, and the heavy loss of life and property in Chechnya had not produced a similiar reaction from NATO. Indeed a distinction was made between what was judged a civil war in Chechnya, and what was considered "ethnic cleansing," in Kosovo. The distinction, no matter how tenuous, could explain Russia's support for Serbia in its war with NATO. It did not clarify what other out of area missions NATO might undertake in the future and it certainly did not clarify the issue of self-determination in the twenty-first century.

Furthermore, the breakup or threatened dissolution of established states is perceived differently in post-colonial and post–Cold War conditions. And whereas sympathy is extended to those peoples who continue to reach for independence, e.g., the Kashmiris, Kurds, Abkhaz, Basque, etc., the fervor with which nations earlier supported secessionist movements has diminished. More inclined to guarantee human rights and political stability, UN peacekeeping missions are concerned with sustaining the status quo rather than offering unrestrained encouragement to separatist expressions. Thus, in 1997, the United Nations called for the creation of a Rapidly Deployable Mission Headquarters that could focus attention on regions of instability before UN peacekeepers were authorized. In the meantime, given the many requests for UN intervention in distant troublespots, a logistics depot has been opened in Brindisi, Italy. A simplified procurement of supplies for ongoing and new missions has been developed, and by 1997, nearly seventy countries had allocated 88,000 soldiers and technical experts for a UN standby force. In fact, a Standby High Readiness Brigade or SHIRBRIG was to be made operational in 1999. Such actions by the United Nations reflected current thinking in the UN that although some new states will be formed as a consequence of breakaway movements, the UN was more inclined to create the necessary conditions so that the parties to a dispute involving self-determination could find ways to reconcile their rival moral claims short of realizing that objective.

Finally, giving credence to a shift in the United Nations attitude toward self-determination, were the complicated arrangements that promised peace in Bosnia-Herzegovina in 1995–97, and in Northern Ireland in 1997–98. Both were examples of a more aggressive use of diplomacy that fell short of recognizing self-determination as an absolute right.[6]

# NOTES

1. A standard treatment of the League mandate system during its first decade is Quincy Wright, *Mandates under the League of Nations* (Chicago: University of Chicago Press, 1930).
2. See "The Immediate Consequences of the War (1939–1945)," in Henri Grimal, *Decolonization: The British, French, Dutch, and Belgian Empires, 1919–1963,* trans. Stephan De Vos (Boulder, CO: Westview Press, 1978), pp. 113–37.
3. Rupert Emerson, "Colonialism, Political Development, and the UN," *International Organization* 19, no. 3 (Summer 1965), p. 486.
4. UN Document S/PV/988, December 18, 1961, pp. 9, 15.
5. Emerson, "Colonialism, Political Development, and the UN," p. 498.
6. See: Gidon Gottlieb, *Nation Against State.* New York: Council on Foreign Relations, 1993.

# SELECTED READINGS

Carpenter, Ted Galen, ed. *Delusions of Grandeur: the United Nations and Global Intervention.* Washington, D.C.: Cato Institute, 1997.

Carter, Gwendolyn M., and Patrick O'Meara, eds. *African Independence: The First Twenty-five Years.* Bloomington: Indiana University Press, 1985.

Danspeckgruber, Wolfgang, with Sir Arthur Watts. *Self-Determination and Self-Administration: A Sourcebook.* Boulder: Lynne Rienner, 1997.

Dore, Isaak I. *The International Mandate System and Namibia.* Boulder, CO: Westview Press, 1985.

Emerson, Rupert. *From Empire to Nation.* Cambridge, MA: Harvard University Press, 1960.

Gottlieb, Gidon. *Nation Against State: A New Approach to Ethnic Conflicts and the Decline of Sovereignty.* New York: Council on Foreign Relations Press, 1993.

Grimal, Henri. *Decolonization: The British, French, Dutch, and Belgian Empires, 1919–1963.* Trans. Stephan De Vos. Boulder, CO: Westview Press, 1978.

Gurr, Ted Robert. *Minorities at Risk: A Global View of Ethnopolitical Conflicts.* Washington DC: U.S. Institute of Peace Press, 1993.

Hall, H. Duncan. *Mandates, Dependencies, and Trusteeship.* Washington, DC: Carnegie Endowment for International Peace, 1948.

Hoffmann, Stanley. *The Ethics and Politics of Humanitarian Intervention.* Notre Dame: University of Notre Dame Press, 1996.

Holland, R. F. *European Decolonization, 1918–1981.* New York: St. Martin's Press, 1985.

Hutchinson, John, and Anthony D. Smith, eds. *Nationalism.* Oxford: Oxford University Press, 1994.

———. *Ethnicity.* Oxford: Oxford University Press, 1996.

Jackson, Robert H. *Quasi-states: Sovereignty, International Relations and the Third World.* Cambridge: Cambridge University Press, 1990.

Murray, James N., Jr. *The United Nations Trusteeship System.* Urbana: University of Illinois Press, 1957.

Oakley, Robert B., Michael J. Dziedzic, and Eliot M. Goldberg, eds. *Policing the New World Disorder: Peace Operations and Public Security.* Washington DC: National Defense University Press, 1998.

Pomerance, Michla. *Self-Determination in Law and Practice: The New Doctrine in the United Nations.* The Hague: Martinus Nijhoff Publishers, 1982.

Reinicke, Wolfgang H. *Global Public Policy: Governing Without Government.* Washington, DC: Brookings Institution Press, 1998.

Sparks, Donald L., and December Green. *Namibia: The Nation after Independence.* Boulder, CO: Westview Press, 1992.

Urquhart, Brian. *Decolonization and World Peace.* Austin: University of Texas Press, 1989.

Wainhouse, David W. *Remnants of Empire: The United Nations and the End of Colonialism.* New York: Harper & Row, 1967.

Wright, Quincy. *Mandates under the League of Nations.* Chicago: University of Chicago Press, 1930.

# 9

## SOCIAL AND TECHNICAL COOPERATION

International violence commands world attention when it breaks out, but economic and social programs command most of the resources of international organizations in their day-to-day operations. Article 55 defines the Charter provisions related to economic and social cooperation and calls for "the creation of conditions of stability and well-being which are necessary for peaceful and friendly relations among nations." Agencies within the UN system carry on a great many such programs, as do several hundred other global and regional intergovernmental organizations. Although these activities are supported primarily because of their contribution to economic and social well-being, they are also frequently justified by their asserted contribution to peace. Organizations for international economic and social cooperation are commonly called functional organizations, and people who advocate this approach to global peace are known as functionalists.

This chapter and the two following chapters will evaluate the activities of the United Nations and related organizations in a number of functional fields. This chapter will focus on human rights, international communication, health, the law of the sea, the environment, education and information, international relief programs, and aid to refugees. International organization for trade and economic development will be examined in Chapters 10 and 11. Because the growth of functional cooperation has been accompanied by the development of a unique body of ideas to justify and explain it, which has had some influence on the course of events, we will preface the discussion of particular activities with a brief review of functionalist theory.[1]

### FUNCTIONAL COOPERATION IN THEORY AND PRACTICE

#### FUNCTIONALIST THOUGHT

Students of international organizations have used a variety of theories and approaches borrowed from studies of other social institutions. Functionalism does not fit this pattern. While not without its intellectual debts, functionalism is almost unique as a body of prescriptions, explanatory concepts, and predictions developed with specific application to international organization. As empirical explanation and prediction, its weaknesses are now widely recognized, but its prescriptive aspects have continuing vitality.

Functionalist thought achieved currency in the early twentieth century as writers began to generalize about the multitude of international organizations for economic and social cooperation that had emerged during the preceding half century.[2] The functionalist persuasion was subsequently given impetus by two world wars and by frustration with the inability of the League's collective security machinery to keep the peace. To those who embraced functionalist ideas, the prospect of organizing "peace by pieces" in specific functional areas appeared more hopeful than military approaches, which had failed repeatedly, and more realizable than visionary schemes for peace through global or regional political federations.

As elaborated by its various spokesmen, functionalism is first of all a prescription for more international cooperation in dealing with economic and social problems. Since most people recognize the desirability of cooperative activity, this aspect of functionalism finds few critics. Functionalists also assert that cooperation in "nonpolitical" matters will promote world peace. This too has a ring of self-evident truth. To the extent that needs are met and problems resolved by cooperation, there will be that much less to fight about. Deprivation and inequality generate frustrations that can find an outlet in international conflict. By providing the means for solving such problems on a global basis, functional activities help eliminate the sources of tensions that lead to war.

The asserted link with peace extends well beyond this commonsense assumption, however, to embrace a theory of individual and social learning. Its key element is the belief that the workshop setting of functional activities provides a school for learning cooperative behavior. As individuals and governments work together for their mutual benefit, they develop habits and attitudes conducive to further cooperation. One successful venture leads to another, and the result is an ever-widening circle of shared interests. The genius of this approach is its avoidance of major challenges to state sovereignty and strongly entrenched national interests. Particular functions—health, mail service, telecommunications, and the like—become the subject of international cooperation only as the shared interests are recognized. The process is gradual and pragmatic, searching out areas of mutuality and binding together those interests which are overlapping. As the edifice of world community is constructed piece by piece, the roots of political conflict wither and the whole area of international relations is infused with learned habits of cooperation.

Functionalists have also argued that performing needed functions at the international level is more efficient because it permits a global attack on worldwide problems, unlimited by the constricting effect of national boundaries. Moreover, the relatively low controversiality of technical activities permits politicians to delegate decision making to experts and professionals, whose main concern is technical efficiency in performing their work. As a side effect, by providing useful services to people around the world, functional organizations can begin to replace national governments as the focus of human loyalties.

Not all of these assumptions appear to be confirmed by practice. Perhaps most important, international discussion of economic and social problems does not necessarily generate good will and cooperation. Some international issues are undoubtedly more controversial than others, but economic and social issues are not always low in controversy. Dispute has raged over Third World attempts to establish a new international economic order, despite their social or economic character. The history of recent adventures in functional cooperation is replete with instances of political wrangling. The process of authoritative value allocation has proved to be inherently political, whether the values are economic, social, or "political" in their content. The technical nature of an activity does not banish the need for value choices or the primacy of self-interest. Nor does the involvement of bureaucrats, however expert or professional, eliminate the push and shove of contending interests, including an interest in building bureaucratic empires. Replacing politicians with bureaucrats may simply be a means of reducing popular control.

Other functionalist assumptions may also be questioned. The functionalist explanation of war, at best, overlooks multiple causative factors. Although social inequality and economic deprivation are contributing causes of some wars, they are not alone an adequate explanation. Experience also raises doubt that cooperative habits learned in one functional context will necessarily be transferred to another, or that a widening sphere of functional cooperation will finally lead to elimination of violent conflict in the so-called political sphere. Functional cooperation has increased, but conflict and the threat of it do not appear to have undergone a corresponding decrease. Time may yet vindicate the functionalist thesis, but recent history offers no assurance that it will. Often-sounded complaints about "politicization" of economic and social agencies suggest that political controversy is more likely to hinder functional cooperation than to be mellowed by it.

Nor has the proliferation of functional activities thus far been accompanied by noticeable transference of loyalties from states to international institutions. The European Union, with its relatively high level of economic integration, has had only a modest impact on national loyalties. As for global agencies, it is almost ludicrous to suggest that the World Bank, the International Monetary Fund, UNESCO, or the World Intellectual Property Organization has become a significant focus of human loyalties (except perhaps for their paid secretariats). With so many international agencies now emphasizing assistance to less developed countries, functional organizations have become engaged in promoting the viability of states rather than diverting loyalties from them.

Functionalism nevertheless retains relevance for the real world of international organizations. Despite its obvious weaknesses, the theory offers useful insights. Learning from past experience is undoubtedly a growth accelerator, and successful functionalist ventures have provided models for new applications. If national loyalties remain firm, functional cooperation nevertheless wins support where it is perceived as genuinely serving individual and national interests.

Of more immediate importance, the functionalist prescription is closely attuned to the facts of international life. With time and space compressed by technology, states are constantly faced with new opportunities to promote welfare by joint action and new challenges to avoid problems created by the closeness. Interdependence is an inescapable fact. In such a world, the functional approach makes sense as a practical endeavor, whatever its theories of institutional development or its contribution to peace.

## THE ORGANIZATION OF FUNCTIONAL COOPERATION

The nineteenth-century system of international economic and social cooperation unfolded without plan or means of central coordination. The inevitable result was a patchwork of international institutions tending toward common structural forms, but each juridically and politically separate. Such unplanned growth is a common affliction of national societies. A nation, however, has a central government that can undertake reorganization when its administrative structure grows too cumbersome. The international system has no central authority capable of rationalizing the random growth of its institutions. As a consequence, the pattern of decentralization has continued largely unabated to the present day.

The impact of the League of Nations on nineteenth-century organizational patterns was to multiply institutions and activities without providing effective overall coordination. The League Covenant (Article 24) extended its sheltering arms to existing "international bureaus established by general treaties" if the parties to the treaties consented, and it also provided that any international bureaus or commissions thereafter established were to be "placed under the direction of the League." Only a half dozen or so of the existing agencies chose to accept League direction.

Despite the problems of coordination, League functional programs were widely recognized as being vigorous, constructive, and worth preserving, and this opinion was reflected in the copious UN Charter prescriptions for economic and social cooperation. The impact of League experience was also evident in the establishment of the Economic and Social Council as a special coordinating organ. This followed closely the report of the 1939 Bruce Committee (chaired by Stanley Bruce of Australia), *The Development of International Cooperation in Economic and Social Affairs,* which recommended the creation of special organs to supervise the work of League committees in economic and social areas.

The principle of decentralization was accepted, however, in the overall system of postwar economic and social collaboration. The UN Charter abandoned the League Covenant's vain hope that all international bureaus and commissions would be placed under the direction of the general organization. Instead, the various "specialized agencies" were authorized to maintain cooperative relationships with the Economic and Social Council and to accept such coordination as might flow from consultation and recommendation.

In practice, decentralized control has characterized many of the UN functional activities established within the United Nations itself. Agencies such as UNICEF, the UN Environmental Program, the UN Relief and Works Agency for Palestine Refugees (UNRWA), and the UN Development Program, though subject to the general supervision of the Assembly, have separate governing boards or advisory bodies and depend heavily on voluntary contributions to support their programs. Their staffs also respond to mandates of their respective governing bodies and the needs of the governments and other agencies that make up the constituencies they serve. Perhaps the very extent and variety of the economic and social programs administered on a global scale preclude truly effective central coordination. Repeated unsuccessful efforts at coordination launched in the Economic and Social Council certainly suggest such a conclusion.

Efforts were made to cope with and coordinate ever more complex social issues at the World Summit for Social Development, which met in Copenhagen in 1995. The conference addressed numerous social issues, notably the intensity and magnitude of worldwide poverty caused by rural and urban drift. Urban poverty was judged the most intractable problem but it nevertheless received less attention than the agrarian scene. The Summit also failed to address forcefully the matter of women's rights, and the NGOs monitoring the proceedings concluded that the conference was too weighted on the intergovernmental side. Acknowledging the need for a follow-up conference, and prodded by the Group of 77, a Special Session of the General Assembly on the Implementation of the Outcome of the Summit was planned for the year 2000 in Geneva. And in May 1998, the Preparatory Committee for the Special Session cited the need to invite all organs and agencies of the United Nations system—including the Bretton Woods institutions, the World Trade Organization, the United Nations Development Program, the International Labor Organization, as well as the non-governmental organizations accredited by the Economic and Social Council to attend United Nations special conferences and summits.

## WHAT FUNCTIONAL ORGANIZATIONS DO

The things done by functional organizations can be classified in a number of ways. The substantive function of an organization—human rights, health, telecommunications, and so on—is a common, even unavoidable, method of classification. Organizational functions can also be usefully classified by reference to the nature of the policy product. Here we will focus on three types of policy output: *rules and standards* for state conduct, *operating programs* that provide services to states and their peoples, and *information,* including *promotional* activities. Most functional organizations engage to some extent in all three, although some are oriented more toward one activity than another.[3]

*Rule-making* takes a variety of forms. In the broadest sense it includes recommendations and standards that depend on voluntary acceptance as well as international treaties having the force of law and authoritative rule-making by the few agencies empowered to bind their members by majority action. Organizations that make rules also attempt to secure some degree of compliance. Most of the implementation takes the form of publicity and moral pressures, or else technical assistance to states whose noncompliance springs from lack of technical capacity rather than lack of will. Functional organizations generally have little power to enforce compliance through coercive sanctions, although noncompliance may in some instances be grounds for expulsion or loss of organizational benefits (such as future eligibility for loans and grants).

*Programs* to provide services, such as refugee relief or development aid, are dependent on funds and other resources available to the organization. The influence of secretariats on operating programs is usually substantial because they have responsibility both to prepare proposals and to administer the approved programs and, being more permanent than national delegates, are repositories of an "institutional memory." Secretariats are typically in league with recipient states, since both have an interest in expanded programs, whereas donor states set the ultimate limits by their willingness—or unwillingness—to contribute the resources.

*Informational and promotional* activities involve the gathering, analysis, and dissemination of information, as well as the airing or propagation of points of view. All organizations have staff that perform these functions. Organizations also provide forums for state representatives and other participants to exchange views and information. Some of this communication is intended simply to inform; much is intended to persuade and promote programs, causes, or points of view.

The discussion that follows will make reference to these functions in examining a number of important social and technical activities within the UN system.

## HUMAN RIGHTS RULE-MAKING

The rights of persons have traditionally been matters of domestic jurisdiction and concern. International protection of individuals has not been completely absent from the law and practice of the modern state system, but until World War II such protection was limited to special groups—primarily diplomatic representatives, consular personnel, and aliens—whose status involved the interests of a foreign sovereign. From time to time, states have also undertaken treaty obligations with respect to their own nationals, as evidenced by the various European treaties from the sixteenth century onward, guaranteeing freedom of worship to religious minorities. As another example, in 1890 the

Brussels Conference produced a treaty providing effective measures to end the slave trade.

In this century the peace architects of Versailles required new states and defeated countries of Eastern Europe to assume treaty guarantees of the linguistic, educational, and other rights of ethnic minority groups incorporated within their territories. Neither the earlier religious guarantees nor the minorities treaties were very effective in securing the rights of persons, and their strictly limited nature underscored the general freedom of a state to deal as it wished with those living within its jurisdiction. The League Covenant went a bit farther in concept, if not in effectiveness, in making the "well-being and development" of subject peoples in mandated territories (Article 22) a matter of international concern and in committing members to "secure just treatment of the native inhabitants" of all their dependent territories (Article 23).

Against this background the UN Charter emphasis on the promotion of human rights, induced in large part by reaction to Nazi atrocities, constitutes a sharp break with tradition. No less than seven references to human rights are found in the Charter—the Preamble, Article 1 (purposes and principles), Article 13 (responsibilities of the Assembly), Article 55 (objectives of economic and social cooperation), Article 56 (members "pledge" to take action for the achievement of the purposes set forth in Article 55), Article 62 (functions and powers of ECOSOC), Article 68 (a commission to promote human rights), and Article 76 (objective of the trusteeship system). The new approach did not take the form of specific legal obligations, but it did assert an international interest in the rights of individuals.

Since 1945 proponents of international action have waged a continuing battle with the conservative forces of national sovereignty, although few countries have been consistent in their support of either camp. Positions on humanitarian principles have often been tinged with political expediency. The Soviet Union, before its demise, consistently displayed a double standard in favor of Socialist states, while the United States sometimes attempted to shield the questionable conduct of authoritarian states in the Western camp. Many Third World countries have persistently condemned the human rights violations of some countries, while overlooking transgressions in other parts of the world. Surveying the record in his 1991 annual report, Secretary-General Pérez de Cuéllar probably struck an accurate balance when he pointed to a "certain dichotomy" in the field of human rights. On the one hand, instruments and procedures for the international protection of human rights have multiplied; on the other, countless "human wrongs are committed in systematic fashion and on a massive scale" with the United Nations often "a helpless witness rather than an effective agent for checking their perpetration."[4]

Kofi Annan repeated and amplified this theme. He cited the difficulties in mounting consistent human rights investigations in the post-Mobutu Democratic Republic of the Congo, the successor state to Zaire. He lamented the helplessness of the international community in preventing terrorist killings of innocent people in Algeria. He acknowledged the need to improve the machinery trying war criminals in the former Yugoslavia and central Africa, and he underlined the responsibility of the United Nations in protecting human rights in all regions of the world. At the annual summit of the Organization of African Unity he declared, "human rights are African rights," and not an imposition or plot by the affluent nations of the Western world. Celebrating Human Rights Day in Tehran in December 1997, he underscored his belief of "all human rights for all" and declared it the theme of the fiftieth anniversary celebrations of the Universal Declaration of Human Rights.[5]

The UN record in dealing with human rights must be assessed in relation to the capacity of international organization to affect the conduct of states in this sensitive area. States, not international agencies, are the primary guarantors of individual rights. Unlike states, the United Nations has no courts to hear the complaints of individuals. Even the International Court of Justice permits only states to be parties to contentious cases brought before it. If a violation is found, the United Nations has no means of providing redress other than negotiation, censure, or, in extreme cases, the levying of sanctions. The Charter authorizes economic and military sanctions only in case of threats to peace and security, and, as discussed in Chapter 5, the consensus required to use them has, until recently, seldom existed.

The difficulty is compounded by disagreement among states on the nature of the rights to be protected and on the priorities among them. Western industrialized democracies have emphasized political and civil rights, such as freedom of speech, religion, and the press, and freedom from arbitrary arrest and imprisonment. Third World states give priority to economic, social, and cultural guarantees—the right to decent food, shelter, clothing, humane working conditions, and education. Many economic and social rights depend for their realization, not on political will, but on adequate resources and efficient economic organization. Others—for example, equal rights for women—may challenge deeply ingrained social custom. Different societies have different values, and the right to food may seem far more important to hungry people than the right to an uncensored press. For these reasons, states guard their sovereign authority to define individual rights and decide what protection shall be given.

The UN role under these circumstances is concerned mainly with formulating standards, encouraging conformity to them, and occasionally condemning egregious lapses—at least with respect to civil and political rights. This is not "enforcement," but it does encourage greater observance. Supplying information and providing forums for exchange of views is one way of encouraging conformity, and technical assistance may be appropriate for a state that desires to achieve a higher standard but lacks experience and the necessary institutional infrastructure. Economic "rights" may also be promoted by technical assistance and financial aid channeled through international organizations. Aside from economic aid and some services rendered directly to persons in need, the United Nations has only an indirect role in promoting human rights. Even the treaty guarantees formulated through the UN system and by other international organizations are not directly enforceable over a state's objection. However, patterns for monitoring compliance established under some of the treaties have provided a significant incentive for states to honor their treaty obligations. To the extent that human rights treaties become part of the domestic law of the signatories, they then become enforceable through internal legal processes.

In a somewhat different context, UN peacekeeping may have a very practical effect on human rights by helping to eliminate the depredations that accompany violent conflict. Namibia, Cambodia, El Salvador, and other beneficiaries of UN peacekeeping undoubtedly enjoy a higher level of well being because of it. These UN activities have been discussed in chapters 5 and 6 under the headings of peacekeeping and dispute settlement but deserve mention here to emphasize the multifaceted character of human rights and their protection.

## SETTING VOLUNTARY NORMS

Voluntary norms are commonly set by an international forum through the declaration of generally applicable rules of behavior. Declaring the rule produces no legal obligation; it simply expresses a goal, an aspiration, a guide to conduct, and perhaps a moral imperative. The most celebrated such statement in the field of human rights is the Universal Declaration of Human Rights, approved by the General Assembly on December 10, 1948, by a vote of 48 to 0, with 8 abstentions (6 Eastern European members, Saudi Arabia, and South Africa). Its thirty articles encompass a broad range of civil, political, economic, social, and cultural rights and reflect the differing aspirations and values that had to be reconciled in order to secure wide agreement for its adoption. The political and civil rights of the old liberalism are joined with the economic and social ideals of the new, while all are hedged with the right of the sovereign state to limit individual rights and freedoms as necessary to meet "the just requirements of morality, public order and the general welfare in a democratic society." Although the practical application of some of the enumerated economic and social rights might require more government control than is consistent with some of the political rights, and others depend on the availability of adequate economic resources, the declaration as a whole is an admirable and appealing distillation of universal human aspirations. It is reproduced in Appendix D.

Other human rights declarations since approved by the Assembly have dealt with more specific subjects such as the rights of children, racial discrimination, territorial asylum, discrimination against women and disabled persons, torture, religious discrimination, rights of aliens, and discrimination against minorities.

In addition to declarations, which are formalized statements of general principles, the UN General Assembly has adopted a number of resolutions on some aspect of human rights, broadly defined. Many deal with economic and social conditions, but some are addressed to particular violations of civil and political rights. Such declarations and resolutions have unquestionably influenced the way governments talk about human rights. They are frequently cited by governments as a standard of behavior, most often when criticizing other governments, and lip service is paid to them both in and out of the United Nations. They have probably brought increased observance of human rights as well, although the impact is difficult to measure. In the short run, most countries do not remedy their conduct in response to UN criticism, and UN action sometimes heightens intransigence. Chile, for example, reacted to UN criticism during the 1970s by holding a national plebiscite to endorse the Pinochet regime, which had been accused of gross human rights violations. In the long run, however, the picture is changing. After decades of UN criticism, South Africa abandoned its apartheid policies and elected a black African president. No longer holding high office, in 1998 Augusto Pinochet was arrested in Great Britain on a charge from Spain that he be tried for crimes against humanity perpetrated during his tenure. Although these developments may have had more to do with economic and political factors than General Assembly resolutions, they none the less represented a new era and a greater disposition to focus on matters of human rights. Even the ill-fated UN intervention in Somalia, the strenuous effort at righting wrongs in Haiti, the concern for the desperate noncombatants of Kosovo and Bosnia, the formation of special tribunals to try those accused of gross violations against the innocent in the former Yugoslavia, as well as the genocide in Rwanda, gave new emphasis to human rights issues, and indeed, prompted the creation of an international criminal court.

Other responses to UN declarations suggest that the long-run effects could eventually be substantial. Many of the principles of these declarations have passed into the law of individual countries through embodiment in constitutions, statutes, and judicial decisions. The Universal Declaration, in particular, has been cited in numerous decisions of domestic courts, has served as a model and inspiration for domestic legislation, and has been mentioned or partially incorporated into more than fifty extant national constitutions. A U.S. federal court has cited the Universal Declaration as evidence that torture committed by an official of a foreign government against one of his own nationals was a violation of international law. Another U.S. court declared the Universal Declaration "a powerful and authoritative statement of the customary international law of human rights."[6] References to human rights declarations in statutes, constitutions, and judicial decisions may in some countries be mere window dressing. In the United States and many other countries, they often are not. Frequent citation does not prove that human rights are being better observed than before, but incorporation of UN declarations into legal instruments and judicial decisions does mean that they are acquiring legal status that may enable them to increase respect for human rights.

## LAWMAKING TREATIES

The United Nations has not been content to let the Universal Declaration filter into national legal systems through the slow and uncertain process of exhortation, example, and action by individual states. When the declaration was adopted in 1948, it was regarded as preliminary to the drafting of a multilateral treaty that would translate its precepts into binding legal obligations. Since that time the organization has drafted multilateral treaties on a variety of special topics as well as preparing two omnibus covenants—the International Covenant on Civil and Political Rights and the International Covenant on Economic, Social, and Cultural Rights—generally paralleling the Universal Declaration.

The process of preparing such treaties is lengthy. Typically, it involves initial consideration in the ECOSOC Commission on Human Rights, reconsideration by the ECOSOC parent body, a third detailed examination in the Third (Social, Humanitarian, and Cultural) Committee of the General Assembly, and final approval by the Assembly in plenary meeting. Alternatively, the United Nations has sponsored special conferences to draft lawmaking treaties, including some in the field of human rights. Treaties take effect when a specified number of states individually sign and ratify the documents in accordance with their respective constitutional requirements.

A number of shorter, special purpose treaties passed through the UN pipeline more quickly than the two general covenants, including conventions on slavery, refugees and stateless persons, genocide (defined as "acts committed with intent to destroy, in whole or part, a national, ethnical, racial, or religious group, as such"), the political rights of women, the nationality of married women, the rights of children, and racial discrimination. A UN convention on Elimination of All Forms of Discrimination against Women took effect in 1981, and a convention proscribing torture was entered into force in June 1987. Table 9-1 gives a list of the principal UN human rights treaties and their current ratification status.

The two general covenants were not approved by the Assembly until December 1966, eighteen years after the adoption of the Universal Declaration, and both remained inoperative until 1976, when the requisite thirty-five ratifications were finally obtained. Originally the provisions of the two covenants were proposed as a single document, but the United States and some other Western countries viewed as inappropriate and impractical the effort to convert economic and social goals into legally enforceable obligations. The traditional freedoms of speech, press, worship, assembly, security of person and property, political participation, and procedural due process are prohibitions against unreasonable and arbitrary government action. Guarantees of an adequate standard of living, education, social security, full employment, medical care, holidays with pay, and a right to leisure, on the other hand, are invitations to a vast expansion of governmental functions with no guarantee that the goals will in fact be attained. It was argued that some states willing to accept treaty obligations for the promotion of political rights would refuse to ratify a treaty including economic and social rights. The answer, over the objections of some, was to write two covenants instead of one.

The United States, spurred by the enthusiasm and dedication of its best-known human rights delegate, Eleanor Roosevelt, played a leading part in drafting the Universal Declaration. Domestic controversy, fueled by fears that UN treaties might override U.S. laws in the field of civil rights, precluded a similar

TABLE 9-1  UN Human Rights Conventions

| Convention (grouped by subject) | Year Opened for Ratification | Year Entered into Force | Number of Ratifications, Accessions, Acceptances (Feb. 1998) |
|---|---|---|---|
| GENERAL HUMAN RIGHTS | | | |
| International Covenant on Civil and Political Rights | 1966 | 1976 | 140 |
| Optional Protocol to the International Covenant on Civil and Political Rights | 1966 | 1976 | 93 |
| Second Optional Protocol to the International Covenant on Civil and Political Rights, Aiming at the Abolition of the Death Penalty | 1989 | 1991 | 31 |
| International Covenant on Economic, Social and Cultural Rights | 1966 | 1976 | 137 |
| RACIAL DISCRIMINATION | | | |
| International Convention on the Elimination of All Forms of Racial Discrimination | 1966 | 1969 | 150 |
| International Convention on the Suppression and Punishment of the Crime of Apartheid | 1973 | 1976 | 101 |
| International Convention against Apartheid in Sports | 1985 | 1988 | 57 |
| RIGHTS OF WOMEN AND CHILDREN | | | |
| Convention on the Political Rights of Women | 1953 | 1954 | 110 |
| Convention on the Nationality of Married Women | 1957 | 1958 | 66 |
| Convention on Consent to Marriage, Minimum Age for Marriage and Registration of Marriages | 1962 | 1964 | 47 |
| Convention on the Elimination of All Forms of Discrimination against Women | 1979 | 1981 | 161 |
| Convention on the Rights of the Child | 1989 | 1990 | 191 |
| SLAVERY AND RELATED MATTERS | | | |
| Slavery Convention of 1926, as amended in 1953 | 1953 | 1955 | 87 |
| Protocol Amending the 1926 Slavery Convention | 1953 | 1953 | 59 |

TABLE 9-1   *(continued)*

| Convention (grouped by subject) | Year Opened for Ratification | Year Entered into Force | Number of Ratifications, Accessions, Acceptances (Feb. 1998) |
|---|---|---|---|
| **Slavery and Related Matters** | | | |
| Supplementary Convention on the Abolition of Slavery, the Slave Trade, and Institutions and Practices Similar to Slavery | 1956 | 1957 | 117 |
| Convention for the Suppression of the Traffic in Persons and the Exploitation of the Prostitution of Others | 1950 | 1951 | 72 |
| **Refugees and Stateless Persons** | | | |
| Convention Relating to the Status of Refugees | 1951 | 1954 | 131 |
| Protocol Relating to the Status of Refugees | 1967 | 1967 | 131 |
| Convention Relating to the Status of Stateless Persons | 1954 | 1960 | 44 |
| Convention on the Reduction of Statelessness | 1961 | 1975 | 19 |
| **Other** | | | |
| Convention on the Prevention and Punishment of the Crime of Genocide | 1948 | 1951 | 124 |
| Convention on the Non-Applicability of Statutory Limitations to War Crimes and Crimes against Humanity | 1968 | 1970 | 43 |
| Convention against Torture and Other Cruel, Inhuman or Degrading Treatment or Punishment | 1984 | 1987 | 104 |
| International Convention on the Protection of the Rights of All Migrant Workers and Members of Their Families | 1990 | not yet in force | 9 |

Source: United Nations Human Rights Website http://www.unhchr.ch/html/menu3/b/a-ccpr.htm

role for the United States in the covenant-drafting process Some domestic opponents of human rights treaties feared that they would water down cherished U.S. rights. Others believed that international economic guarantees might hasten the growth of socialism in the United States. Still others were concerned, with some justification, that international treaty commitments might outlaw racially discriminatory laws and practices then common in many states. To head off a proposed constitutional amendment (the "Bricker Amendment") limiting the President's treaty-making power, the Eisenhower administration assured the Senate that the United States would not sign or ratify the UN human rights covenants. This assurance had its desired domestic effect but at the price of diminished U.S. influence and leadership in the international protection of human rights.

Although discriminatory laws in the United States have since been eliminated by judicial decision and legislative action, the United States has never regained its place in the forefront of international human rights activity. Of the principal UN human rights treaties, until 1986 the United States had ratified only a Supplementary Convention on Slavery and a related protocol, the Convention on the Political Rights of Women, and a protocol relating to the Status of Refugees. The U.S. policy of hostility or indifference to UN human rights treaties was reversed in the executive branch by President Jimmy Carter, who submitted several treaties to the Senate in 1977, urging consent to their ratification. The new interest in human rights survived the Carter administration, and the Senate finally approved the Genocide Treaty in 1988, the International Covenant on Civil and Political Rights in 1992, and the UN Convention Against Torture in 1994, as well as the International Convention on the Elimination of All Forms of Racial Discrimination, also in 1994. The United States is also a signatory to the Convention on Consent to Marriage, Minimum Age for Marriage and Registration of Marriages (1962); the Convention on the Political Rights of Women (1976); the Protocol Relating to the Status of Refugees (1968); the International Covenant on Economic, Social and Cultural Rights (1977); the Convention on the Elimination of All Forms of Discrimination Against Women (1980); and the Convention on the Rights of the Child (1995).

## IMPLEMENTING HUMAN RIGHTS

Any discussion of human rights implementation must take account of the global power structure within which the United Nations operates. International organizations provide important linkages within the system, but the principal centers of power are sovereign states. Whether individual rights are violated or vindicated in the territory of a given state depends mainly on decisions made within that state. A state may legitimately complain if its own nationals are mistreated by foreign governments and sometimes succeed in obtaining redress. But under traditional international law, states have been largely free to treat their own citizens as they will—and this is the source of the most persistent and flagrant human rights violations. The new law of human rights, arising from both treaty and custom, offers people more protection against their own governments, but the tradition of national autonomy remains strong. Pressures by one state on another for better observance of human rights generally stop short of coercive action. The reluctance of states to do more reflects the realities of an international system made up of sovereign entities. If states are thus inhibited, the United Nations is still less able to *enforce* individual rights against the wishes of a recalcitrant state.

Useful things can still be done through international action, however. One helpful, and generally inoffensive, way is to supply information and technical assistance. The United Nations has for years conducted a program of seminars, fellowships, and advisory services for countries requesting special help. The world organization also circulates information about human rights through UN meetings and through studies, reports, and other publications. United Nations discussions of human rights are all too frequently dominated by political polemics, but on some subjects they serve a useful informational function. It is quite probable, for example, that the ECOSOC Commission on the Status of Women has contributed to the extension of political rights to women through its efforts to gather information and exchange views and experiences. In other areas of concern, discussion has been enlightened by special UN studies on such topics as forced labor, slavery, torture, disappearances, summary and arbitrary executions, religious intolerance, protection of persons with mental illnesses, and discrimination in education, employment, and political rights. In addition, national reports on human rights observance are periodically discussed in the ECOSOC Commission on Human Rights.

In dealing with alleged violations of human rights, the United Nations has relied on investigation, discussion, publicity, and censure. These have occurred in a variety of forums, including the General Assembly and its Third Committee, the Economic and Social Council, the Commission on Human Rights, and the Subcommission on Prevention of Discrimination and Protection of Minorities. In a few instances, where marginal national interests have been involved and UN action has been conciliatory, states have reacted favorably to such pressure. Most attempts by the organization to remedy specific violations of human rights have not been efficacious, at least in the short run. Viewed as a deterrent, UN censure seldom outweighs the domestic motivations that lead to rights violations.

Nevertheless, UN organs have persisted in exerting the moral pressure of discussion and recommendation and have strengthened their procedures for doing so. For years the Commission on Human Rights was debarred from taking any action on complaints that particular states were denying human rights. This limitation was modified in 1967, when the commission was authorized to examine information and make studies of situations revealing gross violations of human rights. The procedure was regularized in 1970 with the adoption of

ECOSOC Resolution 1503, permitting the commission to investigate "particular situations which appear to reveal a consistent pattern of gross and reliably attested violations."

The "1503 procedure" has since become the usual means of dealing with the thousands of letters and reports received each year at the United Nations, mainly from private individuals and groups, containing complaints of human rights abuses. Through the screening process most complaints are never acted on because the procedure restricts the commission to matters referred by its Sub-Commission on Prevention of Discrimination and Protection of Minorities, which in turn acts only on a recommendation from a working group of five of its members. Even so, Resolution 1503 has been a step toward more effective UN scrutiny. All such matters remained private until 1978, when the commission began to divulge the names of countries that it had discussed in confidential sessions. Since 1980 the commission has publicly disclosed reports of its investigations or discussions in a number of cases, including complaints against Equatorial Guinea, Bolivia, Cambodia, El Salvador, Guatemala, Nicaragua, the Soviet Union (in Afghanistan), Poland, Romania, Cuba, and Iran. Such "mobilization of shame" has become important in the commission's compliance procedures.

Nongovernmental organizations have been especially active in support of improved UN human rights procedures. While many individuals and groups have communicated with the United Nations from time to time, some of the more active groups—which have their own operations independent of the United Nations—include Amnesty International, the International Commission of Jurists, the International League for Human Rights, the International Federation for Human Rights, and the World Council of Churches. Amnesty International, established in London in 1961, has become widely known for its efforts to publicize and secure the release of political prisoners and to eradicate torture. It is respected as a source of information as well as for its persistence in mobilizing public opinion and encouraging government action to vindicate fundamental human rights.

Some of the human rights treaties have their own provisions for implementation, but most use the same procedures of complaint, investigation, discussion, and censure used by UN bodies outside the treaty framework. Under the International Covenant on Civil and Political Rights, an eighteen-member Human Rights Committee of specialists elected by the parties is empowered to receive reports from states on measures adopted to implement the covenant. The committee studies the reports and transmits its comments to the parties and the Economic and Social Council. In addition, states may authorize the committee to receive and consider communications from other parties alleging nonfulfillment of treaty obligations. No state may bring such a complaint unless it has made an appropriate declaration subjecting itself to the procedure. The committee's powers are limited to discussion and reporting, supplemented by a conciliation procedure with consent of the parties. By accepting an optional protocol to the treaty, states have empowered the committee to consider complaints from private persons within their jurisdiction. Any views expressed by the Committee have only the force of recommendation.

## REGIONAL INSTITUTIONS

A perspective on UN efforts to promote human rights throughout the world may be gleaned from an examination of the regional approaches to human rights in the Americas and Western Europe. The Organization of American States was seven months ahead of the United Nations when it adopted the American Declaration of the Rights and Duties of Man in Bogota, Colombia, in April 1948. The American Declaration was the first international human rights instrument of a general nature, and it led to the creation in 1959 of the Inter-American Commission on Human Rights (IACHR), which held its inaugural session in 1960. From that time through 1997, the Commission convened ninety-seven sessions at its headquarters in Washington D.C. or in different countries of the Western Hemisphere. In 1961, the IACHR began site-visits, observing human rights situations in specific countries and launching investigations where conditions revealed violations of the Declaration. Since that early period through 1997, the IACHR carried out sixty-nine "visits" to twenty-three member states and published forty-four special country reports.

In 1965, the IACHR became expressly authorized to examine complaints or petitions regarding specific cases of human rights violations. By 1998 the Commission had received thousands of petitions, which resulted in 12,000 cases being processed or ordered for processing. The final published reports of the IACHR regarding these individual cases are found in the Annual Reports of the Commission or released independently. In 1969, members of the Organization of American States adopted the American Convention on Human Rights, and it went into force in 1978. As of August 1997, it had been ratified by twenty-five countries (Argentina, Barbados, Brazil, Bolivia, Chile, Colombia, Costa Rica, Dominica, Dominican Republic, Ecuador, El Salvador, Grenada, Guatemala, Haiti, Honduras, Jamaica, Mexico, Nicaragua, Panama, Paraguay, Peru, Suriname, Trinidad and Tobago, Uruguay, and Venezuela). This Convention defines human rights and created the Inter-American Court of Human Rights. It is the responsibility of the IACHR to order the Court to issue "provisional measures" in urgent cases that involve a danger to persons even when a case has not been submitted to the Court. It also submits cases to the Inter-American Court and appears before that body in the litigation of cases. Finally, the IACHR may request advisory opinions from the Court regarding questions of interpretation of the American Convention. In 1997–98, the Commission was charged with processing 800 individual cases to determine if all domestic remedies had been exhausted and if there was still reason to believe justice had not been done. The IACHR may seek to address a case itself, but on occasion it will transfer the case to the Inter-American Court. The Court is located in Costa Rica and is considered an autonomous institution of the Organization of American States. It is comprised of seven judges who are elected by the states that are parties to the

Convention. Judges serve six-year terms and may be re-elected to a second term. The Organization of American States also established an Inter-American Juridical Committee, which consists of eleven judges who function out of Committee headquarters in Rio de Janeiro. Its major task is the codification of international law.

Undoubtedly the most effective arrangement for the international protection of human rights is the European Convention on Human Rights, drafted under the auspices of the Council of Europe and in force since 1953. The council's members have accepted the convention and thereby agreed to submit certain types of human rights controversies to the binding determination of an international body. These states have also approved an optional provision granting individuals and private associations the right to complain. The emphasis is on quiet negotiation to find a "friendly solution" among the parties involved. For states that have ratified an optional protocol conferring jurisdiction on the European Court of Human Rights, the final decision is left to the court.

The successful operation of the convention has rested on a number of circumstances. First, the convention has been limited to traditional civil and political rights already widely guaranteed in Western European countries. Second, the legal systems of the parties have sufficient homogeneity to produce similarity in interpretation and application of the treaty guarantees. Third, the emphasis throughout is on quiet negotiation of settlement, utilizing a judicial or quasi-judicial body as the final arbiter and at no stage providing a public forum for political harassment of one state by another. Fourth, states have seldom used the machinery in their dealings with one another, with the great majority of complaints issuing from individuals. Fifth, petitions by individuals are carefully screened to rule out frivolous or insubstantial complaints.

The maintenance of Council standards in the post-cold war era however, presents significant problems. The former Eastern bloc nations became members of the Council of Europe shortly after the demise of the Soviet Union, and the Russian Federation was made the organization's thirty-ninth member in February 1996. All pledged adherence to the principles safeguarding human rights and to the organs and procedures responsible for assuring compliance. But Russian problems with secessionist Chechnya, and the vicious ethnic conflicts that followed the breakup of the Yugoslav Federation, raised questions that are difficult to answer. What has been a positive record in human rights safeguards has been weakened by these, as well as other human rights incidents in the Baltic states where minorities have been placed at risk. Since the inclusion of the East European states in the Council of Europe, violations of the European Convention on Human Rights have escalated. Moreover, the East European states have not only demonstrated ignorance of the understandings arrived at in the 1993 Vienna World Conference on Human Rights, they have also avoided using their own Court of Conciliation and Arbitration, created in 1994 by the Organization for Security and Cooperation in Europe for purposes of protecting human rights.

## THE DECLARATION OF HUMAN RIGHTS REVISITED

By 1998 fifty years had elapsed since the Universal Declaration of Human Rights was adopted by the United Nations. Representing the first time in history that a document considered to have universal value was formalized by an international organization, it was also the first time that human rights and fundamental freedoms were formulated in detail in an international document. Moreover, the broad-based support for the Declaration hinted at a different future for the more threatened of the world's humanity. Cited as the "Magna Carta" for all the people of the planet, its contents ranged from civil to cultural, to economic, to political and social issues, and amplified the first words of the UN Charter that addressed itself to "We the Peoples." At the World Conference on Human Rights convened in Vienna in June 1993 and attended by 171 nations, a Vienna Declaration and Program of Action was adopted to better integrate the work of governments and non-governmental organizations in meeting the goals of the original declaration as well as subsequent conventions on the elimination of racial discrimination, discrimination against women, and the rights of the child. Calling for a more proactive strategy, the fiftieth anniversary of the declaration provided opportunities for countries to condemn blatant violations of human rights, and more so, to take responsibility and action to deter those violators who till now hid their actions behind a cloak of national sovereignty.

The celebration of the Declaration of Human Rights fell within the Decade of Human Rights Education (1995–2004), and although the document had been translated into 200 languages, additional language versions were judged essential. But more than words, the fiftieth anniversary was used to mobilize civil society and non-governmental organizations in the struggle to achieve basic rights. National committees were formed in scores of states, and grassroots movements energized communities to higher awareness. Moreover, in accordance with recommendations made at the 1993 World Conference on Human Rights for increased coordination within the United Nations system, Secretary-General Kofi Annan reiterated the organization's commitment to the complex issues that involved peacekeeping, protecting the rights of labor and children, safeguarding health and the provision of appropriate education. If there was a core issue around which the United Nations was formed and continued to operate it was the matter of human rights, and although progress since 1948 could no doubt be cited, the fiftieth anniversary celebration of the document was also a painful reminder that people everywhere remained at risk, and too often were confronted by the most dire circumstances.

The plight of people at risk in fact had been noted in the proclamation that established 1993 as the International Year of Indigenous People, and subsequently, the period 1995–2004 as the International Decade of the World's Indigenous People. Noting the disproportionate impact of poverty on indigenous people in countries like Bolivia, Guatemala, Mexico, and Peru, the failure to provide even the most minimal health services was deplored by Latin American community organizations. Using a similar theme, the Australian Institute of Health and Welfare revealed the desperate conditions of the aboriginal children in central Australia that produced an unconscionably high rate of infant mortality. In New Zealand the focus was on the Maori males who were twice as likely as non-Maori males to be affected by heart disease, pneumonia, chronic respiratory problems and infections of the skin. And although regional organizations were more likely to report shortcomings in the area of human rights, the global character of the problems facing indigenous people did not go unnoticed. Much of the difficulty was traced to uncontrolled industrial development and its resultant environmental damage, especially water pollution, the loss of important sources of nutrition such as fish, and exposure to high levels of contaminants. Indigenous folk are also subject to deprivation of property rights, to high unemployment, and to cultural genocide. Native Americans in the United States continued to live out impoverished lives on reservations. Brazil brutalized Indian communities that blocked lucrative mining interests. And the Chiapans of Mexico formed the Zapatista National Liberation Army and took up arms and terror in an effort to protect their domains from encroaching exploiters.

To cite the above is to note that the adoption of the Universal Declaration of Human Rights more than fifty years ago did not terminate the abuses suffered by people around the world. The United Nations system is mindful of its responsibilities but beyond shedding light on grievances, on publicizing salient questions, or prodding nations to improve their performance, it cannot itself make right the many complex wrongs. With the United Nations committed to the cause, the next fifty years must address the implementation of national development programs that are directed at correcting the inequities and gross displays of intolerance that are found in all societies. Only with the forging of new relationships based upon mutual respect and recognition will the profound intentions of the Universal Declaration be realized. The United Nations system exists to promote that ideal, and if the organization's past dedication is a measure, its member states can anticipate even greater pressure to fulfill their stated goals.

## HUMAN RIGHTS, NATO, AND THE TRAGEDY OF KOSOVO

Nowhere at the end of the millennium was the issue of human rights more dramatically or more tragically illustrated than in the plight of the Kosovar Albanians. And nowhere were the senseless struggles that pitted one portion of humanity against another more expressive of the shallowness of civilization than in Kosovo in 1999. Although threatened populations stretched from the Adriatic to the Caucasus and into Russia, through the Mediterranean to Mesopatamia and Africa, eastward to the Asian subcontinent, and onward to Southeast, East and Pacific Asia, it was this area of the Balkans, nestled between parent Serbia, Montenegro, Albania and Macedonia, that in 1999 represented the flashpoint for still another intercontinental conflagration. Blind expressions of nationalism, nourished on ancient ideas and myths of territoriality, culture, and identity, fueled the manifestations of fear and loathing between Serb and Kosovar Albanian. Although called to accept a common political order, Serbs and Albanians shared little except their mutual hate for one another. Their passions held in check during the Josip Broz Tito decades that followed World War II, the great leader's death in 1980 left a power vacuum that no successor was able to fill. Moreover, once a reputed federation managed by strict communist rules of decorum, the repudiation of European communism in 1989–90 further complicated Yugoslavia's feeble efforts at the formation of an unnational state. Denied universal leaders and a cosmopolitan following, let alone a civil society, by the 1980s Yugoslavia's different subnational ethnic claimants to power had stoked the furnaces of separatism and exclusivity. Their demagogic antics fired the passions of their respective peoples and prompted the disintegration of the state. Generations of intermingling, however, had also made the different republics of Yugoslavia more polyglot and their peoples more intertwined. Furthermore, a diplomatic separating out of the different political units with clear territorial boundaries was never attempted. As a consequence, when the break up came it provoked the disastrous ethnic wars which initially enveloped Croatia and Serbia, and then spilled over into Bosnia. The efforts made to form a greater Serbia were matched by those determined to establish a greater Croatia. Bosnia was squeezed between them, and after several years of bloodletting it could only be rescued by the intervention of the NATO alliance led by the United States.

The transatlantic attempt to douse the flames of indiscriminate tribal warfare in the former Yugoslavia was aimed at restoring tranquility to an expanding Europe as much as it was meant to promote and protect human rights in the Balkans. Therefore, NATO, the alliance formed early in the cold war to thwart a perceived Soviet military threat to western Europe, was preserved and ultimately enlarged in order to work its magic under new and different circumstances. Not having fired a shot in anger in its contest with the Soviet Union, NATO's mere presence was believed sufficient to guarantee European stability and security. Moreover, Europe's deeper integration and democratization programs were made dependent on the alliance's continued success in muting the nationalistic drives of its members. Transcending the national frontiers of the member states, NATO shifted its gaze from the protection of state boundaries to that involving the human condition and the safeguarding of human rights. No longer simply a military alliance, NATO's socio-political role legitimized the organization in the post-cold war years and justified its interventionist role in Bosnia. Performing at a virtual supranational level in Bosnia, NATO, in the absence of a more formidable United Nations, assumed a posture that arguably challenged the sovereignty of individual nations.

Hence NATO let it be known it could not ignore the conflict in Kosovo involving Serb forces and those of the Kosovo Liberation Army (KLA). The

NATO governments largely believed the KLA was organized to pressure Belgrade to restore Kosovo's autonomous status which it had withdrawn in 1989. Challenged by the import of the Universal Declaration of Human Rights, and also believing an escalating civil war in the province could provoke a wider European war, NATO again demanded that the Serbs cease their persecution of the Albanian Kosovar majority, grant the province its long denied autonomy, and begin a process of reconciliation between Serbs and Albanians residing within the region. Thus, in October 1998, NATO pressured the Serb government of Slobodan Milosevic to accept an agreement calling for the withdrawal of Yugoslav military and paramilitary forces from Kosovo. Belgrade indicated its willingness to comply but at the same time it launched an offensive against the KLA which quickly impacted the larger Albanian population. With the ethnic conflict intensifying, the NATO governments convened a conference in France in February 1999 between the KLA and members of the Milosevic government. Although the KLA grudingly accepted the peace formula drafted by the alliance, a formula which would have left Kosovo an integral part of Serbia, Belgrade rejected it out of hand because it also called for the stationing of a NATO security force in the province. Arguing NATO was violating Yugoslavia's sovereignty, and that the intrusion would be direct interference in a purely domestic matter, Belgrade refused to yield to NATO demands or threats. The Serbs therefore used the period offered by the deliberations in France to reinforce and expand their military operations in Kosovo. Moreover, Milosevic made the fateful decision to accelerate the program of ethnic cleansing, that is, the forced removal of the Kosovar Albanians.

What followed was Serbia's clear violation of the Universal Declaration of Human Rights, now a centerpiece for European integration and democratization. NATO warned Belgrade, as it had in October 1998, that it was prepared to use force if the Serbs persisted in their ethnic cleansing campaign. In fact, tens of thousands of Albanian Kosovars already had been forced from their homes when NATO reissued its warning in February 1999. Milosevic and his government remained defiant, however, and in fact stepped up their campaign to change Kosovo's demographic character. With NATO's credibility on the line, with the fear that a far greater human tragedy was in the offing, NATO repeated its warning, but neither that threat nor last minute diplomatic efforts could budge the Milosevic government from its declared intention to rid the province of Albanian Kosovars, and with them the KLA as well.

Arguing they could no longer stand by while helpless Kosovars were brutally uprooted and many murdered, in March 1999, NATO air power was directed against Serbia and Montenegro, the latter still an actor in what remained of the Yugoslavian state. NATO air strikes were intended to bring the Serbs back to the conference table but instead they propelled the Belgrade government to move even more rapidly with its program to rid Kosovo province of its Albanian inhabitants. Serb military and paramilitary units moved quickly and systematically, forcing the Albanians from their land and homes, destroying their property, killing and maiming an untold number, notably males between the ages of 16 and 60, and herding the vast majority to border locations where first tens of thousands and then an estimated seven to nine hundred thousand desperate people were forced upon neighboring Albania, Macedonia, and to some extent Montenegro. NATO's stated objective had been to relieve the pressure on the Kosovar Albanians, but quite the reverse had occurred. Confronted with a refugee situation, like none other in recent European memory, NATO also became the central medium in administering to the traumatized throngs that clogged the border areas, and moreover, posed threats to the neighboring countries that lacked the capacity to manage the influx.

Crimes against humanity were cited in countless stories told by the Albanian refugee population and given the new emphasis on the protection of human rights, NATO along with other agencies collected data on war crimes for transmission to the International Criminal Court. Of those identified for future retribution, first on the list was the Serbian leader, Slobodan Milosevic. But although attention was riveted on the plight of the Albanian Kosovars and the need to punish the perpetrators of Europe's foremost human tragedy since the end of World War II, far more was involved. The elevation of human rights over that of state rights was one major aspect of this confrontation, and in this matter the United Nations was a significant symbol as well as actor. But no less important, that is, in the long term, was the forging of a new Atlantic and European Community that was committed to the construction of a trans-Atlantic and European civil society. NATO celebrated its Fiftieth Anniversary in April 1999, and the Washington Summit that was attended by the alliance's heads of state or governments collectively acknowledged their mutual responsibilities in preventing a repetition of the Kosovar tragedy in a Europe reaching for but not yet fully comprehending the depth of its transformation.

## IMPROVEMENT OF LABOR STANDARDS

Closely related to UN action in the field of human rights are the efforts of the International Labor Organization to upgrade labor standards around the world. The ILO has been a force for higher labor standards since its creation in 1919, when Allied statesmen, responding to labor pressures and honoring their wartime commitments to trade union groups, drafted the constitution of the ILO as Part XIII of the Versailles Treaty. The organization has ever since been marked by a vigorous secretariat, known as the International Labor Office, and a unique form of tripartite representation for employer, worker, and government interests in its policy-making bodies. Each member state sends two government delegates, one employers' delegate, and one workers' delegate to the annual meeting of the International Labor Conference, and the same tripartite distribution is found in its fifty-six-member governing body.

Like the United Nations in its human rights programs, the ILO functions by setting standards, giving advice, facilitating the exchange of information, and mobilizing world opinion in support of higher standards. Standards are set through legally binding conventions, subject to state ratification, and through recommendations voicing goals and aspirations that are beyond the reach of some states and hence not proper subjects for lawmaking treaties. The conventions and recommendations taken together are referred to as the International Labor Code. From six conventions and six recommendations adopted by the first International Labor Conference in 1919, the number had grown to 181 conventions and 188 recommendations by 1998. The code extends to nearly every aspect of working conditions—hours, wages, the right to organize and bargain collectively, employment discrimination, workers' compensation, employment security, vocational guidance and training, and occupational safety and health, among others. A number of the conventions and recommendations deal with special abuses, such as slavery and forced labor, or with special categories of workers—women, children, miners, seamen, dockworkers, and sharecroppers. States vary widely in their ratification of conventions. France has ratified more than a hundred, the United States less than twenty.

The ILO has unusually well-developed techniques for encouraging compliance with the code. This is done by a searching annual review of member states' reports, a judicious use of the ILO's powers of investigation, and a procedure for hearing complaints in specific cases. The ILO has seldom been hesitant in pointing out instances of noncompliance and making specific recommendations for remedial action.

In addition to rule-making and implementation, the ILO carries on extensive informational activities through publications, conferences, seminars and fellowships, and technical experts. Its *Yearbook of Labor Statistics* and its quarterly *Official Bulletin* have long been important sources of data on international labor conditions. A monthly *International Labor Review* and numerous special publications provide information on current problems and conditions.

Programs of technical assistance are used to help countries conform to the International Labor Code as well as to promote economic development as a means of providing a social and economic base for improved labor standards. Assistance is provided in areas of ILO interest and expertise, such as vocational training, social security services, occupational health and safety, and labor statistics. Some ILO technical assistance is funded from its own budget, but a larger share draws on resources of the UN Development Program.

The International Labor Organization operates in the same world environment as the United Nations, and it has suffered the effects of political battles between East and West and between North and South. In 1977 the United States withdrew from the organization, after having held continuous membership since 1934. The U.S. dissatisfaction sprang from a number of causes. The United States saw the tripartite principle threatened by delegations from the Soviet bloc and some other states whose employer and labor representatives were, for practical purposes, government representatives under a different label. The United States also objected to what it saw as selective concern for human rights, especially as reflected in actions of the International Labor Conference that pilloried friends of the United States and ignored violations in some other countries. Excessive politicization was also alleged, particularly in using the forum to penalize Israel for actions that had little to do with labor standards and in granting observer status to the Palestine Liberation Organization (PLO) in 1975. As early as 1970 the AFL-CIO, with its strong anti-Communist tradition, had been seriously alienated by the appointment of a Soviet national as an ILO Assistant Director-General.

Loss of the U.S. financial contribution, amounting to 25 percent of the regular budget, caused severe temporary curtailment of ILO programs. The United States returned in 1980, after some signs that the ILO would behave more circumspectly. An Arab proposal to condemn Israel was defeated, labor rights violations in Eastern Europe were given more attention, and procedures were adopted to bolster employer and worker autonomy within the organization. Perhaps more important, the United States concluded that working from within was a more effective method of influencing labor standards and ILO programs than remaining outside the organization. Since returning the United States has maintained a more sympathetic involvement with the organization and in 1988 ratified ILO conventions on forced labor and labor standards in maritime shipping. Two other conventions, dealing with tripartite consultation on international labor standards and labor statistics, have since been ratified. The forced labor treaty was the first ILO convention to be accepted by the United States in thirty-five years.

# RULES IN OTHER FUNCTIONAL SETTINGS

Human rights and labor standards are matters of domestic concern that have traditionally been regulated by individual states. By contrast, many areas of functional cooperation involve interstate contacts that fall beyond the jurisdiction of any single state and must be regulated by international action if they are to be regulated at all. In recognition of this fact, states have submitted a number of their functional relationships to the regulative processes of international organization. Its growth does not necessarily justify the functionalist premise that economic and social cooperation leads to peace, but it does demonstrate that states will subject themselves and their citizens to a degree of international regulation in limited functional areas when self-interest requires it. Some of the more significant ventures in the regulation of international contacts will be briefly examined here.

## Postal Service

Among the best-observed international regulations are those of the Universal Postal Union (UPU), an organization dating from 1874. Under its auspices letters can be delivered anywhere in the world by the most expeditious route at a modest uniform cost and in accordance with generally uniform procedures. The technical nature of UPU's functions is conducive to consensus, and consensus on broad objectives provides the foundation for majority rule within the organization when the goal of complete unanimity cannot be attained. Revisions of the UPU constitution, initiated at meetings of the Congress of the Postal Union, held every five years, become effective upon ratification by two-thirds of member countries. Changes in the rules and regulations governing letter post are effected by a simple majority of the membership, without need for ratification. Between congresses, proposals for amendments to the postal rules are circulated by the bureau (secretariat) and take effect when enough affirmative replies are received. Compliance with the rules is obligatory from the time of their entry into force, with loss of membership privileges as the sanction. Formal approval of changes is not necessary as long as a state in fact observes the regulations. Compliance is generally forthcoming because the benefits of participation outweigh the burdens of compliance.

## TELECOMMUNICATIONS

The work of the International Telecommunication Union is in many respects analogous to that of the UPU, especially its efforts to create a homogeneous global communication system by joint regulation of telegraph, telephone, and radio-telegraph services. The two organizations' methods of legislating and of enforcing compliance are also broadly similar. The ITU conference meets at intervals of five to eight years to make general policy and initiate amendments to the ITU convention. Decisions are reached through unanimous agreement if possible but by simple and qualified majorities when necessary. A state is permitted to ratify amendments with reservations and still remain in good standing, but the penalty for nonratification is loss of its vote in ITU organs after a two-year grace period. As a practical matter, from the date of their entry into force, amendments are treated as provisionally applicable even to nonratifying states. In a number of technical matters, including the important function of radio-frequency regulation, the ITU assigns tasks to specialist, "nonpolitical" experts instead of to negotiating conferences composed of government representatives. This approach differs from that of the UPU and is possible because of the highly technical nature of the tasks.

Compliance with ITU rules, a product of necessity and convenience, has been very high except in the special problem area of radio broadcasting. There the ITU has sometimes been faced with defiance by countries refusing to be limited to the use of frequencies allotted by the ITU's International Frequency Registration Board. If a recalcitrant member broadcasts on a frequency not assigned to it, the ITU may punish the offender by freeing other states to use its assigned frequencies. Interference with authorized radio signals, otherwise known as radio jamming, is another special problem. The practice is clearly in violation of ITU regulations, but it is so entwined with the vital interests of states that ITU sanctions are unable to curb it. When faced with a complaint of radio jamming, the ITU has generally resigned itself to the fact that retaliation through release of frequencies would only add to the confusion and further impair radio transmission. With the end of the cold war, the systematic radio jamming by Eastern European states was discontinued.

## CIVIL AVIATION

In the field of air transportation, international efforts to promote safety, regularity of transport, uniformity, and nondiscrimination are centered in the International Civil Aviation Organization. The rule-making function is exercised principally by the organization's thirty-three-member council, rather than its triennial assembly. Standards approved by a two-thirds vote of the council become effective at a date prescribed by the council unless a majority of states indicate their disapproval during the intervening period. The organization distinguishes between binding *standards,* which are necessary to the safety or regularity of international air navigation, and nonbinding *recommended practices,* which represent desirable goals.

A state that cannot conform to a new standard may notify the council within the time period fixed for raising objections and be released from its legal obligation. If the standard relates to the airworthiness of aircraft or the competence of personnel, however, other states are free to close their airspace to the aircraft of the noncomplying state. The ICAO convention commits all members to the principle of nondiscrimination against the aircraft of any country, but noncompliance with standards revives the discretionary rights of one state against another that would prevail under the rules of customary international law. Compliance with ICAO rules is widespread, and most instances of noncompliance appear to be rooted in lack of economic and technical resources rather than willful disregard of the norms.

ICAO regulation is primarily technical, relating to such matters as air traffic control, communication and navigational aids, safety standards for aircraft, and rules of the air. The organization has not been given the authority to regulate the commercial aspects of civil aviation, including access to the passenger and cargo markets of individual countries. A right jealously guarded by states, the granting of commercial privileges still occurs through bilateral agreement between states.

## HEALTH

Health problems have long been a subject of international regulation. The international health councils established during the nineteenth century in seaport cities of North Africa, the Middle East, and Southeastern Europe—sometimes by the imposition of the more powerful European states—represented an early form of international action to improve sanitary conditions and prevent the spread of epidemics along the channels of commerce. Later the councils were supplemented by multilateral conventions that established rules for quarantine, and other precautionary measures to be taken in ports, and prohibited vessels from leaving port without a clean bill of health. Exchange of information through conferences was put on a more systematic basis in 1907 with the establishment of the International Office of Public Health in Paris, and League health machinery subsequently forged ahead with direct efforts to fight disease and improve world levels of health.

The World Health Organization (WHO), which came into being in 1948 as a specialized agency of the United Nations, has combined and expanded international cooperation in all of these fields. As a regulatory body, the WHO has effective rule-making power in several limited but important areas, including: (1) sanitary and quarantine regulations applicable to ground, sea, and air travel; (2) standardization of medical nomenclature; (3) standards for diagnostic procedures; (4) standards on the safety, purity, and potency of biological and pharmaceutical substances passing in international commerce; and (5) advertising and labeling of such products. When approved by the World Health Assembly, health regulations come into force for all members after a specified period of notice, except for states that specifically object or enter reservations. The WHO constitution gives the Assembly the right to make law by treaty, subject to ratification by member states, but the World Health Organization prefers the regulation approach because it speeds up the process and permits rules to take immediate effect for all member states, barring a formal objection. Beyond these special areas, the WHO may make recommendations on any health-related subject. Research, collection and dissemination of information, and expert advice are also used extensively to upgrade health standards around the world.

Although the preceding discussion has emphasized WHO's rule-making functions, WHO also has extensive programs of health services and technical assistance to developing countries. These include a number of successful campaigns against disease. A concentrated effort to combat malaria, beginning in the mid-1950s, led to its eradication from most of Asia, much of the Americas, and all of Europe. Permanent eradication in Africa was not possible until basic health services were improved. The WHO's success in fighting smallpox was even more spectacular. A campaign in the late 1960s and early 1970s reduced the incidence of smallpox to a rare occurrence in most parts of the world.

An Expanded Program on Immunization (EPI), launched in 1974, provides immunization for children against diphtheria, measles, pertussis (whooping cough), poliomyelitis, tetanus, and tuberculosis. These are a major cause of death and disability in the developing countries. Although not fully successful, the proportion of immunized children worldwide rose from less than 20 percent in the late 1970s to more than 70 percent in the 1990s. The worldwide fight against disease is also aided by WHO's epidemiological intelligence network, which receives reports from member governments immediately upon the outbreak of any case of smallpox, cholera, plague, or yellow fever and transmits the information to health authorities throughout the world by means of daily broadcasts.

A global strategy in support of a "Health for All by the Year 2000" campaign, adopted by the WHO assembly in 1981, had the goal of promoting a world level of health that will permit all persons to lead socially and economically productive lives. Specific objectives included safe water within fifteen minutes' walking distance of every home, immunization against the six EPI diseases, local health care within an hour's travel, and trained personnel to attend childbirth and to care for pregnant mothers and for children up to at least a year old. These goals could not be reached by the year 2000 since neither the WHO nor the poorer countries have the resources to do the job.

The WHO program gathers and reports international statistics, supports national information and education programs, and provides training for medical personnel in member countries. It also seeks to improve national facilities for screening and protecting blood supplies and encourages the establishment and expansion of laboratory facilities for diagnosis and treatment of AIDS. The WHO also has launched a "Tobacco or Health Program," an educational effort emphasizing the harmful effects of tobacco.

In addition to its general health functions, the WHO cooperates with the United Nations and related agencies for the control of narcotics and limiting their use to legitimate medical and scientific needs. Systematic efforts at international control date from the Hague Convention of 1912. International cooperation in this area was expanded by the League and further systematized under UN auspices. The present international regime is based on the Single Convention on Narcotic Drugs, adopted in 1961 to replace a number of earlier treaties and amended by a 1972 protocol; a 1971 Convention on Psychotropic Substances; and the 1988 UN Convention against Illicit Traffic in Narcotic Drugs and Psychotropic Substances. Under the treaties, an International Narcotics Control Board sets acceptable limits for the manufacture and importation of controlled drugs and monitors treaty compliance. The effectiveness of regulation depends largely on the ability and willingness of states to enforce treaty provisions, but international agencies help states remain sensitive to their obligations.

An ECOSOC Commission on Narcotic Drugs is an important forum for discussion of international narcotics problems, and the United Nations maintains research laboratories in several countries. The WHO role is to advise other international agencies on drugs likely to produce addiction and to sponsor research and technical assistance relating to the prevention and treatment of drug addiction.

## THE ENVIRONMENT

When the United Nations Conference on the Human Environment met in Stockholm in June 1972, environmental concerns were barely visible on the international horizon. Only two prime ministers attended. By June 1992, when the United Nations Conference on Environment and Development (UNCED) convened in Rio de Janeiro, the presence of heads of state or government from more than a hundred nations attested that problems of the global environment had achieved high priority on the international agenda.

The current salience of environmental concerns owes much to the 1972 conference. It adopted a Declaration on the Human Environment, setting forth twenty-six principles and one hundred nine action recommendations that still serve as guidelines for UN environmental activities. Perhaps equally important, preparation for the conference induced some ninety states to create new governmental entities, bureaucracies, and intragovernmental consultative mechanisms to deal with the problems to be discussed at Stockholm.[7] In many governments, this organizational response to the conference gave environmental concerns an emphasis they had not previously enjoyed.

The 1972 conference also proposed the establishment of a United Nations Environment Program (UNEP) as a permanent UN agency. UNEP was subsequently created by the UN General Assembly and came into being in 1973, with headquarters in Nairobi, Kenya—the first UN agency to be based in a developing country. The organization has never grown large—employing about 200 professionals with supporting staff—but it has been influential in raising global consciousness and instigating programs for environmental protection.

UNEP is a rule-making agency in the broad sense of "rule-making" as we have defined it. Its fifty-eight-member governing council makes recommendations, proposes standards, and initiates discussions leading to international treaties. In this respect it is comparable to rule-making organizations previously discussed in the areas of human rights, communication, transportation, and health. Rule-making in these and other functional areas can also be viewed through the lenses of a related concept frequently used by international relations theorists, that of *regimes*. The regime concept can be illustrated by application to UNEP and its role in the international system.

*Regimes,* in Stephen D. Krasner's frequently cited definition, are sets of "implicit or explicit principles, norms, rules, and decision-making procedures around which actors' expectations converge in a given area of international relations."[8] An international organization is not itself a regime but rather a structure within a regime that provides procedures for rule-making, dispute resolution, and other forms of interaction from which principles, norms, and rules may emerge. Within a given regime there may be many such structures. The regime actors are likely to include national government officials, staffs of international organizations, and representatives of affected private groups and entities.

Krasner's definition of "regime" leaves considerable room for different views of whether a particular regime has come into existence. "Norms" and "principles" are sometimes difficult to define, and including "implicit' as well as explicit rules within the concept of regime may make the regime itself hard to define with precision. In view of this difficulty, other writers have identified regimes with specific multilateral agreements regulating state conduct (and private conduct as well, through government action) in a given issue area. Thus

Oran Young speaks of specific (and separate) regimes for stratospheric ozone, greenhouse gases, biological diversity, and so on. The international Convention for the Regulation of Whaling and the Agreement on the Conservation of Polar Bears would constitute additional regimes within the broader issue area of the environment.[9] Peter Haas, likewise, treats the Barcelona Convention for the Protection of the Mediterranean Sea Against Pollution as a particular regime within the environmental area.[10]

In this discussion we accept both concepts of a regime. UNEP, using the broader definition, functions within a regime consisting of the "principles, norms, rules, and decision-making procedures" relating to international environmental activities. Participants in this regime include the UNEP secretariat; staffs of other international organizations concerned with environmental impacts (such as the FAO, WHO, and the International Oceanographic Commission); members of environment-oriented NGOs and of the relevant scientific communities; officers of multinational corporations; and officials of national governments—often technical specialists but also, on occasion, participants drawn from high political levels of government.

Though small in size, UNEP has done much to shape the regime in which it operates. Its principal functions are gathering and disseminating information, encouraging governments to adopt environmentally sound policies, and promoting the development of international environmental law. Its information programs are extensive. Among them are the International Register of Potentially Toxic Chemicals (IRPTC), which makes available extensive information on chemical safety; the INFOTERRA computer network, which provides names, addresses, and telex/telephone numbers of thousands of institutions and experts capable of giving answers to environmental questions; and the Global Environmental Monitoring System (GEMS). GEMS coordinates a network of monitoring stations in some 150 countries, providing information on climate and atmospheric conditions, renewable terrestrial resources, ocean and transboundary pollution, and the health consequences of pollution.

UNEP also devotes a substantial portion of its resources to seminars and other training sessions for government officials, as well as to technical cooperation. An important substantive emphasis of UNEP has been the relationship of environmental factors to economic development, health, and human settlements. Much of the technical assistance to developing countries focuses on environmentally sound ways to sustain productivity of forests, animal and plant species, soils, and water supplies.

UNEP activities have also promoted the formation of more specific regimes through the development of international law. This includes the "hard" law of international treaties as well as the "soft" law of guidelines, principles, and standards for environmental management. Both are important. Hard law creates legal obligations; soft law helps build government consensus on appropriate goals and methods. Soft law could be regarded as creating regimes involving a lower level of commitment. Soft law standards have been formulated to provide guidance in such areas as weather modification, offshore mining and drilling, marine pollution from land-based sources, management of hazardous wastes, environmental impact assessment, and exchange of information on chemicals in international trade.

Multilateral treaties create specific regimes involving a relatively high degree of commitment. Some of those adopted with UNEP encouragement include the 1985 Vienna Convention and the 1987 Montreal Protocol (both dealing with protection of stratospheric ozone layer) and the 1989 Basel Convention (trade in hazardous wastes). By 1990 UNEP's regional seas program had resulted in eleven regional conventions for marine environment protection. Two further treaties drafted with UNEP input were opened for ratification at the 1992 UNCED global conference. One, a biodiversity treaty, sought to preserve key plant and animal species by controlling the impact of deforestation, pollution, and misuse of resources. The other, much watered down at U.S. insistence, contained a nonspecific commitment to limit the emission of the greenhouse gases believed to cause global warming. The global warming issue was revisited in Kyoto, Japan, and later in Bonn, Germany, in 1997. The United States again demonstrated reluctance in agreeing to climate treaties that would limit its carbon-dioxide and methane emissions, which were described as one-quarter of the world's total. Fearing threats to the United States economy, American business groups continued to pressure government not to accede to international demands, thus weakening UNEP's role. Nevertheless, and in spite of its difficulty in gaining support from the United States, UNEP has had its successes. Although the desertification campaign failed, its regional seas program and negotiations on atmospheric ozone depletion resulted in international agreements. And given sustained opposition from the larger powers, especially the United States, UNEP has formed alliances with sympathetic nongovernmental organizations, such as the World Commission on Environment and Development. UNEP's budget has increased from $20 million in 1973 to more than $100 million in 1998, but that sum is not significant considering its expanded responsibilities.

The focus on UNEP functions in this discussion does not obscure the fact that UNEP is only one structure within the broad global environmental regime, and but one of a number of international organizations, including the UN General Assembly and ECOSOC, having environmental functions. The vast majority of regime participants have no direct connection with UNEP. UNCED, the most highly publicized environmental meeting of the century, was called by the UN General Assembly and had a structure quite distinct from UNEP. Although it owed something to UNEP initiative and to the international currents that UNEP had helped set in motion, UNCED drew its support and character from many different sources, governmental and nongovernmental. Indeed, while UNCED was meeting in Rio, nearly 4,000 NGOs from 153 countries held their own parallel global forum and eco-fest at a nearby seaside park. This was symbolic of the array of participants in the regime, ranging from the fringes to the very core.

Nevertheless, UNEP occupies a special place in the development of the environmental regime. UNEP's mission has been that of communicator, educator, propagator, coordinator, and broker. If significant change is to occur, it must be effected by those who have the resources. UNEP thus has aimed at creating a regime within which the resources of others can be mobilized in support of environmental preservation. To accomplish this goal it has worked with environmental personnel in other international organizations to develop shared goals and perspectives and often joint activities. Even more important, UNEP has cultivated national constituencies in member states drawn from the scientific community, interested nongovernmental organizations, and public officials with environmental responsibilities. By creating links with national groups, and promoting international contacts among those groups, UNEP has helped to develop shared norms and expectations consonant with its own. At the national level, this transnational constituency has become an effective force in advising and persuading national governments to support UNEP activities. Although most environmental activities are necessarily carried on by other actors, UNEP, through its broker-communicator role, has played a crucial part in shaping the regime.

## The Environment and Sustainable Development

Considering the many challenges facing the world community in the twenty-first century, none will be more important than achieving sustainable equilibrium between economic development, reducing poverty, promoting distributive justice and protecting the planet's resources, commons, and life-support systems. The Nineteenth Special Session of the General Assembly in 1997 underscored the difficulties in achieving cooperation on existing agreements, especially measures outlined during the Earth Summit. Nevertheless, since 1992 there has been a proliferation of new actors in the field of environment and sustainable development which has expanded the base of participation in the United Nations. The world of the twenty-first century will become increasingly more urban and the future of the world's cities and towns will be determined through a synthesis of environmental, social, and economic development issues. The United Nations Commission on Sustainable Development (CSD) has become the central forum for a plethora of specialized agencies seeking answers to questions of balance and harmonization. Moreover, from their joint endeavor has come a veritable proliferation of international environmental conventions, autonomous governing bodies and secretariats.

But while there is identifiable dynamism and achievement, the overall record is not totally positive. Developing country needs for financial resources have not been met, and Official Development Assistance (ODA) from donor governments in the developed world has in fact declined since the Rio Summit. The Global Environmental Facility (GDF) that is concerned with sustainable development projects has not been adequately funded. And while UNDP and the World Bank devote considerably more resources to sustainable development projects and programs, and private or voluntary investment in such activities is also significant, little progress has been made in creating innovative sources of financing for the future. What is needed is a more integrated systemic approach throughout the whole range of United Nations activities. Such a development requires closer interaction between UNEP and the UN Commission on Human Settlements. Also involved is the Inter-Agency Committee on Sustainable Development (IACSD) that includes UNEP and the UN Center for Human Settlements (Habitat), as well as the Governing Council of UNEP and the Commission on Human Settlements that reports to the UN General Assembly.

UNEP, however, is the environmental voice of the United Nations and the principal source of information for the UN Commission on Sustainable Development (CSD). The Nairobi Declaration adopted by the UNEP Governing Council in 1997 called for strengthening UNEP as the world community's coordination center on environmental issues. Only UNEP has the worldwide capacity to monitor and assess environmental matters through its GEMS and GRID programs. So too, UNEP is the central agency concerned with the development of policy and law on environmental questions. It is also the bridge between science and policy making, and maintains an active association with national environmental organizations and agencies. UNEP therefore has been at the center of negotiations that have resulted in the drafting of important treaties that are related to the environment and sustainable development.

## THE LAW OF THE SEA

The oceans constitute 70 percent of the earth's surface. In the past most of this area has been open to all states. Recent developments in the law of the sea have increased national control over large parts of this area through rules expanding the breadth of the territorial sea, creating an "exclusive economic zone" out to 200 miles from a country's coastline and extending national control of seabed resources still farther in many cases. Other proposed rules, if adopted, would establish a world government for the seabed beyond national jurisdiction, a regime that states have been unwilling to accept anywhere else on earth. This is more than just a rule-making exercise to help regulate matters of technical, social, and economic interest. It is a massive experiment in peaceful political and territorial change.

In centuries past the oceans were used for two main purposes—navigation and fishing. Although specific disputes over fisheries and navigation rights sometimes arose, the oceans were treated for the most part as a global commons not subject to the control of any single state. With the increased use of the oceans made possible by new technology, the twentieth century has seen rising demands from states to extend national control over larger and larger ocean areas and the seabed beneath. While oil and fisheries have provided the primary motivation, the extension of national jurisdiction to areas that were formerly part of the high seas necessarily has an impact on navigation rights as well. In addition, intensive use creates problems of depleted fishing resources and increased maritime pollution.

These and other ocean problems have been attacked in a number of international forums. The International Maritime Organization (formerly known as IMCO, Intergovernmental Maritime Consultative Organization), founded in 1948 as a UN specialized agency, has produced important treaties dealing with maritime safety and pollution. The UN Environmental Program (UNEP) encourages global and regional agreements to preserve the ocean environment. A UNESCO-sponsored Intergovernmental Oceanographic Commission promotes and coordinates scientific research, monitoring of the oceans, and international exchange of oceanographic data. The Food and Agriculture Organization conducts research and provides technical assistance on fish as a food resource. The International Labor Organization makes recommendations and sponsors conventions dealing with maritime labor conditions. The International Whaling Commission, through international agreement, jawboning, and economic pressures exerted by sympathetic states, tries to preserve existing stocks of whales from extinction.

*Early Treaty-Drafting Conferences*

While the attack on maritime-related problems has been highly splintered, by far the most ambitious effort to establish rules for the use of the oceans has occurred in UN-sponsored treaty-drafting conferences. As early as 1930 an international conference at The Hague tried to codify the law of the sea in treaty form but failed to reach agreement. In 1958 a UN Conference on the Law of the Sea (UNCLOS I) was more successful. It produced four multilateral treaties—the Convention on the Territorial Sea and the Contiguous Zone, the Convention on the High Seas, the Convention on the Continental Shelf, and the Convention on Fishing and Conservation of the Living Resources of the High Seas—each of which entered into force among the ratifying states during the 1960s. Although the treaties codified much of the existing law of the sea, important issues remained unresolved, including the breadth of the territorial sea and the extent of coastal state jurisdiction over fishing rights.

The conventions on the territorial sea and the contiguous zone, the high seas, and fisheries addressed problems that had been at the heart of ocean law for centuries. They codified long-standing rules of customary international law, adapted to modern circumstances. Jurisdiction over the continental shelf, on the other hand, was a new issue because technology had only recently made possible the exploitation of the oil resources of the ocean floor. The United States started the rush toward national jurisdiction with President Harry Truman's September 1945 proclamation claiming control over the natural resources of the seabed and subsoil of the U.S. continental shelf. Many states followed suit, and the 1958 convention embodied these claims in treaty law. The convention was extremely generous to coastal states, recognizing jurisdiction as far out as developing technology might permit exploitation of seabed resources.

A second UN conference (UNCLOS II), held in 1960, was unable to agree on disputed issues, and in subsequent years national jurisdiction over the oceans continued to expand. Several states, most of them in Latin America, went so far as to claim a territorial sea of two hundred miles, which, if established, would include control over navigation as well as ocean and seabed resources. Others claimed an economic zone of varying distances that would not impinge on navigation rights.

## UNCLOS III

Faced with such diverse and extensive claims to national jurisdiction, the United Nations called a third UN Conference on the Law of the Sea (UNCLOS III). The initial impetus for this renewed UN effort is traceable to a remarkable speech before the 1967 General Assembly by Ambassador Arvid Pardo of Malta. The need for greater uniformity was obvious. The need to reconcile coastal state jurisdictional claims with flag state claims to "freedom of the seas" and every state's interest in what was left of the "global commons" was also apparent. The genius of Pardo's appeal was to join these concerns with the special needs of developing countries for additional sources of financial aid. To achieve these purposes, he proposed to set fixed limits to national jurisdiction and to declare the resources of the seabed and ocean floor beyond those limits "the common heritage of mankind." This common heritage would be managed by a seabed authority empowered to exploit its resources on behalf of mankind, with particular emphasis on the needs of developing countries.

Preparations for the conference lasted six years, and drafting the convention took another nine years, from the first brief session held in December 1973 to the closing session in 1982. The new treaty embraced, modified, and amplified the four treaties drafted in 1958 at UNCLOS I and added important new provisions on an exclusive economic zone (EEZ), the rights of landlocked states, a regime for the common area beyond national jurisdiction, preservation of the marine environment, marine scientific research, and machinery for the settlement of disputes arising under the treaty.

A number of notable changes from previous law are written into the treaty. The breadth of the territorial sea, previously claimed at three, four, six, twelve, and up to 200 miles by different states, and unspecified in the 1958 convention, is fixed at twelve miles, with an additional twelve miles of contiguous zone for enforcing regulations against smuggling. The 1958 convention set the contiguous zone at twelve miles from the coastline. The convention also provides an exclusive economic zone extending 200 miles from the coastline, in which coastal states have control over the economic resources of the sea and the subsoil beneath but not jurisdiction over navigation. A limit is also put on the breadth of the continental shelf. Although various methods of calculation are given, coastal states are guaranteed jurisdiction over the seabed to a distance of

200 nautical miles, with a maximum in some cases of three hundred fifty miles. Any minerals extracted from the continental shelf beyond 200 miles are subject to a royalty, paid to an international authority, primarily for the benefit of developing states. The dispute settlement provisions are also noteworthy. Disputes arising under the law of the sea that are not settled by agreement must be submitted to binding arbitral or judicial procedures. An International Tribunal for the Law of the Sea was created as one such alternative.

The most controversial provisions turned out to be those setting aside the ocean floor beyond national jurisdiction (called the "Area") as the common heritage of mankind and creating an International Sea-Bed Authority to administer it. Under the terms of the treaty, governments and private firms may obtain licenses to conduct mining operations in the Area, subject to fees, royalties, and production regulations. The authority is also empowered to engage in undersea mining through an operating agency known as the "Enterprise," and, as a condition to receiving the permit, national licensees must share technology with the Enterprise and give it first choice of mining tracts to exploit. The authority is to be an autonomous international organization with its own assembly, council, and secretariat, governed by majority vote. A degree of minority protection is provided through requirements for extraordinary majorities on some issues.

Although the United States had earlier indicated that it would accept the seabed provisions of the treaty as part of the overall law of the sea package, the Reagan administration expressed reservations about the sea-bed authority and subsequently refused to sign the convention. The United States objected to the burdensome regulation of private corporations engaged in seabed mining, particularly the costs involved and production limits designed to protect land-based producers of the same minerals. The United States also feared that it would be perpetually outvoted on critical issues by the Third World majority and that treaty amendment provisions might later be used to exclude private enterprise entirely.

In spite of this controversy, however, the Law of the Sea Convention represented the most ambitious scheme of codification and progressive development of international law ever attempted. New limits on the breadth of the territorial sea was assured. So too the rules pertaining to the exclusive economic zone, and the right of transit through international straits that fall within national jurisdictions. In accordance with the provisions of Article 308, the Convention entered into force on November 16, 1994, having acquired the necessary sixty ratifications, although the United States was not one of them. The entry into force of the United Nations Convention on the Law of the Sea and the Agreement relating to the implementation of Part XI of the Convention caused the United Nations to redesign its program of information, advice, and assistance in this field. The United Nations Office of Legal Affairs assisted the various institutions created by the Convention, including the Commission on the Limits of the Continental Shelf, which held its first meeting in June 1997. Moreover, the International Seabed Authority completed its initial organizational work and began to function in 1997. So too the International Tribunal for the Law of the Sea, which opened for serious business in 1998.

## INFORMATION AND PROMOTION

Every international organization gathers and disseminates information. This is an inevitable by-product of meetings, but it is also done systematically. Many organizations sponsor research in their technical areas and hold conferences for the exchange of information among scholars and experts, including representatives of governments and private groups. Many collect and publish statistical data supplied by research or by their members. All publish various reports of their activities.

### "Days," "Years," "Decades," and "World Conferences"

International agencies also engage in promotional activities. Secretariats carry on various "public information" programs designed not only to inform but also to persuade. Speeches made in deliberative bodies have the same objectives. Although efforts at international consciousness-raising and promotion of worthy causes have become commonplace in international organizations, certain techniques repeatedly used by the United Nations merit special emphasis. They are the "day," the "week," the "year," the "decade," and the "world conference."

UN-sponsored days have become legion. Without being exhaustive, a representative list might include the International Day for the Elimination of Racial Discrimination (March 21), the International Day of Innocent Children Victims of Aggression (June 4), World Environment Day (June 5), the International Day against Drug Abuse and Illicit Trafficking (June 26), International Literacy Day (September 8), International Peace Day (third Tuesday of September), World AIDS Day (December 1), Human Rights Day (December 10), International Day for Biological Diversity (December 29) and of course United Nations Day (October 24). The list of weeks is shorter but includes the Week of Solidarity with the Peoples Struggling against Racism and Racial Discrimination (beginning March 21), and Disarmament Week (October 24–30).

Nearly every year is now set aside for the promotion of some worthy cause. Thus 1990 was designated by the General Assembly as International Literacy Year, 1992 as International Space Year, 1993 as the International Year for the World's Indigenous Peoples, and 1994 as the International Year of the Family. The "decade" usually involves a more ambitious undertaking, with proposals for programs to achieve the purposes of the decade and periodic reports on progress. The first such decade was the UN Development Decade, 1961–70. The 1970s were subsequently declared the Second Development Decade, the 1980s the Third, and the 1990s the Fourth. The 1970s and the 1980s were also designated disarmament decades. A Decade to Combat Racism and Racial Discrimination was launched in 1973, and a Second Decade to Combat Racism in 1983. A UN Decade for Women was inaugurated in 1976, and in 1981 an International Drinking Water Supply and Sanitation Decade. A United Nations Decade of Disabled Persons began in 1983 and a World Decade for Cultural Development in 1988. The 1990s, in addition to the Fourth Development Decade, were also set aside for a Third Disarmament Decade, a UN Decade for International Law, an International Decade for the Eradication of Colonialism, and an International Decade for Natural Disaster Reduction.

The world conference approach has already been noted in Chapter 3, in connection with the involvement of private groups with international organizations. Here we emphasize that UN-sponsored world conferences since the early 1970s—on such subjects as the environment, population, human rights, women, housing, energy resources, refugees, and development—have been staged primarily to raise the level of knowledge and international concern. Such meetings have the advantage of focusing on a single subject, commonly for two weeks or longer, and the governmental delegations are more heavily weighted with technical experts than generalist diplomats.

Secretary-General Kofi Annan's call for a Peoples' Millennium Assembly organized around the General Assembly session of the year 2000, captured the attention and provoked the imaginations of creative thinkers all over the world. His concern that the non-governmental organizations, representing the "peoples' interests," and that form the basis for a global civil society, be intimately linked with the organs of the United Nations, addresses a vision that argues for a world body that is as embracing of the world's humanity as it is of its sovereign states. All world conferences, let alone a "Peoples' Millennium Assembly," are preceded by extensive preparation that normally includes negotiations on agreements or declarations to be approved at the conference—and more so, in the spotlight of the world media. The Millennium Assembly lowers the threshhold for a broad range of popular representation and is slated to combine government bureaucracies with private organizations from the social and economic sectors as never before. With global media coverage a certainty, conference participants can be expected to project a wide range of messages, and of all the world conferences sponsored by the United Nations since its inception in 1945, the People's Millennium Assembly adds a new and significant dimension to the United Nations system. (See Figure 9-1.)

## EDUCATION, SCIENCE, AND CULTURE

Among international organizations the UN Educational, Scientific and Cultural Organization (UNESCO) has a special responsibility for the dissemination of information. Its activities are very wide-ranging, which has been a source of both weakness and strength. The strength comes from the capacity to appeal to and gain support from many governmental and private constituencies with

FIGURE 9-1    UN World Conferences, Decades, Years, Weeks, and Annual Days

---

### WORLD CONFERENCES

- World Conference on International Cooperation of Cities and Citizens for Cultivating an Eco-Society (1998)
- United Nations Diplomatic Conference of Plenipotentiaries on the Establishment of an International Criminal Court (1998)
- Third United Nations Conference on the Exploration and Peaceful Uses of Outer Space (UNISPAC III) (1999)
- Review Conference of the States Parties to the Treaty on the Non-Proliferation of Nuclear Weapons (NPT) (2000)
- Second World Conference on Natural Disaster Reduction (2000)
- Tenth United Nations Congress on the Prevention of Crime and the Treatment of Offenders (2000)
- World Conference on Racism and Racial Discrimination, Xenophobia and Related Intolerance (2001)
- Third United Nations Conference on the Least Developed Countries (2001)

---

### INTERNATIONAL DECADES AND YEARS

- 1990s—International Decade for Natural Disaster Reduction
- 1990s—Third Disarmament Decade
- 1990–1999—United Nations Decade of International Law
- 1990–2000—International Decade for the Eradication of Colonialism
- 1991–2000—Fourth United Nations Development Decade
- 1991–2000—Second Transport and Communications Decade in Africa
- 1991–2000—United Nations Decade against Drug Abuse
- 1993–2002—Second Industrial Development Decade for Africa
- 1993–2002—Asian and Pacific Decade of Disabled Persons
- 1993–2003—Third Decade to Combat Racism and Racial Discrimination
- 1994–2004—International Decade of the World's Indigenous People
- 1995–2004—United Nations Decade for Human Rights Education
- 1997–2006—United Nations Decade for the Eradication of Poverty
- 1998—International Year of the Ocean
- 1998—Fiftieth anniversary of the Universal Declaration of Human Rights
- 1999—International Year of Older Persons
- 1999—Centennial of the First International Peace Conference
- 2000—International Year for the Culture of Peace
- 2000—International Year of Thanksgiving
- 2001—International Year of Volunteers

---

### ANNUAL DAYS AND WEEKS

- 8 March—United Nations Day for Women's Rights and International Peace
- 21 March—International Day for the Elimination of Racial Discrimination

FIGURE 9-1    *(continued)*

---

### ANNUAL DAYS AND WEEKS

- 21 March—Beginning Week of Solidarity with the Peoples Struggling against Racism and Racial Discrimination
- 22 March—World Day for Water
- 23 March—World Meteorological Day
- 7 April—World Health Day
- 23 April—World Book and Copyright Day
- 3 May—World Press Freedom Day
- 15 May—International Day of Families
- 17 May—World Telecommunication Day
- 25 May—Beginning Week of Solidarity with the Peoples of All Colonial Territories Fighting for Freedom, Independence and Human Rights
- 31 May—World No-Tobacco Day
- 4 June—International Day of Innocent Children Victims of Aggression
- 5 June—World Environment Day
- 17 June—World Day to Combat Desertification and Drought
- 26 June—International Day against Drug Abuse and Illicit Trafficking
- 26 June—International Day in Support of Victims of Torture
- First Saturday of July—International Day of Cooperatives
- 11 July World Population Day
- 9 August—International Day of the World's Indigenous People
- 8 September—International Literacy Day
- 16 September—International Day for the Preservation of the Ozone Layer
- Third Tuesday of September—International Day of Peace
- Last week in September—World Maritime Day
- 1 October—International Day of Older Persons
- First Monday of October—World Habitat Day
- 9 October—World Post Day
- Second Wednesday of October—International Day for Natural Disaster Reduction
- 16 October—World Food Day
- 17 October—International Day for the Eradication of Poverty
- 24 October—United Nations Day
- 24 October—World Development Information Day
- 24–30 October—Disarmament Week
- 16 November—International Day for Tolerance
- 20 November—Africa Industrialization Day
- 20 November—Universal Children's Day
- 21 November—World Television Day
- 29 November—International Day of Solidarity with the Palestinian People

*(continued)*

FIGURE 9-1  *(continued)*

| ANNUAL DAYS AND WEEKS |
| --- |

- 1 December—World AIDS Day
- 2 December—International Day for the Abolition of Slavery
- 3 December—International Day of Disabled Persons
- 5 December—International Volunteer Day for Economic and Social Development
- 7 December—International Civil Aviation Day
- 10 December—Human Rights Day
- 29 December—International Day for Biological Diversity

SOURCE: UN Publications Service, http//www.un.org/events/refpap37.htm

an interest in one or more of UNESCO's activities. The weakness lies in the dispersion of effort and the limited impact that result from spreading limited resources over a wide area.

A large share of UNESCO's resources has been devoted to technical assistance in education, particularly in programs for the elimination of illiteracy and for training in basic vocational skills essential to economic development. UNESCO had primary responsibility for organizing the 1990 International Literacy Year activities. In addition, UNESCO provides technical assistance for the promotion of the natural sciences and, to a lesser extent, the social sciences, the humanities, mass communication, and the development and preservation of national cultural heritages. It also promotes intergovernmental cooperation in research relating to the environmental sciences and natural resources. All of these programs are slanted heavily toward the needs of developing countries, and most are undertaken with financial assistance from the UN development program.

UNESCO has also produced a number of treaties in areas of concern to it, including an International Convention concerning the Protection of the World Cultural and National Heritage, the Universal Copyright Convention, the Convention on the Free Flow of Educational, Scientific and Cultural Materials, and the Convention against Discrimination in Education.

The strictly informational activities of UNESCO cover a staggering variety of topics. Titles in the catalog of UNESCO and UNESCO-sponsored publications number in the thousands. Periodical publications range in scope from the *UNESCO Courier* (topical themes and events of popular interest) to the *International Social Science Journal, Diogenes* (humanities), *Nature and Resources, Prospects* (education), and *Museum.* These titles are illustrative, not exhaustive. Other publications include bibliographies, reports, histories (including the multivolume *History of Africa* and *History of the Scientific and Cultural Development of Mankind*), translations of literary masterpieces, and special studies on all manner of subjects within UNESCO's fields of interest, as well as valuable statistical documentation in education, the social sciences, library services, mass communication, and other fields.

Another important informational activity, often fostered by means of conferences, is the promotion of interchange among scientists, scholars, and artists. To further this interchange, UNESCO has encouraged the formation of international professional societies and has often supported them through financial subventions. Scholarships and fellowships, educational exchange, elimination of barriers to the free flow of information, and improvement of mass communication systems are other elements of the UNESCO approach to dissemination of information. If UNESCO falls short in its efforts to spread education, science, and culture, it is not from lack of variety in its methods.

With such broad objectives, UNESCO's reach has necessarily exceeded its grasp. Falling short of goals need not bring a negative assessment; the task may simply be larger than the available resources. UNESCO has undoubtedly promoted the production and exchange of information in its various fields of activity, and its technical assistance programs have added something to national resources for education and development. Critics, nevertheless, have faulted the diffusion of its efforts and have suggested that its impact might be greater if its focus were sharper.

In response to these criticisms, UNESCO has tried to set priorities, but the pressures for diffusion of its efforts have been irresistible. First of all, its mandate is very broad—education, science, and culture can be construed to embrace almost anything—and the UNESCO Constitution posits the additional goal of contributing to a more peaceful world. Second, UNESCO constituencies—governmental and private—provide constant pressure for the continuation or addition of programs that benefit them. For two decades or more, the director-general of UNESCO has predominated in setting the direction for UNESCO's programs, and he is responsive to the groups that give him support. These include scientists, scholars, and other private beneficiaries of UNESCO programs and, more important, the prevailing Third World majority in the UNESCO general conference and executive board, whose interests lie in expanding programs. A third reason for diffusion is UNESCO's bureaucracy, with its vested interest in proliferation and expansion. A reversal of the trend would cost some officials their jobs, while other officials might lose perquisites and influence in the constituent communities they serve.

For the developed countries that pay most of the bills, the growth of UNESCO budgets has been a greater source of dissatisfaction than the abstract question of how many programs are too many. The United States, in particular, objected to budgetary increases during the 1970s and early 1980s, claiming the UNESCO director-general and his staff were not exercising sufficient restraint and that the UNESCO council and general conference were not holding him sufficiently accountable. Other problems also seriously eroded U.S. support for UNESCO. From the mid-1970s onward, the United States persistently objected to the "politicization" of UNESCO—particularly as expressed in Arab-sponsored resolutions criticizing Israel for its archaeological activity in Jerusalem and its educational policies in the West Bank, and the attempted exclusion of Israel from participation in UNESCO.

The United States also complained that UNESCO laid emphasis on group rights or "peoples rights," such as self-determination, at the expense of individual rights. A related concern was the Third World demand for a New International Information Order. The New Order was supposed to redress the imbalance and distortion in the flow of world information alleged to result from control of world news and information channels by the developed states. The United States, however, feared that this would legitimize greater government control over the news media.

On December 28, 1983, the United States notified the 161-member UNESCO body that it would withdraw at the end of the twelve-month period required by charter law. Washington accused UNESCO of anti-American and anti-Western policies, but it was equally severe in its condemnation of the organ's financial and budgetary actions. Moreover, UNESCO's Director-General was condemned for championing both the Palestine Liberation Organization as well as the "new world information order," which limited news coverage of Third World countries. The United States formally confirmed its withdrawal from UNESCO on December 19, 1984. Great Britain and Singapore also left the organization in December 1985. (South Africa had withdrawn its membership from UNESCO in 1956 but rejoined in 1994. Portugal left the council in 1972 and returned in 1974. In all, there have been ten withdrawals and seven re-entries since the creation of UNESCO.) Although Washington's annual financial contribution represented 25 percent of UNESCO's budget, UNESCO functioned normally and the U.S. Department of State was pressured to establish a formal observer mission with the organization in 1985. Moreover, the United States continued to administer the International Conventions and Scientific Organizations Fund of the agency. It also remained a member of UNESCO's Universal Copyright Convention and fully participated in its Intergovernmental Copyright Committee.

Although the United States preferred to remain an observer of UNESCO activities, Great Britain rejoined the body in 1997. And indeed, the absence of the United States did not affect UNESCO's membership, which swelled to 186 member states and four associate members in 1998. The aloofness of the United States meant a loss of almost 25 percent of UNESCO's budget but the council made up much of the deficit by introducing a new schedule of payments that called for an increase in contributions by the member states. By 1998, Japan and Germany were the largest contributors to UNESCO, and the annual budget had risen to more than $500 million, with extrabudgetary funds being made available by the United Nations Development Program, the United Nations Population Fund, the United Nations Children's Fund, the United Nations Environment Program, the World Bank and regional banks, the Funds in Trust, and other voluntary contributions from member states. These funds totalled more than $300 million annually. By the end of the century, UNESCO had authorized expenditures to the following sectors: Education 36 percent, Natural Sciences 20.6 percent, Culture 15.8 percent, Communication, Information and Informatics 10.4 percent, Social and Human Sciences 9.6 percent, and Programs and Activities 7.6 percent. In 1998, UNESCO employed 2,200 civil servants, professionals and general staff, about 500 of whom were located in sixty field offices around the world. Moreover, 588 non-governmental organizations maintained official relations with UNESCO, while another 1,200 were occasionally associated. UNESCO also sponsored 4,800 grassroot clubs, associations, and centers that promoted its ideals and performed unofficial tasks. The vitality of UNESCO was also demonstrated by the 165 permanent delegations that were based in the Paris headquarters of the organization. The election of a new Director-General in 1987 and his re-election in 1993 for still another six-year term enabled UNESCO to resolve many of the older complaints registered by the larger contributors. But the United States Congress remained philosophically at odds with the organization, and the general criticism levelled against the United Nations in American political circles suggested the United States would continue to ignore its charter membership in UNESCO.

## OTHER INFORMATION ACTIVITIES

Other international organizations also render informational services on which governments, businesses, the professions, and others throughout the world have come to rely. The Statistical Office of the United Nations, for example, publishes a number of annual basic reference works, including the *Statistical Yearbook,* the *Demographic Yearbook,* the *Yearbook of International Trade Statistics, World Energy Supplies,* and the *Yearbook of National Accounts Statistics.* The *UN Chronicle,* published quarterly (monthly before 1986) by the UN Department of Public Information, contains a review of major UN activities during the preceding quarter. The United Nations also issues periodicals on special subjects such as the *International Review of Criminal Policy* and the *International Social Service Review.* These and other regular UN publications are supplemented by numerous special reports. The specialized agencies likewise produce a flood of facts in their own special fields of competence and interest. When publications are considered together with the many conferences, seminars, and other meetings whose primary function is the spreading of knowledge, the informational services of the United Nations assume a wide scope indeed.

Units within the United Nations having special informational responsibilities include the UN Department of Public Information (DPI), the UN Institute for Training and Research (UNITAR), and the United Nations University. The DPI, with its information centers in many countries, supplies UN publications to the world and carries on a variety of public relations activities designed to present the organization in its most favorable light. In addition to the printed word, the DPI produces programs and public service advertisements for radio and television. UNITAR, established by the General Assembly in 1963, trains individuals for work in economic and social development and conducts training seminars for national government personnel concerned with the work of the United Nations. Its most visible activity is the publication of special studies undertaken by UNITAR staff, often in collaboration with visiting scholars. Since 1975 the United Nations University, with headquarters in Tokyo, has attempted to stimulate research on world problems and has provided fellowships for postgraduate training in collaboration with national research institutes and universities. It is also establishing its own research and training centers, working through networks of cooperating institutions. Both UNITAR and the United Nations University serve as links between the United Nations and the international academic community.

# INTERNATIONALLY ADMINISTERED PROGRAMS

Technical assistance is widely used by international organizations to promote economic, social, and technical goals. Reference has already been made to the technical assistance programs of WHO and UNESCO in areas of their special interest, as well as to UN and ILO assistance in promoting human rights. While some organizations, such as WHO, UNESCO, the ILO, and the Food and Agriculture Organization, have large programs of technical assistance, nearly every UN specialized agency offers technical assistance of some sort, financed variously from its regular budget, the UN development program, voluntary contributions, and other sources. Chapter 11 will discuss aid to developing countries in detail. Here we will briefly examine programs of international organizations for the aid of refugees and other persons in need of emergency relief.

## Emergency Relief

Since World War II international organizations have been continuously involved in programs for the relief of people in distress. If League of Nations efforts to protect refugees during the interwar years are included, the period of continuous involvement begins even earlier. Although the long-term problems of economic development absorb the greater part of UN resources, the organization and its related agencies have compiled a substantial record of accomplishment in meeting the short-term needs of selected groups of people in distress.

### UNRRA

A direct forerunner of UN programs was the UN Relief and Rehabilitation Administration (UNRRA), an agency of the wartime United Nations that operated from November 1943 until its disbandment in June 1947. During this period UNRRA expended nearly $4 billion, and at the peak of its activity it employed 27,800 persons. The initiative, the basic planning, and 70 percent of the funds came from the United States, but the implementation involved the concerted action of many governments. Food, clothing, and medicine supplied by UNRRA filled a critical need of millions in Europe and Asia. In China alone, direct food relief was provided to an estimated ten million people. The process of rehabilitation also extended to the revival of agricultural and industrial production and to the support of public health programs, public education, and other social services. In addition, UNRRA assumed the responsibility of caring for millions of refugees and displaced persons.

UNRRA was terminated somewhat precipitately because the U.S. Congress decided to stop funding the organization. Congressional support had been undermined by persistent charges, not altogether unjustified, of UNRRA inefficiency and "political intrigue" and by a suspicion that the Soviet Union was using UNRRA aid to consolidate its hold on Eastern Europe. Whatever the justification for dumping UNRRA, its demise created an alarming gap in the world's machinery for economic and social defense, and provision was made for the assumption of UNRRA functions by other organizations wherever possible. On the initiative of the UN General Assembly, an International Refugee Organization (IRO) was established to deal with the continuing refugee problem; a UN International Children's Emergency Fund (UNICEF), supported by private donations and voluntary government contributions, was created to administer relief programs for children in the war-devastated areas; and the United Nations itself assumed responsibility for the advisory social welfare services. Portions of the health program were picked up by the World Health Organization.

## Korean Relief and Reconstruction

War in Korea provided the setting for another UN relief operation of substantial proportions. Under a Security Council authorization the UN unified command administered a $450 million program of civilian and refugee relief. The U.S. government contributed more than $400 million of the total sum, and private U.S. agencies provided about half of the remainder. A longer-range program of reconstruction was authorized in December 1950 by a General Assembly resolution that established the UN Korean Reconstruction Agency (UNKRA). By the time UNKRA operations were phased out in 1960, to be replaced by massive amounts of direct U.S. aid, approximately $150 million had been expended for the rehabilitation of the Korean economy and public services. The United States limited itself to 65 percent of the total UNKRA budget. Unlike some countries that absorbed large amounts of UN and U.S. aid, South Korea experienced remarkable postwar economic growth and industrialization.

## UNICEF

The UN International Children's Emergency Fund (UNICEF) was established in 1946 as a temporary organization to administer residual funds left over from

UNRRA. Over the years, the approach that was so satisfactory in assisting the children of war-devastated areas has proved adaptable to the problems of developing countries as well. The General Assembly responded by placing the organization on a permanent basis in 1953. The words *International* and *Emergency* were deleted from the title when it was given permanent status, but the acronym UNICEF was retained in preference to the less pronounceable UNCF. The budget of UNICEF is raised mainly through voluntary government contributions, although a substantial portion comes through private donations and the sale of greeting cards. The fund has its own thirty-nation executive board, elected by ECOSOC, and its executive director and staff are a unit of the UN Secretariat.

The initial program's emphasis on emergency supplies of food, clothing, and medicines has shifted toward emphasis on longer-range programs for the benefit of children. UNICEF is still a source of drugs, insecticides, vaccines, and field equipment for disease-control campaigns, as well as food and medical supplies in emergency situations. But it is no longer simply a supply program. UNICEF's grants-in-aid, usually matched by two or three times as much in local funds, are now available to governments for help in planning projects and training national personnel. As a condition of a grant, a government must agree to conduct the program as part of its permanent services if the need persists. UNICEF does not operate projects of its own, although it supervises the national programs it sponsors. UNICEF-aided projects are often conducted with the advice and cooperation of such other UN agencies as WHO, FAO, UNESCO, and the ILO. Joint endeavors have included mass disease control, family education in better nutrition practices, teacher training and the local production of teaching materials, and the establishment of child welfare services. In the 1980s UNICEF concentrated on programs to reduce infant mortality.

UNICEF still takes on emergency relief assignments. Aided by the International Red Cross, UNICEF coordinated most of the Western humanitarian assistance sent to Cambodia in the wake of its domestic upheavals and the 1978 Vietnamese invasion. In 1989 the UNICEF executive director was appointed as the representative of the UN Secretary-General to mobilize emergency aid to persons displaced by civil war in the Sudan. But in July 1998, the head of UNICEF was compelled to acknowledge the agency's inefficiency in managing the massive relief operation. Members of the Sudan People's Liberation Army, long at war with the Sudanese government, cited rampant corruption within the aid mission, and urged donor nations to investigate claims that Operation Lifeline Sudan, an umbrella organization of the United Nations, had squandered the resources of the mission. UNICEF was charged with failing to serve the interests of the most desperate of Sudan's displaced population, estimated to be as high as 2.6 million. The region of Bahr el-Ghazal located in the southwestern portion of the country was reported to be most heavily impacted by the failure of the mission. Moreover, the negative report was issued at a time when the Rome-based World Food Program had authorized the largest air drops in its history and had just launched a campaign in April 1998, calling for 93,500 tons of food, and again in July, for an additional 51,500 tons of emergency supplies. The admission by UNICEF that it had failed to adequately police the distribution of aid and that corrupt officials and dishonest aid handlers had used the assistance for their own purposes, raised serious questions about the future of the program. Lost in the controversy was the plight of the hungry people of the southern Sudan. UNICEF was poorly equipped to deal with so complicated and massive a problem, and it was situations such as this that induced observers to minimize the work of an organization that in 1965 had made it the recipient of the Nobel Peace Prize.

*Disaster Relief*

Earthquakes, floods, famines, and other natural disasters have commonly evoked emergency aid from international sources, both public and private. Such aid has necessarily been provided on an ad hoc basis because the precipitating event is always unplanned. As early as 1965 the United Nations provided a small fund for use by the Secretary-General in meeting emergency needs arising from natural disasters. An Office of the Disaster Relief Coordinator (UNDRO) was established in 1971 following a particularly disastrous earthquake in Peru and a tidal wave in Bangladesh the preceding year. UNDRO administers a fund for emergency relief, maintained on a continuing basis through voluntary contributions, and applied to disasters resulting from both natural and human causes. It also provides planning assistance to prevent and minimize damage in countries subject to recurring normal disasters. UNDRO is not used to administer larger-scale relief operations, however. When famine reached crisis proportions in Ethiopia and other parts of Africa during the 1980s, the Secretary-General created a special Office of Emergency Operations in Africa (OEOA) to mobilize international aid, while UNDRO served a primarily reporting function. In 1991 the General Assembly established the position of UN Emergency Relief Coordinator at the under-secretary level to coordinate the activities of all UN agencies, including UNDRO, concerned with humanitarian emergency assistance. To ensure availability of adequate resources for use in the initial phase of emergencies, the Assembly authorized the creation of a $50 million revolving fund to be financed by voluntary contributions.

*Reorganization*

In 1997–98, Secretary-General Kofi Annan reorganized UN agencies and programs concerned with a broad range of human needs. He combined the Geneva-based programs on human rights into a single office to ensure greater coordination and strength of purpose, and appointed the President of Ireland as the new Commissioner for Human Rights. A former German Environment Minister was named to head the UN Environment Program, while the senior official of the UN High Commissioner for Refugees was made Emergency Relief Coordinator. Rounding out these changes in key UN positions was the appointment of the Secretary-General of the International Peace Academy to the post of Special Representative for Children in Armed Conflict. Kofi Annan's "quiet revolution" focused on making the United Nations leaner and more effective by consolidating several Secretariat bodies and eliminating waste, fraud, and mismanagement. It also involved shifting resources from administration to development and humanitarian needs. In 1998 it was estimated all the United Nations Funds and Programs, including UNICEF, had $4.6 billion a year to spend on economic and social development, with major concern given to population policies, children, agriculture, food distribution, and refugees.

## REFUGEES

The problem of refugees is not unique to the twentieth century, but sustained intergovernmental cooperation in dealing with it is a hallmark of our era. Governments have tried to regard refugees as a series of temporary problems, each capable of a discrete solution, but from a world perspective the existence of refugees in substantial numbers has become a continuing fact of life.

### Refugees and the League

In 1921 the League of Nations established the office of High Commissioner for Refugees as a temporary agency to deal with the influx of nearly two million refugees from the Russian civil war into countries of Eastern and Central Europe. The hard shell of the problem had scarcely been dented when new streams of Greek, Armenian, and Assyrian refugees began to pour out of Turkey, beginning in 1922. The League High Commissioner was still attempting to cope with these problems when the Nazi persecutions of the 1930s produced a new flow of refugees from the Saar, Austria, and Czechoslovakia. The League agency was intended to be temporary, but the problem was continuous and recurrent.

The homeless multitudes of the interwar period needed legal and political protection as well as relief and assistance with resettlement. The League High Commissioner and his small staff, however, never had the resources to render direct assistance on any significant scale. On a meager budget they could do little more than serve as an advocate with governments, work for uniform standards of legal protection, give advice to national governments, and attempt to coordinate the efforts of public and private agencies engaged in refugee relief. In the legal field one notable contribution was the Nansen passport, named after Fridtjof Nansen, the first League High Commissioner. This was a certificate issued to refugees by a national government on the recommendation of the High Commissioner; it served as the equivalent of a regular passport and greatly facilitated refugee travel throughout Europe.

## Refugees and World War II

World War II produced new millions of homeless people in Europe, and the responsibility for massive relief and repatriation was undertaken by military authorities and UNRRA. Of some eight million refugees and displaced persons in Allied-occupied zones at the time of the German surrender, five to six million were repatriated within a year through the prodigious efforts of military authorities, and numerous others were assimilated or resettled. UNRRA repatriated an additional 750,000 refugees during its lifetime.

## The International Refugee Organization

The IRO began operations in July 1947 as a UN specialized agency. During its term of existence, which expired in February 1952, the IRO spent nearly $400 million in assisting more than 1,600,000 refugees who came under its mandate in Africa, the Americas, Asia, and Europe. Approximately 73,000 were repatriated, and more than a million were resettled abroad through the active advocacy and assistance of the IRO. At the termination of the IRO, most of the refugees remaining from its original mandate were of the "hard core" groups—the sick, the aged, and the infirm—for whom resettlement was especially difficult. A number of states urged that the IRO be continued beyond 1952, but the United States, which underwrote more than half of the IRO budget, insisted on the early termination date, claiming that the problem was small enough to be handled by the countries of asylum and by voluntary organizations.

## The UN High Commissioner

In anticipation of the IRO's demise, the General Assembly created the Office of UN High Commissioner for Refugees (UNHCR) to serve as a continuing focus for UN refugee activities.[11] Commencing operations in 1951, the high commissioner was given the assignment of providing international protection for refugees and assisting governments and voluntary organizations to find permanent solutions through resettlement and assimilation. His present mandate excludes refugees receiving aid from other UN programs (such as the Palestine refugees) and refugees who have the rights of nationals in the country of asylum (for example, refugees from India to Pakistan, and vice versa). Otherwise the mandate extends to nearly all persons outside their country of origin whose "well-founded fear of persecution for reasons of race, religion, nationality, or political opinion" prevents them from seeking the protection of the home country.

The high commissioner's primary responsibility of providing international protection is carried out by promoting the adoption and supervising the application of international conventions and by encouraging governments to take other measures for the benefit of refugees. Of special importance is the 1951 Convention Relating to the Status of Refugees and its 1967 protocol, which codify minimum rights in such matters as freedom of religion, access to courts, the right to work, education, social security, and travel documents. The high commissioner also provides material assistance to refugees from funds made available by voluntary contributions. States party to the 1951 Convention and/or to the 1967 Protocol in 1997 numbered 134. The number of implementing partners representing the non-governmental organizations was 453 in 1997. Fifteen major donor countries traditionally have accounted for about 95 percent of UNHCR's total operating budget. UNHCR's expenditures have risen accordingly, from $3.5 million in 1965, to $544 million in 1990, to $900 million the following year, and to more than $1 billion annually since 1992. The total UNHCR budget for 1997 was $1.22 billion, down from $1.43 billion in 1996. UNHCR's budget is divided into two parts: the basic General Program concerned with refugee protection and assistance; and Special Programs for emergencies, voluntary repatriation operations, and programs for non-refugees. Budgets for major special programs and emergencies in 1995 totalled $863.9 million, including Burundi-Rwanda ($263.3 million) and the former Yugoslavia ($222.7 million). The General Programs budget for 1995 was $428.7 million. In addition to voluntary contributions, UNHCR receives a limited subsidy—less than 2 percent of the total—from the regular budget of the United Nations. These funds are used exclusively for administrative costs.

In the 1980s Africa was the locale of major UN refugee relief efforts. An estimated three million refugees were located in Ethiopia, Somalia, the Sudan, Burundi, Rwanda, Uganda, Tanzania, Zaire, Angola, Zambia, and other African countries, Their needs were highlighted by two International Conferences for Assistance to Refugees in Africa, held in 1981 (ICARA I) and 1984 (ICARA II). In a broader perspective, the refugees were simply one highly visible aspect of the emergency brought on by years of extended drought and other natural disasters, political turmoil, and economic mismanagement that had made Africa the object of world concern and concerted relief efforts. ICARA II specifically recognized that the solution to refugee relief was closely tied to the development and revitalization of African economies.

The ensuing years brought no relief from refugee problems, either to Africa or the rest of the world. In 1985 the number of refugees subject to the mandate of the high commissioner was approximately 9 million. In April 1992 the high commissioner estimated the number to be in excess of 17 million. African refugees were still heavily concentrated in Sudan, Ethiopia, and Somalia, but also in Chad, Angola, Zaire, Mozambique, and most states of sub-Saharan East Africa. The 1985 estimate of 3 million refugees in Africa had become almost 6 million by 1992. Another 7 million were found in Southwest Asia and the Middle East, some 5 to 6 million of them in Pakistan and Iran, refugees from the Afghan civil war. Europe had more than 1 million, most notably in wartorn

Croatia and Bosnia, and more than 1 million were found in Latin America and the Caribbean.

The end of the Cold War therefore brought no respite in the condition, or reduction in the number of refugees. In fact, since 1992, the world's refugee population has swelled to levels never before recorded. According to the UNHCR more than 27 million people were listed as refugees in 1998, and more than 140 countries were involved or associated with this expanding and deepening human tragedy. Thus, what was envisoned as a temporary office with a projected lifespan of three years, fifty years earlier, has become one of the world's principal and permanent humanitarian agencies. The UNHCR remains based in Geneva, Switzerland, but its offices are located in 115 countries. Moreover, its total force of 5,475 (1997) are essentially field workers (4,520 or 83 percent of the total), functioning on a day-to-day basis in some of the most isolated, dangerous places, and under conditions of enormous difficulty. It is not surprising that the selfless nature and devotion to duty of the UNHCR workers has twice brought the Nobel Peace Prize to the agency, first in 1954 and again in 1981.

UNHCR's programs are approved and supervised by an Executive Committee composed of fifty member countries, but it is the agency and its many satellites that must tender to the needs of those fleeing from racial or religious persecution, ethnic or tribal conflict, or because they hold divergent political opinions, and/or have membership in a particular social group. Since the termination of the Cold War, the UNHCR has moved beyond its defined mandate and also provides help to those forced to live in refugee-like situations. This category includes people who have been granted protection on a group basis, e.g., the Kurds of northern Iraq, or on purely humanitarian grounds, e.g., the Hutu from Rwanda who sought refuge in the former Zaire, but who were not formally recognized as refugees. Still another category were the displaced people who fled their homes but did not cross an international border. Such victims of civil war, as in Sarajevo and other besieged Bosnian communities, also received assistance from the UNHCR. Nevertheless, the agency is most concerned with those persons who no longer have the protection of their state, and who are often detached from their families and communities of origin. Like the Kosovar Albanians, subjected to ethnic cleansing in 1999, such persons are particularly vulnerable to violence, and the most vulnerable of all are women, their children, the elderly, and the infirm.

UNHCR work is strictly humanitarian and non-political. The agency not only cares for the world's most destitute population, it also guarantees "international protection," which means no refugee can be involuntarily returned to a country where he or she has reason to fear persecution. UNHCR therefore is currently more inclined to assist large groups of refugees rather than individual cases. Thus, even the Dayton Peace Accords of 1995 authorized UNHCR to develop the modalities for the return of 2 million refugees and displaced persons who had fled Bosnia-Herzegovina. But the end of the Cold War not only provoked the breakup of Yugoslavia and the subsequent civil war, it also created the instabilities that forced some 5 million people in eastern and central Europe to seek asylum in western European countries. In the four years of brutal combat and ethnic cleansing that consumed regions of the former Yugoslavia, some 3.5 million people received assistance from the UNHCR, 2.7 million in Bosnia-Herzegovina alone. Moreover, after diplomacy failed to resolve the Kosovo dilemma, NATO airstrikes against Serbian military installations in March 1999 resulted in the Serbs intensifying their ethnic cleansing campaign against the Albanians living in the region. The flight of hundreds of thousands of Kosovar Albanians to neighboring countries presented still greater problems for the United Nations relief agencies as well as the international community.

The 1995–96 genocide in Rwanda and Burundi created one of the largest concentrations of refugees, with the UNHCR assisting almost 2 million people who fled to Tanzania and Zaire, now the Republic of the Congo. 1.7 million Mozambican refugees have been returned to their regions of origin since 1992 and the UNHCR task was transformed into the rebuilding of their communities. Still another million refugees were created by the civil strife in Liberia, Sierra Leone, and the Central African Republic, while hundreds of thousands more were displaced internally. And so the statistics read on and on; included among them are the 1.8 million Kurds, the tens of thousands of Guatemalans, and the thousands of Tibetans. Nor is peace and tranquility always the experience of refugees in asylum countries. Sexual violence, exploitation and other forms or assault shadow the uprooted. UNHCR staff endeavor to shelter these hapless people from physical harm, but it can only hope to minimize, not eliminate, the horrors.

The UNHCR remains the one beacon of hope for people caught up in circumstances seldom of their own doing; and the agency responds to the most desperate of the world's humanity, providing the basics of human survival, i.e., shelter, food, water, sanitation and medical attention. Indeed, the tents made from blue plastic sheeting supplied by UNHCR have become an all-too-familiar symbol of an all-too-large portion of the world's humanity that remains under great stress.

Given the ubiquitous and persistent character of the world refugee dilemma, there appears little doubt it will be a major United Nations concern well into the twenty-first century. It is therefore contemplated to establish an early-warning system in which an international presence will be created in areas at risk and before communities are uprooted and opposed positions can no longer be reconciled. In 1998, the UNHCR experimented with a "preventive deployment" posture and dispatched specialist teams to the Central Asian republics (of the former Soviet Union), where tensions resulting from independence had caused or threaten to cause fratricidal strife. Acknowledging that the search for long-term solutions was a political matter, to be managed by individual governments, UNHCR sought to purchase the necessary time to allow meaningful negotiations to develop. Where regional organizations are available UNHCR is pleased to encourage their initiatives and it has been especially supportive in its

TABLE 9-2    Estimated number of persons of concern who fall
under the mandate of the UNHCR, by region

| REGION | TOTAL OF CONCERN AS OF JANUARY 1997 |
| --- | --- |
| Africa | 8,091,000 |
| Asia | 7,925,000 |
| Europe | 5,749,000 |
| Latin America | 169,000 |
| North America | 720,000 |
| Oceania | 75,000 |
| Total* | 22,729,000 |

SOURCE: United Nations High Commissioner for Refugees, 1998.

* Totals may not add up due to rounding.

relations with the Commonwealth of Independent States (CIS) as well as the International Congress of Central American Refugees. UNHCR also believes it important to monitor the living and working conditions of returnees after repatriation, and community-based projects have been established to repair roads and bridges, increase the availability of clean water, and improve education and health care. Tools and seed packets also are distributed to resettled farmers to help reactivate the largely agricultural economies as well as help replenish the local food supply. (See Table 9-2 and Table 9-3.)

### Palestine Refugees

Since 1949 a UN Relief and Works Agency for Palestine Refugees in the Near East (UNRWA) has cared for refugee victims of the Arab-Israeli conflict. Over the years it has absorbed more money than any other UN refugee program and yet has brought no final solution. UNRRA, the IRO, and the high commissioner have had the satisfaction of seeing old refugee groups diminish through repatriation, resettlement, and assimilation, even though new needs have arisen from new refugee groups. But UNRWA, which started with approximately nine hundred thousand Arabs who fled their homes in 1948, had more than 3.4 million persons on its rolls in 1998. Of the more than 3.4 million, approximately 1.4 million were in Jordan, 1.2 million in Gaza and the West Bank, and about 350,000 each in Lebanon and Syria. UNRWA education, health, relief services and social programs for the camp refugees covered 40 percent of the total refugee population. The largest service was in the realm of education and it provided nine to ten years of schooling for more than 400,000 pupils in 640 schools throughout the region. UNRWA employed a teaching staff of approximately

TABLE 9-3    Origin of Major Refugee populations and persons in refugee-like situations (10 largest groups)—estimates as of July 1997

| ORIGIN OF MAJOR REFUGEE POPULATIONS AND PERSONS IN REFUGEE-LIKE SITUATIONS (10 LARGEST GROUPS) (1) ESTIMATES AS OF JULY 1997 | | |
|---|---|---|
| COUNTRY OF ORIGIN (2) | MAIN COUNTRIES OF ASYLUM | REFUGEES |
| Afghanistan | Iran/Pakistan/CIS/India | 2,673,000 |
| Liberia | Guinea/Côte d'Ivoire/Ghana/Nigeria | 778,000 |
| Bosnia & Herzegovina (3) | F.R. Yugoslavia/Germany | 673,000 |
| Iraq | Iran/Saudi Arabia/Other Mid East/ Pakistan | 672,000 |
| Somalia | Djibouti/Ethiopia/Kenya/Yemen | 572,000 |
| Rwanda | Burundi/Tanzania/Uganda/Democratic Republic of Congo | 467,000 |
| Sudan | Uganda/Democratic Republic of Congo/Kenya/Ethiopia | 464,000 |
| Burundi | Tanzania/Democratic Republic of Congo | 427,000 |
| Sierra Leone | Guinea/Liberia | 374,000 |
| Eritrea | Sudan | 331,000 |

SOURCE: UNHCR Website—http://www.unhcr.ch/un&ref/numbers/table3.htm

(1) Some 3.2 million Palestinians fall under the mandate of the United Nations Relief and Works Agency for Palestine Refugees in the Near East (UNRWA), and are thus not included in this table. Palestinians who are outside the UNRWA area of operation, for example those in Iraq and Libya, are considered to be of concern to UNHCR.

(2) For a significant number of refugees, particularly in more developed countries, the breakdown by origin is unknown.

(3) The "Others of concern" consist of war affected populations. The decrease during 1996 reflects the disengagement of UNHCR from the distribution of food and a more restricted targeting of beneficiaries, except for shelter, following the end of the conflict.

13,000, virtually all of them Palestinians. UNRWA's health program involved a network of 120 clinics, treating 6 million patients each year, including specialized services in child health. UNRWA's renewable mandate from the General Assembly, the last one in effect til 1999, was funded almost entirely from voluntary contributions from the international community. The list of major donors included members of the European Union, both collectively and individually (especially the Netherlands and Denmark), the United States (the largest single cash-donor country), the Nordic countries, and Japan. Although Saudi Arabia and Kuwait have made contributions, the Arab states, while supporting UNRWA verbally, have not been particularly forthcoming with their donations.

UNRWA's budget for 1997–98 was $312 million, but available operative revenues were only $262 million, necessitating cuts in expenditures, notably in education. Having experienced five consecutive years of budget deficits since 1993, UNRWA's financial problems were both chronic and structural, and although the organization was slated to function through 1999, its long term future was in serious jeopardy. Even an additional $19 million in new pledges received in 1997–98 did not enable the Agency to revoke some of the more severe cuts in its programs, and further austerity measures were deemed essential to assure its perpetuation.

UNRWA became involved in the Middle East peace process in the years following the 1993 accord between Israel and the Palestine Liberation Organization that transformed the latter into the Palestinian Authority (PA) in Gaza and the West Bank. As Israel withdrew from numerous towns and villages in favor of the PA, UNRWA's work was made more, not less, demanding. The Agency developed a working relationship with the PA and on June 24, 1994, an exchange of letters between the Commissioner-General of UNRWA and the Chairman of the Palestine Liberation Organization allowed for a continuation of UNRWA's presence. UNRWA thereupon agreed to provide land, buildings, temporary shelter, and emergency humanitarian aid to assist the PA in establishing its operations in Jericho, the first metropolitan area placed under PLO authority by the Israelis. It subsequently did the same in the additional towns and villages evacuated by the Israelis in 1995 and 1997. From that time forward, UNRWA developed effective relations with the PA in the education, health, relief, and social sectors.

UNRWA also assisted UN delegations in furthering the peace process and its headquarters was moved from Vienna to Gaza in 1995. A new headquarters building was designed in Gaza, but that shift alone involved an estimated $13.5 million. UNRWA continued to expand its mandate and its Commissioner-General undertook the task of paying the salaries of 9,000 members of the Palestinian Police Force. The General Assembly approved that assistance but only through July 1995. UNRWA also accelerated the construction of schools, health clinics, and women's program centers. To make the territories more livable, UNRWA played a role in improving sanitation and roads, and employed 5,500 Palestinian laborers in Gaza alone. All this attention to the West Bank and Gaza did not deflect UNRWA from its other responsibilities, however. The refugee populations in Jordan, Lebanon, and Syria, all had reason to expect UNRWA assistance but the Agency's added responsibilities meant making heavier demands on the donor states. In effect, the promise of a Palestinian homeland had attracted more refugees to the territories, and UNRWA's task was made more, not less, burdensome by the prospects of an enhanced equilibrium in the region. In 1997–98, 35 percent of the Palestinian refugees continued to live in camps in areas either administered by Israel, or by the Palestine Authority on the West Bank and Gaza, as well as Arab host countries.

UNRWA was only one of three primary sources of financial support in the West Bank and Gaza. The Israeli Civil Administration in the territories, and the Palestinian NGOs (among which the most notable was the Harakat Al-Mukawama Al-Islamiya, or HAMAS as it is better known) were the other contributing bodies. The latter's funding came, in major part, from the oil rich

Arab states, which sponsored the development of schools, Koranic classes, health facilities, and other social services. HAMAS also established the Islamic University in Gaza and its financial base was larger than that of UNRWA following the 1991 Gulf War. It was not surprising therefore that both the Israeli authorities and UNRWA found it useful to work in harmony with the Palestinian NGOs, many of which had been organized by HAMAS. The combined efforts of UNRWA, the Israeli government, and the NGOs provided for an annual financial distribution of almost $400 million for education, health, and other social services. Although it continued to employ several thousand teachers and provided schooling for almost half of the region's students in the 1990s, UNRWA activities were more directed toward health care, providing free basic medical services to 940,000 registered refugees, or approximately half the population of the West Bank and Gaza. Since the appearance of the Palestinian Authority (after 1993) in the territories, however, the services rendered the refugee community have been disrupted by the competition, antagonism, and rivalry exhibited by major Palestinian actors. HAMAS only reluctantly accepts subordination to the Palestinian Authority/PLO leadership, and it, often violently, opposes Yasir Arafat's negotiations with the Israeli government. The PA in turn has endeavored to enforce its writ in the territories through harsh measures of governance. Although HAMAS continues to emphasize its role as a deliverer of social services to the refugee population, its acknowledged militancy has made it more difficult to meet its obligations. UNRWA's work in these unsettled conditions therefore is not only more costly, it is considerably more complicated.

# CONCLUSION

The contribution of expanding functional cooperation to international peace and security is highly speculative, but its contribution to economic and social well being is subject to more concrete evaluation. Where interstate transactions have been of a sufficiently technical and noncontroversial character, as in communication and transportation, the UN system has provided widely accepted standards for national conduct. In the field of human rights, where the issue is less one of international cooperation than one of the conduct of the state within its own borders, standards have been set but not well observed. Even here a little progress in securing compliance has been made, and the record of the ILO in upgrading labor standards has been quite respectable. Substantial progress has also been made in creating international legal instruments for environmental protection. In the special area of the law of the sea, UN forums have contributed to a remarkable alteration of rules governing the use of the oceans and seabeds. International agencies have also promoted the exchange of useful information, and the services they render can stand on their own merits. Whereas most human needs are being met by individual and group action organized within a national setting, UN operations have in many local situations provided a significant margin of difference for war victims, refugees, the socially underprivileged, and the economically deprived.

The tradition of decentralization bequeathed to the UN system has continued unabated, along with a steady proliferation of new agencies. This situation has given rise to criticisms of overlapping, duplication of effort, and nonrational overall allocation of resources. There is no world budget for economic and social affairs. The United Nations and each specialized agency sets its own budget and program within the limits that its membership will collectively permit. Entrenched bureaucracies look out for their own bureaucratic interests. The Economic and Social Council was supposed to have a central coordinating function, but in practice it has been limited to discussion and liaison. Theoretically, governments could bring coordination to the system since the same governments for the most part hold membership in all the agencies of the UN system. But national governments are pluralistic institutions as well, and governmental policy toward a particular international function tends to be set by the government department with an interest in that function, whether health, education, the environment, oceans, or international trade. Government representatives to different international agencies often speak with different voices. If governments do not always coordinate their own policies effectively, there is little hope that they will provide effective coordination of the programs of many international agencies.

Some mitigating circumstances exist. Although no organization has the capacity to impose coordination, a degree of coordination has been introduced by cooperation across agency lines. An Administrative Committee on Coordination provides a forum in which representatives of the UN and specialized agency secretariats at the highest level can attempt to achieve a substantive meshing of their programs as well as greater uniformity in administrative matters. An International Civil Service Advisory Board, which serves the entire UN system, has helped establish uniformity in position classification, salaries and allowances, and pensions. Organizations engaged in related activities regularly interact at one another's meetings. Intersecretariat liaison, by means of committees and other devices, is a standard operating procedure.

In defense of the system, one might even argue that the present pluralistic state of international society defies consensus on any rational criteria for overall allocation as between regional and universal levels and among individual programs on the same level. Greater centralization of resource allocation could result in different but not necessarily more rational matching of resources to needs.

The most formidable barriers to improved functional cooperation are in fact political and budgetary, not organizational. North-South divisions, as well as other political conflicts, have impinged on most of the functional activities, often turning their forums into ideological battlegrounds and shaping their programs to meet sometimes unrelated political criteria. Cold war struggles have now subsided, but this has brought no corresponding upsurge in resources devoted to economic and humanitarian cooperation. In the long run, functional cooperation may provide cement for the foundations of world peace, but in the short run, functional growth depends on an expansion of the area of political agreement.

# NOTES

1. Useful commentaries on functionalist theory include James Patrick Sewell, *Functionalism and World Politics* (Princeton: Princeton University Press, 1960); Ernst B. Haas, *Beyond the Nation-State* (Stanford: Stanford University Press, 1964); A. J. R. Groom and Paul Taylor, eds., *Functionalism: Theory and Practice in International Relations* (London: University of London Press, 1975); and Robert E. Riggs and I. Jostein Mykletun, *Beyond Functionalism: Attitudes Toward International Organization in Norway and the United States* (Minneapolis: University of Minnesota Press, 1979). An excellent brief analysis is "The Functional Approach to Peace," in Inis L. Claude, Jr., *Swords into Plowshares,* 4th ed. (New York: Random House, 1971), pp. 378–407. For a recent study of international agencies set in a functionalist context see Mark F. Imber, *The U.S.A., ILO, UNESCO, and IAEA: Politicization and Withdrawal in the Specialized Agencies* (London: Macmillan in association with the Centre for International Policy Studies, University of Southampton, 1989).

2. E.g., Simeon E. Baldwin, "The International Congresses and Conferences of the Last Century as Forces Working toward the Solidarity of the World," *American Journal of International Law* 1 (July 1907), pp. 565–78; Paul S. Reinsch, *Public International Unions, Their Work and Organization: A Study in International Administrative Law* (Boston: Ginn, 1911); J. A. Salter, *Allied Shipping Control: An Experiment in International Administration* (Oxford: Clarendon Press, 1921); and Leonard S. Woolf, *International Government: Two Reports* (New York: Brentano, 1916). International functionalism is now most often identified with the Englishman David Mitrany, especially his small book *A Working Peace System: An Argument for the Functional Development of International Organization,* 1st ed. (London: Royal Institute of International Affairs, 1943). Mitrany published on this theme both before and after 1943.

3. For a more detailed classification of organization functions and decisions, see Robert W. Cox and Harold K. Jacobson, "The Framework for Inquiry," in Cox and Jacobson, *The Anatomy of Influence: Decision Making in International Organization* (New Haven: Yale University Press, 1973), pp. 8–11; and Harold K. Jacobson, *Networks of Interdependence,* 2nd ed. (New York: Alfred A. Knopf, 1984), pp. 81–83.

4. *Report of the Secretary-General,* UN Document A/46/1 (1991), p. 9.

5. United Nations Focus Series, "Secretary-General Sets Course for Long-Awaited UN Revitalization," March 1, 1998, p. 4.

6. *Filartiga* v. *Pena-Irala,* 630 F.2d 876 (2d Cir. 1980); and see also *Rodriguez-Fernandez* v. *Wilkinson,* 505 F. Supp. 787 (D. Ian. 1980), as well as *Siderman* v. *The Republic of Argentina,* 965 F.2d 699 (9th Cir. 1992).

7. John W. McDonald, *Global Environmental Negotiations: The 1972 Stockholm Conference and Lessons for the Future,* The Project on Multilateral Negotiations of The American Academy of Diplomacy and The Paul H. Nitze School of Advanced International Studies, Johns Hopkins University, Working Paper Series WP-2, January 25, 1990, p. 5. See also John G. Ruggie, "On the Problem of 'The Global Problematique': What Roles for International Organizations?" reprinted in Richard A. Falk, Samuel S. Kim, and Saul H. Mendlowitz, *The United Nations and a Just World Order* (Boulder, CO: Westview Press, 1991), p. 459.

8. Stephen D. Krasner, "Structural Causes and Regime Consequences: Regimes as Intervening Variables," in Krasner, ed., *International Regimes* (Ithaca: Cornell University Press, 1983), p. 2.

9. Oran R. Young, "The Politics of International Regime Formation: Managing Natural Resources and the Environment," *International Organization* 43, no. 3 (Summer 1989), pp. 349–76. See also Oran R. Young, *International Cooperation: Building Regimes for Natural Resources and the Environment* (Ithaca: Cornell University Press, 1989).

10. Peter M. Haas, "Do Regimes Matter? Epistemic Communities and Mediterranean Pollution Control," *International Organization* 43, no. 3 (Summer 1989), pp. 377–403.

11. The first two decades of the UNHCR are recounted in Louise W. Holborn, *Refugees—A Problem of Our Time: The Work of the United Nations High Commissioner for Refugees, 1951–1972*, 2 vols. (Metuchen, NJ: Scarecrow Press, 1975). A discussion of more recent activities is found in D. Gallagher, "The Evolution of the International Refugee System," *International Migration Review* 23 (Fall 1989), pp. 579–98. The international legal status of refugees is treated in Guy S. Goodwin-Gill, *The Refugee in International Law* (Oxford: Clarendon Press, 1983).

# Selected Readings

Alston, Philip, ed. *The United Nations and Human Rights: A Critical Appraisal*. Oxford: Clarendon Press, 1995.

Berkov, Robert. *The World Health Organization: A Study in Decentralized International Administration*. Geneva: Librairie E. Droz, 1957.

Buergenthal, Thomas. *Law-Making in the International Civil Aviation Organization*. Syracuse: Syracuse University Press, 1969.

Choucri, Nazli, ed. *Global Changes: Environmental Challenges and Institutional Responses*. Cambridge, MA: MIT Press, 1993.

Codding, George A., Jr. *The Universal Postal Union*. New York: New York University Press, 1964.

Codding, George A., Jr., and Anthony M. Rutkowski. *The International Telecommunications Union in a Changing World*. Dedham, MA: Artech House, 1982.

Conway, Gordon. *The Doubly Green Revolution: Food for All in the 21st Century*. New York: Penguin Books, 1997.

Cox, Kevin R., ed. *Spaces of Globalization: Reasserting the Power of the Local*. New York: Guilford, 1997.

Cox, Robert W., and Harold K. Jacobson. *The Anatomy of Influence: Decision Making in International Organization*. New Haven: Yale University Press, 1973.

Donnelly, Jack. *Human Rights and World Politics*. Boulder, CO: Westview Press, 1992.

Elhance, Aran. *Hydropolitics in the Third World: Conflict and Cooperation in International River Basins*. Washington, DC: US Institute of Peace Press, 1999.

Feld, Werner J., and Robert S. Jordan. *International Organizations: A Comparative Approach*. 2nd ed. Westport, CT: Greenwood Publishing Group, 1988.

Ferris, Elizabeth G., ed. *Refugees and World Politics*. New York: Praeger, 1985.

Finkelstein, Lawrence S. *Politics in the United Nations System*. Durham: Duke University Press, 1988.

Flood, Patrick J. *The Effectiveness of Human Rights Institutions.* Westport, CT: Praeger, 1998.

Forsythe, David P. *Human Rights and World Politics.* Rev. 2nd ed. Lincoln: University of Nebraska Press, 1989.

———. *The Internationalization of Human Rights.* Lexington, MA: D. C. Heath and Company, 1991.

Gibson, John S. *International Organization, Constitutional Law, and Human Rights.* New York: Praeger, 1991.

Groom, A. J. R., and Paul Taylor. *Frameworks for International Cooperation.* London: Pinter Publishers, 1990.

Gustov, Mel. *Global Politics in the Human Interest.* Boulder, CO: Rienner, 1999.

Haas, Ernst B. *Beyond the Nation-State: Functionalism and International Organization.* Stanford: Stanford University Press, 1964.

Haas, Peter M., Robert O. Keohane, and Marc A. Levy, eds. *Institutions for the Earth: Sources of Effective International Environmental Protection.* Cambridge, MA: MIT Press, 1993.

Hill, Martin. *The United Nations System: Coordinating Its Economic and Social Work.* Cambridge: Cambridge University Press, 1978.

Hoogvelt, Ankie. *Globalization and the Postcolonial World: The New Political Economy of Development.* Baltimore: The Johns Hopkins University Press, 1997.

Holborn, Louise W. *The International Refugee Organization.* London: Oxford University Press, 1956.

———. *Refugees—A Problem of Our Time: The Work of the United Nations High Commissioner for Refugees, 1951–1972.* 2 vols. Metuchen, NJ: Scarecrow Press, 1975.

Hoy, Paula. *Players and Issues in International Aid.* West Hartford, CT: Kumarian Press, 1998.

Imber, Mark F. *The U.S.A., ILO, UNESCO, and IAEA: Politicization and Withdrawal in the Specialized Agencies.* London: Macmillan in association with the Centre for International Policy Studies, University of Southampton, 1989.

International Bank for Reconstruction and Development, *World Development Indicators 1998,* Washington, DC: World Bank Publications, 1998.

Karns, Margaret P., and Karen A. Mingst, eds. *The United States and Multilateral Institutions: Patterns of Changing Instrumentality and Influence.* Boston: Unwin Hyman, 1990.

Kaufman, Natalie Hevener. *Human Rights Treaties and the Senate: A History of Opposition.* Chapel Hill: The University of North Carolina Press, 1990.

Lipschutz, Ronnie D. *Global Civil Society and Global Environmental Governance.* Albany: State University of New York Press, 1996.

Meron, Theodore, ed. *Human Rights in International Law: Legal and Policy Issues.* 2 vols. Oxford: Clarendon Press, 1984.

Morrell, James B. *The Law of the Sea: An Historical Analysis of the 1982 Treaty and Its Rejection by the United States.* Jefferson, NC: McFarland and Co., 1991.

Mower, A. Glenn. *Regional Human Rights: A Comparative Study of the West European and Inter-American Systems.* Westport, CT: Greenwood Press, 1991.

Robertson, A. H., and J. G. Merrills. *Human Rights in the World: An Introduction to the Study of the International Protection of Human Rights.* 3rd ed. Manchester: Manchester University Press, 1989.

Sanger, Clyde. *Ordering the Oceans: The Making of the Law of the Sea.* Toronto: University of Toronto Press, 1987.

Savage, James. *The Politics of International Telecommunication Regulation.* Boulder, CO: Westview Press, 1989.

Schaeffer, Robert K. *Understanding Globalization: the Social Consequences of Political, Economic, and Environmental Change.* Lanham, Md.: Rowman and Littlefield, 1997.

Schiff, Benjamin N. *Refugees Unto the Third Generation: UN Aid to Palestinians.* Syracuse: Syracuse University Press, 1995.

Sewell, James P. *UNESCO and World Politics.* Princeton: Princeton University Press, 1975.

Soroos, Marvin S. *The Endangered Atmosphere: Preserving a Global Commons.* Columbia, SC: University of South Carolina Press, 1997.

Storper, Michael. *The Regional World: Territorial Development in a Regional Economy.* New York: Guilford, 1997.

Taylor, Paul, and A. J. R. Groom, eds. *Global Issues in the United Nations' Framework.* London: Macmillan, 1989.

———. *International Institutions at Work.* London: Pinter Publishers, 1988.

Vosti, Stephen A., and Thomas Reardon. *Sustainability, Growth, and Poverty Alleviation.* Baltimore: The Johns Hopkins University Press, 1997.

Wang, James C. F. *Handbook on Ocean Politics and Law.* Westport, CT: Greenwood Press, 1992.

Weiss, Thomas G., and Leon Gordenker. *NGOs, the UN, and Global Governance.* Boulder: Lynne Rienner, 1996.

Wells, Robert N., Jr., ed. *Peace by Pieces—United Nations Agencies and Their Roles: A Reader and Selective Bibliography.* Metuchen, NJ: Scarecrow Press, 1991.

Whitman, J., and D. Pocock, eds. *After Rwanda: The Coordination of United Nations Humanitarian Assistance.* New York: St. Martin's Press, 1996.

Williams, Douglas. *The Specialized Agencies and the United Nations: A System in Crisis.* New York: St. Martin's Press, 1987.

Zarjevski, Yefime. *A Future Preserved: International Assistance to Refugees.* New York: Pergamon Press, 1988.

# 10

## Managing International Trade and Finance

In the UN world of international economic activity, the French aphorism *Plus ça change, plus c'est la même chose* (The more things change, the more they remain the same) seems applicable and appropriate. Within the UN system new programs of economic cooperation have multiplied, but the problems besetting member countries remain. Two-thirds of the world's peoples still live in grinding poverty in the countries of Africa, Asia, Oceania, and Latin America. Millions suffer from malnutrition or are on the verge of starvation. Despite some moderation in birthrates, populations soar and urban centers groan under the influx of millions of unwanted migrants who are no longer able to survive in the countryside. Inflation, in some societies reaching as high as 400 to 500 percent (in a few cases several thousand percent) in a single year, is endemic in the world. Trade has increased tremendously, but serious balance-of-trade and balance-of-payments problems remain for most countries. A heavy load of Third World debt burdens trade and hinders development, creating major problems for lenders and debtors alike. Protectionism continues to plague trade relationships, and the search for monetary and exchange rate stability goes on. The continued existence of these problems emphasizes their difficult nature and the limits of resolving economic issues through international cooperation.

Before examining UN efforts to promote economic growth and well being, we will first present a brief historical perspective on the major economic problems that the UN system (including the UN "family" of specialized agencies and related bodies) was designed to address. This will make possible a more accurate description and a more meaningful evaluation of UN attempts to come to grips with these perplexing problems. In this chapter we are concerned primarily with international trade and finance. The next chapter will focus on the special problems of economic development and modernization in Third World states and on the role of the UN system in meeting these challenges. Both chapters deal with "the interface of politics and economics in the allocation of scarce resources and values," a field of study commonly known as political economy.[1]

# EARLY ECONOMIC MODELS

From the sixteenth century to the latter part of the eighteenth century, a state-dominated system of mercantilism pervaded the economic scene in the Western world. Both domestic and foreign economic activity were regulated and directed by governments in support of state power. Each state sought to enhance its power and security by amassing treasures of precious metals useful to buy off opponents and to hire mercenary troops for military campaigns. The major objective of trade was to achieve a favorable balance that would enable states to enlarge their national treasuries through an international payments system that settled accounts by transfers of gold and silver.

In the latter part of the mercantilist era, a rising class of merchants and entrepreneurs began to demand greater measures of economic freedom. The American Revolution, although justified by the new political doctrines of freedom and democracy, was fundamentally a reaction against the mother country's narrowly restrictive trade and tax policies. These policies were aimed at keeping the colonies functioning within the mercantilist framework as suppliers of cheap raw materials and as a market restricted to high-priced British manufactures. It was not an accident of history that Adam Smith published his *Wealth of Nations* in the same year that the American colonists declared their independence. The new liberalism, grounded in the philosophy of laissez-faire, broke down internal restrictions in European states and, following the Napoleonic Wars, fostered the development of an international trading system embracing the concept of free trade. International market forces replaced the dictates of government officials in shaping national specialization and the direction of trade. Under the new system trade flourished and Europe became an industrial and commercial center for the entire world.

The rebirth of economic nationalism in the twentieth century signaled that the long period of relatively free trade was coming to an end. World War I accelerated this movement, and the economic dislocation and rivalry fostered by four years of hostilities carried over to undermine the efforts of political and economic leaders to return to the relatively stable period of the nineteenth century. Attempts to regain stability centered on restoring the unity formerly provided by the gold standard and the British pound sterling. Neither effort was wholly successful; Britain failed during the 1920s to regain the economic strength it had wasted during the war, and the gold standard, functioning out of the London money market, reflected this weakness. Some semblance of free trade was regained by the latter part of the decade, however, and monetary stability appeared within reach by 1928.

The American stock market crash in 1929 and the deepening world depression of the early 1930s dealt a deathblow to hopes of restoring the stability of the prewar era. They ushered in a period of economic nationalism with an intensity even greater than that of the heyday of mercantilism. The traumatic shock to domestic and international economic institutions produced by the Great Depression was probably matched only by the mass psychological depression that came in its wake. The world of the 1930s was poised on the brink of revolution—economic, social, and political. Millions were unemployed, the economic plant of most countries stagnated, and politicians and statesmen alike groped blindly for solutions to mounting problems. The natural reaction of most leaders was to protect the national economy from foreign competition and to open up bigger foreign markets so as to absorb the growing surpluses resulting from insufficient domestic demand. That these policies of economic nationalism were contradictory made little difference; popular demand for policies of short-range advantage or retaliation could not be resisted.

The multilateral trading system of the nineteenth century, with its relatively low tariffs, virtually disappeared during the 1930s. Although some semblance of a world market economy continued to function, it was rigidly circumscribed by the neo-mercantilist practices of governments. High tariffs became endemic in all countries, and quota restrictions permitting only small amounts of foreign goods to enter the domestic market buttressed the high tariffs in most countries. The use by some countries of currency depreciation to achieve trade advantage was followed by equal or greater depreciation in scores of other countries. Subsidies for domestic producers, state licensing of importers, barter agreements, preferential trade arrangements, quotas, and exchange control were freely used in desperate efforts to stimulate or protect economic activity. Such devices often provided only a brief stimulus, and they were bitterly resented by trading partners as "beggar thy neighbor" policies aimed at improving a nation's economic position at the expense of other nations. Retaliation became the guiding principle for state economic policy, growing ever stronger by feeding on itself. Feeble attempts to arrest the cycle of economic nationalism through League of Nations-sponsored world monetary and trade conferences and the U.S.-sponsored reciprocal trade agreement tariff reduction system produced much verbal support but little action for a return of the trading system from its unilateral and bilateral nature to its former multilateral basis. The division of labor and free trade postulated by Adam Smith as the basis for national productivity disappeared except as ideals for a future world economy.

## REBUILDING THE WORLD ECONOMY

World War II arrested the trend toward the unilateral and bilateral determination of economic policies. Under U.S. leadership the Allies implemented a system of economic cooperation to facilitate the war effort and laid plans for rebuilding a working multilateral trading system when peace was restored. Unlike the laissez-faire economy of the nineteenth century, the new liberalized world economy was to be constructed by building regional and global institutions to facilitate agreement on trade, monetary, and investment matters. The new approach offered a compromise between the requirements of a free-trading system and the growing role of government to provide economic stability.

One individual—John Maynard Keynes, an English economist—assumed a natural leadership in the planning process. Keynes's ideas, expounded in numerous articles and books, placed major emphasis on utilizing the fiscal and monetary policies of government to guide and direct a free enterprise economy. The Great Depression, according to Keynes, had lasted a decade because *government* had failed to provide the policies and programs that could have ended it much sooner. His prescriptions for the continued health of national economies were avidly followed by economic planners and governments, so much so that his theories and approaches led to the coining of the term *Keynesianism* to describe them. Lord Keynes (he was made a member of the British nobility in recognition of his contributions to the field of economics) also functioned as the major planner of the post-World War II global economy. It was his firm belief that government institutions must play a major role in guiding and directing international as well as domestic economic activity. In the absence of world government, cooperative institutions must be constructed so that common policies could be developed that would lend strength and flexibility to the global economy.

Keynes proposed that the central international economic institutions should in effect constitute a three-legged stool created to support the postwar world economy. The first leg was to be the International Monetary Fund (IMF), with responsibility for maintaining currency exchange stability and for helping member nations deal with short-term disequilibriums in their balances of payments. The second leg was to be the International Bank for Reconstruction and Development, with responsibility for aiding in the reconstruction of war-devastated areas and in the modernization of the underdeveloped countries. The third leg, recognized by Keynes and others as politically the most difficult to secure agreement on, was to be an International Trade Organization (ITO) that would reduce or eliminate tariffs and other barriers to trade and would develop a set of rules to govern trade behavior. The three institutions were expected to function within the general framework of the UN system.

But more was needed than optimism and Keynesian plans for a bright new world of plenty. At war's end, the problems created during the era of economic nationalism remained major hurdles to the reestablishment of a multilateral trading system. Added to them were the problems that had grown out of the devastation and dislocation caused by the war itself. Ideological dangers, too, lurked amid the chaos and despair of Europe; the masses were fearful of a short-lived capitalist recovery that would soon return them to the prewar days of unemployment and general depression, and the middle class believed that the danger of communism from within or outside the state was very real. To meet these problems, planners identified six areas needing attention by the new United Nations: (1) the economic recovery of Europe and other areas suffering economic deprivation from the war must be assigned the highest priority; (2) global trade most be returned to a rational basis freed of most of the restrictive encumbrances instituted since 1930; (3) international monetary stability must be achieved through the harmonization of exchange rates and the expansion of international liquidity; (4) regional economic cooperation should be fostered so that critical areas of the world could develop a viable economic unity; (5) international investment must be encouraged so that capital would be available to support the reconstruction of war-devastated areas; and (6) massive transfers of resources and technology from rich to poor societies should be made to provide for the economic development of underdeveloped peoples. The first five of these areas will be discussed in this chapter, and the sixth will be covered in the next.

## Reconstruction of Western Europe

In the spring of 1945, at the end of World War II, the economic plant of Europe was moribund. Heavy shelling and bombing had destroyed industrial and transport facilities, power supplies were low, food was scarce, raw materials were almost nonexistent, and whole populations were dispersed and homeless. The immediate task, the feeding and housing of millions, was directed by the temporary UN Relief and Rehabilitation Administration (UNRRA), which expended almost $4 billion, much of it in direct aid to needy and homeless refugees. Slowly and painfully, displaced persons were sorted out and returned to their homelands, trains started running again, and rebuilding campaigns got underway. But the major problem remained: Where would Europe obtain the huge amounts of capital needed to restore its economic vitality?

## The European Recovery Program

The answer came in a commencement address delivered by Secretary of State George C. Marshall at Harvard University in June 1947, a speech that kindled the spark of hope for millions. Marshall called for a massive injection of U.S. aid into both Western and Eastern Europe, but before the assistance would be granted, Europe had to reach agreement on the amount of aid required and on what each participating state could contribute to the common effort. The Soviet Union rejected the offer to include Eastern Europe in the program and attacked the program as a policy of political interference and economic imperialism. Invited countries that refused to participate included Albania, Bulgaria, Czechoslovakia, Finland, Hungary, Poland, Romania, the Soviet Union, and Yugoslavia. United States' policymakers then began to push the concept of an integrated Western Europe. They believed that integration would not only restore economic viability to the region but would also build political stability and military defense capability on the new economic base. At a major conference called in the summer of 1947 in response to U.S. initiatives, sixteen West European countries worked out a plan for joint recovery, formed a Committee of European Economic Cooperation (CEEC) to determine individual capital needs, and agreed to cooperate in the reduction of barriers to trade and the free movement of labor. From this impetus emerged a European integration movement that was to attain unprecedented objectives of economic and political unity in an area that for centuries had exuded mutual suspicion and hostility through carefully nurtured nationalisms.

The following year the cooperating sixteen nations established the Organization for European Economic Cooperation (OEEC) as a means for jointly implementing the Marshall Plan and building a sound European economy. The initial members of the OEEC were Austria, Belgium, Britain, Denmark, France, Greece, Iceland, Ireland, Italy, Luxembourg, the Netherlands, Norway, Portugal, Sweden, Switzerland, and Turkey. West Germany participated unofficially and became a member when it was granted independence by the occupying countries. To facilitate the expansion of intra-European trade, the OEEC established the European Payments Union (EPU) in 1950 to provide for a common system of payments among its members. The arrangement worked so well that by the late 1950s full convertibility of OEEC currencies was achieved. This signaled that Western Europe had achieved full recovery from the war. The success of the new institutional approach in lifting Europe from despair to prosperity augured well for its global potential.

## THE ATTACK ON TRADE RESTRICTIONS

Early success in promoting Western European cooperation raised hopes that the postwar period might be an appropriate time to launch a major offensive against tariffs and other barriers to trade on a global scale. Tariffs have a depressing effect on world living standards because they violate basic economic principles. An international division of labor with its resulting specialization— the key to higher standards of living in all states—is negated by the artificial restrictions of tariffs, which encourage the development of noncompetitive industries and distort the direction of trade.

Psychological factors have often been more decisive than economic considerations in state decisions to increase barriers to trade. It was the need to change popular attitudes about "protectionism" that presented the most difficult obstacle to proponents of freer trade in the postwar era. The architects of an orderly and relatively free trading system recalled how irresistible public pressures in the United States, following the stock market crash in 1929, had forced the enactment by Congress of the Hawley-Smoot Tariff of 1930, with its viciously high protective rates. They remembered, too, how that U.S. action "exported" the depression to other countries in the trading system by touching off worldwide retaliation that resulted in a cycle of deepening restrictionism powered by fear, rising nationalism, and deteriorating domestic conditions. Between 1930 and 1936, world trade was reduced by two-thirds. To prevent a recurrence of the 1930 tragedy, two needs became obvious: (1) to establish a world trading organization that would provide an orderly, systematic means by which states could carry on their trading activities and devise common policies;

and (2) to use that organization to move the trading world toward freer commercial conditions.

## GATT—An Interim Measure

The United States took the initiative in promoting the first objective by preparing and circulating a preliminary blueprint for the International Trade Organization (ITO). The organization was to be one of three major institutions—along with the World Bank and the International Monetary Fund—to provide support for the postwar world economy. Like the bank and the fund, the ITO was to function as a specialized agency within the overall framework of the United Nations. The ITO charter, known as the Havana Charter after the 1948 UN Conference on Trade and Employment at Havana where it was drafted, represented the most extensive attack theretofore attempted on barriers to trade. Unfortunately for its sponsors, the forces of protectionism prevailed in the U.S. Senate; and the United States, the prime mover at Havana, failed to ratify the charter. Other nations, cognizant that an ITO without the United States would be like an arch without a keystone, also backed away. The first major effort to establish an institutional basis for trade cooperation within the UN system thus fell victim to the U.S. effort to provide leadership in the postwar world without accepting the responsibilities essential to effective leadership.

All hopes for a freer flow of international trade did not die with the ITO, however. While early negotiations for the anticipated ITO were going on, many nations urged an immediate attack on trade barriers through an ad hoc conference that would function as a temporary arrangement until the ITO came into operation. Meeting in Geneva in 1947, twenty-three nations worked out a vast number of bilateral tariff concessions that were written into a final act called the General Agreement on Tariffs and Trade (GATT).

The GATT conference was an adaptation of the reciprocal trade agreement system inaugurated by Secretary of State Cordell Hull in 1934 and subsequently implemented by most of the world's trading nations. That system provided for bilateral negotiations on a selective product-by-product basis, with all tariff reductions based on the principle of reciprocity. Agreements reached through bilateral bargaining sessions were embodied in trade agreements incorporating the most-favored-nation clause, thus making lower tariff rates applicable to all nations participating in the program as well as the two nations that signed the agreement. This application of the nondiscriminatory, most-favored-nation approach made it an outward-looking program aimed at building a liberal trading system. Although numerous trade agreements had been concluded before 1947, tariffs remained generally high and a speeded-up approach was clearly needed to overcome the hiatus of the war period. The GATT conference was the means selected for accelerating the program by providing for multilateral participation in a series of simultaneous bilateral bargaining sessions. Meeting in Geneva, 123 bilateral exchanges were held over a period of six months in which tariff reductions were considered on 50,000 items of commerce. The results of these negotiations were incorporated into a single document, the General Agreement on Tariffs and Trade (GATT), and all concessions became applicable to each of the twenty-three participating countries.

The failure of the ITO had given impetus to the GATT approach and led to the establishment of substitute international machinery. Unlike the ITO, GATT was based on executive agreements rather than a treaty, which means that U.S. participation in GATT did not involve the Senate in the ratification process. GATT's role progressively expanded after 1947, serving four major purposes:

1. It was a forum for negotiations on tariff reduction and the progressive elimination of other barriers to trade.
2. It functioned as a vehicle for developing and articulating new trade policy.
3. It provided a set of rules that governed the conduct of trade policy.
4. It offered a means for interpreting rules and procedures for the adjustment of trade disputes.

GATT operated under the guidance of its informal steering body, the Consultative Group of Eighteen (CG-18), with a membership of nine developed and nine developing countries. Parity between developed and developing states reflected efforts by the industrialized nations to escape from early Third World charges that GATT functioned largely as a Western organization. CG-18 was charged with maintaining a smooth flow of international trade and was responsible for facilitating balance-of-payment adjustments by fostering coordination between GATT and the International Monetary Fund. GATT was never given the full status of a specialized agency of the United Nations, but it functioned in much the same manner and maintained liaison with other UN bodies. Although known for many years as "the rich man's club," GATT's membership of full contracting parties and parties associated with the organization on a limited basis included two-thirds of the world's countries, and its members carried on more than 80 percent of world trade.

The hub of the GATT wheel was the rule against discrimination for imports and exports. Except for established systems of preference, tariffs, quantitative restrictions, and other barriers to trade were to be administered without favor under GATT rules. New systems aimed at establishing complete preference— a customs union, a common market, or a free trade area—were permitted only if their basic purpose was "to facilitate trade between the constituent territories and not to raise barriers to the trade of other . . . parties."

Eight rounds of negotiations to reduce barriers to trade were carried on by GATT.[2] Three of these were major campaigns to reduce tariffs. The so-called Kennedy Round (1964–67), inspired by President John F. Kennedy's leadership in advance planning, was aimed primarily at keeping the European Community open to world trade, which it did successfully. It also reduced the level of tariffs and other impediments to trade by one-third. The Tokyo Round (1973–79) focused special attention on encouraging trade between the developing and developed countries, with special emphasis on the export needs of developing countries. The Uruguay Round began in 1986 with a new session of multilateral negotiations at Punta del Este, Uruguay. Following opening discussions in Uruguay, negotiations were continued at GATT's headquarters in Geneva.

The Uruguay Round was especially important because of the growing threat of protectionism in the world and GATT's efforts to keep global markets open. One of its major obstacles to agreement was trade in agricultural products, since farmers in the United States, Western Europe, and Japan as well as in various Third World countries strongly opposed competition from foreign farm products. In most of these countries, farmers exercised unusually strong political power, typically far in excess of their numbers. These battles carried the Uruguay Round into the 1990s.

Originally concerned only with tariffs, GATT's rules were directed toward limiting the use of quantitative restrictions in imports and other nontariff barriers (NTBs). Import quotas were more rigid barriers to trade than tariffs; a tariff was a tax that increased the price for the consumer, whereas a quota permitted only a fixed number of imports, regardless of consumer demand. Exceptions to the general rule against import quotas included (1) states that suffered from a serious deficit in their balance of payments, (2) developing countries that were using quotas to foster economic advancement, and (3) states that restricted the domestic production and marketing of agricultural and fishery products. Because these exceptions included almost all GATT members (including the United States for the first and third exceptions), emphasis was placed on a requirement for consultation with GATT or the International Monetary Fund prior to the imposition of quotas by any state. Other NTBs included in GATT's oversight function were state licensing, special taxes, and exchange control. Individual countries, such as the United States and Japan, clashed frequently in GATT sessions over the use of NTBs as protectionist replacements for lowered tariffs. GATT was not as successful in eliminating nontariff barriers as it had been in reducing tariff rates. Tariff rates for most products averaged only 2–5 percent of the imported article's value, whereas countries that were not GATT members did not qualify for most-favored-nation treatment and paid pre-GATT tariff rates, many of which doubled the price of the import.

Probably the most useful function performed by GATT was helping to resolve disputes over alleged infractions of its trading rules. The lesson of the 1930s, burned indelibly into the pages of economic history, is that the greatest danger to a liberal trading system is retaliation that touches off a spiral of increasing protectionism. With the past as a guide, every complaint brought to GATT over a violation of rules was treated as a grave matter. Disputing parties were first urged to settle their disagreement bilaterally; failing this, the aggrieved party took the matter to a special GATT panel, which, in consultation with the parties, heard the issues and made a recommendation. Only if the offending state failed to abide by the panel decision did the complaining state retaliate by withdrawing a concession. The resolution of numerous disputes and the absence of major trade wars testify to the effectiveness of GATT's settlement procedures. The success of GATT's dispute settlement process was attributed in many cases to its closed-door sessions, which greatly reduced the pressures of special, protectionist interests.

However, GATT settlement procedures—especially those dealing with nontariff barriers to trade—were sorely strained when world economic conditions took a turn for the worse. There have been eight economic recessions in the West since 1947, and each one took a toll in terms of broken agreements, new trade barriers, political maneuverings, additional trade disputes, and subjective interpretations of existing rules. The recession in the early 1990s caused GATT to suffer all of these on one level of intensity or another. The increasing economic problems besetting the U.S. economy during this period were particularly harmful to world trade because U.S. markets were critical to most of the trading world. When, for example, the growth rate for the United States dipped to $-.07$ percent in 1991, the growth rate of the European Community fell to about 1.2 percent in 1992, and Japan's fell from 5.2 percent in 1990 to approximately 2.0 percent in 1992.

In the early 1990s, a series of events occurred which had a substantial impact on world trade and the operations of GATT. These occurred in the Soviet Union, which broke up into fifteen independent states, and in Eastern Europe, which became free from Soviet control. Almost all of these newly independent states, including Russia, applied for membership in GATT, and most desperately requested and received economic aid for their collapsing economies.

## FROM GATT TO WTO

The Uruguay round of GATT deliberations that began in 1986 was significantly affected by the passing of the Cold War, the fall of communism in Eastern Europe, and the collapse and ultimate demise of the Soviet Union. The world was suddenly a different place in the early 1990s and central concerns moved from security matters to economic issues. The restorative powers of capitalism were never more in evidence as the major trading nations, led by the United States, as well as Japan and a reunified Germany, prompted changes in global behavior not seen since the years immediately following the end of World War II. GATT deliberations now included 125 participating states generating 85 percent of world trade, and in the aftermath of the events noted above, as well as the major role played by the United States in rallying a UN-directed coalition that had liberated Kuwait from Iraqi aggression, the time seemed propitious for a seachange in the relations of nations, most notably in their financial and commercial endeavors. Prompted by the United States, but supported by the world's other dominant economic actors in the G-7 (Japan, Germany, Great Britain, France, Canada, and Italy), the Uruguay Round of negotiations was brought to a conclusion. In 1993 the members of GATT agreed to replace their temporary organization with a permanent one, namely, the World Trade Organization (WTO). WTO was not exactly the ITO envisaged immediately following World War II, but it was nevertheless the most ambitious undertaking yet launched to regulate world trade.

Unlike GATT, which functioned more as a coordinating secretariat, the World Trade Organization was a full-fledged intergovernmental organization with a formal decisionmaking structure at the ministerial level. Organized as a fair-trade policeman, WTO was mandated to manage disputes arising from the trading partners. Functioning equally in overseeing trade in manufactures and agricultural commodities, WTO also was given the power to examine a range of service industries. WTO was made responsible for enforcing rules, which gave it the character of a court, and its dispute procedures were made semi-judicial in character. Quite different from GATT, WTO accepts reports of commercial misbehavior from independent panels. Such reports are immediately actionable and can only be blocked by a consensus opposition. Appeals can be made by countries that seek to neutralize or offset complaints registered against them, but a decision of the WTO appellate body is binding. In sum, WTO members cannot block adverse findings, and if offenders do not comply with panel recommendations, trading partners may demand compensation, or impose their own sanctions.

The U.S. Congress, always sensitive to matters challenging the country's sovereign powers, was less than pleased with the results of the Uruguay Round and the resulting formation of the WTO. Arguing adherence to WTO requirements would elevate the U.S. trade deficit by eliminating tariff revenues, would cancel subsidies to American farmers, could not protect intellectual property, and would hinder not promote fair trade in services, Congressional opposition presented a formidable challenge to the new organization. Not alone in establishing their opposition to WTO, American environmentalists predicted the lowering of protective standards (notably in the matter of preserving the world's fish and marinelife resources). In spite of this opposition, the Clinton administration pressured for acceptance of WTO, citing its positive aspects, and blunting the criticism that suggested a loss of national sovereignty. President Clinton noted the United States retained the right to make and implement its individual policy no matter what the WTO did or ruled. Insisting the United States had nothing to lose and everything to gain from a more open and unrestricted international trading community, Clinton joined other advocates of the organization who believed WTO would generate higher world incomes and that more trade would translate into higher revenues for national coffers, not disruptive tariffs. Overall WTO, it was argued, aimed at liberalizing trade worldwide, and in the United States alone that could mean the creation of 1.5 million new jobs within ten years. The debate was far from over on the issue of WTO, but the United States became a charter member of the new organization and countries not yet members, e.g., China, was eager to join the WTO.

## UNCTAD

The UN Conference on Trade and Development (UNCTAD) owes its existence at least partially to GATT's pre-UNCTAD policies of relative exclusivity. The idea of a new world trade organization started with a developing nations' resolution, adopted by the General Assembly in 1961, calling on the Secretary-General to make preliminary plans for an international trade and development conference. Debated extensively in the Economic and Social Council, the proposal grew out of the developing nations' exasperation over the failure of the developed nations to lower their restrictions on commodity trade. With the slogan "export or die," the Assembly majority pressed ahead with the trade conference despite the objection of seventeen developed nations that it duplicated GATT's work.

The first UN Conference on Trade and Development convened in Geneva in the spring of 1964. Its objective can be summarized as an effort to pressure the developed states into accepting a liberal trade policy as the best means of securing the capital needed to promote economic development. The major economic actors often prefer programs of technical assistance and loans, rather than lowered trade barriers, as the means of aiding developing countries. It is commonly argued that imports from low-wage developing countries compete unfairly with domestic articles produced by higher-priced labor. This viewpoint has much persuasive force in domestic politics, even though it overlooks the basic comparative cost rationale for international trade. Imports and exports exist primarily because countries have either an absolute or comparative advantage in producing particular articles of commerce. If costs were equalized in all states, international trade would become almost an irrelevancy. If each state refused to trade with nations in which labor was cheaper or general costs were lower, very little trade would take place. Moreover, the higher productivity of labor in the advanced states tends to equalize their costs with those of low-wage countries. The developing countries recognized that political muscle was needed to secure economic concessions. Consequently, they functioned within a voting bloc at the conference that came to be known as the Group of 77, or G-77, a caucus corresponding to the number of independent Third World countries in 1964.[3] Regional caucuses and informal contact groups supplemented the major caucus at the conference.

Although no immediate major liberalization of trade resulted from it, the developing states succeeded in placing some of their objectives squarely on the international agenda. As set forth in the final act of the three month conference, they included (1) an increase in their export earnings, (2) a stabilization of primary commodity prices, (3) the attainment of a new specialization based on an international division of labor, and (4) the extension of the most-favored-nation principle to developing states without reciprocity. To assure a continuing forum for these and similar issues, the final act also recommended that UNCTAD be established as a permanent organ of the General Assembly, meeting at least once every three years, with a Trade and Development Board to develop policy between UNCTAD sessions and a permanent secretariat "within the United Nations Secretariat." The Nineteenth General Assembly, dominated by the same Third World majority, obligingly complied (but with only grudging acceptance by the major trading states).

As presently constituted, the Trade and Development Board meets annually and is open to participation by all UNCTAD members. Although the developing states hold a voting majority on the board, the "principal trading states" are also represented on it so that pressures can be applied continuously on them. The headquarters of the UNCTAD secretariat are located at Geneva in proximity to the headquarters of other trade and economic organizations. Since the initial 1964 Geneva meeting, subsequently known as UNCTAD I, major international conferences have been held every three or four years. These have included UNCTAD II in New Delhi (1968), UNCTAD III in Santiago (1972), UNCTAD IV in Nairobi (1976), UNCTAD V in Manila (1979), UNCTAD VI in Belgrade (1983), UNCTAD VII in Geneva (1987), UNCTAD VIII in Colombia (1992), and UNCTAD IX in Midrand, South Africa (1996). The end of the Cold War and the changes in the world economic climate, not the least of which was the formation of the World Trade Organization, markedly reduced the significance of UNCTAD. WTO was seen as the better organization to represent the views and policies of the less developed countries, but the UNCTAD Board continued to hold regular meetings at its United Nations Headquarters. Moreover, the fifteenth executive session of the Board held in Geneva on 27 June 1997 endorsed conclusions resulting from the first sessions of the new UNCTAD commissions on Trade and Goods and Services and Commodities; on Investment, Technology and Related Financial Issues; and on Enterprise, Business Facilitation and Development. UNCTAD's Secretary-General called a special meeting in November 1998 to examine Markets and Development. UNCTAD also took steps to call a Third United Nations Conference on the Less Developed Countries and urged the organization to reject the stringent economic measures imposed by the more developed countries on their fragile systems. To improve its bargaining leverage, UNCTAD nations called for closer cooperation with the United Nations Development Program as well as the need to more effectively interact with subregional intergovernmental organizations. In general, UNCTAD representatives acknowledged the need to reorganize, streamline and upgrade the organization's activities if it expected to have any influence on the globalization of the world's economy.

The Group of 77 has long championed the cause of the less developed countries and it has been keen to support UNCTAD's role as the voice of the poorer nations. This collaboration has produced many voting victories since 1964; nonetheless, it has not changed the basic economic posture of the major, more affluent trading nations, or their relations with the Third World. The two most significant campaigns pressed by the Group of 77 were conducted during the period of the Cold War. The first was aimed at persuading the industrialized states to adopt a generalized system of preferences (GSP) that would improve opportunities for Third World states to sell their products in Western markets. Under the GSP program to encourage Third World experts, the United States and other developed countries allow specified products from the less or least developed countries (LDCs) to enter their markets duty free. The size of the program can be judged by noting that in one year (1988), $18.4 billion of goods entered the United States with no tariff or tax. The U.S. Trade and Tariff Act of 1984 continued the program, but some countries—Korea, Taiwan, and Singapore, for example—"graduated" because of their increased competitiveness. The second campaign sought a drastic reorganization of the world economy through the creation of a New International Economic Order (NIEO). These campaigns, and their impact on development programs, will be discussed in the next chapter. Suffice it now to conclude that UNCTAD has been a political success in producing unity and voting strength for the developing states bloc but that it has done little to alter the basic economic realities in a world market system that favors the rich nations, often at the expense of the poor.

This conclusion was never more significant than during the Asian economic crisis of 1997–98. While seeking to establish the independence of developing countries, UNCTAD's mission also involved the promotion of direct foreign investment (FDI). Focused on expanding the financial capabilities of the developing states, FDI introduced partnerships between local industries and foreign companies. Originally designed to sustain domestic control of national enterprises, in time of economic strain and financial upheaval, however, the opportunities available to foreign interests to exploit local business conditions are legion. Moreover, crisis economies could not manage without outside assistance, and the outsiders were provided a track that enabled them to reap significant rewards from the miseries of the host nations. Thus, although UNCTAD could cite the continued growth of foreign investment capital in spite of the sustained financial crisis, it was not without paying a very high price. UNCTAD's interest in refocusing FDI initiatives offset the reluctance of international investors to risk their capital in nations faced with significant fiscal and monetary problems. UNCTAD's 1998 report on investment distinguished between losses in portfolio investments, that is, stocks and bonds, and direct investment which involved the acquisition, merger, or purchase of a significant share of a business enterprise. The long term commitment of the latter contrasted with the short term aspects of the former, and as a consequence FDI flows were actually less volatile than short term portfolio flows. These differences helped to explain the turnaround in 1999 in many of the Asian crisis areas. The rebound from the devastating collapse that began in Thailand in July 1997 and spread across Asia and then to Russia and Brazil, was slow and painful but nevertheless welcome. Thailand was forecast to achieve economic stability in 1999. South Korea's economy which had contracted by nearly 6 percent in 1998 indicated a 2 percent increase in 1999, following a $58 billion bailout from the international financial community. UNCTAD's promotion of FDI was a major factor in the turnaround, but the developing countries were not oblivious to the fact that their dislocated treasuries meant more aggressive entrepreneurial interests from the United States and Europe could invest or purchase Asian companies with less capital expenditure. Hewlett-Packard for example was able to purchase Samsung's 45 percent share in their local joint venture, while Goodyear Tire and Rubber was able to enter into a global alliance with Japan's Sumitomo Rubber Industries. General Motors also credited Asia's crisis with its ability to increase its stakes in the Suzuki Motor Corporation. In effect, American and European business interests descended upon Asia during the 1997–98 crisis and bought out companies at very good prices.

# PROMOTING REGIONAL INTEGRATION

While plans to establish a global trading system were unfolding, regional integration movements to facilitate trade and economic progress were also under way. These resulted in a spate of new regional organizations, first in Western Europe, then in Latin America and elsewhere. The former are composed of advanced countries that are seeking means to foster economic growth and broaden the base of their prosperity; the latter are composed of developing countries that are trying through the fusion of their trade policies to gain a taste of the kind of prosperity that was accepted as a starting point for the European model. Although contemporary regional organizations represent different levels of cooperation and integration, they have the common objective, supported by various UN programs, of promoting economic well being through regional unity.

## EUROPEAN INTEGRATION

### The European Union

The most economically and politically advanced integration arrangement is the European Union (EU), which originated in 1951 with the Coal and Steel Community. Two additional economic organizations—the European Economic Community (EEC) and the European Atomic Energy Community (EURATOM)—emerged with a unified interorganizational economic decision-making system for the three groups as specified in the 1957 Treaty of Rome. The EU's fifteen members (Belgium, Britain, Denmark, France, Greece, Ireland, Italy, Luxembourg, the Netherlands, Portugal, Spain, Austria, Germany, Finland, and Sweden) have established a common market, a common external tariff, free flow of capital, free migration of workers, as well as many common economic policies and programs.

The EU has a common political structure—consisting of a Council of Ministers, a Commission, a European Parliament, and a Court of Justice. The council, composed of government representatives, is the supreme decision-making body in the EU. The seventeen commissioners are appointed by governments but serve in their individual capacities in administering EU affairs, directing a bureaucracy of 25,000 civil servants in Brussels, Belgium. A commission president chosen by the council serves as chief administrator and makes his voice heard in policy matters as well. The judges, appointed by consent of the governments (at least one per member state), render legal decisions that are binding on (but sometimes ignored by) member states. The parliament must be consulted on all EU directives and regulations adopted by the council. The parliament enjoys veto power over many EU measures. Its members are elected by the people of their states to represent people rather than governments and are seated in the parliament by their political affiliation. Thus, for example, liberals are seated with fellow liberals, conservatives with conservatives from all fifteen member countries, and socialists with all other socialists.

Since the mid-1980s the EU has made major strides toward economic union of the member states, and a higher level of political coordination as well. Much of the renewed integrative energy dates from the Single European Act, signed in 1985 and in force from 1987 as an amendment to the 1957 Treaty of Rome. The Single European Act strengthened the powers of EU organs, eliminating for most issues the veto power that individual governments had previously exercised in the council.

The Single European Act also committed members to complete the internal market by December 31, 1992, with the removal of all barriers to the free movement of money, trade products, workers, and services among the member states. Most aspects of the single market took effect on January 1, 1993, as scheduled.

In the meantime, a December 1991 "summit" meeting of community leaders in Maastricht, The Netherlands, approved the Treaty on European Union providing for even tighter economic and political union, to be achieved in stages and completed no later than 1999. Subject to ratification by individual states, the Maastricht Treaty called for a unified foreign and security policy for the EU as well as a common European citizenship. A common defense policy was set as a goal, but not necessarily to be attained by 1999. The agreement also increased the scope and powers of the EU in dealing with social issues—education, health, the environment, immigration, industrial policy, and consumer protection.

In the economic realm, the Maastricht Treaty provided for completion of the internal market and subsequent creation of an Economic and Monetary Union (EMU). The key EMU agency was to be a European Central Bank (ECB) empowered to regulate EU monetary policy, including the issuance of a new common European currency to replace national currencies such as the German mark, the French franc, and the British pound. The EMU would not necessarily cover the whole European community because membership for each state depended on its meeting stringent, specified conditions that demonstrated a sound economy. European unity, it was believed, was necessary to compete effectively with the United States and Japan in an increasingly competitive world.

Among EU members, Britain has historically been least enthusiastic about concentrating power in the EU at the expense of national control of economic matters, but British Prime Minister John Major gave full government support to ratification of the Maastricht Treaty. This was despite vocal opposition within his ruling Conservative party. A serious challenge to the treaty was raised in June 1992 when Danish voters, in a nonbinding referendum, rejected the treaty. This led to an agreement in the EU council to relax some of the Maastricht requirements most troubling to Denmark and a few other members, without amending the text of the treaty. Therefore, in a later referendum Denmark also gave its approval to Maastricht.

The European Union, which had its origins with the Coal and Steel Community in 1951–52, and developed into a six-nation common market in 1957, added Britain, Denmark, and Ireland in 1973, Greece in 1981, Portugal and Spain in 1986, to assume the role of a European Community or EC. Following the Single European Act (1987) and the Maastricht Treaty, which was signed in 1992 and ratified by the states in 1993, what had been described as a "community" was transformed into a "union," namely, the European Union. Subsequently opened to membership from the European Free Trade nations (EFTA), Norway and Iceland declined the invitation but Finland, Sweden, and Austria accepted, bringing the Union to its fifteen members in 1995. With a number of East European nations waiting their turn for formal admission, the ranks of the European Union were forecast to swell further in the century ahead.

The supreme test of the European Union centered on the creation of a single currency, which became a certainty for eleven of the EU's fifteen member states when the Council of EU Finance Ministers voted its approval on May 1, 1998, and the European Parliament followed suit on May 2. These actions brought the long-anticipated European Monetary Union (EMU) to a point of realization. Germany, France, Italy, the Netherlands, Belgium, Spain, Portugal, Luxembourg, Austria, Finland, and Ireland, all agreed to adopt the Euro as their new uniform currency. (Britain, Sweden, and Denmark delayed their acceptance for another time, and Greece failed to meet the demanding qualifications of membership established by the EU.) In fact the single currency plan, that took effect in January 1999, replaced the currencies of the eleven states. Actual notes and coins, however, were to be introduced over a six-month period commencing in January 2002. At that time the individual currencies of the participating states, a key symbol of state sovereignty, would cease being legal tender.

Although considerable enthusiasm had been created for the EMU and the single currency, and many Europeans acknowledged that a successful Euro would rival the American dollar, and possibly even surpass it as a measure of value (the Euro was said to represent 40 percent of the world's trading area), Europe was far from being a model monetary zone. Noting that its economies were fragmented, its people rooted in their national homelands, its cultures vastly different from one another, its unemployment levels high and politically explosive, and its political powers highly decentralized, the belief persisted that the single currency policy could explode the entire experiment in European integration. Explaining that the United States Federal Reserve can reduce interest rates to encourage economic activity, a European Central Bank sets policy for the eleven nations even though their economies operate on different cycles. Moreover, national governments lose much of their budgetary leverage, and staying in the Euro requires member states to keep their budget deficits below 3 percent of gross domestic product. Therefore, should unemployment deepen and national governments find themselves unable to respond to their own constituents, demand that the Euro be dropped could be the least costly consequence of an unfolding scenario.

Born and shaped by a Cold War that no longer burdened Europeans, the European Union reached for the light of a new era and a new century. The launching of the Euro on January 1, 1999 as a fully fledged currency with the backing of the European System of Central Banks, provided the new Europe with a vitality not witnessed since the formation of the Common Market. Nevertheless, the real test was still to be experienced, that is, when euro-donominated notes and coins phase in on January 1, 2002, and as a consequence, phase out the national currency units of EMU's member states.

## EFTA

An early rival to the emerging European Community—the European Free Trade Association (EFTA)—was established by the Stockholm Convention of 1959. The objectives of EFTA were more simple, viz, to eliminate tariffs and other barriers to trade among members and to harmonize internal production cost factors. EFTA's original members were Austria, Denmark, Great Britain, Norway, Portugal, Sweden, and Switzerland. Known as the "Outer Seven" when the Common Market countries, France, West Germany, Italy, Belgium, the Netherlands, and Luxembourg were called the "inner six," EFTA subsequently saw the defection of Britain, Denmark, Portugal, and later, Austria and Sweden, which joined the "inner six" as it evolved into the European Economic Community, later, the European Community, and finally, the European Union. In the course of its own history EFTA remained focused on the elimination of tariffs and other trade barriers, bringing Finland within its orbit, only to lose it too to the expanding European Union. Iceland, however, joined EFTA in 1970. Offered membership in the European Union, Iceland, like Norway, Switzerland, and subsequently, Lichtenstein, opted to retain their "independence" while they sought to promote their individual as well as collective needs free of the encumbrances of a supranational organization. EFTA nevertheless joined the larger European grouping in a common free trade zone in 1991, and its members pledged more than $2 billion to a special fund to assist in the development of the poorer European countries. Remaining EFTA countries have no voice in the determination of trade policies within the European Union, and although EFTA no longer competes with its continental neighbor, it nevertheless provides a haven for countries that still need to be convinced that greater intimacy is in their interest.

## COMECON

The Communist world's attempt to promote economic development through regional unity took the form of the Council for Mutual Economic Assistance

(CMEA or COMECON). Its members included the Soviet Union and six Eastern European states (Bulgaria, Czechoslovakia, East Germany, Hungary, Poland, and Romania) plus Angola, Cuba, Mongolia, and Vietnam. Established in 1949, its main objective was to foster an integration of Communist economies based on national specialization. COMECON operated through a council and an executive committee supplemented by various committees and commissions. With the fall of Communist regimes in Eastern Europe, COMECON was dissolved in 1991.

## INTEGRATION IN THE AMERICAS, ASIA, AND AFRICA

Numerous integration schemes have appeared in Latin America. The Latin American Integration Association (LAIA, Spanish acronym ALADI), in existence since 1980, has promoted tariff reductions among Mexico and ten South American countries with only modest success. ALADI is a successor to the Latin American Free Trade Association (LAFTA) which had earlier failed to establish a free trade area. Two groups of ALADI members have undertaken stronger commitments, however. The Andean Pact countries (Bolivia, Colombia, Ecuador, Peru, Venezuela) are attempting to create a free trade area. Four others—Argentina, Brazil, Paraguay, and Uruguay—agreed in 1991 to establish a more ambitious Common Market of the South (MERCOSUR).

In Central America, a never very effective Central American Common Market (Costa Rica, El Salvador, Guatemala, Honduras, Panama, Nicaragua) has set a goal of becoming a genuine Central American Economic Community. Simultaneously, these same six countries have agreed with Mexico, Venezuela, and Colombia to form a single free trade area. The more active trade arrangements are the Caribbean Common Market (CARICOM) and the Southern Common Market (MERCOSUR). CARICOM dates back to 1973 and continues to make progress toward more integrative economic union. MERCOSUR, a later creation, has made considerable progress in reducing tariff barriers, negotiating a common external tariff, and in opening its market to other countries and trade associations. MERCOSUR, however, remains a means and not an end and its member states endeavor to make their subregional organization compatible with universalism and globalization. In fact, its spokesmen have addressed the need to make MERCOSUR a "launch pad" into the globalized economic world. MERCOSUR, nevertheless, has given priority to the establishment of a political consultation mechanism that can expedite the exchange of macroeconomic information and help avoid measures that restrict regional trade flows. Keenly interested in matters of agriculture, MERCOSUR attaches considerable importance to the Agriculture Committee of the World Trade Organization and seeks ways to reduce subsidies while at the same time protecting the agricultural sector of the member states.

North America has also become the scene of regional free trade arrangements, with potentially wide impact on U.S.-hemispheric relations. In 1988 the United States and Canada agreed to create a two-nation free trade area, and in

1992 agreement was reached to include Mexico as part of a North American Free Trade Agreement (NAFTA). In spite of heated opposition in the U.S. Congress and from American labor unions, NAFTA entered into force in 1994, establishing a free trade area linking the United States with its first (Canada) and third (Mexico) trading partners. Those opposing NAFTA could not be silenced, however, its critics insisting American jobs would be lost to the country's southern neighbor, and that even the promise of an improved economy in Mexico would not stem the tide of illegal migrants. Proponents of NAFTA anticipated a more stable southern frontier, citing not only greater opportunities for poor Mexicans in Mexico, but a more democratic Mexico. Nevertheless, on the day that NAFTA entered into force, fighting broke out in the southern Mexican state of Chiapas. The rebellious forces were described as the Zapatista National Liberation Army and their demands called for general Mexican government reform, not simply relief for the impoverished state of Chiapas. The Mexican army's fierce response to the Zapatistas neutralized but it did not silence the dissidents. Although both the Mexican and United States governments experienced some degree of embarrassment, Mexico nevertheless rapidly demonstrated an improvement in its economy and a loan given to it by the Clinton administration was repaid sooner than expected, including major interest charges. Mexico's Institutional Revolutionary Party (PRI) has dominated the politics and government of the country since the late 1920s and although there are periodic struggles within the organization, its opposition remains marginalized in spite of electoral victories in 1997–98. Multiparty democracy in Mexico remains a distant goal. NAFTA may project a more democratic Mexico but the symbiotic relationship between PRI and the state remains the principal force behind Mexico's development as a modern nation. The longest continually ruling party in the world, PRI functions through an intricate web of patronage and corruption, and it remains to be determined how NAFTA, albeit a more intimate association with the United States, will influence the course of Mexico's political, let alone its economic development.

A different approach to economic well-being is used by the Organization of Petroleum Exporting Countries (OPEC), an intergovernmental cartel established to promote joint action on production and pricing in the world oil market. The membership of OPEC comprises seven Middle East Arab states (Algeria, Iraq, Kuwait, Libya, Qatar, Saudi Arabia, and the United Arab Emirates), two African states (Gabon and Nigeria), two Asian states (Indonesia and Iran), and two Latin American states (Ecuador and Venezuela). Although the cartel helped produce high levels of income for its members during the 1970s, a steep decline in world oil prices during the 1980s created frictions within OPEC over production and distribution quotas. Harmony within OPEC was also severely challenged by the Iran-Iraq War in the 1980s and the Gulf War of 1991. New oil discoveries, improved conservation measures, the engineering of automobiles requiring less gasoline per mile of use, mild winters attributed to global warming, and a number of technological developments, contributed to a considerable saving of raw petroleum. In addition, the inability of OPEC to discipline its members, and their individual decisions to pump more oil, caused a glut of oil on the open market. Even with Iraq denied the opportunity to freely sell its stocks, the amount of available oil exceeded worldwide demand. The depressed price of oil on the open market caused considerable dislocation in a number of oil-producing states and even more friction among OPEC members. Subsequent efforts by the United Nations Secretary-General and others to relieve the sanctions on Iraq, and notably, to permit Baghdad to sell some of its oil in return for needed food and medicine, was answered affirmatively by the Security Council in 1997 and 1998. The added supply caused the price of oil to drop even lower. OPEC's meeting in March 1999 addressed the problem of too much oil and extremely poor returns, and for the first time in many years, the members appeared agreeable to a new allocation of quotas that they promised to respect.

Other attempts at promoting freer trade on a regional basis include the Association of South-East Asian Nations (ASEAN), which agreed on steps toward an Asian Free Trade Area; the Central African Customs and Economic Union (UDEAC); the Economic Community of West African States (ECOWAS); and an Economic Cooperation Organization composed of Azerbaijan, Iran, Kyrgyzstan, Pakistan, Tajikistan, Turkey, Turkmenistan, and Uzbekistan.

## Why Regional Integration?

The simultaneous development of UN organizations fostering the growth of a world trading system and of regional groupings raises the question whether these developments are complementary or contradictory. Does a regional common market, for example, contribute to global multilateralism, or is it a new form of bloc nationalism that hampers world trade? Does the integration of national economies within regions promote or impede the goal of an orderly world economy? Does it foster political unity or rivalry? In sum, are the benefits of regional economic integration local or global, and what, if any, are its disadvantages?

These questions are difficult to answer with any degree of certainty, but a number of advantages have been claimed for regional economic integration:

1. *Increased trade:* Trade among members will normally expand as governmental barriers are reduced or eliminated.
2. *Lower costs:* The cost of production may decrease if free internal movement of labor and capital is encouraged.
3. *Greater specialization:* A freer market will encourage a regional division of labor and a consequent specialization.
4. *Increased investment:* Investment may be spurred by the mobility of capital and labor and by the expanded demand of a larger market.
5. *Expanded production:* A freer and larger market with close economic ties among members will tend to stimulate production to fill a larger demand.

6. *Monetary stability:* Balance-of-payments disequilibriums with out-side nations may be ameliorated by increased trade within the market. Ultimately, a common currency could resolve most monetary and exchange problems among members.
7. *Greater efficiency:* More highly competitive conditions within the free trade area may result in greater efficiency and higher productivity. Economies of scale from larger production units may result from the expanded market.
8. *Improved terms of trade:* The elimination of artificial barriers to trade within the market area may have the effect of evening out the price ex-change ratio among members. In the trade relations of members with nonmembers, domestic competition may result in lower consumer prices for imports and hence improved terms of trade.
9. *A better bargaining position:* Members as a bloc may substantially in-crease their bargaining power in tariff negotiations with outside states.

To this list, functionalists might add that regional economic arrangements may serve as a base for building political integration. A regional market's insti-tutional machinery, its harmonization of economic policies, and the spillover effect of its successes may help create an awareness within the region of the ad-vantages of the integrative process.

Although the advantages of the regional approach are real and its poten-tiality great, it also has some significant drawbacks. Foremost among these is the basic *discriminatory* nature of a free trade area or common market. Each member of the regional group agrees to give preferential trade treatment to its fellow members. Since other trading nations do not share in this internal re-duction or elimination of trade barriers, they are, ipso facto, the objects of the regional group's discrimination. Trade discrimination, whether direct or indi-rect and however good its intentions, is inimical to the development of global multilateralism.

Within a free trade area or common market, partially dormant forces of the marketplace are awakened. As governments remove their protective mantles, competition becomes keen. If economic growth falters or the business cycle takes an adverse swing, keen competition can turn to cutthroat competition in a battle for survival. Even during prosperity, free trade is most advantageous for the stronger trading partners. If economic freedom within a regional group permits one or several members to attract a major portion of available invest-ment funds and to dominate the marketplace, economic integration will merely serve to accelerate the process of enriching the rich and impoverishing the poor.

Although a common market may stimulate efficiency and productivity, it may also drive marginal producers out of business, a process that could re-dound to the disadvantage of market consumers. The natural forces of a free economy encourage the concentration of business into larger units. This con-centration and the specialization promoted by common policies increase the possibility that business executives will reach an understanding with one another, divide up the market, and raise prices. In the EU, for example, leading industrialists in all member countries supported the common market idea partly because of the opportunities for dividing up the continental market that they believed it would provide. A high and growing incidence of mergers and cartel arrangements in EU countries raises the threat of monopoly pricing that may develop once competition with outside firms has been reduced by the cost differential between members and nonmembers. Although cartels could be brought under government regulation—and the EU's Treaty of Rome (1957) contains provisions that authorize such action—the continental tradition of restrictive marketing practices, augmented by the political power of the giants of industry, militates against it.

A free trade area or common market represents a substantial movement toward laissez-faire. Governmental restrictive and promotional systems are dismantled by common agreement to eliminate artificial cost differentials and restraints on trade within the market. The impact of such policies may be a collapse in the delicately engineered internal equilibrium of power among business, labor, and agriculture.

In a regional group composed of Third World developing states, many of these same infirmities may exist. Extremes in levels of development and economic potentials may bestow even greater favors on the more advanced members of the market than in a group composed wholly of developed states. Although the classical economists argued that free trade would tend to equalize incomes in all states, the evidence negates this theory. Within a free market the state that develops most rapidly will attract additional shares of investment capital and skilled labor from neighboring states. Competitive advantages in a free market tend to increase the rate of industrial development in more advanced states and frustrate the attempts of weaker states to industrialize.

Finally, the development of common market arrangements, whether in developed or developing states, may have an unhealthy impact on the building of a global multilateral system. The very factors that lend strength to a common market system may also limit world trade. Preferential treatment for members' trade, for example, may encourage retaliation by outsiders. The movement to reduce world trade barriers may be stymied by the realization that freer trade with the rest of the world will weaken the rationale for a regional preferential system. In a common market the "invasion" of external capital to surmount the common external tariff by investing "inside" the market causes balance-of-payments disequilibriums and reactions within member countries against foreign domination of their economies. Moreover, the discriminatory features of a free trade area or a common market encourage the development of rival trading blocs. If common markets multiply—and evidence of planning for market arrangements in Asia and Africa lends credence to this assumption—a world of regional blocs may restore much of the rivalry that characterized the economic nationalism of the 1930s.

On balance, the development of regional market arrangements has probably been a healthy one. The objective of using a regional market to promote economic development in the Third World, however, remains largely untested. And as an element related to the problem of political unity, no one has yet been able to unravel the tangled skein of economic factors to produce a definitive explanation of which factors produce closer ties and which invite disunity. Perhaps the main reason that free trade areas and common markets will continue to find favor is the psychological satisfactions that major interest groups derive from them. One observer's evaluation of the European Community in 1963 could, with adaptations, be applied to the creation of most regional economic arrangements since then:

> It is not surprising that everyone sees something for himself in the Rome Treaty—it is all things to all men. The free trader sees a cutting down of the internal barriers to trade. The protectionist sees the building of a new tariff wall around Western Europe. The right wing sees the strengthening of business interests and the possibility of stiffer resistance to wage demands on the grounds of competitive requirements. The left wing looks to the international unity of workers and sees the approach of the ideal of world brotherhood. The federalists see the creation of new supranational powers and the gradual emergence of a federal government. The confederalists look forward to *l'Europe des patries*—the Europe of nation states. The Europeans see the growth of a new European spirit and self-consciousness. The supporters of an Atlantic Community see the development of much broader loyalties. The one thing that is clear is that not all of these views can be right.[4]

## THE PURSUIT OF INTERNATIONAL LIQUIDITY

The removal of barriers to trade through actions by regional organizations, GATT, UNCTAD, and the WTO, may spur the exchange of goods, but another factor—the means of payment for goods received—also determines the volume of the goods exchanged. When business executives in India buy Japanese Toyotas, for example, they must pay for them, not in Indian rupees, but in Japanese yen or in an "international" currency such as the U.S. dollar or the British pound. Foreign currencies needed for carrying on trade are known as foreign exchange. They may be obtained from a free foreign exchange market or, in the case of a state using some form of exchange control, a government agency determines whether the projected transaction warrants the use of scarce foreign exchange. In a free exchange market, the rate of exchange between domestic and foreign currency is determined by supply-and-demand forces similar to those operating in a stock market or a commodity market. In a controlled market, the price of foreign currencies is pegged at an official rate favorable to the exchange control state. This system, often supplemented by a "black market" exchange system, was used in Communist states and in most Third World nations. In the early 1990s, Russia and several other former Communist states changed from a tight, centrally planned economy to a free market system. In some states, this action drastically reduced the exchange value of the nation's currency, producing serious inflation.

One of the main objectives of states in the area of international finance is to accumulate sufficient reserves of foreign currencies to carry them over a lean period. Two types of currencies, distinguished from each other by the role that each plays in relation to international trade and finance, are useful in providing that kind of security. The first type is an international "trading" currency that businesspeople use to carry on their day-to-day transactions in foreign markets. Bankers use trading currency to make loans and investments in most countries of the world. The trading currency is the working currency accepted as an international monetary unit in a world of diverse national currencies. For some years the U.S. dollar has functioned as the major trading currency, with many billions of dollars currently in the hands of foreign bankers and businessmen. Almost all world oil business, for example, has been transacted in U.S. dollars. The second type is a "reserve" currency that provides governments with the means for protecting the value of their national currencies in foreign exchange markets. When the value of a national currency threatens to drop below its parity or stability level, the government purchases quantities of its own currency in the free market using its international reserves. If a national currency becomes overvalued in the free market, the government reverses the process, accumulating reserves in exchange for its national currency. Countries, therefore, need sizable amounts of reserves to keep the value of their national currencies stable. This is especially true of the developed countries of the West, which operate on the basis of a largely free-floating flexible exchange system in which currency values are fixed by supply-and-demand market conditions, as determined in large part by banks and foreign exchange speculation. The international reserves held by countries are in the form of gold, special drawing rights (SDRs), and foreign exchange. The last of these consists mainly of U.S. dollars and the currencies of Britain, France, Germany, Japan, and other Western states.

After World War II the U.S. dollar became the kingpin of the international monetary system for several reasons. For one, the United States was committed to buy gold from foreign monetary authorities or to sell gold to them at the fixed price of $35 an ounce. Because gold was in short supply, U.S. dollars supplemented gold in national reserves, with the understanding that those dollars could be converted into gold. Consequently, all other currencies were tied to the dollar in terms of their exchange relationship with it and to the extent that they held dollars as a reserve currency. The preeminence of the U.S. dollar as a reserve currency was not planned; it occurred because of the willingness of private businesspeople, bankers, and public officials in various countries to hold U.S. dollars as a safe, universal currency. Since the U.S. government was ready to redeem dollar reserves for gold, there was a general acceptance of dollars in lieu of gold in what might be described as a gold-exchange-standard system. The unrivaled prosperity of the United States and the immersion of its business executives in business operations around the globe also helped place the U.S. dollar in the center of the world monetary stage at that time.

The U.S. dollar also became the world's reserve currency because unprecedented numbers of dollars were available to foreign traders and monetary agencies. This bonanza of dollars resulted from a series of annual deficits in the U.S.

balance of payments, which grew in magnitude for forty years. These deficits put hundreds of billions of dollars into foreign hands—much in the form of official reserves—and thus provided the liquidity that fostered a rising level of world trade. In addition, billions of U.S. dollars were exchanged for gold, substantially reducing U.S. gold reserves. United States' policies for many years sought to reduce or eliminate the balance-of-payments deficit and to reduce the outflow of dollars. Had these policies been successful, they would have halted the growth of reserves abroad at the very time when greater international liquidity was needed to support expanding trade and general prosperity. Before the gold-dollar crisis and the challenge of the world debt crisis are examined, a survey of the UN system for creating and safeguarding monetary stability is in order.

## THE ROLE OF THE INTERNATIONAL MONETARY FUND (IMF)

The world's monetary system, weakened during the period of economic nationalism of the 1930s, emerged from World War II in almost complete disarray. To promote a more orderly international payments system, the planners at the Bretton Woods Conference in 1944 drew up Articles of Agreement for an International Monetary Fund. The IMF, the World Bank (also a product of Bretton Woods), and the ill-fated International Trade Organization were to be the three legs of the Keynesian stool on which international economic well being would rest. Although the Soviet Union participated at Bretton Woods, it refused to accept the result. In the official Soviet view, the IMF and the World Bank were merely "crutches" to prolong the life of international capitalism which was doomed in time to collapse by the immutable laws of historic development. This attitude began to change during the Gorbachev years, and in 1991, at President Gorbachev's request, the Soviet Union was invited to form a "special association" with the IMF. Although the Soviet Union did not long survive this invitation, its former republics, as independent states, were subsequently granted full membership in the IMF.

The IMF is one of the sixteen specialized agencies within the United Nations system. Each member of the IMF is represented on its governing board, which meets annually to fix general policy. Day-to-day business is conducted by a 22-member Executive Board chaired by a managing director who is also administrative head of a staff approaching 2,000. Voting in both boards is weighted according to a state's monetary contribution to the IMF, which gives a larger voice to the wealthier states. Members of the executive board cast the vote of the state or states they are appointed to represent.

The main purposes of the IMF, as set forth in its Articles of Agreement, include the following:

1. To promote *international monetary cooperation.*
2. To facilitate the *expansion of international trade.*
3. To promote *exchange stability.*
4. To assist in the establishment of a *multilateral system of payments.*

5. To give *confidence* to members by making its resources available.
6. To *shorten the duration* and *lessen the degree of disequilibrium* in members' balances of payments.

The architects of the Bretton Woods system intended that national currencies should be freely convertible with one another, avoiding the exchange control systems that emerged during the Great Depression and World War II. They also planned to avoid the wildly fluctuating exchange rates of the 1920s and 1930s by requiring each member country to establish and maintain a fixed value for its currency, tied directly or indirectly to the value of gold. The IMF would then help countries maintain their currency values by lending funds to cover temporary balance-of-payments deficits resulting from periods of weak demand for a state's currency. If long periods of either strong or weak demand created a "fundamental disequilibrium" in a state's payments position, that country could, with the IMF's permission, alter its exchange rate to reflect the real value of its currency on international markets. The IMF was not intended to be the principal source of lending to finance international trade but rather to supplement normal commercial sources.

This system reflected the founders' concern that the world not slip back into the financial anarchy of the 1930s or retain strangling wartime controls. As in the proposals for a world trade system, the IMF's originators foresaw a new, orderly world of international finance based on a common code to guide the actions of member states and governed by an international institution that could determine exchange and payments policies. Since 1945 the IMF has contributed to greater financial order, but not without major crises to the system and severe pain to individual countries. Moreover, in the 1970s the IMF was forced to abandon the principle of fixed exchange rates tied to gold, as originally provided in the IMF articles, in favor of floating rates set by market forces.

As the IMF operates today, it administers a code of conduct governing exchange rate policies and restrictions on payments, primarily in the interest of promoting freer exchange of currencies. It is also a forum for government consultation on major monetary questions. Beyond this it seeks to provide exchange stability by two means: influencing currency values and permitting members to draw foreign exchange from the IMF to tide them over periods of serious financial hardship.

The concept underlying the use of the IMF as a pooling arrangement is fairly simple. All members contribute to a common bank of monetary reserves on which they can draw to overcome short-term disequilibriums in their balances of payments. The contributions are based on a quota system set according to a state's national income, gold reserves, and other factors related to ability to contribute. Initially, each member is required to contribute 25 percent of its quota in hard currency (presently, the U.S. dollar, British pound, French franc, German mark, or Japanese yen)—the so-called "credit tranche"—but the remainder can be in its own currency. (Before the mid-1970s, a member had to contribute 25 percent of its initial quota in gold rather than hard currencies, and this was known as the "gold tranche.") Each member has a right to purchase foreign exchange from the IMF in amounts equal to the value of its credit tranche, but the maximum may run much higher by agreement with the IMF. Other lending arrangements supplement the quota system, most designed to meet needs of developing countries. When a state withdraws an amount from the IMF for an emergency, it actually purchases the foreign exchange with its own domestic currency; when it repays the amount, it returns foreign exchange to the IMF for its own currency. In this way, the reserve pool as a revolving fund remains fairly constant in the total value of its holdings, but the amounts of different currencies fluctuate, depending on the demand for them.

The objective underlying the currency pool is to maintain fairly stable exchange values for members' currencies. When a member suffers a short-term deficit in its balance of payments which cannot be financed through commercial banks, purchases of foreign exchange from the IMF are ordinarily expected to carry it through the crisis. The IMF usually attaches conditions to large borrowings, designed to help remedy the problems that produced the large deficit. Such conditions may include commitments by the borrowing state to restrict domestic credit, allow more realistic exchange rates and price levels, balance its budget, and cut subsidies to state enterprises and inefficient sectors of its economy. Borrowers have frequently criticized IMF "conditionality," as it is called, because the financial discipline often has temporarily harsh effects on the domestic economy.

## THE MONETARY AND DEBT CRISES

Over the years the International Monetary Fund has coped with numerous minor problems but has faced three major crises. One of these, involving mainly the Western industrialized and major trading nations, came to a climax in the early 1970s. The second, involving Third World debtor countries, occurred during the 1980s and still persists to some extent. The third struck unexpectedly in 1997 when heretofore successful Asian Rim nations, especially, South Korea, Indonesia, Malaysia, and Thailand confronted financial crises that caused the value of their currencies to plummet, and their economic machinery to virtually shut down. An examination of these three crises will provide the reader with a better understanding of the problems of the international monetary system and the role of the IMF in managing them.

### The Monetary Crisis

The first crisis grew out of the post–World War II international monetary system's dependence on one national currency—the U.S. dollar. As many nations recovered from the economic trauma of the war period, they expanded their export trade and built up huge dollar balances. These balances served as claims against the U.S. gold hoard, which at that time amounted to more than two-thirds of the world's available gold. The gold-dollar exchange system, constructed on the assumption that U.S. dollars were as good as gold because they could be exchanged at the fixed rate of $35 for one fine ounce of gold, began to waver as dollars were rapidly converted into gold.

By 1970 the drain of U.S. dollars and gold into the global economy had become a virtual gusher. All attempts to stanch the outflow of dollars and stabilize the gold-dollar exchange system were of no avail. A more flexible system was needed to supplement the dollar as an international currency supporting the expansion of world trade and providing ready reserves to protect national currencies. In 1969 the International Monetary Fund began to issue special drawing rights (SDRs) to augment the gold and the dollars and other key currencies that were being used as international reserves, with an initial issue of $3 billion. Since SDRs are a form of fiat money, created as bookkeeping entries in the IMF accounting system, they have been called "paper gold." Their value is related to the value of a weighted basket of the currencies of the five leading export nations. SDRs continue to be used today, and periodically the IMF issues additional amounts. Although SDRs are issued to IMF members on the basis of their contributions to the capitalization of the IMF (and hence their voting power), for many years Third World countries have attempted to obtain a larger share, especially for use as developmental capital. This attempt has been resisted by the West, which regards issuance of SDRs as a means for promoting monetary stability rather than for subsidizing economic development.

By 1971 hundreds of billions of U.S. dollars in the world constituted claims against a dwindling supply of U.S. gold and the existing international monetary system was in a state of full crisis. This situation forced the Nixon administration to abandon the official fixed rate of exchange between gold and the dollar. That same year, in a meeting at the Smithsonian Institution in Washington, the ministers of the Group of Ten (a caucusing group composed of the ten leading contributors to the IMF) promulgated the "Smithsonian Agreement," which resulted in a 10 percent devaluation of the U.S. dollar and a realignment of exchange rates. In 1973, after another dollar devaluation, the national currencies of the developed states were permitted to "float" through the workings of a flexible exchange rate system, with occasional individual and collective government interventions in the free exchange market to stabilize currency values. The first crisis was thus overcome by permitting the market mechanism to determine national currency exchange values.

### The Debt Crisis

The second major IMF crisis had its roots in the 1960s and early 1970s, as Third World countries began to borrow more and more foreign capital to fuel the engine of economic growth. With the world oil crisis of the 1970s and the global recession of the early 1980s, what began as a slow, incremental increase in debt became a virtual avalanche. The existence of a full-fledged crisis became apparent in 1982 when Mexico, without prior warning, announced to the industrialized creditor nations and to the world's private banking system that it was unable to make interest payments on its $80 billion debt. Other Third World nations quickly followed with similar admissions of their inability to pay. The debt crisis soon came to be recognized as a threat not only to Third World development but also to economic well being (including bank solvency) in the industrialized countries.

As the crisis mounted and the prospect of a general default in payments increased, the IMF emerged as the lender "of last resort." IMF loans helped provide the means for Third World states to meet payments on their huge debts, but in return the IMF required states to undertake economic reforms that in the short run tended to reduce living standards. The conditions and their sometimes harsh effects were resisted and resented by many of the debtor countries.

In 1985, at a joint meeting of the IMF and the World Bank, U.S. Treasury Secretary James A. Baker III proposed a new global approach to the problem. The Baker Plan, as it was known, called for three kinds of international action: (1) concerted new lending by commercial banks; (2) a program of public loans, principally by international institutions; and (3) pursuit of domestic economic adjustment policies by the debtor countries. The adjustment measures were to include greater fiscal discipline (curbing inflation and government spending), moving government-controlled businesses to the private sector, opening domestic markets to foreign investment, and a general shift toward market-oriented economic policies. Results of the Baker Plan were disappointing because commercial banks were unwilling to make substantial new loans to the highly indebted countries, and many of these countries also lagged in their adjustment efforts.

A problem of such magnitude could not be ignored, and a subsequent U.S. proposal, the "Brady Initiative" (after U.S. Treasury Secretary Nicholas Brady), proved more workable. The 1989 Brady Initiative included measures aimed at debt reduction, rather than merely refinancing old debt, and contemplated a role for all the major lending agencies—international financial institutions, commercial banks, and creditor governments. The IMF and the World Bank were to be key players in the plan by lending new money to debtor countries to finance debt reduction programs. With this new money, the debt reduction was to be accomplished by three principal methods: (1) debt buybacks, by which a debtor country would purchase its own debt at a discount from face value; (2) exchange of old debt, at a discount, for new debt secured by designated assets; and (3) exchange of old debt for new debt (bonds) at face value but at a reduced interest rate. Such exchanges and buybacks were assumed to be possible because the debt was already being sold on international financial markets at a heavy discount. In addition, commercial banks were to be encouraged to provide new lending and accelerated write-offs of portions of existing debt. Creditor governments were also to help by rescheduling, restructuring, and in some cases reducing existing debt and by making new loans to countries with sound reform programs. In all cases, programs of debt reduction were to be conditional on the adoption of appropriate economic reform policies by the debtor country. While implementation of the Brady Initiative did not solve all

Third World debt problems, it provided a reasonable mechanism for debt relief. As a result of its operation, a number of debtor countries—including Mexico—substantially reduced their external debt, and by the early 1990s the world debt problem as a whole began to appear manageable.

*The Pacific Rim Crisis*

The International Monetary Fund acknowledged in a report released in March 1998 that it had failed to anticipate the intensity of the Asian financial crisis that impacted the world economy in the fall of 1997. The crisis shook the economic foundations of South Korea, Thailand, Malaysia, and Indonesia, and revealed serious problems in Japan's economic structure and performance. The IMF staff explained to its 182 member countries that it had not been adequately prepared in analyzing government budgets and in ferreting out inflationary spending, important factors in dealing with the Latin American debt crisis of the 1980s. The IMF cited weak banking systems and the dangers arising from "hot money" across national borders for the Asian crisis. (A similar situation had also contributed to the Mexico crisis of 1995.) The problem was not one of productivity or competition as much as it was caused by unregulated and overly aggressive financial sectors. Unlike some earlier matters that involved the largely less developed states, the Pacific Rim countries were judged success stories and the IMF was cognizant of the tension between itself as a confidential adviser to its members, and as an international watchdog that needs to deal more aggressively with states engaged in financial excesses. The Asian crisis broke new ground because of the depth of the problems and its contagion impact on the world economy. And given the fact that the problem was seen as stretching into the next century, the IMF only had the most preliminary lessons to draw from the experience.

This time the focus of attention was the region of east and southeast Asia, and the affected states were the so-called "Asian Tigers," which were often cited as growth performers. For decades, the envy of the rest of the world, the question arising in 1998—the year of the Tiger—was whether the Asian "miracle" had come to an end or whether these countries could again grow at rates achieved in previous years. Through the 1980s and into the 1990s the high growth performers of east and southeast Asia represented economies expanding between 6 and 8 percent per annum. Social indicators as measured by life expectancy, declines in poverty, and major improvements in education and health standards, all revealed remarkable successes, far above other developing countries. But by far, economic growth was attributed to a variety of policies that included macroeconomic stabilization, strong savings and investment performance, the openness of the economies, and human capital formation. Considering that the "Asian formula" for success was operationalized by institutional structures that were generally held to be sound and professional,—what went wrong? Why was a prolonged period of strong economic performance suddenly, and almost unexpectedly, interrupted?

Economists identified a reversal of capital flows as the immediate reason for the crisis that initially hit Thailand, and then rapidly in turn, Indonesia, Malaysia, and South Korea, four countries whose economic programs had been endorsed by the IMF. All the countries had attracted massive inflows of foreign capital in the years immediately following the end of the Cold War, most of these flows being short-term, they were in part prompted by weak economic growth in Europe and Japan, and made possible by international investors seeking to diversify their activities. These short-term investments could not be adequately managed by the existing domestic financial institutions. Banks invested in property and equity, which caused an inflationary spiral. In Indonesia, it was the private enterprises that became the principal debtors of short-term external debt. In South Korea, it was the banks and their foreign subsidiaries that were the main debtors. And once the solvency of the borrowers was questioned, investors began withdrawing their short-term financing, forcing exchange rates to drop precipitously, and stock values and property prices quickly followed. Problems could not be contained within the national framework and before long they had become regional, and then finally global.

To stop the hemorrhaging, short-term flows were pegged to the exchange rate of the U.S. dollar, but export growth weakened in Indonesia and Thailand, and current account deficits rose. Subsequently, under the pressure of exchange rates, the peg was abandoned and the exchange rate was allowed to float. Although fiscal policy was not the root of the crisis, questions arose concerning accountability of use of public resources. The authorities had failed to act to earlier signs of an overheated economy. In point of fact the crisis was judged a financial sector crisis. The IMF therefore demanded reforms in return for its assistance. IMF noted the need to lift trade restrictions such as trade monopolies. It called for an end to capital controls so that foreign banks could determine the underlying commercial risks in lending. It insisted on transparency in all financial transactions, and the termination of intimacies between government, banks, and corporations that had caused inappropriate investment decisions. Finally, the IMF pointed to poor governance practices that permitted financial institutions and corporations to wallow in license and corruption.

There being no single cure, the IMF aknowledged the necessity of treating each affected nation separately. Currency depreciation had impacted all the countries in the crisis area, and in Indonesia, the hardest hit, depreciation was reported to be between 75 and 80 percent. Thus the IMF called for the closing of all insolvent financial institutions, while the weak ones were to be restructured and recapitalized, with the necessary changes in management. Open economies and the termination of trade monopolies were a given. Moreover, domestic trade in all agricultural products had to be deregulated and restrictive marketing arrangements abolished. In large measure, the affected nations were called upon to liberalize their policies to allow for greater foreigner access, a difficult pill to swallow for each of the nations involved.

The IMF was itself criticized for appearing to bail out lenders who were themselves at fault and who should suffer the consequences of their actions. In reply to its critics the IMF insisted the situation could only worsen, deepen, and spread if nothing were done to arrest the problem. Moreover, so long as the governments concerned were prepared to implement what was acknowledged to be a painful process of reforms, there was no reason to deny support. In this matter there was complete concurrence from the World Bank as well as the Asian Development Bank and bilateral creditors. It was noted, however, that the effort to correct a serious financial crisis in no way prevented foreign investors from incurring losses, nor was this institutional assistance a substitute for continuous private lending.

Indonesia, the worst affected by the crisis, was in line to receive a $43 billion bailout, in installments, so long as the country was in compliance with IMF demands. But Indonesia proved to be the most reluctant of the assisted countries to accept the terms of the IMF. Administered by a government that had been in power since the mid-1960s, the Suharto regime confronted challenges to its rule, and in spite of a re-election process that gave the septugenarian still another term in April 1998, political and social unrest, prompted by economic dislocation, produced the crisis that finally swept the dictator from power in May 1998.

Still another dimension of the IMF equation in confronting the Asian financial crisis was the role played by the U.S. Congress, which stubbornly refused to replenish IMF coffers that had been seriously depleted by the granting of emergency loans. Called upon by President Clinton to approve the transfer of $18 billion to the IMF, the Republican-controlled Congress hesitated in granting the president's wishes, and questioned the operational effectiveness of the IMF before finally releasing the needed funds.

## CRISIS AND MORE CRISIS

The sudden shift to open, market economies, in addition to the economic crash in Pacific/Asia in 1997–98, predictably, had a negative affect on the development of stable societies in several global regions. Russia's experiment with the capitalist system was in trouble from the outset, but by the spring of 1997 it was apparent the state confronted an enormous budget crisis, making it almost impossible for the government to perform its functions. Despite strong efforts by the G-7 and international financial institutions, Russia's economic fundamentals were so weak that in August 1998 the ruble was effectively devalued and the government announced it would default on its debt. Burdened with a Gorbachev debt of enormous proportions, the reformer governments were never able to stabilize fiscal policy. Russian "robber barons" took advantage of the chaos to secret capital outside the country, a sum estimated in 1999 to be four times the amount needed to finance Russia's external debt, and equal to one-quarter export earnings. Ironically, it was the International Monetary Fund's support for the convertibility of the ruble (making Russia attractive to foreign investors) that facilitated the export of capital—the very opposite consequence of what was intended. The "black hole" between expenditures and revenues resulted in a budget deficit that further undermined the credibility of the government. The financial disorder meant payrolls could not be met and both civilian and military employees went unpaid. Contractors providing goods and services did not receive their due and ceased their operations. And to add to the dilemma, the inability to pay payroll taxes needed to support off-budget social welfare projects meant pension funds, disability payments, health and other benefits could not be provided.

The Asian economic crisis also had strong negative affects on Russia as prices on its key exports of oil and other primary commodities fell drastically. Western investors revisited their investments in emerging markets such as Russia and by September 1998, the Moscow stock exchange had lost 80 percent of its value, and more than one-half of listed companies suspended operations. Over-reliance on short-term, high-interest treasury paper to finance the deficit no longer worked, and the pyramid of reforms collapsed and all but eliminated the reformers. A successor government, though deemed to be more conservative, had little leverage in dealing with the immediate problem, nor could it stem the trend toward decentralization of power. With only about ten provinces net contributors to the central budget, the more affluent regions were inclined to retain revenues owed the central government. On the other side of this picture, at least half of Russia's provinces were insolvent and provincial governors sought desperately to shift whatever revenues they had to cover their most urgent local needs.

With economic fundamentals deteriorating, the currency devalued, and little creditworthiness on internal or foreign markets, the central government in 1999 was forced to deal piecemeal with immediate problems. It also blamed the economic debacle on the young reformers on the one side, and the G-7 on the other. Russia, however, could not manage without significant infusions of aid from external sources. If such assistance was not forthcoming, it was argued, the G-7 would be responsible for the ensuing political turmoil. Only the G-7, it was noted, could prevent the exacerbation of the socio-economic situation and stem the tide of inflation that was forecast to rise 300 percent.

Acknowledging they could not turn their back on Russia's plight, the Paris and London Clubs responsible for assisting the country's market economy rescheduled the Russian debt and agreed to reduce their demands on its virtually bankrupt treasury. More important, the United States and the European Union recognized their continuing responsibility in seeing to it that the country's needy received adequate nutrition, that Russia's health sector not be allowed to further unravel, that the educating and training of new Russian elites, especially in business management, be expanded, and that the promotion of civil society through the encouragement provided non-governmental organizations not be neglected.

Thus the Asian economic crisis impacted the Russian scene, and together the twin crises washed up on the shores of the Americas, destabilizing South America's largest nation, Brazil. Like Russia, the IMF was called upon to assist the Brazilian government and a financial package estimated to be between $30 and $40 billion was cobbled together on short notice in October–November

1998. Bolstered by this support, Brazil's business and governmental leaders declared the days of wild overspending and speculation were over, but declaratory statements proved empty when in January 1999 the government revealed attempts to support Brazilian currency values had failed. Again the international financial community was called into play, and again the response was that Brazil must not be allowed to collapse. Unlike Russia, Brazil was a pivotal country in Latin America, and although critics lamented "throwing good money after bad," the first concern was stemming the economic contagion that had spread from Asia, to Russia, to Brazil and Latin America. Not only economic development was threatened, the political stability needed to assure a successful transition to democracy and a more peaceful global condition hung in the balance.

## CONCLUSION

Within the broad framework of the UN system, states have joined together to build institutional structures for economic cooperation. Some structures are integrated with central UN decision machinery represented by the General Assembly, while others are located elsewhere in the system. Despite the emphasis on decentralization, all of the operational units have the primary goal of avoiding a return to narrow and bitter economic nationalism.

The General Agreement on Tariffs and Trade (GATT) illustrates the progress achieved during the Cold War era in building a sturdy international trade and financial system. Starting as a small, limited-membership organization that was dubbed "the rich man's club," GATT approached universalism before it yielded to the WTO. The UN Conference on Trade and Development (UNCTAD) supplemented the work of GATT by providing a forum that was focused on the needs of the developing countries. UNCTAD continues to function within the framework of the World Trade Organization.

In the related field of monetary policy, the International Monetary Fund (IMF) has made an important contribution to exchange rate stability and the financing of international payments' deficits. It has played a central role in dealing with debt crises and has used its resources to encourage "sound" economic policies in member states. Serious problems remain, in individual countries as well as in the global system, but multilateral institutions provide continuing encouragement and assistance for cooperative efforts to deal with them.

Despite past achievements in institution building, the challenge to promote economic well being through international action persists. With two-thirds of the world's peoples living in poverty, international cooperation as heretofore practiced obviously has its limits. Most of these people will share the benefits of global economic cooperation only as their countries progress toward the goal of development and modernization. Here another major structure within the UN system—the World Bank Group—is of central importance. In the next chapter we will turn our attention to the subject of economic development and UN efforts to promote it.

# NOTES

1. The quotation is from David P. Forsythe's "Introduction" to Forsythe, ed., *The United Nations in the World Political Economy* (New York: St. Martin's Press, 1989), p. 1. *Political economy* is an umbrella term for studies that take account of economic factors in politics. In a more specialized sense, political economy is identified with the application of economic theories and methods, particularly theories of rational choice, to political subjects. See, e.g., Roland Vaubel and Thomas D. Willett, *The Political Economy of International Organizations: A Public Choice Approach* (Boulder, CO: Westview Press, 1991).
2. For a discussion of GATT operations see John Starrel, "Trade—To Free or Not to Free, GATT Is the Question," *Europe,* no. 234 (November–December 1982), pp. 4–5. See also John Tessitore and Susan Woolfson, "Trade and the Trading System," *A Global Agenda—Issues before the 46th General Assembly,* New York: University Press of America, 1991, pp. 110–25.
3. For an assessment of the role of the Group of 77, see Marc Williams, *Third World Cooperation: The Group of 77 in UNCTAD* (New York: St. Martin's Press, 1991).
4. Sidney Dell, *Trade Blocs and Common Markets* (New York: Alfred A. Knopf, 1963), pp. 360–61.

# SELECTED READINGS

*Agenda 2000: For a Stronger and Wider Union.* Brussels: European Commission, 1997.

Balassa, Bela. *Change and Challenge in the World Economy.* New York: St. Martin's Press, 1985.

Bergsten, Fred C., and Randall C. Henning. *Global Economic Leadership and the Group of Seven.* Washington, D.C.: Institute for International Economics, 1996.

Burtless, Gary, et al. *Globaphobia: Confronting Fears about Open Trade.* Washington, D.C.: Brookings, 1998.

Chilcote, Ronald H., ed. *Dependency and Marxism—Toward a Resolution of the Debate.* Boulder, CO: Westview Press, 1982.

Eichengreen, Barry. *Globalizing Capital: A History of the International Monetary System.* Princeton: Princeton University Press, 1996.

Ferguson, Tyrone. *The Third World and Decision Making in the International Monetary Fund: The Quest for Full and Effective Participation.* London: Pinter Publishers, 1988.

Forsythe, David P., ed. *The United Nations in the World Political Economy.* New York: St. Martin's Press, 1989.

Frankel, Jeffrey A. *Regional Trading Blocs in the World Trading System.* Washington, D.C.: Institute for International Economics, 1997.

Fry, Maxwell, J. *Money, Interest, and Banking in Economic Development,* 2nd ed. Baltimore: The Johns Hopkins University Press, 1994.

Gilpin, Robert. *The Political Economy of International Relations.* Princeton: Princeton University Press, 1987.

Goldstein, Morris. *The Asian Financial Crisis*. Washington, D.C.: Institute for International Economics, 1998.

Hook, Stephen, W. *Foreign Aid Toward the Millennium*. Boulder: Lynne Rienner, 1996.

Howell, Thomas R., et al., eds. *Conflict Among Nations: Trade Policies in the 1990s*. Boulder, CO: Westview Press, 1992.

Jackson, John H. *The World Trading System*. Cambridge, MA: The MIT Press, 1989.

Jacobson, Harold K. *Networks of Interdependence: International Organizations and the Global Political System*. 2nd ed. New York: Alfred A. Knopf, 1984.

Keohane, Robert O., and Stanley Hoffman, eds. *The New European Community: Decisionmaking and Institutional Change*. Boulder, CO: Westview Press, 1992.

Kihl, Young Whan, and James M. Lutz. *World Trade Issues: Regime, Structure, and Policy*. New York: Praeger, 1985.

Nugent, Neill. *The Government and Politics of the European Community*. 2nd ed. Durham, NC: Duke University Press, 1991.

O'Cleireacain, Seamus. *Third World Debt and International Public Policy*. New York: Praeger, 1990.

Rodrik, Dani. *Has Globalization Gone Too Far?* Washington, D.C.: Institute for International Economics, 1997.

Sbragia, Alberto M., ed. *Euro-Politics: Institutions and Policymaking in the "New" European Community*. Washington, D.C.: The Brookings Institution, 1992.

Schott, Jeffrey J., ed. *The World Trading System: Challenges Ahead*. Washington, D.C.: Institute for International Economics, 1996.

Spero, Joan Edelman. *The Politics of International Economic Relations*. 4th ed. New York: St. Martin's Press, 1990.

Tehranian, Majid. *Global Communication and World Politics: Domination, Development, and Discourse*. Boulder, CO: Rienner, 1999.

Urwin, Derek W. *The Community of Europe: A History of European Integration since 1945*. London: Longman, 1991.

Vaubel, Roland, and Thomas D. Willett. *The Political Economy of International Organizations: A Public Choice Approach*. Boulder, CO: Westview Press, 1991.

Williams, Marc. *Third World Cooperation: The Group of 77 in UNCTAD*. New York: St. Martin's Press, 1991.

# 11

## Promoting Economic Development

Promoting economic development may prove to be the decisive test of functional cooperation. To meet this global challenge, the United Nations, regional international organizations, and individual governments have launched programs aimed at helping the developing or less developed countries (LDCs) to help themselves. In no other field has the United Nations provided programs of such variety and scope. These approaches combine technical assistance and capital loans and grants with a broad range of educational, health, welfare, and internal improvement programs to build a base from which each society may hope to achieve sustainable economic development.

Despite these efforts, economic growth in most developing countries has been slow and has seldom measured up to expectations. This disparity between expectations and realities has in turn produced a dangerous "frustration gap." Next to the problem of avoiding bloody conflict, closing this gap is the major challenge facing the world today.

### PROBLEMS OF DEVELOPMENT

The less developed world covers vast areas of the planet stretching eastward from Latin America through Africa and the Middle East to South and Southeast Asia and the islands of the Pacific littoral. Moreover, many of the new independent republics emerging from the breakup of the Soviet Union, as well as some East European and Balkan states, also fit this description. In meeting the problems of development, states are in some respects like individuals. No two individuals are exactly alike, but individuals living in poverty have many common characteristics and environmental problems that help explain their plight. Ending poverty for individuals depends not only on improving their economic lot but also on changing their thinking, their attitude, their environment—in effect, their whole way of life.

In the years following World War II, improving living standards in the industrialized societies came to be accepted as a natural human condition. This fostered a belief that there was essentially no limit to the ability of energetic human beings to improve their lives. Synonyms for development have included "progress," "modernization," "industrialization," "economic growth," and "societal evolution." Whatever it is called, this question invariably arises: Why cannot the poor nations follow the same route to prosperity as the rich nations? The answer, found throughout this chapter, is: They can, but . . . . It is to the "can" and "but" that we turn our attention.

Leaders of developing countries are generally committed to making the transition to the world reflected in Western material values. What they really want, however, is the kind of production of wealth that the West enjoys, but not necessarily the Western values essential to that goal, such as the work ethic, competitiveness, the elimination of class status, and the freedom that goes along with democracy and capitalism. Yet their societies are slowly giving way to modern demands. Whether such changes will solve their problems and enrich their lives is a moot question; they have caught a vision of plenty through the windows of the Western world, and they want to have a share in it.

After a century of hot and cold wars, new problems have complicated the process of helping Third World countries with their economic development. The "Second World," once thoroughly communist, has now embraced the principles of representative democracy and market capitalism and is attempting to put them into practice. In the process these states are seeking huge amounts of foreign aid from the West. The new potential aid recipients include not only the countries of Eastern Europe but also the former Soviet republics that are now independent states. These states have caught "development fever" and have become direct competitors with the Third World for the economic aid provided by the First World countries and the United Nations.

## A PROFILE OF A LESS DEVELOPED COUNTRY (LDC)

An understanding of the problem of economic development may be promoted by examining a profile of the features that characterize most developing states. Such a picture of a typical developing state's base or starting point will highlight what needs to be done for economic development and will point up the difficulties of doing it. A note of caution is in order, however, since great differences in size, population, resources, power supplies, native skills, and other natural and human variables exist in developing states as diverse as Brazil and Sierra Leone, Nigeria and Afghanistan. Moreover, the profile does not apply to the oil-rich states of the Third World or to the developing states that have made great progress in recent years, such as South Korea, Taiwan, and Singapore.

*First,* and most basic, our profile state is *poor.* Millions of people in the Third World today live in conditions that can be described as absolute poverty, as distinguished from general income inequality. Although all Third World states are "less developed" than states in the First World, the poorest states are often referred to as the "least developed" or the Fourth World.[1] Both the "less" and the "least" developed countries are referred to as LDCs. The World Bank estimates that more than a billion people in the developing world lived in poverty, with incomes of less than $370 a year.

Poverty is a human tragedy for the hundreds of millions struggling to survive it; it is also an economic barrier to the process of development. Economic development is largely a function of turning savings into growth, and people living in grinding poverty have little capacity to save and invest. In addition, developed states are unlikely to invest in societies where mass consumer demand is nonexistent. The problem is circular: Poverty leads to little or no savings, with a resulting low level of investment, which ensures the continuance of poverty. The central challenge of economic development in the poorer countries is finding a way to break this vicious circle.[2]

*Second,* the profile state is located to the *south* of most of the developed countries and has a *tropical* climate. More precisely, the poorest of the developing countries are with few exceptions located south of thirty degrees north latitude, which runs along the southern boundary of the United States and along the northern reaches of the African continent. Tropical jungles, vast mountain ranges, arid deserts, and wild bush country make up great portions of the land masses of these countries, forcing the people to carry on a daily struggle with nature to eke out a bare existence. High temperatures and humidity and soils leached by tropical rains make the job of wresting a living a precarious one. The profile state lacks the energy sources of coal and oil, although potential hydroelectric power sources exist in the form of great tropical rivers that wind through the mountains and jungles. In some Third World countries, tropical forests are being destroyed because wood is the only available energy supply for cooking and heating. Third World countries also suffer economically because of the high shipping costs that result from the great distances separating most of them from the industrial countries, which increase the prices of both their exports and their imports.

*Third,* the profile state is faced with *population growth* that often outpaces gains in productivity. The first benefits of modernization to reach many of the developing nations were drugs and medicines to save lives, chemicals to control mosquitoes and other disease carriers, and water-purifying agents. With better public health and sanitation, death rates plunged while traditionally high birth rates, at least initially, were not much affected. The result was a population explosion that threatened to nullify the economic benefits of modernization in those countries for all but the rich.

Many developing countries have now adopted programs to slow population growth and, with assistance from the United Nations Population Fund (UNFPA), have achieved modest success. Although birth rates are still extremely high in many countries, the 1991 edition of *The State of World Population* reported that birth rates in 1990, for the first time in human history, had declined in every region of the world.[3] According to the United Nations Population Fund (UNFPA), an unprecedented 51 percent of couples in developing countries were using contraception, an increase from 10 percent during the 1960s and 45 percent in the 1980s. Population control programs undoubtedly contributed to this result. In some countries it also reflected the decline in fertility that normally accompanies the stage of development when incomes begin to rise, children are less an economic asset, and many children are no longer necessary to ensure that some survive to care for parents in their old age. On a more somber note, population growth has also been slowed by the increased incidence of diseases such as AIDS and tuberculosis which in some Third World countries are at epidemic levels. In spite of all the efforts and conditions that contributed to decreases in population growth, by 1997, the world population had reached 5.9 billion. (It had stood at less than 2.5 billion when the United Nations was organized in 1945.) China accounted for more than one-fifth of the total with more than 1.2 billion, while India was listed at 968 million and was expected to reach 1 billion by the year 2000, and possibly surpass China in the year 2025. Asia and Africa represented more than 72 percent of the total world population in 1997, and earlier forecasts that total population would attain if not exceed 6.3 billion by the year 2000 retained their validity. Concerned with a variety of population issues, UN conferences on population were held in Rome in 1954, Belgrade in 1964, Bucharest in 1974, Mexico City in 1984, and Cairo in 1994.

*Fourth,* the profile state often lacks the ability to support itself because of the low productivity of *primitive agriculture.* Peasant families painfully tilling their small plots with ancient farming technology or working on large haciendas or plantations for absentee landlords are living symbols of the plight of agriculture in such countries. Much of the profile state's farming is geared to a subsistence level, with little or no effort or capability to develop a cash crop that could earn foreign exchange. Farming is intensive, with peasants crowded onto the arable land in such numbers that the soil's fertility is low. Crop diseases, insects, wild animals and rodents, and unpredictable natural disasters in the form of droughts, floods, and hurricanes can ruin the efforts of months of toil. Remedies have been attempted through land reform and technical assistance, but reform is difficult. Old ways die hard, and resources for changing them are scarce. The continuing flight of people from rural areas to teeming city slums testifies that the problems of low agricultural productivity persist.

*Fifth,* the profile state has a *colonial background* that has helped determine the direction of modernization and continues to affect the thought and action of its people. In many cases the rudimentary physical framework for development was laid out by the colonial power in the nineteenth century and the first half of the twentieth century. Surpassing the influence of that framework, however, is the lasting imprint that colonialism left on the attitudes and emotions of the people. The humiliation and sense of frustration fostered by foreign rule left scars of anti-Westernism that remain today. In such states internal disunity often still exists as a holdover of a carefully cultivated colonial policy of "divide and rule" or as a result of boundary lines drawn by imperial design that sundered established communities or tribes and mixed traditional enemies within the same political unit. In societies lacking most of the internal impulses and capabilities necessary for modernization, the unity produced by the effort to end foreign rule produced a ferment for change that independence and UN programs have encouraged. Self-determination demands combined with retreating colonialism shaped the twentieth century character of the United Nations. But the newly independent states that proudly assumed their roles in the world organization demonstrated particular opposition to domestic movements that used the same logic and demands in seeking their independence from the core entity. Civil wars plagued the new states, and it needs reminding that in 1971 Bangladesh was the first among the post–World War II countries to achieve independence as a consequence of a successful civil war. That war not only caused the dismemberment of a Pakistan state that was barely twenty-five years old, it also reaffirmed Pakistani fears that India, which contributed to the dismemberment, was determined to eliminate the consequences of the 1947 partition of what had been the British Indian empire.

*Sixth,* the profile state is built on the social fabric of a *traditional society.* Custom and tradition provide the social cement, and religion and conservative values provide the guidelines for human action. Small elite groups dominate the society and often oppose virtually all change because change would mean a loss of their status. Rigid class structures immobilize even the able and ambitious individual. Objective conditions of social stagnation are reinforced by group attitudes, requiring a revolution of perspectives as a prelude to modernity. No society completely abandons its traditional culture; transitional societies in a state of vigorous change reshape the old values, resulting in a social, political, and economic restlessness and rootlessness. Interaction between the old and the new may yield turmoil, revolution, or civil war as rival groups offer the people new ideologies imported from foreign sources, each seeking to capture the modernization process and to direct it toward ideologically determined goals.

*Seventh,* the world profile state is characterized by high illiteracy. UN-ESCO's *Compendium of Statistics on Illiteracy: 1995 Edition,* released in 1997 by the Asia/Pacific Cultural Centre for UNESCO, identified nine nations with the highest number of illiterates. They were Bangladesh, Brazil, China, Egypt, India, Indonesia, Mexico, Nigeria, and Pakistan. Together these nine countries contained almost 642 million of the world's more than 1 billion people who were unable to read. Furthermore, educational needs to achieve modernization go beyond basic literacy to include technical, secondary, and university training. A university-trained elite exists in most of the underdeveloped countries, but it is extremely small in number and it consists for the most part of specialists in law, the humanities, and the social sciences. This elite provided the leadership in the march to independence, but a new elite of entrepreneurs, managers, scientists, engineers, and technicians is needed to exploit resources and organize the productive machinery.

*Eighth,* in its trade relations with the rest of the world, the profile state rests on a *weak economic base.* The export trade of most developing countries is based on the production or extraction of one or a few primary commodities.

Living standards beyond the subsistence level provided by local agriculture depend on the export market for these commodities. Foreign exchange earnings needed for buying capital goods from the advanced countries are limited by adverse world market conditions. These include (1) an oversupply of most primary commodities; (2) competition from advanced states with greater productive efficiency; (3) fluctuating prices resulting from speculation among buyers, changes in supply, and other conditions beyond the control of the developing states; (4) the introduction of synthetics and substitutes to replace natural commodities; (5) high shipping costs in getting commodities to distant markets; and (6) in some cases, deteriorating terms of trade resulting in lower prices for primary commodity exports and higher prices for imports of manufactured consumer and capital goods. A recognition that the world economy, as reflected in the foregoing, is stacked against their interests led the LDCs in the 1970s to demand fundamental changes through the creation of a New International Economic Order (NIEO).

*Ninth,* the profile state suffers from *political instability.* Most developing states are, or in the recent past have been, characterized by one-party, authoritarian regimes. The rulers have been of various types—royal autocrat, military strongman, religious figure, nationalist or communist ideologue (or both), among others. In some of the new nations, early attempts to establish democratic systems failed when the promised bounty of independence could not be delivered, and an authoritarian regime was re-instituted. Opposition groups and parties have commonly been nonexistent, suppressed, or present in a highly innocuous form to provide the shadow but not the substance of a democratic system. In some states political activity has been largely confined to the capital city as an arena for infighting among the political elite jockeying for positions of strength or attempting a coup. Throughout much of the Third World, changes of government through free elections have been rare occurrences. Even in this area there has been progress in recent years, epitomized by UN-supervised free elections in Nicaragua, Namibia, and elsewhere. Nevertheless, building political stability remains one of the most difficult and frustrating problems facing the developing states.

*Tenth,* the people of the profile state are disproportionately subjected to epidemic and endemic diseases and other *health* problems. At least in part through the efforts of the World Health Organization, Third World peoples experienced improving health conditions in the decades of the 1950s, 1960s, and 1970s. With the increased use of vaccination and antibiotic drugs, developing countries were better able to combat communicable diseases than the richest nations had been during the 1920s and 1930s. Also, the population explosion produced societies of predominantly young people who enjoyed resistance in many diseases.

In the 1980s, however, the picture slowly but ominously changed. Drought, especially in Africa, spawned famine, which left in its wake reduced resistance to disease. In Africa also, a new disease that was immune to antibiotics emerged.

Western societies, also subjected to this disease on a growing scale, identified it in their laboratories and gave it a name: Acquired Immunodeficiency Syndrome (AIDS). For this new plague there is as yet no preventative vaccine or cure. Treatment is extremely expensive and only delays the onslaught of the deadly infection. The WHO estimates that 30 million people worldwide could be infected by the HIV virus by the year 2000, and other less conservative estimates place the number at 100 million or higher.

In summary, a typical developing state suffers from chronic mass poverty; its location, topography, and climate limit its potential; its predominantly young population threatens to outstrip economic growth; its inefficient economy rests on an outmoded agricultural base; its international debt threatens its financial stability; its customs and traditions thwart change; its colonial background induces contemporary conflicts; its illiteracy rate is high; its competitive position in world trade is poor; its people are largely apolitical; its government is often authoritarian, and in some a new epidemic threatens its ability to focus on development projects. These human and environmental conditions should give rise to little but despair. They are, however, counterbalanced by an overriding urge to develop and by the help offered by other states, regional groups, and international organizations. The counterbalancing forces give some cause for hope.

# A BLUEPRINT FOR ECONOMIC DEVELOPMENT

Governmental action to promote economic growth and modernization requires judicious planning so that strategies will match national needs and capabilities. Careful planning is also needed to ensure that resources provided through international agencies are put to productive use. Government programs cannot, however, provide a shortcut or easy route to modernization. Economic development has always been a slow and painful process. Despite unprecedented amounts of outside help from the United Nations and other sources, the job remains largely one of local initiative and self-help. The long race between rival ideologies and their respective approaches has ended, with capitalism the clear winner in most of the former communist states. But within each developing society there is a still greater race to push development ahead of its two most dangerous competitors—hunger and mass frustration.

## PREPARING THE BASE

Except for certain natural factors not subject to human alteration, most of the characteristics of our profile state are susceptible to change and improvement. The proximate objective of every developing society is to reach the point from which the society will launch itself into an upward trend of steady, sustainable growth.

*Sociological and Political Changes*

An adequate "takeoff" base requires a modernization of social and political institutions and practices. The following changes are fundamental to that objective.

**1. Attitudinal Changes.** In many countries a privileged elite will be challenged to adopt new attitudes favoring a modernization that may threaten its traditional status. The choice, however, is not always between self-instituted change and the status quo. The alternative may be a violent revolt that would sweep away all elements of entrenched privilege, carried out by those in the society whose attitudes have changed more rapidly than those of the elite. Other critical value changes may involve new orientations toward "worldliness" and "getting ahead," the psychic satisfactions of work, the profit incentive, and other sometimes crass but essential motivations to economic advances.

**2. Political Evolution.** Tangible societal changes must proceed apace of changing attitudes. First, a political socialization must occur, taking the form of support for a minimally effective national political system. Government, a distant power that extracts taxes and drafts village youth for military service, must take on a new image through directing and servicing functions. Political leadership must be selected on the basis of abilities and policies rather than inherited status or wealth. A corps of administrators recruited and trained in modern governmental techniques must provide a degree of unity for the entire country, reaching even remote villages.

**3. Educational Development.** Education may be the keystone in building a modern society. Not only do technicians of varying degrees of skills need to be trained, but fundamental learning in the "three R's" must be imparted to a large portion of the population. Schools can serve an integrating function in selecting the best and most compatible traits of the old world to mesh with those of the new world of modernity. As in the advanced states, education must also provide a nationalizing force in developing a single language and in cultivating national myths, traditions, and popular heroes. Beyond the production of a literate, informed citizenry and a trained labor force, elites with secondary and college education must be developed to direct the nation's changeover to a world of business, commerce, industry, and modern administration.

Unfortunately, many developing countries are unable or reluctant to devote the necessary resources to education, and pressures often exist to divert budgetary funds from education to projects that will show more "immediate" results. These countries also suffer from a "brain drain" that occurs when some of their best educated young people study at universities in the West and subsequently decide not to return.

**4. Population Control.** Population control is widely perceived as crucial to developmental success but may in fact be primarily a problem of education. Demographers speak of the self-limiting nature of the population explosion, noting that rising living standards in the advanced nations had the effect of reducing birthrates drastically. If preindustrialization birthrates had continued in Europe during the nineteenth and twentieth centuries, for example, some European countries would now have populations almost ten times larger. But in the developing world of today, the population surge is of such a magnitude that living standards in many countries cannot readily be raised to the point where they constitute a self-limiting control on family size.

One of the major issues confronting the United Nations in its efforts to control population is that of abortion. In the 1980s, the United States declared that it would no longer support UN population control programs in countries such as China where the government administered a proabortion policy. But while U.S. assistance for international population control programs was significantly reduced, it was not until 1994, when conservatives gained control of the U.S. Congress, that efforts at denying American funding to UN population programs reached optimum levels. Congressional attacks on the United Nations became more numerous and the United States delayed meeting its financial obligations. In April 1998, the Congress moved legislation that would allow the government to pay a portion of the country's arrears, but only if the United Nations could demonstrate that the American contribution would not be used for family planning activities. But whether such opposition to birth control and family planning emerges from the United States or elsewhere, the largely technical potentialities of birth control are thwarted by the vast human barriers of politics, ideology, religion, morality, economics, apathy, and ignorance. What has been lost in what has become a passionate debate is the awareness that birth control is a logical answer to the problem of abortion.

In a major program for population control supported by the United Nations, governmental and private organizations in India have distributed birth control information widely and provided the means of contraception. Positive governmental programs may go beyond this approach to encourage smaller families. In the West such programs have included (1) prohibitions against child labor, (2) policies and programs for the emancipation of women, (3) social mobility leading to the economic independence of children from their parents, (4) mechanization of agriculture, and (5) social insurance freeing parents from dependence on children in their old age. When large families become an economic burden rather than an asset, when children can no longer be exploited for economic and dowry purposes, when large families are no longer accepted as a status symbol, populations may be brought under a measure of control. Regardless of the gains made in national income, if population growth exceeds or equals them, no improvement in standards of living can result and frustration and revolutionary zeal may intensify.

*5. Community Development.* Finally, social change in local communities must be stressed. It is not enough that changes occur in the capital city. Villagers must discover that working together can enrich their lives, improve their living conditions, and reduce social barriers. Technical assistance in such fields as agriculture, health, education, the environment, and public works can enable people in local communities, often with local resources, to obtain some of the benefits of modernization. This requires improving individual skills, increasing self-reliance, and learning the benefits and techniques of cooperative activity in the local community.

### Economic Changes

The central objective of modernization in all developing societies is economic betterment. Social and political changes are aimed mainly at making these societies more receptive to and more efficient at promoting economic development. But the economic problem of achieving a modern economy remains: that is, how to move a poor country to the takeoff point for sustainable growth.

What are the economic variables in the development equation? How can an underdeveloped state marshal its forces in a collective economic offensive? A UN delegate once said of economic development that "it was easy enough to recognize what had to be done but difficult to decide how to go about it." Though no two states would proceed in exactly the same way, some common approaches can be suggested as "prescriptions for development." Remember, however, that much controversy exists over the best way to achieve development.

1. *Increase Agricultural Output.* The objectives of greater farm productivity are: (1) a healthier, better-fed, harder-working population; (2) increased foreign exchange earnings through exports; and (3) a savings—extracted from increased output—destined for investment. In the early stages of development, there may be no increase in the peasant's food consumption, but there must be a rise in food production to support a growing urban work force. The most useful means of expanding productivity fall into the category of improved farming technology—modern implements, fertilizers, insect and disease control, good seed stocks, weed control, and scientific farming techniques. In all of these areas, the United Nations has provided leadership, loans, grants, and specific programs. Agrarian reform is another approach that has proved successful in a few societies. Basic to agrarian reform is a land redistribution among the peasants, achieved by splitting up large estates. Although such a redistribution would increase incentives, small holdings are often uneconomic because they cannot take advantage of economies of scale and because mechanization of such holdings is nearly impossible. Peasant cooperatives to encourage joint production, aided by a reform of inheritance laws that would end fragmentation of plots, may provide an answer to this dilemma. Credit to finance purchases of seeds and fertilizer is a critical element in efforts to boost production.

In 1979 the United Nations sought to expand credit for the rural poor through the creation of the International Fund for Agricultural Development (IFAD), which has since dispensed more than $4 billion in project loans. IFAD mobilizes resources for agricultural development and makes them available to developing countries—especially those in the least developed category or

Fourth World—on concessional terms. Much of IFAD's financial support initially came from the oil-producing Arab states and from several Western nations, but Middle East conflicts and a severe drop in oil prices, along with recessions in the West in the early 1980s, and again in the early 1990s, produced severe budget cuts in IFAD's operations.

*2. Develop Simple Industries.* Agricultural production must be supplemented by the development of fishing, mining, and raw material potentials. Most of the new nations have access to the world's oceans and some have sizable inland lakes—both of which are sources for food rich in protein. Expansion in the production of primary commodities may help underdeveloped states to earn critically needed foreign exchange, although lower prices resulting from highly competitive conditions in the world commodity market may negate the benefits of increased production. Increased productivity, however, will enable such states to take advantage of periods of peak demand and high prices when the advanced countries are engaged in high levels of military spending or enjoy economic boom conditions. Finding a receptive market for their products has generally been more difficult for Third World countries than increasing production of primary commodities and other trade products.

*3. Invest in Social Overhead.* A modern economy can be built only on a broad economic base or infrastructure. This means that each less developed country professing modernization as a goal must be prepared to devote human and financial resources to the building of facilities for basic transport, communication, irrigation, and power supplies. The manpower needs to carry out such projects might be available if the labor surplus engaged in inefficient agricultural pursuits could be taken off the land, mobilized into construction units, and utilized in simple "social capital" projects. Added incentives underlying this approach may include reduced unemployment, increased agricultural production as labor-saving techniques are introduced, and an efficient use of foreign exchange to buy machinery from the industrial nations. Psychologically, the personal involvement of thousands of young people in social projects of this kind may help unleash a national pride and a surge of development spirit, thus giving purpose to their lives. Recognizing that the world's youth population would increase from 738 million in 1975 to 1.18 billion by 2000, the United Nations proclaimed the International Youth Year in 1985 as a call for governmental action to produce jobs for young people.

*4. Acquire Technical Skills.* Modern factories and transportation, communication, and power facilities can be operated only with skilled personnel. An industrializing society faces an enormous task in forging a new labor force of energetic and capable workers from a peasant society. Trainees must be supported out of the savings yielded from a surplus of production over consumption. Exceptions to this rule may be found in apprentice-type training programs and in the technical assistance rendered by advanced states or international institutions. New workers must adjust to the strict discipline of industrial life—regular hours, machine-dictated work speeds, the rhythmic monotony of life on a production line. Managerial and administrative personnel will constitute a new elite, culled out of the indigenous population through ruthless competition for unprecedented rewards.

A vast new reservoir of skilled personnel became available with the ending of the East-West cold war in the early 1990s. In the independent countries that were formerly republics of the Soviet Union, in the countries of Eastern Europe that had been under Soviet control since World War II, and in the countries of the West, great reductions in the production of military materials left many individuals with engineering, managerial, and other skills desperately seeking job opportunities. Unfortunately, putting their skills to work for development requires that they be remunerated in convertible ("hard") currency, which is always in short supply in most developing countries.

*5. Foster Industrialization.* The capstone of the needed social, political, and economic changes can be summed up in the word *industrialization.* Industrialization tends to generate greater efficiency and productivity, which in turn results in increased trade and capital accumulation. Industrialization increases the capacity of a society to process primary commodities for marketing and consumption. In the West, nations embarked on policies of colonial expansionism to secure dependable sources of raw materials and new markets for dumping the surplus products. Many leaders in developing states equate development and industrialization, and they stress the latter as the key to growth and prosperity. However, if industries are created before a proper base has been prepared, they will exist precariously in a modernizing enclave while the rest of the country and most of its people sink deeper into poverty. Sometimes overlooked by developing societies are nonindustrialized states with high productivity and living standards, such as New Zealand and the Netherlands.

For a developing state to industrialize, it must import most of the necessary machinery, tools, and skills. Unlike social capital improvements, which often need sheer muscle power, industrial capital can be built locally only *after* some measure of industrialization has occurred. If modernizing states had the time and patience, they could follow the lead of the West in moving from primitive handicraft to increasingly complex machines over a century or more, but their societies demand rapid action. Quite naturally, most leaders of the new nations prefer to hurdle the successive steps of development and start with modern, sophisticated—even automated—factories. Since the more efficient factory uses less labor, the rise of a large, disgruntled, unemployed urban proletariat seems unavoidable and a dangerous by-product of that kind of industrialization. However, experts from advanced nations who urge leaders to build simple, labor-intensive industries may be suspected of having protectionist motives or, worse still, neocolonialist attitudes.

Industrialization, if it occurs, can produce many salutary results for the underdeveloped society. For one thing, manufactured goods become more readily available and cheaper for the masses. Foreign exchange formerly expended on imports of consumer items can be saved. Savings for investment should increase substantially once industrialization has begun, since national income will be higher. Industrialized plants may also contribute to a local fabrication of capital goods. Despite its pitfalls and the problems it may create, industrialization may be a logical route for many developing countries to take in their attempted "great leap forward" to modernization. The extent, however, to which their people may view it as a singularly facile solution to problems of mass poverty is likely to be more an emotional than a rational reaction.

*6. Safeguard the Environment.* Programs to industrialize may be short-term economic successes and yet in the long run prove to be environmental disasters. This issue was brought to a focus in the United Nations Conference on Environment and Development, held at Rio de Janeiro in June 1992, as well as the Conference on Global Warming convened in Kyoto, Japan in 1997. The central message at Rio, Kyoto, as well as the earlier 1972 Stockholm Conference on the Environment, was the need to act globally in dealing with such problems as the destruction of the ozone layer, the greenhouse effect, and the pollution of the oceans.

Many of the most direct and immediate problems, however, continue to be local and regional. In a number of Third World countries, the forests are being denuded of trees as expanding populations desperately seek land for cultivation and fuel for cooking and warmth, The result is often a creeping desertification as forests recede and ultimately disappear. This of course can be a global problem too, since all breathe oxygen generated by the earth's great forests. Pollution or exhaustion of local water resources is also a problem in most parts of the world. Some water supplies have been victims of attempted development. The state of Uzbekistan, a former Soviet republic, is a case in point. Soviet planners, in their efforts to increase crop production, reversed the flow of waters feeding the Aral Sea with fresh water. Once the world's fourth largest lake, it has now turned into a smelly sewer, less than half its former area and one quarter of its volume. As a result, the huge harvest of fish and seafood that supported the Uzbek people for centuries is no more.

While Third World countries embark on ambitious development programs, the thirty most industrialized countries of the West continue to add huge quantities of pollution to the oceans, the land, and the atmosphere. The United States, with about 5 percent of the world's population, produces an estimated 25 percent of global pollution. Some developing states, especially in Africa, have permitted their territory to become a dumping ground for hazardous wastes from Western industrialized states.

The 1992 Rio conference emphasized the need for a new game plan to eliminate poverty without environmental degradation. The catch phrase was "sustainable development," meaning progress that meets the needs of the present while not compromising future generations. Agreements on the ozone layer, global warming, and biodiversity, signed at the conference, indicated modest progress. Another international development of importance was the establishment in 1990 of a Global Environment Facility (GEF) to provide financing for environmental projects associated with the functioning of the World Bank, the IMF, the UN Development Program, and the UN Environment Program. Sponsored by the World Bank, with an initial fund of almost $1 billion, the GEF is specifically concerned with global warming, conservation of biodiversity, ozone-layer damage, and protection of international waters.

In spite of these apparent achievements, however, agreements like those at Kyoto in 1997 whereby the advanced industrialized countries agreed, sometime after the year 2000, to cut by five percent the exhaust emissions from cars, industrial plants, households, and agricultural facilities to stem the global greenhouse warming effect, illustrated the complexities in implementing programs affecting the different nations. The Kyoto agreement could not be made official until it was signed and ratified by 55 states, including those that accounted for at least 55 percent of 1990 carbon dioxide emissions in industrialized countries. At the end of 1998 sixty countries had signed the Protocol, but *only* two— Fiji and Antigua and Barbuda, had actually ratified it! And whereas the United States agreed to sign the document, it also insisted it would not seek ratification until the developing countries pledged "meaningful participation," which meant nothing less than a reduction in the latter's development schedules. In response, the developing countries, led by China, India, and the Group of 77 argued they could not place limits on their growth at such a key moment in their own industrialization, and indeed, while the established industrialized states continued to hold all the advantages. The complexity of this controversy indicated there would be no resolution to the global warming dilemma when the Conference of Parties meets in 2000. Moreover, given intransigence on all sides of the issue, and because the United States accounted for a major portion of the emissions dilemma, the Kyoto Protocol could only be made operational when the U.S. Congress demonstrated a significant change in attitude and ratified the instrument.

## ACQUIRING THE MEANS

Capital accumulation is the *sine qua non* of development. Capital can be defined as the factor of production—along with land and labor, the other factors of production—that takes the form of money or producer goods. Like a catalytic agent in a chemical process, capital, especially in the form of foreign exchange, can produce a desirable reaction between the human and mechanical elements in the economic equation by providing supplies, tools, plant facilities, power, and modern production machines. It can also attract foreign technicians and pay for training local personnel to fill skilled and semiskilled positions. Capital is most useful when it is applied to a carefully prepared social and economic base, when it is invested in sound ventures rather than projects aimed at feeding national egos, and when it is used to produce goods that have a market abroad.

Because Third World leaders believe that capital accumulation will set the pace for industrialization, it has become their main objective. This overriding fascination with capital as the central theme of developmental programs has not always been shared by foreign advisers and planners, or by international institutions and aid-supplying nations. Their restraint is voiced in favor of a "balanced, overall process," but it may also reflect a fear that developing states will be unable to compete effectively in world markets or that, from a narrower viewpoint, industrial development in the Third World may cut into their own foreign markets. Most Western countries, for example, prefer to offer various kinds of development aid, but not capital for industrialization. From their perspective, capital will flow from developed to developing states whenever investment opportunities make such movement profitable, and most capital transfers should therefore be kept in the private sector. Regardless of these caveats, the hunt continues for capital to supply the voracious appetites of the developing nations. Major sources of capital include: (1) local savings, (2) foreign trade, (3) private investment, (4) private loans, and (5) foreign aid. Each of these sources has received various kinds of support from the United Nations.

## Local Savings

Leadership elites within developing states must come to grips with two fundamental economic imperatives. First, domestic consumption must be restrained so that production yields a surplus; second, the surplus or savings must be invested creatively to increase production. A surplus can be provided (1) by raising output but not consumption, (2) by reducing consumption but not output, or (3) by raising output faster than consumption. The first two choices are clearly dangerous to the stability of the state since they could provoke a bitter reaction from workers who either work harder for the same pay or receive pay cuts in the interest of development. In none of the three options will domestic consumption be likely to measure up to popular demand, reflecting the harshness of economic development and the resort in some societies to authoritarian methods to force savings through work pressures and through controlled, subsistence-level standards of living.

Local savings can be accrued through taxation, private profit, profit from socialized industries, expropriation, rationing, or inflation. All involve some ingredients of compulsion or exploitation, but the objective is to move as rapidly as possible to a stage of development where progress is reflected in expanded output and in increased consumption that attracts capital investments from abroad. Local savings, however, have a limited applicability to this early forward movement since the germinal core of industrial goods must come from abroad and thus must be paid for in foreign exchange. Local savings are best fitted for "social overhead" projects, which contribute to the building of an infrastructure base that may help attract foreign capital.

## Foreign Trade

Many Third World countries seek to industrialize by replacing imports with locally produced articles of commerce (the import substitution approach) and by expanding exports. An import substitution strategy increases the role of government in managing the economy and is often implemented through a system of tariffs. Foreign markets, particularly those of the advanced countries of the West, are the major source of capital useful to economic development. During the past forty years, foreign trade earnings have accounted for about 80 percent of the foreign exchange funds of the developing countries as a group. Most of their exports have been primary commodities. Many of the advanced countries followed this same route to industrialization and diversification. In the first half of the nineteenth century, for example, the United States depended heavily on cotton exports to feed the engine of economic growth. Foreign earnings financed a growing textile industry, which in turn increased exports and spurred the growth of related industries, such as iron foundries and machine tool and farm implement manufactures.

The leaders of developing countries, whether they accept this approach or not, believe that the cards are stacked against them in the world of trade realities. *First,* they point out, seesawing demand for primary commodities brought about by war-peace and boom-recession fluctuations in the West has produced chaos in the development of supply sources. *Second,* specialization in primary products tends to perpetuate existing trade patterns and to condemn Third World states to remain dependent on Western markets for their exports, and on Western suppliers for imports of industrial products. *Third,* supplies of primary commodities have tended to exceed demand because of productivity increases in Third World states, the development of primary production in advanced states, the substitution of synthetics for natural products, and a change in consumer demand toward more sophisticated products having a smaller raw material content. Protectionist trade policies, price-support programs for marginal domestic producers, and subsidies for exporters have helped Western states accelerate this trend toward securing primary commodities from local producers. *Fourth,* the terms of trade between the developed and the developing nations have generally tended to favor the former. The terms-of-trade problem involves the prices that developing states receive for their exports in relationship to the prices that they pay for goods and machinery imported from the advanced states. Over the past seventy years the trend has favored higher prices for industrial goods and lower prices for primary commodities, with the exceptions of the periods encompassing World War I, World War II, the Korean War and the Vietnam War. This problem can be illustrated by a simple example: In 1956, Morocco had to export 200 tons of phosphate abroad to pay for one imported truck; in 1963, Morocco had to export 318 tons of phosphate to pay for the same truck.[4] That trend has continued, although phosphate prices have fluctuated over the years. Such marketing conditions have undermined development plans, arrested economic growth, and produced widespread despair in the developing world. Under such conditions, increases in the productivity of Third World countries inescapably lead to greater supplies and lower prices.

With the establishment of UNCTAD in 1964 (see Chapter 10), the Third World had a new forum in which to voice their demands for capital through trade. By 1970 UNCTAD had reached agreement on a generalized system of preferences (GSP), and the next year the West-oriented General Agreement on

Tariffs and Trade (GATT) gave its members authority to offer tariff preferences to LDCs. Today most of the industrialized, market economy countries of the West offer GSP treatment on designated products, in many cases permitting them duty-free entry. In the United States, for example, billions of dollars worth of dutiable imports from developing countries have entered the country duty free each year since the adoption of GSP. Excluded by the United States from GSP treatment were categories such as Communist countries (not many still extant), members of OPEC, countries that have nationalized U.S.-owned properties without compensation, and countries that grant sanctuary to terrorists. Nearly three thousand tariff categories are eligible for duty-free treatment, including many agricultural items, wood and paper products, and a broad range of manufactured articles.

The GSP approach is based on the "infant industry" concept that new industries in the LDCs cannot compete effectively with older, more efficient firms in the industrialized countries. The generalized system of preferences is a means of equalizing the competition and giving the developing states an opportunity to enter the markets of the developed countries. The foreign exchange they earn in this way can be directed into support for economic development programs. Although GSP has been helpful, a shrinking world market for many articles of commerce, growing competition from the developed countries, and the failure to open markets to most Third World goods have kept such gains limited. Increased trade remains the best hope of the developing countries, and the share of developing country exports in the consumption of manufactured goods in the industrial countries has increased substantially since GSP was instituted. The United Nations International Trade Center in Geneva has helped developing countries gain some expertise in carrying on export trade in the international marketplace. Nevertheless, the low prices charged to make their goods competitive, combined with the high prices paid for imports from the industrialized countries, have worked to reduce the amount of net capital available for development projects from trade earnings.

The Third World bloc never believed that GSP alone would solve their trade and development problems. Indeed, it became increasingly clear to the developing states that the existing world economy had to be liquidated and replaced with a new system more favorable to the interests of the LDCs. At the Sixth Special Session of the General Assembly, called in 1974 to deal explicitly with trade and development problems, the Third World's caucusing Group of 77 proclaimed the need to establish a New International Economic Order (NIEO). The existing world economic system, according to NIEO proponents, was hopelessly rigged against the interests and needs of the developing countries. This view was supported by a "dependency theory" that came to be generally accepted throughout the Third World to explain its failure to make rapid development progress. Dependency theorists argue that the world economy is divided into an exploitative northern tier and a dependent southern tier, which is a carryover from the colonial era. Low prices for raw materials and high prices for industrialized goods, they claim, keep the South in bondage. Hence a new system based an economic realities, fairness, and justice is needed. Later that same year, the General Assembly followed up the Special Session Declaration by approving a Charter of Economic Rights and Duties of States, which sought to convert the general principles of NIEO into a statement of the concrete actions needed to implement the new approach.

The demand for NIEO was in essence an attempt by the developing states to restructure the international economic system and provide for the redistribution of the world's wealth. In their view, prices for primary commodities have been kept artificially low and those of industrial goods excessively high in world trade as a result of colonialism and neocolonialism. Moreover, in the general workings of the world economy—interest rates, shipping costs, protectionism, insurance rates, and decisions made in GATT, the IMF, and the World Bank Group, for example—the nations of the West dominated the decision processes. The NIEO program called specifically for more favorable terms of trade, support for international commodity agreements, increased foreign aid, rescheduling of Third World debt, greater control by the LDCs over multinational corporations (MNCs), control over their natural resources, greater availability of technology, and a greater decision-making role for the LDCs, especially in the IMF and World Bank.

By the mid-1980s the leaders of the Third World backed away from their persistent demands for NIEO and began to focus on more immediate and pragmatic issues. With the collapse of the Communist Second World and the consequent loss of Third World bargaining power with the West, most developing countries concluded that working within the system was more feasible than demands to transform it. Furthermore, many less developed states were moving toward a market orientation in their own economies. The revival of the NIEO appears less likely in the climate of the post–cold war world. Moreover, the transformation of GATT into a more inclusive World Trade Organization has drawn a positive response from the LDCs. While the LDCs initially feared the establishment of WTO would work to their disadvantage—indeed enhance their dependency on the more aggressive capitalist states and international business organizations—WTO's apparent emphasis on equity and balance actually provides Third World nations with some needed leverage in their dealings with the contemporary economic giants.

*Private Investment*

Historically, most funds for the development of emergent economies have come from capital transfers in the form of investments by individuals and corporations from capital-surplus countries. The significance of this source was recognized by President George D. Woods of the International Bank when he stressed that "economic development in many countries will never really get into high gear until they find a way to tap the vast resources of capital and know-how that are available in the private sector of the industrialized nations." [5]

The major obstacle, over which the developing countries have little or no control, is the vast lucrative investment market in the advanced countries themselves. Most private investment capital flows through domestic stock exchanges or is invested directly in business expansions in the United States, Western Europe, Japan, Australia, and other relatively "safe" countries. Not only are these countries politically stable and economically viable, but investments are safe from governmental expropriation, skilled labor is available, mass consumer markets provide local outlets for manufactured goods, and conversions of profits into U.S. dollars or other hard currencies and their transfer to investors are a simple matter. These conditions are much harder to find in the developing countries of Africa, Asia, and Latin America.

Unlike the flow of governmental funds, which is determined by political and military objectives, private capital transfer is influenced mainly by commercial considerations. Various UN agencies have searched for answers to the problem of making emergent economies more attractive as investment opportunities. Among the proposals that have been made are: (1) tax exemptions or reductions and governmental investment guarantees by the developed countries; (2) informational, promotional, and technical assistance centers set up by the developing countries and international institutions; (3) cooperation between private investors and local entrepreneurs aimed at encouraging a "reinvestment of profits"; and (4) studies by the International Bank leading to the establishment of international investment insurance, machinery for arbitrating disputes, and guarantees for the securities of developing states in world capital markets.

## Private Loans

Private borrowing is related to private investment but poses some additional problems. As with young married couples, the attraction of consumer goods from the advanced countries may lead newly independent and underdeveloped countries to live beyond their means. In the competition for overseas markets, many private firms may be far too willing to risk loans to facilitate the peddling of their wares. The result may be a growth in private debts that sacrifices future capital needs, raises false expectations of higher living standards, and causes a disastrous inflation within the underdeveloped country. In addition to consumer loans, Third World nations may seek loans to underwrite major development projects, with the expectation that increased foreign exchange earnings will enable them to pay off the loans plus interest over a period of years. If the anticipated expansion in sales in the world market does not occur, both the Third World nations and the lending banks may be in serious trouble. If private loans have been supplemented by loans from national, regional, and UN lending agencies, the recipient governments may find it impossible to come up with the foreign exchange needed for annual payments.

This situation came to pass in the 1980s with the emergence of a Third World debt crisis. As discussed in Chapter 10, Mexico in 1982 was the first major debtor to announce that it could no longer meet its foreign debt payments. The result was a devaluation of the peso and a rescheduling of Mexico's massive debt by the International Monetary Fund (IMF), the Bank for International

Settlements (BIS), and a number of central banks and commercial banks in the United States, Western Europe, and Japan. But Mexico was not alone. By 1983, thirty-four countries were trying to reschedule their foreign debt payments. Rescheduling an international debt means that missed interest and amortization payments are canceled and then added to the aggregate debt owed by the defaulting state, typically with a lengthening of the overall period for the repayment of the debt. Additional loans were granted by the IMF so that hard-pressed debtor countries would not have to default on their loans or have them rescheduled. Such additional loans were granted only on the condition that each recipient country adopt rigorous austerity measures and adhere to stabilization guidelines laid down by the IMF.

Virtually the same scenario was repeated in 1997–98 in East and Southeast Asia, notably among the Asian "tigers," the countries that had been the success stories of the developing world in the 1980s and early 1990s. Zealous, often unbridled enthusiasm and confidence blinded Asian policymakers as well as entrepreneurs to the realities of the marketplace. Heavy competition and a slump in product demand, coupled with financial miscalculations and outright corruption, plunged Thailand, Indonesia, South Korea, and Malaysia into a depressionary swamp from which, without international assistance, they could not expect to extricate themselves. Once again, LDC dependence on the IMF was pronounced. IMF demands were similar to those imposed on Mexico and a host of other states during the 1980s, and the proud and heretofore highriding Asian "tigers" were "encouraged" to follow the dictates of the IMF, no matter how onerous or unpopular they might be.

*Foreign Aid*

Capital inflows in the form of public grants or loans have been a significant development financing source for more than four decades. Foreign economic assistance offers the advantage of reducing the harshness of life in an industrializing society, which must otherwise employ painful methods of economic "forced marches" and compulsorily reduced consumption to achieve a surplus. Regardless of the motivations underlying foreign aid—national self-interest, philanthropy, ideological rivalry, economic dependence, regional growth, or global stability—it has become an established institution of the contemporary state system. For many years the developing states have offered proposals within the UN system for massive transfers of capital, preferably in the form of nonrepayable grants. In the early years of the United Nations, with the example of Marshall Plan successes in Western Europe, Third World spokesmen called for a Special UN Fund for Economic Development (the SUNFED proposal), to which each developed state would contribute 1 percent of its annual gross national product (GNP). Since this was far in excess of most national aid programs, the United States and other capital-surplus countries rejected the SUNFED idea, holding that existing international institutions such as the World Bank were sufficient to meet the need for capital. Moreover, it was clear that the market economy states of the West offered foreign aid predominantly to prepare the LDCs for an infusion of *private* capital. The West viewed foreign aid as a means laying the groundwork for profitable investments, thus providing extensive benefits for both donor and recipient states. Foreign aid, in other words, was to "prepare the base" for investment by building infrastructure, improving health, expanding agriculture, conquering illiteracy, and teaching modern skills. These advancements were expected to attract the private capital needed for meaningful economic growth in the developing state. To funnel capital into the LDCs through intergovernmental programs would tend to promote socialism, not capitalism.

The developing states remained steadfast in their search for capital through foreign aid. Their demands for capital aid resulted in 1956 in the creation of the International Finance Corporation (IFC) as an affiliate of the International Bank for Reconstruction and Development (IBRD).* The new lending institution was authorized to make loans to and investments in private companies in developing countries. In 1960, in response to criticisms by the LDCs that the repayment terms for IBRD and IFC loans were too harsh, the International Development Association (IDA) was established as an affiliate of the World Bank to grant interest-free "soft loans" with long repayment schedules. A third affiliate, the Multilateral Investment Guarantee Agency (MIGA), was established in 1988 to guarantee eligible foreign investments against losses resulting from political risks, as contrasted with commercial, risks. The IFC, IDA, and MIGA, along with the World Bank, are treated in more detail below.

These efforts to placate the developing bloc through operations of the World Bank group failed, and pressures continued to mount for the SUNFED proposal. Finally, in 1966, the Third World bloc had sufficient votes in the General Assembly to raise a two-thirds majority in favor of the SUNFED idea. The creation of the UN Capital Development Fund (UNCDF) capped, under a new title, more than a decade of effort to implement the SUNFED proposal for grants rather than loans. The capital-surplus states of the First World, however, refused to put a single dollar, mark, franc, yen, pound, or other hard currency into the UNCDF, and the Communist countries of the Second World followed their example by likewise refusing to participate. Without an infusion of capital, the United Nations Capital Development Fund lost its prospective utility, and that loss shattered the dream of the developing states bloc that dated back almost to the founding of the United Nations.

Another abortive LDC attempt to secure capital was a proposal to use for development purposes the special drawing rights (SDRs) created by the International Monetary Fund (IMF) to supplement international reserves. The major capital states firmly rejected this proposal. The LDCs also hoped for substantial income from seabed mining under the 1982 Law of the Sea Treaty, but prospects for commercial exploitation of the seabed have receded into the twenty-first century. A breakthrough of sorts did occur outside the United

---

*The origins and role of the World Bank group are discussed more extensively in the latter part of this chapter.

Nations, however. Huge amounts of capital accumulated in the developed states were loaned to the LDCs by commercial banks of the West, but not on concessionary terms. The problems of repayment created by those capital transfers have already been discussed.


# PROMOTING INTERNATIONAL ACTION

The major responsibility for economic development quite naturally falls to the lot of the developing states themselves. Indeed, it would be difficult to discover a single "poor" state whose people did not regard economic betterment as the major objective and whose government did not regard it as the most pressing problem. Yet the need for outside help has become an accepted tenet of international economic orthodoxy and "foreign aid" is widely regarded as a moral and political obligation of developed states. In response to numerous appeals, diverse programs of assistance have been established over a period of more than four decades, starting with the Point Four Program of the United States in 1949. These international efforts, although based on converging interests of donors and recipients, have for the most part been shaped and directed by donor countries and have reflected their political, economic, military, moral, or community interests. This relationship between donors and recipients has produced problems of coordinating aid programs so that they will fit constructively with the developmental plans of the recipients. Major issues have arisen, and these issues have occasionally embroiled relations between giver and receiver.


## Should Donors Use Bilateral or Multilateral Channels?

One such issue involves the means by which aid is funnelled into developing economies. Although most financial aid comes from about a dozen capital-surplus countries, each contributor may use a variety of approaches.

Most donor states favor bilateral aid because they can exercise control over programs by imposing conditions on recipient states. In this way, industries competitive with those of the donor state can be discouraged, economic and social reforms can be encouraged, and counterpart funds can be required. Cold war ideological and political objectives were for many years critical determinants of the direction, kinds, and amount of bilateral aid. Propaganda advantages are also not overlooked by donor governments, since local populations can easily be made aware of the identity of their benefactor. Large amounts of foreign aid may permit the donor state to influence the recipient state's foreign policy, and directed trade patterns together with a need for spare parts may foster its economic dependence.

Most developing countries prefer to receive aid through multilateral channels because this is likely to minimize interference in their domestic and foreign affairs. Exceptions to this preference are found in states that have a close and favorable relationship with major aid-givers. The United Nations probably offers the best hope for a fair and impartial aid program worked out through a partnership of donor and recipient countries, and most LDCs have accorded this approach their full support. Donor countries, however, while participating in various UN aid programs, have chosen to administer most of their aid through bilateral channels so as to retain full control over its distribution.

## Should Capital Transfers Have Priority?

An optimal aid program should match inputs of capital and technical assistance so that balanced growth can occur. This rarely happens even under the very best aid programs. Donor countries, while often generous to a fault in providing technical assistance, are reluctant to provide capital through government channels. But the leaders of the developing countries, under great pressure from their peoples to produce tangible results, clamor for capital.

Some LDCs, such as the oil-producing states of OPEC, have large amounts of capital in the form of foreign exchange, whereas most developing states— especially in Africa—have very little capital and desperately seek to obtain more through United Nations programs. The addition of the former republics of the Soviet Union, now independent states, to the aid seekers has increased the competition for scarce capital aid. Major capital aid programs outside of the UN system are almost wholly motivated by political considerations, such as U.S. aid to Israel and Egypt. Annual contributions to these countries amounting to billions of dollars were promised at the time of the Camp David Accords (1978) and the signing of a peace treaty (1979), and have been sustained through the 1990s.

## Should Aid Funds Be Granted or Loaned?

To give or to lend is a perennial problem facing aid-giving states and international institutions. In bilateral programs the United States has moved from a predominantly grant basis to a basis of mainly making low-interest loans, some at least partly repayable in local currencies. For many years the Soviet Union gave their aid in the form of long-term, low-interest loans, often repayable in local commodities. International institutions such as the World Bank generally extend short-term loans at moderate to high interest rates and expect repayment in hard currency.

Those who favor grants over loans argue that grants are more flexible than loans because they can be used to develop educational and other social overhead facilities, whereas loans must ordinarily be used to expand self-liquidating productive facilities so that interest payments can be made and the principal of the loan amortized. Since grants do not have to be repaid, they have a minimally disturbing impact on the recipient country's balance of payments, unlike hard currency loans, which force the aid-receiving country to increase its exports or decrease its imports to obtain foreign exchange for installment payments. Grants, therefore, permit a better allocation of resources within a state and speed up economic growth by permitting a more rational application of aid funds.

The most compelling argument favoring loans over grants is that the need to repay loans with interest may encourage the recipient countries to devote the borrowed funds to productive projects rather than to monuments or imported luxury goods. Furthermore, within donor countries loans are more acceptable politically than grants.

Like most aid issues, that of loans versus grants poses a somewhat false dichotomy. Both grants and loans are needed in underdeveloped societies—grants to help develop a substantial and suitable infrastructure, loans to provide the capital required for industrial growth and diversification. To increase the capacity of developing states to pay off loans, however, expanding world trade, open markets in the advanced countries, and higher prices for primary commodities are necessary.

# REGIONAL PROGRAMS

Regional groups have also developed aid programs that have been encouraged and supported by the United Nations. Several of the more prominent regional programs will be examined in this section, and then the diverse approaches and programs of the United Nations will be surveyed and evaluated. But one caveat is in order. Regional aid programs may appear to be multilateral in nature, meaning that decisions concerning foreign aid are apparently developed collectively by the members of the group. This is not necessarily true in fact. Although a regional program is proclaimed to be multilateral, it may in fact be largely bilateral because the donor country retains the ultimate decision over which nations receive the aid, what terms and conditions are attached to the aid, and what type of aid is offered.

## THE COLOMBO PLAN

The first regional technical assistance and capital-aid program emerged out of a Commonwealth Conference in 1950 at Colombo, Ceylon (now Sri Lanka). The Colombo Plan initially provided for a development program in which the advanced Commonwealth states—the United Kingdom, Canada, Australia, and New Zealand—furnished half of the needed capital, with the other half supplied by recipient governments in South and Southeast Asia. The United States and Japan later joined as contributors, and the recipients today include not only Commonwealth states but other Asian countries as well. Britain and Canada, however, withdrew as members in 1991, while expressing a continuing interest in the region.

The Colombo Plan represents a balance between a regional and a bilateral approach to development. International machinery has been kept to a minimum. A consultative committee representing all the participating states meets annually to review past activities, plan specific programs for the year ahead, and provide a forum in which recipient nations can lobby for more aid and donors can announce new projects. Contributions take the form of both grants and loans, and all aid funds are provided through bilateral arrangements, although multilateral consultation is a factor in coordinating the program. An auxiliary program of technical assistance operates under the plan through a permanent secretariat at Colombo known as the Council for Technical Cooperation in South and Southeast Asia. Every effort is made to balance inputs of capital with improved absorptive capacities so that balanced growth can occur. Technical cooperation has flourished not only between donor and recipient countries but also among the Asian members themselves. More than $100 billion in loans and grants has been extended to Asian nations for agricultural and developmental purposes since 1950, with significant developmental results in many of the recipient countries. In fact, some of the recipients of Colombo Plan aid, along with other aid programs, have now become donors rather than receivers of aid. This group includes four Asian Tigers—Japan, Singapore, South Korea, and Taiwan.

## THE EUROPEAN DEVELOPMENT FUND AND THE LOMÉ CONVENTIONS

The European Development Fund (EDF) is the principal means by which the European Union provides aid, concessionary finance, and technical assistance to developing countries. The fund was originally established in 1958 to grant financial aid to dependencies of the six nations that founded the European Economic Community or Common Market, but it broadened its concerns and role as the colonies achieved their independence. Operating with a host of United Nations organizations that includes UNDP, UNICEF, and UNRWA, through 1998 EDF assisted thirteen African countries, six Asian countries (in addition to Gaza and the West Bank territories), one in Latin America, and several states of the former Yugoslavia in Europe. The fund began with capital of $581 million for the first five-year period, and for the period 1996–2000 its budget was projected well above $1 billion. Control over dispensing aid from the fund is today exercised by the European Union's Council of Ministers, whose members cast weighted votes on projects recommended by the EU commission. Most of its credits are for improving economic infrastructure, such as railways, ports, roads, telecommunications, and urban development. Modernization of agriculture has had the second highest priority. Since 1964 the fund has also supplied the recipient countries with technical assistance in the form of advice from experts, technicians, economic surveys, and aid for vocational and professional training. Through the Yaoundé Conventions of 1963 and 1967, a free trade area was established between the Europeans and the African Associated States.

In 1975 the aid and trade provisions were extended to include former colonies in the Caribbean and the Pacific as well as Africa, with a treaty signed at Lomé, Togo, by representatives of the EC and forty-six developing states.

Known as the ACP (African, Caribbean, Pacific) states, these LDC partners of the European community were expanded to include sixty-nine states. The arrangements were continued through subsequent agreements (Lomé II, III, and IV). Concluded in 1989, Lomé IV ran from 1990 to 2000. In addition to continuing generalized preferences and other trade concessions, Lomé IV authorized $16 billion in grants and subsidized loans to be disbursed through the European Development Fund and the European Investment Bank. Although the ACP countries have sometimes been disappointed with the amount of financial aid, and trade concessions have occasionally been weakened by escape clauses and other restrictions, the Lomé conventions have been an effective contribution to North-South cooperation.

## European Bank for Reconstruction and Development

The European Bank for Reconstruction and Development (EBRD) was established in 1991 to foster the transition toward market economies and to promote private and entrepreneurial initiatives in those central and eastern European countries that were committed to the principles of multiparty democracy, pluralism, and market economies. The EBRD helps countries implement structural and economic reform that includes de-monopolization, decentralization, and privatization. Its activities promote the private sector, strengthen financial institutions and legal systems, and help develop the infrastructure needed to support free enterprise. EBRD encourages co-financing and foreign direct investment from the public and private sectors, helps mobilize domestic capital, and provides technical cooperation. It works in close cooperation with international financial institutions and a range of international organizations. The bank also promotes sustainable development in all its activities. EBRD has sixty members (fifty-eight countries, the European Union and the European Investment Bank), including twenty-six countries from central and eastern Europe and the Commonwealth of Independent States (CIS). EBRD's initial subscribed capital was in excess of $10 billion, and by 1996, the bank's board of governors had doubled that figure. The powers of EBRD are vested in a Board of Governors, with each member appointing a governor and an alternate. The Board of Governors delegates powers to a more manageable twenty-three-member Board of Directors, elected by the Governors to a three-year term. The Board of Directors are responsible for the operations of the bank. EBRD merges the principles and practices of merchant and development banking, provides funding for private or privatizable enterprises, as well as for physical and financial infrastructure projects that support the private sector. By December 1996, the bank had approved 450 projects, 73 percent of which were in the private sector. EBRD represents the wave of the future and is a critical element in linking democratic politics with economic development. It also demonstrates the transference of development responsibilities from the public sector to free enterprise capital institutions.

# THE ORGANIZATION FOR ECONOMIC COOPERATION AND DEVELOPMENT

The Organization for Economic Cooperation and Development (OECD) is unique as a regional organization fostering technical and developmental assistance because its twenty-four members include only donor nations. The OECD was created in 1961 as an outgrowth of the Organization for European Economic Cooperation (OEEC), which had been established in 1948 to coordinate Marshall Plan aid, and its members are European states plus Australia, New Zealand, Turkey, the United States, and Japan. One of the OECD's initial goals was to expand aid to developing states. This goal could more frankly be explained as an effort by the United States—the main force behind the establishment of the OECD—to encourage European and other member states to carry a larger share of economic development financing.

The OECD pursues its aid-fostering role through a Development Assistance Committee (DAC), which establishes general policies and reviews annually the aid efforts of its members. Each member nation must present and defend its aid-giving programs before all other members in DAC sessions. No aid is offered through the organization's channels, however; in all cases aid is dispensed through bilateral actions or multilateral programs that are part of the UN system. The OECD's role is mainly one of stimulating and harmonizing its members' efforts in providing aid and technical assistance to developing countries, and expanding trade with them. The OECD includes in its membership many of the leading industrial countries of the world, which are also the main aid-givers. Indeed, important initiatives concerning aid-giving activities are usually, if unofficially, agreed upon by the Group of 7 (Britain, Canada, France, Germany, Italy, Japan, and the United States) at their annual G-7 meeting.

# THE ALLIANCE FOR PROGRESS

In the Western hemisphere the most widely heralded regional approach to economic development was the Alliance for Progress program adopted at the Punta del Este Conference of 1961. The Punta del Este Charter provided for an economic alliance between the United States and nineteen governments of Latin America (Cuba's government was excepted), aimed at realizing a steady increase in living standards through joint action. Specifically, the program called for: (1) a substantial inflow of capital to Latin America, targeted at $20 billion over a ten-year period, (2) social and economic reforms within each of the recipient countries, (3) a strengthening of democratic institutions and the role of private enterprise in Latin America, and (4) a stabilization of markets and prices for Latin American primary commodities.

The large capital inflow was predicated on a sizable investment of private capital from North America, Western Europe, and Japan and on annual transfers of public funds from the United States through low- or no-interest loans. Public funds were to be spent on "social overhead" projects, especially in agriculture, education, communications, and transportation, to build sturdy countrywide bases for private investments in industry. Unfortunately for the Alliance, the United States fell short of its aid targets and the massive new private investment also failed to materialize. Nor did social reform move very rapidly. The program petered out before the end of the decade, providing only a shadow of its original promise. Since then the United States has used both bilateral and multilateral channels for aid to Latin America, but never with such fanfare or great pretensions.

## THE REGIONAL BANKS

The regional approach to development assistance is rounded out by three international banks—the Inter-American Development Bank, established in 1959; the African Development Bank, established in 1964; and the Asian Development Bank, established in 1966. As a rule, each of these banks extends loans repayable over twenty-five to thirty years in hard currencies and gives preference to loans that encourage further inflows of public and private capital to its region. Priorities in loans are also given to national, subregional, and regional projects that promote harmonious regional growth and meet the needs of small or less developed countries in the region. The banks have both regional and nonregional members, the bulk of the capital coming from the nonregional states (including the major industrialized countries) for lending within the region. Initially the membership of the African Development Bank was limited to members of the Organization of African Unity in order to avoid outside control. This had the effect, however, of severely limiting the capital resources of the bank, and in 1982 its articles were amended to permit nonregional membership, which greatly expanded its lending operations. In 1997 the banks were lending at the rate of about $5 billion annually for the Inter-American bank, $6 billion for the Asian bank, and $2 billion for the African bank.

In addition to the three regional banks, a number of subregional financial institutions have been established that directly or indirectly relate to the objective of economic development. One of these, the European Investment Bank, an agency of the European Union established in 1958, provides loans for economically distressed areas in Europe as well as associated Third World countries. Two-thirds of European Investment Bank lending is focused on the development of less-favored regions, and special emphasis is given to investment by public-private partnerships and private finance initiatives. Lending by the EIB doubled between 1998 and 2000 in ten Central and East European countries as well as Cyprus. EIB also developed a new borrowing strategy to support the new common European currency, the Euro. EIB's subscribed capital was pegged at between $50 and $60 billion in 1998. In addition, a European Investment Fund was created in June 1994 as an independent international financial institution, bringing together the public and private sectors. EIF was a joint venture between the European Investment Bank, the European

Commission, and a group of banks and financial institutions from all the member states of the European Union. The creation of the EIF involved a de facto amendment to the Union treaty and the mission of the fund was to provide guarantees, essentially to the private or mixed private/public sectors, in support of long-term financing for major infrastructure projects in transport, telecommunications, gas pipelines, optical fibre networks, bridges and tunnels, harbors, airports, and mobile telephone schemes. Other subregional banks include the Central American Bank for Economic Integration (CABEI), which became operational in 1961 as an agency of the Central American Common Market; the East African Development Bank, consisting of Kenya, Tanzania, and Uganda, which was established in 1967; and the Nordic Investment Bank, created in 1967, with five Scandinavian countries as members.

The regional approach to economic development affords a viable compromise between outright bilateralism and a globalism that suffers from a dearth of donor countries and a surfeit of countries in need. Some regional approaches, however, involve only consultation, coordination, and review, leaving the hard decisions on contributions, projects, and priorities to be made bilaterally (and often unilaterally) by the major donor members. The regional banks, with their councils of governors determining basic policies and their boards of directors making loan decisions, more closely approximate models of true multilateralism. But even here multilateralism is modified by a voting system weighted by amounts of capital contributed. Most of the regional and subregional organizations were at least in part a response to cold war pressures. Even without cold war motivations, the major contributors participate because national interests are served. Recipients, so much in need of help, willingly accept bilateral and regional aid on the terms offered. Any increase in the total flow of assistance is welcome. But little doubt remains that most of the developing states prefer assistance to be allotted, administered, and supervised through the truly *international* channels of the United Nations.

# UN PROGRAMS

Economic development has become the major focus of debate in the General Assembly, the Economic and Social Council, and many subsidiary organs of the United Nations. Most UN programs have economic development as their basic objective, and most UN personnel administer development programs. Even such crucial questions as disarmament, collective security, and pacific settlement evoke an avalanche of words paying homage to economic development. Under constant LDC pressures, the developed states have agreed to participate in a variety of global programs.

The UN Charter says very little about economic development. Although economic cooperation is mentioned in a number of contexts, the only reference to economic *development* appears in Article 55, which provides, among other objectives, that "the United Nations shall promote: (a) higher standards of living, full employment, and conditions of economic and social progress and development." The Charter contains no authority to require any governmental or organizational action in the economic field, and aid programs must rest on a foundation of cooperation and voluntary contributions. The organization has in no way been deterred by the Charter's reticence on the subject of economic development, however, and a great variety of UN programs, resembling an "alphabet soup" in their shorthand acronymic symbolization, have been established in three broad categories—planning and research, technical assistance, and capital financing.

## BUILDING SUPPORT FOR DEVELOPMENT

The leaders of most developing countries recognize that the principal responsibility for promoting economic advancement is theirs, that foreign aid and international cooperation are not substitutes for national action. But nations newly launched on programs of modernization lack the experience and sophistication needed to avoid costly mistakes and dead-end objectives. One of the most significant approaches of the United Nations, consequently, has been to create opportunities for a meaningful dialogue between industrialized countries and countries seeking that status, and among the developing countries themselves. The dialogue has been carried on almost endlessly for many years, constituting a novel "school" for imparting desire, knowledge, judgment, and common sense to national purveyors of development schemes. The principal forums for carrying on the dialogue have been the Economic and Social Council (ECOSOC), the General Assembly in regular and special sessions, the Second (Economic and Financial) Committee of the Assembly, the informal forum of UN headquarters, and countless conferences, committees, commissions, and agencies of the UN system.

    The UN dialogue has also been a learning experience for the developed countries. From 1946 onward, the chambers of the United Nations have rung with the clamor of many voices setting forth the views of the world's less fortunate on the urgency of economic development, the causes and cures for poverty, and the responsibilities of the more fortunate to alleviate poverty through substantial aid. The main cleavage between the developing states and the developed states has been over the approach to development, with the Western states advocating gradualist policies tested in their centuries-long development struggles and the developing states demanding rapid progress through shortcuts and massive technical and capital assistance programs. The Communist-bloc states increasingly joined the fray, offering until the late 1980s a socialist pattern as the best means for achieving progress.

    Out of the debates has emerged not only a communication of existing ideas but also new approaches, increased knowledge, and a better understanding of the problems of development. This interchange has been complemented by special studies, by information gathering and analysis conducted by various secretariats, and by widespread publication of the findings. In fact, so extensive has been the research on problems of development that ECOSOC delegates have complained that they are being drowned in a flood of resolutions, reports, and discussions "beyond the analytical capacity and memory of the human brain." In recent years computers have come into common use to help bring some semblance of order out of this chaos. But the search for shortcuts, for new formulas, for sound plans continues.

## The Regional Commissions

On urging from the General Assembly, the Economic and Social Council (ECOSOC) in 1947 established the Economic Commission for Europe (ECE) and the Economic Commission for Asia and the Far East (ECAFE) to give aid to countries devastated by the war. ECAFE became the Economic and Social Commission for Asia and the Pacific (ESCAP) in 1974. Latin American demands that economic development be recognized as a problem of equal significance resulted in the creation of the Economic Commission for Latin America (ECLA) in 1948, later changed to ECLAC with the addition of Caribbean nations in 1984. In 1958 the Economic Commission for Africa (ECA) was established to help plan and organize economic development drives for the new nations of that continent. Lack of regional harmony caused plans for a Middle East regional commission to be temporarily abandoned in the 1960s, but a new Economic and Social Commission for Western Asia (ESCWA) was established in 1974.

While all of the regional commissions foster economic cooperation among their members, each has an emphasis dictated by the special needs of the region. Headquartered in Geneva, the main concern of the Economic Commission for Europe at the time of its establishment (1947) was the rebuilding of Western Europe from the devastation of World War II. With that task completed, the ECE directed its attention to the economic development of the economically weaker members of the European community, and gave priority to economic cooperation between Western European nations and those of the former Soviet bloc in Eastern Europe.

ESCAP has concentrated on economic and social development of the poorer countries of the Asian region. From its Bangkok headquarters the commission has encouraged the creation of such developmental aids as the Asian Free Trade Area, the Mineral Resources Development Center, the International Pepper Community, the Asian Clearing Union, and the Asian Development Bank. It has also sponsored joint development projects, notably Mekong River development and the Asian Highway.

ECLAC, with its central office in Santiago, Chile, has generated wide support in Latin America and is recognized for its contribution to the establishment of the Inter-American Development Bank, the Latin American Free Trade Association, the Central American Common Market, and other cooperative projects. It is also credited with spearheading the creation of UNCTAD within the global UN system. ECLAC has fostered joint action in dealing with the many social problems affecting the modernization drive, such as birth control, child welfare, and housing.

The ECA, established in 1958 with headquarters at Addis Ababa, has in many respects the most difficult task of any regional commission. Its operations have been hampered by the abject poverty of many of its peoples and political rivalries among its members, many of which have ineffective and authoritarian governments. Nevertheless it has helped to establish useful regional organizations in the fields of trade, banking, environmental protection, resource utilization, and political integration. Among these the African Development Bank has been notably well-managed and successful.

The Economic and Social Commission for Western Asia (ESCWA) is primarily a pan-Arab organization, with other countries in the Middle East—Iran, Israel, and Turkey—excluded from membership. When established in 1974, its headquarters were in Lebanon, but because of the war with Israel and much internal strife, the seat of operations was moved to Baghdad, Iraq. The lack of regional harmony had long worked against the establishment of a Middle East Commission, and these problems came to the fore once again when the United Nations undertook military action against the Iraqi regime of Saddam Hussein. Although its headquarters remained in Baghdad, the developmental activities of the commission have yet to materialize.

Membership in the several regional commissions is not limited to states in the geographic region but includes others having special interests in the region. The nonregional members are for the most part industrialized states capable of contributing to the development of the region. The role of the commissions generally has been one of forging a regional outlook among diverse nations with different economic and social systems and, in some cases, with long histories of mutual hostilities. Cooperation within each of the regions has been fostered by numerous conferences, regular exchanges of information, the development of personal and official contacts, and an atmosphere of unity assiduously fostered by each commission's secretariat. Each of the commissions makes annual and special reports to ECOSOC, as well as recommendations to member governments and the specialized agencies on matters falling within their competences. Annual economic surveys of the commissions have served as bases for the development of "country plans" for the distribution of aid by donor countries international organizations, and for the creation of new regional programs, such as the regional banks, common markets, and free trade associations. Annual sessions of the commissions have become major economic planning conferences with broad participation.

*The Development Decades*

Four major UN campaigns to speed Third World development have taken the form of Development Decades for the 1960s, the 1970s, the 1980s, and the 1990s. The first was undertaken in 1961, when the Sixteenth General

Assembly proclaimed a UN Development Decade to dramatize the organization's efforts, to call attention to the need for long-range planning, and to mobilize support for development. The Assembly set a target of raising the annual economic growth rate of developing countries from a 1960 average of about 3.5 percent to a 1970 minimum of 5 percent. The goal was not reached, but subsequent Development Decades continued to dramatize UN development programs and the need for greater efforts.

One major problem has been the failure of many developing countries to carry out economic, political, and social reforms. For another, the flow of development capital has not measured up to expectations. During the first two decades the UN established the primary objective of transferring 1 percent of total GNP from each of the developed states to the developing states. In fact, such assistance fell from 0.51 percent of GNP in 1960 to below 0.40 percent in the 1970s and 1980s. Burgeoning population growth further atrophied program goals by diverting attention within the developing countries to the need for increasing food production to avert mass famine and by emasculating aggregate national gains when measured in terms of per capita standards of living.

In the Third Development Decade the United Nations adopted a New International Development Strategy (NIDS) and also established a Substantial New Program of Action (SNPA) for the least developed countries (LDCs). The New International Development Strategy was aimed at getting each developed country to transfer 0.7 percent of its GNP each year to Third World development assistance. This figure was lower than the 1 percent of GNP demanded in the previous decades, but it was much higher than the actual development aid. SNPA also requested that donor countries contribute an additional 0.15 percent of GNP each year during the 1980s for the benefit of the poorest or least developed countries. It also strongly recommended that the industrialized countries convert their public loans to the poorest countries into outright grants. Supporters of SNPA argued that this would be a realistic approach since the alternative would probably be a general default by these countries.

The Fourth Development Decade was approved by the General Assembly in December, 1990, along with an International Development Strategy to accelerate growth to the year 2000. The strategy emphasized human resources development, entrepreneurship and innovation, and the energetic application of science and technology. The basic plan also called for political systems based on consent and respect for human rights, as well as social and economic rights. Third and Fourth World participants agreed to avoid environmental degradation in their efforts to reduce the economic gap between them and the developed countries.

The Fourth Development Decade came at a propitious moment in the history of the United Nations and its development planning. The cold war was ending, and the developing states foresaw a great decline in world military expenditures which, according to the plan, would allow for the "application of larger resources to the fight against world poverty." As in the past, this optimism was soon shattered by new emerging world economic problems.

*Promoting Industrial Development*

Seven years into the First Development Decade (1967), the General Assembly established the UN Industrial Development Organization (UNIDO) "to promote the industrial development . . . and accelerate the industrialization of the developing countries, with particular emphasis on the manufacturing sector." The establishment of UNIDO reflected the emphasis that the developing states place on industrialization, an emphasis that has not always been shared by the developed states. Opposed by many of the industrialized states, the creation of UNIDO demonstrated the voting power of the Third World in the General Assembly. Not surprisingly, UNIDO has not received heavy financial support from the developed countries.

UNIDO functioned as an "autonomous" organization within the United Nations until January 1, 1986, when it became a UN specialized agency. Its responsibilities are to strengthen, coordinate, and expedite international efforts to promote industrial development, through such activities as research, surveys, training programs, seminars, technical aid, and information exchange. Its main activity, however, is to apply continual pressures on the industrialized states to assist the developing states in their modernization drive. This role follows naturally because UNIDO's governing Industrial Development Board is elected by the General Assembly, and African, Asian, and Latin American states hold a majority of the Assembly seats. Examples of specific projects aided by UNIDO include the production of raw materials from sugarcane waste in Trinidad, the construction of a steel-rolling plant in Jordan, and textile manufacturing in the Sudan. Dr. Abd-El Rahman Khane, Executive Director of UNIDO, has often proclaimed that the organization's goal is to have the Third World account for 25 percent of the world's industrial output by the year 2000. In 1975 it accounted for only 10 percent, and by 1990 it had not yet reached 11 percent. In support of the Industrial Development Decade for Africa, proclaimed in 1980, special attention was focused on Africa, but wars, famine, disease, uncontrolled population growth, lack of skilled labor, and political corruption, have continued to inhibit significant industrial growth.

*The Role of Government: Changing Perspectives*

At the century's end it was apparent expectations had fallen far short of realities. While benefits are not to be discounted, the failures and the limitations demonstrated by the developing states are substantial. Neither international nor regional organizations have achieved for the states what they have been unable to do for themselves. State shortcomings are all too obvious, especially in their lack of capacity to fashion rules and institutions that deliver the necessary goods and services to their citizens. Moreover, sustainable development, whether in economic or social matters, is impossible in the absence of successful governmental structures and processes. The shift away from the too-heavy dependence on the public sector to more assertive non-governmental enterprises does not come naturally. But with government unable to meet the objectives of ever more complex societies, the emphasis has shifted to privatization. Government has been cast in a new set of roles, that of partner, catalyst, and facilitator. Structural adjustment policies demanded by the IMF in the developing nations have aimed at institutionalizing this reorientation, but not without adverse effects visited upon already overburdened populations.

Development, however, is no longer naively viewed as the inevitable consequence of good programs executed by good people. The central role of the state, which appeared to be the answer to the cyclic discontinuities of the marketplace, and the supreme vehicle for the mobilization of human talents, from hindsight, was all too simple. The development administrators were hardly the dedicated public servants anticipated in the literature. Rigid in workways and ignorant of citizen accountability, few countries had the cadres or the circumstances to achieve the desired outcomes. Inadequate experience in self-government exaggerated the roles of arbitrary rulers, and corruption in politics begat corruption in modernization schemes. As a consequence, development faltered or was suspended, and poverty endured and intensified.

Expanded government was a product of two world wars and a great depression in the advanced industrial nations, and it was therefore not surprising that governments came to dominate the developing countries, or that development strategies were fashioned around state-dominant scenarios. It was government that "developed" and became the primary consumer of national resources, but without improving its effectiveness or delivery systems. Government existed to serve its own—not the people's—interest, and nowhere was this better illustrated than in the Second World where communist systems, statecentric and absolutist, came tumbling down in a heap, taking with them one of the world's two vaunted superpowers.

The epochmaking changes of the 1990s can only be compared with events immediately following the century's two catastrophic wars. State-dominated development strategies that followed the Second World War produced state spending at levels that were half the total income of the developed countries and a quarter of the less developed. Thus, even with the new emphasis on privatization, government continued to play a central role. But it was a central role modified by greater popular exposure and scrutiny in matters ranging from taxation to economic policies. Technological changes have opened opportunities to the global marketplace that at the end of the century require public/private sector cooperation and greater transparency in the conduct of public affairs. Less tolerant of government failures, grassroot expression is gaining a more audible voice with the increase in non-governmental organizations. The demand for greater government probity and accountability is matched by insistence that it be more effective in managing public goods such as property rights, physical infrastructure, and basic health and education. In the absence of meaningful government performance, business groups as well as rank and file citizens are less likely to meet their obligations and a vicious circle is created in which little is achieved, frustrations mount, and rebellion is forecast. Especially pronounced in the developing countries, the extreme examples of Somalia, Afghanistan, Rwanda, and Liberia, where states literally ceased to function, have left to international agencies the desperate job of preserving civilization.

The challenges confronting the United Nations system are more complex at the end of the century than they were at its founding. It will require considerably more cooperation among and between the member states whose interest it ultimately is to see to it that the failures of the past are not repeated in the future. Development is a painful experience and progress will not be realized without sacrifice, but the objectives are not beyond reach, and the benefits promise a better future for all the world's people.

## TECHNICAL ASSISTANCE PROGRAMS

Technical assistance, which involves the teaching of skills and new technologies, is an indispensable instrument of any development program. Of the three main legs of the development stool—the infrastructure base, technical competence, and development capital—technical cooperation is the least controversial. It has consumed a sizable portion of the energies and funds of the advanced countries and of UN development programs. The transfer of any skill—from the most rudimentary to the most complex, from teaching a farmer how to wield a steel hoe most effectively to training technicians to run an atomic power plant—falls within the scope of technical assistance. The most significant categories are the technological, managerial, administrative, educational, and medical, in all of which there has been a sharing of skills but a growing scarcity of technicians.

Fortunately, some modern skills were transmitted to societies in the developing states during the nineteenth century and the first half of the twentieth century by the colonialists, missionaries, League of Nations programs, or private business and philanthropic organizations. The first government program of technical assistance on a substantial scale began during World War II, when the United States sought to increase the production of primary commodities essential to the war effort through a major program of technical and cultural exchange with Latin American countries. United States' experts in agriculture, mining, and education accepted in-service posts in Latin America, while large numbers of Latin Americans received training in the United States as medical doctors and technicians, engineers, agronomists, and public administrators. This program was phased out after the war, but in 1949 President Harry S. Truman urged Americans to adopt "a bold new program for making the benefits of our scientific advances and industrial progress available for the improvement and growth of under-developed areas." Set forth in his inaugural address as the last of four policies aimed at achieving peace and security in the world, Point Four was implemented by Congress in the Act for International Development. The act provided for two programs: (1) an expanded program of technical assistance carried out through the United Nations and (2) a bilateral program of technical cooperation. With some changes in titles and administrative procedures, both programs continue today as the world's leading multilateral and bilateral technical assistance programs. In addition, technical assistance can be broken down into two categories: One involves transferring knowledge and skills by sending individuals abroad for training (the "King of Siam" approach), whereas the other imports and uses foreign experts (the "Peter the Great" approach).

## UN Development Program

The U.S. decision in 1949 to offer the underdeveloped world a large-scale technical assistance program led the General Assembly in November of that year to adopt an Expanded Program of Technical Assistance (EPTA). It went beyond the existing meager program and was financed through voluntary contributions rather than through the regular budget. Nine years later, in October 1958, the Assembly complemented the EPTA by establishing a special fund to lay the groundwork for encouraging capital flows into developing states. In November 1965 the Assembly combined the EPTA and special fund into a new UN Development Program (UNDP) to secure a unified approach. Although administratively joined, each maintains a distinctive approach to development within the UNDP.

## Expanded Program of Technical Assistance (EPTA)

EPTA incorporates three main forms of assistance: (1) providing experts, including some from the underdeveloped countries themselves, to train cadres of technicians; (2) awarding fellowships for technical training in advanced countries; and (3) supplying limited amounts of equipment for training and demonstration purposes. Funds for EPTA, as for the special fund, come from voluntary contributions offered at annual pledging conferences. Contributions may be made in both local and hard currencies, but donors may not attach any conditions to the use of their contributions.

Funds are dispensed to approved projects sponsored by the United Nations or by specialized agencies that have been accepted as "participating organizations" of EPTA. Initially the participants included: (1) the International Labor Organization (ILO), (2) the Food and Agriculture Organization (FAO), (3) the UN Educational, Scientific and Cultural Organization (UNESCO), (4) the International Civil Aviation Organization (ICAO), and (5) the World Health Organization (WHO). Six additional organizations subsequently joined the program: (6) the International Telecommunication Union (ITU) and (7) the World Meteorological Organization (WMO), in 1951; (8) the International Atomic Energy Agency (IAEA), in 1959; (9) the Universal Postal Union (UPU), in 1962; (10) the International Maritime Organization (IMO), in 1964; and (11) the World Bank, in 1965. All are represented on the Inter-Agency Consultative Board for the Development Program, which coordinates all UN technical assistance and related programs. The International Monetary Fund, although not participating directly in the program, works closely with the consultative board to deal with balance of payments problems affecting development programs.

Resident representatives in the field assist government in developing sound programs and advise the consultative board on their feasibility in relation to local conditions. Offices around the globe, most of which are organized on a single-country basis, coordinate technical assistance programs, function as "country representatives" for some of the specialized agencies, lend assistance on preinvestment surveys, and serve as a link between the United Nations and the recipient government. The resident representative's office has grown in significance as efforts have increased to achieve a greater measure of coordination and unity of purpose in UN assistance programs.

UN technical assistance programs have been widely recognized as desirable and generally effective. Developing states have for the most part not been critical of the pace of the UN technical assistance program. Rather their complaints have been directed primarily at the shortage of development capital.

## The Special Fund

The special fund was a partial response to demands for capital transfers to supplement technical assistance. It reflected a growing recognition by the advanced states that the fruits of technical assistance would be increased if it were supported by inputs of capital. At that, the special fund was only a compromise falling far short of the perennial demands of the developing states for a massive development fund to provide capital grants and to be replenished annually at a contributory rate of 1 percent of the GNP of each industrialized state.

The special fund embodied the concept of paving the way for increased private, national, and international investment by conducting "pre-investment" surveys, by discovering the wealth-producing potentials of unsurveyed natural resources, by establishing training and research institutes, and by preparing "feasibility reports on the practicability, requirements, and usefulness" of development projects. Although EPTA and the special fund were to be coordinated from the start, the special fund functioned independently in allocating money and determining priorities. The amalgamation of the two in 1966 in the UN Development Program (UNDP) gave some assurance that both programs would operate thereafter under a single source of direction. The UNDP is the world's largest agency for technical cooperation, currently supporting several thousand development projects.

## Other Technical Assistance Programs

The diversity of needs in the developing world has helped spawn a variety of special UN projects, each devoted to an attack on some particular problem of economic development not covered or covered inadequately by the general technical assistance program. To fill a need for top-level administrators in developing societies, an Operational, Executive, and Administrative (OPEX) personnel service was established in 1958 by the General Assembly. Internationally recruited experts are assigned under OPEX to governments, with the proviso that their duties include training nationals to replace them. Another complementary personnel program emerged in 1963, when the General Assembly established the UN Institute for Training and Research (UNITAR). Fully operational by 1966, UNITAR specializes in conducting training seminars for new members of government delegations and their staffs and for individuals in UN-related civil service positions. Its faculty are recruited through fellowship programs and through the voluntary participation of eminent scholars and statesmen.

A number of programs, peripheral yet significant to economic development, complete the UN effort to provide technical assistance. UN conferences on a host of topics such as population control, desertification, science and technology, environmental protection, world fisheries, and the role of women have been convened over the years to foster development attuned to the needs of particular regions and countries. An Industrial Development Center functions as a clearinghouse in the fields of economics and industrial technology, and an Economic Projections and Programming Center develops long-term projections of world economic and industrial trends to facilitate national planning. Both of these centers are located at UN headquarters, although the latter center also operates through regional subcenters.

A World Food Program was undertaken jointly in 1963 by the United Nations and the FAO to provide food for economic and social development projects and to supply food in emergencies. Under this program food aid constitutes a partial substitute for cash wages for workers in such fields as mining, industry, community development, and irrigation. In the field of demography, the UN Population Commission conducts extensive research on population problems affecting the ability of states to develop and has sponsored three World Population Conferences. Other programs that contribute indirectly to technical cooperation include the UNICEF program for fostering the development of future leaders and technicians through food and educational programs for children. The United Nations itself trains political leaders in statesmanship, and Secretariat technicians learn modern administrative techniques. Many other types of aid programs include provisions for technical assistance as well. For example, the International Bank has become active in the field of technical assistance through project preparation, development programming, and the training of senior development officials.

The United Nations University, headquartered in Tokyo, carries on a fellowship program that is linked with national and regional development organizations in more than sixty countries. Under this program it has supplied hundreds of scholars, scientists, and government officials to help fill knowledge gaps in the areas of poverty, famine, and resource management. Some of these fellows are experienced specialists, whereas others are graduate students, mainly from Third World countries.

*The Future of Technical Assistance*

Technical assistance programs enable some nations to help other nations, making all of them better off. The donor countries benefit because the poorer countries make better trading partners as their living conditions improve and because societies moving toward a brighter economic future are less prone to revolutionary violence. There has been little criticism of the principle of technical cooperation, from either the developed or the developing countries. Duplication and overlapping of jurisdictions have abounded in UN programs, however, and between these programs and bilateral and regional programs, and this has sometimes aroused petty jealousies and conflicts. Efforts within the United Nations to coordinate programs have been only partially effective, and future consolidations and partnership arrangements, such as those carried out by EPTA and the special fund through the UN Development Program, are needed in order to employ limited resources and personnel more advantageously. Finally, as already noted, no technical assistance program, no matter how well financed and administered, can achieve major development goals unless capital accumulation, investment, and transfers of technology move forward in tandem with it. We now turn our attention to the UN role of fostering inflows of capital into developing economies to obtain the balance that is so essential for economic development.

# UN DEVELOPMENT FINANCING PROGRAMS: THE WORLD BANK GROUP

Within the UN system, most financial assistance for economic development has been dispensed through loan programs carried on by the World Bank group—the International Bank for Reconstruction and Development (IBRD or "World Bank"), the International Finance Corporation (IFC), the International Development Association (IDA), and the Multilateral Investment Guarantee Agency (MIGA)—and, indirectly, by the International Monetary Fund (IMF). Although all of these function within the broad framework of the UN system, each is involved in its own fund-raising and decision-making operations. Developing states have not given up their attempts to establish an effective capital grants type of UN organization, but they have realistically turned to the World Bank Group and the IMF for capital aid in the form of loans to supplement loans from national, regional, and private sources. International Monetary Fund membership is a prerequisite for joining the World Bank and its affiliates, but a nation can join the IMF without joining the World Bank.

## THE ROLE OF THE WORLD BANK GROUP

Within the UN system, the agencies of the World Bank group, along with the International Monetary Fund, are responsible for most of the capital aid transfers to the developing countries. Coordination between the World Bank agencies and the IMF is provided by the World Bank/IMF Development Committee. The committee functions both as an advisory body to the two boards of governors and as an action body to encourage "foreign capital flows of all kinds" to the developing states. Its membership includes twenty-two finance and development ministers from the two boards of governors.

## The International Bank

From its inception at the 1944 Bretton Woods Conference, the International Bank for Reconstruction and Development (IBRD) was intended to be the central unit in UN lending operations. Since private international capital had virtually disappeared during the 1930s, the World Bank reflected the prevailing attitude that some form of public international financing was essential as a supplement to private loans. Initially the World Bank devoted its resources to the urgent task of restoring Europe's war-torn economies, with only seven loans committed to developing countries by the end of 1949. The pace of development loans quickened, however, rising by billions of dollars in each subsequent decade. In its 1997 fiscal year the World Bank made loan commitments to developing countries valued at $13.99 billion. Within guidelines laid down by member states, the World Bank's lending policies are developed by its board of governors, using a weighted voting system based on subscribed capital. The IBRD makes "hard loans," repayable in convertible currency, and most of its loans have run for five to fifteen or twenty years at less than commercial rates of interest, about 6.8 percent in 1997. Loans are made either to member governments or to private firms with a government guarantee. Loans to private firms have been minimal because firms have found it difficult to obtain their government's guarantee or have preferred not to get involved with governmental red tape. Moreover, the World Bank has no facilities for investigating and administering loan applications from small businesses, and few locally owned large firms exist in the developing states. To meet this problem, the World Bank has granted loans to private banks and loan and investment agencies so that they can relend those funds to private companies and entrepreneurs.

The World Bank is run by bankers, giving it a conservative image that its board of governors regards as a proper one. It operates on sound principles of international finance, and its loan criteria are aimed at protecting its interests and those of its creditors. This image of soundness is necessary since most of the World Bank's loan funds are obtained, not from governments, but from borrowing in private capital markets. Loan applicants must use a "project" approach in which the applicant demonstrates that the loan will finance a carefully planned undertaking that will contribute to the productive and earning capacity of the country. For many years the World Bank frowned on social project loans (for building hospitals and schools or for slum clearance), general-purpose loans, and loans to meet rising debt or to resolve balance-of-payments problems, but it has given such loans some support in recent years. In fact, the

World Bank's lending policies have been substantially modified by its efforts in the latter half of the 1980s and the 1990s to encourage economic growth in major debtor countries of the Third World. For some years the World Bank limited its use of funds to "self-liquidating projects"—projects that would provide revenues large enough to service debt payments—but it now measures the repayment capacity of the nation's entire economy in making its loans. On average, World Bank loans have financed only 25 percent of the cost of projects with other investors often joining the World Bank to provide the balance.

Over the years the World Bank has undergone a change, both in its self-image and in its operations, from a strictly financial institution to that of a development agency intimately concerned with solving problems of economic development. Instead of remaining aloof and merely passing judgment on loan applications, it now assists states in their development planning, helps prepare project proposals, and provides training for senior development officials. Its economic survey missions check resource and investment potentials in member countries and determine priorities for country and regional projects. The World Bank has also participated increasingly in consortium arrangements for financing major projects, with funds provided jointly by global, regional, and local public and private lending institutions. The World Bank has demonstrated that it can use its funds to secure the cooperation of political enemies on a mutually beneficial development plan, as in the joint development of a common river control system by India and Pakistan.

Despite its increased pace of activity, the World Bank has never been able to meet all the capital needs of developing states. For one thing, repayment of loans in hard currencies imposes grave difficulties on borrowing states that do not rank high as foreign exchange earners. At the end of fiscal 1997, six member countries (Bosnia-Herzegovina, Democratic Republic of the Congo, Iraq, Liberia, Sudan, and Syria) and one successor republic of the former Federal Republic of Yugoslavia—the Federated Republic of Yugoslavia (Serbia and Montenegro)—were in nonaccrual status. Of these countries, all but Bosnia-Herzegovina had payments in arrears to the bank. All overdue payments from Bosnia-Herzegovina were cleared in June 1996, but the country remained in nonaccrual status because of the high level of collectibility risk associated with its outstanding debt stock. Loans in nonaccrual status at the end of 1997 amounted to 2.23 percent of the total IBRD portfolio. Many developing states have been overstraining their debt-servicing capacities, and new loans might add to the world debt crisis. Moreover, since economic activity in many developing states is carried on predominantly by private companies, a practical means of making loans to relatively small firms without government guarantees has been considered essential to economic development. This has led some critics to conclude that the World Bank has functioned effectively as an international bank, but that it has not been successful as a development institution. These critics perhaps harken back to the early post–World War II years when the Third World bloc fought vigorously to have the United Nations create a major capital *grants* institution but lost the battle. These weaknesses of the World

Bank, however, have been partly mitigated by the establishment of two additional lending affiliates.

## The International Finance Corporation (IFC)

From the start of the World Bank's operations, many observers recognized that some kind of affiliate was needed to help finance private investment. Such an affiliate would permit the stimulation of private companies by injections of international capital secured mainly from private sources. This kind of financing was provided by the establishment of the International Finance Corporation in 1956, with a startup subscribed capital fund of $78 million. The IFC promotes the flow of capital from world money markets, stimulates the formation of investment capital within member countries, and encourages private enterprise and private investment opportunities. It makes loans and direct equity investment in private companies, including companies owned jointly by local and foreign interests. The IFC, for example, has entered into mixed equity loan commitments in such industries as steel, textiles, cement, jute, pulp, food processing, and pharmaceuticals. From its modest startup fund of $78 million the IFC steadily increased its resources, approving a total of $6.7 billion in 1997. Total project costs for 1997, however, were $17.9 billion. IFC approved 276 projects in eighty-four countries and regions during this period, up from 264 projects in seventy-six countries and regions in 1996. IFC invested funds in eight new countries, including Tajikistan, Moldova, and Eritrea. IFC currently invests across a wide spectrum of sectors from capital markets, infrastructure, agribusiness, petrochemicals, and extractive industries to general manufacturing. Projects range across every geographic region, and opportunities are sought to invest in social service projects such as health care and education.

In an effort to get more private capital flowing into developing states, the IFC in 1989 established the International Securities Group (ISG) to provide investment banking services to clients in Third World countries. Specifically, ISG functions (1) as an advisor in the issuance of securities; (2) as a partner, bringing companies from the developing world to the international capital markets; and (3) as a provider of information to the world investment community on investment opportunities in emerging markets. As a result of IFC/ISG activities, by 1998 there were more than 1,000 companies listed on the stock exchanges in twenty developing countries. In this sense, IFC rejects anything resembling a "welfare" approach and seeks through pure capitalism to encourage economic growth and modernization.

Obviously, the IFC is merely scratching the surface of world needs for public capital to stimulate private investment. Loans to small- and medium-sized firms are not included in its scope of operations, although it has encouraged members to establish local development banks to do this job and has offered to help finance them. The IFC itself has been authorized to borrow large sums from the World Bank. The result is effective but circular: The International Bank secures funds from private capital markets, lends some of these funds to the IFC, which in turn lends some to country development banks, from which the funds finally return through direct loans to private businesses. Are these international and national institutional middlemen really necessary? They obviously are, since they were created in response to urgent needs. Most investors refuse to risk their capital in developing states without governmental guarantee programs. The stage of sustainable growth may finally be reached by a developing country when significant inflows of private funds occur without global, regional, or local institutional stimulation or direct protection. Both the IFC and its International Securities Group affiliate (ISG) are in full pursuit of that objective.

### The International Development Association (IDA)

In response to a growing chorus of demands for a capital grants program and a continuing criticism of the conservative nature of the World Bank's operations, the International Development Association was established in 1960 as a "soft loan" affiliate. The IDA was also a response by the United States (the idea was developed in Congress) to a stepped-up Soviet aid/trade offensive. Although IDA is a separate legal entity and its funds and reserves are separate from those of the International Bank, the management and staff of the two institutions are the same.

The "soft loan" features of IDA pertain to the long period for repayment (fifty years), the slow amortization rate (which begins after a ten-year grace period, with 1 percent of the loan's principal repayable annually during the second ten years and 3 percent payable annually for the remaining thirty years), and the low cost of the loan (no interest but a three-fourths of 1 percent annual service charge). IDA loans are not "soft," however, in one highly significant respect—they must be repaid in "hard" (convertible) foreign exchange. This usually means U.S. dollars or a currency freely convertible into dollars.

Developing states, recognizing the advantages of IDA's terms—especially the provision that no payments on a loan are due for ten years—quickly depleted the initial and subsequent subscriptions. As with World Bank loans, recipients of IDA funds must finance a portion of all loan projects, usually with local currency. IDA's loans go mainly to government agencies in the poorest countries for projects similar to those financed in other developing countries by the World Bank. Whether IDA loans will continue to be paid off when the ten-year grace period ends depends in each case on a country's progress in economic development and its export trade. It will also depend on general world conditions—war or peace, boom or bust, population control or population explosion, the terms of trade, the development of synthetics, changes in consumer tastes, and numerous other unpredictable factors that may either ease repayments or, for all practical purposes, turn loans into grants. IDA lends only to those countries that had a per capita income in 1995 of less than $905 and a lack of financial ability to borrow from the World Bank on market terms.

In 1998, eighty countries were eligible to borrow from IDA. Together these countries were home to 3.2 billion people, comprising 65 percent of the total population of the developing countries. Some 1.2 billion of these people survived on incomes of $1 or less a day. When a country passes the IDA eligibility threshold it can no longer apply for the Bank's interest-free credits and must borrow from the IBRD at market-related rates. Some countries, however, like China and India, are eligible for a combination of IBRD loans and IDA credits. These countries are known as "blend borrowers." In 1998 there were seventeen so-called blend borrowers. Countries that "graduated" from IDA eligibility included Costa Rica, Chile, Indonesia, and Morocco. Since 1960 IDA has loaned almost $100 billion to some ninety countries, and in fiscal year 1997 it disbursed $6 billion.

### The Multilateral Investment Guarantee Agency (MIGA)

A third affiliate of the World Bank, the Multilateral Investment Guarantee Agency (MIGA), came into being through treaty ratification in 1988. MIGA's role is to encourage the flow of private equity capital to developing countries by insuring investments against losses resulting from political risks—war and civil strife, expropriation, government repudiation of contracts, and host government currency restrictions. With equity investments, or risk capital, recipient states have the benefit of capital infusion without incurring debt obligations.

## THE WORLD BANK GROUP: AN EVALUATION

The World Bank group operates on a professional, nonpolitical level. The activities of the World Bank and its three affiliates have benefited almost every developing state, and indications are that the pace of their lending operations will accelerate over the next decade. Yet the group's operations have been subject to extensive criticism. Control of World Bank group operations by Western (former colonial) powers, through a voting system that is weighted on the basis of contributions, has aroused widespread suspicion of its motives and its policies. Critics point out that the World Bank's loan terms are no bargain—that they are usually only slightly easier, and sometimes even harsher, than those of private banks. In many cases states borrow from the World Bank despite its high rates because their low credit rating prevents them from securing private loans. The International Finance Corporation, critics charge, has never gained general acceptance in the advanced donor states or, for that matter, in the developing world, as evidenced by relatively low-level funding and its modest lending activity. Its objective of furthering private investment by meshing capital from both the public and private sectors is a novel approach, but the total resources have been too meager to effectively stimulate growth capitalism within recipient states. The International Development Association has enjoyed a singular success in dispensing funds, probably because it comes closest to the capital grants system unsuccessfully sought by developing states for many years. It is, however, frequently "loaned out," with no loanable funds available until a new pledging conference provides a replenishment.

Despite criticism, the World Bank group has retained the support of its members, whether developed or developing countries. The group's loans have helped more than one hundred countries to finance useful development projects, and it has often successfully encouraged internal financial reforms within borrowing countries. This last role, sometimes referred to as "the art of development diplomacy," may go beyond domestic matters, as in the World Bank's negotiation of the Indus River Agreement between India and Pakistan. Given the continuing capital needs for economic development in the world today and the failure of the UN Capital Development Fund, one can only conclude that the role of the World Bank group will continue to grow.

## CONCLUSION ON ECONOMIC DEVELOPMENT

Where, on balance, do the developing states stand today? What are the prospects for development in the decades beyond 2000? Although more has been done to promote world economic development during the last three decades than in all the past aeons of history, much more has been needed and expected. Progress, if defined as an improvement in mass standards of living, has failed to measure up to optimistic hopes. Agricultural output, while increasing substantially in some developing states, has barely kept pace with population growth, and millions remain undernourished. Famines in Africa during the 1980s and 1990s may be a harbinger for much of the Third World, with the danger that undernourishment in many countries may turn first to serious malnutrition and then to large-scale famine. In the field of housing, millions of new dwellings must be built each year merely to stay abreast of population growth. Education, despite extensive UN and national programs fostered by UNESCO, remains a major problem at all points on the educational scale—too many illiterates, too few trained technicians, and a great paucity of university-trained professionals. Unemployment and underemployment also pose a serious problem in many countries.

Although some countries and subregions have failed to dent the problem of economic stagnation, others have been making determined efforts to join the world of developed states. Some societies have received huge infusions of aid but have failed to use that aid effectively to broaden the base of their economies or to integrate new productive enterprises with the demands of the world market. Efforts of the international community through bilateral, regional, and global programs have been scattered and largely uncoordinated, often characterized by wasteful duplication and overlapping.

Clearly, most developing states prefer to receive aid through UN programs that leave them unencumbered politically and militarily and avoid damage to national egos. The United Nations offers a partnership arrangement with assisted countries, cooperating in planning, developing, and administering aid programs that are somewhat freer of power rivalries than other aid programs. No other organization can provide such a storehouse of development information and experience or possess so many useful contacts beneficial to developing states. The United Nations also provides a natural focus for coordinating development programs, an "agitation chamber" for debating and stimulating action by member states, a forum for the exchange of information and ideas, and a repository of skills that are available to developing states. But the key objective of the great majority of members—obtaining the full support of the developed states for a large-scale capital grants program—has not been realized.

Nevertheless, a still higher profile is forecast for the United Nations system in the twenty-first century. Kofi Annan heads a spirited secretariat team that is committed to new initiatives, and especially to the linkages between the UN and the global business community. Citing the need to address the forces of globalization, United Nations officials are concerned with both the positive and negative dimensions of the new world economy. Cognizant that globalization in its current form can adversely impact the developing nations, the Secretary-General has focused attention on the running North-South debate that highlights differences between the wealthy and poor nations. In the middle of this exchange is the third world's continuing dependency on the United Nations, and the more affluent states' preference for the more intrusive World Bank and International Monetary Fund. Sensitive to the issues behind this controversy, Kofi Annan has noted: "Unless we tackle the underlying distortions and imbalances in the global economy, unless we start the kind of global governance that is needed, we must expect more [political and military] conflicts and even more intractable ones." [6]

The United Nations therefore is engaged in forging even closer ties to the World Bank and IMF, and encourages increased dialogue among global stakeholders. Hence new fora have been fashioned to elevate high-level economic consultations between the Bretton Woods institutions and the United Nations Economic and Social Council. A UN sponsored meeting on finance and development, scheduled for the year 2000, has elevated expectations among developing country spokesmen that the architecture of the world's financial institutions will be redrawn to focus more effort and resources on sustainable development projects and social issues. Differences over whether the United Nations is the proper forum for the airing of views on globalization and debt relief will frame the exchange between the developed and the developing nations, and the latter no doubt will find strength in numbers by rallying around the Group of 77 on the one side, and ECOSOC on the other.

Although determined to avoid the pressure tactics employed by the developing countries, the G-7 states nonetheless have been forced to acknowledge that policies which focus too heavily on free markets and fiscal stringency, the central themes of the IMF and World Bank, failed to work in Pacific-Asia in 1997. In fact those very IMF policies may have contributed to the severity of the Asian economic crisis in 1998–99. Chastened by these events, the G-7 seems more inclined to listen to the concerns of the developing nations. Moreover, no better forum exists for the bridging of North-South differences than the United Nations. Thus, despite their reluctance to mix macroeconomic policymaking with specific financial and fiscal responsibilities, the G-7 of the twenty-first century is more likely to demonstrate flexibility in their relations with the developing countries. In calling for a new development paradigm, the G-7 appears poised to give special attention to social well-being as well as development strategies that emanate from the emergent nations.

As 1998 drew to a close, finance ministers and central bank governors of the G-7 countries publicized a major policy reform to bolster confidence in world financial markets. The central purposes of the policy were to 1) reduce uncertainty about conditions prevailing in specific countries as well as financial markets; and 2) to redistribute the risk of foreign lending to emerging market economies, what had become known as the "moral hazard" issue. The centerpiece for the new policy was the abandonment of secrecy and a new emphasis on total transparency in all fiscal and monetary dealings. Public and private corporations were to be held to a high standard of probity and a newly reconstructed IMF was to be given responsibility for monitoring compliance with strict, international guidelines. For the first time the G-7 nations accepted responsibility for the heavy stress on development projects that had seldom taken into account the most vulnerable groups in society. To rectify this matter the IMF also was called upon to demonstrate greater transparency and accountability.

Closing the distance between the developed and developing nations will require bringing the IMF and World Bank into more intimate association with the Group of 77. And indeed at the dawn of a new century it was the advanced industrial countries that were heard championing the governance of international monetary, financial, and trade systems issues pressed earlier by the developing states at the United Nations. Before leaving his post as U.S. Ambassador to the United Nations in 1998, Bill Richardson cited the parallel forum developing between the United Nations and the Bretton Woods institutions. The new millennium appeared to be the moment to usher in a new approach in the formation of ideas on financing development in the technotronic era.

## NOTES

1. See "Redefining 'Least Developed Country,'" *Development Forum* 19, No. 3 (July–August 1991), p. 9. The UN Committee for Development Planning has defined LDCs as "those low-income countries that are suffering from long-term handicaps to growth, in particular low levels of human resource development and/or severe structural weaknesses." The World Bank, in 1992, defined LDCs as those countries with a per capita income per year of $610 or less. General definitional characteristics for being accepted by the United Nations as a member of the "least developed" or poorest nations include: (1) a per capita gross domestic product (GDP) of approximately $200 a year; (2) a low life expectancy; (3) literacy rates under 20 percent; and (4) a low contribution of manufacturing industries to GDP. It should be remembered that LDCs means "Less Developed Countries" and also "Least Developed Countries," with the former usage referring to the entire group of developing states, whereas the latter refers to the poorest of this group, sometimes referred to as the Fourth World.

    The least developed countries, according to UN classification, include: Afghanistan, Angola, Bangladesh, Benin, Bhutan, Burkina Faso, Burundi, Cambodia, Cape Verde, Central African Republic, Chad, Comoros, Congo, Djibouti, Equatorial Guinea, Ethiopia, Gambia, Ghana, Guinea, Guinea-Bissau, Haiti, Kiribati, Laos, Lesotho, Liberia, Madagascar, Malawi, Maldives, Mali, Mauritania, Mozambique, Myanmar, Nepal, Niger, Rwanda, Samoa, São Tomé and Principe, Sierra Leone, Soloman Islands, Somalia, Sudan, Togo, Tuvalu, Uganda, United Republic of Tanzania, Vanuatu, Yemen, and Zambia.

2. See International Bank for Reconstruction and Development, *World Development Report, 1997* (Washington, DC: IBRD, 1997).

3. "Report Cites Progress on Population Growth," *The Interdependent,* UNA/USA, vol. 17, no. 3 (June/July 1991), p. 4.

4. UN Document E/CONF.46/C.1/S.R. 9, May 1, 1964, p. 8.

5. George D. Woods, "World Bank and Affiliates Examine Pressing Problems of Economic Development," *United Nations Monthly Chronicle* (November 1964), p. 60. This classic statement was made in relation to strengthening the International Finance Corporation so that it could encourage greater use of private resources for development purposes.

6. United Nations, *Development Update,* No. 26, January–February 1999, p. 1.

## SELECTED READINGS

Ali, Sheikh R. *The International Organizations and World Order Dictionary.* Santa Barbara and Oxford, England: ABC-CLIO Press, 1992.

Berg, Robert J. and David F. Gordon, eds. *Cooperation for International Development: The United States and the Third World in the 1990s.* Boulder, CO: Lynne Rienner, 1989.

Culpeper, Roy. *The Multilateral Development Banks: Titans or Behemoths?* Boulder: Lynne Rienner, 1997.

Delvin, Robert. *Debt and Crisis in Latin America*. Princeton: Princeton University Press, 1989.

Fry, Gerald W. and Galen R. Martin. *The International Development Dictionary*. Santa Barbara and Oxford, England: ABC-CLIO Press, 1991.

———. *The International Education of the Development Consultant: Communicating with Peasants and Princes*. Oxford: Pergamon Press, 1989.

Kapur, Devesh, John P. Lewis, and Richard Webb. *The World Bank: Its First Half Century*. Volume I: History. Washington, D.C.: Brookings Institution, 1997.

Keohane, Robert O. and Mary A. Levy, eds. *Institutions for Environmental Aid: Pitfalls and Promise*. Cambridge: MIT Press, 1996.

Kim, Samuel S. *The Quest for a Just World Order*. Boulder, CO: Westview Press, 1984.

Krueger, Anne O. *Perspectives on Trade and Development*. Chicago: University of Chicago Press, 1990.

———, Constantine Michalopoulos, and Vernon W. Ruttan. *Aid and Development*. Baltimore: The Johns Hopkins University Press, 1989.

MacDonald, Scott B., Margie Lindsay, and David L. Crum, eds. *The Global Debt Crisis: Forecasting for the Future*. London: Pinter Publishers, 1990.

Meller, Patricio, ed. *The Latin American Development Debate: Neostructuralism, Neomonetarism, and Adjustment Processes*. Boulder, CO: Westview Press, 1991.

Robinson, Thomas W., ed. *Democracy and Development in East Asia: Taiwan, South Korea, and the Philippines*. Washington, DC: AEI Press, 1991.

Seligson, Mitchell A. and John T. Passe-Smith. *Development and Underdevelopment: The Political Economy of Global Inequality*. Boulder: Lynne Rienner, 1998.

Shihata, Ibrahim F. I., Franziska Tschofen, and Antonio R. Parra, eds. *The World Bank in a Changing World. Selected Essays*. Dordrecht: Martinus Nijhoff Publishers, 1991.

Ward, Barbara. *The Rich Nations and the Poor Nations*. New York: W. W. Norton, 1962.

Weaver, James H., Michael T. Rock and Kenneth Kusterer. *Achieving Broad-Based Sustainable Development*. West Hartford, CT: Kumarian Press, 1996.

*World Development Report 1997*. Oxford: Published for the World Bank by Oxford University Press, 1997.

Young, Oran R. *Global Governance: Drawing Insights from the Environmental Experience*. Cambridge: MIT Press, 1998.

# 12

## Looking Back Toward an Uncertain Future: The United Nations and the Twenty-First Century

If the United Nations did not exist it would have to be invented. As the world's premier international organization it has come to mean all things to the people of the earth, and indeed as the organization prepares to enter the twenty-first century its numerous organs and agencies, programs and projects, embrace virtually every activity associated with life on the planet. In a world divided into nation-states and representing a vast array of interests, it is the United Nations that represents the common humanity of peoples everywhere. But above all, it is the United Nations that nurtures and encourages the positive and constructive interaction between the many governments that speak for the individual states.

Not everyone, however, believes the organization is a "noble experiment" in human cooperation. Indeed, for those who question the ubiquitous character of the United Nations, it continues to be judged a threat rather than a promise. Fearful that the success of the United Nations translates into loss of national power and authority, any delegation of what otherwise is considered exclusive state responsibility supposedly diminishes sovereignty and confuses as well as undermines constitutional order. And nowhere is criticism of the United Nations more vituperative than in the land that conceived it, and on whose soil it is located.

Without the United States, the United Nations is a weak and lesser vehicle and it is not surprising that Americans have been among both the organization's strongest advocates as well as its most staunch critics. The United States throughout its history, but more so in the twentieth century, has been Janus-like in its attitude toward international organization. Americans have at once appealed for a world of accommodative spirit, a global civil society in which diversity is harmonized and celebrated; and at the same time, they have reveled in what is considered a national uniqueness that sets them apart from the many others who inhabit the planet. When the United Nations was in its infancy, this dichotomy was less in evidence. Then, the United States, the only intact major survivor of World War II, set out to remodel the world. And except for the obstacles strewn in its path by the Soviet Union, for a brief period the United Nations was at the virtual beck and call of the United States, its clear and overwhelming majority not yet disturbed by the admission of scores of new nations.

471

The retreat from colonialism by the remaining imperial states, however, transformed the world and the United Nations. What had been an American monopoly quickly faded. While posturing friendship and even alliance with the new countries, the United States found itself in a contest with the Soviet Union, which also sought their favor. Moreover, each new addition to the rolls of the United Nations brought an agenda that reflected its exclusive interests, and oftentimes those interests clashed with others projected by the United States. This latter "rivalry" was best illustrated in the deliberations of the UN General Assembly, the one forum where the lesser powers were positioned to challenge the "mighty" and seek their own advantages.

The United States did not relish being made the target of criticism and verbal abuse, and although it learned to parry each barb directed against it, the United Nations ceased to be the best place from which to pursue American foreign policy. In the 1970s the United States exchanged roles with the Soviet Union, and Washington far more than Moscow availed itself of the veto power in the Security Council. United States' outright rejection of majority decisions and resolutions in the General Assembly, however, illustrated the profound changes occurring in the organization's performance. With the UN no longer a big power instrument, the United States was more inclined to pursue its particular interests outside the purview of the United Nations. Not alone in this matter, the disputes that came before the United Nations were seldom those immediately engaging any of the prominent powers. It is interesting to note that even the UN-sponsored proximity talks that resulted in the Soviet withdrawal from Afghanistan included only Afghanistan and Pakistan. By contrast with the larger powers, therefore, invasions of privacy and sovereignty had become common among the lesser members. The smaller nations, burdened by internal disorder, and in some cases, violated by the aggressive behavior of their neighbors, often welcomed and even invited UN intervention.

The passing of the cold war accentuated the inchoate nature of many of the states born after World War II, and one or more of the Security Council's permanent powers felt compelled to deal with intra-state disturbances in order to prevent their intensification or spread. Representative of the status quo power structure, the major members of the Security Council, but especially the United States, were eager to sustain an equilibrium that was also the basis for their own longevity. But the end of the cold war also pointed to a significant gap in a world divided between "haves" and "have nots." Although Russia replaced the Soviet Union on the Security Council and enjoyed the privileges that went with permanent power status, in other than strategic terms it too had become something not very different from a third world nation. Economically backward, its meager financial contribution to the United Nations dramatized its lesser place among the greater contemporary powers. On the other hand, Japan, which had assumed a United Nations financial responsibility only second to that of the United States, remained outside the select circle. So too Germany, whose unified state and more substantial financial resources had established it as the key actor in Western Europe. But Germany too was prevented from entering the central power structure of the United Nations.

Parallel and often more significant decision making therefore was conducted outside the framework of the United Nations. The G-7 countries that dominated the global economy functioned at a distance from the world organization. Here Japan and Germany could share position with the United States, and Russia's admission to the club that was sometimes described as "G-7 plus one" was more a gesture of realpolitik than recognition that Moscow was an eminent financial actor. Nevertheless, the existence of the G-7 forum and summit added little to the stature of the United Nations. Moreover, the International Monetary Fund and the International Bank for Reconstruction and Development were more likely to respond to the decisions of the G-7 than to those identified with the United Nations. The power of decision therefore remained with the major actors in a wide range of economic or strategic matters, and the United Nations had to content itself with a status that while not inconsequential, nonetheless, was secondary to the actions and maneuvers of the most powerful among the national states.

## THE UNITED NATIONS AND STRUCTURAL REFORM

At century's end, the United Nations continued to reflect internal cleavages as well as unresolved issues between the greater and lesser powers. The organization's structure remained much as it had been designed by its founders and drafters of the Charter. On the one hand, the Security Council remained potentially the most potent UN institution. On the other hand, however, its increased assertiveness, attributed to the termination of ideological rivalry and the introduction of a more formal pragmatism, obscured weaknesses borne of exclusive pursuits. No longer inclined to aggravate civil strife for their own competitive purposes, the permanent Security Council members now saw the necessity for neutralizing intra-state disturbances in the still half-formed nations. Functioning more under Chapter VI Charter directives, however, the Council was less concerned with enforcement than with the creation of conditions wherein the parties to a dispute might find peaceful solutions. UN peacekeeping operations, used sparingly during the cold war era, multiplied as a consequence of this changed attitude, but in authorizing action, the Council imposed heavier responsibilities upon the UN Secretariat and forced the organization into deeper indebtedness. Chapter VII of the UN Charter vests the Security Council with exceptional enforcement powers, and pursuant to Article 43, the permanent powers are called upon to designate standby military units for international duty. Sustained reluctance to operationalize the intent of the article, however, negated the value of Chapter VII powers and blurred the lines between Security Council and General Assembly responsibilities.

Nevertheless, because the Security Council could react more quickly to emerging crises, the General Assembly was largely relieved of its peacekeeping role. Moreover, no longer called upon to operate under the Uniting For Peace Resolution, which was passed to overcome a stalemated Security Council during the 1950 Korean War, the Assembly settled back into its more designated role of debating the great and lesser issues confronting the world community. Still capable of pressuring the great powers, however, or more specifically, of marshaling votes against another member state, the General Assembly's decision in 1998 to confer near-member status on the Palestine Liberation Organization, over the objection of the United States, demonstrated a combative attitude that was little concerned with building harmony between the Assembly and the Council, or more specifically, between the UN and the United States. Clearly, whereas the Security Council remained an instrument of the larger powers, the General Assembly had long before become the voice of the many smaller governments. Finding a balance between the two major organs of the United Nations has always been the task of the UN Secretariat and especially of the Secretary-General. But no matter how accomplished the Secretaries-General, their diplomacy was never sufficient, and it has been obvious for some time that what was needed was nothing less than the restructuring of all the principal organs of the United Nations.

Thus, the argument persisted that the Council should be expanded and that both Japan and Germany should be given permanent power status. Moreover, because membership had increased to new levels, various groups recommended that the current ten nonpermanent members be increased to fourteen or fifteen, while still others pressured for the addition of at least four large states, all drawn from the developing world, and each of which would be considered a permanent member of the Council. These same groups called for terminating the veto power enjoyed by the permanent members. In fact, the new permanent members would be admitted without the right of veto, while the original permanent members would yield that prerogative no later than 2005. But such changes in the operations of the Security Council could only be successful if they were interfaced with similar changes in the General Assembly. Mindful of the sovereign equality principle, nonetheless, the Charter's one-nation, one-vote principle needed amending. Weighted voting had been debated over the lifetime of the organization but it had never received a positive reception. With the organization approaching almost 200 members, however, and with the vast majority of them poor and feeble states, the fiction of state equality, and more important, of equal responsibility, was difficult to sustain. A new voting formula based upon population, economic power, and strategic responsibilities, therefore, would seek to apportion to the member states that degree of influence that they bring to the organization. Moreover, given the greater and growing importance of the non-governmental organizations in the everyday work of the United Nations, it would appear the moment had arrived to consider dividing the UN General Assembly into two houses, with one representing the member states and governments, and the other the international civil society, especially those international organizations representing business, labor, and science.

Despite the merits of such changes and the obvious necessity to prepare the United Nations for the twenty-first century, entrenched interests on all sides militated against their acceptance and adoption. And as the debate continued, the work of the organization followed its more familiar form and pattern. The expansion of UN peacekeeping missions called for more sophisticated methods but the most pressing dilemma was paying for them. Moreover, the failure of UN peacekeeping in Somalia had caused a serious drop in public confidence, especially in the United States, which blamed UN leadership for placing peacekeepers in a no-win situation. When the UN mission in Bosnia-Herzegovina also failed, the United States was even more convinced that only direct and forceful action could save the situation.

The introduction of NATO forces, heavily represented by the United States, replaced a lightly armed UN mission, and the relative success of that NATO operation made possible a return to near normalcy in the embattled region. Moreover, a somewhat aggressive American diplomacy, outside the framework of the United Nations, aimed at guaranteeing the security of all the parties in the former Yugoslavia. NATO intrusion in the Balkans suggested a role for the alliance not conceived during the Cold War. Mention need only be made to NATO maneuvering to deflect Serbia from spreading the civil conflict in Kosovo. Thus, unlike other cold war military pacts that had become dysfunctional, NATO was given an afterlife, and the official and formal enlargement of the alliance in March 1999 to include some of the states of the former Warsaw Pact underlined who and what would be responsible for collective security in an extended region that included a considerable portion of Eurasia as well as the Arab Middle East. Lost in the expanding role of NATO—and particularly, the almost unanimous support given Czech, Hungarian, and Polish membership by the American Congress—was Washington's considerable opposition to updating the United Nations system. Whether in matters of greater or lesser concern, and certainly in the application of collective security, the nation-state prevailed over that of the world organization.

Unable to give more significance to UN collective security instruments, the United Nations has come to anticipate more successful co-deployment programs, and as with NATO's presence in the Balkans, so too it has welcomed the intervention of collective CIS forces in Tajikistan and Georgia, and OAU and ECOWAS troops in Liberia, Sierra Leone, and the Central African Republic. Chastened by its failure to terminate civil conflict, the UN has been forced to acknowledge its limitations, as well as its dependence on individual states, and especially the regional collective security organizations that have more direct linkages, compelling reasons, greater forces, and less encumbered procedures.

But co-deployment is no panacea. NATO's decision to launch an air assault on Serbian military positions in March 1999 illustrated the alliance's difficulties in challenging the policies of a determined foe. The mere presence of NATO was expected to deter individual nations from engaging in behavior deemed disruptive to the security and stability of Europe. Confronted by a stubborn and defiant Yugoslav government, however, neither NATO diplomacy nor air strikes deflected the Serbs from their intended goal. NATO did not seek authorization from the United Nations Security Council for its military campaign against Serbia, and in fact a Russian effort that called for a halt to the attacks was rejected when it came before that body. With the United Nations only marginally represented in the ensuing conflict, with international monitors no longer able to operate within Kosovo, and with the NATO air campaign against Yugoslav installations intensifying, the Serbs were emboldened to accelerate their "ethnic cleansing" pogrom. By the end of April almost one million Albanian residents of Kosovo had been forced to leave their country. Spreading out helter skelter, neither the countries to which they fled, nor the international aid agencies that are constructed to deal with refugee problems, could cope with the human seas approaching, spilling over and inundating the border regions. An impoverished Albania reached out to the largest number of refugees, but Macedonia, Montenegro and Bosnia were reluctant to allow such huge numbers of refugees to domicile, even temporarily, within their lands. Moreover, efforts made by other European countries and the United States to open their doors to fleeing refugees were merely symbolic and did little to relieve the pressure on the impacted states or comfort the vast majority of Kosovars who survived in the most deplorable conditions. Nonetheless, NATO's determination to force the Yugoslav government to cease its actions and permit the refugees to return to Kosovo was matched by an equally determined Serbian leadership that rejected every entreaty. Caught in the middle, the refugees were made dependent on the United Nations High Commissioner for Refugees which assumed the task of administering to the victims of Europe's most terrifying event since the end of World War II. Co-deployment and the new emphasis given to collective security were both tested in this last Balkan war of the twentieth century. Serbia's acceptance of NATO demands in June 1999 came suddenly when Russian and European Union negotiators convinced Belgrade that sustained intransigence would only bring an intensification of the alliance's air campaign. Soon thereafter the UN Security Council authorized the use of an international "peace force" and the return of the Kosovar refugees.

But because the United Nations must defer to outside organizations to keep the peace, it does not mean the organization is without notable achievements. The UN was not constructed with the idea of going it alone. Always an international arrangement between and among and not over the member states, the world body has often provided the legitimacy for a particular operation, and indeed it represents what passes for international morality in a world of amoral, self-interested nation-states. Thus the United Nations can celebrate the many progressive changes that it has been instrumental in making possible. High on the list of accomplishments is the UN role in decolonization, and the phasing out of the Trusteeship Council marks the end of an imperial age that for centuries dominated world history. The suggestion that the Trusteeship format be reinvented so as to give it responsibility for a "global commons" that would oversee the protection of both human rights and the world environment would open still another chapter in the story of life on the planet.

Therefore, while UN achievements have been questionable in addressing intra- and inter-state conflict, the organization stands at the apex of global actions promoting the Universal Declaration of Human Rights and in laying the foundation for economic development, the eradication of diseases, the improvement of nutritional and literacy standards, as well as in advocating the rights of women and children. More responsive to the plight of refugees that have multiplied since the end of the cold war, the United Nations is in the vanguard of operations seeking their protection. So too it is the UN that is concerned with the character of human conflict and the efforts devoted to the creation of an international criminal court centers world attention on the need to isolate the perpetrators of the most brutal crimes.

It is also the United Nations that is the conscience of a world concerned with the destruction of the natural environment and the exploitation of the human condition. The organization desperately seeks answers to issues of sustainability, to global drug-trafficking, and controversial population questions. Contrasted with the work of the individual states, UN agencies have elevated the needs of humanity, and through linkages with non-governmental organizations, they represent key instruments in the formation of a global civil society.

Comprised mainly of citizens' associations, non-governmental organizations, and non-profit groups, international civil society stresses universal education and the promotion of life, liberty, and justice. Kofi Annan's support and desire for a closer working relationship between the United Nations agencies and the non-governmental organizations brings the UN closer to the formation of a Civil Society Forum. The Secretary-General's call for a Peoples Millennium Congress to range alongside the convening of the General Assembly in the year 2000 may yet prove to be the forerunner in the construction of a permanent Peoples Assembly, that is, a second chamber that would be representative of all the world's people and eventually elected by the world's "citizens." Indeed such a model already exists in the formation of the European Parliament. Humanity-centered concerns—such as greater understanding of cultural diversity, the quest for human solidarity, and improving the quality of life—would blend with issues of development and especially sustainable economic welfare. Indeed, it is international civil society that stands between the individual state's insatiable appetite for both strategic and conventional weapons, and their ultimate deployment and use. In a world of competitive and often aggressive nation-states, it is only civil society that so ardently pursues disarmament schemes and demands that governments renounce war as an instrument of national policy. In the final analysis, true transparency in decision making is possible only with a vital and institutionalized international civil society that is rooted in humanitarian values.

## THE REALITIES OF THE GLOBAL CONDITION

But the United Nations is still a long way between purpose and fulfillment, between aspiration and accomplishment. Irrespective of the revolutionary changes that have altered approaches to economic development, indeed, despite the contemporary emphasis on globalized markets and electronic financial transactions, the character of world poverty has not changed. Moreover, all indications point to a widening gulf between the prosperous few and the many abject poor. None of the strategies developed to close this gap have succeeded, whether launched by public or private sectors, or combinations of them. At the beginning of a new century the distribution of wealth is so uneven that the imbalance has raised concerns of a meltdown not only in overall physical growth, but in political cooperation as well. Financial crises sweeping Pacific-Asia in 1998 not only raised questions about how successful globalization schemes are, but also how such schemes pose more complicated challenges to political order and social equilibrium in affluent as well as poor countries. The United Nations is hardly equipped to manage the magnitude of such problems, and even the sovereign states seem to lack capacity to address their scale and complexity.

Given these unresolved dilemmas, disintegrative forces, accelerated by perceived inequities and exclusive behaviors, continue to undermine world order. Internecine as well as cross-border conflicts that were energized by psychological as well as physical deprivation, and exploited by vengeful hate groups, have produced anarchic conditions that ignore international norms of appropriate behavior. Innocent people whose only crime was a belief system or an identity different from that of the majority, continue to be singled out and wantonly abused and murdered. Rwanda's plunge into genocidal fury in the mid-1990s tragically illustrated the critical nature of the condition. Generally speaking, economic disequilibrium and social and psychological insecurities, in addition to malperforming governments, provide ammunition for militant extremist movements that the United Nations confronts with its collective soul, but that it can do little to address without the cooperation of its member states.

Finally, the acquisition of more and deadlier weapons by sundry groups as well as states, further aggravates overall conditions. For instance, the high profile responsibility given to UNSCOM in policing and restricting Iraq's capacity to develop weapons of mass destruction contrasts with UN futility in dealing with the Indian and Pakistan governments following their decisions to defy international treaties aimed at preventing the spread of nuclear weapons. Third world country attempts to join the exclusive nuclear weapons club, and the testing of nuclear devices in defiance of the Comprehensive Nuclear Test Ban Treaty, posed not only a threat to specific regions, but to the international regime dedicated to denying additional countries such capability. The United Nations was not structured to effectively neutralize the many threats mounted by the different nation-states in the post-cold war period. Moreover, the emergence of so many different independent and aggressive actors exposes the organization to more, not fewer problems.

## Fast Changing Times and a Slow Changing United Nations

Pressured from within as well as without, the United Nations, under the leadership of Secretary-General Kofi Annan, introduced reforms aimed at closing the gap between the desirable and the possible, between aspiration and accomplishment, between stated purpose and realizable goals. Since 1997, the reorganization of the UN Secretariat has moved apace, but all internal changes were made dependent on the ability of member states to use the UN more effectively, and through the organization, to overcome differences that divided them from one another. Not prepared to wait for the latter, however, the UN Secretariat was engaged in assessing its strengths and weaknesses, and it has charted new institutional structures that carries the UN's moral import into the new millennium.

For the Secretary-General and his staff of international civil servants, the United Nations remained the only international body representing the collective interest of the world's sovereign states. That reality translated into a universality of rights and obligations not found in any other arena, and where successful, offered the states a predictability of behavior that was undergirded by the rule of law. Guided by reciprocity and standardized rules that were unanimously accepted, it was the only forum where diversity of membership and disparate natural endowments met on an even playing field.

The UN's universal character offered governments unparalleled opportunities for interaction and negotiation, and no other international organization enjoyed so broad a mandate. No other body connected with the variety of issues that burdened the world community. Only the United Nations was conceived to address so wide a spectrum of activities in so many critical areas simultaneously. Nevertheless, the United Nations seldom lived up to its kaleidoscopic billing. And as has been demonstrated, its operational mandate was too easily negated by the sheer lack of resources. Dependent on member states that often refused to honor individual commitments, the organization confronted unbridgeable gaps between needs, delivery, and expectations. Moreover, subject to manipulation by states with narrow agendas, the UN has been too often trapped between its universal mandate and the exclusive interests of its members.

Constructed on the ashes of World War II, the foundation on which the United Nations rested was neither solid nor nourishing. Exposed to cold war rivalries at the outset, the organization split into blocs and alliances that multiplied with the inclusion of the newly independent states. Regionalism and a virulent nationalism prevented the organization from achieving its visionary objectives. Less a futuristic organization, the United Nations came to represent the peculiar interests of the different states that joined its ranks. All sought to maximize opportunities while paying lip service to the organization's universal purpose. Although far from its stated ideal, the United Nations nevertheless prevailed, developed innovative programs, notably in socio-economic areas, and managed to survive the cold war because none of its major members were inclined to abandon it. The end of the cold war, however, focused new attention on the organization and it came under increasing pressure to assume far greater and more complex responsibilities.

High on the list of UN priorities was the need to promote and oversee democratization programs worldwide. Not less a charge was the UN's role in promoting dialogue between rival third world parties, as well as mediating their disputes. Humanitarian services were also made a principal United Nations function. Initially comprised of fifty-one member states in 1946, the International Red Cross was perhaps the most notable non-governmental organization in a world not yet familiar with regional and international institutions and programs. The United Nations was a far simpler organization at its first meeting, and no one that day could have envisaged the 185 nations that currently constitute its membership. Moreover, non-governmental organizations that have come to reflect so much of the work of the organization now number in the thousands, and an expanding international private sector influences the behavior of the world body as never before. The United Nations is compelled to adjust to momentous changes but the organization is limited in what the Secretary-General can do on his own initiative. Major responsibility in managing reform lies with the member states whose jurisdiction controls the restructuring and modernizing of the organization.

The Secretary-General, however, cannot wait for the states to act. It is his office that most symbolizes the United Nations, and it is the Secretary-General who must operationalize the orders and recommendations of the different organs and agencies of the world body. Continuously in the spotlight, the Secretary-General cannot avoid the criticism that is often leveled against the United Nations, and as the world's foremost diplomat, his actions will always be subjected to the swings of violent censure or high praise. Kofi Annan's succession to the office of Secretary-General illustrated the lot of the holder of the office. His predecessor, Boutros Boutros-Ghali was denied an extended term by the opposition mounted solely by the United States, which had judged his management of the office unacceptable, despite overwhelming approval from the organization's member states. Pressured to fill the vacancy, the Security Council, followed by the General Assembly, approved the appointment of Kofi Annan, whose long and intimate association with the UN Secretariat, as well as his apolitical background, propelled him into the office. The new Secretary-General understood full well the need to win the confidence of the United States, as well as the other permanent members of the Security Council. As a representative from the third world he already had the support of a majority of its members. Annan also realized that he had no time to waste in deliberative discussions, and aware that his strongest hand lay in rearranging the Secretariat, he devoted himself to that task.

The Secretary-General's initial directives called for dividing the work of the Secretariat into five core areas. They were: peace and security; economic and social affairs; development cooperation; humanitarian affairs; and human rights. The changes called for alterations in the workways of all UN departments, programs, and funds. Separate executive committees were created for the first four sectors while human rights was judged an integral aspect of each of the others and hence was incorporated within each of the four committees. All units of the United Nations, however, were classified with one or more of the core groups. The purpose of the Executive Committees was to improve the efficiency of each unit by avoiding duplication and by pooling all available resources. Each Executive Committee, therefore, was made responsible for policy development, decision making, and management, as well as authorized to engage in strategic planning. As a follow-on to this reform, the Secretary-General merged the three departments concerned with economic and social affairs into one. A similar consolidation occurred when the three Secretariat bodies serving the intergovernmental forums were also combined into a single department. These reforms produced considerable savings and a negative rate of growth budget for 1998–99. Further cuts in Secretariat staff followed and the result was a 25 percent decline from 1984–85 levels. Secretary-General Annan insisted not a single mandate had been sacrificed by the reductions, and that the objective of the reform was a new, more agile and vibrant administration.

The Secretary-General's call for a greater unity of purpose among the upper echelon of the UN Secretariat raised staff awareness from its more narrowly defined bureaucratic segmentation to a pressing need for collective and strategic thinking. To institutionalize the changes in Secretariat structure and workways, Annan established a Senior Management Group, comprised of the conveners of the four executive Committees and a number of other high-ranking managers. The purpose of the SMG was to directly advise and assist the Secretary-General, who chaired the body and thus maintained hands-on control over all UN Secretariat functions. Annan's substantial experience at UN headquarters, his knowledge of virtually all the departments and agencies, and his general administrative acumen, not only made him the first international civil servant to hold the position, but one of the few people with the vision to lead the United Nations into the twenty-first century. Citing the multidimensional and more complex aspects of the office, Annan surprised no one when he recommended and the General Assembly accepted his recommendation to create the office of the Deputy Secretary-General.

The appointment of the Deputy Secretary-General enhances the ability of the Secretary-General to manage cross-functional sectors and multidimensional emergencies in an increasingly more complex UN system. Most important, it does so while unifying the detailed work of the Secretariat. With a single consolidated Department for Economic and Social Affairs and a single Department of General Assembly Affairs and Conference Services, the organization has been streamlined, its work coordinated, and its expenditures reduced. Similar consolidation has occurred in Human Rights and Emergency Relief. All matters involving the proliferation of weapons, including conventional weapons, have been housed in the Department for Disarmament and Arms Regulation, and considerable effort has gone into consolidating ECOSOC's subsidiary bodies. As a result of all these actions and recommendations, UNDP, UNICEF, UNFPA and other units and agencies were expected to work more efficiently, and a UN Development Assistance Framework was authorized to set common objectives and time frames for program assistance to specific nations. UN "houses" were designated in all countries where the United Nations had ongoing programs, and the first "UN House" was established in South Africa in 1998.

All of these activities were undertaken without amending the UN Charter. Moreover, the Secretary-General was credited with having strengthened the organization; he also appeared to answer the questions raised by the UN's more outspoken critics. More important, these reforms allowed the UN system to function at near optimum levels with a smaller staff and a substantially reduced budget. Furthermore, Annan's appeal for financial assistance from nongovernmental organizations as well as business groups was not intended to bypass the member states, but to supplement the income of the world organization. Indeed, the gesture also acknowledged the increasing significance of the non-states and modified the traditional state-centric vision that has guided the United Nations from its inception. The Annan reforms also were slated to create a new communications strategy that placed the organization and its programs in more direct contact with the world's common folk. Under the Secretary-General's stewardship, it seemed realistic that the Trusteeship Council could be transformed into an open forum for a common humanity, and that a new trusteeship will center attention on safeguarding human rights, maintaining the integrity of the global environment, as well as the earth's common areas (i.e., the oceans, atmosphere, and outer space).

In an organization as complex as the United Nations, reform is manifested in a vast number of changes and modifications, but the real test will not be found in the creation of more efficient committees or cost-saving innovations. The United Nations of the twenty-first century will ultimately be judged by how it measures up to its essential ethos, that is, how it protects, assists, and enhances the lives of the weakest members of global society. While the independent, sovereign states will continue to reinforce their unique qualities and pursue their exclusive and peculiar interests, it is only the United Nations system that stands sentinel over the world's ecosystem; it is only the UN that is charged with improving the lot of the earth's poor, of feeding its hungry, of tending to its sick, and in moment of great urgency, of protecting the most threatened members of the human family.

## TOWARD WORLD ORDER

During the twentieth century the world witnessed the disintegration of colonial empires, two world wars, the rise and decline of the cold war, an almost unbroken series of local conflicts, and a variety of hostile rivalries among nations large and small. Amid these signs of political disintegration, a technological revolution in transportation, communication, and industry has vastly increased the points of social contact across national boundaries and thus the opportunities for both cooperation and hostile collision. At the same time military technology has substantially increased the penalties of resort to organized violence and brought added incentive to avoid at least the most destructive forms of warfare. Faced with the social consequences of technological progress, as they affect international relations, governments have increasingly turned to international organization as a means of eliminating frictions and resolving differences through non-violent means.

More than 100 years of experience with functional international organizations, now greatly augmented by the growth of the UN system, has not produced a global political community. It has, however, produced a practical approach to international cooperation. The processes of international organization are geared to a world in which common problems must be attacked by multilateral means, while making full allowance for local particularisms and national freedom of action. As vessels for common action, these processes have proved adaptable and adequate to bear all of the international cooperation that existing bonds of community will generate. Genuine community, with freedom from oppression and want, still lies at the top of distant peaks. That ideal may be unattainable. But international organization points in that direction, even though, as a human institution, it continues to reflect the divisions and follies of the world in which we live.

## SELECTED READINGS

Annan, Kofi. *The Quotable Kofi Annan: Selections from Speeches and Statements by the Secretary-General.* New York: United Nations Publications, 1998.

Bertrand, Maurice. *The Third Generation World Organization.* Dordrecht: Martinus Nijhoff Publishers, 1989.

Carnegie Commission on Preventing Deadly Conflict. *Preventing Deadly Conflict.* New York: Carnegie Corporation of New York, 1997.

Claude, Inis L., Jr. *States and the Global System.* New York: St. Martin's Press, 1988.

Coate, Roger A. *Unilateralism, Ideology, and U.S. Foreign Policy In and Out of UNESCO.* Boulder, CO: Lynne Rienner Publishing, 1989.

Finger, Seymour Maxwell. *American Ambassadors at the UN: People, Politics, and Bureaucracy in Making Foreign Policy.* New York: Holmes & Meier, 1988.

———, and Joseph R. Harbert, eds. *U.S. Policy in International Institutions.* Rev. ed. Boulder, CO: Westview Press, 1982.

Foreign Affairs Agenda. *The New Shape of World Politics: Contending Paradigms in International Relations.* New York: Council on Foreign Relations and W. W. Norton, 1997.

Franck, Thomas M. *Nation against Nation: What Happened to the U.N. Dream and What the U.S. Can Do about It.* New York: Oxford University Press, 1985.

Fromuth, Peter J., ed. *A Successor Vision: The United Nations of Tomorrow.* New York: UN Association of the United States of America, 1988.

Gati, Toby Trister, ed. *The US, the UN, and the Management of Global Change.* New York: New York University Press, 1983.

Gerson, Allan. *The Kirkpatrick Mission: Diplomacy Without Apology: America at the United Nations, 1981–1985.* New York: The Free Press, 1991.

Karns, Margaret P., and Karen A. Mingst, eds. *The United States and Multilateral Institutions: Patterns of Changing Instrumentality and Influence.* Boston: Unwin Hyman, 1990.

Kegley, Charles W., ed. *The Long Postwar Peace.* New York: HarperCollins Publishers, 1991.

Maynes, Charles W. and Richard S. Williamson. *U.S. Foreign Policy and the United Nations System.* New York: W. W. Norton, 1996.

Muller, Joachim, ed. *Reforming the United Nations: New Initiatives and Past Efforts.* Boston: Kluwer Law International, 1997.

Riggs, Robert E. *US/UN: Foreign Policy and International Organization.* New York: Appleton-Century-Crofts, 1971.

Rosenau, James N. *The United Nations in a Turbulent World.* International Peace Academy, Occasional Paper Series. Boulder, CO: Lynne Rienner Publishing, 1992.

Rosenau, James N., and Ernst-Otto Czempiel, eds. *Governance without Government: Order and Change in World Politics.* Cambridge: Cambridge University Press, 1992.

Yoder, Amos. *The Evolution of the United Nations System.* New York: Crane Russak, 1989.

Zakaria, Fareed. *From Wealth to Power: The Unusual Origins of America's World Role.* Princeton: Princeton University Press, 1998.

# A

# THE COVENANT OF THE LEAGUE OF NATIONS[1]

## THE HIGH CONTRACTING PARTIES,

In order to promote international cooperation and to achieve international peace and security

by the acceptance of obligations not to resort to war,

by the prescription of open, just and honorable relations between nations,

by the firm establishment of the understandings of international law as the actual rule of conduct among Governments, and

by the maintenance of justice and a scrupulous respect for all treaty obligations in the dealings of organized peoples with one another,

Agree to this Covenant of the League of Nations.

## ARTICLE 1. MEMBERSHIP AND WITHDRAWAL

1. The original Members of the League of Nations shall be those of the Signatories which are named in the Annex to this Covenant and also such of those other States named in the Annex as shall accede without reservation to this Covenant. Such accessions shall be effected by a declaration deposited with the Secretariat within two months of the coming into force of the Covenant. Notice thereof shall be sent to all other Members of the League.
2. Any fully self-governing State, Dominion or Colony not named in the Annex may become a Member of the League if its admission is agreed to by two-thirds of the Assembly, provided that it shall give effective guaranties of its sincere intention to observe its international obligations, and shall accept such regulations as may be prescribed by the League in regard to its military, naval and air forces and armaments.
3. Any Member of the League may, after two years' notice of its intention so to do, withdraw from the League, provided that all its international

---

[1] Amendments in italics.

obligations and all its obligations under this Covenant shall have been fulfilled at the time of its withdrawal.

## ARTICLE 2. MAJOR ORGANS

The action of the League under this Covenant shall be effected through the instrumentality of an Assembly and of a Council, with a permanent Secretariat.

## ARTICLE 3. ASSEMBLY

1. The Assembly shall consist of representatives of the Members of the League.
2. The Assembly shall meet at stated intervals and from time to time, as occasion may require, at the Seat of the League or at such other place as may be decided upon.
3. The Assembly may deal at its meetings with any matter within the sphere of action of the League or affecting the peace of the world.
4. At meetings of the Assembly each Member of the League shall have one vote and may have not more than three Representatives.

## ARTICLE 4. COUNCIL

1. The Council shall consist of representatives of the Principal Allied and Associated Powers,[1] together with Representatives of four other Members of the League. These four Members of the League shall be selected by the Assembly from time to time in its discretion. Until the appointment of the Representatives of the four Members of the League first selected by the Assembly, Representatives of Belgium, Brazil, Greece and Spain shall be Members of the Council.
2. With the approval of the majority of the Assembly, the Council may name additional Members of the League, whose Representatives shall always be Members of the Council;[2] the Council with like approval may increase the number of Members of the League to be selected by the Assembly for representation on the Council.[3]
2. bis.[4] *The Assembly shall fix by a two-thirds' majority the rules dealing with the election of the non-permanent Members of the Council, and particularly such regulations as relate to their term of office and the conditions of re-eligibility.*
3. The Council shall meet from time to time as occasion may require, and at least once a year, at the Seat of the League, or at such other place as may be decided upon.
4. The Council may deal at its meetings with any matter within the sphere of action of the League or affecting the peace of the world.

5. Any Member of the League not represented on the Council shall be invited to send a Representative to sit as a member at any meeting of the Council during the consideration of matters specially affecting the interests of that Member of the League.
6. At meetings of the Council, each Member of the League represented on the Council shall have one vote, and may have not more than one Representative.

## ARTICLE 5. VOTING AND MEETING PROCEDURES

1. Except where otherwise expressly provided in this Covenant or by the terms of the present Treaty, decisions at any meeting of the Assembly or of the Council shall require the agreement of all the Members of the League represented at the meeting.
2. All matters of procedure at meetings of the Assembly or of the Council, including the appointment of Committees to investigate particular matters, shall he regulated by the Assembly or by the Council and may be decided by a majority of the Members of the League represented at the meeting.
3. The first meeting of the Assembly and the first meeting of the Council shall be summoned by the President of the United States of America.

## ARTICLE 6. SECRETARIAT, SECRETARY-GENERAL AND EXPENSES

1. The permanent Secretariat shall be established at the Seat of the League. The Secretariat shall comprise a Secretary-General and such secretaries and staff as may be required.
2. The first Secretary-General shall be the person named in the Annex; thereafter the Secretary-General shall be appointed by the Council with the approval of the majority of the Assembly.
3. The secretaries and the staff of the Secretariat shall be appointed by the Secretary-General with the approval of the Council.
4. The Secretary-General shall act in that capacity at all meetings of the Assembly and of the Council.
5. *The expenses of the League shall be borne by the Members of the League in the proportion decided by the Assembly.*

## ARTICLE 7. SEAT, QUALIFICATIONS AND IMMUNITIES

1. The Seat of the League is established at Geneva.
2. The Council may at any time decide that the Seat of the League shall be established elsewhere.
3. All positions under or in connection with the League, including the Secretariat, shall be open equally to men and women.

4. Representatives of the Members of the League and officials of the League when engaged on the business of the League shall enjoy diplomatic privileges and immunities.
5. The buildings and other property occupied by the League or its officials or by Representatives attending its meetings shall be inviolable.

## ARTICLE 8. REDUCTION OF ARMAMENTS

1. The Members of the League recognize that the maintenance of peace requires the reduction of national armaments to the lowest point consistent with national safety and the enforcement by common action of international obligations.
2. The Council, taking account of the geographical situation and circumstances of each State, shall formulate plans for such reduction for the consideration and action of the several Governments.
3. Such plans shall be subject to reconsideration and revision at least every ten years.
4. After these plans shall have been adopted by the several Governments, the limits of armaments therein fixed shall not be exceeded without the concurrence of the Council.
5. The Members of the League agree that the manufacture by private enterprise of munitions and implements of war is open to grave objections. The Council shall advise how the evil effects attendant upon such manufacture can be prevented, due regard being had to the necessities of those Members of the League which are not able to manufacture the munitions and implements of war necessary for their safety.
6. The Members of the League undertake to interchange full and frank information as to the scale of their armaments, their military, naval and air programs and the condition of such of their industries as are adaptable to warlike purposes.

## ARTICLE 9. PERMANENT MILITARY, NAVAL AND AIR COMMISSION

A permanent Commission shall be constituted to advise the Council on the execution of the provisions of Articles 1 and 8 and on military, naval and air questions generally.

## ARTICLE 10. GUARANTIES AGAINST AGGRESSION

The Members of the League undertake to respect and preserve as against external aggression the territorial integrity and existing political independence of all Members of the League. In case of any such aggression or in case of any threat or danger of such aggression the Council shall advise upon the means by which this obligation shall be fulfilled.

## ARTICLE 11. COLLECTIVE ACTION

1. Any war or threat of war, whether immediately affecting any of the Members of the League or not, is hereby declared a matter of concern to the whole League, and the League shall take any action that may be deemed wise and effectual to safeguard the peace of nations. In case any such emergency should arise the Secretary-General shall on the request of any Member of the League forthwith summon a meeting of the Council.
2. It is also declared to be the friendly right of each Member of the League to bring to the attention of the Assembly or the Council any circumstance whatever affecting international relations which threatens to disturb international peace or the good understanding between nations upon which peace depends.

## ARTICLE 12. DISPUTES

1. The Members of the League agree that, if there should arise between them any dispute likely to lead to a rupture, they will submit the matter either to arbitration *or judicial settlement* or to inquiry by the Council, and they agree in no case to resort to war until three months after the award by the arbitrators *or the judicial decision,* or the report by the Council.
2. In any case under this Article the award of the arbitrators *or the judicial decision* shall be made within a reasonable time, and the report of the Council shall be made within six months after the submission of the dispute.

## ARTICLE 13. ARBITRATION OR JUDICIAL SETTLEMENT

1. The Members of the League agree that, whenever any dispute shall arise between them which they recognize to be suitable for submission to arbitration *or judicial settlement,* and which can not be satisfactorily settled by diplomacy, they will submit the whole subject-matter to arbitration *or judicial settlement.*
2. Disputes as to the interpretation of a treaty, as to any question of international law, as to the existence of any fact which, if established, would constitute a breach of any international obligation, or as to the extent and nature of the reparation to be made for any such breach, are declared to be among those which are generally suitable for submission to arbitration *or judicial settlement.*
3. *For the consideration of any such dispute, the court to which the case is referred shall be the Permanent Court of International Justice, established in accordance with Article 14, or any tribunal agreed on by the parties to the dispute or stipulated in any convention existing between them.*
4. The Members of the League agree that they will carry out in full good faith any award *or decision* that may be rendered, and that they will not

resort to war against a Member of the League which complies therewith. In the event of any failure to carry out such an award *or decision*, the Council shall propose what steps should be taken to give effect thereto.

## ARTICLE 14. PERMANENT COURT OF INTERNATIONAL JUSTICE

The Council shall formulate and submit to the Members of the League for adoption plans for the establishment of a Permanent Court of International Justice. The Court shall be competent to hear and determine any dispute of an international character which the parties thereto submit to it. The Court may also give an advisory opinion upon any dispute or question referred to it by the Council or by the Assembly.

## ARTICLE 15. DISPUTES NOT SUBMITTED TO ARBITRATION OR JUDICIAL SETTLEMENT

1. If there should arise between Members of the League any dispute likely to lead to a rupture, which is not submitted to arbitration *or judicial settlement* in accordance with Article 13, the Members of the League agree that they will submit the matter to the Council. Any party to the dispute may effect such submission by giving notice of the existence of the dispute to the Secretary-General, who will make all necessary arrangements for a full investigation and consideration thereof.
2. For this purpose, the parties to the dispute will communicate to the Secretary-General, as promptly as possible, statements of their case with all the relevant facts and papers, and the Council may forthwith direct the publication thereof.
3. The Council shall endeavor to effect a settlement of the dispute, and, if such efforts are successful, a statement shall be made public giving such facts and explanations regarding the dispute and the terms of settlement thereof as the Council may deem appropriate.
4. If the dispute is not thus settled, the Council either unanimously or by a majority vote shall make and publish a report containing a statement of the facts of the dispute and the recommendations which are deemed just and proper in regard thereto.
5. Any member of the League represented on the Council may make public a statement of the facts of the dispute and of its conclusions regarding the same.
6. If a report by the Council is unanimously agreed to by the Members thereof other than the Representatives of one or more of the parties to the dispute, the Members of the League agree that they will not go to war with any party to the dispute which complies with the recommendations of the report.
7. If the Council fails to reach a report which is unanimously agreed to by the members thereof, other than the Representatives of one or more of

the parties to the dispute, the Members of the League reserve to themselves the right to take such action as they shall consider necessary for the maintenance of right and justice.

8. If the dispute between the parties is claimed by one of them, and is found by the Council, to arise out of a matter which by international law is solely within the domestic jurisdiction of that party, the Council shall so report, and shall make no recommendation as to its settlement.

9. The Council may in any case under this Article refer the dispute to the Assembly. The dispute shall be so referred at the request of either party to the dispute, provided that such request be made within 14 days after the submission of the dispute to the Council.

10. In any case referred to the Assembly, all the provisions of this Article and of Article 12 relating to the action and powers of the Council shall apply to the action and powers of the Assembly, provided that a report made by the Assembly, if concurred in by the Representatives of those Members of the League represented on the Council and of a majority of the other Members of the League, exclusive in each case of the Representatives of the parties to the dispute, shall have the same force as a report by the Council concurred in by all the members thereof other than the Representatives of one or more of the parties to the dispute.

## ARTICLE 16. SANCTIONS AND EXPULSION

1. Should any Member of the League resort to war in disregard of its covenants under Articles 12, 13, or 15, it shall *ipso facto* be deemed to have committed an act of war against all other Members of the League, which hereby undertake immediately to subject it to the severance of all trade or financial relations, the prohibition of all intercourse between their nationals and the nationals of the covenant-breaking State, and the prevention of all financial, commercial or personal intercourse between the nationals of the covenant-breaking State and the nationals of any other State, whether a Member of the League or not.

2. It shall be the duty of the Council in such case to recommend to the several Governments concerned what effective military, naval or air force the Members of the League shall severally contribute to the armed forces to be used to protect the covenants of the League.

3. The Members of the League agree, further, that they will mutually support one another in the financial and economic measures which are taken under this Article, in order to minimize the loss and inconvenience resulting from the above measures, and that they will mutually support one another in resisting any special measures aimed at one of their number by the covenant-breaking State, and that they will take the necessary steps to afford passage through their territory to the forces of any of the Members of the League which are cooperating to protect the covenants of the League.

4. Any Member of the League which has violated any covenant of the League may be declared to be no longer a Member of the League by a vote of the Council concurred in by the Representatives of all the other Members of the League represented thereon.

## ARTICLE 17. DISPUTES INVOLVING NON-MEMBERS

1. In the event of a dispute between a Member of the League and a State which is not a Member of the League, or between States not Members of the League, the State or States not Members of the League shall be invited to accept the obligations of membership in the League for the purposes of such dispute, upon such conditions as the Council may deem just. If such invitation is accepted, the provisions of Articles 12 to 16 inclusive shall be applied with such modifications as may be deemed necessary by the Council.
2. Upon such invitation being given, the Council shall immediately institute an inquiry into the circumstances of the dispute and recommend such action as may seem best and most effectual in the circumstances.
3. If a State so invited shall refuse to accept the obligations of membership in the League for the purposes of such dispute, and shall resort to war against a Member of the League, the provisions of Article 16 shall be applicable as against the State taking such action.
4. If both parties to the dispute when so invited refuse to accept the obligations of membership in the League for the purposes of such dispute, the Council may take such measures and make such recommendations as will prevent hostilities and will result in the settlement of the dispute.

## ARTICLE 18. REGISTRATION AND PUBLICATION OF TREATIES

Every treaty or international engagement entered into hereafter by any Member of the League shall be forthwith registered with the Secretariat and shall as soon as possible be published by it. No such treaty or international engagement shall be binding until so registered.

## ARTICLE 19. REVIEW OF TREATIES

The Assembly may from time to time advise the reconsideration by Members of the League of treaties which have become inapplicable, and the consideration of international conditions whose continuance might endanger the peace of the world.

## ARTICLE 20. ABROGATION OF INCONSISTENT OBLIGATIONS

1. The Members of the League severally agree that this Covenant is accepted as abrogating all obligations or understandings *inter se* which are incon-

sistent with the terms thereof, and solemnly undertake that they will not hereafter enter into any engagements inconsistent with the terms thereof.

2. In case any Member of the League shall, before becoming a Member of the League, have undertaken any obligations inconsistent with the terms of this Covenant, it shall be the duty of such Member to take immediate steps to procure its release from such obligations.

## ARTICLE 21. ENGAGEMENTS THAT REMAIN VALID

Nothing in this Covenant shall be deemed to affect the validity of international engagements, such as treaties of arbitration or regional understandings like the Monroe doctrine, for securing the maintenance of peace.

## ARTICLE 22. MANDATES SYSTEM

1. To those colonies and territories which as a consequence of the late war have ceased to be under the sovereignty of the States which formerly governed them and which are inhabited by peoples not yet able to stand by themselves under the strenuous conditions of the modern world, there should be applied the principle that the well-being and development of such peoples form a sacred trust of civilization and that securities for the performance of this trust should be embodied in this Covenant.

2. The best method of giving practical effect to this principle is that the tutelage of such peoples should be intrusted to advanced nations who by reason of their resources, their experience or their geographical position can best undertake this responsibility, and who are willing to accept it, and that this tutelage should be exercised by them as Mandatories on behalf of the League.

3. The character of the mandate must differ according to the stage of the development of the people, the geographical situation of the territory, its economic conditions and other similar circumstances.

4. Certain communities formerly belonging to the Turkish Empire have reached a stage of development where their existence as independent nations can be provisionally recognized subject to the rendering of administrative advice and assistance by a Mandatory until such time as they are able to stand alone. The wishes of these communities must be a principal consideration in the selection of the Mandatory.

5. Other peoples, especially those of Central Africa, are at such a stage that the Mandatory must be responsible for the administration of the territory under conditions which will guarantee freedom of conscience and religion, subject only to the maintenance of public order and morals, the prohibition of abuses such as the slave trade, the arms traffic and the liquor traffic, and the prevention of the establishment of fortifications or military

and naval bases and of military training of the natives for other than police purposes and the defense of territory, and will also secure equal opportunities for the trade and commerce of other Members of the League.

6. There are territories, such as South West Africa and certain of the South Pacific islands, which, owing to the sparseness of their population, or their small size, or their remoteness from the centers of civilization, or their geographical contiguity to the territory of the Mandatory, and other circumstances, can be best administered under the laws of the Mandatory as integral portions of its territory, subject to the safeguards above mentioned in the interests of the indigenous population.

7. In every case of mandate, the Mandatory shall render to the Council an annual report in reference to the territory committed to its charge.

8. The degree of authority, control or administration to be exercised by the Mandatory shall, if not previously agreed upon by the Members of the League, be explicitly defined in each case by the Council.

9. A permanent Commission shall be constituted to receive and examine the annual reports of the Mandatories and to advise the Council on all matters relating to the observance of the mandates.

## ARTICLE 23. SOCIAL RESPONSIBILITIES

Subject to and in accordance with the provisions of international conventions existing or hereafter to be agreed upon, the Members of the League:

(a) will endeavor to secure and maintain fair and humane conditions of labor for men, women and children, both in their own countries and in all countries to which their commercial and industrial relations extend, and for that purpose will establish and maintain the necessary international organizations;

(b) undertake to secure just treatment of the native inhabitants of territories under their control;

(c) will intrust the League with the general supervision over the execution of agreements with regard to the traffic in women and children, and the traffic in opium and other dangerous drugs;

(d) will intrust the League with the general supervision of the trade in arms and ammunition with the countries in which the control of this traffic is necessary in the common interest;

(e) will make provision to secure and maintain freedom of communications and of transit and equitable treatment for the commerce of all Members of the League. In this connection, the special necessities of the regions devastated during the war of 1914–1918 shall be borne in mind;

(f) will endeavor to take steps in matters of international concern for the prevention and control of disease.

## ARTICLE 24. INTERNATIONAL BUREAUS

1. There shall be placed under the direction of the League all international bureaus already established by general treaties if the parties to such treaties consent. All such international bureaus and all commissions for the regulation of matters of international interest hereafter constituted shall be placed under the direction of the League.
2. In all matters of international interest which are regulated by general conventions but which are not placed under the control of international bureaus or commissions, the Secretariat of the League shall, subject to the consent of the Council and if desired by the parties, collect and distribute all relevant information and shall render any other assistance which may be necessary or desirable.
3. The Council may include as part of the expenses of the Secretariat the expenses of any bureau or commission which is placed under the direction of the League.

## ARTICLE 25. PROMOTION OF RED CROSS

The Members of the League agree to encourage and promote the establishment and cooperation of duly authorized voluntary national Red Cross organizations having as purposes the improvement of health, the prevention of disease and the mitigation of suffering throughout the world.

## ARTICLE 26. AMENDMENTS

1. Amendments to this Covenant will take effect when ratified by the Members of the League whose Representatives compose the Council and by a majority of the Members of the League whose Representatives compose the Assembly.
2. No such amendment shall hind any Member of the League which signifies its dissent therefrom, but in that case it shall cease to be a Member of the League.

## ANNEX I. ORIGINAL MEMBERS OF THE LEAGUE OF NATIONS, SIGNATORIES OF THE TREATY OF PEACE

| | |
|---|---|
| United States of America* | South Africa |
| Belgium | New Zealand |
| Bolivia | India |
| Brazil | China |
| British Empire | Cuba |
|    Canada | Czechoslovakia |
|    Australia | Ecuador** |

France
Greece
Guatemala
Haiti
Hedjaz*
Honduras
Italy
Japan
Liberia

Nicaragua
Panama
Peru
Poland
Portugal
Romania
Serb-Croat-Slovene State [Yugoslavia]
Siam
Uruguay

## STATES INVITED TO ACCEDE TO THE COVENANT

Argentine Republic
Chile
Colombia
Denmark
Netherlands
Norway
Paraguay

Persia
Salvador
Spain
Sweden
Switzerland
Venezuela

## ANNEX II. FIRST SECRETARY-GENERAL OF THE LEAGUE OF NATIONS THE HONORABLE SIR JAMES ERIC DRUMMOND, K.C.M.G., C.B.

---

[1] The Principal Allied and Associated Powers were: the United States, the United Kingdom, France, Italy and Japan.

[2] Germany was nominated a permanent Member of the Council on September 8, 1926.

[3] The number of Council members increased from four to six on September 25, 1922, and then to nine on September 8, 1926.

[4] The amendment to Article 4 paragraph 2 came into force on July 29, 1926.

* Did not ratify.

** Did not ratify peace treaty but was admitted to membership in 1934.

# B

## The Charter of the United Nations

**WE THE PEOPLES OF THE UNITED NATIONS DETERMINED**

to save succeeding generations from the scourge of war, which twice in our lifetime has brought untold sorrow to mankind, and

to reaffirm faith in fundamental human rights, in the dignity and worth of the
human person, in the equal rights of men and women and of nations large
and small, and

to establish conditions under which justice and respect for the obligations
arising from treaties and other sources of international law can be maintained, and

to promote social progress and better standards of life in larger freedom,

**AND FOR THESE ENDS**

to practice tolerance and live together in peace with one another as good neighbors, and

to unite our strength to maintain international peace and security, and

to ensure, by the acceptance of principles and the institution of methods, that
armed force shall not be used, save in the common interest, and

to employ international machinery for the promotion of the economic and social advancement of all peoples,

**HAVE RESOLVED TO COMBINE OUR EFFORTS
TO ACCOMPLISH THESE AIMS.**

Accordingly, our respective Governments, through representatives assembled
in the city of San Francisco, who have exhibited their full powers found to be
in good and due form, have agreed to the present Charter of the United Nations
and do hereby establish an international organization to be known as the United
Nations.

# CHAPTER I
## PURPOSES AND PRINCIPLES

ARTICLE 1.

The Purposes of the United Nations are:

1. To maintain international peace and security, and to that end: to take effective collective measures for the prevention and removal of threats to the peace, and for the suppression of acts of aggression and other breaches of the peace, and to bring about by peaceful means, and in conformity with the principles of justice and international law, adjustment or settlement of international disputes or situations which might lead to a breach of the peace;
2. To develop friendly relations among nations based on respect for the principle of equal rights and self-determination of peoples, and to take other appropriate measures to strengthen universal peace;
3. To achieve international cooperation in solving international problems of an economic, social, cultural, or humanitarian character, and in promoting and encouraging respect for human rights and for fundamental freedoms for all without distinction as to race, sex, language, or religion; and
4. To be a center for harmonizing the actions of nations in the attainment of these common ends.

ARTICLE 2.

The Organization and its Members, in pursuit of the Purposes stated in Article 1, shall act in accordance with the following Principles.

1. The Organization is based on the principle of the sovereign equality of all its Members.
2. All Members, in order to ensure to all of them the rights and benefits resulting from membership, shall fulfil in good faith the obligations assumed by them in accordance with the present Charter.
3. All Members still settle their international disputes by peaceful means in such a manner that international peace and security, and justice, are not endangered.
4. All Members shall refrain in their international relations from the threat or use of force against the territorial integrity or political independence of any state, or in any other manner inconsistent with the Purposes of the United Nations.
5. All Members shall give the United Nations every assistance in any action it takes in accordance with the present Charter, and shall refrain from giving assistance to any state against which the United Nations is taking preventive or enforcement action.

6. The Organization shall ensure that states which are not Members of the United Nations act in accordance with these Principles so far as may be necessary for the maintenance of international peace and security.
7. Nothing contained in the present Charter shall authorize the United Nations to intervene in matters which are essentially within the domestic jurisdiction of any state or shall require the Members to submit such matters to settlement under the present Charter; but this principle shall not prejudice the application of enforcement measures under Chapter VII.

## CHAPTER II
## MEMBERSHIP

### ARTICLE 3.

The original Members of the United Nations shall be the states which, having participated in the United Nations Conference on International Organization at San Francisco, or having previously signed the Declaration by United Nations of January 1, 1942, sign the present Charter and ratify it in accordance with Article 110.

### ARTICLE 4.

1. Membership in the United Nations is open to all other peace-loving states which accept the obligations contained in the present Charter and, in the judgment of the Organization, are able and willing to carry out these obligations.
2. The admission of any such state to membership in the United Nations will be effected by a decision of the General Assembly upon the recommendation of the Security Council.

### ARTICLE 5.

A Member of the United Nations against which preventive or enforcement action has been taken by the Security Council may be suspended from the exercise of the rights and privileges of membership by the General Assembly upon the recommendation of the Security Council. The exercise of these rights and privileges may be restored by the Security Council.

### ARTICLE 6.

A Member of the United Nations which has persistently violated the Principles contained in the present Charter may be expelled from the Organization by the General Assembly upon the recommendation of the Security Council.

## CHAPTER III
## ORGANS

### ARTICLE 7.

1. There are established as the principal organs of the United Nations: a General Assembly, a Security Council, an Economic and Social Council, a Trusteeship Council, an International Court of Justice, and a Secretariat.
2. Such subsidiary organs as may be found necessary may be established in accordance with the present Charter.

### ARTICLE 8.

The United Nations shall place no restrictions on the eligibility of men and women to participate in any capacity and under conditions of equality in its principal and subsidiary organs.

## CHAPTER IV
## THE GENERAL ASSEMBLY

### Composition
### ARTICLE 9.

1. The General Assembly shall consist of all the Members of the United Nations.
2. Each Member shall not have more than five representatives in the General Assembly.

### Functions and Powers
### ARTICLE 10.

The General Assembly may discuss any questions or any matters within the scope of the present Charter or relating to the powers and functions of any organs provided for in the present Charter, and, except as provided in Article 12, may make recommendations to the Members of the United Nations or to the Security Council or to both on any such questions or matters.

### ARTICLE 11.

1. The General Assembly may consider the general principles of cooperation in the maintenance of international peace and security, including the principles governing disarmament and the regulation of armaments, and may make recommendations with regard to such principles to the Members or to the Security Council or to both.
2. The General Assembly may discuss any questions relating to the maintenance of international peace and security brought before it by any Member of the United Nations, or by the Security Council, or by a state which

is not a Member of the United Nations in accordance with Article 35, paragraph 2, and, except as provided in Article 12, may make recommendations with regard to any such questions to the state or states concerned or to the Security Council or to both. Any such question on which action is necessary shall be referred to the Security Council by the General Assembly either before or after discussion.

3. The General Assembly may call the attention of the Security Council to situations which are likely to endanger international peace and security.
4. The powers of the General Assembly set forth in this Article shall not limit the general scope of Article 10.

## ARTICLE 12.

1. While the Security Council is exercising in respect of any dispute or situation the functions assigned to it in the present Charter, the General Assembly shall not make any recommendation with regard to that dispute or situation unless the Security Council so requests.
2. The Secretary-General, with the consent of the Security Council, shall notify the General Assembly at each session of any matters relative to the maintenance of international peace and security which are being dealt with by the Security Council and shall similarly notify the General Assembly, or the Members of the United Nations if the General Assembly is not in session, immediately the Security Council ceases to deal with such matters.

## ARTICLE 13.

1. The General Assembly shall initiate studies and make recommendations for the purpose of:
   a. promoting international cooperation in the political field and encouraging the progressive development of international law and its codification;
   b. promoting international cooperation in the economic, social, cultural, educational, and health fields, and assisting in the realization of human rights and fundamental freedoms for all without distinction as to race, sex, language, or religion.
2. The further responsibilities, functions and powers of the General Assembly with respect to matters mentioned in paragraph 1(b) above are set forth in Chapters IX and X.

## ARTICLE 14.

Subject to the provisions of Article 12, the General Assembly may recommend measures for the peaceful adjustment of any situation, regardless of origin, which it deems likely to impair the general welfare or friendly relations among nations, including situations resulting from a violation of the provisions of the present Charter setting forth the Purposes and Principles of the United Nations.

## ARTICLE 15.

1. The General Assembly shall receive and consider annual and special reports from the Security Council; these reports shall include an account of the measures that the Security Council has decided upon or taken to maintain international peace and security.
2. The General Assembly shall receive and consider reports from the other organs of the United Nations.

## ARTICLE 16.

The General Assembly shall perform such functions with respect to the international trusteeship system as are assigned to it under Chapters XII and XIII, including the approval of the trusteeship agreements for areas not designated as strategic.

## ARTICLE 17.

1. The General Assembly shall consider and approve the budget of the Organization.
2. The expenses of the Organization shall be borne by the Members as apportioned by the General Assembly.
3. The General Assembly shall consider and approve any financial and budgetary arrangements with specialized agencies referred to in Article 57 and shall examine the administrative budgets of such specialized agencies with a view to making recommendations to the agencies concerned.

## Voting
## ARTICLE 18.

1. Each member of the General Assembly shall have one vote.
2. Decisions of the General Assembly on important questions shall be made by a two-thirds majority of the members present and voting. These questions shall include: recommendations with respect to the maintenance of international peace and security, the election of the non-permanent members of the Security Council, the election of the members of the Economic and Social Council, the election of members of the Trusteeship Council in accordance with paragraph 1(c) of Article 86, the admission of new Members to the United Nations, the suspension of the rights and privileges of membership, the expulsion of Members, questions relating to the operation of the trusteeship system, and budgetary questions.

3. Decisions on other questions, including the determination of additional categories of questions to be decided by a two-thirds majority, shall be made by a majority of the members present and voting.

ARTICLE 19.

A Member of the United Nations which is in arrears in the payment of its financial contributions to the Organization shall have no vote in the General Assembly if the amount equals or exceeds the amount of the contributions due from it for the preceding two full years. The General Assembly may, nevertheless, permit such a Member to vote if it is satisfied that the failure to pay is due to conditions beyond the control of the Member.

## Procedure
ARTICLE 20.

The General Assembly shall meet in regular annual sessions and in such special sessions as occasion may require. Special sessions shall be convoked by the Secretary-General at the request of the Security Council or of a majority of the Members of the United Nations.

ARTICLE 21.

The General Assembly shall adopt its own rules of procedure. It shall elect its President for each session.

ARTICLE 22.

The General Assembly may establish such subsidiary organs as it deems necessary for the performance of its functions.

## CHAPTER V
## THE SECURITY COUNCIL

### Composition
ARTICLE 23.

1. The Security Council shall consist of eleven[1] Members of the United Nations. The Republic of China, France, the Union of Soviet Socialist Republics, the United Kingdom of Great Britain and Northern Ireland, and the United States of America shall be permanent members of the Security Council. The General Assembly shall elect six[2] other Members of the

---

[1] Expanded to fifteen members by Charter amendment in 1965.

[2] Ten elective members, five chosen each year, provided for by Charter amendment in 1965.

United Nations to be non-permanent members of the Security Council, due regard being specially paid, in the first instance to the contribution of Members of the United Nations to the maintenance of international peace and security and to the other purposes of the Organization, and also to equitable geographical distribution.

2. The non-permanent members of the Security Council shall be elected for a term of two years. In the first election of non-permanent members, however, three shall be chosen for a term of one year. A retiring member shall not be eligible for immediate re-election.
3. Each member of the Security Council shall have one representative.

## Functions and Powers
ARTICLE 24.

1. In order to ensure prompt and effective action by the United Nations, its Members confer on the Security Council primary responsibility for the maintenance of international peace and security, and agree that in carrying out its duties under this responsibility the Security Council acts on their behalf.
2. In discharging these duties the Security Council shall act in accordance with the Purposes and Principles of the United Nations. The specific powers granted to the Security Council for the discharge of these duties are laid down in Chapters VI, VII, VIII, and XII.
3. The Security Council shall submit annual and, when necessary, special reports to the General Assembly for its consideration.

ARTICLE 25.

The Members of the United Nations agree to accept and carry out the decisions of the Security Council in accordance with the present Charter.

ARTICLE 26.

In order to promote the establishment and maintenance of international peace and security with the least diversion for armaments of the world's human and economic resources, the Security Council shall be responsible for formulating, with the assistance of the Military Staff Committee referred to in Article 47, plans to be submitted to the Members of the United Nations for the establishment of a system for the regulation of armaments.

## Voting
ARTICLE 27.

1. Each member of the Security Council shall have one vote.

2. Decisions of the Security Council on procedural matters shall be made by an affirmative vote of seven[3] members.
3. Decisions of the Security Council on all other matters shall be made by an affirmative vote of seven[4] members including the concurring votes of the permanent members; provided that, in decisions under Chapter VI, and under paragraph 3 of Article 52, a party to a dispute shall abstain from voting.

## Procedure
### ARTICLE 28.

1. The Security Council shall be so organized as to be able to function continuously. Each member of the Security Council shall for this purpose be represented at all times at the seat of the Organization.
2. The Security Council shall hold periodic meetings at which each of its members may, if it so desires, be represented by a member of the government or by some other specially designated representative.
3. The Security Council may hold meetings at such places other than the seat of the Organization as in its judgment will best facilitate its work.

### ARTICLE 29.

The Security Council may establish such subsidiary organs as it deems necessary for the performance of its functions.

### ARTICLE 30.

The Security Council shall adopt its own rules of procedure, including the method of selecting its President.

### ARTICLE 31.

Any Member of the United Nations which is not a member of the Security Council may participate, without vote, in the discussion of any question brought before the Security Council whenever the latter considers that the interests of that Member are specially affected.

### ARTICLE 32.

Any Member of the United Nations which is not a member of the Security Council or any state which is not a Member of the United Nations, if it is a party to a dispute under consideration by the Security Council, shall be invited

---

[3] Changed to nine members by Charter amendment in 1965.

[4] Changed to nine members by Charter amendment in 1965.

to participate, without vote, in the discussion relating to the dispute. The Security Council shall lay down such conditions as it deems just for the participation of a state which is not a Member of the United Nations.

## CHAPTER VI
## PACIFIC SETTLEMENT OF DISPUTES

### ARTICLE 33.

1. The parties to any dispute, the continuance of which is likely to endanger the maintenance of international peace and security, shall, first of all, seek a solution by negotiation, enquiry, mediation, conciliation, arbitration, judicial settlement, resort to regional agencies or arrangements, or other peaceful means of their own choice.
2. The Security Council shall, when it deems necessary, call upon the parties to settle their disputes by such means.

### ARTICLE 34.

The Security Council may investigate any dispute, or any situation which might lead to international friction or give rise to a dispute, in order to determine whether the continuance of the dispute or situation is likely to endanger the maintenance of international peace and security.

### ARTICLE 35.

1. Any Member of the United Nations may bring any dispute, or any situation of the nature referred to in Article 34, to the attention of the Security Council or of the General Assembly.
2. A state which is not a Member of the United Nations may bring to the attention of the Security Council or of the General Assembly any dispute to which it is a party if it accepts in advance, for the purposes of the dispute, the obligations of pacific settlement provided in the present Charter.
3. The proceedings of the General Assembly in respect of matters brought to its attention under this Article will be subject to the provisions of Articles 11 and 12.

### ARTICLE 36.

1. The Security Council may, at any stage of a dispute of the nature referred to in Article 33 or of a situation of like nature, recommend appropriate procedures or methods of adjustment.
2. The Security Council should take into consideration any procedures for the settlement of the dispute which have already been adopted by the parties.

3. In making recommendations under this Article the Security Council should also take into consideration that legal disputes should as a general rule be referred by the parties to the International Court of Justice in accordance with the provisions of the Statute of the Court.

## ARTICLE 37.

1. Should the parties to a dispute of the nature referred to in Article 33 fail to settle it by the means indicated in that Article, they shall refer it to the Security Council.
2. If the Security Council deems that the continuance of the dispute is in fact likely to endanger the maintenance of international peace and security, it shall decide whether to take action under Article 36 or to recommend such terms of settlement as it may consider appropriate.

## ARTICLE 38.

Without prejudice to the provisions of Articles 33 to 37, the Security Council may, if all the parties to any dispute so request, make recommendations to the parties with a view to a pacific settlement of the dispute.

## CHAPTER VII
## ACTION WITH RESPECT TO THREATS TO THE PEACE, BREACHES OF THE PEACE, AND ACTS OF AGGRESSION

### ARTICLE 39.

The Security Council shall determine the existence of any threat to the peace, breach of the peace, or act of aggression and shall make recommendations, or decide what measures shall be taken in accordance with Articles 41 and 42, to maintain or restore international peace and security.

### ARTICLE 40.

In order to prevent an aggravation of the situation, the Security Council may, before making the recommendations or deciding upon the measures provided for in Article 39, call upon the parties concerned to comply with such provisional measures as it deems necessary or desirable. Such provisional measures shall be without prejudice to the rights, claims, or position of the parties concerned. The Security Council shall duly take account of failure to comply with such provisional measures.

### ARTICLE 41.

The Security Council may decide what measures not involving the use of armed force are to be employed to give effect to its decisions, and it may call upon the Members of the United Nations to apply such measures. These may include complete or partial interruption of economic relations and of rail, sea, air, postal, telegraphic, radio, and other means of communication, and the severance of diplomatic relations.

## ARTICLE 42.

Should the Security Council consider that measures provided for in Article 41 would be inadequate or have proved to be inadequate, it may take such action by air, sea, or land forces as may be necessary to maintain or restore international peace and security. Such action may include demonstrations, blockade, and other operations by air, sea, or land forces of Members of the United Nations.

## ARTICLE 43.

1. All Members of the United Nations, in order to contribute to the maintenance of international peace and security, undertake to make available to the Security Council, on its call and in accordance with a special agreement or agreements, armed forces, assistance, and facilities, including rights of passage, necessary for the purpose of maintaining international peace and security.
2. Such agreement or agreements shall govern the numbers and types of forces, their degree of readiness and general location, and the nature of the facilities and assistance to be provided.
3. The agreement or agreements shall be negotiated as soon as possible on the initiative of the Security Council. They shall be concluded between the Security Council and Members or between the Security Council and groups of Members and shall be subject to ratification by the signatory states in accordance with their respective constitutional processes.

## ARTICLE 44.

When the Security Council has decided to use force it shall, before calling upon a Member not represented on it to provide armed forces in fulfilment of the obligations assumed under Article 43, invite that Member, if the Member so desires, to participate in the decisions of the Security Council concerning the employment of contingents of that Member's armed forces.

## ARTICLE 45.

In order to enable the United Nations to take urgent military measures, Members shall hold immediately available national air-force contingents for combined international enforcement action. The strength and degree of readiness of these contingents and plans for their combined action shall be determined, within the limits laid down in the special agreement or agreements referred to in Article 43, by the Security Council with the assistance of the Military Staff Committee.

## ARTICLE 46.

Plans for the application of armed force shall be made by the Security Council with the assistance of the Military Staff Committee.

## ARTICLE 47.

1. There shall be established a Military Staff Committee to advise and assist the Security Council on all questions relating to the Security Council's military requirements for the maintenance of international peace and security, the employment and command of forces placed at its disposal, the regulation of armaments, and possible disarmament.
2. The Military Staff Committee shall consist of the Chiefs of Staff of the permanent Members of the Security Council or their representatives. Any Member of the United Nations not permanently represented on the Committee shall be invited by the Committee to be associated with it when the efficient discharge of the Committee's responsibilities requires the participation of that Member in its work.
3. The Military Staff Committee shall be responsible under the Security Council for the strategic direction of any armed forces placed at the disposal of the Security Council. Questions relating to the command of such forces shall be worked out subsequently.
4. The Military Staff Committee, with the authorization of the Security Council and after consultation with appropriate regional agencies, may establish regional sub-committees.

## ARTICLE 48.

1. The action required to carry out the decisions of the Security Council for the maintenance of international peace and security shall be taken by all the Members of the United Nations or by some of them, as the Security Council may determine.
2. Such decisions shall be carried out by the Members of the United Nations directly and through their action in the appropriate international agencies of which they are members.

## ARTICLE 49.

The Members of the United Nations shall join in affording mutual assistance in carrying out the measures decided upon by the Security Council.

ARTICLE 50.

If preventive or enforcement measures against any state are taken by the Security Council, any other state, whether a Member of the United Nations or not, which finds itself confronted with special economic problems arising from the carrying out of those measures shall have the right to consult the Security Council with regard to a solution of those problems.

ARTICLE 51.

Nothing in the present Charter shall impair the inherent right of individual or collective self-defense if an armed attack occurs against a Member of the United Nations, until the Security Council has taken measures necessary to maintain international peace and security. Measures taken by Members in the exercise of this right of self-defense shall be immediately reported to the Security Council and shall not in any way affect the authority and responsibility of the Security Council under the present Charter to take at any time such action as it deems necessary in order to maintain or restore international peace and security.

## CHAPTER VIII
## REGIONAL ARRANGEMENTS

ARTICLE 52.

1. Nothing in the present Charter precludes the existence of regional arrangements or agencies for dealing with such matters relating to the maintenance of international peace and security as are appropriate for regional action, provided that such arrangements or agencies and their activities are consistent with the Purposes and Principles of the United Nations.
2. The Members of the United Nations entering into such arrangements or constituting such agencies shall make every effort to achieve pacific settlement of local disputes through such regional arrangements or by such regional agencies before referring them to the Security Council.
3. The Security Council shall encourage the development of pacific settlement of local disputes through such regional arrangements or by such regional agencies either on the initiative of the states concerned or by reference from the Security Council.
4. This Article in no way impairs the application of Articles 34 and 35.

ARTICLE 53.

1. The Security Council shall, where appropriate, utilize such regional arrangements or agencies for enforcement action under its authority. But no enforcement action shall be taken under regional arrangements or by regional agencies without the authorization of the Security Council, with the exception of measures against any enemy state, as defined in paragraph 2

of this Article, provided for pursuant to Article 107 or in regional arrangements directed against renewal of aggressive policy on the part of any such
state, until such time as the Organization may, on request of the Governments concerned, be charged with the responsibility for preventing further
aggression by such a state.
2. The term enemy state as used in paragraph 1 of this Article applies to any
state which during the Second World War has been an enemy of any signatory of the present Charter.

## ARTICLE 54.

The Security Council shall at all times be kept fully informed of activities undertaken or in contemplation under regional arrangements or by regional agencies for the maintenance of international peace and security.

## CHAPTER IX
## INTERNATIONAL ECONOMIC AND SOCIAL COOPERATION

### ARTICLE 55.

With a view to the creation of conditions of stability and well-being which are
necessary for peaceful and friendly relations among nations based on respect
for the principle of equal rights and self-determination of peoples, the United
Nations shall promote:

a. higher standards of living, full employment, and conditions of economic
   and social progress and development;
b. solutions of international economic, social, health, and related problems;
   and international cultural and educational cooperation; and
c. universal respect for, and observance of, human rights and fundamental
   freedoms for all without distinction as to race, sex, language, or religion.

### ARTICLE 56.

All Members pledge themselves to take joint and separate action in cooperation with the Organization for the achievement of the purposes set forth in
Article 55.

### ARTICLE 57.

1. The various specialized agencies, established by intergovernmental agreement and having wide international responsibilities, as defined in their
   basic instruments, in economic, social, cultural, educational, health and
   related fields, shall be brought into relationship with the United Nations
   in accordance with the provisions of Article 63.

2. Such agencies thus brought into relationship with the United Nations are hereinafter referred to as specialized agencies.

## ARTICLE 58.

The Organization shall make recommendations for the coordination of the policies and activities of the specialized agencies.

## ARTICLE 59.

The Organization shall, where appropriate, initiate negotiations among the states concerned for the creation of any new specialized agencies required for the accomplishment of the purposes set forth in Article 55.

## ARTICLE 60.

Responsibility for the discharge of the functions of the Organization set forth in this Chapter shall be vested in the General Assembly and, under the authority of the General Assembly, in the Economic and Social Council, which shall have for this purpose the powers set forth in Chapter X.

## CHAPTER X
## THE ECONOMIC AND SOCIAL COUNCIL

### Composition
### ARTICLE 61.

1. The Economic and Social Council shall consist of eighteen[5] Members of the United Nations elected by the General Assembly.
2. Subject to the provisions of paragraph 3, six[6] members of the Economic and Social Council shall be elected each year for a term of three years. A retiring member shall be eligible for immediate re-election.
3. At the first election, eighteen members of the Economic and Social Council shall be chosen. The term of office of six members so chosen shall expire at the end of one year, and of six other members at the end of two years, in accordance with arrangements made by the General Assembly.

---

[5] Expanded to twenty-seven members by Charter amendment in 1965 and to fifty-four members by Charter amendment in 1973.

[6] Changed to provide for the election of nine members each year by Charter amendment in 1965 and eighteen members each year by Charter amendment in 1973.

4. Each member of the Economic and Social Council shall have one representative.

## Functions and Powers
### ARTICLE 62.

1. The Economic and Social Council may make or initiate studies and reports with respect to international economic, social, cultural, educational, health, and related matters and may make recommendations with respect to any such matters to the General Assembly, to the Members of the United Nations, and to the specialized agencies concerned.
2. It may make recommendations for the purpose of promoting respect for, and observance of, human rights and fundamental freedoms for all.
3. It may prepare draft conventions for submission to the General Assembly, with respect to matters falling within its competence.
4. It may call, in accordance with the rules prescribed by the United Nations, international conferences on matters falling within its competence.

### ARTICLE 63.

1. The Economic and Social Council may enter into agreements with any of the agencies referred to in Article 57, defining the terms on which the agency concerned shall be brought into relationship with the United Nations. Such agreements shall be subject to approval by the General Assembly.
2. It may coordinate the activities of the specialized agencies through consultation with and recommendations to such agencies and through recommendations to the General Assembly and to the Members of the United Nations.

### ARTICLE 64.

1. The Economic and Social Council may take appropriate steps to obtain regular reports from the specialized agencies. It may make arrangements with the Members of the United Nations and with the specialized agencies to obtain reports on the steps taken to give effect to its own recommendations and to recommendations on matters falling within its competence made by the General Assembly.
2. It may communicate its observations on these reports to the General Assembly.

### ARTICLE 65.

The Economic and Social Council may furnish information to the Security Council and shall assist the Security Council upon its request.

## ARTICLE 66.

1. The Economic and Social Council shall perform such functions as fall within its competence in connection with the carrying out of the recommendations of the General Assembly.
2. It may, with the approval of the General Assembly, perform services at the request of Members of the United Nations and at the request of specialized agencies.
3. It shall perform such other functions as are specified elsewhere in the present Charter or as may be assigned to it by the General Assembly.

## Voting

## ARTICLE 67.

1. Each member of the Economic and Social Council shall have one vote.
2. Decisions of the Economic and Social Council shall be made by a majority of the members present and voting.

## Procedure

## ARTICLE 68.

The Economic and Social Council shall set up commissions in economic and social fields and for the promotion of human rights, and such other commissions as may be required for the performance of its functions.

## ARTICLE 69.

The Economic and Social Council shall invite any Member of the United Nations to participate, without vote, in its deliberations on any matter of particular concern to that Member.

## ARTICLE 70.

The Economic and Social Council may make arrangements for representatives of the specialized agencies to participate, without vote, in its deliberations and in those of the commissions established by it, and for its representatives to participate in the deliberations of the specialized agencies.

## ARTICLE 71.

The Economic and Social Council may make suitable arrangements for consultation with non-governmental organizations which are concerned with matters within its competence. Such arrangements may be made with international organizations and, where appropriate, with national organizations after consultation with the Member of the United Nations concerned.

ARTICLE 72.

1. The Economic and Social Council shall adopt its own rules of procedure, including the method of selecting its President.
2. The Economic and Social Council shall meet as required in accordance with its rules, which shall include provision for the convening of meetings on the request of a majority of its members.

## CHAPTER XI
## DECLARATION REGARDING
## NON-SELF-GOVERNING TERRITORIES

ARTICLE 73.

Members of the United Nations which have or assume responsibilities for the administration of territories whose peoples have not yet attained a full measure of self-government recognize the principle that the interests of the inhabitants of these territories are paramount, and accept as a sacred trust the obligation to promote to the utmost, within the system of international peace and security established by the present Charter, the well-being of the inhabitants of these territories, and, to this end:

a. to ensure, with due respect for the culture of the peoples concerned, their political, economic, social, and educational advancement, their just treatment, and their protection against abuses;
b. to develop self-government, to take due account of the political aspirations of the peoples, and to assist them in the progressive development of their free political institutions, according to the particular circumstances of each territory and its peoples and their varying stages of advancement;
c. to further international peace and security;
d. to promote constructive measures of development, to encourage research, and to cooperate with one another and, when and where appropriate, with specialized international bodies with a view to the practical achievement of the social, economic, and scientific purposes set forth in this Article; and
e. to transmit regularly to the Secretary-General for information purposes, subject to such limitation as security and constitutional considerations may require, statistical and other information of a technical nature relating to economic, social, and educational conditions in the territories for which they are respectively responsible other than those territories to which Chapters XII and XIII apply.

ARTICLE 74.

Members of the United Nations also agree that their policy in respect of the territories to which this Chapter applies, no less than in respect of their metropolitan areas, must be based on the general principle of good-neighborliness, due account being taken of the interests and well-being of the rest of the world, in social, economic, and commercial matters.

## CHAPTER XII
## INTERNATIONAL TRUSTEESHIP SYSTEM

### ARTICLE 75.

The United Nations shall establish under its authority an international trusteeship system for the administration and supervision of such territories as may be placed thereunder by subsequent individual agreements. These territories are hereinafter referred to as trust territories.

### ARTICLE 76.

The basic objectives of the trusteeship system, in accordance with the Purposes of the United Nations laid down in Article I of the present Charter, shall be:

a. to further international peace and security;
b. to promote the political, economic, social, and educational advancement of the inhabitants of the trust territories, and their progressive development towards self-government or independence as may be appropriate to the particular circumstances of each territory and its peoples and the freely expressed wishes of the peoples concerned, and as may be provided by the terms of each trusteeship agreement;
c. to encourage respect for human rights and for fundamental freedoms for all without distinction as to race, sex, language, or religion, and to encourage recognition of the interdependence of the peoples of the world; and
d. to ensure equal treatment in social, economic, and commercial matters for all Members of the United Nations and their nationals, and also equal treatment for the latter in the administration of justice, without prejudice to the attainment of the foregoing objectives and subject to the provisions of Article 80.

### ARTICLE 77.

1. The trusteeship system shall apply to such territories in the following categories as may be placed thereunder by means of trusteeship agreements:
   a. territories now held under mandate;
   b. territories which may be detached from enemy states as a result of the Second World War; and
   c. territories voluntarily placed under the system by states responsible for their administration.
2. It will be a matter for subsequent agreement as to which territories in the foregoing categories will be brought under the trusteeship system and upon what terms.

ARTICLE 78.

The trusteeship system shall not apply to territories which have become Members of the United Nations, the relationship among which shall be based on respect for the principle of sovereign equality.

ARTICLE 79.

The terms of trusteeship for each territory to be placed under the trusteeship system, including any alteration or amendment, shall be agreed upon by the states directly concerned, including the mandatory power in the case of territories held under mandate by a Member of the United Nations, and shall be approved as provided for in Articles 83 and 85.

ARTICLE 80.

1. Except as may be agreed upon in individual trusteeship agreements, made under Articles 77, 79, and 81, placing each territory under the trusteeship system, and until such agreements have been concluded, nothing in this Chapter shall be construed in or of itself to alter in any manner the rights whatsoever of any states or any peoples or the terms of existing international instruments to which Members of the United Nations may respectively be parties.
2. Paragraph 1 of this Article shall not be interpreted as giving grounds for delay or postponement of the negotiation and conclusion of agreements for placing mandated and other territories under the trusteeship system as provided for in Article 77.

ARTICLE 81.

The trusteeship agreement shall in each use include the terms under which the trust territory will be administered and designate the authority which will exercise the administration of the trust territory. Such authority, hereinafter called the administering authority, may be one or more states or the Organization itself.

ARTICLE 82.

There may be designated, in any trusteeship agreement, a strategic area or areas which may include part or all of the trust territory to which the agreement applies, without prejudice to any special agreement or agreements made under Article 43.

ARTICLE 83.

1. All functions of the United Nations relating to strategic areas, including the approval of the terms of the trusteeship agreements and of their alteration or amendment, shall be exercised by the Security Council.

2. The basic objectives set forth in Article 76 shall be applicable to the people of each strategic area.
3. The Security Council shall, subject to the provisions of the trusteeship agreements and without prejudice to security considerations, avail itself of the assistance of the Trusteeship Council to perform those functions of the United Nations under the trusteeship system relating to political, economic, social, and educational matters in the strategic areas.

### ARTICLE 84.

It shall be the duty of the administering authority to ensure that the trust territory shall play its part in the maintenance of international peace and security. To this end the administering authority may make use of volunteer forces, facilities, and assistance from the trust territory in carrying out the obligations towards the Security Council undertaken in this regard by the administering authority, as well as for local defense and the maintenance of law and order within the trust territory.

### ARTICLE 85.

1. The functions of the United Nations with regard to trusteeship agreements for all areas not designated as strategic, including the approval of the terms of the trusteeship agreements and of their alteration or amendment, shall be exercised by the General Assembly.
2. The Trusteeship Council, operating under the authority of the General Assembly, shall assist the General Assembly in carrying out these functions.

## CHAPTER XIII
## THE TRUSTEESHIP COUNCIL

### Composition
### ARTICLE 86.

1. The Trusteeship Council shall consist of the following Members of the United Nations:
   a. those Members administering trust territories;
   b. such of those Members mentioned by name in Article 23 as are not administering trust territories; and
   c. as many other Members elected for three-year terms by the General Assembly as may be necessary to ensure that the total number of members of the Trusteeship Council is equally divided between those Members of the United Nations which administer trust territories and those which do not.
2. Each member of the Trusteeship Council shall designate one specially qualified person to represent it therein.

## Functions and Powers
### ARTICLE 87.

The General Assembly and, under its authority, the Trusteeship Council, in carrying out their functions, may:

a. consider reports submitted by the administering authority;
b. accept petitions and examine them in consultation with the administering authority;
c. provide for periodic visits to the respective trust territories at times agreed upon with the administering authority; and
d. take these and other actions in conformity with the terms of the trusteeship agreements.

### ARTICLE 88.

The Trusteeship Council shall formulate a questionnaire on the political, economic, social, and educational advancement of the inhabitants of each trust territory, and the administering authority for each trust territory within the competence of the General Assembly shall make an annual report to the General Assembly upon the basis of such questionnaire.

## Voting
### ARTICLE 89.

1. Each member of the Trusteeship Council shall have one vote.
2. Decisions of the Trusteeship Council shall be made by a majority of the members present and voting.

## Procedure
### ARTICLE 90.

1. The Trusteeship Council shall adopt its own rules of procedure, including the method of selecting its President.
2. The Trusteeship Council shall meet as required in accordance with its rules, which shall include provision for the convening of meetings on the request of a majority of its members.

### ARTICLE 91.

The Trusteeship Council shall, when appropriate, avail itself of the assistance of the Economic and Social Council and of the specialized agencies in regard to matters with which they are respectively concerned.

## CHAPTER XIV
## THE INTERNATIONAL COURT OF JUSTICE

ARTICLE 92.

The International Court of Justice shall be the principal judicial organ of the United Nations. It shall function in accordance with the annexed Statute, which is based upon the Statute of the Permanent Court of International Justice and forms an integral part of the present Charter.

ARTICLE 93.

1. All Members of the United Nations are *ipso facto* parties to the Statute of the International Court of Justice.
2. A state which is not a Member of the United Nations may become a party to the Statute of the International Court of Justice on conditions to be determined in each case by the General Assembly upon the recommendation of the Security Council.

ARTICLE 94.

1. Each Member of the United Nations undertakes to comply with the decision of the International Court of Justice in any case to which it is a party.
2. If any party to a case fails to perform the obligations incumbent upon it under a judgment rendered by the Court, the other party may have recourse to the Security Council, which may, if it deems necessary, make recommendations or decide upon measures to be taken to give effect to the judgment.

ARTICLE 95.

Nothing in the present Charter shall prevent Members of the United Nations from entrusting the solution of their differences to other tribunals by virtue of agreements already in existence or which may be concluded in the future.

ARTICLE 96.

1. The General Assembly or the Security Council may request the International Court of Justice to give an advisory opinion on any legal question.
2. Other organs of the United Nations and specialized agencies, which may at any time be so authorized by the General Assembly, may also request advisory opinions of the Court on legal questions arising within the scope of their activities.

## CHAPTER XV
## THE SECRETARIAT

The Secretariat shall comprise a Secretary-General and such staff as the Organization may require. The Secretary-General shall be appointed by the General Assembly upon the recommendation of the Security Council. He shall be the chief administrative officer of the Organization.

The Secretary-General shall act in that capacity in all meetings of the General Assembly, of the Security Council, of the Economic and Social Council, and of the Trusteeship Council, and shall perform such other functions as are entrusted to him by these organs. The Secretary-General shall make an annual report to the General Assembly on the work of the Organization.

The Secretary-General may bring to the attention of the Security Council any matter which in his opinion may threaten the maintenance of international peace and security.

1. In the performance of their duties the Secretary-General and the staff shall not seek or receive instructions from any government or from any other authority external to the Organization. They shall refrain from any action which might reflect on their position as international officials responsible only to the Organization.
2. Each Member of the United Nations undertakes to respect the exclusively international character of the responsibilities of the Secretary-General and the staff and not to seek to influence them in the discharge of their responsibilities.

1. The staff shall be appointed by the Secretary-General under regulations established by the General Assembly.
2. Appropriate staffs shall be permanently assigned to the Economic and Social Council, the Trusteeship Council, and, as required, to other organs of the United Nations. These staffs shall form a part of the Secretariat.
3. The paramount consideration in the employment of the staff and in the determination of the conditions of service shall be the necessity of securing

the highest standards of efficiency, competence, and integrity. Due regard shall be paid to the importance of recruiting the staff on as wide a geographical basis as possible.

## CHAPTER XVI
## MISCELLANEOUS PROVISIONS

### ARTICLE 102.

1. Every treaty and every international agreement entered into by any Member of the United Nations after the present Charter comes into force shall as soon as possible be registered with the Secretariat and published by it.
2. No party to any such treaty or international agreement which has not been registered in accordance with the provisions of paragraph 1 of this Article may invoke that treaty or agreement before any organ of the United Nations.

### ARTICLE 103.

In the event of a conflict between the obligations of the Members of the United Nations under the present Charter and their obligations under any other international agreement, their obligations under the present Charter shall prevail.

### ARTICLE 104.

The Organization shall enjoy in the territory of each of its Members such legal capacity as may be necessary for the exercise of its functions and the fulfilment of its purposes.

### ARTICLE 105.

1. The Organization shall enjoy in the territory of each of its Members such privileges and immunities as are necessary for the fulfilment of its purposes.
2. Representatives of the Members of the United Nations and officials of the Organization shall similarly enjoy such privileges and immunities as are necessary for the independent exercise of their functions in connection with the Organization.
3. The General Assembly may make recommendations with a view to determining the details of the application of paragraphs 1 and 2 of this Article or may propose conventions to the Members of the United Nations for this purpose.

# CHAPTER XVII
# TRANSITIONAL SECURITY ARRANGEMENTS

## ARTICLE 106.

Pending the coming into force of such special agreements referred to in Article 43 as in the opinion of the Security Council enable it to begin the exercise of its responsibilities under Article 42, the parties to the Four-Nation Declaration, signed at Moscow, October 30, 1943, and France, shall, in accordance with the provisions of paragraph 5 of that Declaration, consult with one another and as occasion requires with other Members of the United Nations with a view to such joint action on behalf of the Organization as may be necessary for the purpose of maintaining international peace and security.

## ARTICLE 107.

Nothing in the present Chance shall invalidate or preclude action, in relation to any state which during the Second World War has been an enemy of any signatory to the present Charter, taken or authorized as a result of that war by the Governments having responsibility for such action.

# CHAPTER XVIII
# AMENDMENTS

## ARTICLE 108.

Amendments to the present Charter shall come into force for all Members of the United Nations when they have been adopted by a vote of two thirds of the members of the General Assembly and ratified in accordance with their respective constitutional processes by two thirds of the Members of the United Nations, including all the permanent members of the Security Council.

## ARTICLE 109.

1. A General Conference of the Members of the United Nations for the purpose of reviewing the present Charter may be held at a date and place to be fixed by a two-thirds vote of the members of the General Assembly and by a vote of any seven members of the Security Council. Each Member of the United Nations shall have one vote in the conference.
2. Any alteration of the present Charter recommended by a two-thirds vote of the conference shall take effect when ratified in accordance with their respective constitutional processes by two thirds of the Members of the United Nations including all the permanent members of the Security Council.
3. If such a conference has not been held before the tenth annual session of the General Assembly following the coming into force of the present

Charter, the proposal to call such a conference shall be placed on the agenda of that session of the General Assembly, and the conference shall be held if so decided by a majority vote of the members of the General Assembly and by a vote of any seven members of the Security Council.

## CHAPTER XIX
## RATIFICATION AND SIGNATURE

### ARTICLE 110.

1. The present Charter shall be ratified by the signatory states in accordance with their respective constitutional processes.
2. The ratifications shall be deposited with the Government of the United States of America, which shall notify all the signatory states of each deposit as well as the Secretary-General of the Organization when he has been appointed.
3. The present Charter shall come into force upon the deposit of ratifications by the Republic of China, France, the Union of Soviet Socialist Republics, the United Kingdom of Great Britain and Northern Ireland, and the United States of America, and by a majority of the other signatory states. A protocol of the ratifications deposited shall thereupon be drawn up by the Government of the United States of America which shall communicate copies thereof to all the signatory states.
4. The states signatory to the present Charter which ratify it after it has come into force will become original members of the United Nations on the date of the deposit of their respective ratifications.

### ARTICLE 111.

The present Charter, of which the Chinese, French, Russian, English, and Spanish texts are equally authentic, shall remain deposited in the archives of the Government of the United States of America. Duly certified copies thereof shall be transmitted by that Government to the Governments of the other signatory states.

IN FAITH WHEREOF the representatives of the Governments of the United Nations have signed the present Charter.

DONE at the city of San Francisco the twenty-sixth day of June, one thousand nine hundred and forty-five.

# C

# THE UNIVERSAL DECLARATION OF HUMAN RIGHTS

**(ADOPTED DECEMBER 10, 1948)**
**PREAMBLE**

*Whereas* recognition of the inherent dignity and of the equal and inalienable rights of all members of the human family is the foundation of freedom, justice and peace in the world,

*Whereas* disregard and contempt for human rights have resulted in barbarous acts which have outraged the conscience of mankind, and the advent of a world in which human beings shall enjoy freedom of speech and belief and freedom from fear and want has been proclaimed as the highest aspiration of the common people,

*Whereas* it is essential, if man is not to be compelled to have recourse, as a last resort, to rebellion against tyranny and oppression, that human rights should be protected by the rule of law,

*Whereas* it is essential to promote the development of friendly relations between nations,

*Whereas* the peoples of the United Nations have in the Charter reaffirmed their faith in fundamental human rights, in the dignity and worth of the human person and in the equal rights of men and women and have determined to promote social progress and better standards of life in larger freedom,

*Whereas* Member States have pledged themselves to achieve, in cooperation with the United Nations, the promotion of universal respect for and observance of human rights and fundamental freedoms,

*Whereas* a common understanding of these rights and freedoms is of the greatest importance for the full realization of this pledge,

*Now, therefore,*

*The General Assembly*

*Proclaims* this Universal Declaration of Human Rights as a common standard of achievement for all peoples and all nations, to the end that every individual and every organ of society, keeping this Declaration constantly in mind, shall strive by teaching and education to promote respect for these rights and freedoms and by progressive measures, national and international, to secure their universal and effective recognition and observance, both among the peoples of Member States themselves and among the peoples of territories under their jurisdiction.

### ARTICLE 1

All human beings are born free and equal in dignity and rights. They are endorsed with reason and conscience and should act towards one another in a spirit of brotherhood.

### ARTICLE 2

Everyone is entitled to all the rights and freedoms set forth in this Declaration, without distinction of any kind, such as race, colour, sex, language, religion, political or other opinion, national or social origin, property, birth or other status.

Furthermore, no distinction shall be made on the basis of the political, jurisdictional or international status of the country or territory to which a person belongs, whether it be independent, trust, non-self-governing or under any other limitation of sovereignty.

### ARTICLE 3

Everyone has the right to life, liberty and the security of person.

### ARTICLE 4

No one shall be held in slavery or servitude; slavery and the slave trade shall be prohibited in all their forms.

### ARTICLE 5

No one shall be subjected to torture or to cruel, inhuman or degrading treatment or punishment.

### ARTICLE 6

Everyone has the right to recognition everywhere as a person before the law.

ARTICLE 7

All are equal before the law and are entitled without any discrimination to equal protection of the law. All are entitled to equal protection against any discrimination in violation of this Declaration and against any incitement to such discrimination.

ARTICLE 8

Everyone has the right to an effective remedy by the competent national tribunals for acts violating the fundamental rights granted him by the constitution or by law.

ARTICLE 9

No one shall be subjected to arbitrary arrest, detention or exile.

ARTICLE 10

Everyone is entitled in full equality to a fair and public hearing by an independent and impartial tribunal, in the determination of his rights and obligations and of any criminal charge against him.

ARTICLE 11

1. Everyone charged with a penal offence has the right to be presumed innocent until proved guilty according to law in a public trial at which he has had all the guarantees necessary for his defence.
2. No one shall be held guilty of any penal offence on account of any act or omission which did not constitute a penal offence, under national or international law, at the time when it was committed. Nor shall a heavier penalty be imposed than the one that was applicable at the time the penal offence was committed.

ARTICLE 12

No one shall be subjected to arbitrary interference with his privacy, family, home or correspondence, nor to attacks upon his honour and reputation. Everyone has the right to the protection of the law against such interference or attacks.

ARTICLE 13

1. Everyone has the right to freedom of movement and residence within the borders of each State.

2. Everyone has the right to leave any country, including his own, and to return to his country.

## ARTICLE 14

1. Everyone has the right to seek and to enjoy in other countries asylum from persecution.
2. This right may not be invoked in the case of prosecutions genuinely arising from non-political crimes or from acts contrary to the purposes and principles of the United Nations.

## ARTICLE 15

1. Everyone has the right to a nationality.
2. No one shall be arbitrarily deprived of his nationality nor denied the right to change his nationality.

## ARTICLE 16

1. Men and women of full age, without any limitation due to race, nationality or religion, have the right to marry and to found a family. They are entitled to equal rights as to marriage, during marriage and at its dissolution.
2. Marriage shall be entered into only with the free and full consent of the intending spouses.
3. The family is the natural and fundamental group unit of society and is entitled to protection by society and the State.

## ARTICLE 17

1. Everyone has the right to own property alone as well as in association with others.
2. No one shall be arbitrarily deprived of his property.

## ARTICLE 18

Everyone has the right to freedom of thought, conscience and religion; this right includes freedom to change his religion or belief, and freedom, either alone or in community with others and in public or private, to manifest his religion or belief in teaching, practice, worship and observance.

## ARTICLE 19

Everyone has the right to freedom of opinion and expression; this right includes freedom to hold opinions without interference and to seek, receive and impart information and ideas through any media and regardless of frontiers.

ARTICLE 20

1. Everyone has the right to freedom of peaceful assembly and association.
2. No one may be compelled to belong to an association.

ARTICLE 21

1. Everyone has the right to take part in the government of his country, directly or through freely chosen representatives.
2. Everyone has the right of equal access to public service in his country.
3. The will of the people shall be the basis of the authority of government; this will shall be expressed in periodic and genuine elections which shall be by universal and equal suffrage and shall be held by secret vote or by equivalent free voting procedures.

ARTICLE 22

Everyone, as a member of society, has the right to social security and is entitled to realization, through national effort and international co-operation and in accordance with the organization and resources of each State, of the economic, social and cultural rights indispensable for his dignity and the free development of his personality.

ARTICLE 23

1. Everyone has the right to work, to free choice of employment, to just and favourable conditions of work and to protection against unemployment.
2. Everyone, without any discrimination, has the right to equal pay for equal work.
3. Everyone who works has the right to just and favourable remuneration ensuring for himself and his family an existence worthy of human dignity, and supplemented, if necessary, by other means of social protection.
4. Everyone has the right to form and to join trade unions for the protection of his interests.

ARTICLE 24

Everyone has the right to rest and leisure, including reasonable limitation of working hours and periodic holidays with pay.

ARTICLE 25

1. Everyone has the right to a standard of living adequate for the health and well-being of himself and of his family, including food, clothing, housing and medical care and necessary social services, and the right to security in

the event of unemployment, sickness, disability, widowhood, old age or other lack of livelihood in circumstances beyond his control.

2. Motherhood and childhood are entitled to special care and assistance. All children, whether born in or out of wedlock, shall enjoy the same social protection.

## ARTICLE 26

1. Everyone has the right to education. Education shall be free, at least in the elementary and fundamental stages. Elementary education shall be compulsory. Technical and professional education shall be made generally available and higher education shall be equally accessible to all on the basis of merit.
2. Education shall be directed to the full development of the human personality and to the strengthening of respect for human rights and fundamental freedoms. It shall promote understanding, tolerance and friendship among all nations, racial or religious groups, and shall further the activities of the United Nations for the maintenance of peace.
3. Parents have a prior right to choose the kind of education that shall be given to their children.

## ARTICLE 27

1. Everyone has the right freely to participate in the cultural life of the community, to enjoy the arts and to share in scientific advancement and its benefits.
2. Everyone has the right to the protection of the moral and material interests resulting from any scientific, literary or artistic production of which he is the author.

## ARTICLE 28

Everyone is entitled to a social and international order in which the rights and freedoms set forth in this Declaration can be fully realized.

## ARTICLE 29

1. Everyone has duties to the community in which alone the free and full development of his personality is possible.
2. In the exercise of his rights and freedoms, everyone shall be subject only to such limitations as are determined by law solely for the purpose of securing due recognition and respect for the rights and freedoms of others and of meeting the just requirements of morality, public order and the general welfare in a democratic society.

3. These rights and freedoms may in no case be exercised contrary to the purposes and principles of the United Nations.

## ARTICLE 30

Nothing in this Declaration may be interpreted as implying for any State, group or person any right to engage in any activity or to perform any act aimed at the destruction of any of the rights and freedoms set forth herein.

# D
---

## UNITED NATIONS MEMBER STATES

**MEMBER—**(*DATE OF ADMISSION*)

Afghanistan—(*19 Nov. 1946*)
Albania—(*14 Dec. 1955*)
Algeria—(*8 Oct. 1962*)
Andorra—(*28 July 1993*)
Angola—(*1 Dec. 1976*)
Antigua and Barbuda—(*11 Nov. 1981*)
Argentina—(*24 Oct. 1945*)
Armenia—(*2 Mar. 1992*)
Australia—(*1 Nov. 1945*)
Austria—(*14 Dec. 1955*)
Azerbaijan—(*9 Mar. 1992*)
Bahamas—(*18 Sep. 1973*)
Bahrain—(*21 Sep. 1971*)
Bangladesh—(*17 Sep. 1974*)
Barbados—(*9 Dec. 1966*)
Belarus—(*24 Oct. 1945*)

—On 19 September 1991, Byelorussia informed the United Nations that it had changed its name to Belarus.

Belgium—(*27 Dec. 1945*)
Belize—(*25 Sep. 1981*)
Benin—(*20 Sep. 1960*)
Bhutan—(*21 Sep. 1971*)
Bolivia—(*14 Nov. 1945*)
Bosnia and Herzegovina—(*22 May 1992*)
Botswana—(*17 Oct. 1966*)
Brazil—(*24 Oct. 1945*)
Brunei Darussalam—(*21 Sep. 1984*)
Bulgaria—(*14 Dec. 1955*)
Burkina Faso—(*20 Sep. 1960*)

Burundi—*(18 Sep. 1962)*
Cambodia—*(14 Dec. 1955)*
Cameroon—*(20 Sep. 1960)*
Canada—*(9 Nov. 1945)*
Cape Verde—*(16 Sep. 1975)*
Central African Republic—*(20 Sep. 1960)*
Chad—*(20 Sep. 1960)*
Chile—*(24 Oct. 1945)*
China—*(24 Oct. 1945)*
Colombia—*(5 Nov. 1945)*
Comoros—*(12 Nov. 1975)*
Congo—*(20 Sep. 1960)*
Costa Rica—*(2 Nov. 1945)*
Côte d'Ivoire—*(20 Sep. 1960)*
Croatia—*(22 May 1992)*
Cuba—*(24 Oct. 1945)*
Cyprus—*(20 Sep. 1960)*
Czech Republic—*(19 Jan. 1993)*

—Czechoslovakia was an original member of the United Nations from 24 October 1945. In a letter dated 10 December 1992, its permanent representative informed the Secretary-General that the Czech and Slovak Federal Republic would cease to exist on 31 December 1992 and that the Czech Republic and the Slovak Republic, as successor states, would apply for membership in the United Nations. Following the receipt of its application, the Security Council, on 8 January, recommended to the General Assembly that the Czech Republic be admitted to United Nations membership. The Czech Republic was thus admitted on 19 January as a member state.

Democratic People's Republic of Korea—*(17 Sep. 1991)*
Democratic Republic of the Congo—*(20 Sep. 1960)*
Denmark—*(24 Oct. 1945)*
Djibouti—*(20 Sep. 1977)*
Dominica—*(18 Dec. 1978)*
Dominican Republic—*(24 Oct. 1945)*
Ecuador—*(21 Dec. 1945)*
Egypt—*(24 Oct. 1945)*

—(Egypt and Syria were original members of the United Nations from 24 October 1945. Following a plebiscite on 21 February 1958, the United Arab Republic was established by a nation of Egypt and Syria and continued as a single member. On 13 October 1961, Syria, having resumed its status as an independent state, resumed its separate membership in the United Nations. On 2 September 1971, the United Arab Republic changed its name to the Arab Republic of Egypt.

El Salvador—*(24 Oct. 1945)*
Equatorial Guinea—*(12 Nov. 1968)*
Eritrea—*(28 May 1993)*
Estonia—*(17 Sep. 1991)*
Ethiopia—*(13 Nov. 1945)*
Fiji—*(13 Oct. 1970)*
Finland—*(14 Dec. 1955)*
France—*(24 Oct. 1945)*
Gabon—*(20 Sep. 1960)*
Gambia—*(21 Sep. 1965)*
Georgia—*(31 July 1992)*
Germany—*(18 Sep. 1973)*

—The Federal Republic of Germany and the German Democratic Republic were admitted to membership in the United Nations on 18 September 1973. Through the accession of the German Democratic Republic to the Federal Republic of Germany, effective from 3 October 1990, the two German states have united to form one sovereign state.

Ghana—*(8 Mar. 1957)*
Greece—*(25 Oct. 1945)*
Grenada—*(17 Sep. 1974)*
Guatemala—*(21 Nov. 1945)*
Guinea—*(12 Dec. 1958)*
Guinea-Bissau—*(17 Sep. 1974)*
Guyana—*(20 Sep. 1966)*
Haiti—*(24 Oct. 1945)*
Honduras—*(17 Dec. 1945)*
Hungary—*(14 Dec. 1955)*
Iceland—*(19 Nov. 1946)*
India—*(30 Oct. 1945)*
Indonesia—*(28 Sep. 1950)*

—By letter of 20 January 1965, Indonesia announced its decision to withdraw from the United Nations "at this stage and under the present circumstances." By telegram of 19 September 1966, it announced its decision "to resume full cooperation with the United Nations and to resume participation in its activities." On 28 September 1966, the General Assembly took note of this decision and the President invited representatives of Indonesia to take seats in the Assembly.

Iran (Islamic Republic of)—*(24 Oct. 1945)*
Iraq—*(21 Dec. 1945)*
Ireland—*(14 Dec. 1955)*
Israel—*(11 May 1949)*
Italy—*(14 Dec. 1955)*
Jamaica—*(18 Sep. 1962)*

Japan—*(18 Dec. 1956)*
Jordan—*(14 Dec. 1955)*
Kazakhstan—*(2 Mar. 1992)*
Kenya—*(16 Dec. 1963)*
Kuwait—*(14 May 1963)*
Kyrgyzstan—*(2 Mar. 1992)*
Lao People's Democratic Republic—*(14 Dec. 1955)*
Latvia—*(17 Sep. 1991)*
Lebanon—*(24 Oct. 1945)*
Lesotho—*(17 Oct. 1966)*
Liberia—*(2 Nov. 1945)*
Libyan Arab Jamahiriya—*(14 Dec. 1955)*
Liechtenstein—*(18 Sep. 1990)*
Lithuania—*(17 Sep. 1991)*
Luxembourg—*(24 Oct. 1945)*
Madagascar—*(20 Sep. 1960)*
Malawi—*(1 Dec. 1964)*
Malaysia—*(17 Sep. 1957)*

—The Federation of Malaya joined the United Nations on 17 September 1957. On 16 September 1963, its name was changed to Malaysia, following the admission to the new federation of Singapore, Sabah (North Borneo) and Sarawak. Singapore became an independent state on 9 August 1965 and a member of the United Nations on 21 September 1965.

Maldives—*(21 Sep. 1965)*
Mali—*(28 Sep. 1960)*
Malta—*(1 Dec. 1964)*
Marshall Islands—*(17 Sep. 1991)*
Mauritania—*(7 Oct. 1961)*
Mauritius—*(24 Apr. 1968)*
Mexico—*(7 Nov. 1945)*
Micronesia (Federated States of)—*(17 Sep. 1991)*
Monaco—*(28 May 1993)*
Mongolia—*(27 Oct. 1961)*
Morocco—*(12 Nov. 1956)*
Mozambique—*(16 Sep. 1975)*
Myanmar—*(19 Apr. 1948)*
Namibia—*(23 Apr. 1990)*
Nepal—*(14 Dec. 1955)*
Netherlands—*(10 Dec. 1945)*
New Zealand—*(24 Oct. 1945)*
Nicaragua—*(24 Oct. 1945)*
Niger—*(20 Sep. 1960)*
Nigeria—*(7 Oct. 1960)*
Norway—*(27 Nov. 1945)*

Oman—*(7 Oct. 1971)*
Pakistan—*(30 Sep. 1947)*
Palau—*(15 Dec. 1994)*
Panama—*(13 Nov. 1945)*
Papua New Guinea—*(10 Oct. 1975)*
Paraguay—*(24 Oct. 1945)*
Peru—*(31 Oct. 1945)*
Philippines—*(24 Oct. 1945)*
Poland—*(24 Oct. 1945)*
Portugal—*(14 Dec. 1955)*
Qatar—*(21 Sep. 1971)*
Republic of Korea—*(17 Sep. 1991)*
Republic of Moldova—*(2 Mar. 1992)*
Romania—*(14 Dec. 1955)*
Russian Federation—*(24 Oct. 1945)*

—The Union of Soviet Socialist Republics was an original member of the United Nations from 24 October 1945. In a letter dated 24 December 1991, Boris Yeltsin, the President of the Russian Federation, informed the Secretary-General that the membership of the Soviet Union in the Security Council and all other United Nations organs was being continued by the Russian Federation with the support of the 11 member countries of the Commonwealth of Independent States.

Rwanda—*(18 Sep. 1962)*
Saint Kitts and Nevis—*(23 Sep. 1983)*
Saint Lucia—*(18 Sep. 1979)*
Saint Vincent and the Grenadines—*(16 Sep. 1980)*
Samoa—*(15 Dec. 1976)*
San Marino—*(2 Mar. 1992)*
São Tomé and Principe—*(16 Sep. 1975)*
Saudi Arabia—*(24 Oct. 1945)*
Senegal—*(28 Sep. 1960)*
Seychelles—*(21 Sep. 1976)*
Sierra Leone—*(27 Sep. 1961)*
Singapore—*(21 Sep. 1965)*
Slovakia—*(19 Jan. 1993)*

—Czechoslovakia was an original member of the United Nations from 24 October 1945. In a letter dated 10 December 1992, its permanent representative informed the Secretary-General that the Czech and Slovak Federal Republic would cease to exist on 31 December 1992 and that the Czech Republic and the Slovak Republic, as successor states, would apply for membership in the United Nations. Following the receipt of its application, the Security Council, on 8 January, recommended to the General Assembly that the Slovak Republic be admitted to United Nations membership. The Slovak Republic was thus admitted on 19 January as a member state.

Slovenia—*(22 May 1992)*
Solomon Islands—*(19 Sep. 1978)*
Somalia—*(20 Sep. 1960)*
South Africa—*(7 Nov. 1945)*
Spain—*(14 Dec. 1955)*
Sri Lanka—*(14 Dec. 1955)*
Sudan—*(12 Nov. 1956)*
Suriname—*(4 Dec. 1975)*
Swaziland—*(24 Sep. 1968)*
Sweden—*(19 Nov. 1946)*
Syrian Arab Republic—*(24 Oct. 1945)*

—Egypt and Syria were original members of the United Nations from 24 October 1945. Following a plebiscite on 21 February 1958, the United Arab Republic was established by a union of Egypt and Syria and continued as a single member. On 13 October 1961, Syria, having resumed its status as an independent state, resumed its separate membership in the United Nations.

Tajikistan—*(2 Mar. 1992)*
Thailand—*(16 Dec. 1946)*
The former Yugoslav Republic of Macedonia—*(8 Apr. 1993)*

—The General Assembly decided on 8 April 1993 to admit to United Nations membership the state being provisionally referred to for all purposes within the United Nations as "The former Yugoslav Republic of Macedonia" pending settlement of the difference that had arisen over its name.

Togo—*(20 Sep. 1960)*
Trinidad and Tobago—*(18 Sep. 1962)*
Tunisia—*(12 Nov. 1956)*
Turkey—*(24 Oct. 1945)*
Turkmenistan—*(2 Mar. 1992)*
Uganda—*(25 Oct. 1962)*
Ukraine—*(24 Oct. 1945)*
United Arab Emirates—*(9 Dec. 1971)*
United Kingdom of Great Britain and Northern Ireland—*(24 Oct. 1945)*
United Republic of Tanzania—*(14 Dec. 1961)*

—Tanganyika was a member of the United Nations from 14 December 1961 and Zanzibar was a member from 16 December 1963. Following the ratification on 26 April 1964 of Articles of Union between Tanganyika and Zanzibar, the United Republic of Tanganyika and Zanzibar continued as a single member, changing its name to the United Republic of Tanzania on 1 November 1964.

United States of America—*(24 Oct. 1945)*
Uruguay—*(18 Dec. 1945)*
Uzbekistan—*(2 Mar. 1992)*

Vanuatu—*(15 Sep. 1981)*
Venezuela—*(15 Nov. 1945)*
Viet Nam—*(20 Sep. 1977)*
Yemen—*(30 Sep. 1947)*

—Yemen was admitted to membership in the United Nations on 30 September 1947 and Democratic Yemen on 14 December 1967. On 22 May 1990, the two countries merged and have since been represented as one member with the name "Yemen."

Yugoslavia—*(24 Oct. 1945)*
Zambia—*(1 Dec. 1964)*
Zimbabwe—*(25 Aug. 1980)*

---

Source: UN Press Release ORG/1190 (15 Dec. 1994)
Updated 19 June 1998

# E

# NGO Working Group on the Security Council—List of Associated Organizations

### Location of organization headquarters noted
### List current as of September 1996

## ORGANIZING GROUPS

Amnesty International (UK)
Global Policy Forum (US) [secretariat]
International Federation of Human Rights (France)
International Women's Tribune Center (US)
Lawyers Committee for Nuclear Policy (US)
World Council of Churches (Switzerland)
World Federalist Movement (US)

## MEMBER ORGANIZATIONS

Asia Indigenous Women's Network (Philippines)
CAMDUN (UK)
Cairo Institute for Human Rights Studies (Egypt)
Center for Economic and Social Rights (US)
Consumer Unity and Trust Society
Development and Peace Foundation (Germany)
Economists Allied for Arms Reduction (ECAAR) (US)
Global Action on Aging (US)
Global Education Associates (US)
Helsinki Citizens Assembly (Netherlands)
Human Rights Watch (US)
Just World Trust (Malaysia)
Instituto del Tercer Mundo (Uruguay)
International Center for Law in Development (US)
International Student & Youth Movement for the UN (Switzerland)
Medecins san Frontières (France)

Movement for a Better World (US)
Movimento Federalista Europeo (Italy)
NGO Network on Global Governance (Switzerland)
NGO Committee on Disarmament (US)
Nuclear Age Peace Foundation (US)
One World Now (US)
Oxfam International (UK)
PARISHAN (India)
Pax Christi International (Brussels)
Peace Action (US)
Presbyterian UN Office (US)
Public Services International (Switzerland)
Quaker UN Office (US)
Transparency International (Germany)
United Church Board for World Ministries (US)
War and Peace Foundation (US)
Women's Environment & Development Organization (US)
Women's International League for Peace & Freedom (Switzerland)
World Economy, Ecology & Development Association (WEED) (Germany)
Worldwatch Institute (US)

## PARTICIPANTS

Association of the Bar of the City of New York (US)
Caritas Internationalis
Center for the Development of International Law (US)
Center for UN Reform Education (US)
Center of Concern (US)
Church World Service & Witness (US)
Danish UN Association (Denmark)
Earth Media
Economic & Social Human Rights Advocacy Network (ESHRAN) (US)
Fellowship of Reconciliation (US)
Franciscans International
Greenpeace International (Belgium)
Ibn Khaldun Center for Development Studies (Egypt)
International Network of Engineers & Scientists Against Proliferation (IN-ESAP) (Germany)
Institute for Energy and Environmental Research (Germany)
International Fellowship of Reconciliation
International Mohavir Jain Mission
International Physicians for the Prevention of Nuclear War (US/Russia)
International Public Policy Institute (US)
Lions Club (US)
Lutheran World Federation

Medical Mission Sisters
National Association of Women Jurists (US)
Netherlands Committee for the World Conservation Union (Netherlands)
People's Alliance for Social Development (Chile)
People's Solidarity for Participatory Democracy (Rep. Korea)
Philadelphia Yearly Meeting of the Religious Society of Friends (US)
Resultate (Germany)
Temple of Understanding
Union of Concerned Scientists (US)
United Methodist Church (US)
United Nations Association (US)
UNED
Wainwright House (US)
Women's Commission for Refugee Women & Children (US)
World Conference on Religion & Peace (US)
World Court Project (US)
World Federation of United Nations Associations (Switzerland)
World Order Models Project (US)

---

Source: NGO Working Group on the Security Council: List of members, globalpolicy@globalpolicy.org (Global Policy Forum, UN Plaza, New York).

 **is**

A Harcourt Higher Learning Company

Now you will find Harcourt Brace's distinguished innovation, leadership, and support under a different name . . . a new brand that continues our unsurpassed quality, service, and commitment to education.

We are combining the strengths of our college imprints into one worldwide brand: Harcourt

Our mission is to make learning accessible to anyone, anywhere, anytime—reinforcing our commitment to lifelong learning.

We are now Harcourt College Publishers. Ask for us by name.

One Company
"Where Learning Comes to Life."

www.harcourtcollege.com
www.harcourt.com

# NAME INDEX

# SUBJECT INDEX